ALEXANDRE DUMAS.

LIBRARY

OF THE

WORLD'S BEST LITERATURE

Ancient and Modern

CHARLES DUDLEY WARNER

EDITOR

HAMILTON WRIGHT MABIE, LUCIA GILBERT RUNKLE,
GEORGE H. WARNER

ASSOCIATE EDITORS

THIRTY VOLUMES

VOL. IX

NEW YORK

R. S. PEALE AND J. A. HILL

PUBLISHERS

THE ADVISORY COUNCIL

CRAWFORD H. TOY, A. M., LL. D.,
    Professor of Hebrew,   HARVARD UNIVERSITY, Cambridge, Mass.

THOMAS R. LOUNSBURY, LL. D., L. H. D.,
    Professor of English in the Sheffield Scientific School of
                        YALE UNIVERSITY, New Haven, Conn.

WILLIAM M. SLOANE, PH. D., L. H. D.,
    Professor of History and Political Science,
                        PRINCETON UNIVERSITY, Princeton, N. J.

BRANDER MATTHEWS, A. M., LL. B.,
    Professor of Literature, COLUMBIA UNIVERSITY, New York City.

JAMES B. ANGELL, LL. D.,
    President of the   UNIVERSITY OF MICHIGAN, Ann Arbor, Mich.

WILLARD FISKE, A. M., PH. D.,
    Late Professor of the Germanic and Scandinavian Languages
    and Literatures,   CORNELL UNIVERSITY, Ithaca, N. Y.

EDWARD S. HOLDEN, A. M., LL. D.,
    Director of the Lick Observatory, and Astronomer,
                        UNIVERSITY OF CALIFORNIA, Berkeley, Cal.

ALCÉE FORTIER, LIT. D.,
    Professor of the Romance Languages,
                        TULANE UNIVERSITY, New Orleans, La.

WILLIAM P. TRENT, M. A.,
    Dean of the Department of Arts and Sciences, and Professor of
    English and History,
                        UNIVERSITY OF THE SOUTH, Sewanee, Tenn.

PAUL SHOREY, PH. D.,
    Professor of Greek and Latin Literature,
                        UNIVERSITY OF CHICAGO, Chicago, Ill.

WILLIAM T. HARRIS, LL. D.,
    United States Commissioner of Education,
                        BUREAU OF EDUCATION, Washington, D. C.

MAURICE FRANCIS EGAN, A. M., LL. D.,
    Professor of Literature in the
                        CATHOLIC UNIVERSITY OF AMERICA, Washington, D. C.

La

9379

TABLE OF CONTENTS

VOL. IX

———

LIST OF PORTRAITS

IN VOL. IX

JOHN WILLIAM DRAPER

(1811–1882)

THE subject of this sketch was born at St. Helen's, near Liverpool, England, on the 5th of May, 1811. His earliest education was obtained at a Wesleyan Methodist school, but after a time he came under private teachers, with whose help he made rapid progress in the physical sciences, thus showing in his boyhood the natural bent of his mind and the real strength of his intellect. He afterwards studied for a time at the University of London, but in 1833 came to the United States, and three years later graduated at the University of Pennsylvania with the degree of M. D. In 1839 he was elected to the chair of chemistry in the University of New York, a position which he held until his death in 1882.

JOHN WILLIAM DRAPER

Draper's contributions to science were of a high order. He discovered some of the facts that lie at the basis of spectrum analysis; he was one of the first successful experimenters in the art of photography; and he made researches in radiant energy and other scientific phenomena. He published in 1858 a treatise on 'Human Physiology,' which is a highly esteemed and widely used text-book. He died on the 4th of January, 1882.

Draper's chief contributions to literature are three works: 'History of the Intellectual Development of Europe' (1863), a 'History of the American Civil War' (1867–1870), and 'The History of the Conflict between Religion and Science,' which appeared in the International Scientific Series in 1873. Of these works, the one on the intellectual development of Europe is the ablest, and takes a place beside the works of Lecky and Buckle as a contribution to the history of civilization. The history of the Civil War was written too soon after the events described to have permanent historical value. 'The History of the Conflict between Religion and Science' is a judicial presentation of the perennial controversy from the standpoint of the scientist.

Draper's claims to attention as a philosophic historian rest mainly on his theory of the influence of climate on human character and development. He maintains that "For every climate, and indeed for every geographical locality, there is an answering type of humanity"; and in his history of the American Civil War, as well as in his work on the intellectual development of Europe, he endeavored to prove that doctrine. Another theory which is prominent in his principal work is, that the intellectual development of every people passes through five stages; namely, 1, the Age of Credulity; 2, the Age of Inquiry; 3, the Age of Faith; 4, the Age of Reason; 5, the Age of Decrepitude. Ancient Greece, he thinks, passed through all those stages, the age of reason beginning with the advent of physical science. Europe as a whole has now also entered the age of reason, which as before he identifies with the age of physical science; so that everywhere in his historical works, physical influences and the scientific knowledge of physical phenomena are credited with most of the progress that mankind has made. Draper has left a distinct mark upon the scientific thought of his generation, and made a distinct and valuable contribution to the literature of his adopted country.

THE VEDAS AND THEIR THEOLOGY

From 'History of the Intellectual Development of Europe.' Copyright 1876, by Harper & Brothers

THE Vedas, which are the Hindu Scriptures, and of which there are four,— the Rig, Yagust, Saman, and Atharvan,— are asserted to have been revealed by Brahma. The fourth is however rejected by some authorities, and bears internal evidence of a later composition, at a time when hierarchical power had become greatly consolidated. These works are written in an obsolete Sanskrit, the parent of the more recent idiom. They constitute the basis of an extensive literature, Upavedas, Angas, etc., of connected works and commentaries. For the most part they consist of hymns suitable for public and private occasions, prayers, precepts, legends, and dogmas. The Rig, which is the oldest, is composed chiefly of hymns; the other three of liturgical formulas. They are of different periods and of various authorship, internal evidence seeming to indicate that if the later were composed by priests, the earlier were the production of military chieftains. They answer to a state of society advanced from the nomad to the municipal condition. They are based upon an acknowledgment of a universal Spirit, pervading all things. Of this God they therefore necessarily acknowledge the unity: "There is in truth but one Deity, the Supreme Spirit, the Lord of the universe, whose work is the universe." "The God above all gods, who created the earth, the heavens, and waters." The world, thus considered as an emanation of God, is therefore a part of him; it is kept in a visible state by his energy, and would instantly disappear if that energy were for a moment withdrawn. Even as it is, it is undergoing unceasing transformations, everything being in a transitory condition. The moment a given phase is reached, it is departed from, or ceases. In these perpetual movements the present can scarcely be said to have any existence, for as the Past is ending, the Future has begun.

In such a never-ceasing career all material things are urged, their forms continually changing, and returning as it were through revolving cycles to similar states. For this reason it is that we may regard our earth and the various celestial bodies as having had a moment of birth, as having a time of continuance, in which they are passing onward to an inevitable destruction; and that after the lapse of countless ages similar progresses will be made, and similar series of events will occur again and again.

But in this doctrine of universal transformation there is something more than appears at first. The theology of India is underlaid with Pantheism. "God is One because he is All." The Vedas, in speaking of the relation of nature to God, make use of the expression that he is the material as well as the cause of the universe, "the clay as well as the Potter." They convey the idea that while there is a pervading spirit existing everywhere, of the same nature as the soul of man, though differing from it infinitely in degree, visible nature is essentially and inseparably connected therewith; that as in man the body is perpetually undergoing changes, perpetually decaying and being renewed,— or as in the case of the whole human species, nations come into existence and pass away,— yet still there continues to exist what may be termed the universal human mind, so forever associated and forever connected are the material and the spiritual. And under this aspect we must contemplate the Supreme Being, not merely as a presiding intellect, but as illustrated by the parallel case of man, whose mental principle shows no tokens except through its connection with the body: so matter, or nature, or the visible universe, is to be looked upon as the corporeal manifestation of God.

PRIMITIVE BELIEFS DISMISSED BY SCIENTIFIC KNOWLEDGE

From 'History of the Intellectual Development of Europe.' Copyright 1876,
by Harper & Brothers

A s man advances in knowledge, he discovers that of his primi-
tive conclusions some are doubtless erroneous, and many
require better evidence to establish their truth incontest-
ably. A more prolonged and attentive examination gives him
reason, in some of the most important particulars, to change his
mind. He finds that the earth on which he lives is not a floor
covered over with a starry dome, as he once supposed, but a
globe self-balanced in space. The crystalline vault, or sky, is
recognized to be an optical deception. It rests upon the earth
nowhere, and is no boundary at all; there is no kingdom of hap-
piness above it, but a limitless space adorned with planets and
suns. Instead of a realm of darkness and woe in the depths on
the other side of the earth, men like ourselves are found there,
pursuing, in Australia and New Zealand, the innocent pleasures
and encountering the ordinary labors of life. By the aid of such
lights as knowledge gradually supplies, he comes at last to dis-
cover that this our terrestrial habitation, instead of being a
chosen, a sacred spot, is only one of similar myriads, more nu-
merous than the sands of the sea, and prodigally scattered through
space.

Never, perhaps, was a more important truth discovered. All
the visible evidence was in direct opposition to it. The earth,
which had hitherto seemed to be the very emblem of immobility,
was demonstrated to be carried with a double motion, with pro-
digious velocity, through the heavens; the rising and setting of
the stars were proved to be an illusion; and as respects the size
of the globe, it was shown to be altogether insignificant when
compared with multitudes of other neighboring ones — insignifi-
cant doubly by reason of its actual dimensions, and by the
countless numbers of others like it in form, and doubtless like it
the abodes of many orders of life.

And so it turns out that our earth is a globe of about twenty-
five thousand miles in circumference. The voyager who circum-
navigates it spends no inconsiderable portion of his life in
accomplishing his task. It moves round the sun in a year, but
at so great a distance from that luminary that if seen from him,
it would look like a little spark traversing the sky. It is thus

recognized as one of the members of the solar system. Other similar bodies, some of which are of larger, some of smaller dimensions, perform similar revolutions round the sun in appropriate periods of time.

If the magnitude of the earth be too great for us to attach to it any definite conception, what shall we say of the compass of the solar system? There is a defect in the human intellect, which incapacitates us for comprehending distances and periods that are either too colossal or too minute. We gain no clearer insight into the matter, when we are told that a comet which does not pass beyond the bounds of the system may perhaps be absent on its journey for more than a thousand years. Distances and periods such as these are beyond our grasp. They prove to us how far human reason excels imagination; the one measuring and comparing things of which the other can form no conception, but in the attempt is utterly bewildered and lost.

But as there are other globes like our earth, so too there are other worlds like our solar system. There are self-luminous suns, exceeding in number all computation. The dimensions of this earth pass into nothingness in comparison with the dimensions of the solar system, and that system in its turn is only an invisible point if placed in relation with the countless hosts of other systems, which form with it clusters of stars. Our solar system, far from being alone in the universe, is only one of an extensive brotherhood, bound by common laws and subject to like influences. Even on the very verge of creation, where imagination might lay the beginning of the realms of chaos, we see unbounded proofs of order, a regularity in the arrangement of inanimate things, suggesting to us that there are other intellectual creatures like us, the tenants of those islands in the abysses of space.

Though it may take a beam of light a million years to bring to our view those distant worlds, the end is not yet. Far away in the depths of space we catch the faint gleams of other groups of stars like our own. The finger of a man can hide them in their remoteness. Their vast distances from one another have dwindled into nothing. They and their movements have lost all individuality; the innumerable suns of which they are composed blend all their collected light into one pale milky glow.

Thus extending our view from the earth to the solar system, from the solar system to the expanse of the group of stars to

which we belong, we behold a series of gigantic nebular crea-
tions rising up one after another, and forming greater and
greater colonies of worlds.   No numbers can express them, for
they make the firmament a haze of stars.   Uniformity, even
though it be the uniformity of magnificence, tires at last, and we
abandon the survey; for our eyes can only behold a boundless
prospect, and conscience tells us our own unspeakable insignifi-
cance.

But what has become of the time-honored doctrine of the
human destiny of the universe ? — that doctrine for the sake of
which the controversy I have described in this chapter was raised ?
It has disappeared.   In vain was Bruno burnt and Galileo impris-
oned; the truth forced its way, in spite of all opposition, at last.
The end of the conflict was a total rejection of authority and
tradition, and the adoption of scientific truth.

THE KORAN

From 'History of the Intellectual Development of Europe.' Copyright 1876,
by Harper & Brothers

ARABIAN influence, thus imposing itself on Africa and Asia by
military successes, and threatening even Constantinople,
rested essentially on an intellectual basis, the value of
which it is needful for us to consider.   The Koran, which is
that basis, has exercised a great control over the destinies of
mankind, and still serves as a rule of life to a very large portion
of our race.   Considering the asserted origin of this book, — indi-
rectly from God himself, — we might justly expect that it would
bear to be tried by any standard that man can apply, and vin-
dicate its truth and excellence in the ordeal of human criticism.
In our estimate of it, we must constantly bear in mind that it
does not profess to be successive revelations made at intervals
of ages and on various occasions, but a complete production
delivered to one man.   We ought therefore to look for univer-
sality, completeness, perfection.   We might expect that it would
present us with just views of the nature and position of this
world in which we live, and that whether dealing with the spir-
itual or the material, it would put to shame the most celebrated
productions of human genius, as the magnificent mechanism of
the heavens and the beautiful living forms of the earth are

superior to the vain contrivances of man. Far in advance of all that has been written by the sages of India, or the philosophers of Greece, on points connected with the origin, nature, and destiny of the universe, its dignity of conception and excellence of expression should be in harmony with the greatness of the subject with which it is concerned.

We might expect that it should propound with authority, and definitively settle, those all-important problems which have exercised the mental powers of the ablest men of Asia and Europe for so many centuries, and which are at the foundation of all faith and all philosophy; that it should distinctly tell us in unmistakable language what is God, what is the world, what is the soul, and whether man has any criterion of truth; that it should explain to us how evil can exist in a world the Maker of which is omnipotent and altogether good; that it should reveal to us in what the affairs of men are fixed by Destiny, in what by free-will; that it should teach us whence we came, what is the object of our continuing here, what is to become of us hereafter. And since a written work claiming a divine origin must necessarily accredit itself even to those most reluctant to receive it, its internal evidences becoming stronger and not weaker with the strictness of the examination to which they are submitted, it ought to deal with those things that may be demonstrated by the increasing knowledge and genius of man; anticipating therein his conclusions.

Such a work, noble as may be its origin, must not refuse but court the test of natural philosophy, regarding it not as an antagonist but as its best support. As years pass on, and human science becomes more exact and more comprehensive, its conclusions must be found in unison therewith. When occasion arises, it should furnish us at least the foreshadowings of the great truths discovered by astronomy and geology, not offering for them the wild fictions of earlier ages, inventions of the infancy of man. It should tell us how suns and worlds are distributed in infinite space, and how in their successions they come forth in limitless time. It should say how far the dominion of God is carried out by law, and what is the point at which it is his pleasure to resort to his own good providence or his arbitrary will. How grand the description of this magnificent universe, written by the Omnipotent hand! Of man it should set forth his relations to other living beings, his place among them, his privileges and responsibilities. It should not leave him to grope his way through the vestiges of Greek philosophy, and to miss the truth at last; but it should teach him wherein true knowledge consists, anticipating the physical science, physical power, and physical well-being of our own times, nay, even unfolding for our benefit things that we are still ignorant of. The discussion of subjects so many and so high is not outside the scope of a work of such pretensions. Its manner of dealing with them is the only criterion it can offer of its authenticity to succeeding times.

Tried by such a standard, the Koran altogether fails. In its philosophy it is incomparably inferior to the writings of Chakia Mouni, the founder of Buddhism; in its science it is absolutely worthless. On speculative or doubtful things it is copious enough; but in the exact, where a test can be applied to it, it totally fails. Its astronomy, cosmogony, physiology, are so puerile as to invite our mirth, if the occasion did not forbid. They belong to the old times of the world, the morning of human knowledge. The earth is firmly balanced in its seat by the weight of the mountains; the sky is supported over it like a dome, and we are instructed in the wisdom and power of God by being told to find a crack in it if we can. Ranged in stories, seven in number, are the heavens, the highest being the habitation of God, whose throne — for the Koran does not reject Assyrian ideas — is sustained by winged animal forms. The shooting stars are pieces of red-hot stone, thrown by angels at impure spirits when they approach too closely. Of God the Koran is full of praise, setting forth, often in not unworthy imagery, his majesty. Though it bitterly denounces those who give him any equals, and assures them that their sin will never be forgiven; that in the Judgment Day they must answer the fearful question, "Where are my companions about whom ye disputed?"—though it inculcates an absolute dependence on the mercy of God, and denounces as criminals all those who make a merchandise of religion,—its ideas of the Deity are altogether anthropomorphic. He is only a gigantic man, living in a paradise. In this respect, though exceptional passages might be cited, the reader rises from a perusal of the one hundred and fourteen chapters of the Koran with a final impression that they have given him low and unworthy thoughts; nor is it surprising that one of the Mohammedan sects reads it in such a way as to find no difficulty in asserting that "from the crown of the head to the breast God is hollow, and from the breast downward he is solid;" that he "has curled black hair, and roars like a lion at every watch of the night." The unity asserted by Mohammed is a unity in special contradistinction to the Trinity of the Christians, and the doctrine of a Divine generation. Our Savior is never called the Son of God, but always the Son of Mary. Throughout there is a perpetual acceptance of the delusion of the human destiny of the universe. As to man, Mohammed is diffuse enough respecting a future state, speaking with clearness of a resurrection, the Judgment Day, Paradise, the torment of hell, the worm that never dies, the pains that never end; but with all this precise description of the future, there are many errors as to the past. If modesty did not render it unsuitable to speak of such topics here, it might be shown how feeble is his physiology when he has occasion to allude to the origin or generation of man. He is hardly advanced beyond the ideas of Thales. One who is so untrustworthy a guide as to things that are past cannot be very trustworthy as to events that are to come.

Of the literary execution of his work, it is perhaps scarcely possible to judge fairly from a translation. It is said to be the oldest prose composition among the Arabs, by whom Mohammed's boast of the unapproachable excellence of his work is almost universally sustained; but it must not be concealed that there have been among them very learned men who have held it in light esteem. Its most celebrated passages, as those on the nature of God, in Chapters ii., xxiv., will bear no comparison with parallel ones in the Psalms and Book of Job. In the narrative style, the story of Joseph in Chapter xii., compared with the same incidents related in Genesis, shows a like inferiority. Mohammed also adulterates his work with many Christian legends, derived probably from the apocryphal gospel of St. Barnabas; he mixes with many of his own inventions the Scripture account of the temptation of Adam, the Deluge, Jonah and the whale, enriching the whole with stories like the later Night Entertainments of his country, the seven sleepers, Gog and Magog, and all the wonders of genii, sorcery, and charms.

An impartial reader of the Koran may doubtless be surprised that so feeble a production should serve its purpose so well. But the theory of religion is one thing, the practice another. The Koran abounds in excellent moral suggestions and precepts; its composition is so fragmentary that we cannot turn to a single page without finding maxims of which all men must approve. This fragmentary construction yields texts and mottoes and rules complete in themselves, suitable for common men in any of the incidents of life. There is a perpetual insisting on the necessity of prayer, an inculcation of mercy, almsgiving, justice, fasting, pilgrimage, and other good works; institutions respecting conduct, both social and domestic, debts, witnesses, marriage, children, wine, and the like; above all, a constant stimulation to do battle with the infidel and blasphemer. For life as it passes in Asia, there is hardly a condition in which passages from the Koran cannot be recalled suitable for instruction, admonition, consolation, encouragement. To the Asiatic and to the African, such devotional fragments are of far more use than any sustained theological doctrine. The mental constitution of Mohammed did not enable him to handle important philosophical questions with the well-balanced ability of the great Greek and Indian writers; but he has never been surpassed in adaptation to the spiritual wants of humble life, making even his fearful fatalism administer thereto. A pitiless destiny is awaiting us; yet the prophet is uncertain what it may be. "Unto every nation a fixed time is decreed. Death will overtake us even in lofty towers, but God only knoweth the place in which a man shall die." After many an admonition of the resurrection and the Judgment Day, many a promise of Paradise and threat of hell, he plaintively confesses, "I do not know what will be done with you or me hereafter."

The Koran thus betrays a human and not a very noble intellectual origin. It does not however follow that its author was, as is so often asserted, a mere impostor. He reiterates again and again, "I am nothing more than a public preacher." He defends, not always without acerbity, his work from those who even in his own life stigmatized it as a confused heap of dreams, or what is worse, a forgery. He is not the only man who has supposed himself to be the subject of supernatural and divine communications, for this is a condition of disease to which any one, by fasting and mental anxiety, may be reduced.

In, what I have thus said respecting a work held by so many millions of men as a revelation from God, I have endeavored to speak with respect and yet with freedom, constantly bearing in mind how deeply to this book Asia and Africa are indebted for daily guidance, how deeply Europe and America for the light of science.

As might be expected, the doctrines of the Koran have received many fictitious additions and sectarian interpretations in the course of ages. In the popular superstition angels and genii largely figure. The latter, being of a grosser fabric, eat, drink, propagate their kind, are of two sorts, good and bad, and existed long before men, having occupied the earth before Adam. Immediately after death, two greenish livid angels, Monkir and Nekkar, examine every corpse as to its faith in God and Mohammed; but the soul, having been separated from the body by the angel of death, enters upon an intermediate state, awaiting the resurrection. There is however much diversity of opinion as to its precise disposal before the Judgment Day: some think that it hovers near the grave; some, that it sinks into the well Zemzem; some, that it retires into the trumpet of the angel of the resurrection; the difficulty apparently being that any final disposal before the Day of Judgment would be anticipatory of that great event, if indeed it would not render it needless. As to the resurrection, some believe it to be merely spiritual, others corporeal; the latter asserting that the *os coccygis*, or last bone of the spinal column, will serve as it were as a germ; and that, vivified by a rain of forty days, the body will sprout from it. Among the signs of the approaching resurrection will be the rising of the sun in the west. It will be ushered in by three blasts of a trumpet: the first, known as the blast of consternation, will shake the earth to its centre, and extinguish the sun and stars; the second, the blast of extermination, will annihilate all material things except Paradise, hell, and the throne of God. Forty years subsequently, the angel Israfil will sound the blast of resurrection. From his trumpet there will be blown forth the countless myriads of souls who have taken refuge therein, or lain concealed. The Day of Judgment has now come. The Koran contradicts itself as to the length of this day; in one place making it a thousand, in another fifty thousand years. Most Mohammedans incline to adopt the longer period, since angels, genii, men, and animals have to be tried.

As to men, they will rise in their natural state, but naked; white-winged camels, with saddles of gold, awaiting the saved. When the partition is made, the wicked will be oppressed with an intolerable heat, caused by the sun, which, having been called into existence again, will approach within a mile, provoking a sweat to issue from them; and this, according to their demerits, will immerse them from the ankles to the mouth; but the righteous will be screened by the shadow of the throne of God. The Judge will be seated in the clouds, the books open before him, and everything in its turn called on to account for its deeds. For greater dispatch, the angel Gabriel will hold forth his balance, one scale of which hangs over Paradise and one over hell. In these all works are weighed. As soon as the sentence is delivered, the assembly, in a long file, will pass over the bridge Al-Sirat. It is as sharp as the edge of a sword, and laid over the mouth of hell. Mohammed and his followers will successfully pass the perilous ordeal; but the sinners, giddy with terror, will drop into the place of torment. The blessed will receive their first taste of happiness at a pond which is supplied by silver pipes from the river Al-Cawthor. The soil of Paradise is of musk. Its rivers tranquilly flow over pebbles of rubies and emeralds. From tents of hollow pearls the Houris, or girls of Paradise, will come forth, attended by troops of beautiful boys. Each saint will have eighty thousand servants and seventy-two girls. To these, some of the more merciful Mussulmans add the wives they have had upon earth; but the grimly orthodox assert that hell is already nearly filled with women. How can it be otherwise, since they are not permitted to pray in a mosque upon earth?

I have not space to describe the silk brocades, the green clothing, the soft carpets, the banquets, the perpetual music and songs. From the glorified body all impurities will escape, not as they did during life, but in a fragrant perspiration of camphor and musk. No one will complain, "I am weary;" no one will say, "I am sick."

From the contradictions, puerilities, and impossibilities indicated in the preceding paragraphs, it may be anticipated that the faith of Mohammed has been broken into many sects. Of such it is said that not less than seventy-three may be numbered. Some, as the Sonnites, are guided by traditions; some occupy themselves with philosophical difficulties,—the existence of evil in the world, the attributes of God, absolute predestination and eternal damnation, the invisibility and non-corporeality of God, his capability of local motion. . . . But the great Mohammedan philosophers, simply accepting the doctrine of the oneness of God as the only thing of which man can be certain, look upon all the rest as idle fables—having however this political use: that they furnish contention and therefore occupation to disputatious sectarians, and consolation to illiterate minds.

MICHAEL DRAYTON

(1563–1631)

WHILE London still crowded to the new "Theatre" in Shoreditch, the first built in England; while Ben Jonson was still soldiering in the Low Countries; while Marlowe was working out the tragedy that was to revolutionize all stage traditions, and Shakespeare was yet but a "looker-on at greatness,"—there came up from Warwickshire a young man of good family who had served as page in a noble house, who had studied possibly at Oxford, and who in the first flush of manhood aspired to a place among those prodigies who made the later Eliza-
bethan period immortal. This was Michael Drayton, whose gentle birth and breeding, education and talents, knowledge of the world and of men, together with a most sweet and lovable disposition, made him at once welcome in the literary Bohemia of the day. He became the "deare and bosom friend" of Beaumont and Fletcher, and his work received unquestioned honor from his illustrious contemporaries.

MICHAEL DRAYTON

As a child he had demanded of his elders to know what kind of beings poets were, had spent many hours in writing childishly fantastic verses, and had begged of his tutor to make a poet of him. And although he seems to have been poor and to have lived by the gifts of wealthy patrons, he cast in his lot with literature, and cherished no other ambition than that of writing well. His first book, a volume of spiritual poems, or metrical renderings of the Bible, was published in 1590 under the title 'The Harmony of the Church.' It is difficult to see why this commonplace and orthodox performance should have given such umbrage that the Archbishop of Canterbury condemned the entire edition to destruction. Yet this was its fate, with the exception of forty copies which Archbishop Whitgift ordered to be reserved for the ecclesiastical library at Lambeth Palace. Undiscouraged, the poet next produced a cycle of sixty-four sonnets and a collection of pastorals entitled 'Idea: the Shepherd's Garland,' in which under the name "Rowland" he celebrated an early love. It is strange that the intrinsic merit of these verses, and their undoubted popularity, should not have urged Drayton to continue in the same vein. Instead, however, he set about the composition of a series of historical poems which extended over the next twenty-four years, and to which he gave the best energies of his life. Beginning with the epic 'Matilda,' studied from English history, the series was continued by a poem on the 'Wars of the Roses,' afterward enlarged into 'The Barons' Wars.' This was followed by the epic 'Robert, Duke of Normandy.' Destitute of imagination, prolix and tedious, these verses were yet so popular in Drayton's day that in 1612 he began the publication of a poem in thirty books, meant to include the entire chronology and topography of Great Britain, from the earliest times. This was the famous 'Poly-Olbion,' in which, in spite of the inspiring work of his contemporaries, Drayton harked back in spirit to the dreary monotony of the Saxon Chronicle; the detail is so minute, the matter so unimportant, and the absence of discrimination so apparent, that notwithstanding many noticeable beauties of thought and style, it is hard to realize that this poem was a favorite with that brilliant group which had known Shakespeare, and still delighted in Ben Jonson. After issuing eighteen books of 'Poly-Olbion,' his publishers—with whom he was always quarreling, and whom he declared that he "despised and kicked at"—refused to undertake the remaining twelve books of the second part. His friends, however, loyal in their love and praise of him, secured a more complaisant tradesman to bring out the rest of the already famous poem.

Fortunately for his fame, Drayton had in the mean time produced two other volumes of verse, which displayed the real grace and fancifulness of his charming muse. The first of these, 'Poems Lyrical and Pastoral,' included the satire 'The Man in the Moon'; while in the second were printed the 'Ballad of Agincourt,' the most spirited of English martial lyrics, and that delightful fantasy 'Nymphidia, or the Court of Faery,' in which the touch is so light, the fancy so dainty, and the conceit so delicate, that the poem remains immortally fresh and young. Because everybody wrote plays, Drayton turned playwright, and is said to have collaborated with Massinger and Ford. Of his long works, the 'Heroicall Episodes' is perhaps the most readable. His last effort was 'The Muses' Elizium,' published in 1630. A year later he died, and was buried in Westminster, where a monument was erected to him by the Countess of Dorset.

Drayton's place in English literature is with that considerable and not unimportant band who have done somewhat, but whose repute is much more for what they were in their friends' eyes than for what they did. In an age of great intellectual achievement, he yet managed, in spite of the stimulus of kindred minds and his own undoubted gift, to produce little that has sustained the reputation accorded him by his acquaintances. Most of his work lives chiefly to afford pleasing studies for the literary antiquary, to whom the tide of time brings nothing uninteresting. Yet in the art of living, in the unselfish devotion of his powers to his chosen calling, in the graces of affection and the offices of noble friendship, he was so excellent and exemplary that he won and kept the undying regard of the most able men of the most brilliant period of English literature — men who felt a personal and unrequitable loss when he passed away, and who spoke of him always with admiring tenderness.

In person he seems to have been small and dark. He describes himself as of "swart and melancholy face." Yet his talk was most delightful, and a strong proof of his wide popularity appears in the fact that he is quoted not less than one hundred and fifty times in 'England's Parnassus,' published as early as 1600. The tributes of his friends are innumerable, from the "good Rowland" of Barnfield to the "golden-mouthèd Drayton, musicall," of Fitz-Geoffrey, the "man of vertuous disposition, honest conversation, and well-preserved carriage" of Meres, or the tender lines of his friend Ben Jonson:—

> " Do, pious marble, let thy readers know
> What they and what their children owe
> To Drayton's name; whose sacred dust
> We recommend unto thy trust.
> Protect his memory, and preserve his story,
> Remain a lasting monument of his glory.
> And when thy ruins shall disclaim
> To be the treasurer of his name,
> His name, that cannot die, shall be
> An everlasting monument to thee."

SONNET

SINCE there's no help, come, let us kiss and part,—
　　Nay, I have done, you get no more of me;
　And I am glad, yea, glad with all my heart,
　　That thus so clearly I myself can free:
Shake hands forever, cancel all our vows,
　　And when we meet at any time again,
　Be it not seen in either of our brows
　　That we one jot of former love retain.
Now, at the last gasp of Love's latest breath,
　　When, his pulse failing, Passion speechless lies,
When Faith is kneeling by his bed of death,
　　And Innocence is closing up his eyes,—
Now, if thou wouldst, when all have given him over,
From death to life thou mightst him yet recover!

THE BALLAD OF AGINCOURT

FAIR stood the wind for France,
　　When we our sails advance,
　　　Nor now to prove our chance
　　Longer will tarry;
But putting to the main,
At Kaux, the mouth of Seine,
With all his martial train,
　　Landed King Harry.

And taking many a fort,
Furnished in warlike sort,
Marched towards Agincourt
　　In happy hour —
Skirmishing day by day
With those that stopped his way,
Where the French gen'ral lay
　　With all his power,

Which in his height of pride,
King Henry to deride,
His ransom to provide
　　To the King sending;
Which he neglects the while,
As from a nation vile,
Yet, with an angry smile,
　　Their fall portending.

And turning to his men,
Quoth our brave Henry then:—
"Though they to one be ten,
　　Be not amazed;
Yet have we well begun —
Battles so bravely won
Have ever to the sun
　　By fame been raised.

"And for myself," quoth he,
"This my full rest shall be;
England ne'er mourn for me,
　　Nor more esteem me;
Victor I will remain,
Or on this earth lie slain;
Never shall she sustain
　　Loss to redeem me.

"Poitiers and Cressy tell,
When most their pride did swell,
Under our swords they fell;
    No less our skill is
Than when our grandsire great,
Claiming the regal seat,
By many a warlike feat
    Lopped the French lilies."

The Duke of York so dread
The eager vaward led;
With the main Henry sped,
    Amongst his henchmen.
Excester had the rear —
A braver man not there:
O Lord! how hot they were
    On the false Frenchmen!

They now to fight are gone;
Armor on armor shone;
Drum now to drum did groan —
    To hear was wonder;
That with the cries they make
The very earth did shake;
Trumpet to trumpet spake,
    Thunder to thunder.

Well it thine age became,
O noble Erpingham!
Which did the signal aim
    To our hid forces;
When from a meadow by,
Like a storm suddenly,
The English archery
    Struck the French horses,

With Spanish yew so strong,
Arrows a cloth-yard long,
That like to serpents stung,
    Piercing the weather;
None from his fellow starts,
But playing manly parts,
And like true English hearts,
    Stuck close together.

When down their bows they threw,
And forth their bilbows drew,
And on the French they flew,
　　Not one was tardy;
Arms were from shoulders sent;
Scalps to the teeth were rent;
Down the French peasants went;—
　　Our men were hardy.

This while our noble king,
His broadsword brandishing,
Down the French host did ding,
　　As to o'erwhelm it;
And many a deep wound lent,
His arm with blood besprent,
And many a cruel dent
　　Bruisèd his helmet.

Glo'ster, that duke so good,
Next of the royal blood,
For famous England stood,
　　With his brave brother—
Clarence, in steel so bright,
Though but a maiden knight,
Yet in that furious fight
　　Scarce such another.

Warwick in blood did wade;
Oxford the foe invade,
And cruel slaughter made,
　　Still as they ran up.
Suffolk his axe did ply;
Beaumont and Willoughby
Bare them right doughtily,
　　Ferrers and Fanhope.

Upon Saint Crispin's day
Fought was this noble fray,
Which fame did not delay
　　To England to carry;
Oh, when shall Englishmen
With such acts fill a pen,
Or England breed again
　　Such a King Harry?

QUEEN MAB'S EXCURSION

From 'Nymphidia, the Court of Faery'

HER chariot ready straight is made;
    Each thing therein is fitting laid,
        That she by nothing might be stay'd,
            For naught must her be letting:
Four nimble gnats the horses were,
The harnesses of gossamer,
Fly Cranion, her charioteer,
        Upon the coach-box getting.

Her chariot of a snail's fine shell,
Which for the colors did excel,—
The fair Queen Mab becoming well,
        So lively was the limning;
The seat the soft wool of the bee,
The cover (gallantly to see)
The wing of a py'd butterflee,—
        I trow, 'twas simple trimming.

The wheels composed of crickets' bones,
And daintily made for the nonce;
For fear of rattling on the stones,
        With thistle-down they shod it:
For all her maidens much did fear,
If Oberon had chanced to hear
That Mab his queen should have been there,
        He would not have abode it.

She mounts her chariot with a trice,
Nor would she stay for no advice,
Until her maids, that were so nice,
        To wait on her were fitted,
But ran away herself alone;
Which when they heard, there was not one
But hasted after to be gone,
        As she had been diswitted.

Hop, and Mop, and Drap so clear,
Pip, and Trip, and Skip, that were
To Mab their sovereign dear,
        Her special maids of honor;

Fib, and Tib, and Pinck, and Pin,
    Tick, and Quick, and Jill, and Jin,
Tit, and Nit, and Wap, and Win,
    The train that wait upon her.

Upon a grasshopper they got,
And what with amble and with trot,
For hedge nor ditch they sparèd not,
    But after her they hie them.
A cobweb over them they throw,
To shield the wind if it should blow;
Themselves they wisely could bestow,
    Lest any should espy them.

GUSTAVE DROZ

(1832–1895)

USTAVE DROZ enjoyed for a time the distinction of being the most popular writer of light literature in France, and his fame extended throughout Europe and to America, several of his books having been translated into English. Essentially a Parisian of the day,—gay, droll, adroit,—he not only caught and reflected the humor of his countrymen, but with a new, fresh touch, reached below the surface of their volatile emotions. Occasionally striking the note of deeper feeling, he avoided as a rule the more serious sides of life, as well as the sensational tendencies of most of his contemporaries. His friends claimed for him a distinctive *genre*, and on that account presented him as a candidate for the Academy; but he failed of election.

GUSTAVE DROZ

The son of a well-known sculptor, he was born in Paris, and followed the traditions of his family in entering the École des Beaux-Arts, where he developed some aptitude with his brush; but a preference for writing beguiled him from the studio, and an acquaintance with Marcellin the illustrator, founder of La Vie Parisienne, led him to follow literature. At first he was timid, dreading the test of publication, but presently he gave himself up unreservedly to his pen. Within a year he was established as a favorite of the people, and his friend's journal was on the highway to success. For this he wrote a series of sketches of every-day life that were subsequently collected and published in book form, under the titles 'Monsieur, Madame, et Bébé,' 'Entre Nous,' and 'La Cahier Bleu de Mlle. Cibot.' Within two years these books had reached their twentieth edition, and of the first, nearly one hundred and fifty editions have been demanded since it was issued. He has written several novels, the best known of which are 'Babolein,' 'Les Étangs' (The Ponds), and 'Autour d'une Source' (Around a Spring), but they did not fully sustain the reputation gained by his short sketches; a fact which induced him in 1884 to return to his earlier form in 'Tristesses et Sourires' (Sorrows and Smiles), a volume of light dissertations on things grave and gay that at once revived his popularity.

The peculiarity of the work of Gustave Droz is its delicacy both in humor and pathos. He surprised the French by making them all laugh without making any of them wince; the sharp wits of his day were forgotten in the unalloyed enjoyment of his simple quaintness, in which there was neither affectation nor sarcasm. Yet as has been said, he was a Parisian of the Parisians, quick to perceive the ludicrous, ready to weep with the afflicted, and to laugh again with the happy. His studies of children are among his best, on account of their extreme naturalness, and are never uninteresting, despite the simplicity of the incidents and observations on which they are founded. In 'Le Cahier Bleu de Mlle. Cibot' he has used striking colors to paint the petty afflictions that beset most lives; but lest these pictures should leave an unpleasant impression, they are set off by others of a happier sort, making a collection that constitutes a most effective lesson in practical philosophy.

HOW THE BABY WAS SAVED

From 'The Seamstress's Story'

"YES, Ma'm'selle Adèle," said the seamstress, "the real happiness of this world is not so unevenly distributed after all."

Louise, as she said this, took from the reserve in the bosom of her dress a lot of pins, and applied them deftly to the trimming of a skirt which I was holding for her.

"A sufficiently comfortable doctrine," I answered; "but it does seem to me as if some people were born to live and to die unhappy."

"It is only folks who never find anybody to love enough; and I think it's nobody's fault but their own."

"But my good Louise, wouldn't you have suffered much less last year, when you came so near losing your boy, if you hadn't cared so much for him?"

I was only drawing her on, you see; Louise's chat was the greatest resource to me at that time.

"Why, Ma'm'selle Adèle, you are surely joking. You'd as well tell me to cut off my feet to save my shoes. You'll know one of these days—and not so far off neither, maybe—how mighty easy and sensible it would be not to love your children. They *are* a worry, too; but oh the delight of 'em! I'd like to have had anybody tell me not to love my darling because it might grieve me, when he lay there in his mother's lap, with blue lips, gasping for his breath, and well-nigh dead, his face blackish, and his hands like this piece of wax. You could see that everything was going against him; and with his great big eyes he was staring in my face, until I felt as if the child was tugging at my very heart-strings. I kept smiling at him, though, through the tears that blinded me, hard as I tried to hide them. Oh! such tears are bitter salt indeed, Ma'm'selle! And there was my poor husband on his knees, making paper figures to amuse him, and singing a funny song he used to laugh at. Now and then the corners of his mouth would pucker, and his cheeks would wrinkle a little bit under the eyes. You could tell he was still amused, but in such a dreamy way. Oh! our child seemed no longer with us, but behind a veil, like. Wait a minute. You must excuse me, for I can't help crying when I think of it."

And the poor creature drew out her handkerchief and fairly sobbed aloud. In the midst of it however she smiled and said: "Well, that's over now; 'twas nothing, and I'm too silly. And Ma'm'selle, here I've gone and cried upon your mother's dress, and that's a pretty business."

I took her hand in mine and pressed it.

"Aren't you afraid you'll stick yourself, Ma'm'selle? I've got my needle in that hand," she said playfully. "But you did not mean what you said just now, did you?"

"What did I say?"

"That it would be better not to love your children with all your heart, on account of the great anxiety. Don't you know such thoughts are wicked? When they come into your head your mind wants purifying. But I'm sure I beg your pardon for saying so."

"You are entirely right, Louise," I returned.

"Ah! so I thought. And now let me see. Let's fix this ruche; pull it to the left a little, please."

"But about the sick boy. Tell me about his recovery."

"That was a miracle — I ought to say two miracles. It was a miracle that God restored him to us, and a miracle to find anybody with so much knowledge and feeling,— such talent, such a tender heart, and so much, so much —! I'm speaking of the doctor. A famous one he was, too, you must know; for it was no less than Doctor Faron. Heaven knows how he is run

after, and how rich and celebrated he is! Aren't you surprised
to hear that it was he who attended *our* little boy? Indeed, the
wonders begin with that. You may imagine my husband was at
his wits' end when he saw how it was with the child; and all of
a sudden I saw him jump up, get out his best coat and hat, and
put them on.

"'Where are you going?' I asked.

"'To bring Doctor Faron.'

"Why, if he had said, 'To bring the Prime Minister,' it
would have seemed as likely.

"'Don't you believe Doctor Faron is going to trouble himself
about such as we. They will turn you out of doors.'

"But 'twas no use talking, my dear. He was already on the
stairs, and I heard him running away as if the house was on fire.
Fire, indeed; worse, far worse than any fire!

"And there I was, left alone with the child upon my knees.
He wouldn't stay in bed, and was quieter so, wrapped up in his
little blanket. 'Here will he die,' I thought. 'Soon will his
eyes close, and then it will be all over;' and I held my own
breath to listen to his feeble and oppressed pantings.

"About an hour had passed, when I heard a rapid step upon
the stairs (we are poor, and live in attic rooms). The door
opened, and my husband came in, wet with perspiration and out
of breath. If I live a century, I'll not forget his look when he
said:—

"'Well?'

"I answered, 'No worse. But the doctor?'

"'He's coming.'

"Oh, those blessed words! It actually seemed as if my child
were saved already. If you but knew how folks love their little
ones! I kissed the darling, I kissed his father, I laughed, I
cried, and I no longer felt the faintest doubt. It is by God's
mercy that such gleams of hope are sent to strengthen us in our
trials. It was very foolish, too; for something might easily have
prevented the doctor's coming, after all.

"'You found him at home, then?' I asked my husband.

"Then he told me in an undertone what he had done, stop-
ping every now and then to wipe his face and gather breath.

"My husband had scarcely uttered these words," continued
Louise, "when I heard a step on the stairs. It was he! it was

that blessed angel of a doctor, come to help us in our sore distress.

"And what do you think he said in his deep voice when he got into the room?

"'God bless you, my friends, but I nearly broke my neck on those stairs. Where's that child?'

"'Here he is, my dear, darling doctor.' I knew no better way to speak to him, with his dress cravat showing over his greatcoat, and his decorations dangling like a little bunch of keys at his buttonhole.

"He took off his wrappings, stooped over the child, turned him over, more gently even than his mother could have done, and laid his own head first against his back, then against his breast. How I tried to read his eyes! but they know how to hide their thoughts.

"'We must perform an operation here,' says he; 'and it is high time.'

"Just at this moment the hospital doctor came in, and whispered to him, 'I'm afraid you didn't want to be disturbed, sir.'

"'Oh, never mind. I am sorry it wasn't sooner, though. Get everything ready now.'

"But Ma'm'selle Adèle, why should I tell you all this? I'd better mind my work."

"Oh, go on, Louise, go on!"

"Well then, Ma'm'selle, if you believe me, those two doctors — neither of 'em kin, or even friends till then — went to work and made all the preparations, while my husband went off to borrow lights. The biggest one tied a mattress on the table, and the assistant spread out the bright little knives.

"You who have not been through it all, Ma'm'selle, can't know what it is to have your own little one in your lap, to know that those things are to be used upon him to pierce his tender flesh, and if the hand that guides them be not sure, that they may kill him.

"When all was ready, Doctor Faron took off his cravat, then lifted my child from my arms and laid him on the mattress, in the midst of the lamps, and said to my poor man:—

"'You will hold his head, and your wife his feet. Joseph will pass me the instruments. You've brought a breathing-tube with you, my son?'

"'Yes, sir.'

" My husband was as white as a sheet by this; and when I saw him about to take his place with his hands shaking so much, it scared me, so I said: —

" ' Doctor, please let me hold his head!'

" ' But my poor woman, if you should tremble?'

" ' Please let me do it, doctor!'

" ' Be it so, then;' and then added with a bright look at me, and a cheering smile, ' we shall save him for you, my dear; you are a brave little woman and you deserve it.'

" Yes, and save him he did! God bless him! saved him as truly as if he had snatched him from the depths of the river."

" And you didn't tremble, Louise?"

" You may depend on that. If I had, it would have been the last of my child."

" How in the world did you keep yourself steady?"

" The Lord knows; but I was like a rock. When you must, you must, I suppose."

" And you had to behold every detail of that operation?"

" Yes, indeed; and often have I dreamed it over since. His poor little neck laid open, and the veins, which the doctor pushed aside with his fingers, and the little silver tube which he inserted, and all that; and then the face of the child, changing as the air passed into his lungs. You've seen a lamp almost out, when you pour in oil? It was like that. They had laid him there but half alive, with his eyes all but set; and they gave him back to me, pale and with bloodless lips, it is true, but with life in his looks, and breathing — breathing the free, fresh air.

" ' Kiss him, mother,' says the doctor, ' and put him to bed. Cover the place with some light thing or other, and Joseph must stay with you to-night; won't you, Joseph? Ah, well, that's all arranged.'

" He put on his things and wrapped himself up to go. He was shaking hands with my husband, when I seized one hand, and kissed it — like a fool, as I was; but I didn't stop to think. He laughed heartily, and said to my husband, ' Are you not jealous, friend? Your wife is making great advances to me. But I must be off now. Good night, good people.'

" And from that night he always talks so friendly and familiarly to us, not a bit contemptuously either, but as if he liked us, and was glad to be of service to us."

A FAMILY NEW-YEAR'S

From 'Monsieur, Madame, and Baby'

IT IS barely seven o'clock. A pale ray of wan light filters through the double curtains, and some one is already at the door. In the next room I hear the stifled laughs and silvery voice of my little child, who trembles with impatience and begs to come.

"But father dear," he cries, "it's Baby. It's your own little boy—to wish you 'Happy New Year.'"

"Come in, darling; come quick and give me a kiss," I cry.

The door opens, and my boy, with shining eyes and his arms in the air, rushes toward the bed. Long curls, escaping from the nightcap which imprisons his blond head, fall over his forehead. His loose night-shirt, embarrassing his little feet, adds to his impatience and makes him trip at every step. He has crossed the room at last, and stretching his hands toward mine, "Baby wishes you a happy New Year," he says earnestly.

"Poor darling, with his bare feet! Come, dear! Come and get warm under the covers; come and hide in the quilt."

I draw him to me; but at this movement my wife wakes up suddenly. . . . "How you frightened me! I was dreaming that there was a fire, and these voices in the midst of it! You are indiscreet with your cries!"

"*Our* cries! So you forget, dear mamma, that this is New-Year's day. Baby is waiting for you to wake up, and so am I."

I wrap up my little man in the soft quilt, I bury him in the eiderdown, and warm his frozen feet with my hands.

"Mother dear, this is New Year," he cries. He draws our two heads together with his arms, and kisses us anywhere at random, with his fresh lips. I feel his dimpled hand wandering about my neck; his little fingers are entangled in my beard. My mustache pricks the end of his nose. He bursts out laughing, and throws his head back.

His mother, who has recovered from her fright, draws him into her arms. She pulls the bell.

"The year begins well, my dears," she says, "but we need a little light."

"Tell me, mamma, do naughty children have presents at New-Year's?" says the young dissembler, with an eye on the mountain of boxes and packages visible in the corner, in spite of the gloom.

The curtains are drawn apart, the blinds are opened, there is
a flood of daylight, the fire crackles gayly on the hearth, and two
large packages, carefully wrapped up, are placed on the bed. One
is for my wife; the other for the boy.

What is it? What will it be? I have heaped up knots, and
tripled the wrappings; and I watch with delight their nervous
fingers, lost in the strings.

My wife gets impatient, smiles, is vexed, kisses me, and asks
for scissors. Baby on his side bites his lips, pulls with all his
might, and at last asks me to help him. He longs to see through
the paper. Desire and expectation are painted on his face. The
convulsive movement of his hand in the folds of the quilt rustles
the silk, and he makes a sound with his lips as though a savory
fruit were approaching them.

The last paper is off, finally the cover is lifted, there is an
outcry of joy.

"My tippet!"

"My menagerie!"

"Like my muff,— my dear husband!"

"With a real shepherd, on wheels, dear papa, _how_ I love you!"

They hug me, four arms at once wind round and press me
close. I am stirred — a tear comes to my eyes; two come to
those of my wife; and Baby, who loses his head, utters a sob as
he kisses my hand.

How absurd! you will say. I don't know whether it is absurd
or not, but it is charming, I promise you. After all, does not
sorrow wring tears enough from us to make up for the solitary
one which joy may call forth? Life is less happy when one
chances it alone; and when the heart is empty, the way seems
long. It is so good to feel one's self loved; to hear the regular
steps of one's fellow travelers beside one; and to think, "They
are there, our three hearts beat together;" and once a year,
when the great clock strikes the first of January, to sit down be-
side the way with hands clasped together and eyes fixed upon
the dusty unknown road stretching on to the horizon, and to
embrace and say: — "We will always love each other, my dear
ones; you depend upon me and I on you. Let us trust and keep
straight on."

And that is how I explain that we weep a little in looking at
a tippet and opening a menagerie.

Translated by Jane G. Cooke, for 'A Library of The World's Best Literature.'

THEIR LAST EXCURSION

From 'Making an Omelette': from Lippincott's Magazine, 1871, copyrighted

IN THIS strange, rude interior, how refined and delicate Louise
looked, with all her dainty appointments of long undressed
kid gloves, jaunty boots, and looped-up petticoat! While I
talked to the wood-cutters she shielded her face from the fire
with her hands, and kept her eye on the butter beginning to
sing in the pan.

Suddenly she rose, and taking the pan-handle from the old
woman, said, " Let me help you make the omelette, will you ? "
The good woman let go with a smile, and Louise found herself
alone, in the attitude of a fisherman who has just had a nibble.
She stood in the full light of the fire, her eyes fixed on the
melted butter, her arms tense with effort; she was biting her
lips, probably in order to increase her strength.

" It's rather hard on madame's little hands," said the old
man. " I bet it's the first time you ever made an omelette in a
wood-cutter's hut — isn't it, my young lady ? "

Louise nodded yes, without turning her eyes from the ome-
lette.

" The eggs! the eggs!" she suddenly exclaimed, with such a
look of uneasiness that we all burst out laughing — " hurry with
the eggs! The butter is all puffing up! Be quick — or I can't
answer for the consequences. "

The old woman beat the eggs energetically.

" The herbs!" cried the old man. " The lard and salt!" cried
the young ones. And they all set to work chopping, cutting,
piling up, while Louise, stamping with excitement, called out,
" Make haste! make haste!" Then there was a tremendous
bubbling in the pan, and the great work began. We were all
round the fire, gazing with an anxious interest inspired by our
all having had a finger in the pie.

The old woman, on her knees beside a large dish, slipped a
knife under the edge of the omelette, which was turning a fine
brown. " Now, madame, you've only got to turn it over," she
said.

" Just one little quick blow," suggested the old man.

" Mustn't be violent," counseled the young one.

"All at once; up with it, dear!" I said.

"If you all talk at once —"

"Make haste, madame!"

"If you all talk at once I never shall manage it. It is too awfully heavy."

"One quick little blow."

"But I can't; it's going over. Oh gracious!"

In the heat of action, her hood had fallen off. Her cheeks were like a peach, her eyes shone, and though she lamented her fate, she burst into peals of laughter. At last by a supreme effort the pan moved, and the omelette rolled over, somewhat heavily, I confess, into the large dish which the old woman was holding. Never did an omelette look better!

"I am sure the young lady's arms must be tired," said the old man, as he began cutting a round loaf into enormous slices.

"Oh no, not so very," my wife answered with a merry laugh; "only I am crazy to taste my — our omelette."

We had seated ourselves round the table. When we had eaten and drunk with the good souls, we rose and made ready to go home. The sun had set, and the whole family came out of the cabin to see us off and say good-night.

"Don't you want my son to go with you?" the old woman called after us.

It was growing dark and chilly under the trees, and we gradually quickened our pace. "Those are happy people," said Louise. "We will come some morning and breakfast with them, — shan't we? We can put the baby in one of the donkey panniers, and in the other a large pasty and a bottle of wine.— You are not afraid of losing your way, George?"

"No, dear; no fear of that."

"A pasty and a bottle of wine — What is that?"

"Nothing; the stump of a tree."

"The stump of a tree — the stump of a tree," she muttered. "Don't you hear something behind us?"

"It is only the wind in the leaves, or the breaking of a dead branch."

He is fortunate who at night, in the heart of a forest, feels as calm as at his own fireside. You do not tremble, but you feel the silence. Involuntarily you look for eyes peering out of the darkness, and you try to define the confused forms appearing and changing every minute. Something breaks and sounds beneath your tread, and if you stop you hear the distant melancholy howl of your watch-dog, the scream of an owl, and other noises, far and near, not so easily explained. A sense of strangeness surrounds you and weighs you down. If you are alone, you walk faster; if there are two of you, you draw close to your companion. My wife clung to my arm.

"Let us turn wood-cutters. We could build a pretty little hut, simple, but nice enough. I would have curtains to the windows, and a carpet, and put my piano in one corner." She spoke very low, and occasionally I felt my hand tremble on her arm.

"You would soon get enough of that, dearest."

"It isn't fair to say so." And in another minute she went on: — "You think I don't love you, you and our boy? Oh yes, dear, I love you. Yes, yes, yes! The happiness that comes every day can't be expressed: we live on it, so we don't think of it. Like our daily bread — who thinks of that? But when you are thinking of yourself, when you put your head down, and really think, then you say, 'I am ungrateful, for I am happy, and I give no thanks for it.' Or when we are alone together, and walking arm-in-arm, now, at this very moment, — not that I mean only this moment, — I love you, I love you." She put her head down on my arm and pressed it earnestly. "Oh," she said, "if I were to lose you!" She spoke very low, as if afraid. What had frightened her? The darkness and the forest, or her own words?

She went on: — "I have often and often dreamed that I was saying good-by to you. You both cried, and I pressed you so close to my heart that there was only one of us. It was a nightmare, you know, but I don't mind it, for it showed me that my life was in your lives, dear. What is that cracking noise? Didn't you see something just in front of us?"

I answered her by taking her in my arms and folding her to my heart. We walked on, but it was impossible to go on talking. Every now and then she would stop and say, "Hush! hark! No, it is nothing."

At last we saw ahead of us a little light, now visible, now hidden by a tree. It was the lamp set for us in our parlor window. We crossed the stile and were at home. It was high time, for we were wet through.

I brought a huge log, and when the fire had blazed up we sat down in the great chimney-place. The poor girl was shivering.   I took off her boots and held her feet to the fire, screening them with my hands.

"Thanks, dear George, thanks!" she said, leaning on my shoulder and looking at me so tenderly that I felt almost ready to cry.

"What were you saying to me in that horrid wood, my darling?" I asked her, when she was better.

"You are thinking about that? I was frightened, that is all, and when you are frightened you see ghosts."

"We shall be wood-cutters, shan't we?"

And kissing me, with a laugh, she replied: "It is bedtime, Jean of the Woods."

I well remember that walk, for it was our last. Often and often since, at sunset on a dark day, I have been over the same ground; often and often I have stopped where she stood, and stooped and pulled aside the fern, seeking to find, poor fool that I am! the traces of her vanished footsteps. And I have often halted in the clearing under the birches which rained down on us, and there in the shadow I have fancied I caught the flutter of her dress; I have thought I heard her startled note of fright. And on my way home at night, at every step I have found a recollection of her in the distant barking and the breaking branches, as in the trembling of her hand on my arm and the kiss which I gave her.

Once I went into the wood-hut. I saw it all as before,—the family, the smoky interior, the little bench on which we sat,— and I asked for something to drink, that I might see the glass her lips had touched.

"The little lady who makes such good omelettes, she isn't sick, for sure?" asked the old woman.

Probably she saw the tears in my eyes, for she said no more, and I came away.

And so it is that except in my heart, where she lives and is, all that was my darling grows faint and dark and dim.

It is the law of life, but it is a cruel law. Even my poor child is learning to forget, and when I say to him most unwillingly, "Baby dear, do you remember how your mother did this or that?" he answers "Yes"; but I see, alas! that he too is ceasing to remember.

                                  Translation of Agnes Irwin.

HENRY DRUMMOND

(1851–)

ONE of the most widely read of modern essayists, Henry Drummond, was born at Stirling, Scotland, in 1851. Educated for the ministry, he passed through the Universities of Edinburgh and Tübingen, and the Free Church Divinity Hall, and after ordination was appointed to a mission chapel at Malta. The beauty and the historic interest of the famous island roused in him a desire for travel, and in the intervals of his professional work he has made semi-scientific pilgrimages to the Rocky Mountains and to South Africa, as well as lecturing tours to Canada, Australia, and the United States, where his addresses on scientific, religious, and sociological subjects have attracted large audiences.

A man of indefatigable industry, he has published many books, the most widely read of these being 'Natural Law in the Spiritual World,' a study of psychological conditions from the point of view of the Evolutionist. This work has passed through a large number of editions, and been translated into French, German, Dutch, and Norwegian. Scarcely less popular were 'The Greatest Thing in the World' (love), and 'Pax Vobiscum.' In 1894 he published a volume called 'The Ascent of Man,' in which he insists that certain altruistic factors modify the process of Natural Selection. This doctrine elicited much critical commentary from the stricter sects of the scientists, but the new view commended itself at once to the general reader.

HENRY DRUMMOND

The citations here given are selected from Mr. Drummond's book of travels, 'Tropical Africa,' a book whose simplicity and vividness enable the reader to see the Dark Continent exactly as it is.

THE COUNTRY AND ITS PEOPLE

From 'Tropical Africa'

NOTHING could more wildly misrepresent the reality than the
idea of one's school days that the heart of Africa is a
desert. Africa rises from its three environing oceans in
three great tiers, and the general physical geography of these
has been already sketched: — first, a coast line, low and deadly;
farther in, a plateau the height of the Scottish Grampians;
farther in still, a higher plateau, covering the country for thou-
sands of miles with mountain and valley. Now fill in this sketch,
and you have Africa before you. Cover the coast belt with rank
yellow grass; dot here and there a palm; scatter through it a
few demoralized villages; and stock it with the leopard, the
hyena, the crocodile, and the hippopotamus. Clothe the mount-
ainous plateaux next, both of them, with endless forests; not
grand umbrageous forest like the forests of South America, nor
matted jungle like the forests of India, but with thin, rather
weak forest,— with forest of low trees, whose half-grown trunks
and scanty leaves offer no shade from the tropical sun. Nor is
there anything in these trees to the casual eye to remind you
that you are in the tropics. Here and there one comes upon a
borassus or fan-palm, a candelabra-like euphorbia, a mimosa
aflame with color, or a sepulchral baobab. A close inspection
also will discover curious creepers and climbers; and among the
branches strange orchids hide their eccentric flowers. But the
outward type of tree is the same as we have at home — trees
resembling the ash, the beech, and the elm, only seldom so
large except by the streams, and never so beautiful. Day after
day you may wander through these forests, with nothing except
the climate to remind you where you are. The beasts to be sure
are different, but unless you watch for them you will seldom see
any; the birds are different, but you rarely hear them; and as
for the rocks, they are our own familiar gneisses and granites,
with honest basalt dikes boring through them, and leopard-skin
lichens staining their weathered sides. Thousands and thousands
of miles, then, of vast thin forest, shadeless, trackless, voiceless,
— forest in mountain and forest in plain,— this is East Central
Africa.

The indiscriminate praise, formerly lavished on tropical vege-
tation, has received many shocks from recent travelers. In

Kaffir-land, South Africa, I have seen one or two forests fine enough to justify the enthusiasm of arm-chair word-painters of the tropics; but so far as the central plateau is concerned, the careful judgment of Mr. Alfred Russell Wallace respecting the equatorial belt in general (a judgment which has at once sobered all modern descriptions of tropical lands and made imaginative people more content to stay at home) applies almost to this whole area. The fairy labyrinth of ferns and palms, the festoons of climbing plants blocking the paths and scenting the forests with their resplendent flowers, the gorgeous clouds of insects, the gayly plumaged birds, the paroquets, the monkey swinging from his trapeze in the shaded bowers — these are unknown to Africa. Once a week you will see a palm; once in three months the monkey will cross your path; the flowers on the whole are few; the trees are poor; and to be honest, though the endless forest-clad mountains have a sublimity of their own, and though there are tropical bits along some of the mountain streams of exquisite beauty, nowhere is there anything in grace and sweetness and strength to compare with a Highland glen. For the most part of the year these forests are jaded and sun-stricken, carpeted with no moss or alchemylla or scented woodruff, the bare trunks frescoed with few lichens, their motionless and unrefreshed leaves drooping sullenly from their sapless boughs. Flowers there are, small and great, in endless variety; but there is no display of flowers, no gorgeous show of blossom in the mass, as when the blazing gorse and heather bloom at home. The dazzling glare of the sun in the torrid zone has perhaps something to do with this want of color effect in tropical nature; for there is always about ten minutes just after sunset when the whole tone of the landscape changes like magic, and a singular beauty steals over the scene. This is the sweetest moment of the African day, and night hides only too swiftly the homelike softness and repose so strangely grateful to the over-stimulated eye.

Hidden away in these endless forests, like birds' nests in a wood, in terror of one another and of their common foe the slaver, are small native villages; and here in his virgin simplicity dwells primeval man, without clothes, without civilization, without learning, without religion — the genuine child of nature, thought-less, careless, and contented. This man is apparently quite happy; he has practically no wants. One stick, pointed, makes him a spear; two sticks rubbed together make him a fire; fifty sticks tied together make him a house. The bark he peels from them makes his clothes; the fruits which hang on them form his food. It is perfectly astonishing, when one thinks of it, what nature can do for the animal man, to see with what small capital after all a human being can get through the world. I once saw an African buried. According to the custom of his tribe, his entire earthly possessions — and he was an average commoner — were buried with him. Into the grave, after the body, was lowered the dead man's pipe, then a rough knife, then a mud bowl, and last his bow and arrows — the bowstring cut through the middle, a touching symbol that its work was done. This was all. Four items, as an auctioneer would say, were the whole belongings for half a century of this human being. No man knows what a man is till he has seen what a man can be without, and be withal a man. That is to say, no man knows how great man is till he has seen how small he has been once.

The African is often blamed for being lazy, but it is a misuse of words. He does not need to work; with so bountiful a Nature round him it would be gratuitous to work. And his indolence, therefore, as it is called, is just as much a part of himself as his flat nose, and as little blameworthy as slowness in a tortoise. The fact is, Africa is a nation of the unemployed.

THE EAST-AFRICAN LAKE COUNTRY

From 'Tropical Africa'

SOMEWHERE in the Shiré Highlands, in 1859, Livingstone saw a large lake — Lake Shirwa — which is still almost unknown.

It lies away to the east, and is bounded by a range of mountains whose lofty summits are visible from the hills round Blantyre. Thinking it might be a useful initiation to African travel if I devoted a short time to its exploration, I set off one morning, accompanied by two members of the Blantyre staff and a small retinue of natives. Steering across country in the direction in which it lay, we found, two days before seeing the actual water, that we were already on the ancient bed of the lake. Though now clothed with forest, the whole district has obviously been under water at a comparatively recent period, and the shores of Lake Shirwa probably reached at one time to within a few miles of Blantyre itself. On reaching the lake a

very agéd female chief came to see us, and told us how, long,
long ago, a white man came to her village and gave her a pres-
ent of cloth. Of the white man, who must have been Livingstone,
she spoke very kindly; and indeed, wherever David Livingstone's
footsteps are crossed in Africa, the fragrance of his memory seems
to remain.

The waters of Shirwa are brackish to the taste, and undrink-
able; but the saltness must have a peculiar charm for game, for
nowhere else in Africa did I see such splendid herds of the
larger animals as here. The zebra was especially abundant; and
so unaccustomed to be disturbed are these creatures, that with a
little care one could watch their movements safely within a very
few yards. It may seem unorthodox to say so, but I do not
know if among the larger animals there is anything handsomer
in creation than the zebra. At close quarters his striped coat is
all but as fine as the tiger's, while the form and movement of
his body are in every way nobler. The gait, certainly, is not to
be compared for gracefulness with that of the many species of
antelope and deer who nibble the grass beside him, and one can
never quite forget that scientifically he is an ass; but taking him
all in all, this fleet and beautiful animal ought to have a higher
place in the regard of man than he has yet received.

We were much surprised, considering that this region is
almost uninhabited, to discover near the lake shore a native path
so beaten, and so recently beaten, by multitudes of human feet,
that it could only represent some trunk route through the conti-
nent. Following it for a few miles, we soon discovered its
function. It was one of the great slave routes through Africa.
Signs of the horrid traffic became visible on every side; and
from symmetrical arrangements of small piles of stones and
freshly cut twigs, planted semaphore-wise upon the path, our
native guides made out that a slave caravan was actually passing
at the time. We were in fact between two portions of it, the
stones and twigs being telegraphic signals between front and
rear. Our natives seemed much alarmed at this discovery, and
refused to proceed unless we promised not to interfere — a pro-
ceeding which, had we attempted it, would simply have meant
murder for ourselves and slavery for them. Next day from a
hill-top we saw the slave encampment far below, and the ghastly
procession marshaling for its march to the distant coast, which
many of the hundreds who composed it would never reach alive.

Talking of native foot-paths leads me to turn aside for a moment, to explain to the uninitiated the true mode of African travel. In spite of all the books that have been lavished upon us by our great explorers, few people seem to have any accurate understanding of this most simple process. Some have the impression that everything is done in bullock wagons; an idea borrowed from the Cape, but hopelessly inapplicable to Central Africa, where a wheel at present would be as great a novelty as a polar bear. Others, at the opposite extreme, suppose that the explorer works along solely by compass, making a bee-line for his destination, and steering his caravan through the trackless wilderness like a ship at sea. Now, it may be a surprise to the unenlightened to learn that probably no explorer in forcing his passage through Africa has ever, for more than a few days at a time, been off some beaten track. Probably no country in the world, civilized or uncivilized, is better supplied with paths than this unmapped continent. Every village is connected with some other village, every tribe with the next tribe, every State with its neighbor, and therefore with all the rest. The explorer's business is simply to select from this network of tracks, keep a general direction, and hold on his way. Let him begin at Zanzibar, plant his foot on a native foot-path, and set his face towards Tanganyika. In eight months he will be there. He has simply to persevere. From village to village he will be handed on, zigzagging it may be, sometimes, to avoid the impassable barriers of nature or the rarer perils of hostile tribes; but never taking to the woods, never guided solely by the stars, never in fact leaving a beaten track, till hundreds and hundreds of miles are between him and the sea, and his interminable foot-path ends with a canoe on the shores of Tanganyika. Crossing the lake, landing near some native village, he picks up the thread once more. Again he plods on and on, now on foot, now by canoe, but always keeping his line of villages, until one day suddenly he sniffs the sea-breeze again, and his faithful foot-wide guide lands him on the Atlantic seaboard.

Nor is there any art in finding out these successive villages with their intercommunicating links. He *must* find them out. A whole army of guides, servants, carriers, soldiers, and camp-followers accompany him in his march, and this nondescript regiment must be fed. Indian corn, cassava, mawere, beans, and bananas—these do not grow wild even in Africa. Every meal has to be bought and paid for in cloth and beads; and scarcely three days can pass without a call having to be made at some village where the necessary supplies can be obtained. A caravan, as a rule, must live from hand to mouth, and its march becomes simply a regulated procession through a chain of markets. Not however that there are any real markets — there are neither bazaars nor stores in native Africa. Thousands of the villages through which the traveler eats his way may never have victualed a caravan before. But with the chief's consent, which is usually easily purchased for a showy present, the villagers unlock their larders, the women flock to the grinding-stones, and basketfuls of food are swiftly exchanged for unknown equivalents in beads and calico.

The native tracks which I have just described are the same in character all over Africa. They are veritable foot-paths, never over a foot in breadth, beaten as hard as adamant, and rutted beneath the level of the forest bed by centuries of native traffic. As a rule these foot-paths are marvelously direct. Like the roads of the old Romans, they run straight on through everything, ridge and mountain and valley, never shying at obstacles, nor anywhere turning aside to breathe. Yet within this general straightforwardness there is a singular eccentricity and indirectness in detail. Although the African foot-path is on the whole a bee-line, no fifty yards of it are ever straight. And the reason is not far to seek. If a stone is encountered, no native will ever think of removing it. Why should he? It is easier to walk round it. The next man who comes that way will do the same. He knows that a hundred men are following him; he looks at the stone; a moment, and it might be unearthed and tossed aside, but no — he also holds on his way. It is not that he resents the trouble, it is the idea that is wanting. It would no more occur to him that that stone was a displaceable object, and that for the general weal he might displace it, than that its feldspar was of the orthoclase variety. Generations and generations of men have passed that stone, and it still waits for a man with an altruistic idea. But it would be a very stony country indeed — and Africa is far from stony — that would wholly account for the aggravating obliqueness and indecision of the African foot-path. Probably each four miles, on an average path, is spun out, by an infinite series of minor sinuosities, to five or six. Now, these deflections are not meaningless. Each has some history —

a history dating back perhaps a thousand years, but to which all clue has centuries ago been lost. The leading cause probably is fallen trees. When a tree falls across a path no man ever removes it. As in the case of the stone, the native goes round it. It is too green to burn in his hut; before it is dry and the white ants have eaten it, the new detour has become part and parcel of the path. The smaller irregularities, on the other hand, represent the trees and stumps of the primeval forest where the track was made at first. But whatever the cause, it is certain that for persistent straightforwardness in the general, and utter vacillation and irresolution in the particular, the African roads are unique in engineering.

Though one of the smaller African lakes, Shirwa is probably larger than all the lakes of Great Britain put together. With the splendid environment of mountains on three of its sides, softened and distanced by perpetual summer haze, it reminds one somewhat of the Great Salt Lake simmering in the July sun. We pitched our tent for a day or two on its western shore, among a harmless and surprised people who had never gazed on the pallid countenances of Englishmen before. Owing to the ravages of the slaver, the people of Shirwa are few, scattered, and poor, and live in abiding terror. The densest population is to be found on the small island, heavily timbered with baobabs, which forms a picturesque feature of the northern end. These Wa-Nyassa, or people of the lake, as they call themselves, have been driven away by fear, and they rarely leave their lake dwelling unless under cover of night. Even then they are liable to capture by any man of a stronger tribe who happens to meet them, and numbers who have been kidnapped in this way are to be found in the villages of neighboring chiefs. This is an amenity of existence in Africa that strikes one as very terrible. It is impossible for those at home to understand how literally savage man is a chattel, and how much his life is spent in the mere safeguarding of his main asset, *i. e.*, himself. There are actually districts in Africa where *three* natives cannot be sent on a message, in case two should combine and sell the third before they return.

WHITE ANTS

From ⟨Tropical Africa⟩

THE termite or white ant is a small insect, with a bloated, yellowish-white body, and a somewhat large thorax, oblong-shaped, and colored a disagreeable oily brown. The flabby, tallow-like body makes this insect sufficiently repulsive, but it is for quite another reason that the white ant is the worst abused of all living vermin in warm countries. The termite lives almost exclusively upon wood; and the moment a tree is cut or a log sawn for any economical purpose, this insect is upon its track. One may never see the insect, possibly, in the flesh, for it lives underground; but its ravages confront one at every turn. You build your house perhaps, and for a few months fancy you have pitched upon the one solitary site in the country where there are no white ants. But one day suddenly the door-post totters, and lintel and rafters come down together with a crash. You look at a section of the wrecked timbers, and discover that the whole inside is eaten clean away. The apparently solid logs of which the rest of the house is built are now mere cylinders of bark, and through the thickest of them you could push your little finger. Furniture, tables, chairs, chests of drawers, everything made of wood, is inevitably attacked, and in a single night a strong trunk is often riddled through and through, and turned into matchwood. There is no limit, in fact, to the depredation by these insects, and they will eat books, or leather, or cloth, or anything; and in many parts of Africa I believe if a man lay down to sleep with a wooden leg, it would be a heap of sawdust in the morning. So much feared is this insect now, that no one in certain parts of India and Africa ever attempts to travel with such a thing as a wooden trunk. On the Tanganyika plateau I have camped on ground which was as hard as adamant, and as innocent of white ants apparently as the pavement of St. Paul's; and wakened next morning to find a stout wooden box almost gnawed to pieces. Leather portmanteaus share the same fate, and the only substances which seem to defy the marauders are iron and tin.

But what has this to do with earth or with agriculture? The most important point in the work of the white ant remains to be

noted. I have already said that the white ant is never seen.
Why he should have such a repugnance to being looked at is at
first sight a mystery, seeing that he himself is stone blind. But
his coyness is really due to the desire for self-protection; for
the moment his juicy body shows itself above ground there are
a dozen enemies waiting to devour it. And yet the white ant
can never procure any food until it comes above ground. Nor
will it meet the case for the insect to come to the surface under
the shadow of night. Night in the tropics, so far as animal life
is concerned, is as the day. It is the great feeding-time, the
great fighting-time, the carnival of the carnivores, and of all
beasts, birds, and insects of prey, from the least to the greatest.
It is clear then that darkness is no protection to the white ant;
and yet without coming out of the ground it cannot live. How
does it solve the difficulty? It takes the ground out along with
it. I have seen white ants working on the top of a high tree,
and yet they were underground. They took up some of the
ground with them to the tree-top; just as the Esquimaux heap
up snow, building it into the low tunnel-huts in which they live,
so the white ants collect earth, only in this case not from the
surface, but from some depth underneath the ground, and plaster
it into tunneled ways. Occasionally these run along the ground,
but more often mount in endless ramifications to the top of trees,
meandering along every branch and twig, and here and there
debouching into large covered chambers which occupy half the
girth of the trunk. Millions of trees in some districts are thus
fantastically plastered over with tubes, galleries, and chambers of
earth, and many pounds' weight of subsoil must be brought up
for the mining of even a single tree. The building material is
conveyed by the insects up a central pipe with which all the
galleries communicate, and which at the downward end connects
with a series of subterranean passages leading deep into the
earth. The method of building the tunnels and covered ways is
as follows: At the foot of a tree the tiniest hole cautiously
opens in the ground close to the bark. A small head appears,
with a grain of earth clasped in its jaws. Against the tree
trunk this earth-grain is deposited, and the head is withdrawn.
Presently it reappears with another grain of earth; this is laid
beside the first, rammed tight against it, and again the builder
descends underground for more. The third grain is not placed
against the tree, but against the former grain; a fourth, a fifth,

and a sixth follow, and the plan of the foundation begins to suggest itself as soon as these are in position. The stones or grains or pellets of earth are arranged in a semicircular wall; the termite, now assisted by three or four others, standing in the middle between the sheltering wall and the tree, and working briskly with head and mandible to strengthen the position. The wall in fact forms a small moon-rampart, and as it grows higher and higher it soon becomes evident that it is going to grow from a low battlement into a long perpendicular tunnel running up the side of the tree. The workers, safely ensconced inside, are now carrying up the structure with great rapidity, disappearing in turn as soon as they have laid their stone, and rushing off to bring up another. The way in which the building is done is extremely curious, and one could watch the movement of these wonderful little masons by the hour. Each stone as it is brought to the top is first of all covered with mortar. Of course, without this the whole tunnel would crumble into dust before reaching the height of half an inch; but the termite pours over the stone a moist sticky secretion, turning the grain round and round with its mandibles until the whole is covered with slime. Then it places the stone with great care upon the top of the wall, works it about vigorously for a moment or two till it is well jammed into its place, and then starts off instantly for another load.

Peering over the growing wall, one soon discovers one, two, or more termites of a somewhat larger build, considerably longer, and with a very different arrangement of the parts of the head, and especially of the mandibles. These important-looking individuals saunter about the rampart in the most leisurely way, but yet with a certain air of business, as if perhaps the one was the master of works and the other the architect. But closer observation suggests that they are in no wise superintending operations, nor in any immediate way contributing to the structure, for they take not the slightest notice either of the workers or the works. They are posted there in fact as sentries; and there they stand, or promenade about, at the mouth of every tunnel, like Sister Anne, to see if anybody is coming. Sometimes somebody does come, in the shape of another ant; the real ant this time, not the defenseless *Neuropteron*, but some valiant and belted knight from the warlike *Formicidæ*. Singly or in troops, this rapacious little insect, fearless in its chitinous coat of mail, charges down the tree trunk, its antennæ waving defiance to the enemy and its cruel mandibles thirsting for termite blood. The worker white ant is a poor defenseless creature, and blind and unarmed, would fall an immediate prey to these well-drilled banditti, who forage about in every tropical forest in un-numbered legion. But at the critical moment, like Goliath from the Philistines, the soldier termite advances to the fight. With a few sweeps of its scythe-like jaws it clears the ground, and while the attacking party is carrying off its dead, the builders, unconscious of the fray, quietly continue their work. To every hundred workers in a white-ant colony, which numbers many thousands of individuals, there are perhaps two of these fighting men. The division of labor here is very wonderful; and the fact that besides these two specialized forms there are in every nest two other kinds of the same insect, the kings and queens, shows the remarkable height to which civilization in these communities has attained.

But where is this tunnel going to, and what object have the insects in view in ascending this lofty tree? Thirty feet from the ground, across innumerable forks, at the end of a long branch, are a few feet of dead wood. How the ants know it is there, how they know its sap has dried up, and that it is now fit for the termites' food, is a mystery. Possibly they do not know, and are only prospecting on the chance. The fact that they sometimes make straight for the decaying limb argues in these instances a kind of definite instinct; but on the other hand, the fact that in most cases the whole tree, in every branch and limb, is covered with termite tunnels, would show perhaps that they work most commonly on speculation, while the number of abandoned tunnels, ending on a sound branch in a *cul de sac*, proves how often they must suffer the usual disappointments of all such adventurers. The extent to which these insects carry on their tunneling is quite incredible, until one has seen it in nature with his own eyes. The tunnels are perhaps about the thickness of a small-sized gas-pipe, but there are junctions here and there of large dimensions, and occasionally patches of earth-work are found, embracing nearly the whole trunk for some feet. The outside of these tunnels, which are never quite straight, but wander irregularly along stem and branch, resembles in texture a coarse sandpaper; and the color, although this naturally varies with the soil, is usually a reddish brown. The quantity of earth and mud plastered over a single tree is often enormous; and

when one thinks that it is not only an isolated specimen here
and there that is frescoed in this way, but often all the trees of
a forest, some idea will be formed of the magnitude of the
operations of these insects, and the extent of their influence upon
the soil which they are thus ceaselessly transporting from under-
neath the ground.

In traveling through the great forests of the Rocky Mount-
ains or of the Western States, the broken branches and fallen
trunks, strewing the ground breast-high with all sorts of decay-
ing litter, frequently make locomotion impossible.   To attempt
to ride through these Western forests, with their meshwork of
interlocked branches and decaying trunks, is often out of the
question, and one has to dismount and drag his horse after him
as if he were clambering through a wood-yard.   But in an Afri-
can forest not a fallen branch is seen.   One is struck at first at
a certain clean look about the great forests of the interior, a
novel and unaccountable cleanness, as if the forest bed was care-
fully swept and dusted daily by unseen elves.   And so indeed
it is.   Scavengers of a hundred kinds remove decaying animal
matter, from the carcass of a fallen elephant to the broken wing
of a gnat; eating it, or carrying it out of sight and burying
it in the deodorizing earth.   And these countless millions of
termites perform a similar function for the vegetable world,
making away with all plants and trees, all stems, twigs, and
tissues, the moment the finger of decay strikes the signal.   Con-
stantly in these woods one comes across what appear to be sticks
and branches and bundles of fagots, but when closely examined
they are seen to be mere casts in mud.   From these hollow
tubes, which preserve the original form of the branch down to
the minutest knot or fork, the ligneous tissue is often entirely
removed, while others are met with in all stages of demolition.
There is the section of an actual specimen, which is not yet
completely destroyed, and from which the mode of attack may
be easily seen.   The insects start apparently from two centres.
One company attacks the inner bark, which is the favorite mor-
sel, leaving the coarse outer bark untouched, or more usually
replacing it with grains of earth, atom by atom, as they eat it
away.   The inner bark is gnawed off likewise as they go along,
but the woody tissue beneath is allowed to remain, to form a
protective sheath for the second company, who begin work at
the centre.   This second contingent eats its way outward and

onward, leaving a thin tube of the outer wood to the last, as
props to the mine, till they have finished the main excavation.
When a fallen trunk lying upon the ground is the object of
attack, the outer cylinder is frequently left quite intact, and it is
only when one tries to drag it off to his camp-fire that he finds
to his disgust that he is dealing with a mere hollow tube, a few
lines in thickness, filled up with mud.

But the works above ground represent only a part of the
labors of these slow-moving but most industrious of creatures.
The arboreal tubes are only the prolongation of a much more
elaborate system of subterranean tunnels, which extend over large
areas and mine the earth sometimes to a depth of many feet or
even yards.

The material excavated from these underground galleries and
from the succession of domed chambers — used as nurseries or
granaries — to which they lead, has to be thrown out upon the
surface.   And it is from these materials that the huge ant-hills
are reared, which form so distinctive a feature of the African
landscape. These heaps and mounds are so conspicuous that
they may be seen for miles, and so numerous are they and so
useful as cover to the sportsman, that without them in certain
districts hunting would be impossible.   The first things, indeed,
to strike the traveler in entering the interior are the mounds of
the white ant, now dotting the plain in groups like a small
cemetery, now rising into mounds, singly or in clusters, each
thirty or forty feet in diameter and ten or fifteen in height; or
again, standing out against the sky like obelisks, their bare sides
carved and fluted into all sorts of fantastic shapes.   In India
these ant-heaps seldom attain a height of more than a couple of
feet, but in Central Africa they form veritable hills, and contain
many tons of earth.   The brick houses of the Scotch mission-
station on Lake Nyassa have all been built out of a single ants'
nest, and the quarry from which the material has been derived
forms a pit beside the settlement some dozen feet in depth.   A
supply of bricks as large again could probably still be taken
from this convenient depot; and the missionaries on Lake Tan-
ganyika and onwards to Victoria Nyanza have been similarly
indebted to the labors of the termites.   In South Africa the
Zulus and Kaffirs pave all their huts with white-ant earth; and
during the Boer war our troops in Pretoria, by scooping out the
interior from the smaller beehive-shaped ant-heaps and covering

the top with clay, constantly used them as ovens.   These ant-heaps may be said to abound over the whole interior of Africa, and there are several distinct species.   The most peculiar, as well as the most ornate, is a small variety from one to two feet in height, which occurs in myriads along the shores of Lake Tanganyika.   It is built in symmetrical tiers, and resembles a pile of small rounded hats, one above another, the rims depending like eaves, and sheltering the body of the hill from rain. To estimate the amount of earth per acre raised from the water-line of the subsoil by white ants, would not in some districts be an impossible task; and it would be found probably that the quantity at least equaled that manipulated annually in temperate regions by the earthworm.

These mounds, however, are more than mere waste-heaps. Like the corresponding region underground, they are built into a meshwork of tunnels, galleries, and chambers, where the social interests of the community are attended to.   The most spacious of these chambers, usually far underground, is very properly allocated to the head of the society, the queen.   The queen termite is a very rare insect, and as there are seldom more than one or at most two to a colony, and as the royal apartments are hidden far in the earth, few persons have ever seen a queen; and indeed most, if they did happen to come across it, from its very singular appearance would refuse to believe that it had any connection with white ants.   It possesses indeed the true termite head, but there the resemblance to the other members of the family stops; for the size of the head bears about the same proportion to the rest of the body as does the tuft on his Glengarry bonnet to a six-foot Highlander.   The phenomenal corpulence of the royal body in the case of the queen termite is possibly due in part to want of exercise; for once seated upon her throne, she never stirs to the end of her days.   She lies there, a large, loathsome, cylindrical package, two or three inches long, in shape like a sausage, and as white as a bolster.   Her one duty in life is to lay eggs; and it must be confessed she discharges her function with complete success, for in a single day her progeny often amounts to many thousands, and for months this enormous fecundity never slackens. The body increases slowly in size, and through the transparent skin the long folded ovary may be seen, with the eggs, impelled by a peristaltic motion, passing onward for delivery to the workers, who are waiting to carry them to the nurseries, where they are hatched. Assiduous attention meantime is paid to the queen by other workers, who feed her diligently, with much self-denial stuffing her with morsel after morsel from their own jaws. A guard of honor in the shape of a few of the larger soldier ants is also in attendance, as a last and almost unnecessary precaution. In addition finally to the soldiers, workers, and queen, the royal chamber has also one other inmate — the king. He is a very ordinary-looking insect, about the same size as the soldiers, but the arrangement of the parts of the head and body is widely different, and like the queen he is furnished with eyes.

WILLIAM DRUMMOND OF HAWTHORNDEN

(1585–1649)

T SEEMS to be the mission of many writers to illuminate contemporary literature and so to light the way for future students, rather than to make any vital contribution to the achievement of their time. Such writers reflect the culture of their own day and represent its ideals; and although their creative work may be slight, their loss to literature would be serious. Among these lesser men stands that sincere poet, Drummond of Hawthornden. In Scotland under the Stuarts, when the vital energy of the land was concentrated upon politics and theology, native literature was reduced to a mere reflection of the pre-Spenserian classicism of England. Into this waste of correct mediocrity entered the poetry of William Drummond, an avowed and enthusiastic follower of the Elizabethan school, a finished scholar, one of the typical Scottish gentlemen who were then making Scottish history. Courtier and trifler though he was, however, he showed himself so true a poet of nature that his felicities of phrase seem to anticipate the sensuous realism of Keats and his successors.

WILLIAM DRUMMOND

William Drummond, born in 1585, was a cadet of the historic house which in 1357 gave in marriage to King Robert III. the beautiful Annabella Drummond, who was destined to become the ancestress of the royal Stuarts of Scotland and England. In his own day the family, whose head was the Earl of Perth, was powerful in Scottish affairs, and the history of the clan Drummond would be largely a history of the events which led to the Protectorate. Throughout the storm and stress that preceded the civil war Drummond was a loyalist, though at one time he appeared to be identified with the Covenanters. His literary influence, which was considerable, was always thrown on the side of the King, while the term « Drummondism » was a popular synonym for the conservative policy. Throughout the struggle, however, Drummond seems to have been forced into activity by circumstances rather than by choice. He had the instincts of a recluse and a scholar. He delighted in the society

of literary men, and he was much engrossed in philosophical specu-
lations.

In spite of the difficulties of distance, he managed to keep abreast
of the thought of literary London, the London of Drayton and Web-
ster, of Beaumont, Fletcher, Massinger, and Ford.   His chief satisfac-
tion was to know that his own work was not unacceptable to this
brilliant group, and one of the great pleasures of his life was a visit
from Ben Jonson, who, making a walking tour to Scotland, found at
Hawthornden that congenial hospitality in which his soul delighted.
Of this famous visit, as of other important events, Drummond kept a
record, in which he set down his guest's behavior, opinions, and con-
fidential sayings.   Warmly as he admired Jonson's genius, he found
his personality oppressive, and intrusted his criticisms to his diary.
When this was published, more than a century later, the gentle Scot
was accused of bad taste, breach of confidence, and disloyalty to
friendship.   But his defense lies in the fact that the book was meant
for no eyes but his own, and that the intimacy and candor of its
revelations were intended to preserve his recollections of a memorable
experience.

If his environment was not entirely favorable to literary excel-
lences, it is yet very likely that Drummond developed the full meas-
ure of his gift.   He expressed the spirit of the more imaginative
generation which succeeded a hard and fettered predecessor, and it
is for this that literature owes him its peculiar debt.

His career began in his twenty-ninth year with the publication of
an elegy on the death of Henry, Prince of Wales, eldest son of James I.
This poem, under the title 'Tears on the Death of Mœliades,' ap-
peared in 1613, and reached a third edition within a twelvemonth.
Its two hundred lines show the finished versification of the scholar,
with much poetic grace.   It was a product of the Spenserian school,
and emphasized the fact that the representative literature of the land
had abandoned the Scottish dialect for English forms.   Drummond's
second volume of poems commemorated the death of his wife and his
love of her.   It is in this work that the ultimate mood of the poet
appears.   Much beauty of form, a delightful sensitiveness to nature, a
luxuriance of color, and a finely tempered thoughtfulness pervade the
poems.   His next production, celebrating the visit of James I. to his
native land, was entitled 'Forth Feasting,' and represented the
Forth and all its borders as rejoicing in the presence of their King.
To the reader of to-day the panegyric sounds fulsome and the poetry
stilted, and the once famous book has now merely an archaic interest.

Drummond's reputation is based upon the 'Poems,' and upon the
Jeremy-Taylor-like 'Cypress Grove,' published in 1623 in connection
with the religious verses called 'Flowers of Sion.'   'Cypress Grove'

is an essay on death, akin in spirit to the religious temper of the Middle Ages, and in philosophic breadth to the diviner mood of Plato. Only a mind of a high order would have conceived so beautiful and lofty a meditation on the Final Mystery. This brief essay marks the utmost reach of Drummond's mind, and shows the strength of that serene spirituality, which could thus hold its way undisturbed by the sectarian bitterness that fixed a great gulf between England and Scotland. 'The History of the Five Jameses,' which Drummond was ten years in compiling and which was not published until six years after his death, added nothing to his reputation. It lacked alike the diligent minuteness of the chronicler and the broader view of the historian. Many minor papers on the state of religion and politics, chief of which is the political tract 'Irene,' show Drummond's aggressive interest in contemporary affairs. It is not generally known that this gentle scholar was also an inventor of military engines. In 1626 Charles I. engaged him to produce sixteen machines and "not a few inventions besides." The biographers have remained curiously ignorant of this phase of his activity, but the State papers show that the King named him "our faithful subject, William Drummond of Hawthornden." He died in 1649, his death being hastened, it was said, by his passion of grief over the martyrdom of King Charles.

SEXTAIN

THE heaven doth not contain so many stars,
    So many leaves not prostrate lie in woods
When autumn's old and Borcas sounds his wars,
    So many waves have not the ocean floods,
As my rent mind hath torments all the night,
And heart spends sighs when Phœbus brings the light.

Why should I have been partner of the light,
    Who, crost in birth by bad aspéct of stars,
Have never since had happy day or night?
Why was not I a liver in the woods,
Or citizen of Thetis's crystal floods,
    Than made a man, for love and fortune's wars?

I look each day when death should end the wars,
    Uncivil wars, 'twixt sense and reason's light;
        My pains I count to mountains, meads, and floods,
And of my sorrow partners make the stars;
        All desolate I haunt the fearful woods,
    When I should give myself to rest at night.

With watchful eyes I ne'er behold the night,
　　Mother of peace, but ah! to me of wars,
　　　　And Cynthia, queen-like, shining through the woods,
When straight those lamps come in my thought, whose light
　　My judgment dazzled, passing brightest stars,
　　　　And then mine eyes en-isle themselves with floods.

Turn to their springs again first shall the floods,
　　Clear shall the sun the sad and gloomy night,
　　　　To dance about the pole cease shall the stars,
　　　　The elements renew their ancient wars
　　Shall first, and be deprived of place and light,
E'er I find rest in city, fields, or woods.

End these my days, indwellers of the woods,
Take this my life, ye deep and raging floods;
Sun, never rise to clear me with thy light,
Horror and darkness, keep a lasting night;
Consume me, care, with thy intestine wars,
And stay your influence o'er me, bright stars!

In vain the stars, indwellers of the woods,
Care, horror, wars, I call, and raging floods,
　　For all have sworn no night shall dim my sight.

MADRIGAL

This world a-hunting is,
　　The prey poor man, the Nimrod
　　　　fierce is Death;
His speedy greyhounds are
Lust, sickness, envy, care,
　　Strife that ne'er falls amiss,
With all those ills which haunt us while we breathe.
　　Now if by chance we fly
　　Of these the eager chase,
　　Old age with stealing pace
Casts up his nets, and there we panting die.

REASON AND FEELING

I KNOW that all beneath the moon decays,
   And what by mortals in this world is brought,
   In Time's great periods shall return to naught;
That fairest States have fatal nights and days.
I know that all the Muse's heavenly lays,
   With toil of sp'rit, which are so dearly bought,
   As idle sounds, of few or none are sought,—
That there is nothing lighter than vain praise.
   I know frail beauty like the purple flower,
To which one morn oft birth and death affords;
That love a jarring is of minds' accords,
   Where sense and will envassal Reason's power:
Know what I list, all this cannot me move,
But that, alas! I both must write and love.

DEGENERACY OF THE WORLD

WHAT hapless hap had I for to be born
   In these unhappy times, and dying days
   Of this now doting World, when Good decays,
Love's quite extinct, and Virtue's held a-scorn!
   When such are only prized, by wretched ways,
Who with a golden fleece them can adorn;
   When avarice and lust are counted praise,
And bravest minds live orphan-like forlorn!
Why was not I born in that golden age
   When gold was not yet known? and those black arts
   By which base worldlings vilely play their parts,
With horrid acts staining Earth's stately stage?
To have been then, O Heaven! 't had been my bliss;
But bless me now, and take me soon from this.

THE BRIEFNESS OF LIFE

LOOK, how the flower which ling'ringly doth fade,
   The morning's darling late, the summer's queen,
   Spoiled of that juice which kept it fresh and green,
As high as it did raise, bows low the head:
Right so my life, contentment being dead,
   Or in their contraries but only seen,

With swifter speed declines than erst it spread,
    And, blasted, scarce now shows what it hath been.
As doth the pilgrim, therefore, whom the night
    By darkness would imprison on his way,—
Think on thy home, my soul, and think aright,
    Of what's yet left thee of life's wasting day;
Thy sun posts westward, passèd is thy morn,
And twice it is not given thee to be born.

THE UNIVERSE

OF THIS fair volume which we World do name,
    If we the leaves and sheets could turn with care —
Of Him who it corrects and did it frame
    We clear might read the art and wisdom rare,
Find out his power, which wildest powers doth tame,
    His providence, extending everywhere,
    His justice, which proud rebels doth not spare,
In every page and period of the same.
But silly we, like foolish children, rest
    Well pleased with colored vellum, leaves of gold,
Fair dangling ribands, leaving what is best;
    On the great Writer's sense ne'er taking hold;
Or if by chance we stay our minds on aught,
It is some picture on the margin wrought.

ON DEATH

From 'Cypress Grove'

DEATH is a piece of the order of this all, a part of the life of this world; for while the world is the world, some creatures must die and others take life. Eternal things are raised far above this orb of generation and corruption where the First Matter, like a still flowing and ebbing sea, with diverse waves but the same water, keepeth a restless and never tiring current; what is below in the universality of its kind doth not in itself abide. . . . If thou dost complain there shall be a time in the which thou shalt not be, why dost thou not too grieve that there was a time in which thou wast not, and so that thou art not as old as the enlivening planet of Time? . . . The excellent fabric of the universe itself shall one day suffer ruin, or change like ruin, and poor earthlings, thus to be handled, complain!

JOHN DRYDEN.

JOHN DRYDEN

(1631–1700)

BY THOMAS R. LOUNSBURY

OHN DRYDEN, the foremost man of letters of the period following the Restoration, was born at Aldwinkle, a village of Northamptonshire, on August 9th, 1631. He died May 1st, 1700. His life was therefore coeval with the closing period of the fierce controversies which culminated in the civil war and the triumph of the Parliamentary party; that, in turn, to be followed successively by the iron rule of Cromwell, by the restoration of the exiled Stuarts, and the reactionary tendencies in politics that accompanied that event; and finally with the effectual exclusion from the throne of this same family by the revolution of 1688, leaving behind, however, to their successors a smoldering Jacobite hostility that perpetually plotted the overthrow of the new government and later broke out twice into open revolt. All these changes of fortune, with their changes of opinion, are faithfully reflected in the productions of Dryden. To understand him thoroughly requires therefore an intimate familiarity with the civil and religious movements which characterize the whole period. Equally also do his writings, both creative and critical, represent the revolution of literary taste that took place in the latter half of the seventeenth century. It was while he was in the midst of his intellectual activity that French canons of criticism became largely the accepted rules, by which the value of English productions was tested. This was especially true of the drama. The study of Dryden is accordingly a study of the political and literary history of his times to an extent that is correspondingly true of no other English author before or since.

His family, both on the father's and the mother's side, was in full sympathy with the party opposed to the court. The son was educated at Westminster, then under the mastership of Richard Busby, whose relentless use of the rod has made his name famous in that long line of flagellants who have been at the head of the great English public schools. From Westminster he went to Trinity College, Cambridge. There he received the degree of A. B. in January 1654. Later in that same decade — the precise date is not known — he took up his residence in London; and in London the rest of his life was almost entirely spent.

Dryden's first published literary effort appeared in a little volume made up of thirty-three elegies, by various authors, on the death of a youth of great promise who had been educated at Westminster. This was Lord Hastings, the eldest son of the Earl of Huntingdon. He had died of the small-pox. Dryden's contribution was written in 1649, and consisted of but little over a hundred lines. No one expects great verse from a boy of eighteen; but the most extravagant anticipations of sorry performance will fail to come up to the reality of the wretchedness which was here attained. It was in words like these that the future laureate bewailed the death of the young nobleman and depicted the disease of which he died:—

> «Was there no milder way but the small-pox,
> The very filthiness of Pandora's box?
> So many spots, like næves, our Venus soil?
> One jewel set off with so many a foil?
> Blisters with pride swelled, which through his flesh did sprout
> Like rosebuds, stuck in the lily-skin about.
> Each little pimple had a tear in it,
> To wail the fault its rising did commit;
> Which, rebel-like, with its own lord at strife,
> Thus made an insurrection 'gainst his life.
> Or were these gems sent to adorn his skin,
> The cabinet of a richer soul within?
> No comet need foretell his change drew on,
> Whose corps might seem a constellation.»

Criticism cannot be rendered sufficiently vituperative to characterize properly such a passage. It is fuller of conceits than ever Cowley crowded into the same space; and lines more crabbed and inharmonious Donne never succeeded in perpetrating. Its production upsets all principles of prophecy. The wretchedest of poetasters can take courage, when he contemplates the profundity of the depth out of which uprose the greatest poet of his time.

Dryden is, in fact, an example of that somewhat rare class of writers who steadily improve with advancing years. Most poets write their best verse before middle life. Many of them after that time go through a period of decline, and sometimes of rapid decline; and if they live to reach old age, they add to the quantity of their production without sensibly increasing its value. This general truth is conspicuously untrue of Dryden. His first work gave no promise of his future excellence, and it was by very slow degrees that he attained to the mastery of his art. But the older he grew, the better he wrote; and the volume published a few months before his death, and largely composed almost under its shadow, so far from showing the slightest sign of failing power, contains a great deal of the best poetry he ever produced.

As Dryden's relatives were Puritans, and some of them held place under the government, it was natural that upon coming to London he should attach himself to that party. Accordingly it is no surprise to find him duly mourning the death of the great Protector in certain 'Heroic Stanzas Consecrated to the Memory of Oliver Cromwell.' The first edition bears the date of 1659, and so far as we know, the production was Dryden's second venture in poetry. It was written in the measure of Davenant's 'Gondibert,' and is by no means a poor piece of work, though it has been sometimes so styled. It certainly pays not simply a high but a discerning tribute to the genius of Cromwell. Before two years had gone by, we find its author greeting the return of Charles with effusive loyalty, and with predictions of prosperity and honor to attend his reign, which events were soon woefully to belie. The poet has been severely censured for this change of attitude. It is a censure which might be bestowed with as much propriety upon the whole population of England. The joyful expectations to which he gave utterance were almost universal; and no other charge can well be brought against him than that he had the ability and took the occasion to express sentiments which were felt by nearly the entire nation.

From this time on, Dryden appears more and more in the public eye, and slowly but steadily forged his way to the front as the representative man of letters of his time. In 1670 he was appointed to the two distinct offices of poet laureate and historiographer royal. Thenceforward his relations with the court became close, and so they did not cease to be until the expulsion of James II. In 1683 he received a further mark of royal favor, in being made collector of customs of the port of London. In the political controversies which subsequently arose, Dryden's writings faithfully represented the sentiments of the side he had chosen, and expressed their prejudices and aversions not merely with force but also with virulence. His first literary activity, however, was on neutral ground. After eighteen years of compulsory closing, the Restoration opened wide once more the doors of the theatre. Dryden, like every one else possessed of literary ability, began to write for the stage. His first play, a comedy entitled 'The Wild Gallant,' was brought out in February 1663; and for the eighteen years following, it was compositions of such nature that occupied the main portion of his literary life. During that time he produced wholly or in part twenty-two comedies and tragedies. His pieces must from the outset have met with a fair degree of success, otherwise the King's Company would not have entered into a contract with him, as it did in 1667, to furnish for them each year a fixed number of plays, in consideration of his receiving a certain share of the profits of the theatre.

Yet it cannot be said that Dryden was in any respect a dramatist of a high order. As a writer of comedy he was not only inferior to contemporaries and immediate successors like Wycherley, Congreve, Vanbrugh, and Farquhar, but in certain ways he was surpassed by Shadwell, the very man whom he himself has consigned to a disagreeable immortality as the hero of the 'MacFlecknoe.' His comedies are not merely full of obscenity,— which seems to have been a necessary ingredient to suit them to the taste of the age,— but they are full of a peculiarly disagreeable obscenity. One of his worst offenses in this direction, and altogether his most impudent one, was his adaptation for the stage of Shakespeare's 'Tempest.' The two plays are worth reading together for the sake of seeing how easily a pure and perfect creation of genius can be vulgarized in language and spirit almost beyond the possibility of recognition. In his tragedies, however, Dryden was much more successful. Yet even these, in spite of the excellence of occasional passages, do not attain to a high rank. Indeed, thought and expression are at times extravagant, not to say stilted, to an extent which afterward led him himself to make them the subject of ridicule. It was in them, however, during these years that he perfected by degrees his mastery of heroic verse, of which later he was to display the capabilities in a way that had never previously been seen and has never since been surpassed.

A controversy in regard to the proper method of composing plays brought forward Dryden, at an early period in his literary career, as a writer of prose. In this he at once attained unusual eminence. In him appear for the first time united the two characters of poet and of critic. Ben Jonson had in a measure preceded him in this respect; but Jonson's criticism was not so much devoted to the examination of general principles as to the exposure of the hopeless, helpless obtuseness of the men who had a different opinion of his works from what he himself entertained. The questions discussed by Dryden were of a more general nature. With the Stuarts had come in French literary tastes and French literary methods. The age was supposed to be too refined to be pleased with what had satisfied the coarse palates of preceding generations. In stage-writing in particular, the doctrine of the unities, almost uniformly violated by Shakespeare and most of the Elizabethans, was now held up as the only correct method of composition that could be employed by any writer who sought to conform to the true principles of art. Along with this came the substitution in the drama of rhyme for blank verse. Upon the comparative merits of these two as employed in tragedy, arose the first controversy in which Dryden was engaged. This one was with his brother-in-law, Sir Robert Howard; for in 1663 Dryden had become the husband of the daughter of the Earl of Berkshire, thus marrying, as Pope expressed it, "misery in a noble wife." Dryden was an advocate of rhyme; and the controversy on this point began with the publication in 1668 of his 'Essay of Dramatic Poesy.' It was afterward carried on by both parties, in prefaces to the plays they successively published. The prefaces to these productions regularly became later the place where Dryden laid down his critical doctrines on all points that engaged his attention; and whether we agree with his views or not, we are always sure to be charmed with the manner in which they are expressed.

In 1667 Dryden published a long poem entitled 'Annus Mirabilis.' It was in the same measure as the stanzas on Oliver Cromwell. It gave him a good deal of reputation at the time; but though it is far from being a despicable performance, few there are now who read it and still fewer who re-read it. Far different has been the fate of his next work. It was not until 1681, when England was beginning to emerge slowly from the excitement and agitation growing out of the alleged Popish plot, that he brought out his 'Absalom and Achitophel,' without question the greatest combined poetical and political satire to be found in our tongue. Here it was that for the first time he fully displayed his mastery over heroic verse. The notion once so widely prevalent — for the vogue of which, indeed, Dryden himself is mainly responsible — that Waller and Denham brought this verse to perfection, it now requires both extensive and special ignorance of our earlier authors to entertain; but on the other hand, there is no question that he himself imparted to the line a variety, vigor, and sustained majesty of movement such as the verse in its modern form had never previously received. There is therefore a fairly full measure of truth in the lines in which he was characterized by Pope: —

> "Waller was smooth; but Dryden taught to join
> The varying verse, the full resounding line,
> The long majestic march and energy divine."

These lines of Pope, it may be added, exemplify purposely two peculiarities of Dryden's versification, — the occasional use of the triplet instead of the regular couplet, and of the Alexandrine, or line of six feet, in place of the usual line of five.

The poem is largely an attack upon the Earl of Shaftesbury, who in it bears the title of Achitophel. The portrayal of this statesman, which is given in this volume, is ample evidence of that skill of the poet in characterization which has made the pictures he drew immortal. Perhaps even more effective was the description of the

Duke of Buckingham, under the designation of Zimri. For attacking
that nobleman Dryden had both political and personal reasons. Buck-
ingham had now joined the opponents of the court. Ten years previ-
ously the poet himself had been brought by him on the stage, with
the aid of others, in the play called 'The Rehearsal.' His usual
actions had been mimicked, his usual expressions had been put into
the mouth of the character created to represent him, who was styled
Bayes. This title had been given him because Dryden figuratively
wore the bays, or laurel, as poet laureate. The name henceforward
stuck. Dryden's turn had now come; and it was in these following
lines that he drew the unfaded and fadeless picture of this noble-
man, whose reputation even then was notorious rather than famous,
and whose intellect was motley-minded rather than versatile:—

> « Some of their chiefs were princes of the land;
> In the front rank of these did Zimri stand,
> A man so various that he seemed to be
> Not one, but all mankind's epitome:
> Stiff in opinions, always in the wrong,
> Was everything by starts and nothing long,
> But in the course of one revolving moon
> Was chymist, fiddler, statesman, and buffoon;
> Then all for women, painting, rhyming, drinking,
> Besides ten thousand freaks that died in thinking.
> Blest madman, who could every hour employ
> With something new to wish or to enjoy!
> Railing and praising were his usual themes,
> And both, to show his judgment, in extremes:
> So over-violent or over-civil
> That every man with him was God or Devil.
> In squandering wealth was his peculiar art:
> Nothing went unrewarded but desert.
> Beggared by fools whom still he found too late,
> He had his jest, and they had his estate. »

As an example of the loftier and more majestic style occasionally
found in this poem, is the powerful appeal of Achitophel to Absalom.
The latter, it is to be said, stands for the Duke of Monmouth, the
eldest of the illegitimate sons of Charles II. Him many of the so-
called country party, now beginning to be styled Whigs, were
endeavoring to have recognized as the next successor to the throne,
in place of the Roman Catholic brother of the king, James, Duke of
York. As a favorite son of the monarch, he, though then in opposi-
tion, is treated tenderly by Dryden throughout; and this feeling is
plainly visible in the opening of the address to him put into the
mouth of Achitophel, in these words:—

«Auspicious prince, at whose nativity
  Some royal planet ruled the southern sky,
  Thy longing country's darling and desire,
  Their cloudy pillar and their guardian fire,
  Their second Moses, whose extended wand
  Divides the seas and shows the promised land,
  Whose dawning day in every distant age
  Has exercised the sacred prophet's rage,
  The people's prayer, the glad diviner's theme,
  The young men's vision and the old men's dream,—
  Thee savior, thee the nation's vows confess,
  And never satisfied with seeing, bless.»

Dryden followed up the attack upon Shaftesbury with a poem en-
titled 'The Medal.' This satire, which appeared in March 1682, was
called forth by the action of the partisans of the Whig leader in hav-
ing a medal struck commemorating his release from the Tower, after
the grand jury had thrown out the charge of treason which had been
brought against him. Both of these pieces were followed by a host
of replies. Some of them did not refrain from personal attack, which
indeed had a certain justification in the poet's own violence of denun-
ciation. The most abusive of these was a poem by Thomas Shadwell,
entitled 'The Medal of John Bayes.' Such persons as fancy Dryden's
subsequent punishment of that dramatist unwarranted in its severity
should in justice read this ferociously scurrilous diatribe, in which
every charge against the poet that malice or envy had concocted and
rumor had set afloat, was here industriously raked together; and to
the muck-heap thus collected, the intimacy of previous acquaintance
was doubtless enabled to contribute its due quota of malignant asser-
tion and more malignant insinuation. Shadwell was soon supplied,
however, with ample reason to regret his action. Dryden's first and
best known rejoinder is 'MacFlecknoe, or a Satire on the True Blue
Protestant Poet T. S.' This production has always had the reputation
in literature of being the severest personal satire in the language;
but it requires now for its appreciation an intimate acquaintance
with Shadwell's plays, which very few possess. It is further disfig-
ured in places by a coarseness from which, indeed, none of the poet's
writings were certain to be free. Its general spirit can be indicated
by a brief extract from its opening paragraph. Flecknoe, it is to be
said, was a feeble poet who had died a few years before. He is
here represented as having long reigned over the kingdom of dullness,
but knowing that his end was close at hand, determines to settle the
succession to the State. Accordingly he fixes upon his son Shadwell
as the one best fitted to take his place in ruling over the realm of
nonsense, and in continuing the war with wit and sense. The an-
nouncement of his intention he begins in the following words:—

> « — 'Tis resolved, for Nature pleads that he
> Should only rule who most resembles me.
> Shadwell alone my perfect image bears,
> Mature in dullness from his tender years;
> Shadwell alone of all my sons is he
> Who stands confirmed in full stupidity.
> The rest to some faint meaning make pretense,
> But Shadwell never deviates into sense.»

Far more bitter, however, was the renewed attack which a month later Dryden inserted in the two hundred lines he contributed to the continuation of 'Absalom and Achitophel' that was written by Nahum Tate. In this second part, which came out in November 1682, he devoted himself in particular to two of his opponents, Settle and Shadwell, under the names respectively of Doeg and Og — "two fools," he says, in his energetic way, —

> «That crutch their feeble sense on verse;
> Who by my Muse to all succeeding times
> Shall live in spite of their own doggerel rhymes.»

Of Settle, whose poetry was possessed of much smoothness but little sense, he spoke in a tone of contemptuous good-nature, though the object of the attack must certainly have deemed the tender mercies of Dryden to be cruel. It was in this way he was described, to quote a few lines: —

> «Spiteful he is not, though he wrote a satire,
> For still there goes some thinking to ill-nature.
>
> .   .   .   .
>
> Let him be gallows-free by my consent,
> And nothing suffer, since he nothing meant;
> Hanging supposes human soul and reason, —
> This animal's below committing treason:
> Shall he be hanged who never could rebel?
> That's a preferment for Achitophel.
>
> .   .   .   .
>
> Let him rail on; let his invective Muse
> Have four-and-twenty letters to abuse,
> Which if he jumbles to one line of sense,
> Indict him of a capital offense.»

But it was not till he came to the portraiture of Shadwell that he gave full vent to the ferocity of his satire. He taunted him with the unwieldiness of his bulk, the grossness of his habits, with his want of wealth, and finally closed up with some lines into which he concentrated all the venom of his previous attacks: —

> «But though Heaven made him poor, with reverence speaking,
> He never was a poet of God's making;

The midwife laid her hand on his thick skull,
With this prophetic blessing — *Be thou dull;*
Drink, swear, and roar, forbear no lewd delight
Fit for thy bulk; do anything but write.
Thou art of lasting make, like thoughtless men;
A strong nativity — but for the pen;
Eat opium, mingle arsenic in thy drink,
Still thou mayest live, avoiding pen and ink.
I see, I see, 'tis counsel given in vain,
For treason, botched in rhyme, will be thy bane;
Rhyme is the rock on which thou art to wreck;
'Tis fatal to thy fame and to thy neck.

«A double noose thou on thy neck dost pull,
For writing treason and for writing dull;
To die for faction is a common evil,
But to be hanged for nonsense is the devil.
Hadst thou the glories of thy King exprest,
Thy praises had been satires at the best;
But thou in clumsy verse, unlicked, unpointed,
Hast shamefully defied the Lord's anointed.
I will not rake the dunghill of thy crimes,
For who would read thy life that reads thy rhymes?
But of King David's foes be this the doom,—
May all be like the young man Absalom;
And for my foes may this their blessing be,—
To talk like Doeg and to write like thee.»

Refinement of tone is not the distinguishing characteristic of satire of this sort. It does not attack its object by delicate insinuation or remote suggestion. It operates by heavy downright blows which crush by the mere weight and power of the stroke. There was in truth in those days a certain brutality not only permitted but expected in the way men spoke of each other, and Dryden conformed in this as in other respects to the manners and methods of his age. But of its kind the attack is perfect. The blows of a bludgeon which make of the victim a shapeless mass kill as effectively as the steel or poison which leaves every feature undisturbed, and to the common apprehension it serves to render the killing more manifest. At any rate, so long as a person has been done to death, it makes comparatively little difference how the death was brought about; and the object in this instance of Dryden's attack, though a man of no mean abilities, has never recovered from the demolition which his reputation then underwent.

In 1685 Charles II. died, and his brother James ascended the throne. In the following year Dryden went over to the Roman Catholic Church. No act of his life has met with severer censure. Nor can there be any doubt that the time he took to change his religion afforded ground for distrusting the sincerity of his motives. A king was on the throne who was straining every nerve to bring the Church of England once more under the sway of the Church of Rome. Obviously the adoption of the latter faith would recommend the poet to the favor of the bigoted monarch, and tend to advance his personal interests. There is no wonder, therefore, that he should at the time have been accused of being actuated by the unworthiest of reasons, and that the charge should continue to be repeated to our day. Yet a close study of Dryden's life and writings indicates that the step he took was a natural if not an inevitable outcome of the processes through which his opinions had been passing. He had been early trained in the strict tenets of the Puritan party. From these he had been carried over to the loose beliefs and looser life that followed everywhere hard upon the Restoration. By the sentiments then prevailing he was profoundly affected. Nothing in the writings of the first half of his literary life is more marked — not even his flings at matrimony — than the scoffing way in which he usually spoke of the clergy. His tone towards them is almost always contemptuous, where it is not positively vituperative. His famous political satire began with this line —

"In pious times, ere priestcraft did begin;" —

and a little later in the course of the same poem he observed that —

"Fraud was used, the sacrificer's trade,"

the "sacrificer" here denoting the priest. This feeling toward the clergy never in truth deserted him entirely. But no one who reads carefully his 'Religio Laici,' a poem published in 1682, can fail to perceive that even then he had not only drifted far away from the faith of his childhood, but had begun to be tormented and perplexed by the insoluble problems connected with the life and destiny of man, and with his relations to his Creator. The subject was not likely to weigh less heavily upon him in the years that followed. To Dryden, as to many before and since, it may have seemed the easiest method of deliverance from the difficulties in which he found himself involved, to cast the burden of doubts which disquieted the mind and depressed the heart, upon a Church that undertakes to assume the whole responsibility for the man's future on condition of his yielding to it an unquestioning faith in the present.

An immediate result of his conversion was the production in 1687 of one of his most deservedly famous poems, 'The Hind and the Panther.' He began it with the idea of assisting in bringing about the reconciliation between the Panther, typifying the Church of England, and the Hind, typifying the Church of Rome. It is apparent

that before he finished it he saw that the project was hopeless. It is
a poem of over twenty-five hundred lines, of which the opening up to
line 150 is printed in this volume. Part of the passage here cited
contains, without professing it as an object, and probably without
intending it, the best defense that could be made for his change of
religion. The production in its entirety is remarkable for the skill
which its author displayed in carrying on an argument in verse. In
this he certainly had no superior among poets, perhaps no equal.
The work naturally created a great sensation in those days of fierce
political and religious controversy. Both it and its writer were made
the object of constant attack. A criticism, in particular, appeared
upon it in the shape of a dialogue in prose with snatches of verse
interspersed. It is usually known by the title of 'The Town Mouse
and the Country Mouse,' and was exalted at the time by unrea-
soning partisanship into a wonderful performance. Even to the pres-
ent day, this dreary specimen of polemics is described as a very
witty work by those who have never struggled to read it. It was
the production of Charles Montagu, the future Earl of Halifax, and
of Matthew Prior. A story too is still constantly repeated that Dry-
den was much hurt by the attacks of these two young men, to whom
he had been kind, and wept over their ingratitude. If he shed any
tears at all upon the occasion, they must have been due to the morti-
fication he felt that any two persons who had been admitted to his
friendship should have been guilty of twaddle so desperately tedious.

The flight of James and the accession of William and Mary threw
Dryden at once out of the favor of the court, upon which to a large
extent he had long depended for support. As a Jacobite he could
not take the oath of allegiance; but there is hardly any doubt that
under any circumstances he would have been deprived of the offices
of place and profit he held. In the laureateship he was succeeded by
his old antagonist Shadwell; and within a few years he saw the
dignity of the position still further degraded by the appointment to
it of Nahum Tate, one of the worst of the long procession of poetas-
ters who have filled it. Dryden henceforth belonged to the party out
of power. His feelings about his changed relations are shown plainly
in the fine epistle with which he consoled Congreve for the failure
of his comedy of the 'Double Dealer.' Yet displaced and unpen-
sioned, and sometimes the object of hostile attack, his literary su-
premacy was more absolute than ever. All young authors, whether
Whigs or Tories, sought his society and courted his favor; and his
seat at Will's coffee-house was the throne from which he swayed the
literary sceptre of England.

After the revolution of 1688 Dryden gave himself entirely up to
authorship. He first turned to the stage; and between 1690 and 1694

he produced five plays. With the failure in the last-mentioned year
of his tragi-comedy called 'Love Triumphant,' he abandoned writing
for the theatre. The period immediately following he devoted mainly
to his translation of Virgil, which was published in 1697. It was
highly successful; but far more reputation came to him from a large
folio volume that was brought out in November 1699, under the title
of 'Fables.' Its contents consisted mainly of poetical narratives
founded upon certain stories of the 'Decameron,' and of the modern-
ization of some of the 'Canterbury Tales.' In certain ways these have
been his most successful pieces, and have made his name familiar to
successive generations of readers. Of the tales from Boccaccio, that
of 'Cymon and Iphigenia' is on the whole the most pleasing. The
modernizations of Chaucer were long regarded as superior to the
original; and though superior knowledge of the original has effect-
ually banished that belief, there is on the other hand no justification
for the derogatory terms which are now sometimes applied to Dry-
den's versions.

The verse in this volume was preceded by a long critical essay in
prose. Many of its views, especially those about the language of
Chaucer, have been long discarded; but the criticism will always be
read with pleasure for the genial spirit and sound sense which per-
vade it, and the unstudied ease with which it is written. Cowley
and Dryden are in fact the founders of modern English prose; and
the influence of the latter has been much greater than that of the
former, inasmuch as he touched upon a far wider variety of topics,
and for that reason obtained a far larger circle of readers in the
century following his death. There was also the same steady im-
provement in Dryden's critical taste that there was in his poetical
expression. His admiration for Shakespeare constantly improved dur-
ing his whole life; and it is to be noticed that in what is generally
regarded as the best of his plays — 'All for Love,' brought out in the
winter of 1677-78 — he of his own accord abandoned rhyme for blank
verse.

The publication of the 'Fables' was Dryden's last appearance
before the public. In the following year he died, and was buried in
Westminster Abbey by the side of Chaucer and Cowley. After his
death his fame steadily increased instead of diminishing. For a long
period his superiority in his particular line was ungrudgingly con-
ceded by all, or if contested, was contested by Pope alone. His
poetry indeed is not of the highest kind, though usually infinitely
superior to that of his detractors. Still his excellences were those of
the intellect and not of the spirit. On the higher planes of thought
and feeling he rarely moves; to the highest he never aspires. The
nearest he ever approaches to the former is in his later work, where

religious emotion or religious zeal has lent to expression the aid of its intensity. There is a striking example of this in the personal references to his own experiences in the lines cited below from 'The Hind and the Panther.' Something too of the same spirit can be found, expressed in lofty language, in the following passage from the same poem, descriptive of the unity of the Church of Rome as contrasted with the numerous warring sects into which the Protestant body is divided:—

> "One in herself, not rent by schism, but sound,
> Entire, one solid shining diamond,
> Not sparkles shattered into sects like you:
> One is the Church, and must be to be true,
> One central principle of unity.
> As undivided, so from errors free;
> As one in faith, so one in sanctity.
> Thus she, and none but she, the insulting rage
> Of heretics opposed from age to age;
> Still when the giant brood invades her throne,
> She stoops from heaven and meets them half-way down,
> And with paternal thunders vindicates her crown.

>   .   .   .   .   .   .

> "Thus one, thus pure, behold her largely spread,
> Like the fair ocean from her mother-bed;
> From east to west triumphantly she rides,
> All shores are watered by her wealthy tides.
> The gospel sound diffused from Pole to Pole,
> Where winds can carry and where waves can roll,
> The selfsame doctrine of the sacred page
> Conveyed to every clime, in every age."

But though Dryden's poetry is not of the highest class, it is of the very highest kind in its class. Wherever the pure intellect comes into play, there he is invariably excellent. There is never any weakness; there is never any vagueness; there is never any deviation from the true path into aimless digression. His words invariably go straight to the mark, and not unfrequently with a directness and force that fully merit the epithet of "burning" applied to them by the poet Gray. His thoughts always rise naturally out of the matter in hand; and in the treatment of the meanest subjects he is not only never mean, but often falls without apparent effort into a felicity of phrase which holds the attention and implants itself in the memory. The benefit of exercise, for instance, is not a topic that can be deemed highly poetical; but in his epistle on country life addressed to his cousin John Driden, the moment he comes to speak of hunting and its salutary results his expression at once leaves the commonplace, and embodies the thought in these pointed lines:—

« So lived our sires, ere doctors learned to kill,
And multiply with theirs the weekly bill.
The first physicians by debauch were made;
Excess began, and sloth sustains the trade.

.   .   .   .

By chase our long-lived fathers earned their food;
Toil strung the nerves and purified the blood:
But we their sons, a pampered race of men,
Are dwindled down to threescore years and ten.
Better to hunt in fields for health unbought
Than fee the doctor for a nauseous draught.
The wise for cure on exercise depend;
God never made his work for man to mend. »

In a similar way in 'Cymon and Iphigenia' the contempt which Dryden, in common with the Tories of his time, felt for the English militia force, found vent in the following vigorous passage, really descriptive of them and their conduct though the scene is laid in Rhodes: —

« The country rings around with loud alarms,
And raw in fields the rude militia swarms;
Mouths without hands; maintained at vast expense,
In peace a charge, in war a weak defense;
Stout once a month they march, a blustering band,
And ever, but in times of need, at hand:
This was the morn when, issuing on the guard,
Drawn up in rank and file they stood prepared
Of seeming arms to make a short essay,
Then hasten to be drunk, the business of the day. »

In a world where what is feeble in expression is so often supposed to indicate peculiar delicacy; where what is vague is so often deemed peculiarly poetical; and where what is involved and crabbed and hard to comprehend is thought to denote peculiar profundity,—it is a pleasure to turn to a writer with a rank settled by the consensus of successive generations, who thought clearly and wrote forcibly, who knew always what he had to say and then said it with directness and power. There are greater poets than he; but so long as men continue to delight in vividness of expression, in majesty of numbers, in masculine strength and all-abounding vigor, so long will Dryden continue to hold his present high place among English authors.

The writings of Dryden constitute of themselves a literature. They treat of a vast variety of topics in many different departments of intellectual activity. The completest edition of his works was first published in 1808 under the editorship of Walter Scott. It fills twenty-one volumes, the first of which however is devoted to a biography. The notes to this edition are generally excellent; the text is very

indifferent. A revised edition of it has been recently published un-
der the editorship of George Saintsbury. But easily accessible is
a single-volume edition of the poems alone, edited by W. D. Chris-
tie, which furnishes a superior text, and is amply supplied with all
necessary annotations.

Thomas R. Lounsbury.

FROM 'THE HIND AND THE PANTHER'

A MILK-WHITE Hind, immortal and unchanged,
Fed on the lawns and in the forest ranged;
Without unspotted, innocent within,
She feared no danger, for she knew no sin.
Yet had she oft been chased with horns and hounds,
And Scythian shafts, and many wingèd wounds
Aimed at her heart; was often forced to fly,
And doomed to death, though fated not to die.
Not so her young; for their unequal line
Was hero's make, half human, half divine.
Their earthly mold obnoxious was to fate,
The immortal part assumed immortal state.
Of these a slaughtered army lay in blood,
Extended o'er the Caledonian wood,
Their native walk; whose vocal blood arose
And cried for pardon on their perjured foes.
Their fate was fruitful, and the sanguine seed,
Endued with souls, increased the sacred breed.
So captive Israel multiplied in chains,
A numerous exile, and enjoyed her pains.
With grief and gladness mixed, their mother viewed
Her martyred offspring and their race renewed;
Their corps to perish, but their kind to last,
So much the deathless plant the dying fruit surpassed.
Panting and pensive now she ranged alone,
And wandered in the kingdoms once her own.
The common hunt, though from their rage restrained
By sovereign power, her company disdained,
Grinned as they passed, and with a glaring eye
Gave gloomy signs of secret enmity.
'Tis true she bounded by and tripped so light,
They had not time to take a steady sight;

For truth has such a face and such a mien
As to be loved needs only to be seen.
　The bloody Bear, an independent beast,
Unlicked to form, in groans her hate expressed.
Among the timorous kind the quaking Hare
Professed neutrality, but would not swear.
Next her the buffoon Ape, as atheists use,
Mimicked all sects and had his own to chuse;
Still when the Lion looked, his knees he bent,
And paid at church a courtier's compliment.
The bristled baptist Boar, impure as he,
But whitened with the foam of sanctity,
With fat pollutions filled the sacred place,
And mountains leveled in his furious race;
So first rebellion founded was in grace.
But since the mighty ravage which he made
In German forests had his guilt betrayed,
With broken tusks and with a borrowed name,
He shunned the vengeance and concealed the shame,
So lurked in sects unseen.　With greater guile
False Reynard fed on consecrated spoil;
The graceless beast by Athanasius first
Was chased from Nice, then by Socinus nursed,
His impious race their blasphemy renewed,
And Nature's King through Nature's optics viewed;
Reversed they viewed him lessened to their eye,
Nor in an infant could a God descry.
New swarming sects to this obliquely tend,
Hence they began, and here they all will end.
　What weight of ancient witness can prevail,
If private reason hold the public scale?
But gracious God, how well dost thou provide
For erring judgments an unerring guide!
Thy throne is darkness in the abyss of light,
A blaze of glory that forbids the sight.
O teach me to believe thee thus concealed,
And search no farther than thy self revealed;
But her alone for my director take,
Whom thou hast promised never to forsake!
My thoughtless youth was winged with vain desires;
My manhood, long misled by wandering fires,
Followed false lights; and when their glimpse was gone,
My pride struck out new sparkles of her own.
Such was I, such by nature still I am;
Be thine the glory and be mine the shame!

Good life be now my task; my doubts are done;
What more could fright my faith than Three in One?
Can I believe eternal God could lie
Disguised in mortal mold and infancy,
That the great Maker of the world could die?
And after that, trust my imperfect sense
Which calls in question his omnipotence?
Can I my reason to my faith compel,
And shall my sight and touch and taste rebel?
Superior faculties are set aside;
Shall their subservient organs be my guide?
Then let the moon usurp the rule of day,
And winking tapers show the sun his way;
For what my senses can themselves perceive
I need no revelation to believe.
Can they, who say the Host should be descried
By sense, define a body glorified,
Impassible, and penetrating parts?
Let them declare by what mysterious arts
He shot that body through the opposing might
Of bolts and bars impervious to the light,
And stood before his train confessed in open sight.
For since thus wondrously he passed, 'tis plain
One single place two bodies did contain;
And sure the same omnipotence as well
Can make one body in more places dwell.
Let Reason then at her own quarry fly;
But how can finite grasp infinity?

   'Tis urged again, that faith did first commence
By miracles, which are appeals to sense,
And thence concluded, that our sense must be
The motive still of credibility.
For latter ages must on former wait,
And what began belief must propagate.

   But winnow well this thought, and you shall find
'Tis light as chaff that flies before the wind.
Were all those wonders wrought by power Divine
As means or ends of some more deep design?
Most sure as means, whose end was this alone,
To prove the Godhead of the Eternal Son.
God thus asserted: Man is to believe
Beyond what Sense and Reason can conceive,
And for mysterious things of faith rely
On the proponent Heaven's authority.

If then our faith we for our guide admit,
Vain is the farther search of human wit;
As when the building gains a surer stay,
We take the unuseful scaffolding away.
Reason by sense no more can understand;
The game is played into another hand.
Why choose we then like bilanders to creep
Along the coast, and land in view to keep,
When safely we may launch into the deep?
In the same vessel which our Savior bore,
Himself the pilot, let us leave the shore,
And with a better guide a better world explore.
Could he his Godhead veil with flesh and blood
And not veil these again to be our food?
His grace in both is equal in extent;
The first affords us life, the second nourishment.
And if he can, why all this frantic pain
To construe what his clearest words contain,
And make a riddle what he made so plain?
To take up half on trust and half to try,
Name it not faith, but bungling bigotry.
Both knave and fool the merchant we may call,
To pay great sums and to compound the small,
For who would break with Heaven, and would not break for all?
Rest then, my soul, from endless anguish freed:
Nor sciences thy guide, nor sense thy creed.
Faith is the best insurer of thy bliss;
The bank above must fail before the venture miss.

TO MY DEAR FRIEND MR. CONGREVE

On His Comedy Called 'The Double Dealer'

WELL then, the promised hour is come at last;
      The present age of wit obscures the past:
         Strong were our sires, and as they fought they writ;
Conquering with force of arms and dint of wit:
Theirs was the giant race before the flood;
And thus, when Charles returned, our empire stood.
Like Janus, he the stubborn soil manured,
With rules of husbandry the rankness cured;
Tamed us to manners, when the stage was rude,
And boisterous English wit with art endued.

Our age was cultivated thus at length,
But what we gained in skill we lost in strength.
Our builders were with want of genius curst;
The second temple was not like the first;
Till you, the best Vitruvius, come at length,
Our beauties equal, but excel our strength.
Firm Doric pillars found your solid base,
The fair Corinthian crowns the higher space;
Thus all below is strength, and all above is grace.
In easy dialogue is Fletcher's praise;
He moved the mind, but had not power to raise.
Great Jonson did by strength of judgment please,
Yet, doubling Fletcher's force, he wants his ease.
In differing talents both adorned their age,
One for the study, t'other for the stage.
But both to Congreve justly shall submit,
One matched in judgment, both o'ermatched in wit.
In him all beauties of this age we see·
Etherege his courtship, Southern's purity,
The satire, wit, and strength of manly Wycherley.
All this in blooming youth you have achieved;
Nor are your foiled contemporaries grieved.
So much the sweetness of your manners move,
We cannot envy you, because we love.
Fabius might joy in Scipio, when he saw
A beardless Consul made against the law,
And join his suffrage to the votes of Rome,
Though he with Hannibal was overcome.
Thus old Romano bowed to Raphael's fame,
And scholar to the youth he taught became.
      O that your brows my laurel had sustained!
Well had I been deposed, if you had reigned:
The father had descended for the son,
For only you are lineal to the throne.
Thus, when the State one Edward did depose,
A greater Edward in his room arose:
But now, not I, but poetry, is curst;
For Tom the second reigns like Tom the first.
But let them not mistake my patron's part,
Nor call his charity their own desert.
Yet this I prophesy: Thou shalt be seen,
Though with some short parenthesis between,
High on the throne of wit, and seated there,
Not mine — that's little — but thy laurel wear.

Thy first attempt an early promise made;
That early promise this has more than paid.
So bold, yet so judiciously you dare,
That your least praise is to be regular.
Time, place, and action may with pains be wrought,
But genius must be born, and never can be taught.
This is your portion, this your native store:
Heaven, that but once was prodigal before,
To Shakespeare gave as much; she could not give him more.
　　Maintain your post: that's all the fame you need;
For 'tis impossible you should proceed.
Already I am worn with cares and age,
And just abandoning the ungrateful stage:
Unprofitably kept at Heaven's expense,
I live a rent-charge on His providence:
But you, whom every Muse and grace adorn,
Whom I foresee to better fortune born,
Be kind to my remains; and oh, defend,
Against your judgment, your departed friend!
Let not the insulting foe my fame pursue,
But shade those laurels which descend to you:
And take for tribute what these lines express;
You merit more, nor could my love do less.

ODE

TO THE PIOUS MEMORY OF THE ACCOMPLISHED YOUNG LADY

MRS. ANNE KILLIGREW,

EXCELLENT IN THE TWO SISTER ARTS OF POESY AND PAINTING.

THOU youngest virgin daughter of the skies,
　　Made in the last promotion of the blest;
　Whose palms, new-plucked from Paradise,
In spreading branches more sublimely rise,
　Rich with immortal green above the rest:
Whether, adopted to some neighboring star,
　Thou roll'st above us in thy wandering race,
Or in procession fixed and regular
　Moved with the heaven's majestic pace,
　　Or called to more superior bliss,
Thou tread'st with seraphims the vast abyss:
Whatever happy region be thy place,
Cease thy celestial song a little space;

Thou wilt have time enough for hymns divine,
  Since Heaven's eternal year is thine.
Hear then a mortal Muse thy praise rehearse
    In no ignoble verse,
But such as thy own voice did practice here,
  When thy first fruits of poesy were given,
To make thyself a welcome inmate there;
  While yet a young probationer,
    And candidate of Heaven.

    If by traduction came thy mind,
    Our wonder is the less to find
A soul so charming from a stock so good;
Thy father was transfused into thy blood:
So wert thou born into the tuneful strain
(An early, rich, and inexhausted vein).
    But if thy pre-existing soul
  Was formed at first with myriads more,
    It did through all the mighty poets roll
  Who Greek or Latin laurels wore,
And was that Sappho last, which once it was before.
  If so, then cease thy flight, O heaven-born mind!
    Thou hast no dross to purge from thy rich ore:
  Nor can thy soul a fairer mansion find
  Than was the beauteous frame she left behind:
Return, to fill or mend the quire of thy celestial kind.

    May we presume to say that at thy birth
New joy was sprung in heaven, as well as here on earth?
  For sure the milder planets did combine
  On thy auspicious horoscope to shine,
  And even the most malicious were in trine.
    Thy brother angels at thy birth
    Strung each his lyre, and tuned it high,
    That all the people of the sky
  Might know a poetess was born on earth;
    And then, if ever, mortal ears
    Had heard the music of the spheres.
    And if no clustering swarm of bees
  On thy sweet mouth distilled their golden dew,
    'Twas that such vulgar miracles
    Heaven had not leisure to renew:
  For all the blest fraternity of love
Solemnized there thy birth, and kept thy holiday above.

O gracious God! how far have we
Profaned thy heavenly gift of Poesy!
Made prostitute and profligate the Muse,
Debased to each obscene and impious use,
Whose harmony was first ordained above,
For tongues of angels and for hymns of love!
Oh wretched we! why were we hurried down
This lubric and adulterate age,
(Nay, added fat pollutions of our own,)
To increase the steaming ordures of the stage?
What can we say to excuse our second fall?
Let this thy Vestal, Heaven, atone for all:
Her Arethusian stream remains unsoiled,
Unmixed with foreign filth and undefiled;
Her wit was more than man, her innocence a child.

Art she had none, yet wanted none,
For Nature did that want supply:
So rich in treasures of her own,
She might our boasted stores defy:
Such noble vigor did her verse adorn
That it seemed borrowed, where 'twas only born.
Her morals too were in her bosom bred,
By great examples daily fed,
What in the best of books, her father's life, she read.
And to be read herself she need not fear;
Each test and every light her Muse will bear,
Though Epictetus with his lamp were there.
Even love (for love sometimes her Muse exprest)
Was but a lambent flame which played about her breast;
Light as the vapors of a morning dream,
So cold herself, whilst she such warmth exprest,
'Twas Cupid bathing in Diana's stream.

Born to the spacious empire of the Nine,
One would have thought she should have been content
To manage well that mighty government;
But what can young ambitious souls confine?
To the next realm she stretched her sway,
For Painture near adjoining lay,
A plenteous province and alluring prey.
A Chamber of Dependences was framed,
As conquerors will never want pretense,
(When armed to justify the offense,)
And the whole fief in right of Poetry she claimed.

The country open lay without defense;
  For poets frequent inroads there had made,
  And perfectly could represent
The shape, the face, with every lineament,
And all the large demains which the dumb Sister swayed;
  All bowed beneath her government,
Received in triumph wheresoe'er she went.
Her pencil drew whate'er her soul designed,
And oft the happy draught surpassed the image in her mind;
  The sylvan scenes of herds and flocks
  And fruitful plains and barren rocks;
  Of shallow brooks that flowed so clear,
  The bottom did the top appear;
  Of deeper too and ampler floods
  Which, as in mirrors, showed the woods;
  Of lofty trees, with sacred shades
  And perspectives of pleasant glades,
  Where nymphs of brightest form appear,
  And shaggy satyrs standing near,
  Which them at once admire and fear.
  The ruins too of some majestic piece,
Boasting the power of ancient Rome or Greece,
Whose statues, friezes, columns, broken lie,
And, though defaced, the wonder of the eye;
What nature, art, bold fiction, e'er durst frame,
Her forming hand gave feature to the name.
So strange a concourse ne'er was seen before,
But when the peopled Ark the whole creation bore.

The scene then changed; with bold erected look
Our martial King the sight with reverence strook:
For, not content to express his outward part,
Her hand called out the image of his heart:
His warlike mind, his soul devoid of fear,
His high-designing thoughts were figured there,
As when by magic ghosts are made appear.
  Our phœnix Queen was portrayed too so bright
Beauty alone could beauty take so right:
Her dress, her shape, her matchless grace,
Were all observed, as well as heavenly face.
With such a peerless majesty she stands,
As in that day she took the crown from sacred hands;
  Before a train of heroines was seen,
  In beauty foremost, as in rank the Queen.

Thus nothing to her genius was denied,
  But like a ball of fire, the farther thrown,
  Still with a greater blaze she shone,
And her bright soul broke out on every side.
What next she had designed, Heaven only knows:
To such immoderate growth her conquest rose
That Fate alone its progress could oppose.

Now all those charms, that blooming grace,
The well-proportioned shape and beauteous face,
Shall never more be seen by mortal eyes;
In earth the much-lamented virgin lies.
Not wit nor piety could Fate prevent;
Nor was the cruel Destiny content
To finish all the murder at a blow,
To sweep at once her life and beauty too;
  But, like a hardened felon, took a pride
To work more mischievously slow,
  And plundered first, and then destroyed.
O double sacrilege on things divine,
To rob the relic, and deface the shrine!
      But thus Orinda died:
Heaven by the same disease did both translate;
As equal were their souls, so equal was their fate.

Meantime, her warlike brother on the seas
His waving streamers to the winds displays,
And vows for his return with vain devotion pays.
  Ah, generous youth! that wish forbear,
  The winds too soon will waft thee here!
  Slack all thy sails, and fear to come;
Alas! thou knowest not, thou art wrecked at home.
No more shalt thou behold thy sister's face;
Thou hast already had her last embrace.
But look aloft, and if thou ken'st from far,
Among the Pleiads, a new-kindled star,
If any sparkles than the rest more bright,
'Tis she that shines in that propitious light.

When in mid-air the golden trump shall sound,
  To raise the nations under ground;
When in the Valley of Jehoshaphat
The judging God shall close the book of Fate,
  And there the last assizes keep
  For those who wake and those who sleep;

When rattling bones together fly
From the four corners of the sky;
When sinews o'er the skeletons are spread,
Those clothed with flesh, and life inspires the dead;
The sacred poets first shall hear the sound,
And foremost from the tomb shall bound,
For they are covered with the lightest ground;
And straight, with inborn vigor, on the wing,
Like mounting larks, to the new morning sing.
There thou, sweet saint, before the quire shalt go,
As harbinger of Heaven, the way to show,
The way which thou so well hast learned below.

A SONG

FAIR, sweet, and young, receive a prize
    Reserved for your victorious eyes:
    From crowds whom at your feet you see,
  Oh pity and distinguish me!
As I from thousand beauties more
Distinguish you, and only you adore.

  Your face for conquest was designed,
  Your every motion charms my mind;
  Angels, when you your silence break,
  Forget their hymns to hear you speak;
  But when at once they hear and view,
Are loth to mount, and long to stay with you.

  No graces can your form improve,
  But all are lost, unless you love;
  While that sweet passion you disdain,
  Your veil and beauty are in vain:
  In pity then prevent my fate,
For after dying all reprieve's too late.

LINES PRINTED UNDER MILTON'S PORTRAIT

In Tonson's Folio Edition of the 'Paradise Lost,' 1688

THREE poets, in three distant ages born,
    Greece, Italy, and England did adorn.
    The first in loftiness of thought surpassed,
  The next in majesty, in both the last:
  The force of Nature could no farther go;
  To make a third she joined the former two.

ALEXANDER'S FEAST; OR, THE POWER OF MUSIC

A Song in Honor of St. Cecilia's Day: 1697

I

'TWAS at the royal feast for Persia won
    By Philip's warlike son:
    Aloft in awful state
    The godlike hero sate
    On his imperial throne;
His valiant peers were placed around;
Their brows with roses and with myrtles bound:
    (So should desert in arms be crowned.)
    The lovely Thais, by his side,
    Sate like a blooming Eastern bride,
    In flower of youth and beauty's pride.
    Happy, happy, happy pair!
      None but the brave,
      None but the brave,
None but the brave deserves the fair.

CHORUS

    Happy, happy, happy pair!
      None but the brave,
      None but the brave,
None but the brave deserves the fair.

II

    Timotheus, placed on high
    Amid the tuneful quire,
With flying fingers touched the lyre:
    The trembling notes ascend the sky,
    And heavenly joys inspire.
    The song began from Jove,
Who left his blissful seats above,
    (Such is the power of mighty love.)
A dragon's fiery form belied the god:
Sublime on radiant spires he rode,
When he to fair Olympia pressed:
And while he sought her snowy breast,
Then round her slender waist he curled,
And stamped an image of himself, a sovereign of the world.

The listening crowd admire the lofty sound,
A present deity, they shout around;
A present deity, the vaulted roofs rebound:
   With ravished ears
   The monarch hears,
   Assumes the god,
   Affects to nod,
And seems to shake the spheres.

CHORUS

   With ravished ears
   The monarch hears,
   Assumes the god,
   Affects to nod,
And seems to shake the spheres.

III

The praise of Bacchus then the sweet musician sung,
 Of Bacchus ever fair, and ever young.
  The jolly god in triumph comes;
  Sound the trumpets, beat the drums;
   Flushed with a purple grace
   He shows his honest face:
Now give the hautboys breath; he comes, he comes.
  Bacchus, ever fair and young,
   Drinking joys did first ordain;
  Bacchus's blessings are a treasure,
  Drinking is the soldier's pleasure;
   Rich the treasure,
   Sweet the pleasure,
   Sweet is pleasure after pain.

CHORUS

  Bacchus's blessings are a treasure,
  Drinking is the soldier's pleasure;
   Rich the treasure,
   Sweet the pleasure,
   Sweet is pleasure after pain.

IV

 Soothed with the sound, the king grew vain;
  Fought all his battles o'er again;
And thrice he routed all his foes, and thrice he slew the slain.
IX—310

The master saw the madness rise,
His glowing cheeks, his ardent eyes;
And while he heaven and earth defied,
Changed his hand, and checked his pride.
        He chose a mournful Muse,
        Soft pity to infuse;
He sung Darius great and good,
        By too severe a fate,
Fallen, fallen, fallen, fallen,
        Fallen from his high estate,
And weltering in his blood;
Deserted at his utmost need
By those his former bounty fed;
On the bare earth exposed he lies,
•With not a friend to close his eyes.
With downcast looks the joyless victor sate,
Revolving in his altered soul
        The various turn of chance below;
And now and then a sigh he stole,
        And tears began to flow.

CHORUS

Revolving in his altered soul
        The various turns of chance below;
And now and then a sigh he stole,
        And tears began to flow.

V

The mighty master smiled to see
That love was in the next degree;
'Twas but a kindred sound to move,
For pity melts the mind to love.
        Softly sweet, in Lydian measures,
        Soon he soothed his soul to pleasures.
War, he sung, is toil and trouble;
Honor but an empty bubble,
Never ending, still beginning,
        Fighting still, and still destroying:
If the world be worth thy winning,
        Think, oh think it worth enjoying:
Lovely Thais sits beside thee;
        Take the good the gods provide thee;
The many rend the skies with loud applause;
So Love was crowned, but Music won the cause.

The prince, unable to conceal his pain,
      Gazed on the fair
      Who caused his care,
  And sighed and looked, sighed and looked,
  Sighed and looked, and sighed again;
At length, with love and wine at once oppressed,
The vanquished victor sunk upon her breast.

CHORUS

The prince, unable to conceal his pain,
      Gazed on the fair
      Who caused his care,
  And sighed and looked, sighed and looked,
  Sighed and looked, and sighed again;
At length, with love and wine at once oppressed,
The vanquished victor sunk upon her breast.

VI

  Now strike the golden lyre again;
  A louder yet, and yet a louder strain.
  Break his bands of sleep asunder,
And rouse him, like a rattling peal of thunder.
    Hark, hark, the horrid sound
      Has raised up his head;
      As awaked from the dead,
    And amazed, he stares around.
  Revenge, revenge, Timotheus cries,
      See the Furies arise;
      See the snakes that they rear,
      How they hiss in their hair,
And the sparkles that flash from their eyes!
      Behold a ghastly band,
      Each a torch in his hand!
Those are Grecian ghosts, that in battle were slain,
      And unburied remain
      Inglorious on the plain:
      Give the vengeance due
      To the valiant crew.
Behold how they toss their torches on high,
  How they point to the Persian abodes,
And glittering temples of their hostile gods!
The princes applaud with a furious joy;

And the king seized a flambeau with zeal to destroy;
Thais led the way,
To light him to his prey,
And like another Helen, fired another Troy.

CHORUS

And the king seized a flambeau with zeal to destroy;
Thais led the way,
To light him to his prey,
And like another Helen, fired another Troy.

VII

Thus long ago,
Ere heaving bellows learned to blow,
While organs yet were mute,
Timotheus, to his breathing flute
And sounding lyre,
Could swell the soul to rage, or kindle soft desire.
At last divine Cecilia came,
Inventress of the vocal frame;
The sweet enthusiast, from her sacred store,
Enlarged the former narrow bounds,
And added length to solemn sounds,
With Nature's mother wit, and arts unknown before.
Let old Timotheus yield the prize,
Or both divide the crown:
He raised a mortal to the skies;
She drew an angel down.

GRAND CHORUS

At last divine Cecilia came,
Inventress of the vocal frame;
The sweet enthusiast, from her sacred store,
Enlarged the former narrow bounds,
And added length to solemn sounds,
With Nature's mother wit, and arts unknown before.
Let old Timotheus yield the prize,
Or both divide the crown:
He raised a mortal to the skies;
She drew an angel down.

ACHITOPHEL*

From 'Absalom and Achitophel'

THIS plot, which failed for want of common-sense,
    Had yet a deep and dangerous consequence:
    For as when raging fevers boil the blood,
The standing lake soon floats into a flood,
And every hostile humor, which before
Slept quiet in its channels, bubbles o'er;
So several factions from this first ferment
Work up to foam, and threat the government.
Some by their friends, more by themselves thought wise,
Opposed the power to which they could not rise.
Some had in courts been great, and thrown from thence,
Like fiends were hardened in impenitence.
Some, by their monarch's fatal mercy, grown
From pardoned rebels kinsmen to the throne,
Were raised in power and public office high;
Strong bands, if bands ungrateful men could tie.
    Of these the false Achitophel was first;
A name to all succeeding ages curst:
For close designs and crooked councils fit;
Sagacious, bold, and turbulent of wit;
Restless, unfixed in principles and place;
In power unpleased, impatient of disgrace:
A fiery soul, which, working out its way,
Fretted the pigmy body to decay,
And o'er-informed the tenement of clay.
A daring pilot in extremity;
Pleased with the danger, when the waves went high
He sought the storms; but for a calm unfit,
Would steer too nigh the sands to boast his wit.
Great wits are sure to madness near allied,
And thin partitions do their bounds divide;
Else why should he, with wealth and honor blest,
Refuse his age the needful hours of rest?
Punish a body which he could not please;
Bankrupt of life, yet prodigal of ease?
And all to leave what with his toil he won,
To that unfeathered two-legged thing, a son;
Got while his soul did huddled notions try,
And born a shapeless lump, like anarchy.

* Lord Shaftesbury.

In friendship false, implacable in hate;
Resolved to ruin or to rule the State.
To compass this the triple bond he broke,
The pillars of the public safety shook,
And fitted Israel for a foreign yoke:
Then, seized with fear yet still affecting fame,
Usurped a patriot's all-atoning name.
So easy still it proves in factious times,
With public zeal to cancel private crimes.
How safe is treason, and how sacred ill,
Where none can sin against the people's will!
Where crowds can wink, and no offense be known,
Since in another's guilt they find their own!
Yet fame deserved no enemy can grudge;
The statesman we abhor, but praise the judge.
In Israel's courts ne'er sat an Abethdin
With more discerning eyes, or hands more clean,
Unbribed, unsought, the wretched to redress;
Swift of dispatch, and easy of access.
Oh! had he been content to serve the Crown,
With virtues only proper to the gown;
Or had the rankness of the soil been freed
From cockle that oppressed the noble seed;
David for him his tuneful harp had strung,
And heaven had wanted one immortal song.
But wild Ambition loves to slide, not stand,
And Fortune's ice prefers to Virtue's land.
Achitophel, grown weary to possess
A lawful fame, and lazy happiness,
Disdained the golden fruit to gather free,
And lent the crowd his arm to shake the tree.
Now, manifest of crimes contrived long since,
He stood at bold defiance with his prince;
Held up the buckler of the people's cause
Against the Crown, and skulked behind the laws.
The wished occasion of the plot he takes;
Some circumstances finds, but more he makes.
By buzzing emissaries fills the ears
Of listening crowds with jealousies and fears
Of arbitrary counsels brought to light,
And proves the king himself a Jebusite.

MAXIME DU CAMP

(1822–1894)

WHY have I always felt happy, filled with the spirit of content and of infinite independence, whenever I have slept in the tent or in the ruins of foreign lands?" The love of change and adventure has been the spring of Du Camp's life, a life whose events are blended so intimately with his literary achievement, that to know the one is to know the other. This practical man of the world has an imaginative, beauty-loving side to his nature, which craves stimulus from tropical unfamiliar nature and exotic ways.

MAXIME DU CAMP

So, after the usual training of French boys in lycée and college,—"in those hideous houses where they wearied our childhood," as he says,—the just-emancipated youth of twenty-two left his home in Paris for an eighteen-months' trip in the far East. The color and variety of the experience whetted his love of travel, and very soon after his return he began a serious study of photography in view of future plans.

Then came the revolution of 1848, the overthrow of Louis Philippe; and Du Camp had an opportunity to prove his courage and patriotism in the ranks of the National Guard. In his 'Souvenirs de l'Année 1848,' he tells the story with color and interest, and with the forceful logic of an eye-witness.

His bravery and a serious wound won him the red ribbon of the Legion of Honor, bestowed by General Cavaignac. This drew attention to him, and led the minister of public instruction to intrust him a few months later with a mission of exploration to Egypt, Nubia, Palestine, and Asia Minor; a result of which trip was his first literary success. Utilizing his photographic knowledge, he collected a great many negatives for future development. Upon his return he published a volume of descriptive sketches, 'Le Nil, Egypte, et Nubie,' generously illustrated with printed reproductions of these pictures. This first combination of photography and typography was popular, and was speedily imitated, initiative of many illustrated books.

Later, Du Camp's warlike and exploring instincts led him at his own expense into Sicily with Garibaldi, where he collected matter and photographs for 'Les Deux Siciles,' another successful volume. In 1851 he associated with others to found the Revue de Paris, for which he wrote regularly until its suspension in 1858. He has also written a great deal for the Revue des Deux Mondes, in which for several years he continued a series of historical studies upon the government of Paris. The six volumes upon 'Paris: its Organs, its Functions, its Life, during the Second Half of the Nineteenth Century,' form one of his chief achievements. His personal knowledge on the subject, and his access to valuable unpublished documents, give it authoritative value.

In 'Les Ancêtres de la Commune,' and 'Les Convulsions de Paris,' he has accomplished much more in the same line. The latter, a brilliant circumstantial exposition of the Commune, a logical condemnation of its folly and ignorance, brought him gratitude from the French Academy, and aided his election to that body in 1880. For this extensive work on contemporary politics, for his illustrated travels, and his artistic and literary criticism, he is better known than for his two or three novels and volumes of poetry.

Du Camp's may be characterized as a soldierly style, strong, direct, and personal. He loves to retrace old scenes with the later visible sequence of cause and effect. Always straightforward, sometimes bluntly self-assertive, he is sometimes eloquent. Perhaps his great charm is spontaneity.

A STREET SCENE DURING THE COMMUNE

From 'The Convulsions of Paris'

THERE were strange episodes during this terrible evening. At half-past eight, M. Rouville, a Protestant minister, was at home in a house he owns on the Rue de Lille. He heard an alarm, the cry, "Everything is burning! Escape!" Then he went down, saw the street in flames, and the poor people weeping as they escaped. Just as he was returning to rescue a few valuables, some federates rushed into the court, crying, "Hurry! They are setting the place on fire!" He took some money and the manuscript of the sermons he had preached. Mechanically he seized his hat and cane. Then, throwing a last look around the apartment where he had long lived, invoking the memory of the great Biblical destructions familiar to him in Holy Writ, weak and trembling with emotion, he descended the staircase from his home.

There was indescribable tumult in the street, dominated by the cry of women; a shrill wordless involuntary cry of terror, vibrating above the uproar like a desperate appeal to which no supernatural power replied. Pastor Rouville stopped. The house next his own was in flames. They were setting fire to the one opposite. The houses between the Rue de Beaune and the Rue du Bac, red from cellar to garret, were vomiting flame from all the broken windows.

The pastor's family were not at Paris. He was alone with a faithful maid, who did not leave him for a moment. This doubtless determined his resolution, and gave him courage to brave all to save his house. If he had felt his wife and daughter near, he would have thought only of their safety, and would have hastened to get them away from the place, where, he said, « One could die of horror. »

Pastor Rouville is a small man, whose great activity keeps him young and remarkably energetic. He belongs to the strong race of Southern Protestants, which has resisted everything to guard its faith. I should not be surprised if he has had some nimble Cévennole, companion of Jean Cavalier, among his ancestors. Chaplain in the prisons of the Seine, accustomed to sound doubtful spirits, to seek in vicious hearts some intact fibres which could re-attach them to virtue; fervent in faith, eloquent, with a high voice which could rise above the tumult, knowing by experience that there is no obscurity so profound that light cannot be made to penetrate it,— he had remained on duty at his post during the Commune; for the prisoners had more need of spiritual aid, now that the regular administration no longer watched over them. He had been indignant at the incarceration of Catholic priests, and had signed the fine protest demanding the liberty of the archbishop, which the ministers had carried to the Hôtel de Ville.

Alone in the presence of the great disaster which threatened him, he commended his spirit to God, remembering that the little stone of David had killed the giant Philistine, and he decided to fight for his home. He encamped energetically before the door, to forbid access; and using the weapons bestowed upon him by Providence and study, he spoke. The federates stopped before this man, whose simplicity rendered him heroic. One may guess what he said to them: —

"Why strike the innocent and tender, as if they were execrable? Why be enraged with a Protestant, a minister, whose religion, founded on the dogma of free examination, is naturally allied to republican ideas? The faith he teaches is that promulgated by Christ: Christ said to Peter, 'Sheathe thy sword;' he said to men, 'Love one another!' No, the people of Paris, this people whose sufferings have been shared, whose unfortunates have been succored during the siege; this people, so good when not led astray by the wicked; this people will not burn the house of a poor minister, whose whole life has been passed in the exercise of charity."

The pastor must have been eloquent and have spoken with profound conviction, for the federates who were listening to him began to weep, then seized and embraced him. Meantime the tenants of the shops in his house had lowered the iron curtains, which at least was an obstacle against the first throwing of petroleum. This lasted an hour. The federates, evidently softened and touched by the pastor's despair, remained near him and had pity upon him. An old sergeant of the National Guard stayed beside him, as if to bring him help in case of need, and to maintain a little order among his subordinates. Some hope revived in M. Rouville's heart, and he was saying to himself that perhaps his house would be spared, when some young men, wearing the braided caps of officers, arrived as if to inspect the fires. Seeing one house intact, emerging like a little island from an ocean of flames, they exclaimed. The pastor sprang forward and wanted to argue with them. It was trouble wasted. One of these young scamps said to him, "You are an old reactionist: you bore us with your talking. If you don't like it, we will pin you to the wall." Then, turning toward the federates and pointing to the houses on the Rue de Lille, he cried, "All that belongs to the people. The people have the right to burn everything."

This had perhaps decided the fate of the pastor's house, when the sergeant of federates interfered, and addressing the officer said to him, "I have received orders to stop the fire just here." "Show me your order," answered the officer. The sergeant replied, "It is a verbal order." Then there was a lively quarrel between the two men. The sergeant was firm. The officer insisted, and according to the custom of the moment, threatened to have the rebel shot.

The situation was becoming grave, when an incident resolved it. A mounted officer galloped up and ordered all the federates to retreat, because they were about to be surrounded by the troops from Versailles.

Nearly all the National Guards hurried away. The sergeant who had remained near the pastor said, "Get away, scurry, father! You will get yourself killed, and that will not save your camp."

The other officers passed, commanded everything to be burned, and when the sergeant resisted, compelled him to leave. For half an hour the unhappy pastor remained alone, holding back the incendiaries, passing from supplications to threats, and gaining time by every possible artifice. The sergeant returned with tearful eyes, and showed the dismayed pastor a written order to burn the house, sent by his chiefs. Not yet discouraged, the pastor roused the compassion of the old sergeant, and so moved him that the rebel cried, "Ah, well! so much the worse! I'll disobey. No, I won't let your house be burned. They'll shoot me. It's all the same. I deserve to be." Then raising his hand toward the sky, where the stars shone like sparks through the veil of wind-driven smoke, he cried "O my father, I believe in God! Fear nothing; I will stay here. They shan't touch your house. I shall know how to keep off plunderers!"

O strange deceiving people; ready for all crimes, ready for all good actions, according to the voice which speaks to thee and the emotion which carries thee away! This sergeant was indeed thy likeness, and one need not despair of thee, although thou dishearten those who love thee best!

The brandy at the wine merchants'; the ether at the druggists'; the powder and shot forgotten in stations, or secreted in cellars, burst with terrible explosions and scattered flaming coals. The pastor looked at his house, still miraculously intact. He gave it a last look, and departed sobbing. It was eleven o'clock. For three hours in the midst of this furnace he had resisted the incendiaries. His strength was exhausted. The faithful servant, who went back again and again to rescue one thing more from the burning, dragged him away. In the Rue des Saints-Pères they plunged into darkness, all the deeper for the brazier of sparkling lights behind them. They groped their way over the barricades through a shower of bullets. More than once they fell down. Finally, safe and sound despite the dangers braved, they reached the Rue de Seine, near the Rue de Bucy, where they found refuge in a lodging-house.

Next day Pastor Rouville ran towards the Rue de Lille. His
house was standing intact. The old sergeant had kept his word.
What became of this brave man, who at the risk of his life
saved the property of a man whose speech had touched him?
Perhaps he perished. Perhaps he received his due reward. Per-
haps he drags out a wretched life in some workshop of a peni-
tentiary. I know not his fate, nor even his name.

ALEXANDRE DUMAS, SENIOR

(1803?–1870)

BY ANDREW LANG

NO AUTHOR is less capable of being illustrated by extracts than Alexandre Dumas. Writers like Prosper Mérimée or Mr. Robert Louis Stevenson can be not inadequately represented by a short story or a brief scene. Even from Scott's work we can detach 'Wandering Willie's Tale,' or 'The Tapestried Chamber,' or the study of Effie Deans in prison, or of Jeanie Deans before the Queen. But Dumas is invariably diffuse; though, unlike other diffuse talkers and writers, he is seldom tedious. He is long without *longueurs*. A single example will explain this better than a page of disquisition. The present selector had meant to extract Dumas's first meeting with Charles Nodier at the theatre. In memory, that amusing scene appeared to occupy some six pages. In fact, it covers nearly a hundred and thirty pages of the Brussels edition of the 'Memoirs' of Dumas. One reads it with such pleasure that looked back upon, it seems short, while it is infinitely too long to be extracted. In dialogue Dumas is both excellent and copious, so that he cannot well be abbreviated. He is the Porthos of novelists, gigantic, yet (at his best) muscular and not overgrown. For these reasons, extracts out of his romances do no justice to Dumas. To read one of his novels, say 'The Three Musketeers,' even in a slovenly translation, is to know more of him than a world of critics and essayists can teach. It is also to forget the world, and to dwell in a careless Paradise. Our object therefore is not to give an "essence of Dumas," but to make readers peruse him in his own books, and to save them trouble by indicating, among these books, the best.

It is notorious that Dumas was at the head of a "Company" like that which Scott laughingly proposed to form "for writing and publishing the class of books called Waverley Novels." In legal phrase, Dumas "deviled" his work; he had assistants, "researchers," collaborators. He would briefly sketch a plot, indicate the authorities to be consulted, hand his notes to Maquet or Fiorentino, receive their draught, and expand that into a romance. Work thus executed cannot be equal to itself. Many books signed by Dumas may be neglected without loss. Even to his best works, one or other of his assistants was apt to assert a claim. The answer is convincing. Not one of these ingenious men ever produced, by himself, anything that could be mistaken for the work of the master. All his good things have the same stamp and the same spirit, which we find nowhere else. Again, nobody contests his authorship of his own 'Memoirs,' or of his book about his dogs, birds, and other beasts — 'The Story of My Pets.' Now, the merit of these productions is, in kind, identical with many of the merits of his best novels. There is the same good-humor, gayety, and fullness of life. We may therefore read Dumas's central romances without much fear of being grateful to the wrong person. Against the modern theory that the Iliad and Odyssey are the work of many hands in many ages, we can urge that these supposed "hands" never did anything nearly so good for themselves; and the same argument applies in the case of Alexandre Dumas.

A brief sketch of his life must now be given. "No man has had so many of his possessions disputed as myself," says Dumas. Not only his right to his novels, but his right to his name and to legitimate birth, was contested. Here we shall follow his own account of himself in his 'Memoirs,' which do not cover nearly the whole of his life. Alexandre Dumas was born at Villers-Cotterets-sur-Aisne, on July 24th, 1803(?). He lived to almost exactly the threescore and ten years of the Psalmist. He saw the fall of Napoleon, the restoration of the rightful king, the expulsion of the Legitimate monarch in 1830, the Orleans rule, its overthrow in 1848, the Republic, the Empire, and the Terrible Year, 1870–1871. Then he died, in the hour of the sorrow of his

«Immortal and indomitable France.»

Dumas's full name was noble: he was Alexandre Dumas-Davy de la Pailleterie. His family estate, La Pailleterie, was made a marquisate by Louis XIV. in 1707. About 1760 the grandfather of Dumas sold his lands in France, and went to Hayti. There in 1762 was born his father, son of Louise Cossette Dumas and of the Marquis de la Pailleterie. The mother must have been a woman of color; Dumas talks of his father's "mulatto hue," and he himself had undoubted traces of African blood. Yet it appears that the grandparents were duly married. In 1772, his wife having died, the old marquis returned to France. The Revolution broke out, and the father of Alexandre Dumas fought in the armies of the Republic. The cruel mob called him by way of mockery, "Monsieur Humanity," because he endeavored to rescue the victims of their ferocity. He was a man of great courage and enormous physical strength. Napoleon, in honor of one of his feats of arms, called him in a dispatch "The Horatius Cocles of the Republic." He was with Napoleon in

Egypt, where a quarrel arose, as he suspected and opposed the ambition of the future emperor. Though Dumas found a treasure in a bey's house, he honorably presented it to his government. He died in France, a poor man, in 1806.

Dumas was not at home when his father died. He was staying, a child of four, with his cousin Marianne.

« At midnight I was awakened, or rather my cousin and I were awakened, by a great blow struck on the door of our room. By the light of a night lamp I saw my cousin start up, much alarmed. No mortal could have knocked at our chamber door, for the outer doors were locked. [He gives a plan of the house.] I got out of bed to open the door. 'Where are you going, Alexandre?' cried my cousin.

« 'To let in papa, who is coming to say adieu.'

« The girl dragged me back to bed; I cried, 'Adieu, papa, adieu!' Something like a sighing breath passed over my face. . . . My father had died at the hour when we heard the knock! »

This anecdote may remind the reader of what occurred at Abbotsford on the night when Mr. Bullock died in London. Dumas tells another tale of the same kind ('Memoirs,' Vol. xi., page 255: Brussels, 1852). On the night of his mother's death he in vain sought a similar experience. These things "come not by observation"; but Dumas, like Scott, had a mind not untuned to such themes, though not superstitious.

Young Dumas, like most men of literary genius, taught himself to read. A Buffon with plates was the treasure of the child, already a lover of animals. To know more about the beasts he learned to read for his own pleasure. Of mythology he was as fond as Keats. His intellectual life began (like the imaginative life of our race) in legends of beasts and gods. For Dumas was born *un primitif*, as the French say; his taste was the old immortal human taste for romance, for tales of adventure, love, and war. This predilection is now of course often scouted by critics who are over-civilized and under-educated. Superior persons will never share the love of Dumas which was common to Thackeray and Mr. Robert Louis Stevenson. From Buffon he went on to the 'Letters to Émil' (letters on mythology), and to the 'Arabian Nights.' An imaginative child, he knew the "pains of sleep" as Coleridge did, and the terrors of vain imagination. Many children whose manhood is not marked by genius are visionaries. A visionary too was little Dumas, like Scott, Coleridge, and George Sand in childhood. To the material world he ever showed a bold face. "I have never known doubt or despair," he says; his faith in God was always unshaken; the doctrine of immortality he regarded rather with hope than absolute belief. Yet surely it is a corollary to the main article of his creed.

At ten, Dumas went to a private school kept by an Abbé Grégoire. At the Restoration, a boy of twelve, he made and he adhered to an important resolution. He chose to keep his grandmaternal name of Dumas, like his father, and to drop the name and arms of De la Pailleterie, with all the hopes of boons from the restored Royalists. Dumas remained a man of the popular party, though he had certain relations of friendship with the house of Orléans. But he entertained no posthumous hatred of the old monarchy and the old times. His kings are nearly as good, in his romances, as Sir Walter's own, and his Henri III. and Henri IV. may be named with Scott's Gentle King Jamie and Louis XI.

Madame Dumas, marquise as she was by marriage, kept a tobacconist's shop; and in education, Dumas was mainly noted for his calligraphy. Poaching was now the boy's favorite amusement; all through his life he was very fond of sport. Napoleon returned from Elba; Dumas saw him drive through Villers-Cotterets on his way to Waterloo. Soon afterwards came in stragglers; the English, they said, had been defeated at five o'clock on June 18th, but the Prussians arrived at six o'clock and won the battle. What the English were doing between five and six does not appear; it hardly seems that they quitted the field. The theory of that British defeat at Waterloo was never abandoned by Dumas. He saw Napoleon return through Villers-Cotterets. " Wellington, Bülow, Blücher, were but masks of men; really they were spirits sent by the Most High to defeat Napoleon." It is a pious opinion!

At the age of fifteen Dumas, like Scott, became a notary's clerk. About this time he saw 'Hamlet' played, in the version of Ducis. Corneille and Racine had always been disliked by this born romanticist. 'Hamlet' carried him off his feet. Soon afterwards he read Bürger's 'Lenore,' the ballad which Scott translated at the very beginning of his career as an author.

> "Tramp! tramp! along the land they rode,
>   Splash! splash! along the sea;
>   The scourge is red, the spur drops blood,
>   The flashing pebbles flee."

This German ballad, says Scott, " struck him as the kind of thing he could do himself." And Dumas found that the refrain

> "Hurrah, fantôme, les morts vont vite,"

was more to his taste than the French poetry of the eighteenth century. He tried to translate 'Lenore.' Scott finished it in a night; Dumas gave up in despair. But this, he says, was the beginning of his authorship. He had not yet opened a volume of Scott or Cooper, " ces deux grands romanciers." With a friend named Leuven he began to try to write plays (1820–1821). He now poached his way to Paris, defraying his expenses with the game he shot on the road. Shakespeare too was a poacher; let us excuse the eccentricities of genius. He made Talma's acquaintance; he went to the play; he resigned his clerkship: "Paris was my future." Thither he went; his father's name served him with General Foy, and he obtained a little post in the household of the Duc D'Orléans—a supernumerary secretaryship at £60 a year. At the play he met Charles Nodier, reading the rarest of Elzevirs, and at intervals (like Charles Lamb) hissing his own piece! This delightful scene, with its consequences, occupies one hundred and thirty pages!

Dumas now made the acquaintance of Frederic Soulié, and became a pillar of theatres. He began to read with a purpose: first he read Scott; "The clouds lifted, and I beheld new horizons." Then he turned to Cooper; then to Byron. One day he entered his office, crying aloud, "Byron is dead!" "Who is Byron?" said one of his chiefs. Here Dumas breaks off in his 'Memoirs' to give a life of Byron! He fought his first duel in the snow, and won an easy, almost a bloodless victory. For years he and Leuven wrote plays together,—plays which were never accepted.

At last he, Rousseau (not Jean Jacques!), and Leuven composed a piece together. Refused at one house, it was accepted at another: 'La Chasse et l'Amour' (The Chase and Love) was presented on September 22d, 1823. It succeeded. A volume of three short stories sold to the extent of four copies. Dumas saw that he must "make a name" before he could make a livelihood. "I do not believe in neglected talent and unappreciated genius," says he. Like Mr. Arthur Pendennis, he wrote verses "up to" pictures. Thackeray did the same. "Lady Blessington once sent him an album print of a boy and girl fishing, with a request that he would make some verses for it. 'And,' he said, 'I liked the idea, and set about it at once. I was two entire days at it,—was so occupied with it, so engrossed by it, that I did not shave during the whole time.'" So says Mr. Locker-Lampson.

We cannot all be Dumas or Thackeray. But if any literary beginner reads these lines, let him take Dumas's advice; let him disbelieve in neglected genius, and do the work that comes in his way, as best he can. Dumas had a little anonymous success in 1826, a vaudeville at the Porte-Saint-Martin. At last he achieved a serious tragedy, or melodrama, in verse, 'Christine.' He wrote to Nodier, reminding him of their meeting at the play. The author of 'Trilby' introduced him to Taylor; Taylor took him to the Théâtre Français; 'Christine' was read and accepted unanimously.

Dumas now struck the vein of his fortune. By chance he opened a volume of Anquetil, and read an anecdote of the court of Henri III.

This led him to study the history of Saint Megrin, in the Memoirs of L'Estoile, where he met Quelus, and Maugiron, and Bussy d'Amboise, with the stirring tale of his last fight against twelve men. Out of these facts he made his play 'Henri III.,' and the same studies inspired that trilogy of romances 'La Reine Margot' (Queen Margot), 'La Dame de Monsoreau' (The Lady of Monsoreau), and 'Les Quarante-Cinq' (The Forty-Five). These are, with the trilogy of the 'Mousquetaires,' his central works as a romancer, and he was twenty-five when he began to deal with the romance of history. His habit was to narrate his play or novel, to his friends, to invent as he talked, and so to arrive at his general plan. The mere writing gave him no trouble. We shall later show his method in the composition of 'The Three Musketeers.'

'Christine' had been wrecked among the cross-currents of theatrical life. 'Henri III.' was more fortunate. Dumas was indeed obliged to choose between his little office and the stage; he abandoned his secretaryship. In 1829 occurred this "duel between his past and his future." Just before the first night of the drama, Dumas's mother, whom he tenderly loved, was stricken down by paralysis. He tended her, he watched over his piece, he almost dragged the Duc d'Orléans to the theatre. On that night he made the acquaintance of Hugo and Alfred de Vigny. Dumas passed the evening between the theatre and his mother's bedside. When the curtain fell, he was "called on"; the audience stood up uncovered, the Duc d'Orléans and all!

Next morning Dumas, like Byron, "woke to find himself famous." He had "made his name" in the only legitimate way,— by his work. Troubles followed, difficulties with the Censorship, duels and rumors of duels, and the whole romantic upheaval which accompanied the Revolution of 1830. Dumas was attached again to the Orléans household. He dabbled in animal magnetism, which had been called mesmerism, and now is known as hypnotism. The phenomena are the same; only the explanations vary. About 1830 there was a mania for animal magnetism in Paris; Lady Louisa Stuart recounted some of the marvels to Sir Walter Scott, who treated the reports with disdain. When writing his romance 'Joseph Balsamo' (a tale of the French Revolution), Dumas made studies of animal magnetism, and was, or believed himself to be, an adept. The orthodox party of modern hypnotists merely hold that by certain physical means, a state of somnambulism can be produced in certain people. Once in that state, the patients are subject to "suggestion," and are obedient to the will of the hypnotizer. He for his part exerts no "magnetic current," no novel unexplained force or fluid. Some recent French and English experiments are not easily to be reconciled with this hypothesis. Dumas himself believed that he exerted a magnetic force, and without any "passes" or other mechanical means, could hypnotize persons who did not know what he was about, and so were not influenced by "suggestion." In a few cases he held that his patients became clairvoyant; one of them made many political prophecies,— all unfulfilled. Another, in trance, improved vastly as a singer; "her normal voice stopped at *contre-si*. I bade her rise to *contre-re*, which she did; though incapable of it when awake." So far, this justifies the plot of Mr. Du Maurier's novel 'Trilby.' Dumas offers no theory; he states facts, as he says, including "post-hypnotic suggestion."

These experiments were made by Dumas merely as part of his studies for 'Joseph Balsamo' (Cagliostro); his conclusion was that hypnotism is not yet reduced to a scientific formula. In fiction it is already overworked. Dumas got his 'Christine' acted at last. Then broke out the Revolution of 1830. Dumas's description of his activity is "as good as a novel," but too long and varied for condensation. It seems better to give this extract about his life of poverty before his mother died, before fame visited him. (I quote Miss Cheape's translation of the passage included in her 'Stories of Beasts,' published by Longmans, Green and Company.)

HE HAD, in later years, named a cat Mysouff II.

"If you won't think me impertinent, sir," said Madame Lamarque, "I should so like to know what Mysouff means."

"Mysouff just means Mysouff, Madame Lamarque."

"It is a cat's name, then?"

"Certainly, since Mysouff the First was so-called. It is true, Madame Lamarque, you never knew Mysouff." And I became so thoughtful that Madame Lamarque was kind enough to withdraw quietly, without asking any questions about Mysouff the First.

That name had taken me back to fifteen years ago, when my mother was still living. I had then the great happiness of having a mother to scold me sometimes. At the time I speak of, I held a situation in the service of the Duc d'Orléans, with a salary of 1500 francs. My work occupied me from ten in the morning until five in the afternoon. We had a cat in those days, whose name was Mysouff. This cat had missed his vocation; he ought to have been a dog. Every morning I started for my office at half-past nine, and came back every evening at half-past five. Every morning Mysouff followed me to the corner of a particular street, and every evening I found him in the same street, at the same corner, waiting for me. Now the curious thing was that on the days when I had found some amusement elsewhere, and was not coming home to dinner, it was of no use to open the door for Mysouff to go and meet me. Mysouff, in the attitude of the serpent with its tail in its mouth, refused to stir from his cushion. On the other hand, on the days I did come, Mysouff would scratch at the door until some one opened it for him. My mother was very fond of Mysouff; she used to call him her barometer.

"Mysouff marks my good and my bad weather," my dear mother would say: "the days you come in are my days of sunshine; my rainy days are when you stay away."

When I came home I used to see Mysouff at the street corner, sitting quite still and gazing into the distance. As soon as he caught sight of me, he began to move his tail; then as I drew nearer, he rose and walked backward and forward across the pavement with his back arched and his tail in the air. When I reached him, he jumped up upon me as a dog would have done, and bounded and played round me as I walked towards the house; but when I was close to it he dashed in at full speed. Two seconds after, I used to see my mother at the door.

Never again in this world, but perhaps in the next, I shall see her standing waiting for me at the door.

That is what I was thinking of, dear readers, when the name of Mysouff brought back all these recollections; so you understand why I did not answer Madame Lamarque's question.

The life of Dumas after 1830 need not be followed step by step; indeed, for lack of memoirs, to follow it is by no means easy.

Dumas, by dint of successful plays, and later of successful novels, earned large sums of money — £40,000 in one year, it is said. He traveled far and wide, and compiled books of travel. In the forties, before the Revolution of 1848, he built a kind of Abbotsford of his own, named "Monte Cristo," near St. Germains, and joyously ruined himself. "Monte Cristo," like Abbotsford, has been described as a palace. Now, Abbotsford is so far from being a palace that Mr. Hope Scott, when his wife, Scott's granddaughter, inherited the place, was obliged to build an additional wing.

At Monte Cristo Dumas kept but one man-servant, Michel (his "Tom Purdie"), who was groom, keeper, porter, gardener, and everything. Nor did Dumas ruin himself by paying exorbitant prices for poor lands, as Scott did. His collection of books and curios was no rival for that of Abbotsford. But like Scott, he gave away money to right and left, and he kept open house. He was eaten up by parasites, — beggars, poor greedy hangers-on of letters, secretaries, above all by tribes of musical people. On every side money flowed from him; hard as he worked, largely as he earned, he spent more. His very dog brought in thirteen other dogs to bed and board. He kept monkeys, cats, eagles, a vulture, a perfect menagerie. His own account of these guests may be read in 'My Pets'; perhaps the most humorous, good-humored, and amusing of all his works.

The Revolution of 1848 impoverished him and drove him from Monte Cristo; not out of debt to his neighbors. Dumas was a cheerful giver, but did not love to "fritter away his money in paying bills." He started newspapers, such as The Musketeer, and rather lost than gained by a careless editorship. A successful play would enrich him, and he would throw away his gains. He went with Garibaldi on his expedition against the King of Naples, and was received with ingratitude by the Neapolitans.

A friend of Daniel Dunglas Home, the "medium," he accompanied him to Russia, where Home married a lady of a noble and wealthy family. Returned to France, Dumas found his popularity waning. His plays often failed; he had outlived his success and his generation; he had saved nothing; he had to turn in need to his son Alexandre, the famous dramatist. Finally he died, doubting the security of his own fame, in the year of the sorrows of France.

Dumas is described by Michelet as "a force of nature." Never was there in modern literature a force more puissant, more capricious, or more genial. His quantity of mind was out of all proportion to its quality. He could learn everything with ease; he was a skilled cook, a fencer; he knew almost as if by intuition the technique and terminology of all arts and crafts. Ignorant of Greek, he criticized and appreciated Homer with an unmatched zest and appreciation. Into the dry bones of history he breathed life, mere names becoming full-blooded fellow-creatures under his spell. His inspiration was derived from Scott, a man far more learned than he, but scarcely better gifted with creative energy. Like Scott he is long, perhaps prolix; like him he is indifferent to niceties of style, does not linger over the choice of words, but serves himself with the first that comes to hand. Scott's wide science of human nature is not his; but his heroes, often rather ruffianly, are seldom mere exemplary young men of no particular mark. More brilliantly and rapidly than Scott, he indicates action in dialogue. He does not aim at the construction of rounded plots; his novels are chronicles which need never stop while his heroes are alive. His plan is to take a canvas of fact, in memoir or history, and to embroider his fantasies on that. Occasionally the canvas (as Mr. Saintsbury says) shows through, and we have blocks of actual history. His 'Joan of Arc' begins as a romance, and ends with a comparatively plain statement of facts too great for any art but Shakespeare's. But as a rule it is not historical facts, it is the fictitious adventures of characters living in an historical atmosphere, that entertain us in Dumas.

The minute inquirer may now compare the sixteenth-century 'Memoirs of Monsieur D'Artagnan' (fictitious memoirs, no doubt) with the use made of them by Dumas in 'The Three Musketeers' and 'Twenty Years After.' The 'Memoirs' (reprinted by the Librairie Illustrée, Paris) gave Dumas his opening scenes; gave him young D'Artagnan, Porthos, Athos, Aramis, Rosnay, De Treville, Milady, the whole complicated intrigue of Milady, D'Artagnan, and De Vardes. They gave him several incidents, duels, and "local color." By making Milady the wife of Athos, Dumas knotted his plot; he added the journey to England, after the Queen's diamonds; from a subordinate character he borrowed the clerical character of Aramis; a mere hint in the 'Memoirs' suggested the Bastion Saint-Gervais. The discrimination of character, the dialogue, and many adventures, are Dumas's own; he was aided by Maquet in the actual writing. In a similar way, Brantôme and L'Estoile, in their 'Memoirs,' supply the canvas of the tales of the Valois cycle.

The beginner in Dumas will assuredly find the following his best works. For the Valois period, 'The Horoscope' (a good deal neglected), 'Queen Margot,' 'The Lady of Monsoreau,' 'The Forty-Five.' 'Isabeau of Bavière,' an early novel, deals with the anarchy and misery before the coming of Jeanne d'Arc. For Henri II., 'The Two Dianas' is indicated. For the times of Richelieu, Mazarin, Louis XIV., we have 'The Three Musketeers,' 'Twenty Years After,' and 'The Viscount of Bragelonne.' These deal with the youth, middle age, old age, and death of D'Artagnan, Porthos, Athos, and Aramis. The Revolutionary novels, 'Joseph Balsamo,' 'The Queen's Necklace,' and others, are much less excellent. The Regency is not ill done in 'The Regent's Daughter'; and 'The Chevalier of Harmenthal,' with 'Olympe of Cleves,' has many admirers. Quite apart from these is the immense modern fantasy of 'The Count of Monte Cristo'; the opening part alone is worthy of the master. 'The Black Tulip,' so warmly praised by Thackeray, is an innocent little romance of the days of Dutch William. *Les jeunes filles* may read 'The Black Tulip': indeed, Dumas does not sacrifice at all to "the Goddess of Lubricity," even when he describes very lax moralities.

With a knowledge of these books, and of 'My Pets' and the 'Memoirs,' any student will find himself at home in Dumas, and can make wider ranges in that great wilderness of fancy. Some autobiographical details will be found in the novel called 'Ange Pithou.' 'Isaac Laquedem' was meant to be a romance of the Wandering Jew; only two volumes are published. Philosophy a reader will not find, nor delicate analysis, nor "chiseled style"; but he will be in touch with a great sunny life, rejoicing in all the accidents of existence.

A Lang

THE CURE FOR DORMICE THAT EAT PEACHES

From 'The Count of Monte Cristo'

NOT on the same night he had intended, but the next morning, the Count of Monte Cristo went out on the road to Orléans. Leaving the village of Linas, without stopping at the telegraph, which at the moment the count passed threw out its long bony arms, he reached the tower of Montlhéry, situated, as every one knows, upon the highest point of the plain of that name. At the foot of the hill the count dismounted, and began to ascend the mountain by a little winding path about eighteen inches wide; when he reached the summit he found himself stopped by a hedge, upon which green fruit had succeeded to red and white flowers.

Monte Cristo looked for the door of the inclosure, and was not long in finding it. It was a little wooden gate, working on willow hinges, and fastened with a nail and string. The count soon understood its mechanism, and the door opened. He then found himself in a little marvelously well-kept garden, about twenty feet long by twelve wide, bounded on one side by part of the hedge, in which was formed the ingenious machine we have named a door; and on the other by the old tower, covered with ivy and studded with wild flowers. Monte Cristo stopped, after having closed the door and fastened the string to the nail, and cast a look around.

"The man at the telegraph," said he, "must either keep a gardener or devote himself passionately to horticulture." Suddenly he struck himself against something crouching behind a wheelbarrow filled with leaves; the something rose, uttered an exclamation of astonishment, and Monte Cristo found himself facing a man about fifty years old, who was plucking strawberries, which he was placing upon vine-leaves. He had twelve leaves and about as many strawberries, which, on rising suddenly, he let fall from his hand. "You are gathering your crop, sir?" said Monte Cristo, smiling.

"Excuse me, sir," replied the man, raising his hand to his cap; "I am not up there, I know, but I have only just come down."

"Do not let me interfere with you in anything, my friend," said the count; "gather your strawberries, if indeed there are any left."

"I have ten left," said the man, "for here are eleven, and I had twenty-one, five more than last year. But I am not surprised; the spring has been warm this year, and strawberries require heat, sir. This is the reason that, instead of the sixteen I had last year, I have this year, you see, eleven already plucked — twelve, thirteen, fourteen, fifteen, sixteen, seventeen, eighteen. Ah, I miss three! they were here last night, sir — I am sure they were here — I counted them. It must be the son of Mother Simon who has stolen them; I saw him strolling about here this morning. Ah! the young rascal! stealing in a garden; he does not know where that may lead him to."

"Certainly, it is wrong," said Monte Cristo, "but you should take into consideration the youth and greediness of the delinquent."

"Of course," said the gardener, "but that does not make it the less unpleasant. But, sir, once more I beg pardon; perhaps you are an official that I am detaining here?" And he glanced timidly at the count's blue coat.

"Calm yourself, my friend," said the count, with that smile which at his will became so terrible or benevolent, and which this time beamed only with the latter expression; "I am not an inspector, but a traveler, conducted here by curiosity he half repents of, since he causes you to lose your time."

"Ah! my time is not valuable," replied the man, with a melancholy smile. "Still, it belongs to the government, and I ought not to waste it; but having received the signal that I might rest for an hour" (here he glanced at a sun-dial, for there was everything in the inclosure of Montlhéry, even a sun-dial), "and having ten minutes before me, and my strawberries being ripe, when a day longer — by-the-by, sir, do you think dormice eat them?"

"Indeed, I should think not," replied Monte Cristo: "dormice are bad neighbors for us who do not eat them preserved, as the Romans did."

"What! did the Romans eat them?" said the gardener; "eat dormice?"

"I have read so," said the count.

"Really! They can't be nice, though they do say 'as fat as a dormouse.' It is not a wonder they are fat, sleeping all day, and only waking to eat all night. Listen: last year I had four apricots — they stole one; I had one nectarine, only one — well, sir, they ate half of it on the wall; a splendid nectarine — I never ate a better."

"You ate it?"

"That is to say, the half that was left—you understand; it was exquisite, sir. Ah, those gentlemen never choose the worst morsels; like Mother Simon's son, who has not chosen the worst strawberries. But this year," continued the horticulturist, "I'll take care it shall not happen, even if I should be forced to sit up the whole night to watch when the strawberries are ripe." Monte Cristo had seen enough. Every man has a devouring passion in his heart, as every fruit has its worm; that of the man at the telegraph was horticulture. He began gathering the vine-leaves which screened the sun from the grapes, and won the heart of the gardener. "Did you come here, sir, to see the telegraph?" he said.

"Yes, if not contrary to the rules."

"Oh no," said the gardener; "there are no orders against doing so, providing there is nothing dangerous, and that no one knows what we are saying."

"I have been told," said the count, "that you do not always yourselves understand the signals you repeat."

"Certainly, sir; and that is what I like best," said the man, smiling.

"Why do you like that best?"

"Because then I have no responsibility. I am a machine then, and nothing else; and so long as I work, nothing more is required of me."

"Is it possible," said Monte Cristo to himself, "that I can have met with a man that has no ambition? That would spoil my plans."

"Sir," said the gardener, glancing at the sun-dial, "the ten minutes are nearly expired; I must return to my post. Will you go up with me?"

"I follow you." Monte Cristo entered the tower, which was divided into three stages. The lowest contained gardening implements, such as spades, rakes, watering-pots, hung against the wall; this was all the furniture. The second was the usual dwelling or rather sleeping-place of the man; it contained a few poor articles of household furniture, a bed, a table, two chairs, a stone pitcher, and some dry herbs hung up to the ceiling, which the count recognized as sweet-peas, and of which the good man was preserving the seeds, having labeled them with as much care as if he had been a botanist.

"Does it require much study to learn the art of telegraphing, sir?" asked Monte Cristo.

"The study does not take long; it was acting as a supernumerary that was so tedious."

"And what is the pay?"

"A thousand francs, sir."

"It is nothing."

"No; but then we are lodged, as you perceive."

Monte Cristo looked at the room. They passed on to the third stage; it was the room of the telegraph. Monte Cristo looked in turns at the two iron handles by which the machine was worked. "It is very interesting," he said; "but it must be very tedious for a lifetime."

"Yes. At first my neck was cramped with looking at it, but at the end of a year I became used to it; and then we have our hours of recreation, and our holidays when we have a fog."

"Ah, to be sure."

"Those are indeed holidays to me; I go into the garden, I plant, prune, trim, and kill the insects all day long."

"How long have you been here?"

"Ten years, and five as a supernumerary make fifteen."

"You are—"

"Fifty-five years old."

"How long must you serve to claim the pension?"

"Oh, sir, twenty-five years."

"And how much is the pension?"

"A hundred crowns."

"Poor humanity!" murmured Monte Cristo.

"What did you say, sir?" asked the man.

"I was saying it was very interesting."

"What was?"

"All you were showing me. And you really understand none of these signals?"

"None at all."

"And have you never tried to understand them?"

"Never. Why should I?"

"But still there are some signals only addressed to you."

"Certainly."

"And do you understand them?"

" They are always the same."

" And they mean — "

" *Nothing new; You have an hour;* or *To-morrow.*"

" This is simple enough," said the count; " but look! is not your correspondent putting himself in motion ? "

" Ah yes; thank you, sir."

" And what is it saying — anything you understand ? "

" Yes; it asks if I am ready."

" And you reply ? "

" By the same sign, which at the same time tells my right-hand correspondent that I am ready, while it gives notice to my left-hand correspondent to prepare in his turn."

" It is very ingenious," said the count.

" You will see," said the man, proudly; " in five minutes he will speak."

" I have then five minutes," said Monte Cristo to himself; " it is more time than I require. My dear sir, will you allow me to ask you a question ? "

" What is it, sir ? "

" You are fond of gardening ? "

" Passionately."

" And you would be pleased to have, instead of this terrace of twenty feet, an inclosure of two acres ? "

" Sir, I should make a terrestrial paradise of it."

" You live badly on your thousand francs ? "

" Badly enough; but yet I do live."

" Yes; but you have only a small garden."

" True, the garden is not large."

" And then, such as it is, it is filled with dormice, who eat everything."

" Ah! they are my scourges."

" Tell me, should you have the misfortune to turn your head while your right-hand correspondent was telegraphing — "

" I should not see him."

" Then what would happen ? "

" I could not repeat the signals."

" And then ? "

" Not having repeated them, through negligence, I should be fined."

" How much ? "

" A hundred francs."

" The tenth of your income — that would be fine work."

" Ah! " said the man.

" Has it ever happened to you ? " said Monte Cristo.

" Once, sir, when I was grafting a rose-tree. "

" Well, suppose you were to alter a signal, and substitute another ? "

" Ah, that is another case; I should be turned off, and lose my pension. "

" Three hundred francs. "

" A hundred crowns; yes, sir; so you see that I am not likely to do any of these things. "

" Not even for fifteen years' wages ? Come, it is worth thinking about ? "

" For fifteen thousand francs! "

" Yes. "

" Sir, you alarm me. "

" Nonsense! "

" Sir, you are tempting me ? "

" Just so; fifteen thousand francs, do you understand ? "

" Sir, let me see my right-hand correspondent! "

" On the contrary, do not look at him, but on this. "

" What is it ? "

" What! do you not know these little papers ? "

" Bank-notes! "

" Exactly; there are fifteen of them. "

" And whose are they ? "

" Yours, if you like. "

" Mine! " exclaimed the man, half suffocated.

" Yes; yours — your own property. "

" Sir, my right-hand correspondent is signaling. "

" Let him. "

" Sir, you have distracted me; I shall be fined. "

" That will cost you a hundred francs; you see it is your interest to take my bank-notes. "

" Sir, my right-hand correspondent redoubles his signals; he is impatient. "

" Never mind — take these; " and the count placed the packet in the hands of the man. " Now, this is not all, " he said; " you cannot live upon your fifteen thousand francs. "

" I shall still have my place. "

" No! you will lose it, for you are going to alter the sign of your correspondent. "

" Oh, sir, what are you proposing ? "

"A jest!"

"Sir, unless you force me —"

"I think I can effectually force you;" and Monte Cristo drew another packet from his pocket. "Here are ten thousand more francs," he said; "with the fifteen thousand already in your pocket, they will make twenty-five thousand. With five thousand you can buy a pretty little house with two acres of land; the remaining twenty thousand will bring you in a thousand francs a year."

"A garden with two acres of land!"

"And a thousand francs a year."

"Oh heavens!"

"Come, take them!" and Monte Cristo forced the bank-notes into his hand.

"What am I to do?"

"Nothing very difficult."

"But what is it?"

"To repeat these signs;" Monte Cristo took a paper from his pocket, upon which were drawn three signs, with numbers to indicate the order in which they were to be worked.

"There, you see it will not take long."

"Yes; but —"

"Do this, and you will have nectarines and all the rest." The mark was hit: red with fever, while the large drops fell from his brow, the man executed, one after the other, the three signs given by the count; notwithstanding the frightful contortions of the right-hand correspondent, who, not understanding the change, began to think the gardener had become mad. As to the left-hand one, he conscientiously repeated the same signals, which were definitively carried to the Minister of the Interior.

"Now you are rich," said Monte Cristo.

"Yes," replied the man, "but at what a price!"

"Listen, friend," said Monte Cristo. "I do not wish to cause you any remorse; believe me, then, when I swear to you that you have wronged no man, but on the contrary have benefited mankind." The man looked at the bank-notes, felt them, counted them; he turned pale, then red; then rushed into his room to drink a glass of water, but he had no time to reach the water-jug, and fainted in the midst of his dried herbs. Five minutes after the new telegram reached the minister, Debray had the horses put to his carriage, and drove to Danglars's.

"Has your husband any Spanish bonds?" he asked of the baroness.

"I think so, indeed! He has six millions' worth."

"He must sell them at whatever price."

"Why?"

"Because Don Carlos has fled from Bourges, and has returned to Spain."

"How do you know?"— Debray shrugged his shoulders. "The idea of asking how I hear the news!" he said. The baroness did not wait for a repetition; she ran to her husband, who immediately hastened to his agent and ordered him to sell at any price. When it was seen that Danglars sold, the Spanish funds fell directly. Danglars lost five hundred thousand francs; but he rid himself of all his Spanish shares. The same evening the following was read in Le Messager:—

"Telegraphic dispatch. The King, Don Carlos, has escaped the vigilance exercised over him at Bourges, and has returned to Spain by the Catalonian frontier. Barcelona has risen in his favor."

All that evening nothing was spoken of but the foresight of Danglars, who had sold his shares, and of the luck of the stock-jobber, who only lost five hundred thousand francs by such a blow. Those who had kept their shares, or bought those of Danglars, looked upon themselves as ruined, and passed a very bad night. Next morning Le Moniteur contained the following:

"It was without any foundation that Le Messager yesterday announced the flight of Don Carlos and the revolt of Barcelona. The King (Don Carlos) has not left Bourges, and the peninsula is in the enjoyment of profound peace. A telegraphic signal, improperly interpreted owing to the fog, was the cause of this error."

The funds rose one per cent. higher than before they had fallen. This, reckoning his loss, and what he had missed gaining, made the difference of a million to Danglars. "Good!" said Monte Cristo to Morrel, who was at his house when the news arrived of the strange reverse of fortune of which Danglars had been the victim. "I have just made a discovery for twenty-five thousand francs, for which I would have paid a hundred thousand."

"What have you discovered?" asked Morrel.

"I have just discovered the method of ridding a gardener of the dormice that eat his peaches."

THE SHOULDER OF ATHOS, THE BELT OF PORTHOS, AND THE HANDKERCHIEF OF ARAMIS

From 'The Three Musketeers'

FURIOUS with rage, D'Artagnan crossed the ante-room in three strides, and began to descend the stairs four steps at a time, without looking where he was going; when suddenly he was brought up short by knocking violently against the shoulder of a musketeer who was leaving the apartments of M. De Treville. The young man staggered backwards from the shock, uttering a cry, or rather a yell.

"Excuse me," said D'Artagnan, trying to pass him, "but I am in a great hurry."

He had hardly placed his foot on the next step, when he was stopped by the grasp of an iron wrist on his sash.

"You are in a great hurry!" cried the musketeer, whose face was the color of a shroud; "and you think that is enough apology for nearly knocking me down? Not so fast, my young man. I suppose you imagine that because you heard M. De Treville speaking to us rather brusquely to-day, that everybody may treat us in the same way? But you are mistaken, and it is as well you should learn that you are not M. De Treville."

"Upon my honor," replied D'Artagnan, recognizing Athos, who was returning to his room after having his wound dressed, "upon my honor, it was an accident, and therefore I begged your pardon. I should have thought that was all that was necessary. I repeat that I am in a very great hurry, and I should be much obliged if you would let me go my way."

"Monsieur," said Athos, loosening his hold, "you are sadly lacking in courtesy, and one sees that you must have had a rustic upbringing."

D'Artagnan was by this time half-way down another flight; but on hearing Athos's remark he stopped short.

"My faith, monsieur!" exclaimed he, "however rustic I may be, I shall not come to you to teach me manners."

"I am not so sure of that," replied Athos.

"Oh, if I was only not in such haste," cried D'Artagnan; "if only I was not pursuing somebody —"

"Monsieur, you will find me without running after me. Do you understand?"

"And where, if you please?"

"Near Carmes-Deschaux."

"At what hour?"

"Twelve o'clock."

"Very good. At twelve I will be there."

"And don't be late, for at a quarter past twelve I will cut off your ears for you."

"All right," called out D'Artagnan, dashing on down-stairs after his man; "you may expect me at ten minutes before the hour."

But he was not to escape so easily. At the street door stood Porthos, talking to a sentry, and between the two men there was barely space for a man to pass. D'Artagnan took it for granted that he could get through, and darted on, swift as an arrow, but he had not reckoned on the gale that was blowing. As he passed, a sudden gust wrapped Porthos's mantle tight round him; and though the owner of the garment could easily have freed him had he so chosen, for reasons of his own he preferred to draw the folds still closer.

D'Artagnan, hearing the volley of oaths let fall by the musketeers, feared he might have damaged the splendor of the belt, and struggled to unwind himself; but when he at length freed his head, he found that like most things in this world the belt had two sides, and while the front bristled with gold, the back was mere leather; which explains why Porthos always had a cold and could not part from his mantle.

"Confound you!" cried Porthos, struggling in his turn, "have you gone mad, that you tumble over people like this?"

"Excuse me," answered D'Artagnan, "but I am in a great hurry. I am pursuing some one, and —"

"And I suppose that on such occasions you leave your eyes behind you?" asked Porthos.

"No," replied D'Artagnan, rather nettled; "and thanks to my eyes, I often see things that other people don't."

Possibly Porthos might have understood this allusion, but in any case he did not attempt to control his anger, and said sharply: —

"Monsieur, we shall have to give you a lesson if you take to tumbling against the musketeers like this!"

"A lesson, monsieur!" replied D'Artagnan; "that is rather a severe expression."

"It is the expression of a man who is always accustomed to look his enemies in the face."

"Oh, if that is all, there is no fear of *your* turning your back on anybody," and enchanted at his own wit, the young man walked away in fits of laughter.

Porthos foamed with rage, and rushed after D'Artagnan.

"By-and-by, by-and-by," cried the latter; "when you have not got your mantle on."

"At one o'clock then, behind the Luxembourg."

"All right; at one o'clock," replied D'Artagnan as he vanished around the corner.

But he could see no one either in the street he had passed through, or in the one his eager gaze was searching; however slowly the stranger might have walked, he had gone his way, or perhaps into some house. D'Artagnan inquired of everybody he met, but could find nothing at all about him. This chase however did him good in one way; for in proportion as the sweat started out on his forehead, his heart began to cool.

He began to think over the many unlucky things which had happened. It was scarcely eleven in the morning, and yet this morning had already brought him into disgrace with M. Treville, who must think the way D'Artagnan had left him was rather boorish.

Moreover, he had gotten himself into two fierce duels with two men, each able to kill three D'Artagnans; in a word, with two musketeers,—beings he set so high that he placed them above all other men.

It was a sad lookout. To be sure, as the youth was certain to be killed by Athos, he was not much disturbed about Porthos. As hope is the last thing to die in a man's heart, however, he ended by hoping that he might come out alive from both duels, even if dreadfully injured; and on that supposition he scored himself in this way for his conduct:—

"What a rattle-headed dunce I am! That brave and unfortunate Athos was wounded right on that shoulder I ran against head-foremost, like a ram. The only thing that surprises me is that he didn't strike me dead on the spot; he had provocation enough, for I must have hurt him savagely. As to Porthos— oh! as to Porthos—that's a funny affair!"

And the youth began to laugh aloud in spite of himself; looking round carefully, however, to see if his laughing alone in public without apparent cause aroused any suspicion.

IX—312

"As to Porthos, it is funny enough, to be sure, but I am a crazy blockhead all the same. Are people to be run into without warning? No! And have I any right to peep under their cloaks to see what they haven't got? He would have forgiven me, I am sure, if I had said nothing to him about that cursed cloak,—with a double meaning, it is true, but too broad a joke in one of them! Ah! cursed Gascon that I am, I believe I should crack a joke if I was being roasted over a slow fire. Friend D'Artagnan," he went on, speaking to himself with the gentleness he thought fair, "if you get away, which there is not much chance of, I would advise you to practice entire politeness for the future. You must henceforth be admired and quoted as a model of it. To be obliging and civil does not necessarily make a man a coward. Look at Aramis, now: mildness and grace embodied; and did anybody ever dream of calling Aramis a coward? No indeed, and from this instant I will try to model myself after him. And luckily, here he is."

D'Artagnan, walking and soliloquizing, had come within a few steps of the Aiguillon House, and in front of it saw Aramis chatting gayly with three of the King's Guards. Aramis also saw D'Artagnan; but not having forgotten that it was in his presence M. de Treville had got so angry in the morning, and as a witness of the rebuke was not at all pleasant, he pretended not to see him. D'Artagnan, on the other hand, full of his plans of conciliation and politeness, approached the young man with a profound bow accompanied by a most gracious smile. Aramis bowed slightly but did not smile. Moreover, all four immediately broke off their conversation.

D'Artagnan was not so dull as not to see he was not wanted; but he was not yet used enough to social customs to know how to extricate himself dexterously from his false position, which his generally is who accosts people he is little acquainted with, and mingles in a conversation which does not concern him. He was mentally casting about for the least awkward manner of retreat, when he noticed that Aramis had let his handkerchief fall, and (doubtless by mistake) put his foot on it. This seemed a favorable chance to repair his mistake of intrusion: he stooped down, and with the most gracious air he could assume, drew the handkerchief from under the foot in spite of the efforts made to detain it, and holding it out to Aramis, said:—

"I believe, sir, this is a handkerchief you would be sorry to lose?"

The handkerchief was in truth richly embroidered, and had a cornet and a coat of arms at one corner. Aramis blushed excessively, and snatched rather than took the handkerchief.

"Ha! ha!" exclaimed one of the guards, "will you go on saying now, most discreet Aramis, that you are not on good terms with Madame de Bois-Tracy, when that gracious lady does you the favor of lending you her handkerchief!"

Aramis darted at D'Artagnan one of those looks which tell a man that he has made a mortal enemy; then assuming his mild air he said:—

"You are mistaken, gentlemen: this handkerchief is not mine, and I cannot understand why this gentleman has taken it into his head to offer it to me rather than to one of you. And as a proof of what I say, here is mine in my pocket."

So saying, he pulled out his handkerchief, which was also not only a very dainty one, and of fine linen (though linen was then costly), but was embroidered and without arms, bearing only a single cipher, the owner's.

This time D'Artagnan saw his mistake; but Aramis's friends were by no means convinced, and one of them, addressing the young musketeer with pretended gravity, said:—

"If things were as you make out, I should feel obliged, my dear Aramis, to reclaim it myself; for as you very well know, Bois-Tracy is an intimate friend of mine, and I cannot allow one of his wife's belongings to be exhibited as a trophy."

"You make the demand clumsily," replied Aramis; "and while I acknowledge the justice of your reclamation, I refuse it on account of the form."

"The fact is," D'Artagnan put in hesitatingly, "I did not actually see the handkerchief fall from M. Aramis's pocket. He had his foot on it, that's all, and I thought it was his."

"And you were deceived, my dear sir," replied Aramis coldly, very little obliged for the explanation; then turning to the guard who had professed himself Bois-Tracy's friend—"Besides," he went on, "I have reflected, my dear intimate friend of Bois-Tracy, that I am not less devotedly his friend than you can possibly be, so that this handkerchief is quite as likely to have fallen from your pocket as from mine!"

"On my honor, no!"

"You are about to swear on your honor, and I on my word; and then it will be pretty evident that one of us will have lied.

Now here, Montaran, we will do better than that: let each take a half."

"Perfectly fair," cried the other two guardsmen; "the judgment of Solomon! Aramis, you are certainly full of wisdom!"

They burst into a loud laugh, and as may be supposed, the incident bore no other fruit. In a minute or two the conversation stopped, and the three guards and the musketeer, after heartily shaking hands, separated, the guards going one way and Aramis another.

"Now is the time to make my peace with this gentleman," said D'Artagnan to himself, having stood on one side during all the latter part of the conversation; and in this good spirit drawing near to Aramis, who was going off without paying any attention to him, he said:—

"You will excuse me, I hope."

"Ah!" interrupted Aramis, "permit me to observe to you, sir, that you have not acted in this affair as a man of good breeding ought."

"What!" cried D'Artagnan, "do you suppose—"

"I suppose that you are not a fool, and that you knew very well, even though you come from Gascony, that people do not stand on handkerchiefs for nothing. What the devil! Paris is not paved with linen!"

"Sir, you do wrong in trying to humiliate me," said D'Artagnan, in whom his native pugnacity began to speak louder than his peaceful resolutions. "I come from Gascony, it is true; and since you know it, there is no need to tell you that Gascons are not very patient, so that when they have asked pardon once, even for a folly, they think they have done at least as much again as they ought to have done."

"Sir, what I say to you about this matter," said Aramis, "is not for the sake of hunting a quarrel. Thank Heaven, I am not a swashbuckler, and being a musketeer only for a while, I only fight when I am forced to do so, and always with great reluctance; but this time the affair is serious, for here is a lady compromised by you."

"By us, you mean," cried D'Artagnan.

"Why did you give me back the handkerchief so awkwardly?"

"Why did you let it fall so awkwardly?"

"I have said that the handkerchief did not fall from my pocket."

"Well, by saying that you have told two lies, sir; for I saw it fall."

"Oh ho! you take it up that way, do you, Master Gascon? Well, I will teach you how to behave yourself."

"And I will send you back to your pulpit, Master Priest. Draw, if you please, and instantly—"

"Not so, if you please, my good friend; not here, at least. Do you not see that we are opposite Aiguillon House, full of the Cardinal's creatures? How do I know that it is not his Eminence who has honored you with the commission to bring him in my head? Now, I entertain an absurd partiality for my head, it seems to suit my shoulders so finely. I have no objection to killing you, you may be sure, but quietly, in a snug, distant spot, where you will not be able to boast of your death to anybody."

"I agree, but don't be too confident; and take away your handkerchief—whether it belongs to you or somebody else, perhaps you may stand in need of it to bandage up a wound. As a Gascon, I don't put off engagements for prudence's sake."

"Prudence is a virtue useless enough to musketeers, I know, but indispensable to churchmen; and as I am only a temporary musketeer, I hold it best to be prudent. At two o'clock I shall have the honor of expecting you at Treville's. There I will point out the best place and time to you."

The two bowed and separated. Aramis went up the street which led to the Luxembourg; while D'Artagnan, seeing that the appointed hour was coming near, took the road to the Carmes-Deschaux, saying to himself, "I certainly cannot hope to come out of these scrapes alive; but if I am doomed to be killed, it will be by a royal musketeer."

THE DEFENSE OF THE BASTION SAINT-GERVAIS

From 'The Three Musketeers'

WHEN D'Artagnan arrived, he found his three friends all together. Athos was thinking deeply, Porthos was twirling his mustache, and Aramis was reading his prayers out of a beautiful little book bound in blue velvet.

"My faith, gentlemen!" exclaimed he, "I hope that what you have to tell me is very important, or I shall owe you a grudge for dragging me here, out of my bed, after a whole night passed in taking and dismantling a bastion! Ah, it is a thousand pities you were not there! It was warm work!"

"We were somewhere else, where it was not very cold either," replied Porthos, giving his mustache another twist. . . .

"Aramis," said Athos, "didn't you breakfast the other day at Parpaillot's?"

"Yes."

"Were you comfortable there?"

"No, I did not like it at all. It was a fast day, and they had nothing but meat."

"What, no fish to be had in a seaport town?"

"They say," replied Aramis, taking up his book, "that they have all taken to the deep sea, since the Cardinal built that dike."

"That is not what I was asking," replied Athos. "Were you quite free and at your ease, or did any one pay attention to you?"

"Oh, nobody paid any attention to me. And if *that* is your object, Athos, Parpaillot's will suit us very well."

"Let us go at once then," said Athos, "for these walls are like paper."

On the way they met Grimaud [the valet of Athos], whom Athos beckoned silently to follow them. Grimaud, according to his custom, obeyed without a word. The poor fellow had almost forgotten how to speak!

It did not take them long to reach Parpaillot's, but unluckily the hour was ill chosen for a private conference. The *réveille* had just been sounded, and the sleepy soldiers were all pouring into the inn. This state of matters delighted the landlord, but was hardly so agreeable to the four friends, who merely nodded sulkily at the salutations of the crowd.

"If we are not careful," said Athos, rousing himself, "we shall find ourselves landed in some quarrel, which would be highly inconvenient at this moment. D'Artagnan, tell us about your night's work, and then we will tell you about ours."

"Ah yes," said a light-horse soldier, who was slowly sipping a glass of brandy, "you were down at the trenches last night, I think, and I believe you had a brush with the Rochellois."

D'Artagnan looked at Athos, to see if he ought to answer or not.

"My dear fellow," replied Athos, "I don't think you are aware that M. De Busigny did you the honor to address you! Since these gentlemen are interested in last night's affair, tell them about it."

"Is it true that you captured a bastion?" asked a Swiss, who had filled his beer up with rum.

"Yes, monsieur," replied D'Artagnan, "we had that honor. We also introduced a barrel of powder into a corner, which in exploding opened a really beautiful breach; and as the bastion was not built yesterday, the whole building was severely shaken."

"What bastion was it?" said a dragoon, who was holding a goose on the point of his sword, and cooking it at the fire.

"The Bastion Saint-Gervais," replied D'Artagnan; "the Rochellois behind it were always annoying our men."

"And there was a good deal of sharp-shooting?"

"A good deal. We lost five men, and the Rochellois eight or ten."

"But this morning," went on the light-horseman, "they will probably send down some pioneers to rebuild the bastion."

"Yes, probably," answered D'Artagnan.

"Gentlemen," broke in Athos, "I want to propose a bet."

"What bet?" asked the light-horseman.

"I bet you, M. De Busigny, that I and my three friends Porthos, Aramis, and D'Artagnan, will breakfast in the Bastion Saint-Gervais, and will hold it an hour by the clock, against all comers."

Porthos and Aramis looked at each other. They were beginning to understand what Athos had in his head.

"But," objected D'Artagnan, leaning over to whisper to Athos, "we shall be killed without a chance of escape."

"We shall be killed a great deal more certainly if we don't go," replied Athos.

"Ah!" ejaculated Porthos, twirling his mustache, "that is a grand bet."

"I take it," said M. De Busigny; "let us fix the stakes."

"That is easily done," replied Athos. "We are four and you are four. The loser shall give the whole eight a dinner."

"Very well, let us agree to that," said M. De Busigny and the dragoon.

"Your breakfast is ready, gentlemen," broke in the landlord at this instant.

"Then bring it here," answered Athos.

The landlord obeyed, and Athos, making a sign to Grimaud, pointed out a large basket standing in a corner, which he was to fill with wine and food.

"But where are you going to eat it?" asked the landlord.

"What does that matter to you as long as you are paid?" replied Athos, throwing two pistoles on the table. Then, turning to M. De Busigny, he observed:—

"Will you have the kindness, monsieur, to set your watch by mine, or let me set mine by yours?"

"Certainly, monsieur," said the light-horseman, drawing out a beautiful watch incrusted with diamonds; "half-past seven."

"Five-and-twenty minutes to eight. So I am five minutes faster than you;" and bowing to the rest of the company, the four young men took the road to the Bastion Saint-Gervais, followed by Grimaud carrying the basket. He had not the faintest idea where they were going, or what they were to do, but Athos had given his orders, and he always obeyed without questioning.

As long as they were within the camp, the four friends remained silent; but once they had passed the wall of circumvallation, D'Artagnan, who was completely in the dark, thought it was time to ask for an explanation.

"And now, my dear Athos," said he, "will you be good enough to tell me where we are bound for?"

"Why, for the bastion, of course."

"And what are we to do when we get there?"

"I told you before. We are going to breakfast."

"But why didn't we do that at Parpaillot's?"

"Because we had some important matters to discuss, and it was impossible to talk for five minutes at that inn, with all those people coming and going, and perpetually bowing and speaking to you. Here at least," continued Athos, pointing to the bastion, "we shall not be interrupted."

"It seems to me," said D'Artagnan, with the caution which was as much his characteristic as his foolhardy courage, "it seems to me that we might have found some secluded place among the sand-hills on the sea-shore."

"Oh, somebody would have seen, and in a quarter of an hour spies would have informed the Cardinal that we were holding council."

"Yes," said Aramis. "Athos is right. *Animadvertuntur in desertis.*"

"A desert would have done very well," replied Porthos; "but first we should have to find it."

"There is no desert where a bird cannot fly overhead, or a fish jump out of the water, or a rabbit run out of his hole; and bird, fish, and rabbit have all become spies of the Cardinal. Much better to go on with our adventure, which we cannot now give up without dishonor. We have made a bet, and a bet on the spur of the moment; a bet of which I defy any one to guess the true meaning. To win it, we must hold the bastion for an hour. Either they will attack us, or they won't. If we are left unmolested, we shall have plenty of time to talk without any one overhearing us, for I will answer for the walls of this bastion having no ears. If they try to dislodge us, we can talk all the same, and in defending our position shall cover ourselves with glory. You see that from every point of view we have the whip hand."

"Yes," said D'Artagnan, "but most certainly we shall attract some stray bullet."

"My good fellow," remarked Athos, "do you really think that the enemy's bullets are those we have most cause to fear?"

"But surely, if we were embarking on such an expedition, we ought to have brought our muskets?"

"Porthos, you are a goose! What would be the good of burdening ourselves with anything so useless?"

"I should hardly think that a heavy musket, a dozen cartridges, and a powder flask would be useless when one is in the presence of an enemy."

"Dear me!" said Athos, "didn't you hear what D'Artagnan was saying?"

"What did D'Artagnan say?" asked Porthos.

"He said that during last night's attack eight or ten Frenchmen were killed, and as many Rochellois."

"Well?"

"Well, hasn't everybody been too busy ever since to think of stripping the dead bodies?"

"What then?"

"What then? Why, we shall find their muskets, their flasks, and their cartridges, all waiting for us; and instead of four muskets and twelve charges, there will be fifteen pieces and a hundred bullets."

"O Athos," exclaimed Aramis, "you are a great man!"

Porthos nodded approval; only D'Artagnan did not seem to be convinced; and Grimaud appeared to have his doubts, for seeing they were still making for the bastion (which up to that moment he had declined to believe), he plucked his master by the coat.

"Where are we going?" he asked by a sign.

Athos pointed out the bastion.

"But," objected Grimaud, speaking always in pantomime, "we shall leave our bodies there."

Athos raised his hands and eyes to heaven. Grimaud placed his basket on the ground and sat down, shaking his head.

Athos took a pistol from his belt, looked to see if it was well primed, cocked it, and approached the barrel to Grimaud's ear. Grimaud was on his legs again, as if by magic. Athos then signed to him to take up the basket and go on.

Grimaud obeyed.

When they reached the bastion, the four friends turned round and beheld over three hundred soldiers assembled at the gate of the camp; M. De Busigny, the dragoon, the Swiss, and their silent companion forming a group apart.

Athos removed his hat, put it on the edge of his sword, and waved it in the air.

The spectators returned his salute and gave a great hurrah, which penetrated to their ears even at that distance. Then all four disappeared inside the bastion, where Grimaud had preceded them.

THE CONSULTATION OF THE MUSKETEERS

From 'The Three Musketeers'

As Athos had assumed, the bastion was only occupied by a dozen dead men, French and Rochellois.

"Gentlemen," said Athos, to whom the command of the expedition naturally fell, "while Grimaud lays out breakfast, we will begin by picking up the muskets and cartridges, and of course there is nothing in this employment to prevent our talking. Our friends here," he added, pointing to the dead, "will pay no attention to us."

"But after we have made sure they have nothing in their pockets, we had better throw them into the trench," said Porthos.

"Yes," replied Athos, "that is Grimaud's business."

"Well then," said D'Artagnan, "let Grimaud search them, and after he has done so, throw them over the wall."

"He shall do nothing of the sort," replied Athos; "we may find them useful yet."

"You are going mad, my good fellow! Of what use can these dead men be?"

"Don't judge hastily, say the gospel and the Cardinal," replied Athos. "How many guns have we got?"

"Twelve," said Aramis.

"How many charges?"

"A hundred."

"That will do. Now let us load."

They set to work; and as they finished loading the last gun, Grimaud made a sign that breakfast was ready.

By a gesture Athos replied that they were ready also, and then pointed out a pepper-box turret, where Grimaud was to keep watch. To help him pass the time Athos allowed him to take some bread, two cutlets, and a bottle of wine. . . .

"Now," said D'Artagnan, "that there is no chance of our being overheard, I hope you will tell us your secret."

"I trust, gentlemen, to give you both pleasure and glory at once," replied Athos. "I have made you take a charming walk, and now here is an excellent breakfast; while below, as you may see through the loop-holes, are five hundred persons, who consider us to be either lunatics or heroes,—two classes of idiots who have much in common. . . ."

"What is the matter, Grimaud? As the circumstances are grave, I will allow you to speak, but be short, I beg. What is it?"

"A troop."

"How many?"

"Twenty?"

"What are they?"

"Sixteen pioneers, four soldiers."

"How far off?"

"Five hundred paces."

"Then we have just time to finish this fowl and drink your health, D'Artagnan."

A few minutes later the troop hove in sight, marching along a narrow trench that connected the bastion and the town.

"Bah!" said Athos. "It was scarcely worth while disturbing ourselves for a mere handful of rascals armed with pickaxes, hoes, and shovels. Grimaud had only got to make them a sign to return whence they came, and I am sure they would have left us in peace."

"I doubt it," said D'Artagnan, "for they are advancing steadily. And besides the sappers, there are four soldiers and a brigadier, all armed with muskets."

"It is only because they have not seen us," replied Athos.

"Upon my honor," cried Aramis, "I feel quite ashamed to fire on poor devils like that."

"False priest!" exclaimed Porthos, "to have pity on heretics."

"Aramis is right," said Athos. "I will warn them."

"What on earth are you doing?" said D'Artagnan. "You will get yourself shot, my good fellow."

But Athos paid no attention to this remark, and mounting the breach, his hat in one hand and his musket in the other, he addressed the troop, who were so astonished at this unexpected apparition that they halted about fifty paces distant. "Gentlemen," he said, bowing courteously as he spoke, "I am at this moment breakfasting with some friends in the shelter of this bastion. As you know, there is nothing so unpleasant as to be disturbed during your meals; therefore we should be greatly obliged if you would postpone any business you may have here, till we have finished, or else call again. Unless, indeed, you have the happy inspiration to quit the side of rebellion, and to drink, with us, to the health of the King of France."

"Do take care, Athos!" exclaimed D'Artagnan; "don't you see they are aiming at you?"

"Oh, yes, of course," said Athos; "but they are only civilians, who don't know how to shoot; and they will never touch me."

He had scarcely uttered the words when four muskets fired simultaneously. The balls fell round Athos, but not one grazed him.

Four muskets immediately answered, but these were better directed than the others. Three of the soldiers fell dead, and one of the sappers was wounded.

"Grimaud, another musket," said Athos, who was still on the breach. Grimaud obeyed; a second volley was fired; the brigadier and two pioneers fell dead, and the rest of the troop took flight.

"Now we must make a sortie," cried Athos; and the four comrades dashed out of the fort, picked up the muskets belonging to the dead soldiers, and retreated to the bastion, carrying the trophies of their victory. . . .

"To arms!" called Grimaud.

The young men jumped up and ran for their muskets.

This time the advancing troop was composed of twenty or twenty-five men, but they were no longer sappers, but soldiers of the garrison.

"Hadn't we better return to the camp?" said Porthos. "The fight is not equal at all."

"Impossible, for three reasons," said Athos. "First, because we haven't finished breakfast; second, because we have several important things to discuss; and third, because there are still ten minutes before the hour is up."

"Well, anyway," remarked Aramis, "we had better have some plan of campaign."

"It is very simple," replied Athos. "The moment the enemy is within reach, we fire. If they still come on, we fire again, and go on firing as long as our guns are loaded. If any of them are left, and they try to carry the place by assault, we will let them get well into the ditch, and then drop on their heads a piece of the wall, that only keeps poised by a kind of miracle."

"Bravo," cried Porthos. "Athos, you were born to be a general, and the Cardinal, who thinks himself a great commander, is not to be compared to you."

"Gentlemen," replied Athos, "remember, one thing at a time. Cover your man well."

"I have mine," said D'Artagnan.

"And I," said Porthos and Aramis.

"Then fire;" and as Athos gave the word, the muskets rang out and four men fell. Then the drum beat, and the little army advanced to the charge, while all the while the fire was kept up, irregularly, but with a sure aim. The Rochellois however did not flinch, but came on steadily.

When they reached the foot of the bastion, the enemy still numbered twelve or fifteen. A sharp fire received them, but they never faltered, and leaping the trench, prepared to scale the breach.

"Now, comrades!" cried Athos. "Let us make an end of them. To the wall!"

And all four, aided by Grimaud, began to push with their guns a huge block of wall, which swayed as if with the wind, and then rolled slowly down into the trench. A horrible cry was heard, a cloud of dust mounted upwards; and all was silent.

"Have we crushed them all, do you think?" asked Athos.

"It looks like it," answered D'Artagnan.

"No," said Porthos, "for two or three are limping off."

Athos looked at his watch.

"Gentlemen," he said, "an hour has elapsed since we came here, and we have won our bet." . . .

"What is going on in the town?" asked Athos.

"It is a call to arms."

They listened, and the sound of a drum reached their ears.

"They must be sending us an entire regiment," said Athos.

"You don't mean to fight a whole regiment?" said Porthos.

"Why not?" asked the musketeer. "If we had only had the sense to bring another dozen bottles, I could make head against an army!"

"As I live, the drum is coming nearer," said D'Artagnan.

"Let it," replied Athos. "It takes a quarter of an hour to get from here to the town, so it takes a quarter of an hour to get from the town here. That is more than enough time for us to arrange our plans. If we leave this, we shall never find such a good position. . . . But I must first give Grimaud his orders;" and Athos made a sign to his servant.

"Grimaud," said he, pointing to the dead who were lying on the bastion, "you will take these gentlemen and prop them up against the wall, and put their hats on their heads and their guns in their hands."

"Great man!" ejaculated D'Artagnan; "I begin to see."

"You do?" asked Porthos.

"Do *you* understand, Grimaud?" said Aramis.

Grimaud nodded.

"Then we are all right," said Athos. . . .

"On guard!" cried D'Artagnan. "Look at those red and black points moving down there! A regiment, did you call it, Athos?—it is a perfect army!"

"My word, yes!" said Athos, "there they come! How cunning to beat neither drums nor trumpets. Are you ready, Grimaud?"

Grimaud silently nodded, and showed them a dozen dead men, arranged skillfully in various attitudes, some porting arms, some taking aim, others drawing their swords.

"Well done!" exclaimed Athos, "it does honor to your imagination."

"If it is all the same to you," said Porthos, "I should like to understand what is going on."

"Let us get away first," replied D'Artagnan, "and you will understand after."

"One moment, please! Give Grimaud time to clear away the breakfast."

"Ah!" said Aramis; "the red and black specks are becoming more distinct, and I agree with D'Artagnan that we have no time to lose before we regain the camp."

"Very well," rejoined Athos, "I have nothing to say against retreating. The wager was for an hour, and we have been here an hour and a half. Let us be off at once."

The four comrades went out at the back, following Grimaud, who had already departed with the basket.

"Oh!" cried Athos, stopping suddenly, "what the devil is to be done?"

"Has anything been forgotten?" asked Aramis.

"Our flag, man, our flag! We can't leave our flag in the enemy's hands, if it is nothing but a napkin." And Athos dashed again into the bastion, and bore away the flag unhurt, amid a volley of balls from the Rochellois.

He waved his flag, while turning his back on the troops of the town, and saluting those of the camp. From both sides arose great cries, of anger on the one hand and enthusiasm on the other, and the napkin, pierced with three bullet-holes, was in truth transformed into a flag. "Come down, come down!" they shouted from the camp.

Athos came down, and his friends, who had awaited him anxiously, received him with joy.

"Be quick, Athos," said D'Artagnan; "now that we have got everything but money, it would be stupid to get killed."

But Athos would not hurry himself, and they had to keep pace with him.

By this time Grimaud and his basket were well beyond bullet range, while in the distance the sounds of rapid firing might be heard.

"What are they doing?" asked Porthos; "what are they firing at?"

"At our dead men," replied Athos.

"But they don't fire back."

"Exactly so; therefore the enemy will come to the conclusion that there is an ambuscade. They will hold a council, and send an envoy with a flag of truce, and when they at last find out the joke, we shall be out of reach. So it is no use getting apoplexy by racing."

"Oh, I understand," said Porthos, full of astonishment.

"That is a mercy!" replied Athos, shrugging his shoulders, as they approached the camp, which was watching their progress in a ferment of admiration.

This time a new fusillade was begun, and the balls whistled close to the heads of the four victors and fell about their ears. The Rochellois had entered the bastion.

"What bad shooting!" said D'Artagnan. "How many was it we killed? Twelve?"

"Twelve or fifteen."

"And how many did we crush?"

"Eight or ten."

"And not a scratch to show for it."

"Ah, what is that on your hand, D'Artagnan? It looks to me like blood."

"It's nothing," replied D'Artagnan.

"A spent ball?"

"Not even that."

"But what is it, then?" As we have said, the silent and resolute Athos loved D'Artagnan like his own son, and showed every now and then all the anxiety of a father.

"The skin is rubbed off, that is all," said D'Artagnan. "My fingers were caught between two stones — the stone of the wall and the stone of my ring."

"That is what comes of having diamonds," remarked Athos disdainfully. . . .

"Here we are at the camp, and they are coming to meet us and bring us in triumphantly."

And he only spoke the truth, for the whole camp was in a turmoil. More than two thousand people had gazed, as at a play, at the lucky bit of braggadocio of the four friends,— braggadocio of which they were far from suspecting the real motive. The cry of "Long live the musketeers," resounded on all sides, and M. De Busigny was the first to hold out his hand to Athos and to declare that he had lost his wager. The dragoon and the

Swiss had followed him, and all the others had followed the dragoon and the Swiss. There was nothing but congratulations, hand-shakings, embraces; and the tumult became so great that the Cardinal thought there must be a revolt, and sent La Houdinière, his captain of guards, to find out what was the matter.

"Well?" asked the Cardinal, as his messenger returned.

"Well, monseigneur," replied La Houdinière, "it is about three musketeers and a guardsman who made a bet with M. De Busigny to go and breakfast at the Bastion Saint-Gervais, and while breakfasting, held it for two hours against the enemy, and killed I don't know how many Rochellois."

"You asked the names of these gentlemen?"

"Yes, monseigneur."

"What are they?"

"Athos, Porthos, and Aramis."

"Always my three heroes," murmured the Cardinal. "And the guardsman?"

"M. D'Artagnan."

"Always my young rogue! I must gain over these men."

And the same evening, the Cardinal had a conversation with M. De Treville about the morning's exploit, with which the whole camp was still ringing. M. De Treville, who had heard it all at first hand, gave his Eminence all the details, not forgetting the episode of the napkin.

"Very good, M. De Treville," said the Cardinal; "but you must get me that napkin, and I will have three golden lilies embroidered on it, and give as a banner to your company."

"Monseigneur," replied M. De Treville, "that would be an injustice to the guards. M. D'Artagnan does not belong to me, but to M. Des Essarts."

"Then you must take him," said the Cardinal. "As these four brave soldiers love each other so much, they ought certainly to be in the same regiment."

That evening M. De Treville announced the good news to the three musketeers and to D'Artagnan, and invited them all to breakfast the following day.

D'Artagnan was nearly beside himself with joy. As we know, it had been the dream of his life to be a musketeer.

THE MAN IN THE IRON MASK

From 'The Viscount of Bragelonne'

[Dumas adopts the theory that the Man in the Iron Mask was the suppressed twin brother of Louis XIV.]

"WHAT is all this noise?" asked Philippe, turning towards the door of the concealed staircase. And as he spoke a voice was heard saying, "This way, this way. Still a few steps, sire."

"It is M. Fouquet's voice," said D'Artagnan, who was standing near the Queen Mother.

"Then M. D'Herblay will not be far off," added Philippe; but little did he expect to see the person who actually entered.

All eyes were riveted on the door, from which the voice of M. Fouquet proceeded; but it was not he who came through.

A cry of anguish rang through the room, breaking forth simultaneously from the King and the spectators, and surely never had been seen a stranger sight.

The shutters were half closed, and only a feeble light struggled through the velvet curtains, with their thick silk linings, and the eyes of the courtiers had to get accustomed to the darkness before they could distinguish between the surrounding objects. But once discerned, they stood out as clear as day.

So, looking up, they saw Louis XIV. in the doorway of the private stair, his face pale and his brows bent; and behind him stood Fouquet.

The Queen Mother, whose hand held that of Philippe, uttered a shriek at the sight, thinking that she beheld a ghost.

Monsieur staggered for a moment and turned away his head, looking from the King who was facing him to the King who was by his side.

Madame on the contrary stepped forward, thinking it must be her brother-in-law reflected in a mirror. And indeed, this seemed the only rational explanation of the double image.

Both young men, agitated and trembling, clenching their hands, darting flames of fury from their eyes, dumb, breathless, ready to spring at each other's throats, resembled each other so exactly in feature, figure, and even, by pure accident, in dress, that Anne of Austria herself stood confounded. For as yet the truth had not dawned on her. There are some torments that we all instinctively reject. It is easier far to accept the supernatural, the impossible.

That he should encounter such obstacles had never for one moment occurred to Louis. He imagined he had only to show himself, for the world to fall at his feet. The Sun-king could have no rival; and where his rays did not fall, there must be darkness —

As to Fouquet, who could describe his bewilderment at the sight of the living portrait of his master? Then he thought that Aramis was right, and that the new-comer was every whit as much a king as his double, and that after all, perhaps he had made a mistake when he had declined to share in the *coup d'état* so cleverly plotted by the General of the Jesuits.

And then, it was equally the blood royal of Louis XIII. that Fouquet had determined to sacrifice to blood in all respects identical; a noble ambition, to one that was selfish. And it was the mere aspect of the pretender which showed him all these things.

D'Artagnan, leaning against the wall and facing Fouquet, was debating in his own mind the key to this wonderful riddle. He felt instinctively, though he could not have told why, that in the meeting of the two Louis XIV.s lay the explanation of all that had seemed suspicious in the conduct of Aramis during the last few days.

Suddenly Louis XIV., by nature the most impatient of the two young men, and with the habit of command that was the result of training, strode across the room and flung open one of the shutters. The flood of light that streamed through the window caused Philippe involuntarily to recoil, and to step back into the shelter of an alcove.

The movement struck Louis, and turning to the Queen he said:

"Mother, do you not know your own son, although every one else has denied his King?"

Anne trembled at his voice and raised her arms to heaven, but could not utter a single word.

"Mother," retorted Philippe in his quietest tones, "do you not know your own son?"

And this time it was Louis who stepped back.

As for Anne, pierced to the heart with grief and remorse, she could bear it no longer. She staggered where she stood, and unaided by her attendants, who seemed turned into stone, she sank down on a sofa with a sigh.

This spectacle was too much for Louis. He rushed to D'Artagnan, whose brain was going round with bewilderment, and who clung to the door as his last hope.

"To me, musketeer! Look us both in the face, and see which is the paler, he or I."

The cry awoke D'Artagnan from his stupor, and struck the chord of obedience strong in the bosom of every soldier. He lifted his head, and striding straight up to Philippe laid his hand on his shoulder, saying quietly:—

"Monsieur, you are my prisoner."

Philippe remained absolutely still, as if nailed to the floor, his eyes fixed despairingly on the King who was his brother. His silence reproached him as no words could have done, with the bitterness of the past and the tortures of the future.

And the King understood, and his soul sank within him. His eyes fell, and drawing his brother and sister-in-law with him, he hastily quitted the room; forgetting in his agitation even his mother, lying motionless on the couch beside him, not three paces from the son whom for the second time she was allowing to be condemned to a death in life.

Philippe drew near to her, and said softly:—

"If you had not been my mother, madame, I must have cursed you for the misery you have caused me."

D'Artagnan overheard, and a shiver of pity passed through him. He bowed respectfully to the young prince, and said:—

"Forgive me, monseigneur; I am only a soldier, and my faith is due to him who has left us."

"Thank you, M. D'Artagnan. But what has become of M. D'Herblay?"

"M. D'Herblay is safe, monseigneur," answered a voice behind them; "and while I am alive and free, not a hair of his head shall be hurt."

"M. Fouquet!" said the prince, smiling sadly.

"Forgive me, monseigneur," cried Fouquet, falling on his knees; "but he who has left the room was my guest."

"Ah!" murmured Philippe to himself with a sigh, "you are loyal friends and true hearts. You make me regret the world I am leaving. M. D'Artagnan, I will follow you."

As he spoke, Colbert entered and handed to the captain of the musketeers an order from the King; then bowed, and went out.

D'Artagnan glanced at the paper, and in a sudden burst of wrath crumpled it in his hand.

"What is the matter?" asked the prince.

"Read it, monseigneur," answered the musketeer.

And Philippe read these words, written hastily by the King himself:—

"M. D'Artagnan will conduct the prisoner to the Îles Sainte-Marguerite. He will see that his face is covered with an iron mask, which must never be lifted on pain of death."

"It is just," said Philippe; "I am ready."

"Aramis was right," whispered Fouquet to D'Artagnan, "this is as good a king as the other."

"Better," replied D'Artagnan; "he only needed you and me."

A TRICK IS PLAYED ON HENRY III. BY AID OF CHICOT

From 'The Lady of Monsoreau'

THE King and Chicot remained quiet and silent for the next ten minutes. Then suddenly the King sat up, and the noise he made roused Chicot, who was just dropping off to sleep.

The two looked at each other with sparkling eyes.

"What is it?" asked Chicot in a low voice.

"Do you hear that sighing sound?" replied the King in a lower voice still. "Listen!"

As he spoke, one of the wax candles in the hand of the golden satyr went out; then a second, then a third. After a moment, the fourth went out also.

"Oh, oh!" cried Chicot, "that is more than a sighing sound." But he had hardly uttered the last word when in its turn the lamp was extinguished, and the room was in darkness, save for the flickering glow of the dying embers.

"Look out!" exclaimed Chicot, jumping up.

"He is going to speak," said the King, shrinking back into his bed.

"Then listen and let us hear what he says," replied Chicot, and at the same instant a voice which sounded at once both piercing and hollow, proceeded from the space between the bed and the wall.

"Hardened sinner, are you there?"

"Yes, yes, Lord," gasped Henri with chattering teeth.

"Dear me!" remarked Chicot, "that is a very hoarse voice to have come from heaven! I feel dreadfully frightened; but never mind!"

"Do you hear me?" asked the voice.

"Yes, Lord," stammered Henri; "and I bow before your anger."

"Do you think you are carrying out my will by performing all the mummeries you have taken part in to-day, while your heart is full of the things of this world?"

"Well said!" cried Chicot; "you touched him there!"

The King's hands shook as he clasped them, and Chicot went up to him.

"Well," murmured Henri, "are you convinced now?"

"Wait a bit," answered Chicot.

"What do you want more?"

"Hush! listen to me. Creep softly out of bed, and let me take your place."

"Why?"

"Because then the anger of the Lord will fall first upon me."

"And do you think I shall escape?"

"We will try, anyway;" and with affectionate persistence he pushed the King out of bed, and took his place.

"Now, Henri," he said, "go and lie on my sofa, and leave all to me."

Henri obeyed; he began to understand Chicot's plan.

"You are silent," continued the voice, "which proves that your heart is hardened."

"Oh, pardon, pardon, Lord!" exclaimed Chicot, imitating the King's nasal twang. Then, stretching himself out of bed, he whispered to the King, "It is very odd, but the heavenly voice does not seem to know that it is Chicot who is speaking."

"Oh!" replied Henri, "what do you suppose is the meaning of that?"

"Don't be in a hurry; plenty of strange things will happen yet!"

"Miserable creature that you are!" went on the voice.

"Yes, Lord, yes!" answered Chicot. "I am a horrible sinner, hardened in crime."

"Then confess your sins, and repent."

« I acknowledge,» said Chicot, «that I dealt wickedly by my cousin Condé, whose wife I betrayed; and I repent bitterly.»

« What is that you are saying?» cried the King. « There is no good in mentioning that. It has all been forgotten long ago.»

« Oh, has it?» replied Chicot; «then we will pass on to something else.»

« Answer,» said the voice.

« I acknowledge,» said the false Henri, «that I behaved like a thief toward the Poles, who had elected me their king, in stealing away to France one fine night, carrying with me all the crown jewels; and I repent bitterly.»

« Idiot!» exclaimed Henri, «what are you talking about now? Nobody remembers anything about that.»

« Let me alone,» answered Chicot, «I must go on pretending to be the King.»

« Speak,» said the voice.

« I acknowledge,» continued Chicot, «that I snatched the throne from my brother D'Alençon, who was the rightful heir, since I had formally renounced my claims when I was elected King of Poland; I repent bitterly.»

« Rascal!» cried the King.

« There is yet something more,» said the voice.

« I acknowledge to have plotted with my excellent mother, Catherine de' Medicis, to hunt from France my brother-in-law the King of Navarre, after first destroying all his friends, and my sister Queen Marguerite, after first destroying all her lovers; and I repent bitterly.»

« Scoundrel! Cease!» muttered the King, his teeth clenched in anger.

« Sire, it is no use trying to hide what Providence knows as well as we do.»

« There is a crime unconfessed that has nothing to do with politics,» said the voice.

« Ah, now we are getting to it,» observed Chicot dolefully; «it is about my conduct, I suppose?»

« It is,» answered the voice.

« I cannot deny,» continued Chicot, always speaking in the name of the King, «that I am very effeminate, very lazy; a hopeless trifler, an incorrigible hypocrite.»

« It is true,» said the voice.

"I have behaved ill to all women, to my own wife in particular; and such a good wife too."

"A man should love his wife as himself, and above all the world," cried the voice angrily.

"Oh dear!" wailed Chicot in despairing tones; "then I certainly have sinned terribly."

"And by your example you have caused others to sin."

"That is true, sadly true."

"You very nearly sent that poor Saint-Luc to perdition."

"Bah!" said Chicot, "are you sure I did not send him there quite?"

"No; but such a fate may befall both of you if you do not let him go back to his family at break of day."

"Dear me!" said Chicot to the King, "the voice seems to take a great interest in the house of Cossé."

"If you disobey me, you will suffer the same torments as Sardanapalus, Nabuchodnosor, and the Marshal De Retz."

Henry III. gave a loud groan; at this threat he became more frightened than ever.

"I am lost," he ejaculated wildly; "I am lost. That voice from on high will be my death-warrant."

ALEX. DUMAS, FILS.

ALEXANDRE DUMAS, JUNIOR

(1824–1895)

BY FRANCISQUE SARCEY

E SHALL not say much about the life of Alexandre Dumas the younger. The history of a great writer is the history of his works. He was born in Paris, on July 27th, 1824. His name on the register of births appears as "Alexandre, son of Marie Catherine Lebay, seamstress." He was not acknowledged by his father until he had reached his sixth year, March 7th, 1830. I emphasize this particular because it had great influence on the bent of his genius. During all his life Dumas was haunted by a desire of rehabilitating illegitimate children, of creating a reaction against their treatment by the Civil Code and the prejudice which makes of them something little better than outcasts in society.

"When seven years old," he himself says, "I entered as a boarder the school of Monsieur Vauthier, on Rue Montagne Saint-Geneviève. Thence I passed, about two years later, to the Saint-Victor School; the principal was Monsieur Goubaux, a friend of my father, with whom he collaborated under the *nom de plume* of Dinaux. This school, which numbered two hundred and fifty boarding pupils, and with the rather strange habits which I tried to depict in 'The Clémenceau Case,' occupied all the ground covered to-day by the Casino de Paris and the 'Pôle-Nord' establishment. When about fifteen I left the Saint-Victor School for Monsieur Hénon's school, which was situated in the Rue de Courcelles and has now disappeared. It is in the Collège Bourbon (now the Lycée Condorcet) that I received all my instruction, as the pupils of the two schools where I lived attended the college classes. I never belonged to any of the higher State schools,—I have not even the degree of bachelor."

At the end of his years of study he returned to his father. He did not stay there more than six months. The rather tumultuous life which he saw in the house disturbed his proud mind, already filled with serious yearnings.

"You have debts," his father said to him. "Do as I do: work, and you will pay them."

Such was indeed the young man's intention. His first work was a one-act play in verse, 'The Queen's Jewel,' which no one, assuredly, would mention to-day but for his signature. The date was 1845, and the author was then twenty-one. Other works by him were published at various times in the Journal des Demoiselles.

"I was," he has said, "the careless, lazy, and spoilt child of all my father's friends. I believed in the eternity of youth, of strength, of joy. I spent the whole day laughing, the whole night sleeping, unless I had some reason for writing verses."

About 1846 he set resolutely to work. He turned to novel-writing, which seemed to him to offer greater facilities for reaching the public and greater chances of immediate income than dramatic composition. Only two of his novels have survived: 'La Dame aux Camélias' ('Camille': 1848), because from this book came the immortal drama by the same title; and 'The Clémenceau Case,' because the author wrote it when he was in complete possession of his talent, and because moreover it is a first-rate work.

It was in 1852 that the Vaudeville Theatre gave the first performance of 'Camille,' the fortune of which was to be so extraordinary. For two or three years the play had been tossed from theatre to theatre. Nobody wanted it. To the ideas of the time it seemed simply shocking, and the play was still forbidden in London after its performances in France were numbered by the hundreds.

There is this special trait in 'Camille'—it was a work all instinct with the spirit of youth. Dumas twenty years later sadly said: "I might perhaps make another 'Demi-Monde'; I could not make another 'Camille.'" There existed, indeed, other works which have all the fire and charm of the twentieth year. 'Polyeucte' is Corneille's masterpiece; his 'Cid' breathes the spirit of youth: Corneille at forty could not have written the 'Cid.' Racine's first play is 'Andromaque': Beaumarchais's is the 'Barber of Seville'; Rossini, when young, enlivened it with his light and sparkling airs. Fifteen years later he himself wrote his 'William Tell,' a higher work, but a work which was not young.

If the theatrical managers had recoiled from 'Camille' in spite of the great names that recommended it, it is because it was cut after a pattern to which neither they nor the public were accustomed; it is because it contained the germ of a whole dramatic revolution. Now, the author was not a theatrical revolutionist. He had not said to himself, "I am going to throw down the old fabric of the drama, and erect a new one on its ruins." To tell the truth, he had no idea of what he was doing. He had witnessed a love drama. He had thrown it still throbbing upon the stage, without any regard for the dramatic conventions which were then imposed upon playwrights, and which were almost accepted as laws. He had simply depicted what he had seen. All the managers, attached as they were to the

old customs, and respectful of the traditions, had trembled with hor-
ror when they saw moving around Camille the ignoble Prudence, the
idiotic Duc de Varville, the silly Saint-Gaudens. But the public—
though the fact was suspected neither by them nor by the public
itself—yearned for more truth upon the boards. When 'Camille'
was presented to them, the play-goers uttered a cry of astonishment
and joy: that was the thing! that was just what they wanted!
From that day, which will remain as a date in the history of the
French stage, the part of Camille has been performed by all the
celebrated actresses. The part has two sides: one may see in it a
degraded woman who has fallen profoundly in love, rather late in
life; one may also see in it a woman, already poetical in her own
nature, suddenly carried away by a great passion into the sacred
regions of the Ideal.

Almost any young man in Dumas's place would have lost his head
after so astounding a success, and might not have resisted the temp-
tation of at once working out the vein. For on coming out of the
theatre after the first performance, the author had all the managers
at his feet, and the smallest trifle was sure to be accepted if it only
had his signature. But he had learned, by the side of "a prodigal
father," the art of husbanding his talent. He declined to front the
footlights again, save with a work upon which he had been able to
bestow all the care and labor it deserved: he waited a year before
he gave, at the Gymnase theatre, 'Diane de Lys.'

'Diane de Lys' undoubtedly pleased the public, but its success was
not exactly brilliant. It is full of great qualities, it is strongly con-
ceived, constructed with rare power and logic, but it added nothing
to his reputation. The play as a whole seemed long and melancholy.
It is a curious subject for critical study, as one of the stages in which
the genius of the author stopped awhile, on its way to higher works.
It will leave no great trace in his career.

Two years later he gave at the Gymnase theatre—I do not dare
to say his masterpiece, but certainly the best constructed and most
enjoyable play he ever wrote, 'Le Demi-Monde' (The Other Half-
World). In this play he discovered and defined the very peculiar
world of those women who live on the margin of regular "society,"
and try to preserve its tone and demeanor. What scientific and
strong construction are here! What an admirable disposition of the
scenes, both flexible and logical! And through the action, which
moves on with wonderful straightforwardness and breadth, how many
portraits, drawn with a steady hand, each one bearing such distinctive
features that you would know them if you met them on the street!
Olivier de Jalin, the refined Parisian, the dialectician of the play,
who is no other than Dumas himself; Raymond de Nanjac, handsome

and honest, but not keen or Parisian; and that giddy Valentine de Sanctis, whose head turns with the wind, whose tongue cannot rest one moment; and especially Suzanne d'Ange, so witty, so complex, so devious in her motions, so *roublarde*, as a Parisian of to-day would say.

Between 'The Demi-Monde,' and 'La Question d'Argent' (The Money Question), which followed, Dumas spent two years at work. 'La Question d'Argent' is a favorite play with the connoisseurs; but its reception by the public was of the coldest. It is a noteworthy fact that plays turning upon money have never been successful. Le Sage's 'Turcaret' is a dramatic masterpiece: it never had the luck to please the crowd. Dumas's Jean Giraud is, however, a very curiously studied character. The author has represented in him the commonest type of the shady money-man, the unconscious rascal. And very skillfully he made an individual out of that general type, by giving to Jean Giraud a certain rough good-nature; the appearance of a good fellow, with a certain degree of fineness; a mixture of humility and self-conceit, of awkwardness and impudence, and even some ideas as to the power of money that do not lack dignity, and some real liberality of sentiment and act,—for wealth alone, though acquired by ignominious means, suggests and dictates to the great robbers some advantageous movements which the small rascal cannot indulge in: and around this Turcaret of the Second Empire how many pictures of honest people, every one of whom, in his or her way, is good and fine!

One year later Dumas carried to the Gymnase, his favorite theatre, 'Le Fils Naturel' (The Natural Son); and the next year 'Un Père Prodigue' (A Prodigal Father; known also in English through a free adaptation as 'My Awful Dad').

In 'Le Fils Naturel' Dumas for the first time wrote a theme-play, a kind of work in which he was to become a master. Hitherto we have seen him drawing pictures of manners. To be sure, philosophical considerations on the period depicted are not wanting, but the play has not the form and does not assume the movement of a thesis. It does not take up one special trait of our social order, one of our worldly prejudices, in order to show its strong and weak sides. 'Le Fils Naturel' is the work of a moralist as well as of a playwright; or rather, it is the work of a playwright who was a born moralist.

'Un Père Prodigue' originally excited great curiosity. It escaped no one that in his Count Fernand de la Rivonnière, Dumas had shown us some traits of his illustrious father, who *had* been a prodigal father; and that he had depicted himself in Viscount André. Every one made comparisons; some, of course, accused the author of filial disrespect. The accusation was ridiculous, and he did not even answer it. He had so well disguised the persons, he had transported them into such different surroundings, that no one could recognize in them their true prototypes. Then — and this is no small praise — if Count de la Rivonnière is guilty of one fault, that of throwing to the wind his fortune, he is a most amiable nobleman, full of broad ideas and generous sentiments,— has a warm heart. The fourth act, in which the father sacrifices himself in order to save his son's life, is pathetic in the extreme. But nothing equals the first act, which is a model of animated and picturesque composition. No one ever painted in more vivid colors the pillage of a household, and a family without so much as a shadow of discipline. It is an accumulation of small details, not one of which is of an indifferent nature, and which, taken together, drive into our minds the idea that this nobleman, so well-mannered, so charming in conversation, so sober for himself, is running to ruin as gayly as he can.

For four years after the production of 'Un Père Prodigue' Dumas wrote nothing. But in 1864 he reappeared at the Gymnase with a strange play, 'L'Ami des Femmes' (A Friend of the Sex), which completely failed. After 'L'Ami des Femmes' there was another interruption, not of Dumas's labors but of his dramatic production. Perhaps he was sick of an art which had caused him a cruel disappointment. He turned again to novel-writing, and published (1866) 'L'Affaire Clémenceau' (The Clémenceau Case), the success of which was not as great as he had hoped. In France, when a man is superior in one specialty people will not let him leave it. He is not allowed to be at once an unequaled novelist and a first-rate dramatist.

At that time Dumas hesitated which road to follow. An incident which created a great deal of comment threw him back towards the stage, and towards a new form of comedy.

M. Émile de Girardin, one of the best known publicists of the Second Empire, had bethought himself, when over fifty years of age, and knowing nothing of this kind of work, to write a play. He had been a great friend of Dumas père, and had kept up the most affectionate intercourse with his son. He had asked him to fit his play for the stage. It possessed one really dramatic idea. Dumas, in order to oblige his father's friend, made out of it 'Le Supplice d'une Femme' (A Woman's Torture). Émile de Girardin, who was self-conceited and somewhat despotic, refused to recognize his offspring in the bear that Dumas had licked. He declined to sign the play: "Neither shall I," Dumas retorted.

'A Woman's Torture' was acted at the Comédie Française with extraordinary success. This success was for Dumas a warning and a lesson. 'A Woman's Torture' was a three-act play, short, concise, panting, which hurried to the *coup de théâtre* of the second act, upon which the drama revolved, and rushed to its conclusion. The time of five-act comedies, with ample expositions, copious developments, philosophical disquisitions, curious and fanciful episodes, was gone. Henceforth the dramatist had to deal with a hurried and *blasé* public, which, taking dinner at eight, could give to the theatre but a short time, and an attention disturbed by the labor of digestion. 'A Woman's Torture,' which lasted only an hour and a half, and proceeded only by rapid strokes, was exactly what that public wanted. After that time Dumas wrote only three-act and one-act plays; using four acts only for 'Les Idées de Madame Aubray' (Madame Aubray's Ideas); and these four acts are very short. In 1867 this play announced Dumas's return to the stage; and Dumas is here more paradoxical than he had ever been. His theme looked like a wager not simply against bourgeois prejudices, but even against good sense, and, I dare to say, against justice. This wager was won by Dumas, thanks to an incredible display of skill. He took up the thesis a second time in 'Denise,' and won his wager again, but with less difficulty. In 'Denise' the lover struggles only against social prejudices, and allows himself to be carried away by one of those emotional fits which disturb and confound human reason. In 'Madame Aubray's Ideas' the triumph is one of pure logic.

'Une Visite de Noces' (A Wedding Call) and 'La Princesse Georges' followed rather closely on 'Madame Aubray's Ideas.' 'A Wedding Call'!—what a thunderbolt then! It was of but one act, *but* one act the effect of which was prodigious, the echo of which is still heard. Time and familiarity have now softened for us the too sharp outlines of this bitter play. It has been acknowledged a masterpiece. It is certainly one of the boldest works of this extraordinary magician, who, thanks to his unerring skill and to the dazzling wit of his dialogue, brought the public to listen to whatever he chose to put upon the stage. It seemed that, like a lion tamer in the arena, Dumas took pleasure in belaboring and exasperating this many-headed monster, in order to prove to his own satisfaction that he could subdue its revolts.

'La Princesse Georges' is a work of violent and furious passion. We find in it Madame de Terremonde, the good woman who adores her husband, but who adores him with fury, who wants him all to herself, and who, when sure that she is betrayed, passes from the most exasperated rage to tears and despair. There is in the first act a scene of exposition which has become celebrated. No one ever so rapidly mastered the public; no one ever from the first stroke so painfully twisted the heart of the spectators.

Let us pass rapidly over 'La Femme de Claude' (Claude's Wife: 1873). Of all his plays it is the one Dumas said he liked best, the one he most passionately defended with all sorts of commentaries, letters, prefaces, etc.; the one which he insisted on having revived, a long time after it had failed. To my mind that play was a mistake: and the public, in spite of Dumas's arguments, in spite of the protests of the critics, who are often very glad to distinguish themselves by not yielding to the common voice,—the public insisted on agreeing with me.

Only a few months later, Dumas brilliantly retrieved himself with 'Monsieur Alphonse.' His Madame Guichard is the most cheerfully vulgar type of the *parvenue* which any one ever dared to put upon the stage. She can hardly read and write; she is no longer young, and she is "to boot" very proud of her money; she has no tact and no taste; but at heart she is a good sort of woman. Her morality is as primitive as her education. But deceit disgusts her; she hates but one thing, she says,—lying. She is not troubled by conventionalities, and her speech has all the color and energy of popular speech. But see! Dumas in depicting this woman preserved exquisite measure. Madame Guichard says many pert and droll things; she never utters a coarse word. Her language is picturesque; it is free from slang. Hers is a vulgar nature, but she does not offend delicate ears by the grossness of her utterance. Dumas never drew a more living picture; she is the joy of this rather sad play.

All that remain to be reviewed are 'L'Étrangère,' 'La Princesse de Bagdad,' and 'Françillon'; all of which were given at the Comédie Française. 'L'Étrangère' is indeed a melodrama, with an admixture of comedy. Had he gone further in that direction, Dumas might have made a new sort of play, which would perhaps have reigned a long time on the stage. But after this trial, successful though it was, he stopped. 'La Princesse de Bagdad' entirely failed. 'Françillon' was Dumas's last success at the Comédie Française.

After 1887 Dumas gave nothing to the stage. He had completed a great five-act play, 'The Road to Thebes,' which the manager of the Comédie Française hoped every year to put on the boards. Dumas kept promising it; but either from distrust of himself or of the public, or from fatigue, or fear of meeting with failure, he asked for new delays, until the day when he declared that not only the play would not be acted during his life, but that he would not even allow it to be acted after his death.

This death he saw coming, with sad but calm eyes. It was a sorrow for us to see this man, whom we had known so quick and alert, grow weaker every day, showing the progress of disease in his shriveled features and body. The complexion had lost all color, the cheeks had become flaccid, the eye had no life left.

On October 1st, 1895, he wrote to his friend Jules Claretie:— "Do not depend upon me any more; I am vanquished. There are moments when I mourn my loss, as Madame D'Houdetot said when dying." He was at Puys, by the seaside, when he wrote that despairing letter. He returned to Marly, there to die, surrounded by his family, on November 28th, 1895, in a house which he loved and which had been bequeathed to him years before by an intimate friend.

His loss threw into mourning the world of letters, and the whole of Paris. People discovered then — for death loosens every tongue and every pen — how kind and generous in reality was Dumas, who had often been accused of avarice by those who contrasted him with his father; how many services he had discreetly rendered, how open his hand always was. His constant cheerfulness and good-nature had finally caused him to be forgiven for his wit, which was sarcastic and cutting, and for his success, which had thrown so many rivals into the shade. This witty man, who was always obliging and even tender-hearted, had no envy, and gave his applause without a shadow of reserve to the successes of others. Every young author found in him advice and support; he did not expect gratitude, and therefore was soured by no disappointment. He was a good man, partly from nature, partly from determination; for he deemed that, after all, the best way to live happy in this world is to make happy as many people as possible.

If in this long essay I have not spoken of Dumas as a moralist, it is because, in my opinion, in spite of all that has been said, Dumas was a dramatist a great deal more than a philosopher. In his comedies he discussed a great many moral and social questions, without giving a solution for any; or rather, the solutions that he gave were due not to any set of fixed principles, but to the conclusion which he was preparing for this play or that. He said, indifferently, "Kill her" or "Forgive her," according to the requirements of the subject which he had selected; and he would afterwards write a sensational preface with a view to demonstrate that the solution this time given by him was the only legitimate one. These prefaces are very amusing reading; for he wrote them with all the fire of his nature, and he had the gift of movement. But they were a strange medley of incongruous and contradictory statements. Every idea that he expresses can be grasped and understood; but it is impossible to see how it agrees with those that precede and follow. It is a chaos of clear ideas.

Dumas was not a philosopher, but an agitator. He stirred up a great many questions; he drew upon them our distracted attention; he compelled us to think of them. Therein he did his duty as a dramatist.

He gave much thought to the fate of woman in our civilization. We may say, however, that though loving her much, he still more

feared her, and I shall even add, despised her. All his characters
who have the mission of defending morality and good sense are very
attentive to her, but keep her at arm's-length. They are affectionate
counselors, not lovers. They hold her to be a frail being, who must
be controlled and guided. Some one has said that there was in
Dumas something of the Catholic priest. It is true. He was to
women a lay director of conscience.

He was a great connoisseur of pictures and a great art lover.
Music, I think, is the only art that did not affect him much. He was
a dazzling talker; his plays teem with bright sayings; his conversa-
tion sparkled with them. I did not know him in his prime, when he
delighted his friends and companions by his unceasing flow of spirits.
I became intimate with him only later. If you knew how to start
him, he simply coruscated. I never knew any one, save Edmond
About, who was as witty, and who, like About, always paid you back
in good sounding coin.

Dumas was a member of the French Academy. He had not
wished for that honor, because it had been denied to his father. He
desired, in his reception speech, to call up the great spirit of this
illustrious father and make it share his academician's chair. He had
this joy; the two Dumas were received on the same day. Their two
names will never perish.

Francisque Sarcey

[The editors have been compelled, for lack of space, to leave out
that part of M. Sarcey's valuable essay which is a professional anal-
ysis of several of Dumas's plays, and which would be of interest,
chiefly, to special students of the French drama and stage.]

THE PLAYWRIGHT IS BORN—AND MADE

From the Preface to 'A Prodigal Father'

OF ALL the various forms of thought, the stage is that which
nearest approaches the plastic arts—inasmuch as we can-
not work in it unless we know its material processes; but
with this difference: that in the other arts one learns these pro-
cesses, while in play-writing one guesses them; or to speak more
accurately, they are in us to begin with.

One can become a painter, a sculptor, a musician, by sheer
study: one does not become a dramatic author in this fashion. A

caprice of nature makes your eye in such a way that you can see a thing after a particular manner, not absolutely correct, but which must nevertheless appear, to any other persons that you wish to have so think, the only correct point of view. The man really called to write for the stage reveals what is an extremely rare faculty, in his very first attempts,— say in a farce in school, or a drawing-room charade. There is a sort of science of optics and of perspective that enables one to draw a personage, a character, a passion, an impulse of the soul, with a single stroke of the pen. Dramatic *cheating of the eye* is so complete that often the spectator, when he is a mere reader of the play, desiring to give himself once more the same emotion that he has felt as one of the audience, not only cannot recapture that emotion in the written words before him, but often cannot even distinguish the passage where the emotion lies hid. It was a word, a look, a silence, a gesture, a purely atmospheric combination, that held him spellbound. So comes in the genius of the playwright's trade, if those two words can be associated. One may compare writing for the stage in relation to other phases of literature, as we compare ceiling painters with [painters of] pictures for the wall or the easel. Woe to the painter if he forget that his composition is to be looked at from a distance, with a light below it!

A man without merit as a thinker, a moralist, a philosopher, an author, may turn out to be a dramatic author of the first class; that is to say, in the work of setting in motion before you the purely external movements of mankind; and on the other hand, to become in the theatre the thinker, the moralist, the philosopher, or the author to whom one listens, one must indispensably be furnished with the particular and natural qualities of a man of much lower grade. In short, to be a master in the art of writing for the stage, you must be a poor hand in the superior art. . . .

That dramatic author who shall know mankind like Balzac, and who shall know the theatre like Scribe, will be the greatest dramatic author that has ever existed.

Translated for 'A Library of the World's Best Literature,' by E. Irenæus Stevenson

AN ARMED TRUCE

From 'A Friend of the Sex'

[The following conversation in the first act of the play takes place in the pleasant morning-room of a country-house near Paris, the home of M. and Madame Leverdet. M. Leverdet is asleep in his chair. The speakers are Madame Leverdet, a coquettish, sprightly lady approaching middle age, and young M. De Ryons, a friend and neighbor. Madame Leverdet is determined to marry off De Ryons advantageously, and as soon as possible. Unfortunately he is a confirmed bachelor, not to say woman-hater, whose cynicism is the result of severely disappointing experiences. Under that cynicism there is however genuine respect and even chivalry as to the right sort of woman,— the superior and sincere type, which he does not happen often to encounter.]

MADAME LEVERDET — Let us come to serious topics while we are alone, my friend.

De Ryons — And apropos of them?

Madame Leverdet — Are you willing to be married off yet?

De Ryons [*with a start of terror*] — Pardon me, my dear lady! At what hour can I take the first train for Paris?

Madame Leverdet — Now listen to me, at least.

De Ryons — What! Here it is two years since I have called on you; I come to make you a little visit of a morning, in all good friendship, with the thermometer forty, centigrade; I am totally unsuspecting; all I ask is to have a little lively chat with a clever woman — and see how you receive me.

Madame Leverdet [*continuing*] — A simple, charming young girl —

De Ryons [*interrupting her, and in the same tone*] — — musical, speaks English, draws nicely, sings agreeably, a society woman, a domestic woman,— all at the choice of the applicant.

Madame Leverdet [*laughing*] — Yes, and pretty and graceful and rich; and, by-the-by, one who finds you a charming fellow.

De Ryons — She is quite right there. I shall make a charming husband — I shall; I know it. Only thirty-two years old; all my teeth, all my hair (no such very common detail, the way young men are nowadays); lively, sixty thousand livres income as a landed proprietor — oh, I am an excellent match: only unfortunately I am not a marrying man.

Madame Leverdet — And why not, if you please?

De Ryons [*smiling*] — It would interfere severely with my studies.

Madame Leverdet — What sort of studies?

De Ryons — My studies of — woman.

Madame Leverdet — Really! I don't understand you.

De Ryons — What! Do you not know that I am making women my particular, my incessant study, and that I am reckoning on leaving some new and very interesting documents dealing with that branch of natural history? — a branch very little understood just at present, in spite of all that has been written on the topic. My friend, I cannot sacrifice the species to the individual; I belong to science. It is quite impossible for me to give myself wholly and completely — as one certainly should do when he marries — to one of those charming and terrible little carnivora for whose sake men dishonor themselves, ruin themselves, kill themselves; whose sole preoccupation, in the midst of the universal carnage that they make, is to dress themselves now like umbrellas and now like table bells.

Madame Leverdet [*scornfully*] — So you really think you understand women, do you?

De Ryons — I rather think I do. Why, just as you see me this instant, at the end of five minutes' study or conversation I can tell you to what class a woman belongs, — whether to the middle class, to women of rank, artists, or whatever you please; what are her tastes, her characteristics, her antecedents, the state of her heart, — in a word, everything that concerns my special science.

Madame Leverdet — Really! Will you have a glass of water?

De Ryons — Not yet, thank you.

Madame Leverdet — I suppose, then, you are under the impression that you know me too.

De Ryons — As if I did not!

Madame Leverdet — Well, and I am — what?

De Ryons — Oh, you are a clever woman. It is for that reason that I call on you [*aside:* every two years].

Madame Leverdet — Will you kindly give me the sum of your observations in general? You can tell me so much, since I am a clever woman.

De Ryons — The true, the true, the true sum?

Madame Leverdet — Yes.

De Ryons — Simply that woman of our day is an illogical, subordinate, and mischief-making creature. [*In saying this De Ryons draws back and crouches down as if expecting to be struck.*]

Madame Leverdet — So then, you detest women?

De Ryons—I? I detest women? On the contrary, I adore them; but I hold myself in such a position toward them that they cannot bite me. I keep on the outside of the cage.

Madame Leverdet—Meaning by that—what?

De Ryons—Meaning by that, that I am a friend of the sex; for I have long perceived that just as truly as women are dangerous in love, just so much are they adorable in friendship, with men;—that is to say, with no obligations, and therefore no treasons; no rights, and in consequence no tyrannies. One assists, too, as a spectator, often as a collaborator, in the comedy of love. A man under such conditions sees before his nose the stage tricks, the machinery, the changes of scenes, all that stage mounting so dazzling at a distance and so simple when one is near by. As a friend of the sex and on a basis of friendship, one estimates the causes, the contradictions, the incoherences, of that phantasmagoric changeableness that belongs to the heart of a woman. So you have something that is interesting and instructive. Under such circumstances a man is the consoler, and gives his advice; he wipes away tears; he brings quarrelsome lovers together; he asks for the letters that must be returned; he hands back the photographs (for you know that in love affairs photographs are taken only in order to be returned, and it is nearly always the same photograph that serves as many times as may be necessary. I know one photograph that I have had handed back by three different men, and it ended its usefulness by being given for good and all to a fourth one, who was— not single). . . . In short, you see, my dear madam, I am above all the friend of those women—who have known what it is to be in love. And moreover inasmuch, just as Rochefoucauld says, as women do not think a great deal of their first experience,— why, one fine day or another—

Madame Leverdet—You prove to be the second one.

De Ryons—No, no; I have no number, I! A well-brought-up woman never goes from one experience of the heart to another one, without a decent interval of time, more or less long. Two railroad accidents never come together on the same railway. During the *intervals* a woman really needs a friend, a good confidant; and it is then that I turn up. I let her tell me all the melancholy affairs in question; I see the unhappy victim in tears after the traitor has called; I lament with her, I weep with her, I make her laugh with me: and little by little I replace the delinquent without her seeing that I am doing so. But then I know very well that I am without importance, that I am a mere politician of the moment, a cabinet minister without a portfolio, a sentimental distraction without any consequences; and some fine day, after having been the confidential friend as to past events, I become the confidential friend as to future ones,— for the lady falls in love for the second time with somebody who knows nothing of the first experience, who will never know anything about it, and who of course must be made to suppose he represents the first one. Then I go away for a little time and leave them to themselves, and then I come back like a new friend to the family. By-and-by, when the dear creature is reckoning up the balance-sheet of her past, when her conscience pours into her ear the names that she would rather not remember, and my name comes with the others, she reflects an instant,— and then she says resolutely and sincerely to herself, "Oh, *he* does not count!" My friend, I am always the one that does not count, and I like it extremely.

Madame Leverdet [*indignantly*]— You are simply a monster!

De Ryons— Oh no, oh no, oh no, I am not!

Madame Leverdet— According to your own account, you have no faith in women. . . . Wretch! Ungrateful creature! And yet it is woman who inspires all the great things in this life.

De Ryons— But somehow forbids us to accomplish them.

Madame Leverdet— Go out from here, my dear De Ryons, and never let me see you again.

De Ryons [*rising promptly and making a mocking bow*]— My dear lady —

Madame Leverdet— No, I will *not* shake hands with you.

De Ryons— Then I shall die of chagrin — that's all about it.

Madame Leverdet— Do you know how you will end, you incorrigible creature? When you are fifty years old you will have rheumatism.

De Ryons— Yes, or sciatica. But I shall find some one who will embroider me warm slippers.

Madame Leverdet— Indeed you will not! You will marry your cook.

De Ryons— That depends on how well she cooks. Again farewell, dear madam.

Madame Leverdet— No, stay one moment.

De Ryons— It is you who are keeping me; so look out.

Madame Leverdet— Let me have really your last word on the whole matter.

De Ryons — It is very easily given. There are just two kinds of women: those who are good women, and those who are not.

Madame Leverdet — Without fine distinctions?

De Ryons — Without fine distinctions.

Madame Leverdet — What is one to do in the case of those who are not — good women?

De Ryons — They must be consoled.

Madame Leverdet — And those who are?

De Ryons — They must be guaranteed against being anything else; and as to that process of guarantee I have taken a patent.

Madame Leverdet — Come now, if you are playing in parlor theatricals, say so. What are you trying to be,— Lovelace or Don Quixote?

De Ryons — I am neither the one nor the other. I am a man who, having nothing else to do, took to studying women just as another man studies beetles and minerals, only I am under the impression that my scientific study is more interesting and more useful than that of the other savant — because we meet your sex everywhere. We meet the mother, the sister, the daughter, the wife, the woman who is in love; and it is important to be well informed upon such an eternal associate in our lives. Now I am a man of my time, exercised over one theory or another, hardly knowing what he must believe, good or bad, but inclined to believe in good when occasion presents itself. I respect women who respect themselves. . . . It is not I who created the world, I take it as I find it. . . . And as to marriage, the day when I shall find a young girl with the four qualities of goodness of heart, sound health, thorough self-respect, and cheerfulness,— the squaring of the conjugal hypothenuse,— then I count for nothing all my long term of waiting; like the great Doctor Faust, I become young again, and such as I am, I give myself to her. My friend, if this same young girl of whom you have been speaking (and by the way, I know her just as well as you do) really unites these conditions,— I do not believe she does so, though I shall see very soon,— why then, I will marry her to-morrow — I will marry her to-night. But in the mean time, as I have positively nothing to do,— if you happen to know a self-respecting woman who needs to be kept from a bit of folly . . . why, I am wholly at your service.

Translated for 'A Library of the World's Best Literature,' by E. Irenæus Stevenson

TWO VIEWS OF MONEY

From 'The Money Question'

[The following passage occurs in the first act of Dumas's play. The characters include the young parvenu Jean Giraud, the aristocratic M. De Cayolle, and several others, all guests in the drawing-room of the country-house of Madame Durieu. In course of the conversation Giraud refers to his father, at one time a gardener on the estate of M. De Charzay.]

JEAN GIRAUD—Oh, yes, yes, I have got along in the world, as people say. There are people who blush for their fathers; I make a brag of mine—that's the difference.

René de Charzay—And what is Father Giraud nowadays? Oh, I beg your pardon—

Jean—Don't be embarrassed—we keep on calling him Father Giraud all the same. He is a gardener still, only he gardens on his own account. He owns the house that your father was obliged to sell a while ago. My father has never had but one idea,—our Father Giraud,—and that is to be a land-owner; I bought that piece of property for him, and so he is as happy as a fish in the water. If you like, we will go and take breakfast with him to-morrow morning. He will be' delighted to see you. How things change, eh? There, where a while ago we were the servants, now we are the masters; though we are not so very proud, for all that.

Countess Savelli [*aside*]—He has passed the Rubicon of parvenus! He has confessed his father! Now nothing can stop his way!

Jean [*to De Charzay*]—I have wanted to see you for a long time, but I have not been sure how you would meet me.

René—I would have met you with pleasure, as my uncle would have met you. One cannot utter reproaches to a man who has made his own fortune, except when he has made it by dishonest means; a man who owes it to his intelligence and his probity, who uses it worthily, everybody is ready to meet kindly, as you are met here.

Jean—Sir, it is not necessary that a man should use his fortune nobly, provided it is made—that is the main thing!

Madame Durieu—Oh, oh, M. Giraud! there you spoil everything that you have said.

Jean — I don't say that of my own case, madam, but I say just what I say,— money is money, whatever may be the kind of hands where it sticks. It is the sole power that one never disputes. You may dispute virtue, beauty, courage, genius; but you can't dispute money. There is not one civilized being, rising in the morning, who does not recognize the sovereignty of money, without which he would have neither the roof which shelters him, nor the bed in which he sleeps, nor the bread that he eats. Whither are bound these masses of people crowding in the streets?— from the employé sweating under his too heavy burden, to the millionaire hurrying down to the Bourse behind his two trotters? The one is running after fifteen sous, the other after one hundred thousand francs. Why do we all have these shops, these railroads, these factories, these theatres, these museums, these lawsuits between brothers and sisters, between fathers and sons, these revelations, these divisions in families, these murders? All for pieces, more or less numerous, of that white or yellow metal which people call silver or gold. And pray who will be the most thought of at the end of this grand race after money? The man who brings back the most of it. Ah, nowadays a man has no business to have more than one object in life — and that is to become as rich as possible! For my part, that has always been my idea; I have carried it out: I congratulate myself on it. Once upon a time everybody found me homely, stupid, a bore; to-day everybody finds me handsome, witty, amiable,— and the Lord knows if *I* am witty, amiable, handsome! On the day when I might be stupid enough to let myself be ruined, to become plain "Jean" as before, there would not be enough stones in the Montmartre quarries to throw at my head. But there, that day is a good way off, and meantime many of my business acquaintances have been ruined for the sake of keeping me from ruin. The last word, too, the greatest praise that I could give to wealth, certainly is, that such a circle as I find myself in at present has had the patience to listen so long to the son of a gardener, who has no other right to their attention than the poor little millions that he has made.

Durieu [*aside*] — It is all absolutely true, every word that he has been saying — gardener's son that he is! He sees our epoch just as it really is.

Madame Durieu — Come now, my dear M. De Cayolle, what do you think of what M. Giraud has been telling us?

Cayolle — I think, madam, that the theories of M. Giraud are sound, but sound only as to that society in which M. Giraud has lived until now: a world of speculation, whose one object naturally ought to be to make money. As to wealth itself, it brings about infamous things, but it also brings about great and noble things. In that respect it is like human speech: a bad thing for some people, a good thing for others, according to the use they make of it. This obligation of our state of society that makes a man wake up each morning with taking thought of the necessary sum for his personal wants, lest he take what does not belong to him, has created the finest intelligence of all the ages! It is simply to this need of money every day that we owe Franklin, who began the world by being a printer's apprentice; Shakespeare, who used to hold horses at the door of the theatre which later he was going to immortalize; Machiavelli, who was secretary to the Florentine republic at fifteen crowns a month; Raphael, the son of a mere dauber; Jean Jacques Rousseau, a notary's clerk and an engraver,— one who did not have a dinner every day; Fulton, once upon a time a mechanic, who gave us steam: and so many others. Had these same people been born with an income of half a million livres apiece, there would have been a good many chances that not one of them would ever have become what he did become. [*To M. Giraud.*] This race after wealth, of which you speak, M. Giraud, has good in it: even if it enriches some silly people or some rascals, if it procures for them the consideration of those in a humble station of life,— of the lower classes, of those who have cash relations with society, on the other hand there is a great deal of good in the spur given to faculties which would otherwise remain stationary; enough good to pardon some errors in the distribution of wealth. Just in proportion as you enter into the true world of society — a world which is almost unknown to you, M. Giraud — you will find that a man who is received there is received only in proportion to his personal value. Look around here where we are, without taking the trouble to go any further, and you will see that money has not the influence you ascribe to it. For proof, here is Countess Savelli, with half a million francs income, who in place of dining out with millionaires besieging her house every day, comes quietly here to dine with our friends the Durieus, people without title, poor people measured by her fortune; and she comes here for the pleasure of meeting M. De Charzay,

who has not more than a thousand crowns income, but who,
for all the millionaires in the world, would never do a thing
a man ought not to do; and she meets here M. De Roncourt,
who has a business of fifteen hundred francs because he gave
up his fortune to creditors who were not his own creditors.
There is Mademoiselle De Roncourt, who sacrificed her dowry
to the same sentiment of honor; yonder is Mademoiselle Durieu,
who would never be willing to become the wife of any other
than an honest man, even if he had for his rivals all the Crœ-
suses present and to come; and last of all, one meets me here,—
a man who has for money (in the acceptation that you give the
word) the most profound contempt.   Now, M. Giraud, if we lis-
tened to you for so long a time, it is because we are well-bred
people, and besides, you talk very well; but there has been no
flattery for your millions in our attention, and the proof is that
everybody has been listening to me a longer time than to you,—
listening to me, who have not like you a thousand-franc note
to put along with every one of my phrases!

Jean—Who is that gentleman who has just been speaking?

Durieu—That is M. De Cayolle.

Jean—The railway director?

Durieu—Yes.

Jean [*going to M. De Cayolle*]—M. De Cayolle, I hope you
will believe that I am very glad to meet you.

Cayolle—I dare say you are, monsieur. [*M. De Cayolle as he
utters the words turns his back upon Giraud and steps aside.*]

Translated for 'A Library of the World's Best Literature,' by E. Irenæus
Stevenson

M. DE RÉMONIN'S PHILOSOPHY OF MARRIAGE

From 'L'Étrangère'

MADAME DE RUMIÈRES—See here, now, Rémonin, you who
claim to explain everything as a learned man—can you
solve this proposition? Why is it that with all the quan-
tity of love in this world, there are so many unhappy marriages?

M. Rémonin—I could give you a perfect explanation, my
dear lady, if you were not a woman.

Madame de Rumières—You mean that the explanation is not
decent?

M. Rémonin — No, I mean that it is a matter based on the abstract. . . . It is this. The reason why marriages are rarely happy, in spite of the "quantity of love" in question, is because love and marriage, scientifically considered, have no relationship. They belong to two sorts of things, completely differing. Love is of the physical. Marriage is a matter of chemistry.

Madame de Rumières — Explain yourself.

Rémonin — Certainly. Love is an element of the natural evolution of our being; it comes to us of itself in course of our life, at one time or another, independent of all our will, and even without a definite object. The human creature can wish to be in love before really loving any one! . . . But marriage is a social combination, an adjustment, that refers itself to chemistry, as I have said; since chemistry concerns itself with the action of one element on another and the phenomena resulting: . . . to the end of bringing about family life, morality, and labor, and in consequence the welfare of man, as involved in all three. Now, so often as you really can conform to the theory of such a blending of things, so long as you happen to have effected in marriage such a combination of the physical *and* chemical, all goes well; the experiment is happy, it results well. But if you are ignorant or maladroit enough to seek and to make a combination of two refractory chemical forces in the matrimonial experiment, then in the place of a fusion you will find you have only inert forces; and the two elements remain there, together but unfused, eternally opposed to each other, never able to be united! . . . Or else there is not merely inertia — there are shocks, explosions, catastrophes, accidents, dramas. . . .

Madame de Rumières — Have you ever been in love?

M. Rémonin — I? My dear marquise, I am a scientist — I have never had time! And you?

Madame de Rumières — I have loved my children. M. de Rumières was a charming man all his life; but he didn't expect me really to love him. My son tells me his affairs of the heart; . . . my daughter has already made me a grandmother. . . . I have little to reproach myself as to my past life, and now I look on at the lives of others, sometimes much interested. I am like the subscribers to the Opéra, who know the whole repertory by heart, but who can always hear some passages with pleasure and who encourage the débutants.

Condensed and translated for 'A Library of the World's Best Literature,' by E. Irenæus Stevenson.

REFORMING A FATHER

From 'A Prodigal Father'

[The ensuing dialogue occurs in the first act of the play. The Count de Ravonnières and his son André reside together in their comfortable bachelor's establishment in Paris, and are devotedly attached to one another. The count, unfortunately, has only grown more careless of money, more a gay man of the world, as he has grown older; and blessed with a youthfulness of physique and temperament that nothing impairs, he is as thriftless as he is fascinating. His son, accordingly, has had to be the economist of their resources, which are at a dangerous ebb. As the scene opens, the count is preparing to take luncheon, with Joseph, the confidential servant of the house, in attendance.]

Joseph — Monsieur is served.

 Count de Ravonnières —Very well. You will please go to my florist Lemoine, the Opera florist,—you know who I mean,—and tell him to send, to-day, with my card,—he has a lot of cards of mine in advance,—to Mademoiselle Albertine de la Borde, 26 or 28 Rue de la Paix — I don't exactly remember the number that the lady gave me —

Joseph — No. 26.

Count — Ah! You know her address, do you?

Joseph — Yes, sir.

Count — To send her a bouquet of white lilacs and roses. And I don't need you any more: go at once. [*Joseph bows, and hands the Count a large envelope.*] What's all this?

Joseph — Some law papers that have come in your absence, sir, which I did not think ought to be forwarded to Dieppe.

Count [*without taking the papers*] — Quite right. Has my son seen them?

Joseph — No, sir.

Count —Very well; don't let him see them. Put them away with the others.

Joseph — May I beg monsieur to say a good word for me to his son?

Count — As to what, Joseph?

Joseph —Your son, sir, has just told me to look out for another situation; and I am so attached to the family —

Count — Oh, I will straighten all that out; if my son sends you away I will take you into our service again. Come now, get off to my florist; be quick about it.

As Joseph *goes out,* André *enters. He does not at first perceive his father, but on turning toward the table discovers him.*

André—Ah! you are here, are you?

Count—Yes, I have been here during an hour; and moreover, a very agreeable person has been doing the honors of your establishment on my behalf.

André—It is a fine time to talk about agreeable persons! You are a very agreeable person—

Count—What in the world is the matter with you?

André—I am perfectly furious.

Count—Against whom?

André—Against you.

Count—Why? What have I been doing?

André—You have drawn on me at sight this draft here.

Count—Oh yes, I know very well what that means. It comes from London; it is to pay for the boat, you know.

André—Oh yes, it comes from London, and it is to pay for the boat! That is no excuse for it. And what about the boat, if you please?

Count—But my dear fellow, they had no business to present it until the 15th.

André—Well?

Count—Why, to-day *is* the 15th!

André—You ought to know it.

Count—I thought that to-day was only the 14th! Have you paid it?

André—Of course.

Count—Ah! then I owe you six thousand francs. That's all there is to the matter.

André—Yes, that's all! But you never said a word to me about it; I had no money in the house: I had to send to our man of business. May I beg of you in the future to be so good as to—

Count—Poor boy! poor boy! Really, between ourselves, you would have done a great deal better (as it is a month since you have seen me, and since you are really very fond of me) to embrace me in meeting me again, rather than to say all these things to me that you have been saying!

André [*embracing his father heartily*]—Oh, of course they make no difference, when it comes to *that!*

Count—Your second impulse is a very good one; but you ought to have begun with it. All the same, I do not in the less ask pardon for the inconvenience that I have caused you, my boy. [*Takes some bank-notes from his pocket.*] Here are your six thousand francs, and [*holding out the remainder of the notes to André*] since you need money, help yourself.

André—Where in the world does that money come from?

Count—Oh, it is some money that I have received.

André—There was none coming to you from anywhere!

Count—There is always something to come to one, if he looks around carefully. And now let us speak of serious things.

André—Yes, by all means. Father, are you not disposed to settle down?

Count—What do you mean by "settle down"?

André—To save money, for one thing.

Count—Save money! I should be charmed to do so; but I really do not see how we can do it. We certainly live as modestly as possible. This house belongs to us; we have only four saddle horses, four carriage horses, a couple of extra horses for evening service (we could not get along with less), two coachmen, two valets, two grooms, one cook. Why, we haven't even a housekeeper.

André—No, we only want that!

Count—We never receive any except masculine society; we certainly are not extravagant as to the table. Look at me here: I am breakfasting this minute on two eggs and a glass of water. It seems to me that with our fortune—

André—Our fortune? Would you like to know in what condition our fortune is?

Count—You ought to know better than I, since it is you who have had the running of affairs since your majority.

André—Well then, I *do* know the expenses; and let me tell you that you have counted up only those that are part of our life in Paris, and you have not said a syllable of those that belong to our country one.

Count—Those that belong to our country one! Those are all just so much economy.

André—So then the place at Vilsac is just so much economy?

Count—Of course. We get everything from it, from eggs up to oxen.

André—Yes, and even to wild boars, when it suits you to shoot one. Now be so good as to consider the place at Vilsac, which you call a matter of economy. First of all, it brings us in absolutely nothing.

Count—It never has brought us in anything.

André—It is mortgaged for two hundred thousand francs.

Count—That happened when I was young.

André—Are you under the impression that there comes a time when mortgages wear themselves out? I wish they did. But I am afraid that you deceive yourself; and in the mean time, you are paying every year a mortgagor's interest. Furthermore, at Vilsac—

Count—Where, remember, we spend September, October, November, all of which is positively an economy—

André—Furthermore, as to Vilsac, this summer place where we pass September, October, and November,—all of which is positively an economy,—the proof of its being an economy is that here we are in the middle of September, and we are just setting out for Dieppe.

Count—For one time only, by chance! And moreover, we will have to go down to Vilsac by the end of the month, for I have asked those fellows to come down there for the shooting.

André—Yes, in this economical country place, where you have asked all those gentlemen to come down for the shooting, at the end of the month—

Count—Really, one would be bored to death without that!

André—In this same economical establishment, I say, you have twelve keepers.

Count—Quite true; but it is one of the best preserves in France, and really, there are so many poachers—

André—You have two masters of hounds, you have ten horses, —in short, a whole hunting equipage; and I don't speak of the indemnities that you pay year by year, if only for the rabbits that you kill.

Count—The fact is, there *are* thousands of rabbits; but shooting rabbits is such fun!

André—Add to that the entertainments that it occurs to you to give every now and then, with fireworks and so on, during the evening.

Count—Oh, yes, but that pleases all the peasants of the neighborhood, who adore me; between ourselves it *is* rather—

Oh, my dear boy! if I had only been rich, what fine things I would have done! In France, people do not know how to spend money. In Russia it is quite another matter! Now, there you have people who understand how to give an entertainment. But then what can anybody do with two hundred thousand livres for an income?

André — Father, one can do exactly what you have done, — one can ruin himself.

Count — What! ruin himself?

André — Yes. When my mother died your personal fortune brought you, as you say, an income of two hundred thousand livres; and the money which my mother left to me, of which you have had the use until I came of age, amounted to a hundred and twenty thousand livres.

Count — I certainly have made an accounting to you in the matter.

André — A perfectly exact one, only —

Count — Only — ?

André — Only in doing so you have seriously impaired your own capital.

Count — Why did you not say that to me at the time?

André — Because I too — I was thinking of nothing but spending money.

Count — You ought to have warned me about this before now.

André — But I — I was doing then just what I see you doing; I was taking life exactly as you had taught me to take it.

Count — André, I hope that is not a reproach.

André — God bless me, no. I am only saying to you why I have not looked after your interests better than you have ever done so yourself.

Count — Very good. Then I am going to explain to you why I brought you up —

André — Not worth while, my dear father. There is no good in going back to that, and I know quite well —

Count — On the contrary, you know nothing at all about the matter, and you will please allow me to speak. It will be a consolation. You are perfectly right as to things that have no common-sense in them; and if I have brought you up after a certain manner, it is just because I myself suffer from a different kind of education. *I* was brought up very severely; at twenty-two years I knew nothing of life. I was born, I was kept hanging on at Vilsac, with my father and my mother, who were saints on earth, with my great-uncle, who had the gout, and with my tutor, who was an abbé. I was born with a constitution like iron. I went hunting day by day for whole months, on foot or on horseback. I ate my meals like an ogre. I rode every sort of a horse, and I was a swordsman like St. George himself. As for other things, my dear fellow, there was no use dreaming about them: I had not a crown in my pocket. The other sex— well, I had heard it said that there was a world of women some- where, but I certainly did not know where it was. One day my father asked me if I was willing to marry, and I cried out, "Oh yes, yes!" with such an explosion that my father himself could not help laughing— he who never laughed. I was presented to a young girl, virtuous and beautiful; and I fell in love with her with a passion which at first fairly frightened the delicate and timid creature. Such was your mother, my dear André, and to her I owe the two happiest years of my life; it is true that I owe to her also my greatest grief, for at the end of those two years she died. But it must be said, either to the blame or to the praise of nature, that organizations such as mine are proof against the severest shocks. At twenty-four years I found my- self rich, a widower, free to do what I pleased, and thrown— with a child a year old— into the midst of this world called Paris, of which I knew nothing whatever. Ought I to have condemned you to this sort of life that I had led at Vilsac, and which had been for me so often an intolerable bore? No, I obeyed my real nature. I gave you my qualities and my shortcomings, without reckoning closely in the matter; I have sought in your case your affection rather than your obedience or your respect. I have never taught you economy, it is true, but then I did not know anything about that myself; and besides, I had not a busi- ness and a business name to leave you. To have everything in common between us, one heart and one purse, to be able to give each other everything and say everything to each other,— that has been our motto. The puritans will think that they have a right to blame this intimacy as too close: let them say so if they choose. We have lost, it seems, some hundreds of thousands of francs; but we have gained this,— that we can always count upon each other, you upon me and I upon you. Either of us will be ready at any moment to kill himself for the other, and that is the most important matter between a father and a son;

all the rest is not worth the trouble that one takes to reason about it. Don't you think I am right?

André — All that is true, my dear father! and I am just as much attached to you as you are to me. Far be it from me to reproach you; but now in my turn I want to make a confession to you. You are an exception in our society; your fettered youth, your precocious widowerhood, are your excuses, if you need any. You were born at a time when all France was in a fever, and when the individual, as well as the great mass of people, seemed to be striving to spend by every possible means a superabundance of vitality. Urged toward active life by nature, by curiosity, by temperament, you have cared for things that were worth caring for, — for them only; for entertaining yourself, for hunting, for fine horses, for the artist world, for people of rank and distinction. In such an environment as this you have paid your tribute to your country, you have paid the debt of your rank in life and of your name. But I, on the other hand, like almost all my generation, brought in contact with a fashionable world from the time that I began life, — I, born in an epoch of lassitude and transition, — I led for a while this life by mere imitation in laziness. . . . It is a kind of existence that no longer amuses me; and moreover, I can tell you that it never did amuse me. To sit up all night turning over cards; to get up at two o'clock in the afternoon, to have horses put to the carriage and go for the drive around the Lake, or to ride horseback; to live by day with idlers and to pass my evenings with such parasites as your friend M. De Tournas — all that seems to me the height of foolishness. And at the bottom of your own thoughts you think just as I do. So now, now that you really have got to a serious explanation of affairs, let us reach a real irrevocable determination of them. Are you willing to let me arrange your life for you in the future exactly as I would wish to arrange my own life? Are you willing to have confidence in me, and after having brought me up in your way, are you willing that in turn, while there is still time for it, I should — bring you up in mine?

Count — Yes, go on.

André — Very well, — to severe diseases strong remedies. You think a great deal of our Vilsac estate?

Count — I was born there. I should not be sorry to end my days there.

André— Very well. We will keep Vilsac for you, and find money in some other way to pay off the mortgage.

Count— How?

André— That's my business; only you must send away the two piqueurs, and six of the keepers.

Count— Poor fellows!

André— And only four horses are to be kept. No more entertainments are to be given, no more fireworks. You will entertain only two or three intimate friends now and then,— if we find as many friends as that among all those that are about us nowadays here,— and you will stay at Vilsac seven or eight months of the year.

Count— Alone?

André— Wait a little. I have not finished yet. This house where we are must be sold. We must put out of doors these servants, who are just so many thieves; and we will keep at Paris only a very modest stopping-place.

Count— Will you kindly allow me to get my breath?

André— Don't stir, or my surgical operation will not be successful. Now that your debts are paid there will be left to you —

Count— There will be left to me —

André— Forty thousand livres income, and as much for me,— no more; and with all that, during three or four years you will not have the capital at your disposition.

Count— Heavens, what a smash!

André— Are you willing to accept my scheme?

Count— I must.

André— Very well, then: sign these papers!

Count— What are they?

André— They are papers which I have just got from the notary, and which I have been expecting to make you sign while at Dieppe and send to me; but since you are here —

Count [*signs*]— Since I am here, I may as well sign at once: you are quite right,— there you are.

André— Very well; now as, according to my notions, just as much as you are left to yourself you will slip back into the same errors as in the past —

Count— What are you going to do further?

André— Guess.

Count —- You are going to forbid —

André—Are you out of your senses? I am going to marry you off.

Count—Marry me off!

André—Without permission.

Count—And how about yourself?

André—I am going to marry myself off—afterwards. You must begin as an example.

Count—André, do you know something?

André—What?

Count—Some one has told you the very thing I have had in mind.

André—Nobody has told me anything.

Count—Your word on it?

André—My word on it.

Count—Explain yourself. You, all by yourself, have had this idea of marriage?

André—I myself.

Count—Deny now the sympathy between us!

André—Well?

Count—It exists [*putting his arms around his son*]. There, embrace me!

André—And you accept?

Count—As if I would do anything else!

Translated for 'A Library of the World's Best Literature,' by E. Irenæus
Stevenson

MR. AND MRS. CLARKSON

From 'L'Étrangère'

[These scenes, the final ones of the drama, occur in the private drawing-room of Catherine, the young Duchess of Septmonts. Mr. Clarkson, a wealthy American man of business, a Californian, has just received a note from the Duke of Septmonts, a blasé young roué of high family, requesting him to call at once. He has come, in some bewilderment, to find the duke. Mr. Clarkson has only a formal acquaintance with the duke, but Mrs. Clarkson, who resides much of the time in Paris, acting as Mr. Clarkson's business representative, knows the duke confidentially. The Duchess of Septmonts receives Clarkson.]

M R. CLARKSON—I beg your pardon, madam, for having insisted on making my way in here; but a few moments ago I found on returning to my house, a letter from your husband. It asked me for a rendezvous as soon as possible, without giving me a reason for it. I find M. de Septmonts not at home. May I ask you if you know how I can be of service to him?

Catherine — I was under the impression that in his letter, M. de Septmonts explained to you the matter in which he wishes your assistance.

Clarkson — No.

Catherine — Did not his letter contain another letter, sealed, which he purposed leaving in your hands?

Clarkson — No.

Catherine — Are you really telling me the truth?

Clarkson — I never lie, madam: I have too much business on my hands; it would mix me up quite too much in my affairs.

Catherine — Then perhaps it is to Mrs. Clarkson that my husband has intrusted that letter.

Clarkson — No. She would have mentioned it; for I told her that I had received a line from the Duke, and was on my way to this house.

Catherine — Perhaps your wife did not tell you — all.

Clarkson — She has no earthly reason to conceal anything from me!

Catherine — True! I know very well that she is your wife only in name; she told me as much when I was at her house yesterday.

Clarkson — Really! She must be very much pleased with you, for she does not talk readily about her personal affairs.

Catherine — Unfortunately, it is quite otherwise as far as I am concerned; she has not hidden from me the fact that she detests me, and that she will do me all the injury she possibly can.

Clarkson — You? Injury? For what reason? Pray, what have you done to her?

Catherine — Nothing! I have known her only two days. Nevertheless —

Clarkson — Nevertheless —

Catherine — What I was going to say is not my secret, sir, it is hers, and she alone has the right to tell it to you. But as to this letter that my husband has told my father he has sent to you — it is I who wrote that letter. You may as well know, too, that it was abstracted from my possession; and moreover, that with that letter any one can indeed do me all the mischief with which your wife, Mrs. Clarkson, has threatened me,

Clarkson [*very gravely*]—Then we must know at once if my wife has that letter. I will write her to come here immediately and join us—that I have something very important to communicate to her—here. Are you willing to have her come? [*He writes while he speaks.*]

Catherine—Certainly.

Clarkson—Then we can have a general explanation. You may be sure, madam, that I shall never lend my hand to anything that means harm to you, or to any woman: I come from the country where we respect women.

Catherine [*rings the bell, and says to a servant who answers it*]—See that this letter is sent immediately. Be careful that it does not go astray. It is not my letter. This gentleman has written it. [*Exit servant.*]

Clarkson—And now, madam, do you know why M. de Septmonts wishes to have an interview with me?

Catherine—Yes, I can guess. It concerns me, perhaps; but I have no right to discuss the matter. It is something which belongs to the Duke, and he alone has the right to impart it to you. All I can do is to beg of you to have all details thoroughly explained to you, and to look into them very carefully.

A Servant *enters*

Servant—M. le Duc has come in; he will be glad to have Mr. Clarkson come to him.

Clarkson—Very good. [*Going.*] I bid you good evening, madam.

Catherine [*to the servant*]—Wait a moment. [*Going to Clarkson and speaking in a low voice.*] Suppose I were to ask you a very great service.

Clarkson—Ask it, madam.

Catherine—Suppose I were to ask you to say to my husband that you are waiting for him here in this drawing-room—that you will be glad to speak with him *here*.

Clarkson—Nothing but that? With great pleasure. [*To the servant.*] Say to M. de Septmonts that I shall be obliged if he will join me—here. [*Servant goes out.*]

Catherine—I shall leave you; for if I know what is going to be discussed in this interview, I neither could nor should take part in it; but whatever may come of it, I shall never forget that you have done everything that you could do as a courtesy to me,—and that you are a gentleman. [*Exit Catherine.*]

Clarkson [*alone*]—Charming! She is charming, that little woman; but may I be hanged if I understand one word of what is going on here.

The Duke of Septmonts *comes in hastily, and advances to* Clarkson

Septmonts—I have just come from your house, Mr. Clarkson. Mrs. Clarkson told me you were here. I returned at once. Pardon me for troubling you. If when I came in I asked you to come to my own drawing-room, and have thus troubled you once more, it is because I was told you were expecting me here, with the duchess. This is her private parlor; and as what we have to say is a matter for men—

Clarkson—Therefore the duchess went to her own room when your return here was announced.

Septmonts—Mr. Clarkson, did *she* tell the servant that you would prefer to hold our conversation here?

Clarkson—No, I told him.

[*Septmonts goes to the door of the room by which Catherine went out, and closes the portière.*]

Clarkson [*in a scornful aside*]—What an amount of mystery and precaution!

Septmonts—The matter is this, Mr. Clarkson. I must fight a duel to-morrow morning. This duel can terminate only in the death of one or other of the contestants. I am the insulted one, therefore I have the choice of weapons. I choose the sword.

Clarkson—Do you fence well?

Septmonts—I believe I am one of the best fencers in Paris. But another friend on whom I could count is one of those men of the world who discuss all the details of an affair, and with whom the preliminaries of such a meeting might last several days. I want to get through with the matter at once.

Clarkson—Ah! The fact is, you *do* give an importance and a solemnity to such things in France that we don't understand, we Americans, who settle the question in five minutes on the first corner of the street, in the sight of everybody.

Septmonts—That is just the reason that I allowed myself to apply to you, Mr. Clarkson. Now, are you disposed to be present as my second?

Clarkson — Bless me, with all my heart! Besides, when I mentioned your letter to Mrs. Clarkson she told me to do all I could to serve you. Have you and my wife known each other long?

Septmonts — About four years; and I owe your wife a great deal, morally speaking. I have no desire to conceal the fact. I was not yet married when I met Mrs. Clarkson. One day I had lost a large sum at play, — a hundred and fifty thousand francs, — which I did not have, and tried in vain to procure; for at that time I was completely ruined. Mrs. Clarkson very generously lent me the sum, and I repaid it, with interest equivalent to the capital.

Clarkson — But as you were ruined, duke, how could you pay this large capital and this large interest? Did your father or mother die? In France the death of parents is a great resource, I know.

Septmonts — No. I was an orphan, and I had no expectations. I married.

Clarkson — Ah, true! You French people make much of marriages for money! It's a great advantage over us Americans, who only marry for love. Now with us, in such a case as yours, a man goes into some business or other; he goes to mining; he works. But every country has its own customs. I beg your pardon for interrupting you. After all, it doesn't concern me. Come back to our duel.

Septmonts I have a letter here in my hands —

Clarkson — Ah! You have a letter in your hands —

Septmonts — A letter which compromises my wife —

Clarkson — Ah! I am completely at your service. I belong to the sort of men who do not admit any compromises in matters of that kind.

Septmonts — I may be killed — one has to look ahead. If I lose my life, I lose it by having been so injured by my wife that I intend to be revenged on her.

Clarkson — And how?

Septmonts — I wish that the contents of this letter, which I have in my possession, shall become public property if I am killed.

Clarkson [*coldly*] — Ah! And how can I serve you as to that?

Septmonts — I will intrust this sealed letter to you. [*He takes the letter from his pocket.*] Here it is.

Clarkson [*still more coldly*] — Very well.

Septmonts — Now, if I survive, you will restore it to me as it is. If not, then in the trial which will follow, you will read it in a court. I wish the letters to become public. Then it will be known that I avenged my honor under a feigned pretext; and M. Gérard and the duchess will be so situated that they will never be able to see each other again.

Clarkson — Nonsense! Once dead, what does it matter to you?

Septmonts — I am firm there. Will you kindly accept the commission?

Clarkson [*in a formal tone*] — Surely.

Septmonts — Here is the letter.

Clarkson [*takes it and holds it as he speaks*] — But, duke, now that I think about it, when this trial occurs it is probable, even certain, that I shall not be in France. I was expecting to leave Paris on business to-morrow morning at the latest. I can wait until to-morrow evening to please you, and to help you with this duel of yours; but that is really all the time I can spare.

Septmonts — Very well; then you will have the goodness to give this letter to Mrs. Clarkson with the instructions I have just given you, and it will be in equally good hands.

Clarkson [*looking at the letter*] — All right. A blank envelope. What is there to indicate that this letter was addressed to M. Gérard?

Septmonts — The envelope with his name on it is inside.

Clarkson — You found this letter?

Septmonts — I found it — before it was mailed.

Clarkson — And as you had your suspicions you — opened it?

Septmonts — Yes.

Clarkson — I beg your pardon for questioning you so, but you yourself did me the honor to say that you wished me to be *fully* informed. Do you know whether the sentiments between M. Gérard and the duchess were of long standing?

Septmonts — They date from before my marriage.

Clarkson [*looking toward the apartment of the duchess*] — Oh, I see. That is serious!

Septmonts — They loved each other, they wanted to marry each other, but my wife's father would not consent.

Clarkson [*reflectively*] — M. Gérard wanted to marry her, did he?

Septmonts — Yes; but when he learned that Mademoiselle Mauriceau was a millionaire, as he had nothing and had no title other than his plain name Gérard, he withdrew his pretensions.

Clarkson — That was a very proper thing for the young man to do. It doesn't surprise me!

Septmonts — Yes; but now, Mr. Clarkson, this young gentleman has come back —

Clarkson — And is too intimate a friend to your wife?

Septmonts — Ah, I do not say that!

Clarkson — What do you say, then?

Septmonts — That as the letter in question gives that impression, the situation amounts to the same thing as far as a legal process is concerned.

Clarkson [*thoughtfully and coldly*] — Oh-h-h!

Septmonts — Don't you agree with me, Mr. Clarkson?

Clarkson — No, not at all. I can understand revenge on those who have injured us, but not on those who haven't done so. And I don't like vengeance on a woman anyway, even when she is guilty; and certainly not when she is innocent; and you owe your wife a great deal — between ourselves, you owe your wife a great deal, duke. I understand now why, for once, your father-in-law M. Mauriceau sides with his daughter and M. Gérard against you. He is sure they both are innocent. By-the-by, does M. Mauriceau also know of this letter?

Septmonts — Yes. He even tried to take it from me by force.

Clarkson — Why did he not take it?

Septmonts — Ah, because you see, I had the presence of mind to tell him that I did not have it any longer — that I had sent it to you!

Clarkson [*ironically*] — That *was* very clever!

Septmonts — And then when M. Gérard had challenged me, M. Mauriceau thought he would make an impression by saying to him before me, " I will be your second."

Clarkson — Well, is that the whole story?

Septmonts — Yes.

Clarkson — Very well, my dear sir: to speak frankly, all those people whom you characterize so slightingly seem to me the right kind of people — excellent people. Your little wife seems to be the victim of prejudices, of morals, and of combinations about which we mere American savages don't know anything at all. In our American society, which of course I can't compare with yours, as we only date from yesterday,— if Mademoiselle Mauriceau had loved a fine young fellow like M. Gérard, her father would have given her to the man she loved; or if he had refused that, why she would have gone quite simply and been married before the justice of the peace! Perhaps her father wouldn't have portioned her; but then the husband would have worked, gone into business, and the two young people would have been happy all the same. As to your M. Gérard here, he is an honest man and a clever one. We like people who work, we Americans, and to whatever country they belong, we hold them as compatriots — because we are such savages, I suppose. So you understand that I don't at all share your opinion of this question.

Septmonts — And so speaking, you mean — ?

Clarkson — That if I give you this explanation, it is because I think I understand that in paying me the honor of choosing me as a second, you thought that the men of my country were less clear-sighted, less scrupulous than the men of yours. In short, duke, you thought I would lend my hand to all these social pettinesses, these little vilenesses which you have just recounted with a candor that honors you.

Septmonts —Do you happen to remember, Mr. Clarkson, that you are talking to *me* — in this way?

Clarkson — To you. Because there are only two of us here! But if you like, we will call in other people to listen.

Septmonts — Then, sir, you tell me to my face —

Clarkson — I tell you to your face that to squander your inheritance — to have gambled away money you did not have — to borrow it from a woman without knowing when or how you could return it — to marry in order to pay your debts and continue your dissipations — to revenge yourself now on an innocent woman — to steal letters — to misapply your skill in arms by killing a brave man — why, I tell you to your face that all that is the work of a rascal, and that therefore a rascal you are. Oh, what astonishes me is that fifty people haven't told you so already, and that I have had to travel three thousand leagues to inform you on the subject! For you don't seem to have ever suspected it, and you don't look thoroughly convinced even now.

Septmonts [*controlling himself with the greatest difficulty*] — Mr. Clarkson, you know that I cannot call you to account until I have settled with your friend M. Gérard. You take a strange advantage of the fact, sir. But we shall meet again. Please re-turn me the paper you have had from me.

Clarkson — Your wife's letter? Never in the world! As it was addressed to M. Gérard, it belongs to M. Gérard. I intend to give it to M. Gérard. If *he* wants to return it to you, I won't stand in the way; but I doubt whether he will return it.

Septmonts — You will fight me, then, you mean?

Clarkson — Oh! as for that; yes, fight as much as you like.

Septmonts — Very well; when I have finished with the other, you and I will have our business together.

Clarkson — Say the day after to-morrow, then?

Septmonts — The day after to-morrow.

Clarkson — Stop; I must start off by to-morrow night, at the latest.

Septmonts — You can wait. And while waiting, leave me!

Clarkson — Duke, do I look like a man to whom to say "leave" in that tone, and who goes? Now look at me; it isn't hard to see what I have decided. I don't mean you to fight with Gérard before you have fought with me. If Gérard kills you, I shan't have the pleasure of crossing swords with "one of the first fencers in Paris," which it will amuse me to do. If you kill him, you cause irreparable misfortunes. If you think I'm going to let you kill a man who has saved me twenty-five per cent. in the cost of washing gold, you are mistaken! Come, prove you are brave, even when you aren't sure of being the stronger! Go and get a good pair of swords from your room (since the sword is your favorite weapon — mine, too, for the matter of that), and follow me to those great bare grounds back of your house. On my way here I was wondering why in goodness's name they were not utilized. In the heart of the city they must be worth a good deal! We will prove it. As for seconds, umpires of the point of honor, we'll have the people who pass by in the street — if any do pass.

[*Septmonts rushes in a fury toward the door, but when there stretches his hand toward the bell. Clarkson throws himself between him and the bell.*]

Clarkson — Ah! no ringing, please! Don't play the Louis XV. gentleman, and order your servants to cudgel a poor beggar! or as sure as my name is Clarkson, I'll slap your face, sir, before all your lackeys!

Septmonts—Very well, so be it! I *will* begin with you. [*Angrily hastens from the room for the weapons.*]

Clarkson— Quite right! [*Looking coolly at his watch.*] Let me see; why, perhaps I *can* get away from Paris this evening after all. [*He goes calmly out at the back toward the darkened garden.*]

[*The Duchess of Septmonts has pulled aside the portière and looks toward the door by which her husband and Mr. Clarkson have gone out. She is very much agitated, and can hardly walk. She rings the bell, and then makes an effort to appear calm. The servant comes in.*]

Catherine [*tremulously, to the servant*]— Ask my father to come here, immediately. [*The servant goes out. Catherine looks toward the window and makes a movement to go to it.*] No, I will not look out! I will not know anything! I do not know anything; I have *heard* nothing; the minutes that that hand marks upon the clock, no one knows what they say to me. One of them will decide my life! Even if I had heard nothing, things would take the turn that they have, and I should merely be amazed in knowing of them. Instead of knowing nothing, I have merely to remember nothing. But no, no,— I am trying in vain to smother the voice of my own conscience! What I am doing is wicked. From the moment that I have known anything about this, I am an accomplice; and if one of these two men is killed he has been killed with my consent. No, I cannot and I will not. [*She runs toward the door. As she does so Mrs. Clarkson enters hastily.*] You, you, madam!

Mrs. Clarkson—Were you not really expecting me to-day, madam? My husband sends me a note to say that you— and he— wish to speak to me immediately.

Catherine— Madam, since Mr. Clarkson has written you, there has occurred a thing which neither your husband, nor I, nor you yourself could foresee.

Mrs. Clarkson—What do you mean?

Catherine—While my husband the duke has been explaining to Mr. Clarkson the reasons of the duel,— which you, you, madam, have provoked,— your husband, who did not find these reasons either sufficient or honorable, has undertaken to defend us— Gérard, yes, Gérard, and me,— and so very forcibly, that at this instant—

Mrs. Clarkson— They are fighting?

Catherine— Yes, yes, only a few steps away from here!

Mrs. Clarkson — Ah! That sounds like Clarkson! [*She takes a step toward the door.*]

Catherine — Madam, that duel must not go on.

Mrs. Clarkson — Why not?

Catherine — I will not permit these two men to lose their lives on my account.

Mrs. Clarkson — You? What difference does it make to you? They are not doing anything but what they chose to do. "Hands off," as the officials at the gaming-tables say when the ball has stopped rolling. You have wished to be free, haven't you? and you are perfectly right; you never said so to anybody, but you begged it all the same of One who can do anything. He has heard your prayer, and he has made use of me to save you; of me, who have been anxious to destroy you! That is justice; and do you think that I object — I who am to be the loser? In the game that I play with Destiny, every time I make up my mind that God is against me, I bow my head and throw up the game. I don't fear any one except God. He is on your side. Let us talk no more about it.

[*Just as she is speaking the last words, Clarkson comes in. He is very grave.*]

Mrs. Clarkson — See there. You are a widow.

Clarkson [*to Mrs. Clarkson*] — My dear Noémi, will you be so kind as to hand that paper to our friend the duchess. She will perhaps feel some embarrassment in taking it directly from my hand — and it is a thing that must be returned to her. Such was the last wish of her husband; he really did not have time to tell me as much, but I fancy that I guess it right.

[*Mrs. Clarkson calmly takes the letter and goes to Catherine.*]

Mrs. Clarkson — I once said to your friend M. Rémonin that if I lost my game I would lose like one who plays fair. Madam, it was through me that your marriage came to pass; and now it is through me that your marriage — is dissolved. [*Turning to Clarkson.*] And now, Clarkson, my dear, let us get out of this. You are a good and a brave fellow. I will go anywhere with you. I have had enough of Europe — things here are too small. Do you know, I really believe I am going to find myself in love with you! Come, let us go! I am positively smothering.

Clarkson — Yes, let us go.

[*At the moment that Mr. and Mrs. Clarkson are going out, servants and police officials, accompanied by a commissioner of the police service, appear in the door. Clarkson is pointed out.*]

Commissioner — I beg your pardon, monsieur, — there seems to have been — a murder here.

Clarkson — Oh no, monsieur, not at all a murder — only a duel.

Commissioner — And am I to understand, monsieur, that it is you who —

Clarkson — Oh yes, monsieur, it is I. You have come to take me into custody?

Commissioner — Yes, monsieur.

Clarkson — What a ridiculous country! I am ready to follow you, monsieur. But I am an American citizen. I shall give you bail — but of course, the law before anything. . . .

Mrs. Clarkson — Reckon on me, Clarkson. *I* shall take charge of this matter.

Clarkson — How are you going to do that?

Mrs. Clarkson — Oh, that's my affair.

[*Mrs. Clarkson crosses the stage and whispers a word to the commissioner. The commissioner bows very respectfully. Mrs. Clarkson goes out.*]

Commissioner [*to Dr. Rémonin*] — You are a doctor, monsieur?

Rémonin — Yes, monsieur.

Commissioner — Will you have the goodness to give a certificate of death?

Rémonin [*significantly*] — With great pleasure!

Translated for 'A Library of the World's Best Literature,' by E. Irenæus Stevenson

GEORGE. DU MAURIER

(1834–1896)

GEORGE LOUIS PALMELLA BUSSON DU MAURIER was born in Paris on March 6th, 1834, and his early life was passed there. His father was a Frenchman, who had married an Englishwoman in Paris. The Du Mauriers came of an old family in Brittany, Du Maurier's grandfather having been a small *rentier*, who derived his living from glass-works. During Du Maurier's childhood his parents removed to Belgium and thence to London. At seventeen years of age he tried for a degree at the Sorbonne in Paris, but was not successful; and he was put, much against his will, to study chemistry under Dr. Williamson at University College, London. Du Maurier's father, whose characteristics are described in 'Peter Ibbetson,' was an amateur of science. It has been hinted by the son that certain unlucky experiments, which were the result of the elder Du Maurier's fancy for the natural sciences, considerably impaired the family fortunes. The father had bent his heart on the son's being a man of science, but the son's tastes were all for art. He did therefore little good in his chemical studies.

GEORGE DU MAURIER

Du Maurier's father died in 1856, and he then devoted himself definitely to art. He worked at the British Museum, and made considerable progress there. He next went to Paris, and lived the life which he has described in 'Trilby.' In 1857 he attended the Academy at Antwerp, and studied under De Kaiser and Van Lerius. His severe studies at Antwerp had the result that his sight was seriously impaired, and he lost the use of his left eye. After two years of enforced idleness he went to London to seek his fortune. An old acquaintance of his student life in Paris introduced him to Charles Reade, who in turn introduced him to Mark Lemon, the editor of Punch. Through these acquaintances he obtained employment in drawing for Once a Week, Punch, and the Cornhill Magazine. On the death of Leech in 1864 he was regularly attached to the staff of Punch, and till the time of his death continued to work

for that periodical with ever-increasing success. It is not too much
to say that for many years Punch was chiefly and mainly Du Maurier.
He early marked out for himself an entirely new path, which was not
in the direction of caricature or broad comedy; grace, sentiment, and
wit, rather than fun, were the characteristics of his work. He con-
fined himself almost entirely to society, so that his field was a nar-
rower one than that of some of his coadjutors. He had not, for
instance, the masculine breadth of Leech, who represented with great
strength and humor the chief characters of English life,—the parson,
the soldier, the merchant, the farmer, etc.

Du Maurier was almost entirely a carpet knight. He drew Lon-
don society, and a certain phase of London society. The particular
society which he represented is of very recent existence. Thirty
years ago there was but one society in London. This was simply the
ancient aristocratic society of England, which gathered in London in
the season. It is true that there was an artistic society in London
at that time, but it was quite apart and of little general recognition
or influence. But since then there has come up in London a society
made up chiefly of artists, professional people, and successful mer-
chants (having moreover its points of contact with the old society),
which is very strong and influential. It is this which Du Maurier
knew, and which he represented. Even here, however, the types he
has selected for description were very special. But they were pre-
sented with so much grace and charm that the public never tired of
them. To his type of woman he was especially faithful: the tall
woman with long throat and well-defined chin, much resembling the
figures of Burne-Jones and Rossetti, only somewhat more mundane.
We have the same woman in the heroine of 'Trilby.'

Though Du Maurier, before beginning 'Peter Ibbetson,' had never
written a book, he had had considerable literary experience, for he
is said to have spent as much time upon the construction of the dia-
logues which accompanied his pictures as upon the pictures them-
selves. The story of 'Peter Ibbetson' he had often related to his
friends, who had urged him to write it down. This he finally did,—
at the special instance, it is said, of Henry James. It appeared in
Harper's Magazine in 1891. 'Trilby' was published in 1894 in Har-
per's Magazine, and at once attained a great popular success. The
publishers estimate that about 250,000 copies of the book have been
sold. Du Maurier had sold the book outright for £2,000, but when it
became apparent that the work was to be a success, the publishers
admitted the author to a royalty, paying at one time $40,000. They
also shared with him the large sums paid for the dramatization of
the work. For 'The Martian,' his last novel, he received £10,000
outright. This also was published in Harper's Magazine.

It is perhaps too early to pass judgment upon the merits of these works. They have, no doubt, grave faults. The story of 'Peter Ibbetson' has been completed when it is but two-thirds told. The remaining portion of the book is a dream. This is of course a dangerous reversal of the usual method of the story-teller, which is to make dreams seem like facts. The hypnotic part of 'Trilby' is said by the professional authorities on the subject to be bad science. The hypnotism in 'Trilby' was perhaps a journalist's idea, that subject being much talked of at the time the book was written. Du Maurier, it need hardly be said, was by training a journalist, although the training had been of the pencil rather than of the pen. The literary style of the novels is curious. It makes no pretensions to finish; the grammar even is sometimes at fault. But on the other hand, it has decided merits. It is particularly easy, flowing, and simple. These are not the qualities we should have expected from the nature of Du Maurier's literary training. The brief dialogues which he has for so many years appended to his sketches in 'Punch' would have educated, we should have thought, the qualities of brevity and point rather than those of ease and fullness. Certain peculiarities of the style cannot be defended, but the author produces his effects in spite of such solecisms. This is true of the matter of his stories as well as of the style. They are at many points inartistically constructed; but the stuff is good, and the works therefore hold their own in spite of these drawbacks. They certainly have one virtue, which is most necessary to the success of any work of the imagination: they have reality. We believe as we read, and continue to believe after we have ceased reading, that the Major and Mimsey and Taffy and Trilby are real persons. They are real to us because they have in the first case been real to their creator. It is possible, however, that the pictures which accompany the text may increase the strength of the illusion.

No book, in recent years at any rate, has had so instantaneous and prodigious a popular success as 'Trilby.' Popularity is always hard to explain with any certainty. It seems to be a quality in the warp and woof of the mind of the man that has it. One condition appears to be that he shall be in sympathy with the minds of the mass of his fellow-beings. There was such a sympathy in Du Maurier's case; and to be more particular, his kindly and friendly enthusiasm was a quality to commend him to men. He had a power of enjoying beauty in his fellow-beings. Then he had had a long education in the qualities that make popularity. He had long studied the art of pleasing. It is not improbable that in these novels, which were intended for the American public, he may have played upon certain of our national susceptibilities. We in this country like to have our literature taken seriously by the European. It may be that Du Maurier may have had an inkling of this, for it is curious to note how much of our poetry appears in these novels. Du Maurier had a very nice taste in poetry, a genuine enthusiasm for it which it is heartily to be wished were shared by all college professors of English literature. Thus, he could not have chosen better lines than those which Peter Ibbetson was in the habit of reciting to Mimsey, 'The Water-fowl' of Bryant,— perhaps the most perfect poem ever produced in this country,— a poem so "beautifully carried," as Matthew Arnold once described it to the present writer. Poe's beautiful and musical lines, written by him at fourteen,—'Helen, thy beauty is to me,'— are also made use of. We have a good deal of Longfellow and other American writers. 'Ben Bolt' is of course an American song. These appeals to our national predilections may have influenced us. But the interest and curiosity of our practical and hard-working American public in the Bohemian art life of the Latin Quarter was also, no doubt, a chief cause of the popularity of 'Trilby.'

Du Maurier did not live long to enjoy his success. He had always been known to his friends as a sensitive man, this quality being ascribed to ill health. Ill health was no doubt a chief cause of the vexation with which he received certain comments upon his books, in some cases inspired by envy of his success. Many of his recent contributions to Punch have been at the expense of the unsuccessful author, and have supported the thesis that ill success was not an indubitable proof of genius. When Lord Wolseley asked him what would be the title of his next novel, he said 'Soured by Success.' He died in London on October 8th, 1896.

AT THE HEART OF BOHEMIA

From 'Trilby.' Copyright 1894, by Harper & Brothers

AND then— well, I happen to forget what sort of a day this particular day turned into, about six of the clock.

If it was decently fine, the most of them went off to dine at the Restaurant de la Couronne, kept by the Père Trin, in the Rue de Monsieur, who gave you of his best to eat and drink for twenty sols Parisis, or one franc in the coin of the empire. Good distending soups, omelets that were only too savory, lentils, red and white beans, meat so dressed and sauced and seasoned that you didn't know whether it was beef or mutton, flesh, fowl, or good red herring,— or even bad, for that matter,— nor very greatly care.

And just the same lettuce, radishes, and cheese of Gruyère or Brie as you got at the Trois Frères Provençaux (but not the same butter!). And to wash it all down, generous wine in wooden "brocs," that stained a lovely æsthetic blue everything it was spilled over.

And you hobnobbed with models, male and female, students of law and medicine, painters and sculptors, workmen and blanchisseuses and grisettes, and found them very good company, and most improving to your French, if your French was of the usual British kind, and even to some of your manners, if these were very British indeed. And the evening was innocently wound up with billiards, cards, or dominoes at the Café du Luxembourg opposite; or at the Théâtre du Luxembourg, in the Rue de Madame, to see funny farces with screamingly droll Englishmen in them; or still better, at the Jardin Bullier (la Closerie des Lilas), to see the students dance the cancan, or try and dance it yourself, which is not so easy as it seems; or best of all, at the Théâtre de l'Odéon, to see Fechter and Madame Doche in the 'Dame aux Camélias.'

Or if it were not only fine, but a Saturday afternoon into the bargain, the Laird would put on a necktie and a few other necessary things, and the three friends would walk arm-in-arm to Taffy's hotel in the Rue de Seine, and wait outside till he had made himself as presentable as the Laird, which did not take very long. And then (Little Billee was always presentable) they would, arm-in-arm, the huge Taffy in the middle, descend the Rue de Seine and cross a bridge to the Cité, and have a look in at the Morgue. Then back again to the quays on the Rive Gauche by the Pont Neuf, to wend their way westward; now on one side to look at the print and picture shops and the magasins of bric-à-brac, and haply sometimes buy thereof, now on the other to finger and cheapen the second-hand books for sale on the parapet, and even pick one or two utterly unwanted bargains, never to be read or opened again.

When they reached the Pont des Arts they would cross it, stopping in the middle to look up the river towards the old Cité and Notre Dame, eastward, and dream unutterable things and try to utter them. Then turning westward, they would gaze at the glowing sky and all it glowed upon — the corner of the Tuileries and the Louvre, the many bridges, the Chamber of Deputies, the golden river narrowing its perspective and broadening its bed, as it went flowing and winding on its way between Passy and Grenelle to St. Cloud, to Rouen, to the Havre, to England perhaps—where *they* didn't want to be just then; and they would try and express themselves to the effect that life was uncommonly well worth living in that particular city at that particular time of the day and year and century, at that particular epoch of their own mortal and uncertain lives.

Then, still arm-in-arm and chatting gayly, across the courtyard of the Louvre, through gilded gates well guarded by reckless imperial Zouaves, up the arcaded Rue de Rivoli as far as the Rue Castiglione, where they would stare with greedy eyes at the window of the great corner pastry-cook, and marvel at the beautiful assortment of bonbons, pralines, dragées, marrons glacés —saccharine, crystalline substances of all kinds and colors, as charming to look at as an illumination; precious stones, delicately frosted sweets, pearls and diamonds so arranged as to melt in the mouth; especially, at this particular time of the year, the monstrous Easter eggs of enchanting hue, enshrined like costly jewels in caskets of satin and gold; and the Laird, who was well read in his English classics and liked to show it, would opine that " they managed these things better in France."

Then across the street by a great gate into the Allée des Feuillants, and up to the Place de la Concorde—to gaze, but quite without base envy, at the smart people coming back from the Bois de Boulogne. For even in Paris " carriage people " have a way of looking bored, of taking their pleasure sadly, of having nothing to say to each other, as though the vibration of so many wheels all rolling home the same way every afternoon had hypnotized them into silence, idiocy, and melancholia.

And our three musketeers of the brush would speculate on the vanity of wealth and rank and fashion; on the satiety that follows in the wake of self-indulgence and overtakes it; on the weariness of the pleasures that become a toil—as if they knew all about it, had found it all out for themselves, and nobody else had ever found it out before!

Then they found out something else—namely, that the sting of healthy appetite was becoming intolerable; so they would betake themselves to an English eating-house in the Rue de la Madeleine (on the left-hand side near the top), where they would renovate their strength and their patriotism on British beef and beer, and household bread, and bracing, biting, stinging yellow

mustard, and horseradish, and noble apple-pie, and Cheshire
cheese; and get through as much of these in an hour or so as
they could for talking, talking, talking; such happy talk! as full
of sanguine hope and enthusiasm, of cocksure commendation or
condemnation of all painters, dead or alive, of modest but firm
belief in themselves and each other, as a Paris Easter egg is full
of sweets and pleasantness (for the young).

And then a stroll on the crowded, well-lighted boulevards,
and a bock at the café there, at a little three-legged marble table
right out on the genial asphalt pavement, still talking nineteen
to the dozen.

Then home by dark old silent streets and some deserted
bridge to their beloved Latin Quarter, the Morgue gleaming
cold and still and fatal in the pale lamplight, and Notre Dame
pricking up its watchful twin towers, which have looked down
for so many centuries on so many happy, sanguine, expansive
youths walking arm-in-arm by twos and threes, and forever talk-
ing, talking, talking. . . .

The Laird and Little Billee would see Taffy safe to the door
of his *hôtel garni* in the Rue de Seine, where they would find
much to say to each other before they said good-night — so much
that Taffy and Little Billee would see the Laird safe to *his* door,
in the Place St. Anatole des Arts. And then a discussion would
arise between Taffy and the Laird on the immortality of the
soul, let us say, or the exact meaning of the word "gentleman,"
or the relative merits of Dickens and Thackeray, or some such
recondite and quite unhackneyed theme, and Taffy and the Laird
would escort Little Billee to *his* door, in the Place de l'Odéon,
and he would re-escort them both back again, and so on till any
hour you please.

Or again, if it rained, and Paris through the studio window
loomed lead-colored, with its shiny slate roofs under skies that
were ashen and sober, and the wild west wind made woeful music
among the chimney-pots, and little gray waves ran up the river
the wrong way, and the Morgue looked chill and dark and wet,
and almost uninviting (even to three healthy-minded young
Britons), they would resolve to dine and spend a happy evening
at home.

Little Billee, taking with him three francs (or even four),
would dive into back streets and buy a yard or so of crusty
new bread, well burned on the flat side, a fillet of beef, a litre

of wine, potatoes and onions, butter, a little cylindrical cheese called "bondon de Neufchâtel," tender curly lettuce, with chervil, parsley, spring onions, and other fine herbs, and a pod of garlic, which would be rubbed on a crust of bread to flavor things with.

Taffy would lay the cloth English-wise, and also make the salad, for which, like everybody else I ever met, he had a special receipt of his own (putting in the oil first and the vinegar after); and indeed, his salads were quite as good as everybody else's.

The Laird, bending over the stove, would cook the onions and beef into a savory Scotch mess so cunningly that you could not taste the beef for the onions — nor always the onions for the garlic!

And they would dine far better than at le Père Trin's, far better than at the English Restaurant in the Rue de la Madeleine — better than anywhere else on earth!

And after dinner, what coffee, roasted and ground on the spot, what pipes and cigarettes of "caporal," by the light of the three shaded lamps, while the rain beat against the big north window, and the wind went howling round the quaint old mediæval tower at the corner of the Rue Vieille des Mauvais Ladres (the old street of the bad lepers), and the damp logs hissed and crackled in the stove!

What jolly talk into the small hours! Thackeray and Dickens again, and Tennyson and Byron (who was "not dead yet" in those days); and Titian and Velasquez, and young Millais and Holman Hunt (just out); and Monsieur Ingres and Monsieur Delacroix, and Balzac and Stendhal and George Sand; and the good Dumas! and Edgar Allan Poe; and the glory that was Greece and the grandeur that was Rome. . . .

Good, honest, innocent, artless prattle — not of the wisest, perhaps, nor redolent of the very highest culture (which by the way can mar as well as make), nor leading to any very practical result; but quite pathetically sweet from the sincerity and fervor of its convictions, a profound belief in their importance, and a proud trust in their lifelong immutability.

Oh happy days and happy nights, sacred to art and friendship! oh happy times of careless impecuniosity, and youth and hope and health and strength and freedom — with all Paris for a playground, and its dear old unregenerate Latin Quarter for a workshop and a home!

CHRISTMAS IN THE LATIN QUARTER

From 'Trilby.' Copyright, 1894, by Harper & Brothers

CHRISTMAS was drawing near.

There were days when the whole Quartier Latin would veil its iniquities under fogs almost worthy of the Thames Valley between London Bridge and Westminster, and out of the studio window the prospect was a dreary blank. No Morgue! no towers of Notre Dame! not even the chimney-pots over the way —not even the little mediæval toy turret at the corner of the Rue Vieille des Mauvais Ladres, Little Billee's delight!

The stove had to be crammed till its sides grew a dull deep red, before one's fingers could hold a brush or squeeze a bladder; one had to box or fence at nine in the morning, that one might recover from the cold bath and get warm for the rest of the day!

Taffy and the Laird grew pensive and dreamy, childlike and bland; and when they talked, it was generally about Christmas at home in merry England and the distant land of cakes, and how good it was to be there at such a time—hunting, shooting, curling, and endless carouse!

It was Ho! for the jolly West Riding, and Hey! for the bonnets of Bonnie Dundee, till they grew quite homesick, and wanted to start by the very next train.

They didn't do anything so foolish. They wrote over to friends in London for the biggest turkey, the biggest plum-pudding, that could be got for love or money, with mince-pies, and holly and mistletoe, and sturdy, short, thick English sausages, half a Stilton cheese, and a sirloin of beef — two sirloins, in case one should not be enough.

For they meant to have a Homeric feast in the studio on Christmas Day — Taffy, the Laird, and Little Billee — and invite all the delightful chums I have been trying to describe; and that is just why I tried to describe them — Durien, Vincent, Antony, Lorrimer, Carnegie, Petrolicoconose, l'Zouzou, and Dodor!

The cooking and waiting should be done by Trilby, her friend Angèle Boisse, M. et Mme. Vinard, and such little Vinards as could be trusted with glass and crockery and mince-pies; and if that was not enough, they would also cook themselves and wait upon each other.

When dinner should be over, supper was to follow, with scarcely any interval to speak of; and to partake of this, other guests should be bidden—Svengali and Gecko, and perhaps one or two more. No ladies!

For as the unsusceptible Laird expressed it, in the language of a gillie he had once met at a servants' dance in a Highland country-house, "Them wimmen spiles the ball!"

Elaborate cards of invitation were sent out, in the designing and ornamentation of which the Laird and Taffy exhausted all their fancy (Little Billee had no time).

Wines and spirits and English beers were procured at great cost from M. E. Delevigne's, in the Rue St. Honoré, and liqueurs of every description — chartreuse, curaçoa, ratafia de cassis, and anisette; no expense was spared.

Also truffled galantines of turkey, tongues, hams, rillettes de Tours, pâtés de foie gras, "fromage d'Italie" (which has nothing to do with cheese), saucissons d'Arles et de Lyon, with and without garlic, cold jellies, peppery and salt — everything that French charcutiers and their wives can make out of French pigs, or any other animal whatever, beast, bird, or fowl (even cats and rats), for the supper; and sweet jellies and cakes, and sweetmeats, and confections of all kinds, from the famous pastry-cook at the corner of the Rue Castiglione.

Mouths went watering all day long in joyful anticipation. They water somewhat sadly now at the mere remembrance of these delicious things — the mere immediate sight or scent of which in these degenerate latter days would no longer avail to promote any such delectable secretion. Hélas! ahimè! ach weh! ay de mi! eheu! οἴμοι — in point of fact, *alas!*

That is the very exclamation I wanted.

Christmas eve came round. The pieces of resistance and plum-pudding and mince-pies had not yet arrived from London — but there was plenty of time.

Les trois Angliches dined at le Père Trin's, as usual, and played billiards and dominoes at the Café du Luxembourg, and possessed their souls in patience till it was time to go and hear the midnight mass at the Madeleine, where Roucouly, the great baritone of the Opéra Comique, was retained to sing Adam's famous Noël.

The whole Quarter seemed alive with the réveillon. It was a clear frosty night, with a splendid moon just past the full, and most exhilarating was the walk along the quays on the Rive Gauche, over the Pont de la Concorde and across the Place thereof, and up the thronged Rue de la Madeleine to the massive Parthenaic place of worship that always has such a pagan, worldly look of smug and prosperous modernity.

They struggled manfully, and found standing and kneeling room among that fervent crowd, and heard the impressive service with mixed feelings, as became true Britons of very advanced liberal and religious opinions; not with the unmixed contempt of the proper British Orthodox (who were there in full force, one may be sure).

But their susceptible hearts soon melted at the beautiful music, and in mere sensuous *attendrissement* they were quickly in unison with all the rest.

For as the clock struck twelve, out pealed the organ, and up rose the finest voice in France:

> "Minuit, Chrétiens! c'est l'heure solennelle
> Où l'Homme-Dieu descendit parmi nous!"

And a wave of religious emotion rolled over Little Billee and submerged him; swept him off his little legs, swept him out of his little self, drowned him in a great seething surge of love — love of his kind, love of love, love of life, love of death, love of all that is and ever was and ever will be — a very large order indeed, even for Little Billee.

And it seemed to him that he stretched out his arms for love to one figure especially beloved beyond all the rest — one figure erect on high, with arms outstretched to him, in more than common fellowship of need: not the sorrowful Figure crowned with thorns, for it was in the likeness of a woman; but never that of the Virgin Mother of our Lord.

It was Trilby, Trilby, Trilby! a poor fallen sinner and waif, all but lost amid the scum of the most corrupt city on earth. Trilby, weak and mortal like himself, and in woeful want of pardon! and in her gray dove-like eyes he saw the shining of so great a love that he was abashed; for well he knew that all that love was his, and would be his forever, come what would or could.

> "Peuple, debout! Chante ta délivrance!
> *Noël! Noël! Voici le Rédempteur!*"

So sang and rang and pealed and echoed the big deep metallic baritone bass — above the organ, above the incense, above everything else in the world — till the very universe seemed to shake with the rolling thunder of that great message of love and forgiveness!

Thus at least felt Little Billee, whose way it was to magnify and exaggerate all things under the subtle stimulus of sound, and the singing human voice had especially strange power to penetrate into his inmost depths — even the voice of man!

And what voice but the deepest and gravest and grandest there is, can give worthy utterance to such a message as that, — the epitome, the abstract, the very essence of all collective humanity's wisdom at its best!

«DREAMING TRUE»

From 'Peter Ibbetson.' Copyright, 1891, by Harper & Brothers

A s I SAT down on a bench by the old willow (where the rat lived), and gazed and gazed, it almost surprised me that the very intensity of my desire did not of itself suffice to call up the old familiar faces and forms, and conjure away these modern intruders. The power to do this seemed almost within my reach: I willed and willed and willed with all my might, but in vain; I could not cheat my sight or hearing for a moment. There they remained, unconscious and undisturbed, those happy, well-mannered, well-appointed little French people, and fed the gold and silver fish; and there with an aching heart I left them.

Oh, surely, surely, I cried to myself, we ought to find some means of possessing the past more fully and completely than we do. Life is not worth living for many of us, if a want so desperate and yet so natural can never be satisfied. Memory is but a poor rudimentary thing that we had better be without, if it can only lead us to the verge of consummation like this, and madden us with a desire it cannot slake. The touch of a vanished hand, the sound of a voice that is still, the tender grace of a day that is dead, should be ours forever at our beck and call, by some exquisite and quite conceivable illusion of the senses.

Alas! alas! I have hardly the hope of ever meeting my beloved ones again in another life. Oh, to meet their too dimly remembered forms in this, just as they once were, by some trick of my own brain! To see them with the eye, and hear them with the ear, and tread with them the old obliterated ways as in a waking dream! It would be well worth going mad, to become such a self-conjurer as that.

I GOT back to my hotel in the Rue de la Michodière.

Prostrate with emotion and fatigue, the tarantella still jingling in my ears, and that haunting, beloved face, with its ineffable smile, still printed on the retina of my closed eyes, I fell asleep.

And then I dreamed a dream, and the first phase of my real, inner life began!

All the events of the day, distorted and exaggerated and jumbled together after the usual manner of dreams, wove themselves into a kind of nightmare and oppression. I was on my way to my old abode; everything that I met or saw was grotesque and impossible, yet had now the strange, vague charm of association and reminiscence, now the distressing sense of change and desolation.

As I got near to the avenue gate, instead of the school on my left there was a prison; and at the door a little thick-set jailer, three feet high and much deformed, and a little deformed jaileress no bigger than himself, were cunningly watching me out of the corners of their eyes, and toothlessly smiling. Presently they began to waltz together to an old familiar tune, with their enormous keys dangling at their sides; and they looked so funny that I laughed and applauded. But soon I perceived that their crooked faces were not really funny; indeed, they were fatal and terrible in the extreme, and I was soon conscious that these deadly dwarfs were trying to waltz between me and the avenue gate for which I was bound — to cut me off, that they might run me into the prison, where it was their custom to hang people of a Monday morning.

In an agony of terror I made a rush for the avenue gate, and there stood the Duchess of Towers, with mild surprise in her eyes and a kind smile — a heavenly vision of strength and reality.

"You are not dreaming true!" she said. "Don't be afraid — those little people don't exist! Give me your hand and come in here."

And as I did so she waved the troglodytes away, and they vanished; and I felt that this was no longer a dream, but something else — some strange thing that had happened to me, some new life that I had woke up to.

For at the touch of her hand my consciousness, my sense of being I, myself, which hitherto in my dream (as in all previous dreams up to then) had been only partial, intermittent, and vague, suddenly blazed into full, consistent, practical activity — just as it is in life, when one is well awake and much interested in what is going on; only with perceptions far keener and more alert.

I knew perfectly who I was and what I was, and remembered all the events of the previous day. I was conscious that my real body, undressed and in bed, now lay fast asleep in a small room on the fourth floor of an *hôtel garni* in the Rue de la Michodière. I knew this perfectly; and yet here was my body too, just as substantial, with all my clothes on; my boots rather dusty, my shirt collar damp with the heat, for it was hot. With my disengaged hand I felt in my trousers pocket; there were my London latch-key, my purse, my penknife; my handkerchief in the breast pocket of my coat, and in its tail pockets my gloves and pipe-case, and the little water-color box I had bought that morning. I looked at my watch; it was going, and marked eleven. I pinched myself, I coughed, I did all one usually does under the pressure of some immense surprise, to assure myself that I was awake; and I *was*, and yet here I stood, actually hand in hand with a lady to whom I had never been introduced (and who seemed much tickled at my confusion); and staring now at her, now at my old school.

The prison had tumbled down like a house of cards, and lo! in its place was M. Saindou's *maison d'éducation*, just as it had been of old. I even recognized on the yellow wall the stamp of a hand in dry mud, made fifteen years ago by a day boy called Parisot, who had fallen down in the gutter close by, and thus left his mark on getting up again; and it had remained there for months, till it had been whitewashed away in the holidays. Here it was anew, after fifteen years.

The swallows were flying and twittering. A yellow omnibus was drawn up to the gates of the school; the horses stamped and neighed, and bit each other, as French horses always did in those days. The driver swore at them perfunctorily.

A crowd was looking on — le Père et la Mère François, Madame Liard the grocer's wife, and other people, whom I remembered at once with delight. Just in front of us a small boy and girl were looking on, like the rest, and I recognized the back and the cropped head and thin legs of Mimsey Seraskier.

A barrel organ was playing a pretty tune I knew quite well, and had forgotten.

The school gates opened, and M. Saindou, proud and full of self-importance (as he always was), and half a dozen boys whose faces and names were quite familiar to me, in smart white trousers and shining boots, and silken white bands round their left arms, got into the omnibus, and were driven away in a glorified manner — as it seemed — to heaven in a golden chariot. It was beautiful to see and hear.

I was still holding the duchess's hand, and felt the warmth of it through her glove; it stole up my arm like a magnetic current. I was in Elysium; a heavenly sense had come over me that at last my periphery had been victoriously invaded by a spirit other than mine — a most powerful and beneficent spirit. There was a blessed fault in my impenetrable armor of self, after all, and the genius of strength and charity and loving-kindness had found it out.

"Now you're dreaming true," she said. "Where are those boys going?"

"To church, to make their *première communion*," I replied.

"That's right. You're dreaming true because I've got you by the hand. Do you know that tune?"

I listened, and the words belonging to it came out of the past, and I said them to her, and she laughed again, with her eyes screwed up deliciously.

"Quite right — quite!" she exclaimed. "How odd that you should know them! How well you pronounce French for an Englishman! For you are Mr. Ibbetson, Lady Cray's architect?"

I assented, and she let go my hand.

The street was full of people — familiar forms and faces and voices, chatting together and looking down the road after the yellow omnibus; old attitudes, old tricks of gait and manner, old forgotten French ways of speech — all as it was long ago. Nobody noticed us, and we walked up the now deserted avenue.

The happiness, the enchantment of it all! Could it be that I was dead, that I had died suddenly in my sleep, at the hotel in the Rue de la Michodière? Could it be that the Duchess of Towers was dead too—had been killed by some accident on her way from St. Cloud to Paris? and that, both having died, so near each other, we had begun our eternal after-life in this heavenly fashion?

That was too good to be true, I reflected; some instinct told me that this was not death, but transcendent earthly life—and also, alas! that it would not endure forever!

I was deeply conscious of every feature in her face, every movement of her body, every detail of her dress,—more so than I could have been in actual life,—and said to myself, "Whatever this is, it is no dream." But I felt there was about me the unspeakable elation which can come to us only in our waking moments when we are at our very best; and then only feebly, in comparison with this, and to many of us never. It never had to me, since that morning when I had found the little wheelbarrow.

I was also conscious, however, that the avenue itself had a slight touch of the dream in it. It was no longer quite right, and was getting out of drawing and perspective, so to speak. I had lost my stay—the touch of her hand.

"Are you still dreaming true, Mr. Ibbetson?"

"I am afraid not quite," I replied.

"You must try by yourself a little—try hard. Look at this house; what is written on the portico?"

I saw written in gold letters the words "Tête Noire," and said so.

She rippled with laughter, and said, "No, try again;" and just touched me with the tip of her finger for a moment.

I tried again, and said "Parvis Notre Dame."

"That's rather better," she said, and touched me again; and I read, "Parva sed Apta," as I had so often read there before in old days.

"And now look at that old house over there," pointing to my old home; "how many windows are there in the top story?"

I said seven.

"No; there are five. Look again!" and there were five; and the whole house was exactly, down to its minutest detail, as it had been once upon a time. I could see Thérèse through one of the windows, making my bed.

"That's better," said the duchess; "you will soon do it—it's very easy—*ce n'est que le premier pas!* My father taught me;

you must always sleep on your back with your arms above your head, your hands clasped under it and your feet crossed, the right one over the left, unless you are left-handed; and you must never for a moment cease thinking of where you want to be in your dream till* you are asleep and get there; and you must never forget in your dream where and what you were when awake. You must join the dream on to reality. Don't forget. And now I will say good-by; but before I go, give me both your hands, and look round everywhere as far as your eye can see.»

It was hard to look away from her; her face drew my eyes, and through them all my heart; but I did as she told me, and took in the whole familiar scene, even to the distant woods of Ville d'Avray, a glimpse of which was visible through an opening in the trees; even to the smoke of a train making its way to Versailles, miles off; and the old telegraph, working its black arms on the top of Mont Valérien.

"Is it all right?" she asked. "That's well. Henceforward, whenever you come here, you will be safe as far as your sight can reach,—from this spot,—all through my introduction. See what it is to have a friend at court! No more little dancing jailers! And then you can gradually get farther by yourself.

"Out there, through that park, leads to the Bois de Boulogne—there's a gap in the hedge you can get through; but mind and make everything plain in front of you—*true*, before you go a step farther, or else you'll have to wake and begin it all over again. You have only to will it, and think yourself as awake, and it will come—on condition, of course, that you have been there before. And mind, also, you must take care how you touch things or people—you may hear, see, and smell; but you mustn't touch, nor pick flowers or leaves, nor move things about. It blurs the dream, like breathing on a window-pane. I don't know why, but it does. You must remember that everything here is dead and gone by. With you and me it is different; we're alive and real—that is, *I* am; and there would seem to be no mistake about your being real too, Mr. Ibbetson, by the grasp of your hands. But you're *not;* and why you are here, and what business you have in this my particular dream, I cannot understand; no living person has ever come into it before. I can't make it out. I suppose it's because I saw your reality this afternoon, looking out of the window at the Tête Noire, and you are just a stray figment of my over-tired brain — a very agreeable figment, I admit; but you don't exist here just now — you can't possibly; you are somewhere else, Mr. Ibbetson; dancing at Mabille, perhaps, or fast asleep somewhere, and dreaming of French churches and palaces, and public fountains, like a good young British architect — otherwise I shouldn't talk to you like this, you may be sure!

"Never mind. I am very glad to dream that I have been of use to you, and you are very welcome here, if it amuses you to come — especially as you are only a false dream of mine, for what else *can* you be? And now I must leave you: so good-by."

She disengaged her hands and laughed her angelic laugh, and then turned towards the park. I watched her tall straight figure and blowing skirts, and saw her follow some ladies and children into a thicket that I remembered well, and she was soon out of sight.

I felt as if all warmth had gone out of my life; as if a joy had taken flight; as if a precious something had withdrawn itself from my possession, and the gap in my periphery had closed again.

Long I stood in thought, with my eyes fixed on the spot where she had disappeared; and I felt inclined to follow, but then considered this would not have been discreet. For although she was only a false dream of mine, a mere recollection of the exciting and eventful day, a stray figment of my over-tired and excited brain — a *more* than agreeable figment (what else *could* she be!) — she was also a great lady, and had treated me, a perfect stranger and a perfect nobody, with singular courtesy and kindness; which I repaid, it is true, with a love so deep and strong that my very life was hers to do what she liked with, and always had been since I first saw her, and always would be as long as there was breath in my body! But this did not constitute an acquaintance without a proper introduction, even in France — even in a dream. Even in dreams one must be polite, even to stray figments of one's tired, sleeping brain.

And then what business had *she* in *this*, *my* particular dream — as she herself had asked of me?

But *was* it a dream? I remembered my lodgings at Pentonville, that I had left yesterday morning. I remembered what I was — why I came to Paris; I remembered the very bedroom at the Paris hotel where I was now fast asleep, its loudly ticking clock, and all the meagre furniture. And here was I, broad awake and conscious in the middle of an old avenue that had long ceased to exist — that had been built over by a huge brick edifice covered with newly painted trellis-work. I saw it,—this edifice,—myself, only twelve hours ago. And yet here was everything as it had been when I was a child; and all through the agency of this solid phantom of a lovely young English duchess, whose warm gloved hands I had only this minute been holding in mine! The scent of her gloves was still in my palm. I looked at my watch; it marked twenty-three minutes to twelve. All this had happened in less than three-quarters of an hour!

Pondering over all this in hopeless bewilderment, I turned my steps towards my old home, and to my surprise, was just able to look over the garden wall, which I had once thought about ten feet high.

Under the old apple-tree in full bloom sat my mother, darning small socks; with her flaxen side-curls (as it was her fashion to wear them) half concealing her face. My emotion and astonishment were immense. My heart beat fast. I felt its pulse in my temples, and my breath was short.

At a little green table that I remembered well sat a small boy, rather quaintly dressed in a bygone fashion, with a frill round his wide shirt collar, and his golden hair cut quite close at the top, and rather long at the sides and back. It was Gogo Pasquier. He seemed a very nice little boy. He had pen and ink and copy-book before him, and a gilt-edged volume bound in red morocco. I knew it at a glance; it was 'Elegant Extracts.' The dog Médor lay asleep in the shade. The bees were droning among the nasturtiums and convolvulus.

A little girl ran up the avenue from the porter's lodge and pushed the garden gate, which rang the bell as it opened, and she went into the garden, and I followed her; but she took no notice of me, nor did the others. It was Mimsey Seraskier.

I went and sat at my mother's feet, and looked long in her face.

I must not speak to her nor touch her — not even touch her busy hand with my lips, or I should "blur the dream."

I got up and looked over the boy Gogo's shoulder. He was translating Gray's Elegy into French; he had not got very far, and seemed to be stumped by the line —

"And leaves the world to darkness and to me."

Mimsey was silently looking over his other shoulder, her thumb in her mouth, one arm on the back of his chair. She seemed to be stumped also; it was an awkward line to translate.

I stooped and put my hand to Médor's nose, and felt his warm breath. He wagged his rudiment of a tail, and whimpered in his sleep. Mimsey said:—

"Regarde Médor, comme il remue la queue! *C'est le Prince Charmant qui lui chatouille le bout du nez.*"

Said my mother, who had not spoken hitherto:—

"Do speak English, Mimsey, please."

O my God! My mother's voice, so forgotten, yet so familiar, so unutterably dear! I rushed to her and threw myself on my knees at her feet, and seized her hand and kissed it, crying, "Mother, mother!"

A strange blur came over everything; the sense of reality was lost. All became as a dream—a beautiful dream, but only a dream; and I woke.

BARTY JOSSELIN AT SCHOOL

From 'The Martian'

From Harper's Magazine. Copyright, 1896, by Harper & Brothers

INDEED, even from his early boyhood, he was the most extraordinarily gifted creature I have ever known, or even heard of; a kind of spontaneous humorous Crichton to whom all things came easily—and life itself as an uncommonly good joke. During that summer term of 1847 I did not see very much of him. He was in the class below mine, and took up with Laferté and little Bussy-Rabutin, who were first-rate boys, and laughed at everything he said, and worshiped him. So did everybody else, sooner or later; indeed, it soon became evident that he was a most exceptional little person.

In the first place, his beauty was absolutely angelic, as will be readily believed by all who have known him since. The mere sight of him as a boy made people pity his father and mother for being dead!

Then he had a charming gift of singing little French and English ditties, comic or touching, with his delightful fresh young pipe, and accompanying himself quite nicely on either piano or guitar without really knowing a note of music. Then he could draw caricatures that we boys thought inimitable, much funnier than Cham's or Bertall's or Gavarni's, and collected and treasured up. I have dozens of them now—they make me laugh still, and bring back memories of which the charm is indescribable; and their pathos to me!

And then how funny he was himself, without effort, and with a fun that never failed! He was a born buffoon of the graceful kind,—more whelp or kitten than monkey—ever playing the fool, in and out of season, but somehow always apropos; and French boys love a boy for that more than anything else; or did in those days.

.   .   .   .

His constitution, inherited from a long line of frugal seafaring Norman ancestors (not to mention another long line of well-fed, well-bred Yorkshire squires), was magnificent. His spirits never failed. He could see the satellites of Jupiter with the naked eye; this was often tested by M. Dumollard, maître de mathématiques (et de cosmographie), who had a telescope, which, with a little good-will on the gazer's part, made Jupiter look as big as the moon, and its moons like stars of the first magnitude.

His sense of hearing was also exceptionally keen. He could hear a watch tick in the next room, and perceive very high sounds to which ordinary human ears are deaf (this was found out later); and when we played blindman's buff on a rainy day, he could, blindfolded, tell every boy he caught hold of—not by feeling him all over like the rest of us, but by the mere smell of his hair, or his hands, or his blouse! No wonder he was so much more alive than the rest of us! According to the amiable, modest, polite, delicately humorous, and ever tolerant and considerate Professor Max Nordau, this perfection of the olfactory sense proclaims poor Barty a degenerate! I only wish there were a few more like him, and that I were a little more like him myself!

By the way, how proud young Germany must feel of its enlightened Max, and how fond of him, to be sure! *Mes compliments!*

But the most astounding thing of all (it seems incredible, but all the world knows it by this time, and it will be accounted for later on) is that at certain times and seasons Barty knew by an infallible instinct *where the north was*, to a point. Most of my readers will remember his extraordinary evidence as a witness in the "Rangoon" trial, and how this power was tested in open court, and how important were the issues involved, and how he refused to give any explanation of a gift so extraordinary.

It was often tried at school by blindfolding him, and turning him round and round till he was giddy, and asking him to point out where the North Pole was, or the North Star, and seven or eight times out of ten the answer was unerringly right. When he failed, he knew beforehand that for the time being he had lost the power, but could never say why. Little Doctor Larcher could never get over his surprise at this strange phenomenon, nor explain it; and often brought some scientific friend from Paris to test it, who was equally nonplussed.

When cross-examined, Barty would merely say:—

"Quelquefois je sais—quelquefois je ne sais pas—mais quand je sais, je sais, et il n'y pas à s'y tromper!"

Indeed, on one occasion that I remember well a very strange thing happened; he not only pointed out the north with absolute accuracy, as he stood carefully blindfolded in the gymnastic ground, after having been turned and twisted again and again— but still blindfolded, he vaulted the wire fence and ran round to the refectory door, which served as the home at rounders, all of us following; and there he danced a surprising dance of his own invention, that he called 'La Paladine,' the most humorously graceful and grotesque exhibition I ever saw; and then, taking a ball out of his pocket, he shouted, "À l'amandier!" and threw the ball. Straight and swift it flew, and hit the almond tree, which was quite twenty yards off; and after this he ran round the yard from base to base, as at "la balle au camp," till he reached the camp again.

"If ever he goes blind," said the wondering M. Mérovée, "he'll never need a dog to lead him about."

"He must have some special friend above!" said Madame Germain (Mérovée's sister, who was looking on).

Prophetic words! I have never forgotten them, nor the tear that glistened in each of her kind eyes as she spoke. She was a deeply religious and very emotional person, and loved Barty almost as if he were a child of her own.

Such women have strange intuitions.

Barty was often asked to repeat this astonishing performance before skeptical people — parents of boys, visitors, etc. — who had been told of it, and who believed he could not have been properly blindfolded; but he could never be induced to do so.

There was no mistake about the blindfolding — I helped in it myself; and he afterwards told me the whole thing was "aussi simple que bonjour" if once he felt the north — for then, with his back to the refectory door, he knew exactly the position and distance of every tree from where he was.

"It's all nonsense about my going blind and being able to do without a dog," he added; "I should be just as helpless as any other blind man, unless I was in a place I knew as well as my own pocket — like this play-ground! Besides, *I* shan't go blind; nothing will ever happen to *my* eyes — they're the strongest and best in the whole school!"

He said this exultingly, dilating his nostrils and chest; and looked proudly up and around, like Ajax defying the lightning.

"But what *do* you feel when you feel the north, Barty — a kind of tingling?" I asked.

"Oh — I feel where it is — as if I'd got a mariner's compass trembling inside my stomach — and as if I wasn't afraid of anybody or anything in the world — as if I could go and have my head chopped off and not care a fig."

"Ah, well — I can't make it out — I give it up," I exclaimed.

"So do I," exclaims Barty.

"But tell me, Barty," I whispered — "*have* you — have you *really* got a — a — *special friend above?*"

"Ask no questions and you'll get no lies," said Barty, and winked at me one eye after the other — and went about his business, and I about mine.

WILLIAM DUNBAR

(1465 ?–1530 ?)

PICTURESQUE figure in a picturesque age is that of William Dunbar, court minstrel to James IV., and as Sir Walter Scott declared, "a poet unrivaled by any that Scotland has ever produced." Little of his personal history is known. Probably he was a native of East Lothian, a member of the family of the Earl of March, and a graduate of St. Andrews University about the year 1479. After his college days he joined the order of Franciscans and became a mendicant friar, preaching the queer sermons of his time, and begging his way through England and France. Yet in these pilgrimages the young scholar learned useful habits of self-denial, saw new phases of human character, and above all enjoyed that close communion with nature which is the need of the poet. Over and over there is a reflection of this life in that fanciful verse, which has caught the color of the morning hours when the hedgerows are wet and the grass dewy, when the wild roses scent the roadside and the lark is at matins — verse full of the joy of life and the hope of youth.

After some years of this vagabond life, Dunbar left the Franciscans and attached himself to the court, where he speedily became a favorite. His day was one of pageant and show, of masque and spectacle, and into its gay assemblage of knights and courtiers, ladies and great nobles, Dunbar fitted perfectly. When an embassy was sent to England to negotiate the royal marriage with Margaret Tudor, Dunbar went along, being specially accredited by the king. He became a favorite with the young Princess, and a poem written in honor of the city of London, and one descriptive of the Queen's Progress, afford a faithful and valuable memorial of this mission. History is fortunate when she secures a poet as her scribe. Dunbar is principally known by his three poems 'The Thistle and the Rose,' 'The Golden Targe,' and 'The Dance of the Seven Deadly Sins.'

The first of these is an allegory celebrating the nuptials of the king. It suggests of course the allegories of Chaucer; but Dunbar's muse is his own, and the poem springs fresh and clear from native fonts. The poet represents himself as awakened by Aurora on a spring morning and told to do homage to May. Through the symbolism of the court of Nature, who crowns the Lion and Eagle, commissions the Thistle and Rose as her handmaidens, and orders their praises sung by the assembled birds of earth, the political significance of the allegory appears. But 'The Thistle and the Rose,' which is thus made to illustrate the union between the two great houses of Scotland and England, is far more than the poem of an occasion. It is full of the melody and fragrance of spring, saturated with that sensuous delight which at this bountiful season fills the veins of Nature. Here Dunbar is no longer the court laureate, but the begging friar, wandering through the green lanes and finding bed and board under the free skies.

'The Golden Targe' is more artificial in construction. It is another allegory, descriptive of an encounter between Cupid and Reason, who is defended by a golden targe or shield from the attacks of love. Here again the rural landscape forms a background to his mimic action. Amazons dressed in green fight the battle of Cupid, and vanquish Reason, then magically vanish and leave the poet to awake from his dream. 'The Golden Targe' was a poem to be read in the royal presence, when the court assembled after a day's hunting or an afternoon of archery; but it is filled with the ethereal loveliness which only the true poet beholds.

It is in 'The Dance of the Seven Deadly Sins' that Dunbar touches the note of seriousness, which characterizes his race and his individual genius. This satire is not so unsparing an indictment as the vision of Piers Ploughman, and yet it provokes inevitable comparison with the older poem. In a dream the poet sees heaven and hell opened. It is the eve of Ash Wednesday, and the Devil has commanded a dance to be performed by those spirits that had never received absolution. In obedience to this command the Seven Deadly Sins present a masque before his Satanic Majesty, and it is in the description of this grisly performance that Dunbar reveals a new aspect of power. The comedy here is not comic, but grotesque and horrid. The vision of the Scot is the vision that came to the poets of the 'Inferno' and 'Paradise Lost,' and it shows that his imagination was capable of the loftiest flights.

After the melancholy day of Flodden Field, the Scottish laureateship ceased to exist, but it is remarkable that so prominent a man as Dunbar should so completely have disappeared from contemporary view that his subsequent career and the time of his death are matters of doubt. His period is given as between the years 1465 and 1530, but these dates are only approximate.

Had Dunbar held his genius in hand as completely as did Chaucer, his accomplishment would doubtless have been greater than it was. Yet his place in literature is that of one of the most important poets of the fifteenth century, the age of Caxton and book-making, the time of that first flush of radiance which ushered in the full day of Spenser and Shakespeare.

THE THISTLE AND THE ROSE

QUHEN Merche wes with variand windis past,
   And Appryle had, with her silver schouris,
      Tane leif at Nature with ane orient blast,
   And lusty May, that muddir is of flouris,
   Had maid the birdis to begyn thair houris
Amang the tendir odouris reid and quhyt,
Quhois armony to heir it wes delyt:

In bed at morrow, sleiping as I lay,
   Me thocht Aurora with hir cristall ene
In at the window lukit by the day,
   And halsit me, with visage paill and grene;
   On quhois hand a lark sang fro the splene:—
Awalk, luvaris, out of you slomering;
Sé hou the lusty morrow dois up spring.

Me thocht fresche May befoir my bed up stude,
   In weid depaynt of mony diverss hew,
Sobir, benyng, and full of mansuetude,
   In brycht atteir of flouris forgit new,
   Hevinly of color, quhyt, reid, broun and blew,
Balmit in dew, and gilt with Phebus bemys;
Quhyll all the house illumynit of her lemys.

Slugird, sche said, awalk annone for schame,
   And in my honour sum thing thou go wryt;
The lark hes done the mirry day proclame,
   To raise up luvaris with confort and delyt;
   Yit nocht incressis thy curage to indyt,
Quhois hairt sum tyme hes glaid and blisfull bene,
Sangis to mak undir the levis grene.

Than callit sche all flouris that grew on feild,
   Discirnyng all thair fassionis and effeiris,
Upone the awfull Thrissil sche beheld,
   And saw him kepit with a busche of speiris;
   Considering him so able for the weiris,
A radius croun of rubeis sche him gaif,
And said, In feild go furth and fend the laif:

And sen thou art a King, thou be discreit;
   Herb without vertew thow hald nocht of sic pryce
As herb of vertew and of odour sueit;

And lat no nettill vyle, and full of vyce,
   Hir fallow to the gudly flour-de-lyce;
Nor latt no wyld weid, full of churlicheness,
Compair hir till the lilleis nobilness.

Nor hald non udir flour in sic denty
   As the fresche Rois, of cullour reid and quhyt:
For gife thow dois, hurt is thyne honesty;
   Considring that no flour is so perfyt,
   So full of vertew, plesans, and delyt,
So full of blisful angeilik bewty,
Imperiall birth, honour and dignité.

FROM 'THE GOLDEN TARGE'

BRYGHT as the stern of day begouth to schyne
   Quhen gone to bed war Vesper and Lucyne,
     I raise, and by a rosere did me rest:
Up sprang the goldyn candill matutyne,
With clere depurit bemes cristallyne
   Glading the mery foulis in thair nest;
   Or Phebus was in purpur cape revest
Up raise the lark, the hevyn's menstrale fyne
   In May, in till a morrow myrthfullest.

Full angelliko thir birdis sang thair houris
Within thair courtyns grene, in to thair bouris,
   Apparalit quhite and red, wyth blomes suete;
Anamalit was the felde with all colouris,
The perly droppis schuke in silvir schouris;
   Quhill all in balme did branch and levis flete,
   To part fra Phebus did Aurora grete;
Hir cristall teris I saw hyng on the flouris
   Quhilk he for lufe all drank up with his hete.

For mirth of May, wyth skippis and wyth hoppis,
The birdis sang upon the tender croppis,
   With curiouse notis, as Venus chapell clerkis;
The rosis yong, new spreding of their knoppis,
War powderit brycht with hevinly beriall droppis,
   Throu bemes rede, birnyng as ruby sperkis;
   The skyes rang for schoutyng of the larkis.

NO TREASURE AVAILS WITHOUT GLADNESS

B<small>E MERRY</small>, man, and tak not sair in mind
    The wavering of this wretchit warld of sorrow;
  To God be humble, and to thy friend be kind,
  And with thy neighbour gladly lend and borrow:
  His chance to-nicht, it may be thine to-morrow;
Be blyth in heart for ony aventúre;
  For oft with wise men't has been said aforrow
Without Gladnéss availis no Treasúre.

Mak thee gude cheer of it that God thee sendis,
  For warldis wrak but weilfare nocht availis;
Nae gude is thine, save only that thou spendis,
  Remenant all thou brukis but with bailis:
  Seek to soláce when sadness thee assailis;
In dolour lang thy life may not indure,
  Wherefore of comfort set up all thy sailis;
Without Gladnéss availis no Treasúre.

Follow on pitý, flee trouble and debate,
  With famous folkis hald thy company;
Be charitáble and humble in thine estate,
  For warldly honour lastis but a cry:
  For trouble in erd tak no mélancholý;
Be rich in patience, give thou in guids be puir;
  Who livis merry he livis michtily;
Without Gladnéss availis no Treasúre.

Thou sees thir wretches set with sorrow and care
  To gather guids in all their livis space;
And when their bags are full, their selves are bare,
  And of their riches but the keeping has:
  While others come to spend it that has grace,
Whilk of thy winning no labour had nor cure.
  Tak thou example, and spend with merriness;
Without Gladnéss availis no Treasúre.

Though all the work that e'er had living wicht
  Were only thine, no more thy part does fall
But meat, drink, clais, and of the lave a sicht,
  Yet to the Judge thou sall give compt of all;
  Ane reckoning richt comes of ane ragment small:
But just and joyous, do to none injúre,
  Ane Truth sall mak thee strang as ony wall;
Without Gladnéss availis no Treasúre.

JEAN VICTOR DURUY

(1811–1894)

URUY, whose monumental works upon Grecian and Roman history have been worthily reproduced in England under the editorship of Professor Mahaffy, and in America in sumptuous illustrated editions, was a figure of the first importance both in the educational and in the distinctly literary history of France, throughout nearly half the present century. He became one of the «Immortals» in 1884, succeeding to the chair of Mignet; but his 'History of Ancient Greece,' which was published in 1862, had been already crowned by the Academy. His more extensive 'History of the Grecian People,' published in 1885–1887, won from the Academy the Jean Renaud prize of 10,000 francs.

He was born September 11th, 1811, of a family employed in the Gobelins tapestry works in Paris. His predilection for study secured him an opportunity to enter the College of Sainte-Barbe, whence he passed to the Normal School.

When he was twenty-two he began teaching history, first at Rheims, and then in the College of Henry IV. in Paris. Here he began his literary work, mostly upon

JEAN VICTOR DURUY

school-books, of which he wrote many, mainly historical and geographical. He received the degree of Doctor of Letters in 1853, and became successively Inspector of the Academy of Paris, Master of Conferences at the Normal School, Professor of History at the Polytechnic School, and Inspector-General of Secondary Instruction. During the whole of this period he had been engaged with secondary classes, and had become strongly impressed by the faulty condition of the primary and secondary schools. In 1863 Louis Napoleon put him at the head of the educational system of the empire as Minister of Public Instruction. This appointment gave him the opportunity to carry out numerous and important secularizing reforms which brought him into sharp collision with the clerical party. He held his post as minister for six years — six years of struggle with the parsimonious disposition of the administration upon the one hand, and with the hostile clericals upon the other.

The measures in which he was especially interested were the reorganization of the Museum of Natural History, the extension of scientific study, the introduction of the study of modern and contemporary history in the lyceums (a dreadful experiment, according to his opponents), gratuitous and compulsory primary education, the improvement of the night schools, and popular classes for adults. He was to a large extent successful in all these, except in the direction of compulsory education. The efforts which he made to improve the instruction given to young girls brought upon him the tempest. The bishops, with Monsignor Dupanloup of Orléans at their head, raised a veritable crusade, and Pope Pio Nono himself at length entered the hostile ranks. Probably in part because of this conflict, he was superseded in 1869 and was made a member of the Senate, from which he retired to private life, and the prosecution of his literary labors on the fall of the empire, in the following year. He died in 1894.

As an author his style is clear and direct. Among his numerous works the most important are the two great histories, for which, as for other achievements, honors were heaped upon him. In these he laid particular stress upon the *milieu*—the conditions of place, time, and race. Consequently he has therein written the history of the Greek and Roman peoples, and not merely the history of Greece and Rome,—and has pictured them, so far as possible, as they looked and felt and thought and acted. He exhibits, for example, the growth of the magnificent power of Rome, and its decadence; and shows the all-conquering empire subdued to the manners, the gods, and the institutions of the conquered. And worse:—"They had become enamored of the arts, the letters, and the philosophy of Greece, and dying Greece had avenged itself by transmitting to them the corruption which had dishonored its old age."

The drift of his argument appears in this paragraph, in which he sums up his story of the Eternal City:—"In the earlier portion of its history may be seen the happy effects of a progressively liberal policy; in the later the baneful consequences of absolute power, governing a servile society through a venal administration."

THE NATIONAL POLICY

From the 'History of Rome'

THE Roman power, till then confined to the West, was now to penetrate into another universe,—that of the successors of Alexander. The eternal glory of Rome, the immense benefaction by which she effaces the memory of so many unjust wars, is to have reunited those two worlds that in all former ages were divided in interest, and strangers to each other; is to have mingled and fused the brilliant but corrupt civilization of the East with the barbaric energy of the West. The Mediterranean became a Roman lake,—*mare nostrum*, they said,—and the same life circulated on all its shores, called for the first and the last time to a common existence.

In this work were employed a century and a half of struggles and diplomacy; for Rome, working for a patient aristocracy and not for a man, was not compelled to attain her end at a bound. Instead of rearing suddenly one of those colossal monarchies formed like the statue of gold with feet of clay, she founded slowly an empire which fell only under the weight of years and of the Northern hordes. After Zama she could have attempted the conquest of Africa, but she left Carthage and the Numidians to enfeeble each other. After Cynoscephalæ and Magnesia, Greece and Asia were all ready for the yoke, but she accorded them fifty years more of liberty. This was because, along with the pride of the Roman name and the necessity for dominion, she always retained some of her ancient virtues. The Popiliuses were more numerous than the Verreses. Now she preferred to rule the world; later she will put it to pillage. Thus, wherever Rome saw strength she sent her legions; all power was broken; the ties of States and leagues were shattered; and when her soldiers were recalled they left behind them only weakness and anarchy. But the task of the legions accomplished, that of the Senate began. After force came craft and diplomacy. Those senators, grown old amidst the terrors of the second Punic war, seemed now to have less pleasure in arms than in the game of politics,—the first, in all ages, of Italian arts.

Several other causes dictated this policy of reserve. Against the Gauls, the Samnites, Pyrrhus, and Hannibal,—in other words, for the defense of Latium and of Italy,— Rome had employed all her strength; it was then a question of her existence: whereas, in the wars with Greece and with Asia, her ambition and her pride alone were interested; and wisdom demanded that some relaxation be given to the plebeians and the allies. The Senate had moreover too many affairs on its hands—the wars with Spain, with Corsica, with Cisalpina, and with Istria—to admit of its becoming deeply involved in the East. Therefore two legions only will fight Philip and Antiochus—that will suffice to conquer, but would be too little to despoil them. Furthermore, the Senate believed that in penetrating into this Greek world, where an old glory concealed so much weakness, they could not accord too much to prudence. These pitiless enemies of the Volscians and the Samnites will not proceed in their next wars by exterminating their adversaries and wasting their country. "It was not with such a purpose," said they, "that they came to pour out their blood; they took in hand the cause of oppressed Greece." And that language and that policy they will not change after victory. The first act of Flamininus, on the day after Cynoscephalæ, was to proclaim the liberty of the Greeks. All who bore that respected name seemed to have the right to Roman protection; and the little Greek cities of Caria, and of the coasts of Asia and Thrace, received with astonishment their liberty from a people that they hardly knew. All were captivated by this apparent generosity. None perceived that in restoring independence to the cities and States, Rome wished to break up the confederations that sought to reorganize and would perhaps have given new force to Greece. In isolating them and attaching them to herself by grateful ties, she placed them almost insensibly under her influence. She made allies of them; and every one knows what the allies of Rome became. Thus the Senate was so well satisfied with this policy, which created division everywhere and awakened extinct rivalries, that for half a century it followed no other.

RESULTS OF THE ROMAN DOMINION

From the ‹ History of Rome ›

ALTHOUGH in literature Rome was but the echo of Greece, she civilized all the Western world, for which the Greeks had done nothing. Her language, out of which sprang the various languages of the Romance nations, is in case of need a means of communication among scholars of all countries, and her books will always remain — a wise selection being made — the best for the higher culture of the mind. They have merited above all others the title of *litteræ humaniores*, the literature by which men are made. A cardinal, reading the ‹ Thoughts of Marcus Aurelius › (written in Greek, it is true, but written by a Roman), exclaimed, "My soul blushes redder than my scarlet at sight of the virtues of this Gentile."

Suppose Rome destroyed by Pyrrhus or Hannibal, before Marius and Cæsar had driven the German tribes back from Gaul: their invasion would have been effected five centuries sooner; and since they would have found opposed to them only other barbarians, what a long night would have settled down upon the world!

It is true that when the Roman people had laid hands upon the treasures of Alexander's successors, the scandal of their orgies exceeded for a century anything that the East had ever seen; that their amusements were sanguinary games or licentious plays; that the Roman mind, after receiving a temporary benefit from Greek philosophy, went astray in Oriental mysticism; and that finally, after having loved liberty, Rome accepted despotism, as if willing to astonish the world as much by her great corruption as she did by the greatness of her empire.

But can we say that no other age or nation has known servility of soul, licentiousness in public amusements, and the conspicuous depravity in morals that is always to be seen where indolence and wealth are united?

To the legacies left by Rome which have now been enumerated, we must add another, which ranks among the most precious. Notwithstanding the poetic piety of Virgil, and Livy's official credulity, the dominant note of Latin literature is the indifference of Horace, when it is not the daring skepticism of

Lucretius. To Cicero, Seneca, Tacitus, and the great jurisconsults, the prime necessity was the free possession of themselves, that independence of philosophic thought which they owed to Greece. This spirit, begotten of pure reason, was almost stifled during the Middle Ages. It reappeared when antiquity was recovered. From that day the renascent world set forward again; and in the new path France, heir of Athens and of Rome, was long her guide — for art in its most charming form, and for thought, developed in the light.

Upon a medal of Constantine his son presents to him a globe surmounted by a phœnix, symbol of immortality. For once the courtiers were not in the wrong. The sacred bird which springs from her own ashes is a fitting emblem of this old Rome, dead fifteen centuries ago, yet alive to-day through her genius: *Siamo Romani.*

TORU DUTT

(1856–1877)

N 1874 there appeared in the Bengal Magazine an essay upon Leconte de Lisle, which showed not only an unusual knowledge of French literature, but also decided literary qualities. The essayist was Toru Dutt, a Hindu girl of eighteen, daughter of Govin Chunder Dutt, for many years a justice of the peace at Calcutta. The family belonged to the high-caste cultivated Hindus, and Toru's education was conducted on broad lines. Her work frequently discloses charming pictures of the home life that filled the old garden house at Calcutta. Here it is easy to see the studious child poring over French, German, and English lexicons, reading every book she could lay hold of, hearing from her mother's lips those old legends of her race which had been woven into the poetry of native bards long before the civilization of modern Europe existed. In her thirteenth year Toru and her younger sister were sent to study for a few months in France, and thence to attend lectures at Cambridge and to travel in England. A memory of this visit appears in Toru's little poem, 'Near Hastings,' which shows the impressionable nature of the Indian girl, so sensitive to the romance of an alien race, and so appreciative of her friendly welcome to English soil.

After four years' travel in Europe the Dutts returned to India to resume their student life, and Toru began to learn Sanskrit. She showed great aptitude for the French language and a strong liking for the French character, and she made a special study of French romantic poetry. Her essays on Leconte de Lisle and Joséphin Soulary, and a series of English translations of poetry, were the fruit of her labor. The translations, including specimens from Béranger, Théophile Gautier, François Coppée, Sully-Prud'homme, and other popular writers, were collected in 1876 under the title 'A Sheaf Gleaned in French Fields.' A few copies found their way into Europe, and both French and English reviewers recognized the value of the harvest of this clear-sighted gleaner. One critic called these poems, in which Toru so faithfully reproduced the spirit of one alien tongue in the forms of another, transmutations rather than translations.

But marvelous as is the mastery shown over the subtleties of thought and the difficulties of translation, the achievement remains that of acquirement rather than of inspiration. But Toru's English renditions of the native Indian legends, called 'Ancient Ballads of

Hindustan,' give a sense of great original power. Selected from much completed work left unpublished at her too early death, these poems are revelations of the Eastern religious thought, which loves to clothe itself in such forms of mystical beauty as haunt the memory and charm the fancy. But in these translations it is touched by the spirit of the new faith which Toru had adopted. The poems remain, however, essentially Indian. The glimpses of lovely landscape, the shining temples, the greening gloom of the jungle, the pink flush of the dreamy atmosphere, are all of the East, as is the philosophic calm that breathes through the verses. The most beautiful of the ballads is perhaps that of 'Savitri,' the king's daughter who by love wins back her husband after he has passed the gates of death. Another, 'Sindher,' re-tells the old story of that king whose great power is unavailing to avert the penalty which follows the breaking of the Vedic law, even though it was broken in ignorance. Still another, 'Prehlad,' reveals that insight into things spiritual which characterizes the true seer or "called of God." Two charming legends, 'Jogadhya Uma,' and 'Buttoo,' full of the pastoral simplicity of the early Aryan life, and a few miscellaneous poems, complete this volume upon which Toru's fame will rest.

A posthumous novel written in French makes up the sum of her contribution to letters. 'Le Journal de Mlle. D'Arvers' was found completed among her posthumous papers. It is a romance of modern French life, whose motive is the love of two brothers for the same girl. The tragic element dominates the story, and the author has managed the details with extraordinary ease without sacrificing either dignity or dramatic effect. The story was edited by Mademoiselle Bader, a correspondent of Toru, and her sole acquaintance among European authors. In 1878, the year after the poet's death, appeared a second edition of 'A Sheaf Gleaned in French Fields' containing forty-three additional poems, with a brief biographical sketch written by her father. The many translators of the 'Sakoontala' and of other Indian dramas show how difficult it is for the Western mind to express the indefinable spirituality of temper that fills ancient Hindu poetry. This remarkable quality Toru wove unconsciously into her English verse, making it seem not exotic but complementary, an echo of that far-off age when the genius of the two races was one.

JOGADHYA UMA

"SHELL BRACELETS, ho! Shell bracelets, ho!
    Fair maids and matrons, come and buy!"
  Along the road, in morning's glow,
    The peddler raised his wonted cry.
The road ran straight, a red, red line,
    To Khigoram, for cream renowned,
Through pasture meadows where the kine,
    In knee-deep grass, stood magic bound
And half awake, involved in mist
    That floated in dun coils profound,
Till by the sudden sunbeams kist,
    Rich rainbow hues broke all around.

"Shell bracelets, ho! Shell bracelets, ho!"
    The roadside trees still dripped with dew
And hung their blossoms like a show.
    Who heard the cry? 'Twas but a few;
A ragged herd-boy, here and there,
    With his long stick and naked feet;
A plowman wending to his care,
    The field from which he hopes the wheat;
An early traveler, hurrying fast
    To the next town; an urchin slow
Bound for the school; these heard and passed,
    Unheeding all,—"Shell bracelets, ho!"

Pellucid spread a lake-like tank
    Beside the road now lonelier still;
High on three sides arose the bank
    Which fruit-trees shadowed at their will;
Upon the fourth side was the ghat,
    With its broad stairs of marble white,
And at the entrance arch there sat,
    Full face against the morning light,
A fair young woman with large eyes,
    And dark hair falling to her zone;
She heard the peddler's cry arise,
    And eager seemed his ware to own.

"Shell bracelets, ho! See, maiden, see!
    The rich enamel, sunbeam-kist!

Happy, oh happy, shalt thou be,
    Let them but clasp that slender wrist;
These bracelets are a mighty charm;
    They keep a lover ever true,
And widowhood avert, and harm.
    Buy them, and thou shalt never rue.
Just try them on!"—She stretched her hand.
    "Oh, what a nice and lovely fit!
No fairer hand in all the land,
    And lo! the bracelet matches it."

Dazzled, the peddler on her gazed,
    Till came the shadow of a fear,
While she the bracelet-arm upraised
    Against the sun to view more clear.
Oh, she was lovely! but her look
    Had something of a high command
That filled with awe. Aside she shook
    Intruding curls, by breezes fanned,
And blown across her brows and face,
    And asked the price; which when she heard
She nodded, and with quiet grace
    For payment to her home referred.

"And where, O maiden, is thy house?
    But no,—that wrist-ring has a tongue;
No maiden art thou, but a spouse,
    Happy, and rich, and fair, and young."
"Far otherwise; my lord is poor,
    And him at home thou shalt not find;
Ask for my father; at the door
    Knock loudly; he is deaf, but kind.
Seest thou that lofty gilded spire,
    Above these tufts of foliage green?
That is our place; its point of fire
    Will guide thee o'er the tract between."

"That is the temple spire."—"Yes, there
    We live; my father is the priest;
The manse is near, a building fair,
    But lowly to the temple's east.
When thou hast knocked, and seen him, say,
    His daughter, at Dhamaser Ghat,
Shell bracelets bought from thee to-day,
    And he must pay so much for that.

Be sure, he will not let thee pass
    Without the value, and a meal.
If he demur, or cry alas!
    No money hath he,—then reveal;

"Within the small box, marked with streaks
    Of bright vermilion, by the shrine,
The key whereof has lain for weeks
    Untouched, he'll find some coin,—'tis mine.
That will enable him to pay
    The bracelet's price.   Now fare thee well!"
She spoke; the peddler went away,
    Charmed with her voice as by some spell;
While she, left lonely there, prepared
    To plunge into the water pure,
And like a rose, her beauty bared,
    From all observance quite secure.

Not weak she seemed, nor delicate;
    Strong was each limb of flexile grace,
And full the bust; the mien elate,
    Like hers, the goddess of the chase
On Latmos hill,—and oh the face
    Framed in its cloud of floating hair!
No painter's hand might hope to trace
    The beauty and the glory there!
Well might the peddler look with awe,
    For though her eyes were soft, a ray
Lit them at times, which kings who saw
    Would never dare to disobey.

Onward through groves the peddler sped,
    Till full in front, the sunlit spire
Arose before him.   Paths which led
    To gardens trim, in gay attire,
Lay all around.   And lo! the manse,
    Humble but neat, with open door!
He paused, and blessed the lucky chance
    That brought his bark to such a shore.
Huge straw-ricks, log huts full of grain,
    Sleek cattle, flowers, a tinkling bell,
Spoke in a language sweet and plain,
    "Here smiling Peace and Plenty dwell."

Unconsciously he raised his cry,
    "Shell-bracelets, ho!"   And at his voice

Looked out the priest, with eager eye,
　　And made his heart at once rejoice.
"Ho, *Sankha* peddler! Pass not by,
　　But step thou in, and share the food
Just offered on our altar high,
　　If thou art in a hungry mood.
Welcome are all to this repast!
　　The rich and poor, the high and low!
Come, wash thy feet, and break thy fast;
，　Then on thy journey strengthened go."

"Oh, thanks, good priest! Observance due
　　And greetings! May thy name be blest!
I came on business, but I knew,
　　Here might be had both food and rest
Without a charge; for all the poor
　　Ten miles around thy sacred shrine
Know that thou keepest open door,
　　And praise that generous hand of thine.
But let my errand first be told:
　　For bracelets sold to thine this day,
So much thou owest me in gold;
　　Hast thou the ready cash to pay?

"The bracelets were enameled,— so
　　The price is high."—"How! Sold to mine?
Who bought them, I should like to know?"
　　"Thy daughter, with the large black eyne,
Now bathing at the marble ghat."
　　Loud laughed the priest at this reply,
"I shall not put up, friend, with that;
　　No daughter in the world have I;
An only son is all my stay;
　　Some minx has played a trick, no doubt:
But cheer up, let thy heart be gay,
　　Be sure that I shall find her out."

"Nay, nay, good father! such a face
　　Could not deceive, I must aver;
At all events, she knows thy place,
　　'And if my father should demur
To pay thee,'—thus she said,—'or cry
　　He has no money, tell him straight
The box vermilion-streaked to try,
　　That's near the shrine.'"—"Well, wait, friend, wait!"

The priest said, thoughtful; and he ran
    And with the open box came back:—
"Here is the price exact, my man,—
    No surplus over, and no lack.

"How strange! how strange! Oh, blest art thou
    To have beheld her, touched her hand,
Before whom Vishnu's self must bow,
    And Brahma and his heavenly band!
Here have I worshiped her for years,
    And never seen the vision bright;
Vigils and fasts and secret tears
    Have almost quenched my outward sight;
And yet that dazzling form and face
    I have not seen, and thou, dear friend,
To thee, unsought-for, comes the grace:
    What may its purport be, and end?

"How strange! How strange! Oh, happy thou!
    And couldst thou ask no other boon
Than thy poor bracelet's price? That brow
    Resplendent as the autumn moon
Must have bewildered thee, I trow,
    And made thee lose thy senses all."
A dim light on the peddler now
    Began to dawn; and he let fall
His bracelet-basket in his haste,
    And backward ran, the way he came:
What meant the vision fair and chaste;
    Whose eyes were they,—those eyes of flame?

Swift ran the peddler as a hind;
    The old priest followed on his trace;
They reached the ghat, but could not find
    The lady of the noble face.
The birds were silent in the wood;
    The lotus flowers exhaled a smell,
Faint, over all the solitude;
    A heron as a sentinel
Stood by the bank. They called,—in vain;
    No answer came from hill or fell;
The landscape lay in slumber's chain;
    E'en Echo slept within her shell.

Broad sunshine, yet a hush profound!
    They turned with saddened hearts to go;

Then from afar there came a sound
    Of silver bells;—the priest said low,
"O Mother, Mother, deign to hear.
    The worship-hour has rung; we wait
In meek humility and fear.
    Must we return home desolate?
Oh come, as late thou cam'st unsought,
    Or was it but some idle dream?
Give us some sign, if it was not;
    A word, a breath, or passing gleam."

Sudden from out the water sprung
    A rounded arm, on which they saw
As high the lotus buds among
    It rose, the bracelet white, with awe.
Then a wide ripple tost and swung
    The blossoms on that liquid plain,
And lo! the arm so fair and young
    Sank in the waters down again.
They bowed before the mystic Power,
    And as they home returned in thought,
Each took from thence a lotus flower
    In memory of the day and spot.

Years, centuries, have passed away,
    And still before the temple shrine
Descendants of the peddler pay
    Shell-bracelets of the old design
As annual tribute. Much they own
    In lands and gold,—but they confess
From that eventful day alone
    Dawned on their industry, success.
Absurd may be the tale I tell,
    Ill-suited to the marching times;
I loved the lips from which it fell,
    So let it stand among my rhymes.

OUR CASUARINA-TREE

LIKE a huge python, winding round and round
    The rugged trunk, indented deep with scars
    Up to its very summit near the stars,
A creeper climbs, in whose embraces bound
    No other tree could live. But gallantly

The giant wears the scarf, and flowers are hung
In crimson clusters all the boughs among,
    Whereon all day are gathered bird and bee;
And oft at night the garden overflows
With one sweet song that seems to have no close,
Sung darkling from our tree, while men repose.

Unknown, yet well known to the eye of faith!
    Ah, I have heard that wail far, far away
    In distant lands, by many a sheltered bay,
When slumbered in his cave the water wraith,
    And the waves gently kissed the classic shore
Of France or Italy, beneath the moon,
When earth lay trancèd in a dreamless swoon;
    And every time the music rose, before
Mine inner vision rose a form sublime,
Thy form, O tree! as in my happy prime
I saw thee in my own loved native clime.

But not because of its magnificence
    Dear is the Casuarina to my soul:
    Beneath it we have played: though years may roll,
O sweet companions, loved with love intense,
    For your sakes shall the tree be ever dear!
Blent with your images, it shall arise
In memory, till the hot tears blind mine eyes.
    What is that dirge-like murmur that I hear
Like the sea breaking on a shingle beach?
It is the tree's lament, an eerie speech,
That haply to the Unknown Land may reach.

When first my casement is wide open thrown
    At dawn, my eyes delighted on it rest;
    Sometimes,—and most in winter,—on its crest
A gray baboon sits statue-like alone,
    Watching the sunrise; while on lower boughs
His puny offspring leap about and play;
And far and near kokilas hail the day;
    And to their pastures wend our sleepy cows;
And in the shadow, on the broad tank cast
By that hoar tree, so beautiful and vast,
The water-lilies spring, like snow enmassed.

JOHN S. DWIGHT

(1813–1893)

OHN SULLIVAN DWIGHT was born in Boston, Massachusetts, May 13th, 1813. After graduation at Harvard in 1832, he studied at the Divinity School, and for two years was pastor of a Unitarian church in Northampton, Massachusetts. He then became interested in founding the famous Brook Farm community, which furnished Hawthorne with the background for 'The Blithedale Romance'; and he is mentioned in the preface to this book with Ripley, Dana, Channing, Parker, etc. This was a "community" scheme, undertaken by joint ownership in a farm in West Roxbury near Boston; associated with the names of Hawthorne, Emerson, George William Curtis, and C. A. Dana,—a scheme which Emerson called "a perpetual picnic, a French Revolution in small, an age of reason in a patty-pan." This community existed seven years, and to quote again from Emerson,—"In Brook Farm was this peculiarity, that there was no head. In every family is the father; in every factory a foreman; in a shop a master; in a boat the skipper: but in this Farm no authority; each was master or mistress of their actions; happy, hapless anarchists."

Here Mr. Dwight edited The Harbinger, a periodical published by that community; taught languages and music, besides doing his share of the manual labor. In 1848 he returned to Boston and engaged in literature and musical criticism; and in 1852 he established Dwight's Journal of Music, which he edited for thirty years. Many of his best essays appeared in the Atlantic Monthly, and he contributed to various periodicals.

He was one of the pioneers of scholarly, intelligent, original, and literary musical criticism in America, and he possessed fine general attainments and a distinct style. It is because of his clear perception of the indispensableness of the arts—and especially of the art of music—to life, and because of his clear statement of their vital relationship, that his work belongs to literature.

MUSIC AS A MEANS OF CULTURE

From the Atlantic Monthly, 1870, by permission of Houghton, Mifflin
and Company

WE AS a democratic people, a great mixed people of all races, overrunning a vast continent, need music even more than others. We need some ever-present, ever-welcome influence that shall insensibly tone down our self-asserting and aggressive manners, round off the sharp, offensive angularity of character, subdue and harmonize the free and ceaseless conflict of opinions, warm out the genial individual humanity of each and every unit of society, lest he become a mere member of a party, or a sharer of business or fashion. This rampant liberty will rush to its own ruin, unless there shall be found some gentler, harmonizing, humanizing culture, such as may pervade whole masses with a fine enthusiasm, a sweet sense of reverence for something far above us, beautiful and pure; awakening some ideality in every soul, and often lifting us out of the hard hopeless prose of daily life. We need this beautiful corrective of our crudities. Our radicalism will pull itself up by the roots, if it do not cultivate the instinct of reverence. The first impulse of freedom is centrifugal,— to fly off the handle,— unless it be restrained by a no less free impassioned love of order. We need to be so enamored of the divine idea of unity, that that alone — the enriching of that — shall be the real motive for assertion of our individuality. What shall so temper and tone down our "fierce democracy"? It must be something better, lovelier, more congenial to human nature than mere stern prohibition, cold Puritanic "Thou shalt *not!*" What can so quickly magnetize a people into this harmonic mood as music? Have we not seen it, felt it?

The hard-working, jaded millions need expansion, need the rejuvenating, the ennobling experience of joy. Their toil, their church, their creed perhaps, their party livery, and very vote, are narrowing; they need to taste, to breathe a larger, freer life. Has it not come to thousands, while they have listened to or joined their voices in some thrilling chorus that made the heavens seem to open and come down? The governments of the Old World do much to make the people cheerful and contented; here it is all *laissez-faire*, each for himself, in an ever keener strife of competition. We must look very much to music to do this good work for us; we are open to that appeal; we can forget ourselves in that; we blend in joyous fellowship when we can sing together; perhaps quite as much so when we can listen to-gether to a noble orchestra of instruments interpreting the high-est inspirations of a master. The higher and purer the character and kind of music, the more of real genius there is in it, the deeper will this influence be.

Judge of what can be done, by what already, within our own experience, has been done and daily is done. Think what the children in our schools are getting, through the little that they learn of vocal music,—elasticity of spirit, joy in harmonious co-operation, in the blending of each happy life in others; a rhythmical instinct of order and of measure in all movement; a quickening of ear and sense, whereby they will grow up suscep-tible to music, as well as with some use of their own voices, so that they may take part in it; for from these spacious nurseries (loveliest flower gardens, apple orchards in full bloom, say, on their annual *fête* days) shall our future choirs and oratorio cho-ruses be replenished with good sound material. . . .

We esteem ourselves the freest people on this planet; yet per-haps we have as little real freedom as any other, for we are the slaves of our own feverish enterprise, and of a barren theory of discipline, which would fain make us virtuous to a fault through abstinence from very life. We are afraid to give ourselves up to the free and happy instincts of our nature. All that is not pursuit of advancement in some good, conventional, approved way of business, or politics, or fashion, or intellectual reputation, or professed religion, we count waste. We lack *geniality;* nor do we as a people understand the meaning of the word. We ought to learn it practically of our Germans. It comes of the same root with the word *genius.* Genius is the spontaneous principle; it is free and happy in its work; it is artist and not drudge; its whole activity is reconciliation of the heartiest pleasure with the purest loyalty to conscience, with the most holy, universal, and disinterested ends. Genius, as Beethoven gloriously illustrates in his Choral Symphony (indeed, in all his symphonies), finds the keynote and solution of the problem of the highest state in " Joy," taking his text from Schiller's Hymn. Now, all may not be geniuses in the sense that we call Shakespeare, Mozart, Raphael, men of genius. But all should be partakers of this spontaneous, free, and happy method of genius; all should live childlike, genial lives, and not wear all the time the consequential livery of their unrelaxing business, nor the badge of party and profession, in every line and feature of their faces. This genial, childlike faculty of social enjoyment, this happy art of life, is just what our countrymen may learn from the social " Liedertafel " and the summer singing-festivals of which the Germans are so fond. There is no element of national character which we so much need; and there is no class of citizens whom we should be more glad to adopt and own than those who set us such examples. So far as it is a matter of culture, it is through art chiefly that the desiderated genial era must be ushered in. The Germans have the sentiment of art, the feeling of the beautiful in art, and consequently in nature, more developed than we have. Above all, music offers itself as the most available, most popular, most influential of the fine arts,— music, which is the art and language of the feelings, the sentiments, the spiritual instincts of the soul; and so becomes a universal language, tending to unite and blend and harmonize all who may come within its sphere.

Such civilizing, educating power has music for society at large. Now, in the finer sense of culture, such as we look for in more private and select "society," as it is called, music in the salon, in the small chamber concert, where congenial spirits are assembled in its name — good music of course — does it not create a finer sphere of social sympathy and courtesy? Does it not better mold the tone and manners from within than any imitative "fashion" from without? What society, upon the whole, is quite so sweet, so satisfactory, so refined, as the best musical society, if only Mozart, Mendelssohn, Franz, Chopin, set the tone! The finer the kind of music heard or made together, the better the society. This bond of union only reaches the few; coarser, meaner, more prosaic natures are not drawn to it. Wealth and fashion may not dictate who shall be of it. Here congenial spirits meet in a way at once free, happy, and instructive, meet with an object which insures "society"; whereas so-called society, as such, is often aimless, vague, modifying and fatiguing, for the want of any subject-matter. Here one gets ideas of beauty which are not mere arbitrary fashions, ugly often to the eye of taste. Here you may escape vulgarity by a way not vulgar in itself, like that of fashion, which makes wealth and family and means of dress its passports. Here you can be as exclusive as you please, by the soul's light, not wronging any one; here learn gentle manners, and the quiet ease and courtesy with which cultivated people move, without in the same process learning insincerity.

Of course the same remarks apply to similar sincere reunions in the name of any other art, or of poetry. But music is the most social of them all, even if each listener find nothing set down to his part (or even hers!) but *tacet*.

We have fancied ourselves entertaining a musical house together, but we must leave it with no time to make report or picture out the scene. Now, could we only enter the chamber, the inner sanctum, the private inner life of a thoroughly musical person, one who is wont to *live* in music! Could we know him in his solitude! (You can only know him in yourself, unless he be a poet and creator in his art, and bequeath himself in that form in his works for any who know how to read.) If the best of all society is musical society, we go further and say: The sweetest of all solitude is when one is alone with music. One gets the best of music, the sincerest part, when he is alone. Our poet-philosopher has told us to secure solitude at any cost; there's nothing which we can so ill afford to do without. It is a great vice of our society, that it provides for and disposes to so little solitude, ignoring the fact that there is more loneliness in company than out of it. Now, to a musical person, in the mood of it, in the sweet hours by himself, comes music as the nearest friend, nearer and dearer than ever before; and he soon finds that he never was in such good company. I doubt if symphony of Beethoven, opera of Mozart, Passion Music of Bach, was ever so enjoyed or felt in grandest public rendering, as one may feel it while he recalls its outline by himself at his piano (even if he be a slow and bungling reader and may get it out by piecemeal). I doubt if such an one can carry home from the performance, in presence of the applauding crowd, nearly so much as he may take to it from such inward, private preparation.

Are you alone? What spirits can you summon up to fill the vacancy, and people it with life and love and beauty! Take down the volume of sonatas, the arrangement of the great Symphony, the recorded reveries of Chopin, the songs of Schubert, Schumann, Franz, or even the chorals, with the harmony of Bach, in which the four parts blend their several individual melodies together in such loving service of the whole, that the plain people's tune becomes a germ unfolding into endless wealth and beauty of meaning; and you have the very essence of all prayer, and praise, and gratitude, as if you were a worshiper in the ideal church. Nothing like music, then, to banish the benumbing ghost of ennui. It lends secret sympathy, relief, expression, to all one's moods, loves, longings, sorrows; comes nearer to the soul or to the secret wound than any friend or healing sunshine from without. It nourishes and feeds the hidden springs of hope and love and faith; renews the old conviction of life's springtime,— that the world is ruled by love, that God is good, that beauty is a divine end of life, and not a snare and an illusion. It floods out of sight the unsightly, muddy grounds of life's petty, anxious, doubting moments, and makes immortality a present fact, lived in and realized. It locks the door against the outer world of discords, contradictions, importunities, beneath the notice of a soul so richly occupied: lets "Fate knock at the door" (as Beethoven said in explanation of his symphony),— Fate and the pursuing Furies,— and even welcomes them, and turns them into gracious goddesses,— Eumenides! Music, in this way, is a marvelous elixir to keep off old age. Youth returns in solitary hours with Beethoven and Mozart. Touching the chords of the 'Moonlight Sonata,' the old man is once more a lover; with the *andante* of the 'Pastoral Symphony' he loiters by the shady brookside, hand in hand with his fresh heart's first angel. You are past the sentimental age, yet you can weep alone in music,— not weep exactly, but find outlet more expressive and more worthy of your manly faith.

A great grief comes, an inconsolable bereavement, a humiliating, paralyzing reverse, a blow of Fate, giving the lie to your best plans and bringing your best powers into discredit with yourself; then you are best prepared and best entitled to receive the secret visitations of these tuneful goddesses and muses.

> "Who never ate his bread in tears,
> He knows you not, ye heavenly powers!"

So sings the German poet. It is the want of inward, deep experience, it is innocence of sorrow and of trial, more than the lack of any special cultivation of musical taste and knowledge, that debars many people — naturally most young people, and all who are what we call shallow natures — from the feeling and enjoyment of many of the truest, deepest, and most heavenly of all the works of music. Take the Passion Music of Bach, for instance; if you can sit down alone at your piano and decipher strains and pieces of it when you *need* such music, you shall find that in its quiet quaintness, its sincerity and tenderness, its abstinence from all striving for effect, it speaks to you and entwines itself about your heart, like the sweetest, deepest verses in the Bible; when "the soul muses till the fire burns."

Such a panacea is this art for loneliness. But sometimes too it may intensify the sense of loneliness, only for more heavenly relief at last. Think of the deep composer, of lonely, sad Beethoven, wreaking his pain upon expression in those impatient chords and modulations, putting his sorrows into sonatas, and wringing triumph always out of all! Look at him as he was then,— morose, they say, and lonely and tormented; look where he is now, as the whole world knows him, feels him, seeks him for its joy and inspiration — and who can doubt of immortality?

Now, in such private solace, in such solitary joys, is there not culture? Can one rise from such communings with the good spirits of the tone-world and go out, without new peace, new faith, new hope, and good-will in his soul? He goes forth in the spirit of reconciliation and of patience, however much he may hate the wrong he sees about him, or however little he accept authorities and creeds that make war on his freedom. The man who has tasted such life, and courted it till he has become acclimated in it, whether he be of this party or that, or none at all; whether he be believer or "heretic," conservative or radical, follower of Christ by name or "Free Religionist,"— belongs to the harmonic and anointed body-guard of peace, fraternity, good-will; his instincts have all caught the rhythm of that holy march; the good genius leads, he has but to follow cheerfully and humbly. For somehow the minutest fibres, the infinitesimal atoms of his being, have got magnetized as it were into a loyal, positive direction towards the pole-star of unity; he has grown attuned to a believing, loving mood, just as the body of a violin, the walls of a music hall, by much music-making become gradually seasoned into smooth vibration.

GEORGE EBERS.

GEORG MORITZ EBERS

(1837–)

EORG EBERS, distinguished as an Egyptian archæologist and as a historical novelist, was born in Berlin in 1837. At ten years of age he was sent to school in Keilhau, where under the direction of Froebel he was taught the delights of nature and the pleasure of study. His university career at Göttingen was interrupted by a long and serious illness. During his convalescence he pursued with avidity his study of Egyptian archæology, and with neither dictionary nor grammar to help him in the mastery of hieroglyphics, he acquired to some degree this ancient language. Later, under the learned Lepsius, he became a thorough and brilliant scholar in the science which is his specialty. It was at this epoch that he wrote 'An Egyptian Princess,' for the purpose of realizing to himself a period which he was studying. Thirteen years later his second work, 'Uarda,' was published. When restored to health, he launched himself with enthusiasm on the life of a university professor. He taught for a time at Jena, and in 1870 removed to Leipsic. He has made several journeys into Egypt, sharing his experiences with the public.

'The Egyptian Princess' is Ebers's most representative romance. It is perhaps the subtle quality of popularity, rather than exceptional merit, which has insured its success. The scene of the story is laid at the time when Egypt drew its last free breath, unconscious that at the very height of its intellectual vigor its national life was to be cut off; the time when Amasis held the throne of the Pharaohs, and Cambyses was king of Persia. 'Uarda' gives a picture of Egypt under one of the Rameses. 'Homo Sum,' a tale of the desert anchorites in the fourth century, is filled with the spirit of the early Christians. In the story of 'Die Schwestern' (The Sisters) Ebers takes the reader to Memphis, the temple of Serapis, and the palace of the Ptolemies. The ethical element enters largely into the novel 'Der Kaiser' (The Emperor), of Christianity in the time of Hadrian.

In the 'Frau Bürgermeisterin' (The Burgomaster's Wife), Ebers leaves behind him the world of antiquity, and deals with the heroic struggle against the Spanish rule made in 1547 by the city of Leyden. 'Gred,' a long and quiet novel, most carefully executed, is a minute picture of middle-class Nürnberg, some centuries ago. 'Ein Wort' (A Word: Only a Word) also stands apart from the historical romances. It is a psychological and ethical story, working out the development of inconspicuous character. Both in 'Serapis' and 'The Bride of the Nile,' the victory of Christianity over heathenism is celebrated. Not less interesting than his fiction is his book of travels called 'Durch Gosen zum Sinai' (Through Goshen to Sinai). In 1889, on account of his health, Ebers resigned his professorship. He now passes his winters in Munich, where his life is that of a scholar and a writer.

THE ARRIVAL AT BABYLON

From 'An Egyptian Princess'

SEVEN weeks later, a long line of chariots and riders of every description wound along the great highway that led from the west to Babylon, the gigantic city which could be seen from a long distance.

Nitetis, the Egyptian princess, sat in a gilt four-wheeled chariot, called a "Harmamaxa." The cushions were covered with gold brocade; the roof was supported by wooden columns; its sides could be closed by means of curtains.

Her companions, the Persian nobles, the dethroned King of Lydia and his son, rode by the side of her chariot. Fifty carriages and six hundred sumpter-horses followed, and a regiment of Persian soldiers on splendid horses preceded the procession.

The road lay along the Euphrates, through luxuriant fields of wheat, barley, and sesame, which yielded two or even three hundredfold. Slender date-palms, with heavy clusters of fruit, stood in the fields, which were intersected in all directions by canals and conduits. Although it was winter, the sun shone warm and clear in the cloudless sky. The mighty river was crowded with barges and boats, which brought the produce of the Armenian highlands to the Mesopotamian plain, and forwarded to Babylon the greater part of the wares which were brought to Thapsacus from Greece.

Engines, pumps, and water-wheels poured refreshing moisture on the fields and plantations along the banks, which were dotted with numerous villages. Everything indicated that the capital of a civilized and well-governed country was close at hand.

The carriage and suite of Nitetis stopped before a long building of brick covered with bitumen, by the side of which grew numerous plane-trees. Crœsus was helped from his horse, approached the carriage of the Egyptian princess, and cried to her: — "We have reached the last station-house. The high tower that stands out against the horizon is the famous tower of Bel, like your Pyramids one of the greatest achievements of mortal hands. Before the sun sets we shall reach the brazen gates of Babylon. Permit me to help you from the carriage, and to send your women to you into the house. To-day you must dress yourself according to the custom of Persian queens, so that you may be pleasant in the eyes of Cambyses. In a few hours you will stand before your husband. How pale you are! See that your women skillfully paint joyous excitement on your cheeks. The first impression is often decisive, and this is the case with your future husband, more than with any one else. If, as I do not doubt, you please him at first sight, you have won his heart forever. If you displease him, he will, in accordance with his rough habits, scarcely deign to look on you again with kindness. Courage, my daughter. Above all things, remember what I have taught you."

Nitetis wiped away a tear, and returned: — "How shall I thank you for all your kindness, Crœsus, my second father, my protector and adviser! Oh, do not ever desert me! When the path of my poor life passes through sorrow and grief, remain my guide and protector, as you have been during this long journey over dangerous mountain passes. Thank you, my father, thank you a thousand times."

With these words, the girl put her beautiful arms round the old man's neck and kissed him like an affectionate daughter.

When she entered the court of the gloomy house, a man came towards her, followed by a train of Asiatic serving-women. The leader, the chief eunuch, one of the most important Persian court officials, was tall and stout. There was a sweet smile on his beardless face; valuable rings hung from his ears; his arms and legs, his neck, his long womanish garments, were covered with gold ornaments, and his stiff artificial curls were surrounded by a purple fillet, and sent forth a pungent odor. Boges, for this was the eunuch's name, bowed respectfully to the Egyptian and said, holding his fleshy hand covered with rings before his mouth: — "Cambyses, the ruler of the world, sends me to meet you, O queen, that I may refresh your heart with the dew of his greetings. He further sends to you through me, his poorest slave, the garments of Persian women, that you may approach the gate of the Achæmenidæ in Median dress, as beseems the wife of the greatest of rulers. These women your servants await your commands. They will transform you from an Egyptian emerald into a Persian diamond." Boges drew back, and with a condescending movement of his hand allowed the host of the inn to present the princess with a most tastefully arranged basket of fruit.

Nitetis thanked both men with friendly words, entered the house, and tearfully put off the robes of her home; the thick plait, the mark of an Egyptian princess, was unfastened, and strange hands clad her in Median fashion.

Meanwhile her companions commanded a meal to be prepared. Nimble servants fetched chairs, tables, and golden utensils from the wagon; the cooks bustled about, and were so ready and eager to help each other that soon, as if by magic, a splendidly laid table where nothing was wanting, down to the very flowers, awaited the hungry travelers.

The same luxury had been displayed during the whole journey, for the sumpter-horses that followed the royal travelers carried every imaginable convenience, from gold-woven water-proof tents down to silver footstools, and the carts that accompanied them bore bakers, cooks, cup-bearers, carvers, men to prepare ointment, wreath-winders, and hair-dressers.

Well-appointed inns were established at regular intervals along the high-road. Here the horses that had fallen on the way were replaced by fresh ones, shady trees offered a pleasant shelter from the heat of the sun, and on the mountains the fires of the inns protected the traveler from cold and snow.

The Persian inns, which resembled our post-houses, were first established by Cyrus the Great, who sought to shorten the enormous distances between the different parts of his realm by means of well-kept roads. He had also organized a regular postal service. At every station the riders with their knapsacks found substitutes on fresh horses ready for instant departure, who, after receiving the letters which were to be forwarded, galloped off post-haste, and when they reached the next inn threw their knapsacks to other riders who stood in readiness. These couriers were called Angares, and were considered the swiftest horsemen in the world.

When the company, who had been joined by Boges the eunuch, rose from table, the door of the inn opened. A longdràwn sigh of admiration was heard, for Nitetis stood before the Persians in the splendid Median court dress, proudly exultant in the consciousness of her beauty, and yet suffused with blushes at her friends' astonishment.

The servants involuntarily prostrated themselves in the Asiatic manner, but the noble Achæmenidæ bowed low and reverently. It was as if the princess had laid aside all shyness with the simple dress of her home, and assumed the pride and dignity of a queen with the silken garments, heavy with gold and jewels, of a Persian princess.

The deep respect which had just been shown her seemed to please her. With a condescending movement of her hand she thanked her admiring friends; then she turned to the chief eunuch and said to him kindly but proudly:—"You have done your duty. I am not dissatisfied with the robes and the slaves you have provided for me. I shall duly praise your care to my husband. Meanwhile, receive this golden chain as a sign of my gratitude."

The powerful overseer of the king's wives kissed her hand and silently accepted the gift. None of his charges had yet treated him with such pride. All the wives whom Cambyses had owned till now were Asiatics, and as they were acquainted with the full power of the chief eunuch, they were accustomed to do all they could to win his favor by means of flattery and submission.

Boges again bowed low to Nitetis; but without paying any further attention to him, she turned to Crœsus and said in a low tone:—"I cannot thank you, my gracious friend, with word or gift for what you have done for me; it will be owing to you alone if my life at this court becomes, if not happy, at least peaceful." Then she continued in a louder voice, audible to her traveling companions:—"Take this ring, which has not left my hand since our departure from Egypt. Its value is small, its significance great. Pythagoras, the noblest of all the Greeks, gave it to my mother when he came to Egypt to listen to the wise teachings of our priests. She gave it to me when I left home. There is a seven engraved on this simple turquoise. This number, which is indivisible, represents the health of body and soul, for nothing is less divisible than health. If but a small portion of the body suffers, the whole body is ill; if one evil thought nestles in our heart, the harmony of the soul is disturbed. Whenever you look at this seven, let it remind you that I wish you perfect enjoyment of bodily health, and the continuance of that benignity which makes you the most virtuous and therefore the most healthy of men. No thanks, my father, for I should remain in your debt though I should restore to Crœsus the wealth of Crœsus. Gyges, take this Lydian lyre of ivory, and when its strings give forth music, remember the giver. To you, Zopyrus, I give this chain, for I have noticed that you are the most faithful friend of your friends, and we Egyptians put bonds and ropes into the fair hands of our goddess of love and friendship, beautiful Hathor, as a symbol of her binding qualities. To you, Darius, the friend of Egyptian lore and the starry firmament, I give for a keepsake this golden ring, on which you will find the Zodiac engraved by a skillful hand. Bartja, my dear brother-in-law, you shall receive the most precious treasure I possess. Take this amulet of blue stone. My sister Tachot put it round my neck when for the last time I pressed a kiss upon her lips before we fell asleep. She told me this talisman would bring sweet happiness in love to him who wore it. She wept as she spoke, Bartja. I do not know what she was thinking of, but I hope I am carrying out her wish when I lay this treasure in your hand. Think that Tachot is giving it to you through me her sister, and think sometimes of the garden of Sais."

She had spoken in Greek till then. Now she turned to the servants, who were waiting at a respectful distance, and said in broken Persian:—"You too must accept my thanks. You shall receive a thousand gold staters. Boges," she added, turning to the eunuch, "I command you to see that the sum is distributed not later than the day after to-morrow! Lead me to my carriage, Crœsus!"

The old man hastened to comply with her request. While he conducted Nitetis to the carriage, she pressed his arm against her breast and whispered, "Are you satisfied with me, my father?"

"I tell you, maiden," returned the old man, "you will be the first at this court after the king's mother, for true regal pride is on your brow, and you possess the art of doing great things with small means. Believe me, a trifling gift, chosen as you can choose, will cause greater pleasure to a nobleman than a heap of gold flung down before him. The Persians are accustomed to bestow and to receive costly gifts. They know how to enrich one another. You will teach them to make each other happy. How beautiful you are! Is that right, or do you desire higher cushions? But what is that! Do you not see clouds of dust rolling hither from the town? That must be Cambyses, who is coming to meet you. Keep yourself upright, girl. Above all, try to bear your husband's glance and return it. Few can bear the fire of his eye. If you succeed in meeting it without fear or embarrassment, you have conquered. Courage, courage, my daughter! May Aphrodite adorn you with her loveliest charms! To horse, my friends! I think the King is coming to meet us."

Nitetis sat very erect in the golden carriage, and pressed her hands on her heart. The cloud of dust came nearer and nearer. Now bright sunbeams were reflected in the weapons of the approaching host, and darted from the cloud of dust like lightning from a stormy sky. Now the cloud divided, and figures could be distinguished; now the approaching procession vanished behind the thick bushes at a turn of the road; and now, not a hundred feet away, the galloping riders were seen distinctly as they approached nearer and nearer.

The whole procession seemed to consist of a gay crowd of horses, men, purple, gold, silver, and jewels. More than two hundred riders, all on snow-white Nisæan steeds, whose bridles and caparisons glittered with gold bells and buckles, feathers, tassels, and embroidery, were followed by a man who was often carried away by the powerful coal-black horse on which he rode, but who generally proved to the unmanageable, foaming animal that he was strong enough to tame its wildness. The rider, whose knees pressed the horse so that the animal trembled and panted, wore a garment with a scarlet and white pattern, which was embroidered with silver eagles and falcons. His trousers were of purple, his boots of yellow leather. He wore a golden belt round his waist, in which was a short dagger-like sword, whose hilt and sheath were incrusted with jewels. The rest of his dress resembled Bartja's. His tiara also was surrounded by the blue-and-white fillet of the Achæmenidæ. Thick jet-black hair streamed from it. A thick beard of the same color covered the whole lower portion of his hale, rigid face. His eyes were even darker than his hair and beard, and glittered with a fire that burned instead of warming. A deep red scar, caused by the sword of a Massagetian warrior, marked the lofty brow, large aquiline nose, and thin lips of the rider. His whole bearing bore the stamp of great power and immoderate pride.

Nitetis could not turn her eyes from his form. She had never seen any one like him. She thought she saw the essence of all manliness in the intensely proud face. It seemed to her as if the whole world, but especially she herself, had been created to serve this man. She feared him, and yet her humble woman's heart longed to cling to this strong man as the vine clings to the elm. She did not know whether the father of all evil, terrible Seth, or the giver of all light, great Ra, was to be imagined in this form.

As light and shade alternate when the heavens are clouded at noon, so did deep red and ashy pallor appear on her face. She forgot the precepts of her fatherly friend; and yet when Cambyses forced his wild snorting steed to stand still by the side of her carriage, she gazed breathlessly into the flashing eyes of the man, for she knew that he was the King, though no one had told her.

The stern face of the ruler of half the world softened more and more, the longer she, urged by a strange impulse, endured his piercing glance. At last he waved his hand in welcome and rode towards her companions, who had dismounted, and who either prostrated themselves in the dust before the King, or stood bowing low, in accordance with Persian custom, hiding their hands in the sleeves of their garments.

Now he himself sprang from his horse. At the same time all his followers swung themselves out of the saddle. The carpet-bearers in his train spread, quick as thought, a heavy purple carpet on the road, so that the King's foot should not touch the dust. A few seconds later, Cambyses greeted his friends and relations with a kiss.

Then he shook Crœsus's hand, and ordered him to mount again and accompany him to Nitetis as interpreter.

The highest dignitaries hastened up and helped the King to mount. He gave the signal, and the whole procession moved on. Crœsus rode beside Cambyses by the golden carriage.

"She is beautiful, and pleasing to my heart," cried the Persian to his Lydian friend. "Now translate to me faithfully what she says in answer to my questions, for I understand only Persian, Babylonian, and Median."

Nitetis had understood his words. Inexpressible joy filled her heart, and before Crœsus could answer the King she said in a low tone, in broken Persian, "How shall I thank the gods, who let me find favor in your eyes? I am not ignorant of the language of my lord, for this noble old man has instructed me in the Persian language during our long journey. Pardon me if I can answer in broken words only. My time for instruction was short, and my understanding is only that of a poor ignorant maiden."

The usually stern King smiled. His vanity was flattered by Nitetis's eagerness to gain his approbation, and this diligence in a woman seemed as strange as it was praiseworthy to the Persian, who was used to see women grow up in ignorance and idleness, thinking of nothing but dress and intrigue.

He therefore answered with evident satisfaction, "I am glad that I can speak to you without an interpreter. Continue to try to learn the beautiful language of my fathers. My companion Crœsus shall remain your teacher in the future."

"Your command fills me with joy," said the old man, "for I could not desire a more grateful or more eager pupil than the daughter of Amasis."

"She confirms the ancient fame of Egyptian wisdom," returned the King; "and I think that she will soon understand and accept with all her soul the teachings of the magi, who will instruct her in our religion."

Nitetis looked down. The dreaded moment was approaching. She was henceforth to serve strange gods in place of the Egyptian deities.

Cambyses did not observe her emotion, and continued: — "My mother Cassandane shall initiate you in your duties as my wife. I will conduct you to her myself to-morrow. I repeat what you accidentally overheard: you please me. Look to it that you keep my favor. We will try to make you like our country; and because I am your friend I advise you to treat Boges, whom I sent to meet you, graciously, for you will have to obey him in many things, as he is the superintendent of the harem."

"He may be the head of the women's house," returned Nitetis. "But it seems to me that no mortal but you has a right to command your wife. Give but a sign and I will obey, but consider that I am a princess, and come from a land where weak woman shares the rights of strong men; that the same pride fills my breast which shines in your eyes, my beloved! I will gladly obey you the great man, my husband and ruler; but it is as impossible for me to sue for the favor of the unmanliest of men, a bought servant, as it is for me to obey his commands."

Cambyses's astonishment and satisfaction increased. He had never heard any woman save his mother speak like this, and the subtle way in which Nitetis unconsciously recognized and exalted his power over her whole existence satisfied his self-complacency. The proud man liked her pride. He nodded approvingly and said, "You are right. I will have a special house prepared for you. I alone will command you. The pleasant house in the hanging gardens shall be prepared for you to-day."

"I thank you a thousand times!" cried Nitetis. "If you but knew how you delight me by your gift! Your brother Bartja told me much of the hanging gardens, and none of the splendors of your great realm pleased us as much as the love of the king who built the green mountain."

"To-morrow you will be able to enter your new dwelling. Tell me how you and the Egyptians liked my envoys?"

"How can you ask! Who could become acquainted with noble Crœsus without loving him? Who could help admiring the excellent qualities of the young heroes, your friends? They have become dear to our house, especially your beautiful brother Bartja, who won all hearts. The Egyptians are averse to strangers, but whenever Bartja appeared among them a murmur of admiration arose from the gaping throng."

At these words the King's face grew dark. He gave his horse a heavy blow, so that it reared, turned its head, galloped in front of his retinue, and in a few minutes reached the walls of Babylon. . . .

The walls seemed perfectly impregnable, for they were two hundred cubits high, and their breadth was so great that two carriages could easily pass each other. Two hundred and fifty high towers surmounted and fortified this huge rampart. A greater number of these citadels would have been necessary if Babylon had not been protected on one side by impenetrable marshes. The enormous city lay on both sides of the Euphrates. It was more than nine miles in circumference, and the walls protected buildings which surpassed even the pyramids and the temples of Thebes and Memphis in size. . . .

Nitetis looked with astonishment at this huge gate; with joyful emotion she gazed at the long wide street, which was festively decked in her honor.

JOSÉ ECHEGARAY

(1832–)

THE period of political disorder and disturbance which followed the revolution of 1868 in Spain was also a period of disorder and decline for the Spanish stage. The drama — throwing off the fetters of French classicism that paralyzed inspiration at the beginning of the century — had revived for a time. But after its rejuvenescence of the glories of the Golden Age of Spanish literature, uniting a new beauty of form with truth to nature in the Classic-Romantic School, it sank into a debasement hitherto unknown.

JOSÉ ECHEGARAY

Meretricious sentiment, dullness, or buffoonery, chiefly of foreign production, occupied the scene before adorned by the imagination, the wisdom, and the wit, of a Zorilla, a Tamayo, a Ventura de la Vega.

It was at this period of dramatic decadence that Echegaray appeared to revive once more the romantic traditions of the Spanish stage, peopling it again with noble and heroic figures, — in whom, however, the chivalric spirit of the Middle Ages is at times strangely joined to the casuistic modern conscience. The explanation of this is perhaps to be found in part in the mental constitution of the dramatist, in whom the analytic and the imaginative faculties are united in marked degree, and who had acquired a distinguished reputation as a civil engineer long before he entered the lists as an aspirant for dramatic honors. Born in Madrid in 1832, his earlier years were passed in Murcia, where he took his degree of bachelor of arts, applying himself afterward with notable success to the study of the exact sciences. Returning to Madrid, after enlarging his knowledge of his profession of civil engineer by practical study in various provinces of Spain, he was appointed a professor in the School of Engineers, where he taught theoretical and applied mathematics, finding time however for the production of important scientific works, and for the study of political economy and general literature. On the breaking out of the revolution of 1868 he joined actively in the movement, taking office under the new government as Director of Public Works, and holding

a ministerial portfolio.   He took office a second time in 1872, and
later filled the post of Minister of Finance, which he resigned on the
proclamation of the Republic.   Retiring from public life, he went to
Paris; and while there wrote, being then a little past forty, his first
dramatic work, 'The Check-Book,' a domestic drama in one act,
which was represented anonymously in Madrid two years later, when
the author for the third time held a ministerial portfolio.

'The Check-Book' was followed in rapid succession by a series of
productions whose titles, 'La Esposa del Vengador' (The Avenger's
Bride), 'La Ultima Noche' (The Last Night), 'En el Puño de la
Espada' (In the Hilt of the Sword), 'Como Empieza y Como Acaba'
(How it Begins and How it Ends), sufficiently indicate their charac-
ter.   They are of unequal merit, but all show dramatic power of
a high order.   But on the representation in 1877 of 'Locura o
Santidad?' (Madman or Saint?), the fame of the statesman and the
scientist was completely and finally eclipsed by that of the dramatist,
in whom the press and public of Madrid unanimously recognized
a new and vital force in the Spanish drama.   In this tragedy the
keynote of Echegaray's philosophy is clearly struck.   Moral perfec-
tion, unfaltering obedience to the right, is the end and aim of man;
and the catastrophe is brought about by the inability of the hero to
make those nearest to him accept this ideal of life.   "Then virtue is
but a lie," he cries, when the conviction of his moral isolation is
forced upon him; "and you, all of you whom I have most loved in
this world, perceiving what I regarded as divinity in you, are only
miserable egoists, incapable of sacrifice, a prey to greed and the
mere playthings of passion!   Then you are all of you but clay; you
resolve yourselves to dust and let the wind of the tempest carry you
off! . . .   Beings shaped without conscience or free-will are simply
atoms that meet to-day and separate to-morrow.   Such is matter —
then let it go!"

But the punishment of sin, in Echegaray's moral code, is visited
upon the innocent equally with the guilty; and the guilty are never
allowed to escape the retributive consequences of their wrong-doing.
The pessimistic coloring of the picture would be at times unendur-
ably oppressive, were it not relieved and lightened by the moral
dignity of the hero.   Echegaray's pessimism is, so to say, altruistic,
never egoistic; and the compensating sense of righteousness vindi-
cated rarely fails to explain, if not to justify, his darkest scenes.

Judged by the canons of art, Echegaray's dramatic productions
will be found to have many imperfections.   But their defects are the
defects of genius, not of mediocrity, and spring generally from an
excess of imagination, not from poverty of invention or faulty insight.
The plot is often overweighted with an accumulation of incidents,

and the means employed to bring about the desired end are often lacking in verisimilitude. Synthetic rather than analytic in his methods, and a master in producing contrasts, Echegaray captivates the imagination by arts which the cooler judgment not seldom condemns. His characters too are not always inhabitants of the real world, and not infrequently act contrary to the laws which govern it. The secondary characters are too often carelessly drawn, sometimes being mere shadowy outlines, while an altogether disproportionate part of the development of the plot is intrusted to them.

On the other hand, in the world of the passions Echegaray treads with secure step. Its labyrinthine windings, its depths and its heights, are all familiar to him. Here every accent uttered is the accent of truth; every act is prompted by unerring instinct. Nothing is false; nothing is trivial; nothing is strained. The elemental forces of nature seem to be at work, and the catastrophe results as inevitably from their action as if decreed by fate.

The genius of Echegaray, which in its irregular grandeur and its ethical tendency has been not inaptly likened by a Spanish critic to that of Victor Hugo, rarely descends from the tragic heights on which it achieved its first and its greatest triumphs; but that its range has been limited by choice, not nature, is abundantly proved in the best of his lighter productions, 'Un Critico Incipiente' (An Embryo Critic). Of his achievement in tragedy the culminating point was reached — after a second series of noteworthy productions, among them 'Lo Que no Puede Decirse' (What Cannot be Told), 'Mar Sin Orillas' (A Shoreless Sea), and 'En el Seno de la Muerte' (In the Bosom of Death) — in 'El Gran Galeoto' (The Great Galeoto), represented in 1881 before an audience which hailed its author as a "prodigy of genius," a second Shakespeare. Other notable works followed, — 'Conflicto entre Dos Deberes' (Conflict between Two Duties), 'Vida Alegre y Muerte Triste' (A Merry Life and a Sad Death), 'Lo Sublime en lo Vulgar' (The Sublime in the Commonplace); but 'El Gran Galeoto' has remained thus far its author's supreme dramatic achievement. In its title is personified the evil speaking which not always with evil intent, sometimes even with the best motives, slays, with a venom surer than that of the adder's tongue, the reputation which it attacks; turning innocence itself by its contaminating power into guilt.

FROM 'MADMAN OR SAINT?'

[Don Lorenzo, a man of wealth and position living in Madrid, has discovered that he is the son, not as he and all the world had supposed, of the lady whose wealth and name he has inherited, but of his nurse Juana, who dies after she has revealed to him the secret of his birth. In consequence he resolves publicly to renounce his name and his possessions, although by doing so he will prevent the marriage of his daughter Inez to Edward, the son of the Duchess of Almonte. The mother will consent to Don Lorenzo's renunciation of his possessions but not of his name, as this would throw a stigma on Inez's origin. He refuses to listen either to the reasoning or to the entreaties of his wife, the duchess, Edward, and Dr. Tomás. Finally they are persuaded that he is mad, and Dr. Tomás calls in a specialist to examine him. The specialist, with two keepers, arrives at the house at the same time with the notary, whom Don Lorenzo has sent for to make before him a formal act of renunciation of his name and possessions.]

Don Lorenzo *enters and stands listening to* Inez

Don Lorenzo [*aside*] — "Die," she said!

Edward — You to die! No, Inez, not that; do not say that.

Inez — And why not? If I do not die of grief — if happiness could ever visit me again — I should die of remorse.

Lorenzo [*aside*] — "Of remorse!" She! "If happiness could ever visit her again!" What new fatality floats in the air and hangs threateningly above my head? Remorse! I have surprised another word in passing! I traverse rooms and halls, and I go from one place to another, urged by intolerable anguish, and I hear words that I do not understand, and I meet glances that I do not understand, and tears greet me here and smiles there, and no one opposes me, and every one avoids me or watches me. [*Aloud.*] What is this? What is this?

Inez [*hurrying to him and throwing herself into his arms*] — Father!

Lorenzo — Inez! How pale you are! Why are your lips drawn as if with pain? Why do you feign smiles that end in sighs! — How lovely in her sorrow! And I am to blame for all!

Inez — No, father.

Lorenzo — How cruel I am! Ah! you think it, although you do not say it.

Edward — Inez is an angel. Rebellious thoughts can find no place in her heart; but who that sees her can fail to think it and to say it?

Lorenzo — No one; you are right.

Edward [*with energy*] — If I am right, then you are wrong.

Lorenzo — I am right also. There is something more pallid than the pallid brow of a lovesick maiden; there is something sadder than the sad tears that fall from her beautiful eyes; something more bitter than the smile that contracts her lips; something more tragic than the death of her beloved.

Edward [*with scornful vehemence*] — And what is that pallor, what are those tears, and what the tragedies you speak of?

Lorenzo — Insensate! [*Seizing him by the arm.*] The pallor of crime, the tears of remorse, the consciousness of our own vileness.

Edward — And it would be vile, and criminal, and a source of remorse, to make Inez happy?

Lorenzo [*despairingly*] — It ought not to be so — but it would! [*Pause.*] And this it is that tortures me. This is the thought that is driving me mad!

Inez — No, father, do not say that! Follow the path you have marked out for yourself, without thought of me. What does it matter whether I live or die?

Lorenzo — Inez!

Inez — But do not vacillate — and above all, let no one see that you vacillate; let your speech be clear and convincing as it is now; let not anger blind you. Be calm, be calm, father; I implore it of you in the name of God.

Lorenzo — What do you mean by those words? I do not understand you.

Inez — Do I rightly know myself what I mean? There — I am going. I do not wish to pain you.

Edward [*to Lorenzo*] — Ah, if you would but listen to your heart; if you would but silence the cavilings of your conscience.

Inez [*to Edward*] — Leave him in peace — come with me; do not anger him, or you will make him hate you.

Lorenzo — Poor girl! She too struggles, but she too will conquer! [*With an outburst of pride.*] She will show that she is indeed my daughter!

[*Inez and Edward go up the stage; passing the study door, Inez sees the keepers and gives a start of horror.*]

Inez — What sinister vision affrights my gaze! — No, father, do not enter there.

IX—320

Edward— Come, come, my Inez!

Inez [*to her father*] — No, no, I entreat you!

Lorenzo [*approaching her*] — Inez!

Inez— Those men there — look!

[*Inez stretches out her hand toward the study; Don Lorenzo stands and follows her gaze. At this moment the keepers, hearing her cry, show themselves between the curtains.*]

Edward [*leading Inez away*] — At last!

.   .   .   .

Lorenzo— Now I am more tranquil! The wound is mortal! I feel it here in my heart! I thank thee, merciful God!

Dr. Tomás *and* Dr. Bermúdez *enter and stop to observe* Don Lorenzo.

Dr. Tomás— There he is — sitting in the arm-chair.

Dr. Bermúdez— Unfortunate man!

Lorenzo [*rising, aside*]— Ah, miserable being! Still cherishing impossible hopes. Impossible? And what if they honestly believe that I— [*Despairingly*] Ah! If they loved me they would not believe it. [*Pause.*] Did I not hear Inez — the child of my heart — speak of remorse? Why should she speak of remorse? [*Aloud, with increasing agitation.*] They are all wretches! They would almost be glad that I should die. But no: I will not die until I have fulfilled my duty as an honorable man; until I have put the climax to my madness.

Dr. Tomás [*laying his hand on Don Lorenzo's shoulder*] — Lorenzo —

Lorenzo [*turning, recognizes him and draws back angrily*] — He!

Dr. Tomás— Let me present to you Dr. Bermúdez, one of my best friends. [*Pause. Don Lorenzo regards both strangely.*]

Dr. Bermúdez [*to Dr. Tomás, in a low voice*]— See the effort he makes to control himself; he is vaguely conscious of his condition — there is not a doubt left on my mind.

Lorenzo— One of your best friends — one of your best friends —

Dr. Bermúdez [*aside to Dr. Tomás*]— The idea is escaping him, and he is striving to retain it.

Lorenzo [*ironically*] — If he is one of your best friends, then your loyalty is a guarantee for his.

Dr. Bermúdez [*aside, to Dr. Tomás*] — At last he has found the word. But notice how unnatural is the tone of his voice. [*Aloud.*] I have come to be a witness, according to what Dr. Tomás tells me, of a very noble action.

Lorenzo — And of an act of base treachery also.

Dr. Tomás — Lorenzo!

Dr. Bermúdez [*aside, to Dr. Tomás*] — Let him go on talking.

Lorenzo — And of an exemplary punishment.

Dr. Bermúdez [*aside to Dr. Tomás*] — A serious case, my friend, a serious case.

Lorenzo [*to Dr. Tomás*] — Call everybody: those of the household and strangers alike. Let them assemble here, and here await my orders, while I go to fulfill my duty yonder. What are you waiting for?

Dr. Bermúdez [*aside, to Dr. Tomás*] — Let him have his way; call them.

[*Dr. Tomás rings a bell; a servant enters, to whom he speaks in a low voice and who then goes out.*]

Lorenzo — It is the final trial; I could almost feel pity for the traitors. Ah! I am sustained by the certainty of my triumph. Be still, my heart. There they are — there they are. I do not wish to see them. To treat me thus who loved them so dearly! — I do not wish, and yet my eyes turn toward them — seeking them — seeking them!

. . . .

Lorenzo — Inez! It cannot be! She! no, no. It cannot be! My child!

[*Hurries towards her with outstretched arms. Inez runs to him.*]

Inez — Father!

[*Dr. Bermúdez hastens to interpose, and separates them forcibly.*]

Dr. Bermúdez — Come, come, Don Lorenzo; you might hurt your daughter seriously.

Lorenzo [*seizing him by the arm and shaking him violently*] — Wretch! Who are you to part me from my child?

Dr. Tomás — Lorenzo!

Edward — Don Lorenzo!

Angela — My God!

[*The women group themselves instinctively together, Inez in her mother's arms, the duchess beside them. Dr. Tomás and Edward hasten to free Bermúdez from Don Lorenzo's grasp.*]

Lorenzo [*aside, controlling himself*]—So! The imbeciles think it is another access of madness! Ha, ha, ha! [*Laughing with suppressed laughter. All watch him.*]

Dr. Bermúdez [*aside to Dr. Tomás*]—It is quite clear.

Angela [*aside*]—Oh, my poor Lorenzo!

Inez [*aside*]—My poor father!

Lorenzo [*aside*]—Now you shall see how my madness will end. Before I leave this house, with what pleasure will I turn that doctor out of it. Courage! The coming struggle inspires me with new strength. What! Is a man to be declared mad because he is resolved to do his duty? Ah, it cannot be! Humanity is neither so blind nor so base as that. Enough! I must be calm. Treachery has begun its work; then let the punishment begin too. [*Aloud.*] The hour has come for me to perform a sacred duty, though a most painful one. It would be useless to ask you to witness formalities which the law requires, but which you would only find irksome. The representative of the law awaits me in yonder room; and in obedience to another and a higher law, I am going now to renounce a fortune which is not mine, and a name which neither I nor my family can conscientiously bear longer. After this is done I will return here, and with my wife, and—and my daughter—and let no one seek to dissuade me from my purpose, for it would be in vain— I will leave this house which has been for me in the past the abode of love and happiness, but which is to-day the abode of treachery and baseness. Gentlemen [*to Dr. Tomás and Dr. Bermúdez*], lead the way; I beg you to do so.

[*All slowly enter the study. On the threshold Lorenzo casts a last look at Inez.*]

Translation made for 'A Library of the World's Best Literature,' by Mary J. Serrano

FROM 'THE GREAT GALEOTO'

[In the scenes which are here cited the poison of slander begins to work. Don Severo, uttering the anonymous gossip of the world, has implanted in the mind of his middle-aged brother Don Julian the first suspicion of the honor of his young wife Teodora and the loyalty of his adopted son Ernest. Teodora, who has been warned by Mercedes, Don Severo's wife, overhears the accusing words of her brother-in-law, who is talking with her husband in an inner apartment; and horror-struck, is about to fly from the room.]

Julian [*inside*] — Let me go!

Mercedes [*inside*] — No, for Heaven's sake!

Julian — It is they. I will go!

Teodora [*to Ernest*] — Go! go!

Severo [*to Ernest*] — You shall give me satisfaction for this!

Ernest — I will not refuse it.

Enter Julian, *pale and disordered; wounded and seemingly in a dying condition, supported by* Mercedes. Don Severo *stations himself at the right,* Teodora *and* Ernest *remain in the background.*

Julian — Together! Where are they going? — Stop them! They shun my presence! Traitors!

[*He makes a movement as if to rush toward them, but his strength fails him and he totters.*]

Severo [*hurrying to his assistance*] — No, no.

Julian — They deceived me — they lied to me! Wretches! [*While he is speaking, Mercedes and Severo lead him to the arm-chair on the right.*] There — look at them — she and Ernest! Why are they together?

Teodora and Ernest [*separating*] — No!

Julian — Why do they not come to me? Teodora!

Teodora [*stretching out her arms, but without advancing*] — My Julian!

Julian — Here, on my heart! [*Teodora runs to Julian and throws herself into his arms. He presses her convulsively to his breast. Pause.*] You see! — You see! [*To his brother.*] I know that she deceives me! I press her in my arms — I might kill her if I would — and she would deserve it — but I look at her — *I look at her* — and I cannot!

Teodora — Julian!

Julian — And he? [*Pointing to Ernest.*]

Ernest — Sir! —

Julian — And I loved him! Be silent and come hither. [*Ernest advances.*] You see she is still mine. [*Presses her closer.*]

Teodora — Yours — yours!

Julian — Do not act a part! Do not lie to me!

Mercedes — For God's sake! [*Trying to calm him.*]

Severo — Julian!

Julian [*to both*] — Peace. Be silent. [*To Teodora.*] I divined your secret. I know that you love him. [*Teodora and Ernest try to protest, but he will not let them.*] Madrid knows it too — all Madrid!

Ernest — No, father.

Teodora — No.

Julian — They would still deny it! When it is patent to all! When I feel it in every fibre of my being, for the fever that consumes me has illuminated my mind with its flame!

Ernest — All these fancied wrongs are the offspring of a fevered imagination, of delirium! Hear me, sir —

Julian — You will lie to me again!

Ernest — She is innocent! [*Pointing to Teodora.*]

Julian — I do not believe you.

Ernest — By my father's memory I swear it!

Julian — You profane his name and his memory by the oath.

Ernest — By my mother's last kiss —

Julian — It is no longer on your brow.

Ernest — By all you hold most sacred, father, I swear it, I swear it!

Julian — Let there be no oaths, no deceitful words, no protests.

Ernest — Well, then, what do you wish?

Teodora — What do you wish?

Julian — Deeds!

Ernest — What does he desire, Teodora? What would he have us do?

Teodora — I do not know. What can we do, what can we do, Ernest?

Julian [*watching them with instinctive distrust*] — Ah, would you deceive me to my very face? You are laying your plans together, wretches! Do I not see it?

Ernest — These are the imaginings of fever.

Julian — Fever, yes! The fire of fever has consumed the bandage with which you both blindfolded me, and at last I see clearly! And now why do you gaze on each other? why, traitors? Why do your eyes shine, Ernest? Speak. Their brightness is not the brightness of tears. Come nearer — nearer still.

[*Draws Ernest to him, bends his head, and so forces him to his knees. Don Julian thus remains between Teodora, who stands at his side, and Ernest, who kneels at his feet. Don Julian passes his hand over Ernest's eyes.*]

Julian — I was right — It is not with tears! They are dry!

Ernest — Pardon! — Pardon!

Julian — You ask my pardon? Then you confess your guilt.

Ernest — No!

Julian — Yes!

Ernest — It is not that!

Julian — Then look into each other's eyes before me.

Severo — Julian!

Mercedes — Sir!

Julian [*to Teodora and Ernest*] — You are afraid, then? You do not love each other like brother and sister, then? If you do, prove it! Let your souls rise to your eyes and in my presence mingle their reflection there, that so I may see, watching them closely, if that brightness is the brightness of light or of fire. You too, Teodora — I will have it so. Come — both; nearer still!

[*Forces Teodora to kneel before him, draws their faces together, and compels them to look at each other.*]

Teodora [*freeing herself by a violent effort*] — Oh no!

Ernest [*also tries to release himself, but Julian holds him in his grasp*] — I cannot!

Julian — You love each other! You love each other! I see it clearly! [*To Ernest.*] Your life!

Ernest — Yes.

Julian — Your blood!

Ernest — All!

Julian [*keeping him on his knees*] — Remain there.

Teodora — Julian! [*Restraining him.*]

Julian — Ah, you defend him, you defend him.

Teodora — Not for his sake.

Severo — In Heaven's name —

Julian [*to Severo*] — Silence! Bad friend! bad son! [*Holding him at his feet.*]

Ernest — Father!

Julian — Disloyal! Treacherous!

Ernest — No, father.

Julian — Thus do I brand you as a traitor on the cheek — now with my hand, soon with my sword! [*With a supreme effort he raises himself and strikes Ernest on the face.*]

Ernest [*rises to his feet with a terrible cry and retreats, covering his face with his hands*] — Ah!

Severo — Justice! [*Stretching out his hand toward Ernest.*]

Teodora — My God! [*Hides her face with her hands and falls into a chair.*]

Mercedes [*to Ernest, exculpating Julian*] — It was delirium!

[*These four exclamations in rapid succession. A moment of stupor; Julian still standing and regarding Ernest, Mercedes and Severo trying to calm him.*]

Julian — It was not delirium, it was chastisement, by Heaven! What! Did you think your treachery would go unpunished, ingrate!

Mercedes — Let us go, let us go!

Severo — Come, Julian.

Julian — Yes, I am going.

[*Walks with difficulty toward his room, supported by Severo and Mercedes, stopping from time to time to look back at Ernest and Teodora.*]

Mercedes — Quick, Severo!

Julian — Look at them, the traitors! It was justice! Was it not justice? So I believe.

Severo — For God's sake, Julian! For my sake!

Julian — You, you alone, of all the world, have loved me truly. [*Embraces him.*]

Severo — Yes, I alone!

Julian [*stops near the door and looks at them again*] — She weeps for him — and does not follow me. She does not even look at me; she does not see that I am dying — yes, dying!

Severo — Julian!

Julian — Wait, wait! [*Pauses on the threshold.*] Dishonor for dishonor! — Farewell, Ernest! [*Exeunt Julian, Severo, and Mercedes.*]

Translation made for 'A Library of the World's Best Literature,' by Mary J. Serrano

THE EDDAS

(ICELANDIC; NINTH TO THIRTEENTH CENTURIES)

BY WILLIAM H. CARPENTER

THE fanciful but still commonly believed meaning of the word "Edda," which even many of the dictionaries explain as "great-grandmother," does not, after all, inaptly describe by suggestion the general character of the work to which it is given. The picture of an ancient dame at the fireside, telling tales and legendary lore of times whose memory has all but disappeared, is a by no means inappropriate personification, even if it has no other foundation. In point of fact, 'Edda' as the title of a literary work has nothing whatsoever to do with a great-grandmother, but means "the art of poetry," "poetics"; and only by an extension of its original use does it belong to all that is now included under it.

There are in reality two 'Eddas,' which are in a certain sense connected in subject-material, but yet in more ways than one are wholly distinct. As originally applied, the name now used collectively unquestionably belonged to the one, variously called, to distinguish it from the other, the 'Younger Edda,' on account of the relative age of its origin; the 'Prose Edda,' since in its greater part it is written in prose; and the 'Snorra Edda,' the Edda of Snorri, from the author of the work in its original form. In contradistinction to this, the other is called the 'Elder Edda,' the 'Poetical Edda,' and from the name of its once assumed author, the 'Sæmundar Edda,' the Edda of Sæmund.

Legitimately and by priority of usage, the name 'Edda' belongs to the first-named work alone. In the form in which it has ultimately come down to us, this is the compilation of many hands at widely different times; but in its most important and fundamental parts it was undoubtedly either written by the Icelander Snorri himself, or under his immediate supervision.

Snorri Sturluson, its author, both from the part he played in national politics in his day and from his literary legacy to the present, is altogether the most remarkable man in the history of Iceland. He was born in 1179, his father, Sturla Thordarson, being one of the most powerful chieftains of the island. As was the custom of the time, he was sent from home to be fostered, remaining away until his foster-father's death, or until he was nineteen years old; his own father in the meantime having died as well. He entered upon active life with but little more than his own ambition to further him; but through his brother's influence he made the following year a brilliant marriage, and thus laid the foundation of his power, which thereafter steadily grew. In 1215 Snorri was elected "Speaker of the Law" for the Commonwealth. At the expiration of his term of service in the summer of 1218 he went to Norway, where he was received with extraordinary hospitality both by King Hakon, who made him his liegeman, and by the King's father-in-law, Earl Skuli. On the authority of some of the sagas, he is said to have promised the latter at this time to use his influence to bring Iceland under the dominion of Norway. Two years later he returned to Iceland, taking back with him as a present from the King a ship and many other valuable gifts. In 1222 he was again made "Speaker of the Law," which post he now held continuously for nine years.

Iceland, as the Commonwealth neared its end, was torn apart by the jealous feuds of the chieftains. A long series of complications had aroused a bitter hostility to Snorri among his own relatives. In 1229, he found it necessary to ride to the Althing at the head of eight hundred men. The matter did not then come to an open rupture, but in 1239 it finally resulted in a regular battle, in which Snorri's faction was worsted. To avoid consequences he immediately after fled to Norway. Unwisely, he here gave his adherence to Earl Skuli, now at odds with the King, and thereby incurred the active displeasure of the latter; who, evidently fearing the use of Snorri's power against him, forbade him by letter to return to Iceland. The command was disregarded, however, and he presently was back again in his native land. In 1240 Skuli was slain, and shortly afterward King Hakon seems to have resolved upon Snorri's death. Using Arni, a son-in-law of the Icelander, as a willing messenger, he sent a letter to Gissur, another son-in-law, between whom and his father-in-law an active feud was on foot, demanding that he send the latter a prisoner to Norway, or if that were impossible, to kill him. Gissur accordingly, with seventy men at his back, came to Snorri's farmstead Reykjaholt on the night of the 22d of September, 1241, when the old chieftain was mercilessly slain in the cellar, where he had taken refuge, by an unknown member of the band.

In spite of his political life, Snorri found opportunity for abundant literary work. The 'Icelandic Annals' say that he "compiled the 'Edda' and many other books of historical learning, and Icelandic sagas." Of these, however, only two have come down to us: his 'Edda' and the sagas of the Norse kings, known since the seventeenth century as the 'Heimskringla,' the best piece of independent prose literature, and in its bearing the most important series of sagas, of all the number that are left to attest the phenomenal literary activity of the Icelanders.

Snorri's 'Edda'—both as he, the foremost poet of his day, originally conceived it, and with its subsequent additions—is a handbook for poets, an *Ars poetica*, as its name itself signifies. That it served its purpose as a recognized authority is discoverable from the references to it in later Icelandic poets, where "rules of Edda," "laws of Edda," "Eddic art," and "Edda" are of frequent occurrence, as indicating an ideal of poetical expression striven for by some and deprecated by others. As Snorri wrote it, the 'Edda' was an admirably arranged work in three parts: the 'Gylfaginning,' a compendium of the old mythology, the knowledge of which in Snorri's day was fast dying out; the 'Skáldskaparmál,' a dictionary of poetical expressions, many of which, contained in ancient poems, were no longer intelligible; and the 'Háttatal,' a poem or rather series of poems, exemplifying in its own construction the use and kinds of metre. As it has come down to us, it has been greatly added to and altered. A long preface filled with the learning of the Middle Ages now introduces the whole; the introductions and conclusions of the parts of the work have been extended; several old poems have been included; a Skáldatal, or list of skalds, has been added, as have also several grammatical and rhetorical tracts,—some of which are of real historical value.

With regard to matter and manner, the parts of Snorri's 'Edda' are as follows:—The 'Gylfaginning' (the Delusion of Gylfi) is a series of tales told in answer to the questions of Gylfi, a legendary Swedish king, who comes in disguise to the gods in Asgard to learn the secret of their power. By way of illustration it quotes, among other poetical citations, verses from several of the lays of the 'Elder Edda.' The 'Skáldskaparmál' (Poetical Diction) is also in great part in the form of questions and answers. It contains under separate heads the periphrases, appellatives, and synonyms used in ancient verse, which are often explained by long tales; and like the preceding part, it also is illustrated by numerous poetical quotations here, particularly from the skalds. The 'Háttatal' (Metres), finally, consists of three poems: the first an encomium on the Norwegian king Hakon, and the others on Earl Skuli. It exemplifies in not fewer than one hundred and two strophes the use of as many kinds of metre, many of them being accompanied by a prose commentary of greater or less length.

That Snorri really wrote the work as here described seems to be undoubted, although there is no trace of it as a whole until after his death. At what period of his career it arose, can however merely be conjectured. We only know with certainty the date of the 'Háttatal'; that may not unlikely have been the nucleus of the whole, which falls undoubtedly between 1221 and 1223, shortly after the return from the first visit to Norway. The oldest manuscript of the 'Snorra Edda,'—now in the University Library at Upsala, Sweden,—which was written before 1300, assigns the work to him by name; and the 'Icelandic Annals,' as has already been stated, under the year of his death corroborate the statement of his authorship of "the Edda" —that is, of course, of this particular 'Edda,' for there can be no thought of the other.

Snorri's poetical work outside of the 'Edda' is represented only by fugitive verses. An encomium that he wrote on the wife of Earl Hakon has been lost. As a poet, Snorri undoubtedly stands upon a lower plane than that which he occupies as a historian. He wrote at a time when poetry was in its decline in Iceland; and neither in the 'Háttatal' nor in his other verse, except in form and phraseology, of which he had a wonderful control, does he rise to the level of a host of earlier skalds. It is his critical knowledge of the old poetry of Norway and Iceland that makes his 'Edda' of such unique value, and particularly as no small part of the material accessible to him has since been irrevocably lost. Snorri's 'Edda,' in its very conception, is a wonderful book to have arisen at the time in which it was written, and in no other part of the Germanic North in the thirteenth century had such a thing been possible. It is not only, however, as a commentary on old Norse poetry that it is remarkable. Its importance as a compendium of the ancient Northern mythology is as great,—one whose loss nothing could supplant. As a whole, it is of incalculable value to the entire Germanic race for the light that it sheds upon its early intellectual life, its ethics, and its religion.

The history of the 'Elder Edda' does not go back of the middle of the seventeenth century. In 1643 the Icelandic bishop Brynjolf Sveinsson sent as a present to Frederick III. of Denmark several old Icelandic vellums, among which was the manuscript, dating, according to the most general assignment, from not earlier than 1350; since called the 'Codex Regius' of the 'Edda.' Not a word is known about its previous history. As to when it came into the hands of the bishop, or where it was discovered, he has given us no clew whatsoever. He had nevertheless not only a name ready for it, but a distinct theory of its authorship, for he wrote on the back of a copy that he had made, "Edda Sæmundi Multiscii" (the Edda of Sæmund the Wise).

Both Bishop Brynjolf's title for the work and his assumption as to the name of its author—for both are apparently his—are open to criticism. The name 'Edda' belongs, as we have seen, to Snorri's book; to which it was given, if not by himself, certainly by one of his immediate followers. It is not difficult, however, to explain its new application. Snorri's 'Edda' cites, as has been mentioned, a number of single strophes of ancient poems, many of which were now found to be contained in Brynjolf's collection in a more or less complete form. This latter was, accordingly, not unnaturally looked upon as the source of the material of Snorri's work; and since its subject-matter too was the old poetry, it was consequently an earlier 'Edda.' Subsequently the title was extended to include a number of poems in the same manner found elsewhere; and 'Edda' has since been irretrievably the title both of the old Norse lays and of the old Norse *Ars poetica*, to which it more appropriately belongs.

The attribution of the work to Sæmund was even less justifiable. Sæmund Sigfusson was an Icelandic priest, who lived from 1056 to 1133. As a young man he studied in Germany, France, and Italy, but came back to Iceland about 1076. Afterward he settled down as priest and chieftain, as was his father before him, on the paternal estate Oddi in the south of Iceland, where he lived until his death. Among his contemporaries and subsequently he was celebrated for his great learning, the memory of which has even come down to the present day in popular legend, where like learned men elsewhere he is made an adept in the black art, and many widely spread tales of supernatural power have clustered locally about his name. Sæmund is the first writer among the Icelanders of whom we have any information; and besides poems, he is reputed to have written some of the best of the sagas and other historical works. It is not unlikely that he did write parts of the history of Iceland and Norway in Latin, but nothing has come down to us that is with certainty to be attributed to him. There is however no ancient reference whatsoever to Sæmund as a poet, and it is but a legend that connects him in any way with the Eddic lays. Internal criticism readily yields the fact that they are not only of widely different date of origin, but are so unlike in manner and in matter that it is idle to suppose a single authorship at all. Nor is it possible that Sæmund, as Bishop Brynjolf may have supposed was the case, even collected the lays contained in this 'Edda.' It is on the contrary to be assumed that the collection, of which Brynjolf's manuscript is but a copy, arose during the latter half of the twelfth century, in the golden age of Icelandic literature; a time when attention was most actively directed to the past, when many of the sagas current hitherto only as oral tradition were given a permanent form, and historical works of all sorts were written and compiled.

The fact of the matter is, that here is a collection of old Norse poems, the memory of whose real time and place of origin has disappeared, and whose authorship is unknown. Earlier commentators supposed them to be of extreme age, and carried them back to the very childhood of the race. Modern criticism has dispelled the illusions of any such antiquity. It has been proved, furthermore, that the oldest of the poems does not go back of the year 850, and that the youngest may have been written as late as 1200. As to their place of origin, although all have come to us from Iceland, by far the greater number of them apparently originated in Norway; several arose in the Norse colonies in Greenland; and although the whole collection was made in Iceland, where alone many of them had been remembered, but two are undoubtedly of distinct Icelandic parentage. With regard to their authorship, results are less direct. Folk-songs they are not in the proper sense of the word, in that in their present shape they are the work of individual poets, who made over in versified form material already existing in oral tradition. Only a small part of the ancient poetry that arose in this way has been preserved. From prose interpolations which supply breaks in the continuity of the lays in the 'Elder Edda' itself, as well as from isolated strophes of old poems, else unknown, quoted in Snorri's 'Edda,' and from the citation and use of such poetical material in sagas and histories,— we know for a certainty that many other lays in the ancient manner once existed that have now been for all time lost.

Brynjolf's manuscript contains, whole or in part, as they are now considered to exist, thirty-two poems. From other sources six poems have since been added, presumably as ancient as the lays of the 'Codex Regius,' so that the 'Elder Edda' is made up of thirty-eight poems, not all of which, however, are even reasonably complete. In form they are in alliterative verse, but three different metres being represented, all the simplest and least artificial of the many kinds used by the Norsemen. In content the lays fall under three heads: they are mythic, in that they contain the myths of the old heathen religion of the Norsemen; ethic, in that they embody their views of life and rules of living; or they are heroic, in that they recount the deeds of legendary heroes of the race.

The mythic poems of the 'Edda,' taken together, give us a tolerably complete picture of the Northern mythology in the Viking Age; although some of them were not written until after the introduction of Christianity, and are therefore open to the imputation of having been to a greater or less extent affected by its teachings. The oldest poems of the collection are mythical in character. In some of them a particular god is the principal figure. Several of them, like the 'Vafthrúdnismál,' the 'Grímnismál,' 'Baldrs Draumar,' and the 'Hárbardsljód,' in this way are particularly devoted to Odin, whose supremacy they show over all other beings, and whose part they

describe in the government of the universe; in others, like the
'Hymiskvida,' the 'Thrymskvida,' and the 'Alvísmál,' Thor occu-
pies the prominent part in his strife with the giants; single ones have
other gods as their principal actors, like Skirnir, the messenger of
Frey, in the 'Skírnismál,' Loki, the god of destruction, in the 'Loka-
senna,' or Heimdall, the guardian of the rainbow bridge which
stretched from heaven to earth, in the 'Rígsthúla.' A few of them
are both mythic and heroic at the same time, like the 'Lay of
Völund,' which tells of the fearful revenge of the mythical smith
upon the Swedish king; or the 'Song of Grotti,' the magical mill,
which ground what was wished, first peace and gold for its owner,
King Frodi of Denmark, but later so much salt on the ship of
Mysing, who had conquered the king and taken it away, that all
together sunk into the sea, which henceforth was salt. By far the
greater of the mythic lays is the long but fragmentary poem 'Vö-
luspá,' the 'Prophecy of the Sibyl,' which is entitled to stand not
only at the head of the Eddic songs but of all old Germanic poetry,
for the beauty and dignity of its style, its admirable choice of
language, and the whole inherent worth of its material. Its purpose
is to give a complete picture, although only in its most essential
features, of the whole heathen religion. It contains in this way the
entire history of the universe: the creation of the world out of chaos;
the origin of the giants, the dwarfs, of gods, and of men; and ends
with their destruction and ultimate renewal. The Sibyl is repre-
sented at the beginning in an assemblage of the whole human race,
whom she bids be silent in order that she may be heard. Many of
the strophes, even in translation, retain much of their inherent dig-
nity and poetic picturesqueness:—

> « There was in times of old
> where Ymir dwelt,
> nor land nor sea,
> nor gelid waves;
> earth existed not,
> nor heaven above;
> there was a chaotic chasm,
> and verdure nowhere.

> « Before Bur's sons
> raised up heaven's vault,
> they who the noble
> mid-earth shaped,
> the sun shone from the south
> on the structure's rocks;
> then was the earth begrown
> with green herbage.

« The sun from the south,
  the moon's companion,
  her right hand cast
  round the heavenly horses:
  the sun knew not
  where she had a dwelling:
  the moon knew not
  what power he possessed;
  the stars knew not
  where they had station.»

The gods thereupon gave the heavenly bodies names, and ordained the times and seasons. This was the golden age of the young world, before guilt and sin had come into it; a time of joy and beneficent activity. A deed of violence proclaimed its approaching end, and out of the slain giants' blood and bones the dwarfs were created. The gods then made the first man and woman, for whom the Norns established laws and allotted life and destiny. The use of gold was introduced, and with it its attendant evils; the Valkyries come, and the first warfare occurs in the world; the gods' stronghold is broken, and Odin hurls his spear among the people. In rapid succession follow the pictures of the awful ills that happen to gods and men, which finally end in Ragnarök, the twilight of the gods, and the conflagration of the universe. This however is not the end. The Sibyl describes the reappearance of the green earth from the ocean. The gods again come back, and a new golden age begins of peace and happiness which shall endure forever.

Scarcely inferior to the 'Völuspá' for the importance of its material is the ethical poem or rather collection of poems called the 'Hávamál,' the 'Speech of the High One,'—that is, of Odin the supreme god. The poem consists of sententious precepts and epigrammatic sayings, which ultimately have been set together to form a connected, though scarcely systematic, philosophy of life. The whole is naturally attributed to Odin, the source of all wisdom, the father and giver of all things. A part of the poem is the oldest of all the Eddic lays, and the whole of it was at hand early in the tenth century. Although many of its maxims show a primitive state of society, as a whole they are the experience of a people more advanced in culture than we are apt to fancy the Norsemen of the Viking Age, who could nevertheless philosophize at home as sturdily as they fought abroad. The morality of the 'Hávamál' is not always our morality, but many of its maxims are eternally true. Its keynote, again and again repeated, is the perishability of all earthly possessions, and the endurance alone of fairly won fame:—

« Cattle die,
    kindred die,
    we ourselves also die;
    but the fair fame
    never dies
    of him who has earned it. »

The heroic poems of the 'Elder Edda' recount as if belonging to a single legendary cycle what originally belonged to two; the one of Northern origin, the other the common property of the whole Germanic race. They are the Helgi poems on the one hand, and the Völsung poems on the other. Together they tell the "Story of the North," and come nearest to forming its greatest epic; it is the same story which Wagner has set to music as immortal in his 'Ring of the Nibelung,' — although the principal source of his material is the prose 'Völsunga Saga' and not the 'Edda,' — and which in a form much later than the Icelandic versions is also told in the German 'Nibelungenlied.'

The Helgi poems are only loosely connected with the story of Sigurd the Völsung, and originally, but without doubt long before they were committed to writing, had no connection with it at all. As they now stand at the head of the heroic lays they are made to tell the deeds of early members of the Völsung race; namely, of Helgi Hjörvard's son, and Helgi Hundingsbane, who is said to have been named after him. The latter the 'Edda' makes the son of Sigmund the Völsung, and consequently an elder brother of Sigurd, the hero of the subsequent cycle of poems. To these last they are joined by a prose piece ending with a description of Sigurd's parentage and birth, and his own personality, which the poems themselves do not give at length.

The remaining poems, fifteen in all, tell the old Germanic story of Sigurd, the Siegfried of the Nibelungenlied, in the most ancient form in which it has come down to us. As contained in the 'Edda' it is a picture of great deeds, painted in powerful strokes which gain in force by the absence of carefully elaborated detail. In various ways it is unfortunate that the lays composing the cycle are not more closely consecutive; a difficulty that was felt by the earliest editors of the manuscript, who endeavored to bring the poems and fragments of poems then extant into some sort of connection, by the interpolation of prose passages of various lengths wherever it was considered necessary to the intelligibility of the story. As it is however there is even yet, and cannot help but be, on account of the differences in age, authorship, and place of origin of the lays, an inherent lack of correlation. Many of the poems overlap, and parts of the action are told several times and in varying form.

The Sigurd poems belong to a time prior to the introduction of Christianity, as is incontestably proved by the genuine heathen spirit that throughout pervades them. Their action is in the early days, when the gods walked upon earth and mixed themselves in human affairs. The real theme of the epic which the lays form is the mythical golden hoard, and with it the fated ring of the Nibelung, owned originally by the dwarf Andvari, from whom it is wrung by the gods in their extremity. Andvari curses it to its possessors, and it is cursed again by the gods, who are forced to deliver it up to Hreidmar as blood-money for his son, whom Loki had slain. Fafnir and Regin, the brothers of the slain Ottur, demand of their father their share of the blood-fine, and when this is refused, Hreidmar is killed while asleep, and Regin is driven away by Fafnir, who then in the guise of a dragon lies upon the golden hoard to guard it. Egged on by Regin, Sigurd slays Fafnir, and Regin also when he learns that he intends treachery.

Sigurd gives the ring of Andvari, taken from the hoard, to the Valkyrie Brynhild, as a pledge of betrothal; and when in the likeness of Gunnar the Nibelung,—having by wiles forgotten his former vows,—he rides to her through the fire, the ring is given back to him by Brynhild, who does not recognize him. The fatal ring is now given by Sigurd to his wife, Gudrun the Nibelung, who in a moment of anger shows it to Brynhild and taunts her with a recital of his history. Brynhild cannot bear to see the happiness of Gudrun, and does not rest until Sigurd is slain; and in slaying him, Guthorm, the youngest of the Nibelungs, is killed, struck down by the sword of the dying Sigurd. Brynhild, who will not outlive Sigurd, perishes on her own sword. Gudrun is subsequently, against her will, wedded to Atli the Hun. Gunnar and Högni, her brothers, the two remaining Nibelungs, are invited to visit Atli, when they are straightway fallen upon, their followers are killed, and they are bound. They are asked to give up the golden hoard, whose hiding-place was known to them alone; but Gunnar first demands the death of his brother Högni, and then triumphantly tells Atli that the treasure is forever hidden in the Rhine,—where, he only knows. He is cast into a serpent pit, and dies. Atli's sons and Gudrun's are slain by their mother, changed by the madness of grief at the slaughter of her brothers into an avenging Fury, and Atli himself and his men are burned in the hall. Carried then by the sea, into which she has hurled herself, Gudrun comes to the land of King Jonakr, who makes her his wife. Swanhild, the daughter of Sigurd and Gudrun, had been married to King Jörmunrek, but coming under unjust suspicion, is trodden to death by horses; and Gudrun dies of a broken heart, with a prayer to Sigurd upon her lips. Last of all, the sons of Gudrun and Jonakr, who, incited by their mother, had been sent out to avenge their sister, are stoned to death; and the curse only ceases to work when there is nothing more left for it to wreak itself upon.

It is a story of great deeds, whose motives are the bitter passions of that early time before the culture of Christianity had softened the hearts of men. The psychological truthfulness of its characters, however, in spite of their distance from to-day, is none the less unmistakable; and we watch the action with bated breath, as they are hurried on by a fate as relentless and inevitable as any that ever pursued an Œdipus. They are not the indistinct and shadowy forms which in many early literatures seem to grope out toward us from the mists of the past, whose clinging heaviness the present is unable wholly to dispel, but are human men and women who live and act; and the principal characters, particularly, in this way become the realities of history, instead of what they actually are, the creations of legend and myth.

Many of the poems of the 'Edda' have been several times translated into English. Notable renderings are those by Dean Herbert, and by William Morris in the translation of the 'Völsunga Saga,' by Magnusson and Morris. The only metrical version of all the lays is that of Benjamin Thorpe (London, 1866). A literal translation of the entire extant old poetry of the North is contained in Vigfusson's monumental work, the 'Corpus Poeticum Boreale.' The 'Snorra Edda' has been translated by G. W. Dasent (Stockholm, 1842); by I. A. Blackwell in 'Northern Antiquities' (London, 1847); and by R. B. Anderson (Chicago, 1880).

Wm H. Carpenter.

FROM THE 'SNORRA EDDA'

THOR'S ADVENTURES ON HIS JOURNEY TO THE LAND OF THE GIANTS

From 'Northern Antiquities': Bohn's Library (London), 1878

ONE day the god Thor set out, in his car drawn by two he-goats, and accompanied by Loki, on a journey. Night coming on, they put up at a peasant's cottage, when Thor killed his goats, and after flaying them put them in the kettle. When the flesh was sodden, he sat down with his fellow-traveler to supper, and invited the peasant and his family to partake of

the repast. The peasant's son was named Thjalfi, and his daugh-
ter Röska. Thor bade them throw all the bones into the goats'
skins, which were spread out near the fireplace; but young
Thjalfi broke one of the shank-bones with his knife, to come at
the marrow. Thor having passed the night in the cottage, rose
at the dawn of day; and when he was dressed took his mallet
Mjölnir, and lifting it up, consecrated the goats' skins, which he
had no sooner done than the two goats reassumed their wonted
form, only that one of them now limped in one of its hind legs.
Thor, perceiving this, said that the peasant or one of his family
had handled the shank-bone of this goat too roughly, for he saw
clearly that it was broken. It may readily be imagined how
frightened the peasant was, when he saw Thor knit his brows,
and grasp the handle of his mallet with such force that the joints
of his fingers became white from the exertion. Fearing to be
struck down by the very looks of the god, the peasant and his
family made joint suit for pardon, offering whatever they pos-
sessed as an atonement for the offense committed. Thor, seeing
their fear, desisted from his wrath and became more placable,
and finally contented himself by requiring the peasant's children,
Thjalfi and Röska, who became his bond-servants, and have fol-
lowed him ever since.

Leaving his goats with the peasant, Thor proceeded eastward
on the road to Jötunheim, until he came to the shores of a vast
and deep sea, which having passed over, he penetrated into a
strange country along with his companions, Loki, Thjalfi, and
Röska. They had not gone far before they saw before them an
immense forest, through which they wandered all day. Thjalfi
was of all men the swiftest of foot. He bore Thor's wallet, but
the forest was a bad place for finding anything eatable to stow
in it. When it became dark, they searched on all sides for a
place where they might pass the night, and at last came to a
very large hall, with an entrance that took up the whole breadth
of one of the ends of the building. Here they chose them a
place to sleep in; but towards midnight were alarmed by an
earthquake, which shook the whole edifice. Thor, rising up,
called on his companions to seek with him a place of safety. On
the right they found an adjoining chamber, into which they en-
tered; but while the others, trembling with fear, crept into the
furthest corner of this retreat, Thor remained at the doorway
with his mallet in his hand, prepared to defend himself whatever

might happen.   A terrible groaning was heard during the night, and at dawn of day Thor went out and observed lying near him a man of enormous bulk, who slept and snored pretty loudly. Thor could now account for the noise they had heard over night, and girding on his Belt of Prowess, increased that divine strength which he now stood in need of.   The giant, awakening, rose up, and it is said that for once in his life Thor was afraid to make use of his mallet, and contented himself by simply asking the giant his name.

"My name is Skrymir," said the other; "but I need not ask thy name, for I know thou art the god Thor.   But what hast thou done with my glove?"   And stretching out his hand Skrymir picked up his glove, which Thor then perceived was what they had taken over night for a hall, the chamber where they had sought refuge being the thumb.   Skrymir then asked whether they would have his fellowship, and Thor consenting, the giant opened his wallet and began to eat his breakfast.   Thor and his companions having also taken their morning repast, though in another place, Skrymir proposed that they should lay their provisions together, which Thor also assented to.   The giant then put all the meat into one wallet, which he slung on his back and went before them, taking tremendous strides, the whole day, and at dusk sought out for them a place where they might pass the night, under a large oak-tree.   Skrymir then told them that he would lie down to sleep.   "But take ye the wallet," he added, "and prepare your supper."

Skrymir soon fell asleep, and began to snore strongly, but incredible though it may appear, it must nevertheless be told that when Thor came to open the wallet he could not untie a single knot, nor render a single string looser than it was before. Seeing that his labor was in vain, Thor became wroth, and grasping his mallet with both hands while he advanced a step forward, launched it at the giant's head.   Skrymir, awakening, merely asked whether a leaf had not fallen on his head, and whether they had supped and were ready to go to sleep.   Thor answered that they were just going to sleep, and so saying, went and laid himself down under another oak-tree.   But sleep came not that night to Thor, and when he remarked that Skrymir snored again so loud that the forest re-echoed with the noise, he arose, and grasping his mallet launched it with such force that it sunk into the giant's skull up to the handle.   Skrymir, awakening, cried out:—

"What's the matter? did an acorn fall on my head? How fares it with thee, Thor?"

But Thor went away hastily, saying that he had just then awoke, and that as it was only midnight, there was still time for sleep. He however resolved that if he had an opportunity of striking a third blow, it should settle all matters between them. A little before daybreak he perceived that Skrymir was again fast asleep, and again grasping his mallet, dashed it with such violence that it forced its way into the giant's cheek up to the handle. But Skrymir sat up, and stroking his cheek, said:—

"Are there any birds perched on this tree? Methought when I awoke some moss from the branches fell on my head. What! art thou awake, Thor? Methinks it is time for us to get up and dress ourselves; but you have not now a long way before you to the city called Utgard. I have heard you whispering to one another that I am not a man of small dimensions; but if you come into Utgard you will see there many men much taller than myself. Wherefore I advise you, when you come there, not to make too much of yourselves, for the followers of Utgard-Loki will not brook the boasting of such mannikins as ye are. The best thing you could do would probably be to turn back again; but if you persist in going on, take the road that leads eastward, for mine now lies northward to those rocks which you may see in the distance."

Hereupon he threw his wallet over his shoulders and turned away from them into the forest, and I could never hear that Thor wished to meet with him a second time.

Thor and his companions proceeded on their way, and towards noon descried a city standing in the middle of a plain. It was so lofty that they were obliged to bend their necks quite back on their shoulders, ere they could see to the top of it. On arriving at the walls they found the gateway closed, with a gate of bars strongly locked and bolted. Thor, after trying in vain to open it, crept with his companions through the bars, and thus succeeded in gaining admission into the city. Seeing a large palace before them, with the door wide open, they went in and found a number of men of prodigious stature sitting on benches in the hall. Going further, they came before the King, Utgard-Loki, whom they saluted with great respect. Their salutations were however returned by a contemptuous look from the King, who after regarding them for some time said with a scornful smile:—

"It is tedious to ask for tidings of a long journey, yet if I do not mistake me, that stripling there must be Aku-Thor. Perhaps," he added, addressing himself to Thor, "thou mayest be taller than thou appearest to be. But what are the feats that thou and thy fellows deem yourselves skilled in? for no one is permitted to remain here who does not in some feat or other excel all men."

"The feat I know," replied Loki, "is to eat quicker than any one else; and in this I am ready to give a proof against any one here who may choose to compete with me."

"That will indeed be a feat," said Utgard-Loki, "if thou performest what thou promisest; and it shall be tried forthwith."

He then ordered one of his men, who was sitting at the further end of the bench, and whose name was Logi, to come forward and try his skill with Loki. A trough filled with flesh-meat having been set on the hall floor, Loki placed himself at one end and Logi at the other, and each of them began to eat as fast as he could, until they met in the middle of the trough. But it was soon found that Loki had only eaten the flesh, whereas his adversary had devoured both flesh and bone, and the trough to boot. All the company therefore adjudged that Loki was vanquished.

Utgard-Loki then asked what feat the young man who accompanied Thor could perform. Thjalfi answered that he would run a race with any one who might be matched against him. The King observed that skill in running was something to boast of, but that if the youth would win the match he must display great agility. He then arose and went with all who were present to a plain where there was good ground for running on, and calling a young man named Hugi, bade him run a match with Thjalfi. In the first course, Hugi so much outstripped his competitor that he turned back and met him, not far from the starting-place.

"Thou must ply thy legs better, Thjalfi," said Utgard-Loki, "if thou wilt win the match; though I must needs say that there never came a man here swifter of foot than thou art."

In the second course, Thjalfi was a full bow-shot from the goal when Hugi arrived at it.

"Most bravely dost thou run, Thjalfi," said Utgard-Loki, "though thou wilt not, methinks, win the match. But the third course must decide."

They accordingly ran a third time, but Hugi had already reached the goal before Thjalfi had got half-way. All who were present then cried out that there had been a sufficient trial of skill in this kind of exercise.

Utgard-Loki then asked Thor in what feats he would choose to give proofs of that dexterity for which he was so famous. Thor replied that he would begin a drinking match with any one. Utgard-Loki consented, and entering the palace, bade his cup-bearer bring the large horn which his followers were obliged to drink out of, when they had trespassed in any way against established usage. The cup-bearer having presented it to Thor, Utgard-Loki said:—

"Whoever is a good drinker will empty that horn at a single draught, though some men make two of it; but the most puny drinker of all can do it at three."

Thor looked at the horn, which seemed of no extraordinary size, though somewhat long; however, as he was very thirsty, he set it to his lips, and without drawing breath, pulled as long and as deeply as he could, that he might not be obliged to make a second draught of it; but when he set the horn down and looked in, he could scarcely perceive that the liquor was diminished.

"'Tis well drunken," exclaimed Utgard-Loki, "though nothing much to boast of; and I would not have believed, had it been told me, that Asa-Thor could not take a greater draught; but thou no doubt meanest to make amends at the second pull."

Thor without answering went at it again with all his might; but when he took the horn from his mouth it seemed to him as if he had drunk rather less than before, although the horn could now be carried without spilling.

"How now! Thor," said Utgard-Loki: "Thou must not spare thyself more, in performing a feat, than befits thy skill; but if thou meanest to drain the horn at the third draught thou must pull deeply; and I must needs say that thou wilt not be called so mighty a man here as thou art among the Æsir, if thou showest no greater powers in other feats than methinks will be shown in this."

Thor, full of wrath, again set the horn to his lips and exerted himself to the utmost to empty it entirely; but on looking in, found that the liquor was only a little lower; upon which he resolved to make no further attempt, but gave back the horn to the cup-bearer.

"I now see plainly," said Utgard-Loki, "that thou art not quite so stout as we thought thee; but wilt thou try any other feat?— though methinks thou art not likely to bear any prize away with thee hence."

"I will try another feat," replied Thor; "and I am sure such draughts as I have been drinking would not have been reckoned small among the Æsir; but what new trial hast thou to propose?"

"We have a very trifling game here," answered Utgard-Loki, "in which we exercise none but children. It consists in merely lifting my cat from the ground; nor should I have dared to mention such a feat to Asa-Thor, if I had not already observed that thou art by no means what we took thee for."

As he finished speaking, a large gray cat sprang on the hall floor. Thor, advancing, put his hand under the cat's belly, and did his utmost to raise him from the floor; but the cat, bending his back, had — notwithstanding all Thor's efforts — only one of his feet lifted up; seeing which, Thor made no further attempt.

"This trial has turned out," said Utgard-Loki, "just as I imagined it would; the cat is large, but Thor is little in comparison with our men."

"Little as ye call me," answered Thor, "let me see who amongst you will come hither, now I am in wrath, and wrestle with me."

"I see no one here," said Utgard-Loki, looking at the men sitting on the benches, "who would not think it beneath him to wrestle with thee: let somebody, however, call hither that old crone, my nurse Elli, and let Thor wrestle with her if he will. She has thrown to the ground many a man not less strong and mighty than this Thor is."

A toothless old woman then entered the hall, and was told by Utgard-Loki to take hold of Thor. The tale is shortly told. The more Thor tightened his hold on the crone the firmer she stood. At length, after a very violent struggle, Thor began to lose his footing, and was finally brought down upon one knee. Utgard-Loki then told them to desist, adding that Thor had now no occasion to ask any one else in the hall to wrestle with him, and it was also getting late. He therefore showed Thor and his companions to their seats, and they passed the night there in good cheer.

The next morning, at break of day, Thor and his companions dressed themselves and prepared for their departure. Utgard-

Loki then came and ordered a table to be set for them, on which there was no lack of either victuals or drink. After the repast Utgard-Loki led them to the gate of the city, and on parting asked Thor how he thought his journey had turned out, and whether he had met with any men stronger than himself. Thor told him that he could not deny but that he had brought great shame on himself. "And what grieves me most," he added, "is that ye call me a man of little worth."

"Nay," said Utgard-Loki, "it behoves me to tell thee the truth, now thou art out of the city; which so long as I live and have my way thou shalt never re-enter. And by my troth, had I known beforehand that thou hadst so much strength in thee, and wouldst have brought me so near to a great mishap, I would not have suffered thee to enter this time. Know, then, that I have all along deceived thee by my illusions: first in the forest, where I arrived before thee, and there thou wert not able to untie the wallet, because I had bound it with iron wire, in such a manner that thou couldst not discover how the knot ought to be loosened. After this, thou gavest me three blows with thy mallet; the first, though the least, would have ended my days had it fallen on me, but I brought a rocky mountain before me which thou didst not perceive, and in this mountain thou wilt find three glens, one of them remarkably deep. These are the dints made by thy mallet. I have made use of similar illusions in the contests ye have had with my followers. In the first, Loki, like hunger itself, devoured all that was set before him; but Logi was in reality nothing else than ardent fire, and therefore consumed not only the meat but the trough which held it. Hugi, with whom Thjalfi contended in running, was Thought; and it was impossible for Thjalfi to keep pace with that. When thou in thy turn didst try to empty the horn, thou didst perform, by my troth, a deed so marvelous that had I not seen it myself I should never have believed it. For one end of that horn reached the sea, which thou wast not aware of, but when thou comest to the shore thou wilt perceive how much the sea has sunk by thy draughts, which have caused what is now called the ebb. Thou didst perform a feat no less wonderful by lifting up the cat; and to tell thee the truth, when we saw that one of his paws was off the floor, we were all of us terror-stricken; for what thou tookest for a cat was in reality the great Midgard serpent that encompasseth the whole earth, and he was then barely long enough to inclose it between his head and tail, so high had thy hand raised him up towards heaven. Thy wrestling with Elli was also a most astonishing feat, for there was never yet a man, nor ever shall be, whom Old Age — for such in fact was Elli — will not sooner or later lay low if he abide her coming. But now, as we are going to part, let me tell thee that it will be better for both of us if thou never come near me again; for shouldst thou do so, I shall again defend myself by other illusions, so that thou wilt never prevail against me."

On hearing these words, Thor in a rage laid hold of his mallet and would have launched it at him; but Utgard-Loki had disappeared, and when Thor would have returned to the city to destroy it, he found nothing around him but a verdant plain. Proceeding therefore on his way, he returned without stopping to Thrúdváng.

Translation of I. A. Blackwell.

THE LAY OF THRYM

From the 'Elder Edda'

WROTH was Vingthor,
    when he awoke,
        and his hammer
missed;
his beard he shook,
his forehead struck,
the son of earth
felt all around him;

And first of all
these words he uttered:—
"Hear now, Loki!
what I now say,
which no one knows
anywhere on earth,
nor in heaven above:
the As's hammer is stolen!"

They went to the fair
Freyja's dwelling,
and he these words
first of all said:—

"Wilt thou me, Freyja,
thy feather-garment lend,
that perchance my hammer
I may find?"

FREYJA

"That I would give thee,
although of gold it were,
and trust it to thee,
though it were of silver."

Flew then Loki —
the plumage rattled —
until he came beyond
the Æsir's dwellings,
and came within
the Jötun's land.

On a mound sat Thrym,
the Thursar's lord;
for his greyhounds
plaiting gold bands,
and his horses'
manes smoothing.

THRYM

"How goes it with the Æsir?
How goes it with the Alfar?
Why art thou come alone
to Jötunheim?"

LOKI

"Ill it goes with the Æsir,
Ill it goes with the Alfar.
Hast thou Hlorridi's
hammer hidden?"

THRYM

"I have Hlorridi's
hammer hidden
eight rasts
beneath the earth;
it shall no man

get again,
unless he bring me
Freyja to wife."

Flew then Loki —
the plumage rattled —
until he came beyond
the Jötun's dwellings,
and came within
the Æsir's courts;
there he met Thor,
in the middle court,
who these words
first of all uttered: —

"Hast thou had success,
as well as labor?
Tell me from the air
the long tidings.
Oft of him who sits
are the tales defective,
and he who lies down
utters falsehood."

LOKI

"I have had labor
and success:
Thrym has thy hammer,
the Thursar's lord.
It shall no man
get again,
unless he bring him
Freyja to wife."

They went the fair
Freyja to find;
and he those words
first of all said: —
"Bind thee, Freyja,
in bridal raiment:
we two must drive
to Jötunheim."

Wroth then was Freyja,
and with anger chafed;
all in Æsir's hall

beneath her trembled;
in shivers flew the famed
Brisinga necklace:
"Know me to be
of women lewdest,
if with thee I drive
to Jötunheim."

Straightway went the Æsir
all to council,
and the Asynjur
all to hold converse;
and deliberated
the mighty gods,
how they Hlorridi's
hammer might get back.

Then said Heimdall,
of Æsir brightest —
he well foresaw
like other Vanir —
"Let us clothe Thor
with bridal raiment,
let him have the famed
Brisinga necklace.

"Let by his side
keys jingle,
and woman's weeds
fall round his knees,
but on his breast
place precious stones,
and a neat coif
set on his head."

Then said Thor,
the mighty As:—
"Me the Æsir will
call womanish,
if I let myself be clad
in bridal raiment."

Then spake Loki,
Laufey's son:—
"Do thou, Thor! refrain
from such-like words;

forthwith the Jötuns will
Asgard inhabit,
unless thy hammer thou
gettest back.»

Then they clad Thor
in bridal raiment,
and with the noble
Brisinga necklace;
let by his side
keys jingle,
and woman's weeds
fall round his knees;
and on his breast
placed precious stones,
and a neat coif
set on his head.

Then said Loki,
Laufey's son:—
«I will with thee
as a servant go;
we two will drive
to Jötunheim.»

Straightway were the goats
homeward driven,
hurried to the traces;
they had fast to run.
The rocks were shivered,
the earth was in a blaze;
Odin's son drove
to Jötunheim.

Then said Thrym,
the Thursar's lord:—
«Rise up, Jötuns!
and the benches deck,
now they bring me
Freyja to wife,
Njörd's daughter,
from Noatun.

«Hither to our court let bring
gold-horned cows,
all-black oxen,

for the Jötuns' joy.
Treasures I have many,
necklaces many;
Freyja alone
seemed to me wanting.»

In the evening
they early came,
and for the Jötuns
beer was brought forth.
Thor alone an ox devoured,
salmons eight,
and all the sweetmeats
women should have.
Sif's consort drank
three salds of mead.

Then said Thrym,
the Thursar's prince:—
«Where hast thou seen brides
eat more voraciously?
I never saw brides
feed more amply,
nor a maiden
drink more mead.»

Sat the all-crafty
serving-maid close by,
who words fitting found
against the Jötun's speech:—
«Freyja has nothing eaten
for eight nights,
so eager was she
for Jötunheim.»

Under her veil he stooped,
desirous to salute her,
but sprang back
along the hall:—
«Why are so piercing
Freyja's looks?
Methinks that fire
burns from her eyes.»

Sat the all-crafty
serving-maid close by,
who words fitting found

against the Jötun's speech:—
"Freyja for eight nights
has not slept,
so eager was she
for Jötunheim."

In came the Jötun's
luckless sister;
for a bride-gift
she dared to ask:—
"Give me from thy hands
the ruddy rings,
if thou wouldst gain
my love,
my love
and favor all."

Then said Thrym,
the Thursar's lord:—
"Bring the hammer in,
the bride to consecrate;
lay Mjöllnir
on the maiden's knee;
unite us each with other
by the hand of Vör."

Laughed Hlorridi's
soul in his breast,
when the fierce-hearted
his hammer recognized.
He first slew Thrym,
the Thursar's lord,
and the Jötun's race
all crushed;

He slew the Jötun's
aged sister,
her who a bride-gift
had demanded;
she a blow got
instead of skillings,
a hammer's stroke
for many rings.
So got Odin's son
his hammer back.

Translation of Benjamin Thorpe in 'The Edda of Sæmund the Learned'

OF THE LAMENTATION OF GUDRUN OVER SIGURD DEAD

FIRST LAY OF GUDRUN

GUDRUN of old days
   Drew near to dying,
   As she sat in sorrow
   Over Sigurd;
Yet she sighed not
Nor smote hand on hand,
Nor wailed she aught
As other women.

Then went earls to her,
Full of all wisdom,
Fain help to deal
To her dreadful heart:
Hushed was Gudrun
Of wail, or greeting,
But with heavy woe
Was her heart a-breaking.

Bright and fair
Sat the great earls' brides,
Gold-arrayed
Before Gudrun;
Each told the tale
Of her great trouble,
The bitterest bale
She erst abode.

Then spake Giaflaug,
Giuki's sister:—
"Lo, upon earth
I live most loveless,
Who of five mates
Must see the ending,
Of daughters twain
And three sisters,
Of brethren eight,
And abide behind lonely."

Naught gat Gudrun
Of wail or greeting,
So heavy was she

For her dead husband;
So dreadful-hearted
For the King laid dead there.

Then spake Herborg,
Queen of Hunland:—
"Crueler tale
Have I to tell of,
Of my seven sons
Down in the Southlands,
And the eighth man, my mate,
Felled in the death-mead.

"Father and mother,
And four brothers,
On the wide sea
The winds and death played with;
The billows beat
On the bulwark boards.

"Alone must I sing o'er them,
Alone must I array them,
Alone must my hands deal with
Their departing;
And all this was
In one season's wearing,
And none was left
For love or solace.

"Then was I bound
A prey of the battle,
When that same season
Wore to its ending;
As a tiring-may
Must I bind the shoon
Of the duke's high dame,
Every day at dawning.

"From her jealous hate
Gat I heavy mocking;
Cruel lashes
She laid upon me;
Never met I
Better master
Or mistress worser
In all the wide world."

Naught gat Gudrun
Of wail or greeting,
So heavy was she
For her dead husband;
So dreadful-hearted
For the King laid dead there.

Then spake Gullrond,
Giuki's daughter:—
"O foster-mother,
Wise as thou mayst be,
Naught canst thou better
The young wife's bale."
And she bade uncover
The dead King's corpse.

She swept the sheet
Away from Sigurd,
And turned his cheek
Toward his wife's knees:—
"Look on thy loved one,
Lay lips to his lips,
E'en as thou wert clinging
To thy King alive yet!"

Once looked Gudrun—
One look only,
And saw her lord's locks
Lying all bloody,
The great man's eyes
Glazed and deadly,
And his heart's bulwark
Broken by sword-edge.

Back then sank Gudrun,
Back on the bolster;
Loosed was her head-array,
Red did her cheeks grow,
And the rain-drops ran
Down over her knees.

Then wept Gudrun,
Giuki's daughter,
So that the tears flowed
Through the pillow;
As the geese withal

That were in the home-field,
The fair fowls the may owned,
Fell a-screaming.

Then spake Gullrond,
Giuki's daughter:—
"Surely knew I
No love like your love
Among all men,
On the mold abiding;
Naught wouldst thou joy in
Without or within doors,
O my sister,
Save beside Sigurd."

Then spake Gudrun,
Giuki's daughter:—
"Such was my Sigurd
Among the sons of Giuki,
As is the king leek
O'er the low grass waxing,
Or a bright stone
Strung on band,
Or a pearl of price
On a prince's brow.

"Once was I counted
By the king's warriors
Higher than any
Of Herjan's mays;
Now am I as little
As the leaf may be,
Amid wind-swept wood,
Now when dead he lieth.

"I miss from my seat,
I miss from my bed,
My darling of sweet speech.
Wrought the sons of Giuki,
Wrought the sons of Giuki,
This sore sorrow;
Yea, for their sister
Most sore sorrow.

"So may your lands
Lie waste on all sides,

As ye have broken
Your bounden oaths!
Ne'er shalt thou, Gunnar,
The gold have joy of;
The dear-bought rings
Shall drag thee to death,
Whereon thou swarest
Oath unto Sigurd.

"Ah, in the days bygone,
Great mirth in the home-field,
When my Sigurd
Set saddle on Grani,
And they went their ways
For the wooing of Brynhild!
An ill day, an ill woman,
And most ill hap!"

Then spake Brynhild,
Budli's daughter:—
"May the woman lack
Both love and children,
Who gained greeting
For thee, O Gudrun!
Who gave thee this morning
Many words!"

Then spake Gullrond,
Giuki's daughter:—
"Hold peace of such words,
Thou hated of all folk!
The bane of brave men
Hast thou been ever;
All waves of ill
Wash over thy mind;
To seven great kings
Hast thou been a sore sorrow,
And the death of good-will
To wives and women."

Then spake Brynhild,
Budli's daughter:—
"None but Atli
Brought bale upon us;
My very brother,
Born of Budli,

« When we saw in the hall
Of the Hunnish people
The gold a-gleaming
On the kingly Giukings;
I have paid for that faring
Oft and fully,
And for the sight
That then I saw. »

By a pillar she stood
And strained its wood to her;
From the eyes of Brynhild,
Budli's daughter,
Flashed out fire,
And she snorted forth venom,
As the sore wounds she gazed on
Of the dead-slain Sigurd.

William Morris in 'The Story of the Völsungs and Niblungs': translated by
Magnusson and Morris, London, 1870

THE WAKING OF BRUNHILDE ON THE HINDFELL BY SIGURD

From 'The Story of Sigurd the Völsung,' by William Morris

HE LOOKETH, and loveth her sore, and he longeth her spirit to
    move,
And awaken her heart to the world, that she may behold him
    and love.
And he toucheth her breast and her hands, and he loveth her pass-
    ing sore;
And he saith, "Awake! I am Sigurd;" but she moveth never the
    more.

Then he looked on his bare bright blade, and he said, "Thou—what
    wilt thou do?
For indeed as I came by the war-garth thy voice of desire I knew."
Bright burnt the pale blue edges, for the sunrise drew anear,
And the rims of the Shield-burg glittered, and the east was exceed-
    ing clear:
So the eager edges he setteth to the Dwarf-wrought battle-coat
Where the hammered ring-knit collar constraineth the woman's
    throat;
But the sharp Wrath biteth and rendeth, and before it fail the rings,
And, lo, the gleam of the linen, and the light of golden things;

Then he driveth the blue steel onward, and through the skirt, and
 out,
Till naught but the rippling linen is wrapping her about;
Then he deems her breath comes quicker and her breast begins to
 heave,
So he turns about the War-Flame and rends down either sleeve,
Till her arms lie white in her raiment, and a river of sun-bright
 hair
Flows free o'er bosom and shoulder and floods the desert bare.

Then a flush cometh over her visage and a sigh upheaveth her
 breast,
And her eyelids quiver and open, and she wakeneth into rest;
Wide-eyed on the dawning she gazeth, too glad to change or smile,
And but little moveth her body, nor speaketh she yet for a while;
And yet kneels Sigurd moveless, her wakening speech to heed,
While soft the waves of the daylight o'er the starless heavens speed,
And the gleaming rims of the Shield-burg yet bright and brighter
 grow,
And the thin moon hangeth her horns dead-white in the golden glow.
Then she turned and gazed on Sigurd, and her eyes met the Völ-
 sung's eyes,
And mighty and measureless now did the tide of his love arise.
For their longing had met and mingled, and he knew of her heart
 that she loved,
As she spake unto nothing but him, and her lips with the speech-flood
 moved:—

"Oh, what is the thing so mighty that my weary sleep hath torn,
And rent the fallow bondage, and the wan woe over-worn?"

He said, "The hand of Sigurd and the Sword of Sigmund's son,
And the heart that the Völsungs fashioned, this deed for thee have
 done."

But she said, "Where then is Odin that laid me here alow?
Long lasteth the grief of the world, and man-folk's tangled woe!"

"He dwelleth above," said Sigurd, "but I on the earth abide,
And I came from the Glittering Heath the waves of thy fire to ride."

But therewith the sun rose upward and lightened all the earth,
And the light flashed up to the heavens from the rims of the glo-
 rious girth; . . .

Then they turned and were knit together; and oft and o'er again
They craved, and kissed rejoicing, and their hearts were full and fain.

ALFRED EDERSHEIM

(1825–1889)

AMONG writers on Biblical topics Dr. Alfred Edersheim occupies a unique place. Bred in the Jewish faith, he brought to his writings the traditions of his ancestry. The history of the Children of Israel was a reality to him, who had known the Talmud and the Old Testament through the lessons of his boyhood, and had been taught to reverence the Hebrew sacred rites handed down through the ages. All the intangible, unconscious religious influences of his youth entered into the work of his manhood. And although this converted Rabbi wrote as a Christian, yet the Bible stories were colored and vivified for him by his Jewish sympathies. Thus his work had the especial value of a double point of view.

Born in Vienna in 1825 of German parents, he studied at the university of his native city and in Berlin, finishing his theological education in Edinburgh. He became a minister of the Free Church of Scotland in 1849, passing over to the Church of England in 1875. In 1881 he received from Oxford an honorary A. M., and was for a time lecturer on the Septuagint at the university. He died in Mentone, France, on March 16th, 1889.

The earlier writings of Dr. Edersheim consist almost entirely of translations from the German, and of Jewish stories written for educational purposes. Of his later works the most important are 'The Bible History,' his largest work, in seven volumes; 'The Temple, its Ministers and Services as they were at the Time of Christ'; 'Sketches of Jewish Social Life in the Days of Christ'; and a 'History of the Jewish Nation after the Destruction of Jerusalem under Titus.' From the evangelical point of view, his 'Life and Times of Jesus the Messiah' is of final authority, brilliantly exemplifying his peculiar fitness to be the interpreter of Jewish life and thought at the period of the rise of Christianity. He presents not only the story of the Christ of the Gospels, but draws a picture of the whole political and social life of the Jews, and of their intellectual and religious condition — a picture which his Rabbinical learning and his race sympathies make authentic. He wrote English with unaffected directness, embodying in the simplest forms the results of his wide scholarship. His books have a very wide and constant sale.

THE WASHING OF HANDS

From 'The Life and Times of Jesus the Messiah'

THE externalism of all these practices [ceremonial practices of the Hebrews] will best appear from the following account which the Talmud gives of "a feast." As the guests enter, they sit down on chairs, and water is brought to them, with which they wash one hand. Into this the cup is taken, when each speaks the blessing over the wine partaken of before dinner. Presently they all lie down at table. Water is again brought them, with which they now wash both hands, preparatory to the meal, when the blessing is spoken over the bread, and then over the cup, by the chief person at the feast, or else by one selected by way of distinction. The company respond by *Amen*, always supposing the benediction to have been spoken by an Israelite, not a heathen, slave, nor law-breaker. Nor was it lawful to say it with an unlettered man, although it might be said with a Cuthæan (heretic, or Samaritan,) who was learned. After dinner the crumbs, if any, are carefully gathered — hands are again washed, and he who first had done so leads in the prayer of thanksgiving. The formula in which he is to call on the rest to join him by repeating the prayers after him is prescribed, and differs according to the number of those present. The blessing and the thanksgiving are allowed to be said not only in Hebrew, but in any other language.

In regard to the position of the guests, we know that the uppermost seats were occupied by the Rabbis. The Talmud formulates it in this manner: That the worthiest lies down first, on his left side, with his feet hanging down. If there are two "cushions" (divans), the next worthiest lies at his feet; if there are three cushions, the third worthiest lies above the first (at his left), so that the chief person is in the middle. The water before eating is first handed to the worthiest, and so in regard to the washing after meat. But if a very large number are present, you begin after dinner with the least worthy till you come to the last five, when the worthiest in the company washes his hands, and the other four after him. The guests being thus arranged, the head of the house, or the chief person at table, speaks the blessing and then cuts the bread. By some it was not deemed etiquette to begin till after he who had said the prayer had done so, but this does not seem to have been the rule among the Palestinian Jews. Then, generally, the bread was dipped into salt or something salted, etiquette demanding that where there were two they should wait one for the other, but not where there were three or more.

This is not the place to furnish what may be termed a list of *menus* at Jewish tables. In earlier times the meal was no doubt very simple. It became otherwise when intercourse with Rome, Greece, and the East made the people familiar with foreign luxury, while commerce supplied its requirements. Indeed, it would scarcely be possible to enumerate the various articles which seem to have been imported from different, and even distant, countries.

To begin with: The wine was mixed with water, and indeed, some thought that the benediction should not be pronounced till the water had been added to the wine. According to one statement two parts, according to another three parts, of water were to be added to the wine. Various vintages are mentioned: among them a red wine of Saron, and a black wine. Spiced wine was made with honey and pepper. Another mixture, chiefly used for invalids, consisted of old wine, water, and balsam; yet another was "wine of myrrh"; we also read of a wine in which capers had been soaked. To these we should add wine spiced either with pepper or with absinthe, and what is described as vinegar, a cooling drink made either of grapes that had not ripened, or of the lees. Besides these, palm wine was also in use. Of foreign drinks, we read of wine from Ammon and from the province Asia, the latter a kind of "must" boiled down. Wine in ice came from Lebanon; a certain kind of vinegar from Idumæa; beer from Media and Babylon; barley wine (*zythos*) from Egypt. Finally, we ought to mention Palestinian apple cider, and the juice of other fruits. If we adopt the rendering of some, even liqueurs were known and used.

Long as this catalogue is, that of the various articles of food, whether native or imported, would occupy a much larger space. Suffice it that as regarded the various kinds of grain, meat, fish, and fruits, either in their natural state or preserved, it embraced almost everything known to the ancient world. At feasts there was an introductory course, consisting of appetizing salted meat, or of some light dish. This was followed by the dinner itself, which finished with dessert (*aphikomon* or *terugima*), consisting of pickled olives, radishes and lettuce, and fruits, among which even preserved ginger from India is mentioned. The most diverse and even strange statements are made as to the healthiness, or the reverse, of certain articles of diet, especially vegetables. Fish was a favorite dish, and never wanting at a Sabbath meal. It was a saying that both salt and water should be taken at every meal, if health was to be preserved. Condiments, such as mustard or pepper, were to be sparingly used. Very different were the meals of the poor. Locusts—fried in flour or honey, or preserved—required, according to the Talmud, no blessing; since the animal was really among the curses of the land. Eggs were a common article of food, and sold in the shops. Then there was a milk dish, into which people dipped their bread. Others who were better off had a soup made of vegetables, especially onions, and meat; while the very poor would satisfy the cravings of hunger with bread and cheese, or bread and fruit, or some vegetables, such as cucumbers, lentils, beans, peas, or onions.

At meals the rules of etiquette were strictly observed, especially as regarded the sages. Indeed, there are added to the Talmud two tractates, one describing the general etiquette, the other that of "sages," of which the title may be translated as 'The Way of the World' (*Derech Erez*), being a sort of code of good manners. According to some, it was not good breeding to speak while eating. The learned and most honored occupied not only the chief places, but were sometimes distinguished by a double portion. According to Jewish etiquette, a guest should conform in everything to his host, even though it were unpleasant. Although hospitality was the greatest and most prized social virtue, which, to use a rabbinic expression, might make every home a sanctuary and every table an altar, an unbidden guest, or a guest who brought another guest, was proverbially an unwelcome apparition. Sometimes, by way of self-righteousness, the poor were brought in, and the best part of the meal ostentatiously given to them. At ordinary entertainments, people were to help themselves. It was not considered good manners to drink as soon as you were asked, but you ought to hold the cup for a little in your hand. But it would be the height of rudeness either to wipe the plates, to scrape together the bread, as though you had not had enough to eat, or to drop it, to the inconvenience of your neighbor. If a piece were taken out of a dish, it must of course not be put back; still less must you offer from your cup or plate to your neighbor. From the almost religious value attaching to bread, we scarcely wonder that these rules were laid down: not to steady a cup or plate upon bread, nor to throw away bread, and that after dinner the bread was to be carefully swept together. Otherwise, it was thought, demons would sit upon it. 'The Way of the World' for sages lays down these as the marks of a rabbi: that he does not eat standing; that he does not lick his fingers; that he sits down only beside his equals — in fact, many regarded it as wrong to eat with the unlearned; that he begins cutting the bread where it is best baked, nor ever breaks off a bit with his hand; and that when drinking, he turns away his face from the company. Another saying was, that the sage was known by four things: at his cups, in money matters, when angry, and in his jokes. After dinner, the formalities concerning hand-washing and prayer, already described, were gone through, and then frequently aromatic spices burnt, over which a special benediction was pronounced. We have only to add that on Sabbaths it was deemed a religious duty to have three meals, and to procure the best that money could obtain, even though one were to save and fast for it all the week. Lastly, it was regarded as a special obligation and honor to entertain sages.

We have no difficulty now in understanding what passed at the table of the Pharisee. When the water for purification was presented to him, Jesus would either refuse it, or if, as seems more likely at a morning meal, each guest repaired by himself for the prescribed purification, he would omit to do so, and sit down to meat without this formality. No one who knows the stress which Pharisaism laid on this rite would argue that Jesus might have conformed to the practice. Indeed, the controversy was long and bitter between the Schools of Shammai and Hillel, on such a point as whether the hands were to be washed *before* the cup was filled with wine, or *after* that, and where the towel was to be deposited. With such things the most serious ritual inferences were connected on both sides. A religion which spent its energy on such trivialities must have lowered the moral tone. All the more that Jesus insisted so earnestly, as the substance of his teaching, on that corruption of our nature which Judaism ignored and on that spiritual purification which was needful for the reception of his doctrine, — would he publicly and openly set aside ordinances of man which diverted thoughts of purity into questions of the most childish character. On the other hand, we can also understand what bitter thoughts must have filled the mind of the Pharisee whose guest Jesus was, when he observed his neglect of the cherished rite. It was an insult to himself, a defiance of Jewish law, a revolt against the most cherished traditions of the synagogue. Remembering that a Pharisee ought not to sit down to a meal with such, he might feel that he should not have asked Jesus to his table.

MARIA EDGEWORTH

(1767–1849)

HE famous author of Irish novels and didactic tales was the daughter of Richard Lovell Edgeworth and his first wife Anna Ehrs, and was born at Black Bourton, Oxfordshire, January 1st, 1767. When she was twelve years old the family settled on the estate at Edgeworth's-town, County Longford, Ireland, which was her home during the remainder of her long life. It was a singularly happy family circle, of which Maria was the centre. Her father married four times, and had twenty-two children, on whom he exercised his peculiar educational ideas. He devoted himself most particularly to Maria's training, and made her his most confidential companion. Several of her works were written in conjunction with her father, and over almost all he exercised a supervision which doubtless hindered the free expression of her genius. Her first publication, 'Letters to Literary Ladies,' on the education of women, appeared in 1795. This was followed by educational and juvenile works illustrating the theories of Mr. Edgeworth: 'The Parent's Assistant,' 'Practical Education' (a

MARIA EDGEWORTH

joint production), supplemented later by 'Early Lessons'; 'Rosamond,' 'Harry and Lucy,' and a sequel to the 'Parent's Assistant.' In 1800 appeared 'Castle Rackrent,' the first of her novels of Irish life, and her best known work; soon followed by 'Belinda,' and the well-known 'Essay on Irish Bulls,' by her father and herself. Miss Edgeworth's reputation was now established, and on a visit to Paris at this time she received much attention. Here occurred the one recorded romance of her life, the proposal of marriage from Count Edelcrantz, a Swedish gentleman. On her return she wrote 'Leonora.' In 1804 she published 'Popular Tales'; in 1809 the first series of 'Fashionable Tales.' These tales include 'Almeria' and 'The Absentee,' considered by many critics her masterpiece. 'Patronage' was begun years before as 'The Freeman Family.' In 1817 she published 'Harrington' and 'Ormond,' which rank among her best works. In the same year her father died, leaving to her the completion of his 'Memoirs,' which appeared in 1820. Her last novel, 'Helen,' published in 1834, shows no diminution of her charm and grace. With occasional visits to Paris and London, and a memorable trip to Scotland in 1823, when she was entertained at Abbotsford, she lived serene and happy at Edgeworth's-town until her sudden death, May 21st 1849.

Miss Edgeworth was extremely small, not beautiful; but a brilliant talker and a great favorite in the exclusive society to which she everywhere had access. Her greatest success was in the new field opened in her Irish stories, full of racy, rollicking Irish humor, and valuable pictures of bygone conditions,— for the genial peasant of her pages is now rarely found. Not the least we owe her is the influence which her national tales had on Sir Walter Scott, who declared that her success led him to do the same for his own country in the Waverley Novels. Miss Edgeworth's style is easy and animated. Her tales show her extraordinary power of observation, her good sense, and remarkable skill in dialogue, though they are biased by the didactic purpose which permeates all her writings. As Madame de Staël remarked, she was "lost in dreary utility." And doubtless this is why she just missed greatness, and has been consigned to the ranks of "standard" authors who are respectfully alluded to but seldom read. The lack of tenderness and imagination was perhaps the result of her unusual self-control, shown in her custom of writing in the family sitting-room, and so concentrating her mind on her work that she was deaf to all that went on about her. Surely some of the creative power of her mind must have been lost in that strenuous effort. Her noble character, as well as her talents, won for her the friendship of many distinguished people of her day. With Scott she was intimate, Byron found her charming, and Macaulay was an enthusiastic admirer. In her recently edited letters are found many interesting and valuable accounts of the people she met in the course of her long life.

Miss Edgeworth's life has been written by Helen Zimmern and Grace A. Oliver; her 'Life and Letters,' edited by Augustus J. C. Hare, appeared in 1895. 'Pen Portraits of Literary Women,' by Helen Gray Cone and Jeannette L. Gilder, contains a sketch of her.

SIR CONDY'S WAKE

From 'Castle Rackrent'

WHEN they were made sensible that Sir Condy was going to leave Castle Rackrent for good and all, they set up a whillaluh that could be heard to the farthest end of the street; and one fine boy he was, that my master had given an apple to that morning, cried the loudest; but they all were the same sorry, for Sir Condy was greatly beloved among the childher, for letting them go a-nutting in the demesne without saying a word to them, though my lady objected to them. The people in the town, who were the most of them standing at their doors, hearing the childher cry, would know the reason of it; and when the report was made known the people one and all gathered in great anger against my son Jason, and terror at the notion of his coming to be landlord over them, and they cried, "No Jason! no Jason! Sir Condy! Sir Condy! Sir Condy Rackrent forever!" and the mob grew so great and so loud I was frightened, and made my way back to the house to warn my son to make his escape or hide himself, for fear of the consequences. Jason would not believe me till they came all round the house and to the windows with great shouts; then he grew quite pale, and asked Sir Condy what had he best do? "I'll tell you what you'd best do," said Sir Condy, who was laughing to see his fright: "finish your glass first; then let's go to the window and show ourselves, and I'll tell 'em, or you shall if you please, that I'm going to the lodge for change of air for my health, and by my own desire, for the rest of my days." "Do so," said Jason who never meant it should have been so, but could not refuse him the lodge at this unseasonable time. Accordingly Sir Condy threw up the sash and explained matters, and thanked all his friends, and bid 'em look in at the punch-bowl, and observe that Jason and he had been sitting over it very good friends; so the mob was content, and he sent 'em out some whisky to drink his health, and that was the last time his Honor's health was ever drunk at Castle Rackrent.

The very next day, being too proud, as he said to me, to stay an hour longer in a house that did not belong to him, he sets off to the lodge, and I along with him not many hours after. And there was great bemoaning through all O'Shaughlin's Town,

which I stayed to witness, and gave my poor master a full account
of when I got to the lodge. He was very low and in his bed
when I got there, and complained of a great pain about his
heart; but I guessed it was only trouble, and all the business,
let alone vexation, he had gone through of late; and knowing
the nature of him from a boy, I took my pipe, and while smok-
ing it by the chimney, began telling him how he was beloved
and regretted in the county, and it did him a deal of good to
hear it. "Your Honor has a great many friends yet, that you
don't know of, rich and poor in the country," says I; "for as I
was coming along the road, I met two gentlemen in their own
carriages, who asked after you, knowing me, and wanted to
know where you was, and all about you, and even how old I
was: think of that!" Then he wakened out of his doze, and be-
gan questioning me who the gentlemen were. And the next
morning it came into my head to go, unknown to anybody, with
my master's compliments, round to many of the gentlemen's
houses where he and my lady used to visit, and people that I
knew were his great friends, and would go to Cork to serve him
any day in the year, and I made bold to try to borrow a trifle
of cash from them. They all treated me very civil for the most
part, and asked a great many questions very kind about my
lady and Sir Condy and all the family, and were greatly sur-
prised to learn from me Castle Rackrent was sold, and my mas-
ter at the lodge for health; and they all pitied him greatly, and
he had their good wishes, if that would do, but money was a
thing they unfortunately had not any of them at this time to
spare. I had my journey for my pains, and I, not used to walk-
ing, nor supple as formerly, was greatly tired, but had the satis-
faction of telling my master, when I got to the lodge, all the
civil things said by high and low.

"Thady," says he, "all you've been telling me brings a
strange thought into my head: I've a notion I shall not be long
for this world anyhow, and I've a great fancy to see my own
funeral afore I die." I was greatly shocked at the first speak-
ing, to hear him speak so light about his funeral, and he to all
appearances in good health, but recollecting myself answered:—
"To be sure it would be as fine a sight as one could see, I
dared to say, and one I should be proud to witness; and I did
not doubt his Honor's would be as great a funeral as ever Sir
Patrick O'Shaughlin's was, and such a one as that had never

been known in the county before or since." But I never thought
he was in earnest about seeing his own funeral himself, till the
next day he returns to it again. "Thady," says he, "as far as
the wake goes, sure I might without any great trouble have the
satisfaction of seeing a bit of my own funeral." "Well, since
your Honor's Honor's so bent upon it," says I, not willing to
cross him, and he in trouble, "we must see what we can do."
So he fell into a sort of a sham disorder, which was easy done,
as he kept his bed and no one to see him; and I got my shister,
who was an old woman very handy about the sick, and very
skillful, to come up to the lodge to nurse him; and we gave out,
she knowing no better, that he was just at his latter end, and it
answered beyond anything; and there was a great throng of peo-
ple, men, women, and children, and there being only two rooms
at the lodge, except what was locked up full of Jason's furniture
and things, the house was soon as full and fuller than it could
hold, and the heat and smoke and noise wonderful great; and
standing among them that were near the bed, but not thinking
at all of the dead, I was startled by the sound of my master's
voice from under the greatcoats that had been thrown all at
top, and I went close up, no one noticing. "Thady," says he,
"I've had enough of this; I'm smothering, and can't hear a word
of all they're saying of the deceased." "God bless you, and lie
still and quiet," says I, "a bit longer; for my shister's afraid of
ghosts and would die on the spot with fright, was she to see
you come to life all on a sudden this way without the least
preparation." So he lays him still, though well-nigh stifled, and
I made all haste to tell the secret of the joke, whispering to one
and t'other, and there was a great surprise, but not so great as
we had laid out it would. "And aren't we to have the pipes
and tobacco, after coming so far to-night?" said some; but they
were all well enough pleased when his Honor got up to drink
with them, and sent for more spirits from a shebean-house,
where they very civilly let him have it upon credit. So the
night passed off very merrily, but to my mind Sir Condy was
rather upon the sad order in the midst of it all, not finding there
had been such a great talk about himself after his death as he
had always expected to hear.

SIR MURTAGH RACKRENT AND HIS LADY

From ‹Castle Rackrent›

Now it was that the world was to see what was *in* Sir Patrick. On coming into the estate he gave the finest entertainment ever was heard of in the country; not a man could .stand after supper but Sir Patrick himself, who could sit out the best man in Ireland, let alone the three kingdoms itself. He had his house, from one year's end to another, as full of company as ever it could hold, and fuller; for rather than be left out of the parties at Castle Rackrent, many gentlemen, and those men of the first consequence and landed estates in the country,— such as the O'Neils of Ballynagrotty, and the Moneygawls of Mount Juliet's Town, and O'Shannons of New Town Tullyhog,— made it their choice often and often, when there was no moon to be had for love nor money, in long winter nights, to sleep in the chicken-house, which Sir Patrick had fitted up for the purpose of accommodating his friends and the public in general, who honored him with their company unexpectedly at Castle Rackrent; and this went on I can't tell you how long: the whole country rang with his praises — long life to him! I'm sure I love to look upon his picture, now opposite to me; though I never saw him, he must have been a portly gentleman — his neck something short, and remarkable for the largest pimple on his nose, which by his particular desire is still extant in his picture, said to be a striking likeness though taken when young. He is said also to be the inventor of raspberry whisky; which is very likely, as nobody has ever appeared to dispute it with him, and as there still exists a broken punch-bowl at Castle Rackrent in the garret, with an inscription to that effect   a great curiosity. A few days before his death he was very merry; it being his Honor's birthday, he called my grandfather in, God bless him! to drink the company's health, and filled a bumper himself, but could not carry it to his head on account of the great shake in his hand; on this he cast his joke, saying:—" What would my poor father say to me if he was to pop out of the grave and see me now? I remember when I was a little boy, the first bumper of claret he gave me after dinner, how he praised me for carrying it so steady to my mouth. Here's my thanks to him — a bumper toast." Then he fell to singing the favorite song he learned from his father —

for the last time, poor gentleman; he sung it that night as loud and as hearty as ever, with a chorus:—

«He that goes to bed, and goes to bed sober,
    Falls as the leaves do,
Falls as the leaves do, and dies in October;
But he that goes to bed, and goes to bed mellow,
    Lives as he ought to do,
Lives as he ought to do, and dies an honest fellow.»

Sir Patrick died that night: just as the company rose to drink his health with three cheers, he fell down in a sort of fit, and was carried off; they sat it out, and were surprised, on inquiry in the morning, to find that it was all over with poor Sir Patrick. Never did any gentleman live and die more beloved in the country by rich and poor. His funeral was such a one as was never known before or since in the county! All the gentlemen in the three counties were at it; far and near, how they flocked! My great-grandfather said that to see all the women even in their red cloaks, you would have taken them for the army drawn out. Then such a fine whillaluh! you might have heard it to the farthest end of the county, and happy the man who could get but a sight of the hearse! But who'd have thought it? just as all was going on right, through his own town they were passing, when the body was seized for debt: a rescue was apprehended from the mob, but the heir, who attended the funeral, was against that for fear of consequences, seeing that those villains who came to serve acted under the disguise of the law; so, to be sure, the law must take its course, and little gain had the creditors for their pains. First and foremost, they had the curses of the country; and Sir Murtagh Rackrent, the new heir, in the next place, on account of this affront to the body, refused to pay a shilling of the debts, in which he was countenanced by all the best gentlemen of property, and others of his acquaintance. Sir Murtagh alleging in all companies, that he all along meant to pay his father's debts of honor, but the moment the law was taken of him there was an end of honor to be sure. It was whispered (but none but the enemies of the family believed it) that this was all a sham seizure to get quit of the debts, which he had bound himself to pay in honor.

It's a long time ago, there's no saying how it was, but this for certain: the new man did not take at all after the old gentleman; the cellars were never filled after his death, and no open house or anything as it used to be; the tenants even were sent away without their whisky. I was ashamed myself, and knew not what to say for the honor of the family; but I made the best of a bad case, and laid it all at my lady's door, for I did not like her anyhow, nor anybody else; she was of the family of the Skinflints, and a widow; it was a strange match for Sir Murtagh; the people in the country thought he demeaned himself greatly, but I said nothing: I knew how it was; Sir Murtagh was a great lawyer, and looked to the great Skinflint estate; there however he overshot himself; for though one of the co-heiresses, he was never the better for her, for she outlived him many's the long day — he could not see that, to be sure, when he married her. I must say for her, she made him the best of wives, being a very notable stirring woman, and looking close to everything. But I always suspected she had Scotch blood in her veins; anything else I could have looked over in her from a regard to the family. She was a strict observer for self and servants of Lent, and all fast days, but not holy days. One of the maids having fainted three time the last day of Lent, to keep soul and body together we put a morsel of roast beef in her mouth, which came from Sir Murtagh's dinner, — who never fasted, not he; but somehow or other it unfortunately reached my lady's ears, and the priest of the parish had a complaint made of it the next day, and the poor girl was forced as soon as she could walk to do penance for it, before she could get any peace or absolution, in the house or out of it. However, my lady was very charitable in her own way. She had a charity school for poor children, where they were taught to read and write gratis, and where they were kept well to spinning gratis for my lady in return; for she had always heaps of duty yarn from the tenants, and got all her household linen out of the estate from first to last; for after the spinning, the weavers on the estate took it in hand for nothing, because of the looms my lady's interest could get from the linen board to distribute gratis. Then there was a bleach-yard near us, and the tenant dare refuse my lady nothing, for fear of a law suit Sir Murtagh kept hanging over him about the water-course.

With these ways of managing, 'tis surprising how cheap my lady got things done, and how proud she was of it. Her table, the same way, kept for next to nothing, — duty fowls, and duty turkeys, and duty geese came as fast as we could eat 'em, for my lady kept a sharp lookout, and knew to a tub of butter everything the tenants had, all round. They knew her way, and what with fear of driving for rent and Sir Murtagh's lawsuits, they were kept in such good order, they never thought of coming near Castle Rackrent without a present of something or other — nothing too much or too little for my lady: eggs, honey, butter, meal, fish, game, grouse, and herrings, fresh or salt, all went for something. As for their young pigs, we had them, and the best bacon and hams they could make up, with all young chickens in spring; but they were a set of poor wretches, and we had nothing but misfortunes with them, always breaking and running away. This, Sir Murtagh and my lady said, was all their former landlord Sir Patrick's fault, who let 'em all get the half-year's rent into arrear; there was something in that, to be sure. But Sir Murtagh was as much the contrary way; for let alone making English tenants of them, every soul, he was always driving and driving and pounding and pounding, and canting and canting and replevying and replevying, and he made a good living of trespassing cattle; there was always some tenant's pig, or horse, or cow, or calf, or goose trespassing, which was so great a gain to Sir Murtagh that he did not like to hear me talk of repairing fences. Then his heriots and duty work brought him in something; his turf was cut, his potatoes set and dug, his hay brought home, and in short, all the work about his house done for nothing; for in all our leases there were strict clauses heavy with penalties, which Sir Murtagh knew well how to enforce: so many days' duty work of man and horse from every tenant he was to have, and had, every year; and when a man vexed him, why, the finest day he could pitch on, when the cratur was getting in his own harvest, or thatching his cabin, Sir Murtagh made it a principle to call upon him and his horse; so he taught 'em all, as he said, to know the law of landlord and tenant.

As for law, I believe no man, dead or alive, ever loved it so well as Sir Murtagh. He had once sixteen suits pending at a time, and I never saw him so much himself; roads, lanes, bogs, wells, ponds, eel weirs, orchards, trees, tithes, vagrants, gravel pits, sand pits, dung-hills, and nuisances,— everything upon the face of the earth furnished him good matter for a suit. He used to boast that he had a law suit for every letter in the alphabet. How I used to wonder to see Sir Murtagh in the midst of the

papers in his office! Why, he could hardly turn about for them.
I made bold to shrug my shoulders once in his presence, and
thank my stars I was not born a gentleman to so much toil and
trouble; but Sir Murtagh took me up short with his old proverb,
"Learning is better than house or land." Out of forty-nine suits
which he had, he never lost one but seventeen; the rest he
gained with costs, double costs, treble costs sometimes; but even
that did not pay. He was a very learned man in the law, and
had the character of it; but how it was I can't tell, these suits
that he carried cost him a power of money: in the end he sold
some hundreds a year of the family estate: but he was a very
learned man in the law, and I know nothing of the matter, ex-
cept having a great regard for the family; and I could not help
grieving when he sent me to post up notices of the sale of the
fee-simple of the lands and appurtenances of Timoleague. "I
know, honest Thady," says he to comfort me, "what I'm about
better than you do; I'm only selling to get the ready money
wanting to carry on my suit with spirit with the Nugents of
Carrickashaughlin."

He was very sanguine about that suit with the Nugents of
Carrickashaughlin. He could have gained it, they say, for cer-
tain, had it pleased Heaven to have spared him to us, and it
would have been at the least a plump two thousand a year in
his way; but things were ordered otherwise,— for the best, to be
sure. He dug up a fairy mount against my advice, and had no
luck afterward. Though a learned man in the law, he was a
little too incredulous in other matters. I warned him that I
heard the very Banshee that my grandfather heard under Sir
Patrick's window a few days before his death. But Sir Murtagh
thought nothing of the Banshee, nor of his cough with a spitting
of blood,— brought on, I understand, by catching cold in attend-
ing the courts, and overstraining his chest with making himself
heard in one of his favorite causes. He was a great speaker,
with a powerful voice; but his last speech was not in the courts
at all. He and my lady, though both of the same way of think-
ing in some things, and though she was as good a wife and
great economist as you could see, and he the best of husbands
as to looking into his affairs, and making money for his family,—
yet I don't know how it was, they had a great deal of sparring
and jarring between them. My lady had her privy purse, and
she had her weed ashes, and her sealing money upon the signing

of all the leases, with something to buy gloves besides; and besides, again, often took money from the tenants, if offered properly, to speak for them to Sir Murtagh about abatements and renewals.   Now the weed ashes and the glove money he allowed her clear perquisites; though once when he saw her in a new gown saved out of the weed ashes, he told her to my face (for he could say a sharp thing) that she should not put on her weeds before her husband's death.   But in a dispute about an abatement, my lady would have the last word, and Sir Murtagh grew mad; I was within hearing of the door, and now I wish I had made bold to step in.   He spoke so loud the whole kitchen was out on the stairs.   All on a sudden he stopped, and my lady too.   Something has surely happened, thought I — and so it was, for Sir Murtagh in his passion broke a blood-vessel, and all the law in the land could do nothing in that case.   My lady sent for five physicians, but Sir Murtagh died, and was buried. She had a fine jointure settled upon her, and took herself away, to the great joy of the tenantry.   I never said anything one way or the other, while she was part of the family, but got up to see her go at three o'clock in the morning.   "It's a fine morning, honest Thady," says she; "good-by to ye," and into the carriage she stepped, without a word more, good or bad, or even half a crown; but I made my bow, and stood to see her safe out of sight, for the sake of the family.

ANNE CHARLOTTE LEFFLER EDGREN

(1849–1892)

ANNE CHARLOTTE LEFFLER EDGREN, afterwards Duchess of Cajanello, was born in Stockholm, October 1st, 1849. She was the most prominent among contemporary women writers of Sweden, and won for herself an eminent position in the world of letters, not only for the truthfulness of her delineation of life, but for the brilliancy of her style and her skill in using her material. The circumstances of her early life were comfortable and commonplace. She was the only daughter of a Swedish rector, and from her mother, also the daughter of a clergyman, she inherited her literary tendencies. From her parents and her three devoted brothers she received every encouragement, but with wise foresight they restrained her desire to publish her early writings; and it was not until her talent was fully developed that her first book, a collection of stories entitled 'Händelsvis' (By Chance), appeared in 1869, under the pseudonym of "Carlot." In 1872 she was married to Gustav Edgren, secretary of the prefecture in Stockholm; and though fitting and harmonious, this marriage was undoubtedly one of convenience, brought about by the altered circumstances of her life.

In 1873 she published the drama 'Skådespelerskan' (The Actress), which held the stage in Stockholm for an entire winter, and this was followed by 'Pastorsadjunkten' (The Curate), 1876, and 'Elfvan' (The Elf), 1880, the latter being even more than usually successful. Her equipment as a dramatist was surprisingly slender, as until the time of her engagement to Mr. Edgren she had never visited the theatre, and necessarily was absolutely ignorant of the technique of the stage. Nevertheless, her natural dramatic instincts supplied the defects of a lack of training, and her plays met with almost universal success. The theme of all her dramas, under various guises, is the same,— the struggle of a woman's individuality with the conventional environment of her life. Mrs. Edgren herself laments that she was born a woman, when nature had so evidently intended her for a man.

Her first work to be published under her own name was in 1882,— a collection of tales entitled 'Ur Lifvet' (From Life), which were received with especial applause. Her works were translated into Danish, Russian, and German, and she now became widely known as one of the most talented of Swedish writers. In 1883 appeared a second volume of 'From Life'; and still later, in 1889, yet another under the same title. These later stories betrayed a boldness of thought and expression not before evinced, and placed the author in the ranks of the radicals. The drama 'Sanna Kvinnor' (Ideal Women) appeared in 1883; 'Huru Man Gör Godt' (How We do Good) in 1885; and in 1888, in collaboration with Sónya Kovalévsky, 'Kampen för Lyckan' (The Struggle for Happiness).

In company with her brother, Professor Mittag-Leffler, she attended a Mathematical Congress in Algiers, in the early part of the year 1888; and upon the return journey through Italy she made the acquaintance of Signor Pasquale del Pezzo, subsequently Duke of Cajanello, a mathematician and friend of her brother, and professor in the University of Naples. Mrs. Edgren was married to the Duke of Cajanello in 1890, after the dissolution of her marriage with Mr. Edgren. After this event she published a romance which attracted a great deal of attention, called 'Kvinlighet och Erotik' (Womanliness and Erotics), 1890, and among others the drama 'Familjelycka' (Domestic Happiness), and 'En Räddende Engel' (A Rescuing Angel), with which last she achieved her greatest dramatic success. Her last work was a biography of her intimate friend Sónya Kovalévsky. While in the midst of her literary labors, and in the fullness of her powers, she died suddenly at Naples, October 21st, 1893.

The subjects of her writings are the deepest questions of life. Her special theme is the relation between men and women, and in her studies of the question she has given to the world a series of types of wonderful vividness and accuracy. The life that she knows best is the social life of the upper classes; and in all her work, but particularly in her dramas, she treats its problems with a masculine vigor and strength. Realism sometimes overshadows poetry, but the faithfulness of her work is beyond question.

OPEN SESAME

"IT WAS once upon a time"—so the fairy stories begin.
At that particular time there was a government clerk, not precisely young, and a little moth-eaten in appearance, who was on his way home from the office the day after his wedding.

On the wedding day itself he had also sat in the office and written until three o'clock. After this he had gone out, and as usual eaten his frugal midday meal at an unpretending restaurant in a narrow street, and then had gone home to his upper chamber in an old house in the Österlånggata, in order to get his somewhat worn dress coat, which had done good and faithful service for twelve years. He had speculated a good deal about buying a new coat for his wedding day, but had at last arrived at the conclusion that, all in all, it would be a superfluous luxury.

The bride was a telegraph operator, somewhat weakly, and nervous from labor and want, and of rather an unattractive exterior. The wedding took place in all quietness at the house of the bride's old unmarried aunt, who lived in Söder. The bride had on a black-silk dress, and the newly married pair drove home in a droschke.

So the wedding day had passed, but now it was the day after. From ten o'clock on he had sat in his office, just as on all other days. Now he was on the way home—his own home!

That was a strange feeling; indeed, it was such an overpowering feeling that he stood still many times on the way and fell into a brown study.

A memory of childhood came into his mind.

He saw himself as a little boy, sitting at his father's desk in the little parsonage, reading fairy tales. How many times had he read, again and again, his favorite story out of the Arabian Nights of 'Ali Baba and the Forty Thieves!' How his heart had beaten in longing suspense, when he stood with the hero of the story outside the closed door of the mountain and called, first gently and a little anxiously, afterwards loudly and boldly: "Sesame, Sesame! Open Sesame!"

And when the mountain opened its door, what splendor! The poor room of the parsonage was transformed into the rich treasure chamber of the mountain, and round about on the walls gleamed the most splendid jewels. There were, besides horses and carriages, beautifully rigged ships, weapons, armor—all the

best that a child's fantasy could dream. His old father looked
in astonishment at his youngest child, it was so long since he
himself had been a child, and all the others were already grown
up. He did not understand him, but asked him half reprovingly
what he was thinking about, that his eyes glistened so.

Thus he also came to think about his youth, about his student
years at Upsala. He was a poet, a singer; he had the name of
being greatly gifted, and stood high in his comrades' estimation.
What if any one had told him at that time that he should end as
a petty government clerk, be married to a telegraph operator,
and live in the Repslagaregata in Söder! Bah! Life had a
thousand possibilities. The future's perspective was illimitable.
Nothing was impossible. No honor was so great that he could
not attain it; no woman so beautiful that he could not win her.
What did it signify that he was poor, that he was only named
Andersson, and that he was the eighth child of a poor parson,
who himself was peasant-born? Had not most of the nation's
gifted men sprung from the ranks of the people? Yes, his en-
dowments, they were the magic charm, the "Open Sesame!"
which were to admit him to all the splendors of life.

As to how things, later on, had gone with him, he did not
allow himself to think. Either his endowments had not been as
great as he had believed, or the difficulties of living had stifled
them, or fortune had not been with him: enough, it had hap-
pened to him as to Ali Baba's wicked brother Casim, who stood
inside the mountain only to find out to his horror that he had
forgotten the magic charm, and in the anguish of death beat
about in his memory to recall it. That was a cruel time—but
it was not worth while now to think about it longer.

Rapidly one thought followed upon another in his mind. Now
he came to think upon the crown princess, who had made a royal
entrance into the capital just at this time. He had received per-
mission to accompany his superiors and stand in the festal pavil-
ion when she landed. That was a glorious moment. The poet's
gifts of his youth were not far from awakening again in the
exaltation of the moment; and had he still been the young
applauding poet of earlier days, instead of the neglected govern-
ment clerk, he would probably have written a festal poem and
sent it to the Post.

For it was fine to be the Princess Victoria at that moment.
It was one of the occasions that life has not many of. To be

nineteen years old, newly married to a young husband, loved and loving, and to make a ceremonious entry into one's future capital, which is in festal array and lies fabulously beautiful in the autumn sun, to be greeted with shouts of joy by countless masses of men, and to be so inexperienced in life that one has no presentiment of the shadows which hide themselves back of this bright picture — yes, that might indeed be an unforgettable moment; one of those that only fall to the lot of few mortals, so that they seem to belong more to the world of fable than to reality! Had the magic charm, "Open Sesame!" conjured up anything more beautiful?

And yet! yet!— The government clerk had neared his home and stood in front of his own door. No, the crown prince was surely not happier when he led his bride into his rejoicing capital, than was he at this moment. He had found again the long-lost magic charm. The little knob there on the door — that was his "Open Sesame!" He needed only to press upon it, when the mountain would again open its treasures to him — not weapons and gleaming armor as in his childhood — not honors and homage and social position as in his youth — no, something better than all these. Something that forms the kernel itself of all human happiness, upon the heights of life as well as in its most concealed hiding-places — a heart that only beat for him, his own home, where there was one who longed for him — a wife! Yes, a wife whom he loved, not with the first passion of youth, but with the tenderness and faithfulness of manhood.

He stood outside his own door; he was tired and hungry, and his wife waited for him at the midday meal; that was, to be sure, commonplace and unimportant — and yet it was so wonderfully new and attractive.

Gently, cautiously as a child who had been given a new plaything, he pressed upon the little knob on the door — and then he stood still with restrained breath and listened for the light quick step that approached.

It was just as though in his childhood he stood outside the mountain and called, first gently and half in fear, and then loudly and with a voice trembling with glad expectation, "Sesame, Sesame! Open Sesame!"

Translated for 'A Library of the World's Best Literature,' by William H. Carpenter

A BALL IN HIGH LIFE

From 'A Rescuing Angel'

THE counselor's wife sat down on the sofa with her hands folded in her lap. Arla remained standing a little farther away, so that the green lamp-shade left her face in shadow.

"My little girl," began her mother in a mild voice, "do not feel hurt, but I must make a few remarks on your behavior to-night. First of all, you will have to hold yourself a little straighter when you dance. This tendency to droop the head looks very badly. I noticed it especially when you danced with Captain Lagerskiöld — and do you know, it looked almost as if you were leaning your head against his shoulder."

Arla blushed; she did not know why, but this reproach hurt her deeply.

"The dancing-teacher always said that to dance well one must lean toward one's partner," she objected in a raised voice.

"If that is so, it is better not to dance so well," answered her mother seriously. "And another thing. I heard you ask Mr. Örn to excuse you. And you danced the cotillon after all."

"I suppose one has a right to dance with whom one pleases."

"One never has a right to hurt others; and besides, you said to Mr. Örn that you were tired out and not able to dance again. How could you then immediately after — "

"Captain Lagerskiöld leads so well," she said, lifting her head, and her mother saw that her eyes were shining. "To dance with him is no exertion."

Her mother seemed inclined to say something, but hesitated.

"Come a little nearer," she said. "Let me look at you."

Arla came up, knelt down on a footstool, hid her face in her mother's dress, and began to cry softly.

"I shall have to tell you, then," said her mother, smoothing her hair. "Poor child, don't give yourself up to these dreams. Captain Lagerskiöld is the kind of a man that I should have preferred never to have asked to our house. He is a man entirely without character and principles — to be frank, a bad man."

Arla raised her tear-stained face quickly.

"I know that," she said almost triumphantly. "He told me so himself."

Her mother was silent with astonishment, and Arla continued, rising, "He has never had any parents nor any home, but has always been surrounded with temptations. And," she went on in a lower voice, "he has never found any one that he could really love, and it is only through love that he can be rescued from the dark powers that have ruled his life."

She repeated almost word for word what he had said. He had expressed himself in so commonplace a way, and she was so far from suspecting what his confession really meant, that she would not have been able to clothe them in her own words. She had only a vague impression that he was unhappy and sinful — and that she should save him. Sinful was to her a mere abstract idea: everybody was full of sin, and his sin was very likely that he lived without God. He had perhaps never learned to pray, and maybe he never went to church or took the communion. She knew that there were men who never did. And then perhaps he had been engaged to Cecilia, and had broken the engagement when he saw that he did not really love her.

"And all this he has told you already!" exclaimed her mother, when she got over her first surprise. "Well then, I can also guess what he said further. Do you want me to tell you? You are the first girl he has really loved — you are to be his rescuing angel —"

Arla made a faint exclamation.

"You do not suppose I have been listening?" asked her mother. "I know it without that; men like this always speak so when they want to win an innocent girl. When I was young I had an admirer of this kind — that is not an uncommon experience."

Not uncommon! These words were not said to her only; other men had said the same before this to other young girls! Oh! but not in the same way, at any rate! thought Arla. As he had said them — with such a look — such a voice — no, nobody else could ever have done that.

"And you didn't understand that a man who can make a young girl a declaration of love the first time he sees her must be superficial and not to be trusted?" continued her mother.

"Mamma does not know what love is," thought Arla. "She does not know that it is born in a moment and lasts for life. She has of course never loved papa; then they would not be so matter-of-fact now."

"And what did you answer?" asked her mother.

Arla turned away. "I answered nothing," she said in a low voice.

The mother's troubled face grew a little brighter.

"That was right," she said, patting her on the cheek. "Then you left him at once."

Arla was on the point of saying, "Not at once," but she could not make this confession. Other questions would then follow, and she would be obliged to describe what had happened. Describe a scene like this to her mother, who did not know what love was! That was impossible! So she said yes, but in so weak and troubled a voice that her mother at once saw it was not true. This was not Arla's first untruth; on the contrary, she had often been guilty of this fault when a child. She was so shy and loving that she could not stand the smallest reproach, and a severe look was enough to make her cry; consequently she was always ready to deny as soon as she had made the slightest mistake. But when her mother took her face between her hands and looked straight into her eyes, she saw at once how matters stood, for the eyes could hide nothing. And since Arla grew older she had fought so much against this weakness that she had almost exaggerated her truthfulness. She was now as quick to confess what might bring displeasure on herself, as if she were afraid of giving temptation the slightest room.

The mother, who with deep joy had noticed her many little victories over herself, was painfully impressed by this relapse. She could not now treat Arla as she had done when she was a little girl. Instead of this, she opened the Bible by one of the many book-marks, with a somewhat trembling hand.

"Although it is late, shall we not read a chapter together, as we always do before we go to bed?" she asked, and looked up at her daughter.

Arla stepped back, and cast an almost frightened glance at the little footstool where she had been sitting at her mother's knee every evening since she was a little girl. All this seemed now so strange — it was no longer herself, it was a little younger sister, who used to sit there and confess to her mother all her dreams and all her little sorrows.

"I don't want to — I cannot read to-night."

Her mother laid the book down again, gave her daughter a mild, sad look and said, "Then remember, my child, that this was the consequence of your first ball."

Arla bent her head and left the room slowly. Her mother let her go: she found it wisest to leave her to herself until her emotion had somewhat worn itself out.   Arla would not go into her own room; she dreaded Gurli's chatter; she had to be alone to get control over her thoughts.   In the drawing-room she found her father.

"Is mamma in her room?" he asked.

"Yes."

"Is she alone?   Are the children asleep?"

"Yes, mamma is alone."

"Well!   Good-night, my girl."   He kissed her lips and went into the bedroom.

Arla opened a window in the drawing-room to let out the hot air, and then began to walk up and down wrapped in a large shawl, enjoying the clear cold winter moonlight, which played over the snow and hid itself behind the trees in the park outside the window.   There they were to meet to-morrow!   Oh, if only he had said now, at once!   If only she could slip out now in her thin gown, and he could wrap his cape around her to keep her warm — she did not remember that the men of to-day did not wear capes like Romeo — and if then they could have gone away together — far, far away from this prosaic world, where nobody understood that two hearts could meet and find each other from the first moment.

She was not left alone long; a door was opened, light steps came tripping, and a white apparition in night-gown stood in the full light of the moonbeam.

"But Arla, are you never, never coming?"

"Why, Gurli dear, why aren't you asleep long ago?"

"Eh? do you think I can sleep before I have heard something about the ball?   Come in now; how cold it is here!"

She was so cold that she shivered in her thin night-gown, but clung nevertheless to her sister, who was standing by the window.

"Go; you are catching cold."

"I don't care," she said, chattering.   "I am not going till you come."

Arla was, as usual, obliged to give in to the younger sister's strong will.   She closed the window and they went into their room, where Gurli crept into bed again and drew the cover up to her very chin.   Arla began to unfasten her dress and take the flowers out of her hair.

"Well, I suppose you had a divine time," came a voice from the bed behind chattering teeth.   There was nothing to be seen of Gurli but a pair of impatient dark eyes, under a wilderness of brown hair.

Arla was sitting at the toilet-table, her back to her sister.

"Oh yes," she said.

"I see on your card that you danced two dances with Captain Lagerskiöld. I suppose he dances awfully well, eh?"

"Do you know him?" asked Arla, and turned on the chair.

"Oh yes, I do. Didn't he ask for me?"

"Yes, now I remember. He said he had seen you with the children on the coasting-hill. You must have been a little rude to him?"

The whole head came out above the cover now.

"Rude! how?"

"He said something about your being so pert."

"Pert? Oh, *what* a fib you do tell!" cried Gurli, and sat up in bed with a jump.

"I don't usually tell stories," said Arla with wounded dignity, but blushed at the same time.

"Oh yes, you do now, I am sure you do. I don't believe you, if you don't tell me word for word what he said. Who began talking of me? And what did he say? And what did you say?"

"You had better tell me why you are so much interested in him," said Arla in the somewhat superior tone of the elder sister.

"That is none of your business. I will tell you that I am no longer a little girl, as you seem to think. And even though I am treated like a child here at home, there are others who— who—"

"Are you not a child?" said Arla. "You are not confirmed yet."

"Oh, is that it? That 'confirmation' is only a ceremony, which I submit to for mamma's sake. And don't imagine that it is confirmation which makes women of us; no indeed, it is something else."

"What then?" asked Arla, much surprised.

"It is—it is—love," burst out Gurli, and hid her head under the covers.

"Love! But Gurli, how you do talk! What do you know about that? You, a little schoolgirl!"

"Don't say 'little schoolgirl'—that makes me furious," cried Gurli, as she pushed the cover aside with both hands and jumped out on the floor. "Then you are much more of a schoolgirl than I. Is there perhaps any man who has told you that he loves you? Is there?"

"Oh, but Gurli, what nonsense," said Arla laughing outright. "Has really one of Arvid's friends —"

"Arvid's friends!" repeated Gurli with an expression of indescribable contempt. "Do you think such little boys would dare? Ph! I would give them a box on the ear,— that would be the quickest way of getting rid of such little whipper-snappers. No indeed; it is a man, a real *man* — a man that any girl would envy me."

She was so pretty as she stood there in her white gown, with her dancing eyes and thick hair standing like a dark cloud around her rosy young face, that a light broke on Arla, and a suspicion of the truth flashed through her mind.

"It is not possible that you mean — of course you don't mean — him — that you just spoke of — Captain Lagerskiöld?"

"And what if it *were* he!" cried Gurli, who in her triumph forgot to keep her secret. Arla's usual modest self-possession left her completely at this news.

"Captain Lagerskiöld has told you that he loves you!" she cried with a sharp and cutting voice, unlike her usual mild tone. "Oh, how wicked, how wicked!"

She hid her face in her hands and burst out crying.

Gurli was frightened at her violent outbreak. She must have done something awful, that Arla, who was always so quiet, should carry on so. She crept close up to her sister, half ashamed and half frightened, and whispered:— "He has only said it once. It was the day before yesterday, and I ran away from him at once — I thought it was so silly, and —"

"Day before yesterday!" cried Arla and looked up with frightened, wondering eyes. "Day before yesterday he told you that he loved you?"

"Yes; if only you will not be so awfully put out, I will tell you all about it. He used to come up to the coasting-hill a great deal lately, and then we walked up and down in the park and talked, and when I wanted to coast he helped me get a start, and drew my sleigh up-hill again. At first I did not notice him much, but then I saw he was very nice — he would look at me sometimes for a long, long time — and you can't imagine how he does look at one! And then day before yesterday he began by saying that I had such pretty eyes — and then he said that such a happy little sunbeam as I could light up his whole life, and that if he could not meet me, he would not know what to do — "

"Gurli!" cried Arla, and grasped her sister's arm violently. "Do you love him?"

Gurli let her eyes wander a little, and looked shy.

"I think I do — I have read in the novels Arvid borrowed in school — only don't tell mamma anything about it; but I have read that when you are in love you always have such an awful palpitation of the heart when *he* comes — and when I merely catch sight of him far off on the hill in Kommandörsgatan, I felt as if I should strangle."

"Captain Lagerskiöld is a bad, bad man!" sobbed Arla, and rushed out of the room, hiding her face in her hands.

The counselor's wife was still up and was reading, while her husband had gone to bed. A tall screen standing at the foot of the bed kept the light away from the sleeper. The counselor had just had a talk with his wife, which most likely would keep her awake for the greater part of the night; but he had fallen asleep as soon as he had spoken to the point.

"You must forgive me that I cannot quite approve your way of fulfilling your duties as hostess," he had said when he came in to her.

His wife crossed her hands on the table and looked up at him with a mild and patient face.

"You show your likes and dislikes too much," he continued, "and think too little of the claims of social usage. For instance, to pay so much attention to Mrs. Ekström and her daughters — "

"It was because nobody else paid any attention to them."

"But even so, my dear, a drawing-room is not a charity institution, I take it. Etiquette goes before everything else. And then you were almost rude to Admiral Hornfeldt's wife, who is one of the first women in society."

"Forgive me; but I cannot be cordial to a woman for whom I have no respect."

The counselor shrugged his shoulders with a gesture of great impatience.

"I wish you could learn to see how wrong it is to let yourself be influenced by these moral views in society."

His wife was silent; it was her usual way of ending a conversation which she knew could lead to no result, since each kept his own opinion after all.

"Did you notice Arla?" asked the counselor.

"Yes. Why?"

"Did you not see that she made herself conspicuous by taking such an interest in this outlived Lagerskiöld?"

"I asked you not to invite Captain Lagerskiöld," said his wife mildly.

"The trouble is not there," interrupted her husband; "but the trouble is that your daughter is brought up to be a goose who understands nothing. That is the result of your convent system. Girls so guarded are always ready to fall into the arms of the first man who knows somewhat how to impress them."

This was the counselor's last remark before he fell asleep. It awakened a feeling of great bitterness and hopelessness in his wife. Her heart felt heavy at the thought of all the frivolity, all the impurity into which her girls were to be thrown one after another. When Arla, in whose earnestness and purity of character she had so great a confidence, had shown herself so little proof against temptation, what then would become of Gurli, who had such dangerous tendencies? And the two little ones who were now sleeping soundly in the nursery?

"To what use is then all the striving and all the prayers?" she asked herself. "What good then does it do to try to protect the children from evil, if just this makes them more of a prey to temptation?"

She laid her arms on the table and rested her forehead on her hands. The awful question "What is the use of it? what is the use of it?" lay heavy upon her.

Then there came a soft knock at her door; it was opened a little, and a timid voice whispered, "Is mamma alone? May I come in?"

A ray of happiness came into the mother's face.

"Come in, my child," she whispered, and stretched out her hands toward her. "Papa sleeps so soundly, you need not be afraid of waking him."

Arla came in on tiptoe, dressed in white gown and dressing-sack and with her hair loose. There were red spots on her cheeks, and her eyes were swollen from crying. She knelt down gently beside her mother, hid her face in her mother's dress, and whispered in a voice trembling with suppressed tears, "Will you read to me now, mamma?"

Translated for 'A Library of the World's Best Literature,' by Olga Flinch

JONATHAN EDWARDS

(1703–1758)

BY EGBERT C. SMYTH

PROBABLY for most persons the influence of Edwards will longest survive through his wonderful personality. "From the days of Plato," says a writer in the Westminster Review, "there has been no life of more simple and imposing grandeur." There are four memoirs. The earliest is from Samuel Hopkins, D. D., a pupil and intimate friend. It "has the quaint charm of Walton's Lives." The second, by Sereno Edwards Dwight, D. D., is much more complete. He first brought to light the remarkable early papers on topics in physics, natural history, and philosophy. Dr. Samuel Miller's, in Sparks's 'Library of American Biography,' is mainly a brief compend. The latest Life is by Professor Alexander V. E. Allen, D. D. It endeavors to show "what he [Edwards] thought, and how he came to think as he did," and is an interesting and important contribution to a critical study of his works. There is still need of an adequate biography, which can only be written in connection with a thorough study of the manuscripts. A

JONATHAN EDWARDS

more full and critical edition of Edwards's writings is also much to be desired.

Edwards's first publication (1731) was a sermon preached in Boston on 'God Glorified in Man's Dependence.' The conditions under which it was produced afford striking contrasts to those attendant upon Schleiermacher's epoch-making 'Reden über Religion'; but the same note of absolute dependence upon God is struck by each with masterly power. A yet more characteristic and deeply spiritual utterance was given in the next published discourse, entitled 'A Divine and Supernatural Light Immediately Imparted to the Soul by the Spirit of God, Shown to be both a Scriptural and Rational Doctrine' (1734). These two sermons are of primary significance for a right understanding of their author's teaching. All is of God; faith is sensibleness of what is real in the work of redemption; this reality

is divinely and transcendently excellent; this quality of it is revealed
to the soul by the Holy Spirit, and becomes the spring of all holi-
ness. "The central idea of his system," says Henry B. Smith, "is
that of spiritual life (holy love) as the gift of divine grace." All of
Edwards's other writings may be arranged in relation to this princi-
ple,—as introductory, explicative, or defensive.

When the sermon on the 'Reality of Spiritual Light' was delivered,
the movement had begun which, as afterwards extended from North-
ampton to many communities in New England and beyond, is known
as "The Great Awakening." The preaching of Edwards was a promi-
nent instrumentality in its origination, and he became its most effect-
ive promoter and champion, and no less its watchful observer and
critic. Among the published (1738) sermons which it occasioned
should be specially mentioned those on 'Justification by Faith Alone,'
'The Justice of God in the Damnation of Sinners,' 'The Excellency
of Jesus Christ,' 'The Distinguishing Marks of a Work of the Spirit
of God, applied to that uncommon operation that has lately appeared
on the minds of many of the people of New England: with a partic-
ular consideration of the extraordinary circumstances with which this
work is attended' (1741). The same year (1741) appeared the sermon
on 'Sinners in the Hands of an Angry God.' Some five years previ-
ous, moved by the notice taken in London by Dr. Watts and Dr.
Guise of the religious revival in Northampton and several other
towns, and by a special request from Rev. Dr. Colman of Boston,
Edwards prepared a careful 'Narrative,' which, with a preface by
the English clergymen just named, was published in London in 1737,
and the year following in Boston. The sermon on the 'Distinguish-
ing Marks of a Work of the True Spirit of God' was followed by the
treatise entitled 'Some Thoughts Concerning the Present Revival of
Religion, and the way in which it ought to be acknowledged and pro-
moted' (1742); and four years later, by the elaborate work on 'Re-
ligious Affections.' The latter sums up all that Edwards had learned,
through his participation in the movement whose beginnings and
early stages are described in the 'Narrative,' and by his long-con-
tinued and most earnest endeavor to determine the true hopes of the
spiritual life which had enlisted and well-nigh absorbed all the pow-
ers of his mind and soul. It is a religious classic of the highest
order, yet, like the 'De Imitatione Christi,' suited only to those who
can read it with independent insight. They who can thus use it will
find it inexhaustible in its strenuous discipline and spiritual richness,
light, and sweetness. Its chief defect lies in its failure to discover
and unfold the true relation between the natural and the spiritual,
and to recognize the stages of Christian growth, the genuineness and
value of what is still "imperfect Christianity."

The "revival," with the endeavor to discover and apply the tests of a true Christian life, brought into prominence as a practical issue the old question of the proper requirements for church membership. The common practice failed to emphasize the necessity of spiritual regeneration and conversion, as upheld by Edwards and his followers. The controversy became acute at Northampton, and combined with other issues, resulted in his dismissal from his pastorate. His meek yet lofty bearing during this season of partisan strife and bitter animosity has commanded general admiration. Before he closed the contest he published two works which, in the Congregational churches, settled the question at issue in accordance with his principles — viz., 'An Humble Inquiry into the Rules of the Word of God concerning the Qualifications requisite to a Complete Standing and Full Communion in the Visible Christian Church,' and 'Misrepresentations Corrected and Truth Vindicated in a Reply to the Rev. Solomon Williams's Book,' etc.

The reply to Williams was written and published after Edwards's removal to Stockbridge. The period of his residence there (1751-1758, January) was far from tranquil. His conscientious resistance to schemes of pecuniary profit in the management of the Indian Mission there, brought upon him bitter opposition. For six months he was severely ill. In the French and Indian war a frontier town like Stockbridge was peculiarly exposed to alarm and danger. Yet at this time Edwards prepared the treatises on the 'Freedom of the Will,' the 'Ultimate End of Creation,' the 'Nature of Virtue,' and 'Original Sin.' The first was published in 1754, the others after his death (1758), as were many of his sermons, the 'History of Redemption,' and extracts from his note-book ('Miscellaneous Observations,' 'Miscellaneous Remarks'). Early in 1758, having accepted the presidency of the College of New Jersey, he removed to Princeton, where he died March 22d.

That with enfeebled health, and under the conditions of his life at Stockbridge, he should have prepared such works as those just enumerated, is a striking evidence of his intellectual discipline and power. It would probably have been impossible even for him, but for the practice he had observed from youth of committing his thoughts to writing, and their concentration on the subjects handled in these treatises. A careful study of his manuscript notes would probably be of service for new and critical editions, and would seem to be especially appropriate, since only the work on the 'Freedom of the Will' was published by its author.

It is impossible in the space of this sketch to analyze these elaborate treatises, or to attempt a critical estimate of their value. Foregoing this endeavor, I will simply add a few suggestions occasioned principally by some recent studies, either of the originals or copies of unpublished manuscripts.

Edwards's published works consist of compositions prepared with reference to some immediate practical aim. When called to Princeton he hesitated to accept, lest he should be interrupted in the preparation of "a body of divinity in an entire new method, being thrown into the form of a history." It was on his "mind and heart," "long ago begun," "a great work." The beginnings of it are preserved in the 'History of Redemption' posthumously published, but this was written as early as 1739, as a series of sermons, and without thought of publication. The volume of miscellanies, also published after his death, are extracts from his note-book, arranged by the editor. Nowhere has Edwards himself given a systematic exposition of his conception of Christianity. The incompleteness of even the fullest edition of his works increases the liability of misconstruction. It would not be suspected, for instance, to what extent his mind dealt with the conception of God as triune, or with the Incarnation.

His published works show on their face his relation to the religious questions uppermost in men's minds during his lifetime. "He that would know," writes Mr. Bancroft, "the workings of the New England mind in the middle of the last century and the throbbings of its heart, must give his days and nights to the study of Jonathan Edwards." And Professor Allen justly adds, "He that would understand . . . the significance of later New England thought, must make Edwards the first object of his study." Besides these high claims to attention, one more may be made. The greatness of Edwards's character implies a contact of his mind with permanent and the highest truth — a profound knowledge and consciousness of God. Human and therefore imperfect, colored by inherited prepossessions, and run into some perishable molds, his thought is pervaded by a spiritual insight which has an original and undying worth. It is not unlikely that the future will assign him a higher rank than the past.

In one of the earliest, if not the first of his private philosophical papers, the essay entitled 'Of Being,' may be found the key to his fundamental conceptions. An exposition of his system, wrought out from this point of view, will show that he has a secure and eminent position among those who have contributed to that spiritual apprehension of nature and man, of matter and mind, of the universe and God, which has ever marked the thinking and influence of the finest spirits and highest teachers of our race.

Edwards was born October 5th, 1703, in East Windsor, Connecticut. He was the son of Rev. Timothy and Esther Stoddard Edwards; was graduated at Yale College in 1720; studied theology at New Haven; from August 1722 to March 1723 preached in New York; from 1724

to 1726 was a tutor at Yale; on the 15th of February, 1727, was or-
dained at Northampton, Massachusetts; in 1750 was dismissed from
the church there, and in 1751 removed to Stockbridge, Massachusetts.
He was called to Princeton in 1757, and died there March 22d, 1758.

Egbert C. Smyth.

FROM NARRATIVE OF HIS RELIGIOUS HISTORY

FROM about that time I began to have a new kind of appre-
hensions and ideas of Christ, and the work of redemption,
and the glorious way of salvation by him. An inward
sweet sense of these things at times came into my heart, and
my soul was led away in pleasant views and contemplations of
them. And my mind was greatly engaged to spend my time
in reading and meditating on Christ, on the beauty and excel-
lency of his person, and the lovely way of salvation by free grace
in him. . . .

Not long after I first began to experience these things, I gave
an account to my father of some things that had passed in my
mind. I was pretty much affected by the discourse we had
together; and when the discourse was ended I walked abroad
alone, in a solitary place in my father's pasture, for contempla-
tion. And as I was walking there and looking upon the sky and
clouds, there came into my mind so sweet a sense of the glori-
ous majesty and grace of God as I know not how to express. I
seemed to see them both in a sweet conjunction; majesty and
meekness joined together: it was a sweet, and gentle, and holy
majesty; and also a majestic meekness; an awful sweetness; a
high, and great, and holy gentleness.

After this my sense of divine things gradually increased, and
became more and more lively, and had more of that inward
sweetness. The appearance of everything was altered; there
seemed to be, as it were, a calm, sweet cast, or appearance of
divine glory, in almost everything. God's excellency, his wisdom,
his purity and love, seemed to appear in everything; in the sun,
moon, and stars, in the clouds and blue sky, in the grass, flowers,

trees, in the water and all nature; which used greatly to fix my mind. I often used to sit and view the moon for a long time, and in the day spent much time in viewing the clouds and sky, to behold the sweet glory of God in these things; in the meantime singing forth, with a low voice, my contemplations of the Creator and Redeemer. And scarce anything among all the works of nature was so sweet to me as thunder and lightning; formerly nothing had been so terrible to me. Before, I used to be uncommonly terrified with thunder, and to be struck with terror when I saw a thunder-storm rising; but now, on the contrary, it rejoiced me. I felt God, if I may so speak, at the first appearance of a thunder-storm; and used to take the opportunity at such times to fix myself in order to view the clouds and see the lightnings play and hear the majestic and awful voice of God's thunder, which oftentimes was exceedingly entertaining, leading me to sweet contemplations of my great and glorious God. While thus engaged it always seemed natural for me to sing or chant forth my meditations, or to speak my thoughts in soliloquies with a singing voice.

My sense of divine things seemed gradually to increase, till I went to preach at New York, which was about a year and a half after they began; and while I was there I felt them very sensibly, in a much higher degree than I had done before. My longings after God and holiness were much increased. . . .

Holiness, as I then wrote down some of my contemplations on it, appeared to me to be of a sweet, pleasant, charming, serene, calm nature, which brought an inexpressible purity, brightness, peacefulness, and ravishment to the soul. In other words, that it made the soul like a field or garden of God, with all manner of pleasant flowers; enjoying a sweet calm and the gently vivifying beams of the sun. The soul of a true Christian, as I then wrote my meditations, appeared like such a little white flower as we see in the spring of the year; low and humble on the ground, opening its bosom to receive the pleasant beams of the sun's glory; rejoicing as it were in a calm rapture; diffusing around a sweet fragrancy; standing peacefully and lovingly in the midst of other flowers round about; all in like manner opening their bosoms, to drink in the light of the sun. There was no part of creature-holiness, that I had so great a sense of its loveliness, as humility, brokenness of heart, and poverty of spirit; and there was nothing that I so earnestly longed for. My heart panted after this — to lie low before God, as in the dust; that I might be nothing, and that God might be All; that I might become as a little child.

RESOLUTIONS

"Resolved, Never to do any manner of thing, whether in soul or body, less or more, but what tends to the glory of God; nor be nor suffer it, if I can possibly avoid it."

"Resolved, To live with all my might while I do live."

"Resolved, When I think of any theorem in divinity to be solved, immediately to do what I can towards solving it, if circumstances do not hinder."

"Resolved, To endeavor to my utmost to deny whatever is not most agreeable to a good and universally sweet and benevolent, quiet, peaceable, contented and easy, compassionate and generous, humble and meek, submissive and obliging, diligent and industrious, charitable and even, patient, moderate, forgiving and sincere temper; and to do at all times what such a temper would lead me to; and to examine strictly, at the end of every week, whether I have so done."

"On the supposition that there was never to be but one individual in the world, at any one time, who was properly a complete Christian, in all respects of a right stamp, having Christianity always shining in its true lustre, and appearing excellent and lovely, from whatever part and under whatever character viewed: Resolved, To act just as I would do, if I strive with all my might to be that one, who should live in my time."

"I observe that old men seldom have any advantage of new discoveries, because they are beside the way of thinking to which they have been so long used: Resolved, If ever I live to years, that I will be impartial to hear the reasons of all pretended discoveries, and receive them if rational, how long soever I have been used to another way of thinking. My time is so short that I have not time to perfect myself in all studies: Wherefore resolved, to omit and put off all but the most important and needful studies."

WRITTEN ON A BLANK LEAF IN 1723

THEY say there is a young lady [in New Haven] who is beloved of that Great Being who made and rules the world, and that there are certain seasons in which this Great Being, in some way or other invisible, comes to her and fills her mind with exceeding sweet delight, and that she hardly cares for anything except to meditate on him — that she expects after a while to be received up where he is, to be raised up out of the world and caught up into heaven; being assured that he loves her too well to let her remain at a distance from him always. There she is to dwell with him, and to be ravished with his love and delight forever. Therefore, if you present all the world before her, with the richest of its treasures, she disregards it and cares not for it, and is unmindful of any pain or affliction. She has a strange sweetness in her mind, and singular purity in her affections; is most just and conscientious in all her conduct; and you could not persuade her to do anything wrong or sinful, if you would give her all the world, lest she should offend this Great Being. She is of a wonderful sweetness, calmness, and universal benevolence of mind; especially after this great God has manifested himself to her mind. She will sometimes go about from place to place, singing sweetly; and seems to be always full of joy and pleasure; and no one knows for what. She loves to be alone, walking in the fields and groves, and seems to have some one invisible always conversing with her.

THE IDEA OF NOTHING

From 'Of Being'

A STATE of absolute nothing is a state of absolute contradiction. Absolute nothing is the aggregate of all the absurd contradictions in the world; a state wherein there is neither body nor spirit, nor space, neither empty space nor full space, neither little nor great, narrow nor broad, neither infinitely great space nor finite space, nor a mathematical point, neither up nor down, neither north nor south (I do not mean as it is with respect to the body of the earth or some other great body, but no contrary point nor positions or directions), no such thing as either here or there, this way or that way, or only one way. When we go about to form an idea of perfect nothing we must shut out all these things; we must shut out of our minds both space that has something in it, and space that has nothing in it. We must not allow ourselves to think of the least part of space, never so small. Nor must we suffer our thoughts to take sanctuary in a mathematical point. When we go to expel body out of our thoughts, we must cease not to leave empty space in the room of it; and when we go to expel emptiness from our thoughts, we must not think to squeeze it out by anything close, hard, and solid, but we must think of the same that the sleeping rocks dream of; and not till then shall we get a complete idea of nothing.

THE NOTION OF ACTION AND AGENCY ENTERTAINED BY MR. CHUBB AND OTHERS

From the 'Inquiry into the Freedom of the Will,' Part iv., §2

So that according to their notion of the act, considered with regard to its consequences, these following things are all essential to it: viz., That it should be necessary, and not necessary; that it should be from a cause, and no cause; that it should be the fruit of choice and design, and not the fruit of choice and design; that it should be the beginning of motion or exertion, and yet consequent on previous exertion; that it should be before it is; that it should spring immediately out of indifference and equilibrium, and yet be the effect of preponderation; that it should be self-originated, and also have its original from something else; that it is what the mind causes itself, of its own will, and can produce or prevent according to its choice or pleasure, and yet what the mind has no power to prevent, precluding all previous choice in the affair.

So that an act, according to their metaphysical notion of it, is something of which there is no idea. . . . If some learned philosopher who had been abroad, in giving an account of the curious observations he had made in his travels, should say he had been in Tierra del Fuego, and there had seen an animal, which he calls by a certain name, that begat and brought forth itself, and yet had a sire and dam distinct from itself; that it had an appetite and was hungry, before it had a being; that his master, who led him and governed him at his pleasure, was always governed by him and driven by him where he pleased; that

when he moved he always took a step before the first step; that
he went with his head first, and yet always went tail foremost;
and this though he had neither head nor tail: it would be no
impudence at all to tell such a traveler, though a learned man,
that he himself had no idea of such an animal as he gave an
account of, and never had, nor ever would have.

EXCELLENCY OF CHRIST

WHEN we behold a beautiful body, a lovely proportion and
beautiful harmony of features, delightful airs of counte-
nance and voice, and sweet motions and gestures, we are
charmed with it, not under the notion of a corporeal but a men-
tal beauty. For if there could be a statue that should have ex-
actly the same, that could be made to have the same sounds and
the same motions precisely, we should not be so delighted with
it, we should not fall entirely in love with the image, if we knew
certainly that it had no perception or understanding. The reason
is, we are apt to look upon this agreeableness, those airs, to be
emanations of perfections of the mind, and immediate effects of
internal purity and sweetness. Especially it is so when we love
the person for the airs of voice, countenance, and gesture, which
have much greater power upon us than barely colors and propor-
tion of dimensions. And it is certainly because there is an analogy
between such a countenance and such airs and those excellencies
of the mind,—a sort of I know not what in them that is agree-
able, and does consent with such mental perfections; so that we
cannot think of such habitudes of mind without having an idea
of them at the same time. Nor can it be only from custom; for
the same dispositions and actings of mind naturally beget such
kind of airs of countenance and gesture, otherwise they never
would have come into custom. I speak not here of the cere-
monies of conversation and behavior, but of those simple and
natural motions and airs. So it appears, because the same habi-
tudes and actings of mind do beget [airs and movements] in gen-
eral the same amongst all nations, in all ages.

And there is really likewise an analogy or consent between
the beauty of the skies, trees, fields, flowers, etc., and spiritual
excellencies, though the agreement be more hid, and require a
more discerning, feeling mind to perceive it than the other.

Those have their airs, too, as well as the body and countenance of man, which have a strange kind of agreement with such mental beauties. This makes it natural in such frames of mind to think of them and fancy ourselves in the midst of them. Thus there seem to be love and complacency in flowers and bespangled meadows; this makes lovers so much delight in them. So there is a rejoicing in the green trees and fields, and majesty in thunder beyond all other noises whatever.

Now, we have shown that the Son of God created the world for this very end, to communicate himself in an image of his own excellency. He communicates himself, properly, only to spirits; and they only are capable of being proper images of his excellency, for they only are properly *beings*, as we have shown. Yet he communicates a sort of a shadow, a glimpse, of his excellencies to bodies, which, as we have shown, are but the shadows of beings, and not real beings. He who by his immediate influence gives being every moment, and by his spirit actuates the world, because he inclines to communicate himself and his excellencies, doth doubtless communicate his excellency to bodies, as far as there is any consent or analogy. And the beauty of face and sweet airs in men are not always the effect of the corresponding excellencies of mind; yet the beauties of nature are really emanations or shadows of the excellencies of the Son of God.

So that when we are delighted with flowery meadows and gentle breezes of wind, we may consider that we see only the emanations of the sweet benevolence of Jesus Christ. When we behold the fragrant rose and lily, we see this love and purity. So the green trees, and fields, and singing of birds are the emanations of his infinite joy and benignity. The easiness and naturalness of trees and vines are shadows of his beauty and loveliness. The crystal rivers and murmuring streams are the footsteps of his favor, grace, and beauty. When we behold the light and brightness of the sun, the golden edges of an evening cloud, or the beauteous bow, we behold the adumbrations of his glory and goodness; and in the blue sky, of his mildness and gentleness. There are also many things wherein we may behold his awful majesty: in the sun in his strength, in comets, in thunder, in the hovering thunder-clouds, in ragged rocks and the brows of mountains. That beauteous light with which the world is filled in a clear day is a lively shadow of his spotless holiness, and happiness, and delight, in communicating himself; and doubtless this is a reason that Christ is so often compared to those things and called by their names,—as, the Sun of Righteousness, the Morning Star, the Rose of Sharon, the Lily of the Valley, the apple-tree amongst the trees of the wood, a bundle of myrrh, a roe, or a young hart. By this we may discover the beauty of many of those metaphors and similes which to an unphilosophical person do seem so uncouth.

In like manner, when we behold the beauty of man's body in its perfection we still see like emanations of Christ's divine perfections; although they do not always flow from the mental excellencies of the person that has them. But we see far the most proper image of the beauty of Christ when we see beauty in the human soul.

Corol. I. From hence it is evident that man is in a fallen state; and that he has naturally scarcely anything of those sweet graces which are an image of those which are in Christ. For no doubt, seeing that other creatures have an image of them according to their capacity, so all the rational and intelligent part of the world once had according to theirs.

Corol. II. There will be a future state wherein man will have them according to his capacity. How great a happiness will it be in Heaven for the saints to enjoy the society of each other, since one may see so much of the loveliness of Christ in those things which are only shadows of beings. With what joy are philosophers filled in beholding the aspectable world. How sweet will it be to behold the proper image and communications of Christ's excellency in intelligent beings, having so much of the beauty of Christ upon them as Christians shall have in heaven. What beautiful and fragrant flowers will those be, reflecting all the sweetnesses of the Son of God! How will Christ delight to walk in this garden among those beds of spices, to feed in the gardens, and to gather lilies!

THE ESSENCE OF TRUE VIRTUE

From 'The Nature of True Virtue,' Chapters i, ii

TRUE virtue most essentially consists in benevolence to being in general. Or perhaps, to speak more accurately, it is that consent, propensity, and union of heart to being in general, which is immediately exercised in a general good-will. . . .

A benevolent propensity of heart to being in general, and a temper or disposition to love God supremely, are in effect the same thing. . . . However, every particular exercise of love to a creature may not *sensibly* arise from any exercise of love to God, or an explicit consideration of any similitude, conformity, union or relation to God, in the creature beloved.

The most proper evidence of love to a created being arising from that temper of mind wherein consists a supreme propensity of heart to God, seems to be the agreeableness of the kind and degree of our love to God's end in our creation, and in the creation of all things, and the coincidence of the exercises of our love, in their manner, order, and measure, with the manner in which God himself exercises love to the creature in the creation and government of the world, and the way in which God, as the first cause and supreme disposer of all things, has respect to the creature's happiness in subordination to himself as his own supreme end. For the true virtue of created beings is doubtless their highest excellency and their true goodness. . . . But the true goodness of a thing must be its agreeableness to its end, or its fitness to answer the design for which it was made. Therefore they are good moral agents whose temper of mind or propensity of heart is agreeable to the end for which God made moral agents. . . .

A truly virtuous mind . . . above all things seeks the glory of God. . . . This consists in the expression of God's perfections in their proper effects,—the manifestation of God's glory to created understandings; the communication of the infinite fullness of God to the creature; the creature's highest esteem of God, love to and joy in him; and in the proper exercises and expressions of these. And so far as virtuous mind exercises true virtue in benevolence to created beings, it chiefly seeks the good of the creature; consisting in its knowledge or view of God's glory and beauty, its union with God, uniformity and love to him, and joy in him. And that disposition of heart, that consent, union, or propensity of mind to being in general which appears chiefly in such exercises, is virtue, truly so called; or in other words, true grace and real holiness. And no other disposition or affection but this is of the nature of virtue.

GEORGES EEKHOUD

(1854-)

L A JEUNE BELGIQUE» is more than a school; it is a literary movement, which began about the year 1880. The aim of this group of writers is to found a national literature, which uses the French language and technique for the expression of the Flemish or Walloon spirit, and the peculiar sentiment and individuality of the Belgian race which has developed between the more powerful nations of France and Germany. In the words of William Sharp:—

«To one who has closely studied the whole movement in its intimate and extra-national bearings, as well as in its individual manifestations and aberrations, its particular and collective achievement in the several literary *genres*, there is no question as to the radical distinction between Belgic and French literature. Whether there be a great future for the first, is almost entirely dependent on the concurrent political condition of Belgium. If Germany were to appropriate the country, it is almost certain that only the Flemish spirit would retain its independent vitality, and even that probably only for a generation or two. But if Belgium were absorbed by France, Brussels would almost immediately become as insignificant a literary centre as is Lyons or Bordeaux, or be, at most, not more independent of Paris than is Marseilles. Literary Belgium would be a memory, within a year of the hoisting of the French tricolor from the Scheldt to the Liège. Meanwhile, the whole energy of ‹Young Belgium› is consciously or unconsciously concentrated in the effort to withstand Paris.»

Among the leading spirits of "La Jeune Belgique" are Maurice Maeterlinck, Georges Eekhoud, Camille Lemonnier, Georges Rodenbach, J. K. Huysmans, Auguste Jenart, Eugene Demolder, and a number of others, who have distinguished themselves in fiction and poetry. Their works are generally inspired by the uncompromising sense of the reality of ordinary life, which would sometimes be repulsive if it were not for their brilliant style and psychological undercurrent.

This school of literature is somewhat analogous to that of the Flemish painting. Nature is always an important accessory to the development of the action; and therefore the landscapes and the *genre* pictures are given with a rapid and sure touch and in a vivid and high key,—so high that at times the colors are almost crude. The reader of these Belgian writers often feels, in consequence, that he is looking at a series of paintings which are being explained by a narrator.

Of all these writers, Georges Eekhoud, whom Mr. Sharp calls «the Maupassant of the Low Countries,» is the one who has made the greatest effort to model his work upon the style of the contemporary French authors. He was born in Antwerp, May 27th 1854. His literary career was begun as an editor of the Precursor, in Antwerp, but he soon became associated with L'Étoile Belge as literary editor. In 1877 he published his first volume, entitled ‘Myrtes et Cyprès.’ This was succeeded by a second book of poetry, ‘Zigzags Poétiques et Pittoresques,’ which appeared in 1879. Among the most admired of these poems are ‘La Mare aux Sangues,’ ‘Nina,’ ‘Raymonne,’ and the strong ‘La Guigne.’

French critics say that his diction lacks polish, but that he has strength, color, and a talent for description. His novels are — ‘Kees Doorik’ (1884), ‘Les Kermesses’ (1884), ‘Les Milices de Saint-François’ (1886), ‘Les Nouvelles Kermesses’ (1887), and ‘La Nouvelle Carthage’ (1888). The latter is considered his most brilliant novel, and won for him the quinquennial prize of 5,000 francs given for French literature in Belgium. It is a vivid picture of Antwerp, with vigorous and highly colored descriptions of its middle-class citizens, enriched by centuries of continued prosperity. In general, Eekhoud is naturalistic, and intent only on painting life as he sees and feels it. His other books include — ‘Cycle Patibulaire’ (1892); ‘Au Siècle de Shakespeare,’ a valuable book on the English literature of the Elizabethan period (1893); and ‘Mes Communions’ (1895).

EX–VOTO

From ‘The Massacre of the Innocents, and Other Tales by Belgian Writers’:
copyright 1895, by Stone & Kimball

THE country I know and love best does not exist for the tourist, and neither guide nor doctor ever dreams of recommending it. This reassures me, for I love my country selfishly, exclusively. The land is ancient, flat, the home of fogs. With the exception of the Polder *schorres*, the district fertilized by the overflowing of the river, few districts are cultivated. A single canal from the Scheldt irrigates its fields and plains, and occasional railways connect its unfrequented towns.

The politician execrates it, the merchant despises it, it intimidates and baffles legions of bad painters.

Poets of the boudoir! virtuosi! This flat country will always elude your descriptions! For you, landscape painters, there is no inspiration to be gained here. O chosen land, neither thou nor thy secret can be seen at a glance! The degenerate folk who pass through this country feel nothing of its healthy, intoxicating charm, or are only wearied in the midst of this gray peaceful nature, unrelieved by hill or torrent; and still less sympathy have they with the country louts who stare at them with placid bovine eyes.

The people remain robust, uncouth, obstinate, and ignorant. No music stirs me like the Flemish from their lips. They mouth it, drawl it, linger lovingly over the guttural syllables, while the harsh consonants fall heavily as their fists. They move slowly, swingingly, bent-shouldered and heavy-jawed; like bulls, they are at once fierce and taciturn. Never shall I meet more comely, firm-bosomed lassies, never see eyes more appealing, than those of this dear land of mine. Under their blue *kiel* the brawny lads swagger well content; though when in drink, if dispute arises, rivalry may drive them into fatal conflicts. The *tierendar* ends many a quarrel without further ado; and as the combatants cut and hack, their faces preserve that dogged smile of the old Germans who fought in the Roman arenas. During the kermesses they over-eat themselves, they get drunk, dance with a kind of *gauche* solemnity, embrace their sweethearts without much ceremony, and when the dance is over, gratify themselves with all manner of excesses.

One and all, they are slow to give themselves away; but once gained, their affection is unalterable.

Those who depict them thick-set, laughter-loving, misshapen boors, do not know this race. The Campine peasantry recall rather the brown shepherd folk of Jordaens than the pot-house scenes by Teniers, a great man who slandered his Perck rustics.

They preserve the faith of past centuries, undertake pilgrimages, respect their *pastoor*, believe in the Devil, in the wizard, in the evil eye, that *jettatura* of the North. So much the better. These yokels fascinate me. I prefer their poetic traditions, the legends drawled out by an old *pachteresse* in the evening hours, to the liveliest tale of Voltaire, and their clan-narrowness and religious fanaticism stir me more than the patriotic declamations and the insipid civic rhodomontade of the journalist. Splendid and glorious rebels, these Vendéans of ours; may philosophy and civilization long forget them. When the day of equality, dreamed

of by geometric minds, comes, they will disappear also, my
superb brutes; hunted down, crushed by invasion, but to the end
unyielding to Positivist influences. My brothers, utilitarianism
will do away with you, you and your rude remote country!

Meanwhile, I who have your hot rebel blood coursing in my
veins, I who shall not survive you, am fain to steep my spirit in
yours, to be at one with you in all that is rude and savage in
you, to stupefy myself at great casks of brown ale at the fairs,
with you to raise up my voice when the clouds of incense rise
like smoke above your sacred processions, to seat myself in silence
beside your smoky hearths or to wander alone across the desolate
sand-dunes at the hour when the frogs croak, and when the dis-
traught shepherd, become an incendiary and a lost man, grazes
his flock of fire across the heaths. . . .

At the beginning of the June of 1865, I had just reached my
eleventh birthday and made my first communion with the Frères
de la Miséricorde at M——. One morning I was called into the
parlor; there I found the father superior and my uncle, who told
me that he would take me to Antwerp to see my father. At the
idea of this unexpected holiday and the prospect of embracing
my kind parent, who had been a widower for five years and to
whom I was now everything, I did not notice my uncle's serious
looks nor the pitying glances of the monk.

We set off. The train did not go fast enough for my liking.
However, we arrived at last. To ring the door-bell of the sim-
ple little house; to embrace Yana the servant; to submit to the
caresses of good Lion, a splendid brown spaniel, to race up-stairs
with him four steps at a time, to bound into the familiar bed-
room, then two words:—"Father!—George!"—to feel myself
lifted up and pressed against his heart; to be devoured with
kisses, my lips seeking his in the big fair beard: these actions
followed one another rapidly; but transient as they were, they
are forever graven on my memory. What a long time the dear
man held me in his arms! He looked at me with tender admi-
ration, repeating, "What a big boy you have grown, my Jurgen,
my Krapouteki!" and he repeated a whole string of impossible
but adorable pet names he had invented for me, and among
which he interspersed caresses. It was still early in the morning.

When I entered, followed by Lion, Yana, and finally by my
uncle, the least member of the four, my father was in his dress-
ing-gown, but was about to dress.

He looked splendid to me. His color was fresh, but too flushed about the cheek-bones, I was told afterwards; his eyes sparkled — sparkled too much; his voice was a little hoarse, but sweet, caressing, despite its grave tone, — a tone never to be forgotten by me.

He was then forty-six. I see his tall figure rise before me now, with his well-set limbs; and his kind face still smiles on me in my dreams.

My uncle clasped his hand.

"You see that I keep my word, Ferdinand. Here's the little scamp himself!"

"Thank you, Henry. Pardon the trouble I have caused you. . . . You will laugh at me; but if you had not brought him, I should have gone to the convent myself to-day. . . . I should have scorned the doctor's régime and prescriptions. . . . You do not know, Georgie. . . . I have not been very well. . . . Oh, a mere nothing; a small ailment, a neglected cold. . . . A slight cold, was it not, Yana? . . . I have lost it, as you see. . . . Ah! my boy, what good it does me to see you! . . . What fun we shall have! We are going out into the country at once. . . . I have prepared a surprise for you."

I listened enchanted — oh the selfishness of childhood! The promise of this expedition made me deaf to his cough — a dry, convulsive cough which he tried to stifle by holding his silk handkerchief to his mouth. Neither did I notice — or rather I did notice but attached no importance to — the bottles of medicine and pill-boxes which stood on the chimney-piece and on the bed-table. A bottle of syrup had just been opened, and a drop remained in the silver spoon. Yana held a prescription in her hand, which had been written that morning. A heavy odor of opiates and other drugs filled the room. These details only recurred to me afterwards.

My uncle took leave.

"Above all, no imprudence!" he said to my father. "You promise me? Be back in town before the dew falls. . . . I will take George to school again to-morrow morning."

"Set your mind at rest; we will be wise!" replied my father, excited and preoccupied, thinking only of his child.

I believe that he was not sorry to find himself alone with me, and as the prospect of returning to M——, evoked by the old officer, had saddened me, he took me on his knee.

"Courage! little one," he said. "It is not for long. I feel
too lonely since the death of your poor mother. I have told my
family that in the future I do not intend to be separated from
you . . . You have made your first communion, . . . you are big,
. . . you shall go back to school for a week, just time to pack
up and to settle in our new quarters. . . . Come, there, I am
betraying the secret . . . Never mind, after all, I may as well
tell you everything now. I have bought a pretty little house,
almost a farmstead, three miles from here. . . . We are going to
live in the country, like peasants, to wear sabots and smocks.
Hey? That will make you grow. . . . What do you say to it?
. . . We shall be always together."

I clapped my hands, and jumped round the room.

"What joy! Always we two, is that it? Then we shall be
always together. Is it really true?"

"Really true."

We sealed this understanding in a long embrace.

An hour later my father, Yana, and I stepped into a landau
at the door.

It was one of those enervating equinoctial days when the
warmth and the intense quietness affect one almost to tears.
The sun, in a beautiful Flemish sky of pale, soft turquoise, had
dispersed the morning mist.

"Look at him, sir," said Yana, pointing to me; "he is as
happy as a king!"

"Now is the time to take in a plentiful supply of air," re-
marked my father; "one only needs to open one's mouth!"

I opened mine quite wide, as if I were yawning.

What a difference, too, between this air and the air at school;
even that which one breathed out of doors in the cloistered
court, shut in by four forbidding high walls, sweating with damp
and decaying with mildew.

Seated with my back to the coachman, my hands on my
father's knee, I uttered exclamations of surprise and besieged
him with questions. He sat back in the carriage, shielded from
the wind by his big overcoat. Yana sat beside him; Lion ran on
in advance.

Passing along the chief street of the suburb, we came out
into the open country. The tufts of young leaves gave a sweet
freshness to the hoary trunks of the great beech-trees which
lined the road. In place of the yellow withered grass in the

meadows, there was a vivid emerald carpet; splendid cows, with well-rounded flanks and dewlaps reaching the ground, nibbled the tender shoots. The full rows of young corn promised a plentiful harvest. Between a double hedge of weeping-willows and alders ran silvery waters, swollen by the melting of the late snows. When we passed a flower-garden the scent of lilac filled the dreamy air. Gates with gilt knobs opened on avenues of elms and oaks; sloping lawns led up to a castle, whose terrace was ornamented with clipped and modeled orange-trees. The majestic passing of a pair of big swans or the scurry of hare-brained ducks stirred the stagnant pond, and left wakes amid the flags and water-lilies.

Moss-grown farmsteads, flanked by barns with green shutters fixed to the red bricks, draw-wells, chickens picking about on the manure-heaps,—these were my chief delight. Sometimes a countryman's cart with its white awning stood on one side for us to pass.

We drove through Deurne, then through Wyneghem.

For the third time a slender spire lifted its gray-slated point into the opaline sky.

" S'Gravenwezel tower! " exclaimed Yana.

" S'Gravenwezel! But that is your village! " I cried. " Are we going to live there ? "

The good creature smiled in the affirmative.

Some few moments later, the driver, directed by Yana, stopped in front of a lonely farm, a quarter of an hour away from the rest of the long, straggling village.

" This is my parents' home! " she said.

I can still see the little one-storied farmhouse, with its overhanging thatched roof, festooned with stone-crop, a white chalk cross on the brickwork to protect it from lightning. At sound of the carriage, the whole household ran to the door. There was Yana's father, a short, thick-set sexagenarian, bent but still healthy-looking, his face wrinkled like old parchment, with a stiff beard and bright eyes; the mother, a buxom woman about ten years younger, very active despite her stoutness; then a host of brothers and sisters, varying from twenty-five to fifteen; the boys bold, dark, curly-headed, muscular, square-set fellows; the girls fresh-looking, tanned by the sun, all like Yana their elder sister, who, to my mind, was the most charming *boerine annversoise* that one could imagine, with her dark hair, her big emerald-green eyes and sweeping lashes. In honor of S'Gravenwezel kermesse,—sounds of which could already be heard in the distance,—they said, but more in honor of our visit, the men wore their Sunday trousers, and bright blue smocks coquettishly gathered at the neck. The women had taken out their lace caps with big wings, the head-dresses with silver pins, woolen dresses, and large silk handkerchiefs which crossed over the breast and fell in a point behind. The good people complimented my father on his appearance. "That is Mynheer's son,—Jonkheer Jorss!" In a few moments I had made friends with these simple cordial folk, and particularly with a fine lad of nineteen—"onze Jan" (our Jean), said Yana—on the eve of drawing lots for the conscription.

When his sister laid the table,—for we were to stay to dinner there,—he offered to show me the orchard, the garden, and the stables. I accepted joyfully. I could no longer keep still. Jean, with my hand in his, took me first to the cows. As they lay down, chained up in their sheds, they lowed piteously. The dung-strewn bedding shone with bronze and old-gold, and the far end of the stable resembled a picture by Rembrandt—at least, it is thus that I recall to-day that reddish-brown half-light. That I might be better able to admire the animals, he roused them with a kick. They got up lazily, sulkily. He told me their names and their good points. That big black one, with the spot between her eyes, was Lottekè; this big glutton chewing the early clover was called La Blanche. Jan persuaded me to pat them. They rubbed their horns against the posts which divided them. The boy told me that they were excellent milkers. I counted six in all. A strong smell of milk filled the air, warm with all this breathing, heaving animality. Jan promised to take me to work in the fields with him when I came to live in the village. I should dig the ground and become a real peasant, a *boer* like himself. *Boer Jorss*, he called me, laughing. But I took this prospect of country life quite seriously; I admired the fine figure, the proud healthy bearing, of this young peasant. I in my turn should grow like that, I thought. A career such as his awaited me! That was better than wearing a frock-coat and a black hat, than growing pale and fevered over books and copies, and seeing nothing of beautiful nature except what can be found in a suburb: weeds growing over waste places and patches of sky amid spotted roofs!

He took me also to the garden, an oblong inclosure with well-kept paths, and planted with sunflowers, peonies, and hollyhocks. The beds were edged with strawberry plants, the fruit just ripening. The kind lad promised me the first that were gathered.

We were called back to the house, while I was making the acquaintance of Spits the watch-dog. The kermesse meal awaited us. At the express request of my father, who threatened to eat nothing, the family, at least the men, sat down with us. As to the women, they all pretended to wait on us. My eyes wandered with delight around this room, so new to me; the alcoves where the parents and older members of the family slept, receded into the wall and were hidden by flowered curtains; the wide chimney-piece was ornamented with a crucifix and plates imprinted with historical subjects; a branch of consecrated box hung below; then there were enormous spits and the imposing chimney-hook.

Yana placed on the table a tureen of cabbage and bacon soup, the smell of which would have aroused the appetite of the dead

We all made the sign of the cross, bowed our heads and clasped our hands over the soup-basins, the savory smell from which rose towards the smoky beam like the perfume of incense. For some seconds nothing was audible save the lowing of the cows from the sheds, the buzzing of flies on the window-panes, and the striking of S'Gravenwezel clock, which rang out midday with the silvery, melancholy chimes of village bells.

What a delicious meal we had! My father thought of all the most expressive adjectives in the patois to express the merits of the soup, I sang the praises of the eggs which served as a golden frame to the red-and-white slices of ham. A mountain of mealy potatoes disappeared beneath our lively forks. I had a healthy country appetite!

Yana, who was touched, declared that her master had not eaten so much for a month.

We were obliged to taste all the products of the farm: butter, milk, cream cheese, early vegetables, and fruit. I laughed at Yana, who had thought it necessary to bring provisions. She did not know the parental hospitality! But I no longer made fun of her forethought when she brought out the contents of the wonderful basket: two bottles of old wine and a plum tart of her own making, which she placed triumphantly in the middle of the table. They all drank to my father's health, to mine, and to our happy stay in S'Gravenwezel.

"It is settled, then, that in a week's time you shall come to my house-warming, you hear, all of you!" said my father definitely. . . . "And now, Djodgy, we must be going, for you are longing to see our nest." . . .

Jan came with us. He walked behind with his sister. Lion ran backwards and forwards, showing his joy by his wild leaps and bounds, and chasing the small animals which he raised among the rye.

Poppies and cornflowers already lit up the changing ears of corn with their bright color, and white or brown butterflies flitted above like animated flowers. We had followed a path which ran across the cornfields, behind Ambroes farm, to the left of the high road. Some minutes later we skirted a little oak wood, and immediately behind it my father pointed our home out to me.

Simple cottage! you haunt me still, above all in springtime, when the air is warm and soft as on that memorable day. . . . Your white walls will ever be to me a sad though sweet and loving memory.

The little house was simple and quiet as possible. There was one story only, and it contained but four rooms. An out-house with hen-roost, which would serve as a shed for the gardener, stood on one side. Yana's brother had for the time being put into it a pretty white kid, which bleated loudly at our approach; he ran to set it free.

Fruit-trees covered the wall facing south. The inclosure, encircled by a hedge of beech, was half orchard, half pleasure garden, and covered an area of three thousand metres. In front of the house was a square lawn, divided by a path from the gate to the front door. Leafy copses of plantain, chestnuts, American oaks, and birches, offered delightful retreats on either side of the house for reading or dreaming. As we went round the grounds, my father explained with animation the improvements which he projected. Here was to be a clump of rhododendrons, here a bed of Orléans roses, there a grove of lilacs. He consulted me with a feverish "Hey?" He was excited, unreserved; rarely had I seen him in such high spirits. Since the death of my mother his beautiful, sonorous, and contagious laugh had been heard no more.

Chattering thus, we came to a mound at the bottom of the garden, from which we could see a corner of the village; the spire emerging from a screen of limes, the crossed sails of a silent mill perched on a grassy knoll, farms scattered among corn-fields and meadows, until the plain was lost in the horizon.

"Look, George," he said, "this will be our world in future. . . . It will be good for us both to live here; for if I need solace, you will gain equally. . . . No more confinement, my dear little fellow; we are rich enough to live in the country as phi-losophers. . . . And when I am gone . . . for one must provide for everything. . . ." He stopped. I remember that a broken-winded barrel organ ground out a polka behind the screen of limes which shut off the village.

My father had suddenly become serious, and the solemnity of his last words moved me deeply. Then that distant melancholy air made me shudder. When he had finished speaking, he coughed for a long time.

We were seated on the slope, our backs to the house, facing the vast plain, the silence of which was rendered more over-whelming by the jarring notes of the barrel organ.

"Father," I murmured, as if in prayer, "what do you mean?"

In reply he drew me towards him, took my head in his hands and looked at me long, his eyes lost in mine; then he embraced me, attempted to smile, and said:—

"It is nothing. I am well, am I not? Why do my family worry me with their advice? Indeed, they will frighten me with their long faces and perpetual visits. . . . To-day at least I have escaped from them. . . . We two are alone . . . free! Soon it will be always so!"

Despite this reanimation, an inexpressible agony wrung my heart, and I made no effort to escape from this influence, which I felt to be due to our deep sympathy.

Regret was already mingled with my delight; and on this exquisite afternoon there was that heart-rending sense of things which have been and will never be again—never.

I threw my arms round my father's neck, and made no other reply to his last words. It required a mutual effort to break the silence; neither of us made the effort. In the distance the organ continued to grind out the tune as if it too were choked with sobs.

Thus we remained for long, until the day waned.

"Is it not time to go back, sir?"

Yana's interruptions aroused us. Silently my father got up, and with my hand still in his we passed through the graying

country, where the twilight already created fantastic shadows. At
about a hundred yards from the house he turned round, and
made me look once more at the little corner of earth, the hermi-
tage which was to shelter us.

"We will call it Mon Repos!" he said, and he moved on.

Mon Repos! How he lingered over those three syllables.
Even thus are certain nocturnes of Chopin prolonged.

When we reached Ambroes farm, we took affectionate fare-
well of Yana's family. My father thanked them for their wel-
come, and reminded them of his invitation. He gave Jan a few
further instructions about the garden; the lad stood cap in hand,
his dark eyes expressive of vivid sympathy.

Yet another "au revoir"; then the carriage drove away, and
we turned our backs on the dear village.

Was it still the kermesse organ which obsessed me, lingering
above all other sounds, growing fainter and fainter but never
quite dying away? And why did I ceaselessly repeat to myself,
whatever the music, these three unimportant syllables "Mon
Repos"?

The sun was setting when we reached the gates of the town.
Country masons, white and dusty, with tools over their shoulder
and tins hanging by their side, walked rapidly to the villages
which we had left behind. Happy workmen! They were wise
to go back to the village, and to leave the hideous slums of
West Antwerp to their town comrades.

A fresh breeze had risen which stirred the tops of the aspens.
The purple light on the horizon beyond the ramparts grew faint.
During the whole drive my father remained sunk in prostration;
his hands, which I stroked, were moist; now burning, now icy.
He roused himself from this painful torpor only to slip his hand
through my hair, and to smile at me as never friend has smiled
since.

Yana too looked sad now, and pretended that it was the
dust which caused her to wipe her eyes continually with her
handkerchief.

I was tired, overcome with so much open air, but I could not
fall asleep that night. I dreamed with open eyes of the events
of the day, of the farm, of good-natured Jan, of the happy meal,
of the kid, of the coming day when I should be "*boer Jorss*," as
the kind fellow said. . . . I was happy, but from time to time
a fit of terrible coughing from the next room stifled me, and

then I recalled the scene in the garden, our silence against the jarring sound of the organ, and later these two words "Mon Repos." I did not close my eyes until the morning.

When I awoke, my uncle was already waiting for me. He was an old officer and adhered to military time only.

"We must be off!" he said in his gruff, harsh voice. "You must go back to work, my lad."

Must I go away again? Why this week's separation? What did my uncle's authoritative tone mean in my father's house, in *our* house? Why did Yana look at him respectfully but sullenly? I did not guess the horrible but absolute necessity for this intrusion; it exasperated me.

What a bitter leave-taking! And that, too, for a week's separation only. It was in vain that my uncle made fun of our tears. I clung to my beloved father, and he had not the strength to repel me. The impatient officer tore me at last from his embrace.

"The train does not wait!" he grumbled. "Were there ever such chicken-hearted people!"

I was indignant.

"No, not at parting from you," I said to my unsympathetic relation, . . . "but from him!"

"Djodgy! Djodgy!" my father tried to say in a tone of reproach. "Forgive him, Henry. . . . Au revoir! In a week's time! . . . Be good ever."

This time Yana no longer tried to hide her tears. Lion moved sadly from one to another, and his human eyes appeared to say, "Stay with him."

But nothing would move my obdurate uncle. We drove away in the same carriage which had taken us the day before to S'Gravenwezel.

We waved to one another as long as the carriage was in the street.

In a week I should see him again!

In a week he was dead!

But I have forgotten nothing.

Thus it is, ever since then, that I love, I adore this Flemish country as my heritage from him who loved it above all others; from him, the sole human being who never wrought me any ill. These vast pale-blue horizons, often veiled with mist or fog, gleam before me again as that tearful smile which I caught for the last time upon his dear face.

KORS DAVIE

From 'The Massacre of the Innocents, and Other Tales by Belgian Writers':
copyrighted 1895, by Stone & Kimball

I T WAS fair-time, yet Rika Let, the young dairymaid of *baes* Verhulst, was sad. She had worked so hard all August that this morning, before mass, the *baezine* had given her a bright florin and spoken kindly to her: —

"Rika, it is fair-time for every one. Enjoy yourself, my girl. Here is something to buy yourself a neckerchief at the fair, a bright-colored one with fringe to cross over your breast." . . .

Rika accepted her mistress's present. Alone in her garret above the stable, she turned the shining coin over and over, but hesitated to exchange it for some coveted trifle at Suske Derk's stall, down there by the church. Great tears sprang to her eyes, eyes which were faintly tinged with green. What sorrow filled the heart of this fair young girl of eighteen summers?

"Ah," she sighed, "if only one of the village lads would take me to the fair and give me a gay kerchief! But who cares for poor Rika? Our lads woo other girls, better born and richer than I am! *Baezine* Verhulst knew that, or she would not have given me money to buy a thing which the poorest laborer, or even the humblest thresher, gives gladly to his sweetheart to-day. . . . Who will dance this evening with Rika Let at the Golden Swan? . . . No one. . . . No, *baezine* Verhulst, it is not a fête day for every one!"

Tears rested on her fair lashes as the morning dew clings to the bearded ears of corn. Mechanically she looked at herself in a piece of glass which hung beneath a little Notre-Dame of Montaigu. She was not plainer than many of her companions who were admired by the ardent and happy lovers. Ugly — Rika! No indeed. Fair as the August cornfields of the Verhulsts were her tresses. Her lips were red and full as ripe cherries. If you feel aught of the charm of the young peasant girls of our country, you would admire Rika.

She dressed herself in her simple Sunday clothes; a little collar and flat cap, both of dazzling whiteness; a skirt and bodice, unsoiled by any speck of dust.

The bell sounded for mass.

Go and pray, Rika! Who can say? the good God mayhap will unseal the eyes of the blind gallants of Viersel.

She told her beads so earnestly, that a friend had to remind her when the service was at an end.

Outside the church a crowd of gay youths, with crossed arms and flowers between their lips, watched the blushing procession of girls who were to be their partners in the evening. Sympathetic glances were exchanged, and with a smile or a simple movement of the head a meeting was arranged, a promise confirmed, a consent given. Eager hearts throbbed under the blue smocks, the many-colored kerchiefs; but no glance sought to attract the bright eyes of the orphan girl, not one of those young hearts beat in unison with hers.

To reach the farm, Rika had to pass through the fair. Suske Derk had displayed her wares. Rika did not even deign to look at them. The mercer called to her:—

"Ha! my pretty devotee! Won't you even wear a scapulary?"

At midday there was a great feast at the Verhulst farm in honor of the fair. Masters, friends, and servants, all with big appetites, seated themselves round a table laden with enormous dishes, brought in by the farmer's wife and Rika. A savory smell filled the large room; the steam dimmed the copper ornaments on the chimney-piece, the crucifix, the candlesticks, the big plates, which were the pride of the cleanly Rika. At first the guests, speechless, gravely and solemnly satisfied their hunger. Then came the bumpers to wash down the viands, for mealy Polder potatoes make one thirsty. As the tankards were re-filled, tongues were loosed, and jokes piquant as the waters of the Scheldt flew apace.

Rika in her turn sat down to the table, but the sorrow at her heart robbed her of appetite, and she ate little. The lively guests, distressed by her silence, attributed it to arrogance, and turned their attention elsewhere. Later they would rejoin their buxom wenches, and think no more of the poor little soul tormented with the desire for love.

The more the day advanced, the less Rika thought of purchasing a fichu at Suske Derk's stall; she would rather return the florin to her mistress! Bugles and screeching fiddles could be heard from the Golden Swan.

Houpsa! rich and poor hasten to the dance, some in shoes, others in sabots. *Lourelourela!* The quadrilles form. The couples hail their vis-à-vis across the room. All is ready. They set off. . . .

Rika alone is absent from the ball. Seated on the threshold of the barn, the sound of the brass and wind instruments, the patter of feet, the laughter and oaths, reach her ear.

The low-roofed houses of the village fade slowly in the twilight. The church steeple rises heavenward as the watchful finger of God; at its base lies the Golden Swan; against the four red-curtained windows the figures of the dancing couples are outlined black as imps.

Rika could not tear herself away from this scene. Her heart, till now pure as the veil of a first communicant, was filled with bitter thoughts.

Marvelous tales were told of Zanne Hokespokes. The little old woman possessed some wonderful secrets; she could give rot to sheep, make cows run dry, and poison nurses' milk. She could see the fate of those who consulted her in cards and in coffee-grounds. She could recall the fickle lover to the side of the deserted maiden. Perhaps she could find a sweetheart for lonely Rika?

Unholy thoughts rose with the oppressive mists of the evening. They grew in the solitude, in the remoteness from others' joy. The ungainly couples danced up and down, black as imps, against the four red windows. The music grated and jarred; but for the last hour the village steeple, which rose heavenward as the watchful finger of God, had been lost in the darkness.

Would it be well to take advantage of the absence of her master and mistress and consult the fortune-teller? No one would meet her. All the village was at the Golden Swan.

Holy Virgin! how they are enjoying themselves! Among the whirling couples Rika saw two figures intertwined, their faces so close that their lips must meet!

Yes, she would have recourse to the spells of the old woman Hokespokes, whatever might happen. She had still the bright coin in her pocket. This and the few coppers which she had saved would suffice.

The sorceress lived in a clay hut deep in the dark woods of Zoersel. The peasants avoided these woods and passed through them in broad daylight only, making the sign of the cross. At nightfall weird melancholy sounds, which seemed to come from another world, murmured in the tree-tops. It took an hour to reach the cottage from Viersel. Rika calculated that she could be home before midnight. Her master and mistress would not return earlier than that. She overcame her last fears, and set out bravely towards the lonely heath.

"In this bag, little one, are the ashes of the tooth of a corpse; the tooth was picked up in the cemetery of Safftingen, the village that was submerged by the Scheldt; therein is also a mushroom, called 'toadstool,' gathered at the foot of the tree on which Nol Bardaf the cobbler was hanged. Next full moon, on a cloudless night, sprinkle the magic powder at the foot of your bed, and prick the mushroom deeply with a hairpin, uttering these words three times:—'I command thee, charmed plant, to bring me the man who shall wound me as I wound thee!' Then go to bed with the mushroom under your pillow, and wait in perfect quiet without speaking. The beloved one will appear. Open your eyes, but above all things neither speak nor move. You must even hold your breath. If he leaves you, do not try to detain him. You will see him again, and will then become his wife."

Thus spoke Zanne Hokespokes.

Rika followed the instructions of the sorceress. She waited several days for the fine cloudless night, and when the full moon rose she did as the witch had bidden her.

"I command thee, charmed thing, to bring me the man who shall wound me as I wound thee!"

Once — twice — thrice.

Rika, with wide-open eyes and strained ear, lay in bed eagerly awaiting the promised vision. Shadow became substance in the garret, which was bathed in the silvery-blue beams of the moon. The silence was so overwhelming that Rika thought she heard the sound of the white light as it fell on the bare floor.

Now she regretted her traffic with a servant of the Devil, now she rejoiced at the prospect of seeing *him*, the man who would love her; but again she feared that he might not come.

The yard door swung on its hinges. A hasty, heavy step crossed the court without disturbing the watch-dog. *He* opened the kitchen door. *Clope! Clope!* rapidly he climbed the ladder which led to the attic. Terror seized Rika; she stifled a cry, as the trap-door opened.

There he was in her room; a soldier, a young artilleryman. He passed by her unnoticed in the white light of the moon.

Ah! Rika loves him at first sight; it is he for whom she has waited. He has a round face, curly auburn hair, a well-cut mouth, a slightly aquiline nose, with dilating nostrils, a square chin, and broad shoulders. A fine mustache covers his upper lip. He wears a brigadier's braids on his sleeve, and spurs on his heels. What mad race has he been running? His broad chest rises and falls, he gasps for breath, and throws himself down on the only stool. Rika longs to rush to him, to wipe the sweat from his brow. As if overpowered, he loosens his tunic, unclasps his belt, and exposes his fine chest. Somewhat rested, oblivious of Rika, he scrutinizes his uniform from head to foot, and notices that one of the buttonholes of his boot-strap is torn. He takes off the strap, and with a knife which he draws from his pocket makes a fresh hole in the leather. Then he readjusts the strap to the trouser.

Rika observed all these movements. More and more she admired his military bearing and the ease with which he moved. Animated by his run, the soldier's face struck her as more expressive than the faces of the other fellows of her acquaintance, even than the faces of the scornful Odo and Freek, the Verhulsts' two sons, whom she had once admired.

The stranger re-buttoned his coat, fastened his belt, put his cap on his head, and left the room with the same quick firm step. She dared not call to him and hold out her arms. The door closed.

The sound of his footsteps, the clank of his sword, were lost in the distance. To Rika a memory only remained.

Has it not all been a dream, poor impressionable little thing?

No; a moment ago he sat quite near Rika's bed.

By the wan light of the moon she saw a sparkling object, the knife which he had just used; here was her proof. She could no longer doubt. She picked up the knife, pressed the still-open blade to her lips, and as her breath dulled the steel, she wiped it, kissed it again; twenty times she repeated the same childish trick.

Truly the good Zanne Hokespokes keeps her word. The pretty knife with its tortoise-shell handle will henceforth be a pledge for Rika. Her fingers lovingly caressed the blade, as if they stroked the mustache of the brigadier; she would fain see her reflection in the dark eyes of the beloved one, as she saw it in the shining metal.

Her eyes grew weary with gazing on the bright surface; she was compelled to lie down. She slept and dreamt of her soldier visitor, with the precious knife clasped to her breast.

TARATA! Tarata! Tarata!

"Wake up, Kors Davie! . . . Perhaps you're sorry to leave the barracks! Confound it! the fellow snores as if he did not care for his holiday!"

Brigadier Warner Cats, Davie's fellow-countryman and comrade, tired of speaking, shook Kors roughly, as the bugle sounded the réveille. Kors sat up, stretched himself, appeared astonished, and rubbed his eyes with his fists.

"That's strange! Pouh! What a vile dream!" he muttered with a yawn. "Comrade, just listen: I was out in the country, very much against my will, I assure you. . . . A horrible old woman pursued me with repeated blows. We crossed heath and swamp; my shoulder-belt and my sword caught in the thickets; my skin was scratched with thorns. . . . I flew over ditches three yards wide to escape from my persecutor. But the wicked old woman galloped after me and belabored me incessantly. . . . I was too much of a coward to turn and face her. . . . Oh! that race by starlight! . . . I almost hated our beloved Campine, . . . for all this happened in La Bruyère. . . . But I'll be hanged if I know where! . . . Oh! my legs, my poor legs. . . . You'll not believe, but I'm as exhausted . . . "

"Pouh! Pouh!" interrupted the faithful Warner Cats. . . . "Dreams are lies! so my grandmother used to say. You'll have forgotten all about these phantoms by the time you're beyond the ramparts, on the way to our beautiful Wildonck, these phantoms will all vanish. . . . Be done with grumbling. . . . Hang nightmares, if only the awakening is sweet!"

Kors got up, packed his kit, folded his blankets, and cheered by the thought of his holiday, hummed a soldier's tune.

As he felt in his pocket he stopped suddenly. "Good heavens! I could have sworn that I put it in my waistcoat pocket."

"What? What's up now, you grumbling devil?" asked Warner.

"Dash it! Begga Leuven's penknife, . . . my Begga. . . . The pretty knife which she bought me for my fête day when I was last in Antwerp."

"Well?"

"I cannot find it! . . . There's a fine state of things. . . . What will Begga say? I wanted to show her the little treasure still bright and new. The dear soul will never forgive my carelessness."

"Nonsense! she'll give you another. . . . Besides, it is not lucky to give knives; they cut the bonds of love!" Warner added gravely; "they bring misfortune."

"In the mean time, the bother is that I've lost the knife. Damn it!"

He turned his pockets inside out in vain.

"Well, I suppose I must make the best of it," he said at last.

When he was ready, he shook hands with his comrade and took up his bundle.

"Au revoir!" said Warner. "Remember me to all friends, and drink a pint to my health next Sunday at Maus Walkiers. Don't forget to go and see my old parents, and tell them that my purse is as flat as a pancake. Remember me also to Stans the wheelwright."

"Good. Are these all my orders?"

Davie hastened into the street.

Having left the town by the Vieux-Dieu fort, he followed the treeless military road on a hot July morning. When he came within sight of the spire of Wommelghem, he turned off by the short cut which led to Ranst and Broechem. Here the copses and brushwood protected him from the intense heat of the sun. He walked sharply, cap in hand, the sweat standing on his brow. Over his shoulder he carried his bundle, tied in a red handkerchief and fastened to a stick which he had cut on the way. He stopped for a drink of beer at the toll-houses and cross-roads, chatted with the barmaids if they took his fancy, then went happily on. Towards midday he had passed through or skirted four villages, and was a mile only from the home where his father and Begga awaited him. As he recalled the bright healthy face of his young sweetheart, the remembrance of his bad dream and of the loss of the knife came back to him. Confounded knife! Kors could not separate the thought of Begga from the lost treasure, and by a strange contradiction of human nature he was almost angry with the poor girl, because she had bought him this pocket-knife which had now come between them. This ungenerous conclusion more and more took possession of him. So preoccupied was he that he forgot to look where he was going. Suddenly he noticed that he had gone astray

He was about to cross a bridge over the Campine canal, though this bridge did not really lie in his route. Beyond it, trees lined the road on either side for a great distance. Between

the trunks could be seen vast meadows, which stretched towards
an immense purple heath, bathed in soft mist. Four fine cows
stood knee-deep in the meadow-grass which fringed the banks of
the canal; not far from the cows a young girl with a branch in
her hand sat on the slope guarding them.

He called to her:—

"Hi, Mietje, come here!"

She sprang up, and jumped lightly over the fence, but when
she came within a few yards of the stranger she stopped, looked
at him for a moment, covered her face with her hands, and
turned to go away. In a few rapid strides the soldier overtook
her, and caught her gently by the arm. He was secretly flattered
by the embarrassment of the young peasant girl. Silent, but
blushing red as a poppy, she looked down, and the blue-green of
her eyes could be seen beneath the fair lashes. She tried to turn
away and escape the scrutiny of the gallant.

"Bless me, what a pretty little puss!" he exclaimed. "Tell
me, my beautiful one, where do such dainty maidens come from?"

"I come from Viersel," she replied, in a very timid voice.

"Then we are neighbors, and almost fellow-villagers, for I live
at Wildonck, and was on my way thither."

"You will never reach it, if you follow this road."

"Egad! I don't deny it, my pretty one! A moment ago I
thought myself a fool for losing my way. Now I bless my stu-
pidity."

She did not reply to this compliment, but flushed crimson.

He would not set her free. The vision of Begga, sullen and
displeased at the loss of the knife, grew fainter and fainter. In
this frame of mind he welcomed the stranger gladly, as a pleas-
ant diversion from the thoughts which had tormented him just
before.

"What is your name, my flower of Viersel?"

"Hendrika Let—Rika."

"That has always been one of my favorite names. It was my
mother's. Do your parents live far from here?"

"My parents! I never knew them. I am a servant at *boer*
Verhulst's, whose farm you see down there, a short distance away
behind the alder-trees."

"You do not ask my name, Rika?"

She was burning to know the name of the beloved one, for
he was indeed the brilliant visitor of the enchanted night. She

stilled the throbbing of her beating heart, and pretended to show only the polite indifference which an honest girl would feel to an agreeable passer-by who accosted her on the road.

"You shrug your shoulders and pout, Rika! Of what interest is a soldier's name to you? Probably he is a bad fellow, as the curé preaches,— a spendthrift, a deceiver of women. Well, I will tell you all the same. I am Cornelis Davie, otherwise Kors, Kors the Black, now brigadier in the first battery of the fifth regiment of artillery, stationed at Fort IV., at Vieux-Dieu, near Antwerp. In two months I shall return to Wildonck for good, and take up the management of the Stork Farm, for old Davie has worked long enough. Then, Rika, Kors Davie will marry. Can you not suggest some girl for him, my sweet Rika? Do you think he will find some fair ones to choose from at Viersel?"

"I think you are getting further and further away from Wildonck!" said the coquette.

It was true; they had walked along together, and the canal was now far behind them.

"You rogue!" said Kors, a little annoyed. "Why need you remind me of the moment of parting?"

"If you follow this road, you may perhaps arrive to-morrow. Farewell, my soldier. My cows may go astray as you have."

The happy girl pretended to move away. This time he seized her round the waist, and holding her in his arms, repeated again and again, "You are beautiful, Rika!"

"If our Viersel lads saw you so foolish, they would laugh at you. Are there no girls at Wildonck, or in the town?"

"The devil take the lads of Viersel, the girls of Wildonck, and the women of Antwerp! I will win you from all the men in your village, sweet one! you are more beautiful to me than all the girls of my native place! Rika, if you will consent, our marriage shall be fixed."

"This love will not last."

He pressed her more closely to him.

"Let me go, let me go, brigadier, or I shall scream. You have surely been drinking. There are several inns between here and your fort, are there not? What would people say if they met me with you? Ah! to the right there is a road which branches off and will take you home. Be off! Good-night!"

The susceptible Davie had now forgotten the very existence of the fair and prudent Begga Leuven.

"Well, if it must be, I will go!" he said, in a firm yet tender voice. "But one word more, Rika. If I return in three days' time; if I repeat then that I love you madly; if I ask you to be my wife, will you refuse me?"

"Cornelis Davie is making fun of Rika Let; land-owners do not marry their farm servants."

"I swear that I am in earnest! I have one desire, one wish only. Rika, when I return in three days' time, on Monday, will you meet me here?"

A feeble consent was wrung from her.

When Kors tried to kiss her lips, she had not the strength to resist; she returned his kiss passionately.

Then, not without a pang, he walked rapidly in the direction of the foot-path, not daring to look back.

Breathless with excitement and triumph, Rika followed him with her eyes, until he was lost behind a leafy clump of oaks.

It was fair-time again, but now Rika Let was happy; she dined at Viersel with her former employers the Verhulsts, accompanied by her husband, the fine Kors Davie of Wildonck, Kors the Black, the owner of the Stork Farm.

Poor old Davie had fretted and died! Ah! the sorcery of old Zanne Hokespokes was indeed potent; she had changed the loyal Kors into an undutiful son and a faithless lover. Poor Begga was helpless against the spells of the Devil. Nothing could do away with the power of the incantation. "Do not be unhappy, sweet Begga! Marry tall Milè, the lock-keeper; he has neither the money nor the manly bearing of the ex-brigadier, but he will love you better."

It was just a year ago, to the day, since Rika Let consulted the witch. The poor dairymaid had reaped ample revenge for the slights cast upon her. She wished to pay a visit to the Verhulsts and introduce her rich husband to them, for the Verhulsts' wealth was nothing compared to that of the Davies.

Rika was gorgeously dressed. Think, *baezine* Verhulst, of offering her a woolen kerchief from Suske Derk's stall! Feel the silk of her dress; it cost ten francs a yard, neither more nor less. The lace on her large fête-cap is worth the price of at least three fat pigs, and the diamond heart, a jewel which belonged to the late *baezine* Davie, the mother of Kors, hanging round her throat on a massive gold chain, is more valuable than all your trinkets!

At midday there was feasting at the Verhulsts' farm in honor of the fair, and more especially to welcome the Davies. Masters, friends, plowmen and haymakers, all with good appetite, seated themselves round a table laden with enormous dishes brought in by the farmer's wife and Rika's successor.

The obsequious Madame Verhulst overpowered her former servant with attention.

"*Baezine* Davie, take one of these *carbonades?* They are soft as butter. . . . A slice of ham? It's fit for a king. Or perhaps you will have some more of this chine, which has been specially kept for your visit? Or a spoonful of saffron rice? It melts in the mouth."

"You are very kind, Madame Verhulst, but we breakfasted late just before starting. . . . Kors, have our horses been fed?"

"Do not be afraid, *baezine* Davie; Verhulst will see to that himself."

Kors, who was more and more in love with his wife, presided at the men's end of the table; near him sat Odo and Freek Verhulst, who had formerly treated Rika so disdainfully. Kors, well shaven, rubicund, merry, and wearing a dark-blue smock-frock, looked lovingly and longingly in the direction of his wife.

A savory smell filled the large room, the steam dimmed the copper ornaments on the chimney-piece, the crucifix, the candlesticks, the plates, which were formerly the pride of the cleanly Rika.

At first the guests gravely and solemnly satisfied their hunger, without saying a word. Then came the bumpers to wash down the viands, for mealy Polder potatoes make one thirsty! As the tankards were re-filled, tongues were loosed, and jokes piquant as the waters of the Scheldt flew apace.

Later, coffee, together with white bread and butter, sprinkled with currants, was served for the ladies. The men bestirred themselves unwillingly. Silently and solemnly they filled their pipes and smoked, while the old gossips and white-capped young girls chattered like magpies. The low-roofed houses of the village, which stand at the foot of the steeple pointing upward as the watchful finger of God, fade in the gathering twilight.

Before the bugles and violins struck up in the Golden Swan, whither *baezine* Davie was longing to go with her husband, the proud Rika took him by the arm and showed him round the Verhulsts's farm. After visiting the cowsheds, the stables, the pig-sties, and the dairy, they climbed to the garret where Rika used to sleep. The same little camp bed stood there, the same broken mirror, the solitary rickety stool. A feeling of emotion, mingled perhaps with remorse, overcame the pretty farmer's wife at sight of the familiar objects, and she threw herself into her husband's arms. The young farmer kissed her passionately over and over again. Rika sat on his knee with his arms around her, and they were oblivious to all save their love. . . .

Below in the court-yard shrill voices called to them; it was time for the dances.

"There is no need to hasten, is there, my Rika?"

"Kors, my well-beloved," Rika said at last with a sigh, after a long and delicious silence, "do you not remember this room?"

"What a strange question, little woman! you know this is the first time I have crossed the threshold!"

"Are you certain?"

She laughed, amused at his puzzled, half-angry, half good-natured look.

"Have you ever lost anything, Kors?" she persisted.

"Be done with riddles! Rather let us go and dance," replied Kors, relieved for the moment by the strident tones of the music, and the sound of dancing.

Houps! Lourelourela! Rich and poor joined in the dance, their figures outlined like black imps against the red windows of the Golden Swan.

"One word more," said Rika, catching hold of Kors's blouse; "have you no recollection of a little thing which you lost one night on a journey?"

"No more enigmas for me, sweet one; let us be off. My feet itch for the dance."

"Must I remind you?—look!"

She drew Begga Leuven's knife from her pocket.

He turned and held out his hand. At touch of the knife, the remembrance of that strange night came back to him. Again he saw the hideous old woman who pursued him with blows; he crossed heath and swamp, his sword caught in the brushwood; he ran until he was breathless. . . . But now he understood more than he did on that morning when he told his nightmare to his loyal friend Warner Cats, the intimate friend whom he had lost in consequence of his willful marriage. . . . He recognized this accursed garret, where he had lost the pretty knife, a present from his first lover. Reason returned, and with it all his pure and holy passion for Begga. She who was called *baezine* Davie had won him by sorcery. To kiss her lips he forsook Begga, his gentle comrade; later, he was deaf to the curses of his grandfather, he was indifferent when Begga married tall Milè, and he shed no tears at the grave of the father whose death was brought about by his disgraceful marriage.

And she, the abominable accomplice of the sorceress, still clung to him,—the vampire!

The pale moon had risen, and now bathed the attic in silver rays tinged with blue.

Rika sank to the ground beneath the unrecognizing glance of Kors; she stretched out her hands to ward off what she felt must come.

In Black Kors's contracted, bloodless hand, the open knife shone as on the night of the charm.

Between two harsh and vibrating strains of music which came from the Golden Swan, a discordant burst of laughter echoed across the silent tragic plain surrounding Verhulst Farm.

At that moment, Kors in a fit of delirium plunged the knife into Rika's breast. . . . She fell without uttering a cry.

Did not the incantation run:—"I command thee, charmed plant, to bring me the man who will wound me as I wound thee"?

EDWARD EGGLESTON

(1837–)

DWARD EGGLESTON was born at Vevay, Indiana, December 10th, 1837. His father was a native of Amelia County, Virginia, and was of a family which migrated from England to Virginia in the seventeenth century, and which became one of much distinction in the State. A brief biography of Mr. Eggleston lately published affords some information as to his early years. He was a sufferer from ill health as a child. He had repeatedly to be removed from school for this cause, and he spent a considerable part of his boyhood on farms in Indiana, where he made acquaintance with that rude backwoods life which he has described in 'The Hoosier Schoolmaster' and other stories. An important incident of his youth was a visit of thirteen months which he paid to his relations in Virginia in 1854. This opportunity of making acquaintance under such favorable circumstances with slave society, must have been of great value to one who was to make American history the chief pursuit of his life. In 1856 he went to Minnesota, and there lived a frontier life to the great improvement of his health. The accounts we have

EDWARD EGGLESTON

of him show him to have had the ardent and energetic character which belongs to the youth of the West. When not yet nineteen years old he became a Methodist preacher in that State. Later, ill health forced him again to Minnesota, where with the enthusiasm of a young man he traveled on foot, shod in Indian moccasins, in winter and summer preaching to the mixed Indian and white populations on the Minnesota River.

Mr. Eggleston's literary career began, while he was still preaching, with contributions to Western periodicals. Having written for the New York Independent, he was offered in 1870 the place of literary editor of that paper, and the following year became its editor-in-chief. He was afterwards editor of Hearth and Home, to the columns of which journal he contributed 'The Hoosier Schoolmaster,' a story that has been very popular. He wrote a number of other novels, 'The End of the World,' 'The Mystery of Metropolisville,' 'The

Circuit Rider,' 'Roxy,' etc. In January 1880, while on a visit to Europe, he began to make plans for a 'History of Life in the United States.' He had always had a strong taste for this subject, a keen natural interest in history being evident here and there in his stories. His historical researches were carried on in many of the chief libraries of Europe and the United States. A result of these studies was the thirteen articles on 'Life in the Colonial Period' published in the Century Magazine. These, however, were but preliminary studies to the work which he intended should be the most important of his life. The first volume of this work, 'The Beginners of a Nation,' was published in 1896.

This work does not pretend to be a particular account of colonial history. It is an attempt rather to describe the colonial individual and colonial society, to state the succession of cause and effect in the establishment of English life in North America, and to describe principles rather than details,—giving however as much detail as is necessary to illustrate principles. The volume of 1896 contains chapters on 'The James River Experiments' and 'The Procession of Motives' which led to colonization. Book ii. of this volume is upon the Puritan migration, and has chapters on the rise of Puritanism in England, on the Pilgrim migration, and the great Puritan exodus. Book iii. receives the name of 'Centrifugal Forces in Colony Planting,' and contains accounts of Lord Baltimore's Maryland colony, of Roger Williams, and the 'New England Dispersions,' by which is meant the establishment of communities in Connecticut and elsewhere. In the sketch of Lord Baltimore, the courtier and friend of kings, we have a striking contrast with the type of men who led the Puritan migrations. There were odd characters in those days; and a court favorite and worldling who, after having feathered his nest, is willing to make two such voyages to Newfoundland as his must have been, and to spend a winter there, all out of zeal for the establishment of his religion in the Western wilds, is certainly a person worthy of study.

The play of the forces that produced emigration, and their relations to the migrations, are described very clearly by the author. People did not emigrate when they were happy at home. Thus, Catholic emigration was small under Laud, when English Catholics were beginning to think that the future was theirs; just as Puritan emigration, vigorous under Laud, dwindled with the days of the Puritan triumph in England. We have in 'The James River Experiments' a good example of the writer's method. The salient and significant facts are given briefly, but with sufficient fullness to enable the reader to have a satisfactory grasp of the matter; and where some principle or general truth is to be pointed out, the author sets this forth strongly. For instance, in describing the motives of colonization in Virginia, he shows how these motives were in almost all cases delusions; how a succession of such delusions ran through the times of Elizabeth and James; and how colonization succeeded in the end only by doing what its projectors had never intended to do. The Jamestown emigrants expected to find a passage to India, to discover gold and silver, to raise wine and silk. But none of these things were done. Wines and silk indeed were raised. It is said that Charles I.'s coronation robe was made of Virginian silk, and Mr. Eggleston tells us that Charles II. certainly wore silk from worms hatched and fed in his Virginian dominions. But these industries, although encouraged to the utmost by government, could not be made to take root. On the other hand, a determined effort was made to discourage the production of tobacco. James I. wrote a book against the culture of that pernicious "weed," as he was the first to describe it. But the hardy plant held its own and flourished in spite of the royal disfavor. Nor were the colonists more successful in their political intentions. Especially interesting, in view of recent discussions, is the account given of the communistic experiments which belonged to the early history of the American colonies. In Virginia all the products of the colony were to go into a common stock. But after twelve years' trial of this plan, there was a division of the land among the older settlers. The pernicious character of the system had been demonstrated. "Every man sharked for his own bootie," says a writer on Virginia in 1609, "and was altogether careless of the succeeding penurie." The two years of communism in the Plymouth colony was scarcely more successful. Bradford, finding that the matter was one of life and death with the colony, abolished the system, although the abolition was a revolutionary stroke, in violation of the contract with the shareholders.

This idea, that the outcome was to be very different from the intentions, appears not only in the striking chapter on 'The Procession of Motives,' but crops up again and again in other parts of the book. Thus, the ill success which attended the government of the colonies from London resulted in the almost unconscious establishment of several independent democratic communities in America. This happened in Virginia and Plymouth. The Massachusetts Bay Colony, however, was self-governing from the start.

But although causes and principles are matters of chief interest with Mr. Eggleston, his book is full of a picturesqueness which is all the more effective for being unobtrusive. The author has not that tiresome sort of picturesqueness which insists on saying the whole thing itself. The reader is credited with a little imagination, and that faculty has frequent opportunity for exercise. It is charmed by

IX—327

the striking passage in which is described the delight of the emi-
grants of the Massachusetts Bay Colony, when, after having set sail
from England, they found themselves upon the open sea for the first
time without the supervision, or even the neighborhood, of bosses.
We know the sense of freedom which the broad and blue ocean
affords to us all; what must have been that feeling to men who had
scarcely ever had an hour of life untroubled by the domination of an
antagonistic religious authority! Every day, for ten weeks together,
they had preaching and exposition. "On one ship," says Mr. Eggles-
ton, "the watches were set to the accompaniment of psalm-singing."

The candor and fair-mindedness of this work is one of its special
merits. We have an indication of this quality in the author's refusal
to accept the weak supposition, common among writers upon Ameri-
can history, that the faults of our ancestors were in some way more
excusable than those of other people. He says in his Preface:—"I
have disregarded that convention which makes it obligatory for a
writer of American history to explain that intolerance in the first
settlers was not just like other intolerance, and that their cruelty and
injustice were justifiable under the circumstances." Other very im-
portant characteristics are sympathy, warmth of heart, and moral
enthusiasm. Nor is the work wanting in an adequate literary merit.
The style, especially in the later chapters, is free, simple, nervous,
and rhythmical.

Little has been said of Mr. Eggleston's novels in the course of
these remarks. But the qualities of his historical writing appear in
his novels. The qualities of the realistic novelist are of great use to
the historian, when the novelist has the thoroughness and the indus-
try of Mr. Eggleston. By the liveliness of his imagination, he suc-
ceeds in making history as real as fiction should be. Mr. Eggleston's
novels deserve the popularity they have attained. They are them-
selves, particularly those which describe Western life, valuable con-
tributions to history. The West, we may add, is Mr. Eggleston's
field. His most recent novel, 'The Faith Doctor,' the scene of which
is laid in New York, is very inferior to his Western stories. Of
these novels probably the best is 'The Graysons,' a book full of
its author's reality and warmth of human sympathy; of this book the
reader will follow every word with the same lively interest with
which he reads 'The Beginners of a Nation.'

ROGER WILLIAMS: THE PROPHET OF RELIGIOUS FREEDOM

From 'The Beginners of a Nation': copyright 1896, by Edward Eggleston

LOCAL jealousy and sectarian prejudice have done what they could to obscure the facts of the trial and banishment of Williams. It has been argued by more than one writer that it was not a case of religious persecution at all, but the exclusion of a man dangerous to the State. Cotton, with characteristic verbal legerdemain, says that Williams was "enlarged" rather than banished. The case has even been pettifogged in our own time by the assertion that the banishment was only the action of a commercial company excluding an uncongenial person from its territory. But with what swift indignation would the Massachusetts rulers of the days of Dudley and Haynes have repudiated a plea which denied their magistracy! They put so strong a pressure on Stoughton, who said that the assistants were not magistrates, that he made haste to renounce his pride of authorship and to deliver his booklet to be officially burned; nor did even this prevent his punishment. The rulers of "the Bay" were generally frank advocates of religious intolerance; they regarded toleration as a door set open for the Devil to enter. Not only did they punish for unorthodox expressions, they even assumed to inquire into private beliefs. Williams was only one of scores bidden to depart on account of opinion.

The real and sufficient extenuation for the conduct of the Massachusetts leaders is found in the character and standards of the age. A few obscure and contemned sectaries — Brownists, Anabaptists, and despised Familists — in Holland and England had spoken more or less clearly in favor of religious liberty before the rise of Roger Williams, but nobody of weight or respectable standing in the whole world had befriended it. All the great authorities in Church and State, Catholic and Protestant, prelatical and Puritan, agreed in their detestation of it. Even Robinson, the moderate pastor of the Leyden Pilgrims, ventured to hold only to the "toleration of tolerable opinions." This was the toleration found at Amsterdam and in some other parts of the Low Countries. Even this religious sufferance, which did not amount to liberty, was sufficiently despicable in the eyes of that intolerant age to bring upon the Dutch the contempt of Christendom. It was a very qualified and limited toleration, and one from which Catholics and Arminians were excluded. It seems to have been that practical amelioration of law which is produced more effectually by commerce than by learning or religion. Outside of some parts of the Low Countries, and oddly enough of the Turkish Empire, all the world worth counting decried toleration as a great crime. It would have been wonderful indeed if Massachusetts had been superior to the age. "I dare aver," says Nathaniel Ward, the New England lawyer-minister, "that God doth nowhere in his Word tolerate Christian States to give tolerations to such adversaries of his Truth, if they have power in their hands to suppress them." To set up toleration was "to build a sconce against the walls of heaven to batter God out of his chair," in Ward's opinion.

This doctrine of intolerance was sanctioned by many refinements of logic, such as Cotton's delicious sophistry that if a man refused to be convinced of the truth, he was sinning against conscience, and therefore it was not against the liberty of conscience to coerce him. Cotton's moral intuitions were fairly suffocated by logic. He declared that men should be compelled to attend religious service, because it was "better to be hypocrites than profane persons. Hypocrites give God part of his due, the outward man, but the profane person giveth God neither outward nor inward man." To reason thus is to put subtlety into the *cathedra* of common-sense, to bewilder vision by legerdemain. Notwithstanding his natural gift for devoutness and his almost immodest godliness, Cotton was incapable of high sincerity. He would not specifically advise Williams's banishment, but having labored with him round a corner according to his most approved ecclesiastical formula, he said, "We have no more to say in his behalf, but must sit down;" by which expression of passivity he gave the signal to the "secular arm" to do its worst, while he washed his hands in innocent self-complacency. When one scrupulous magistrate consulted him as to his obligation in Williams's case, Cotton answered his hesitation by saying, "You know they are so much incensed against his course that it is not your voice, nor the voice of two or three more, that can suspend the sentence." By such shifty phrases he shirked responsibility for the results of his own teaching. Of the temper that stands alone for the right, nature had given him not a jot. Williams may be a little too severe, but he has some truth when he describes Cotton on this occasion as "swimming with the stream of outward credit and profit," though nothing was further from Cotton's conscious purpose than such worldliness. Cotton's intolerance was not like that of Dudley and Endicott, the offspring of an austere temper; it was rather the outgrowth of his logic and his reverence for authority. He sheltered himself behind the examples of Elizabeth and James I., and took refuge in the shadow of Calvin, whose burning of Servetus he cites as an example, without any recoil of heart or conscience. But the consideration of the character of the age forbids us to condemn the conscientious men who put Williams out of the Massachusetts theocracy as they would have driven the Devil out of the garden of Eden. When, however, it comes to judging the age itself, and especially to judging the Puritanism of the age, these false and harsh ideals are its sufficient condemnation. Its government and its very religion were barbarous; its Bible, except for mystical and ecclesiastical uses, might as well have closed with the story of the Hebrew judges and the imprecatory Psalms. The Apocalypse of John, grotesquely interpreted, was the one book of the New Testament that received hearty consideration, aside from those other New Testament passages supposed to relate to a divinely appointed ecclesiasticism. The humane pity of Jesus was unknown not only to the laws, but to the sermons of the time. About the time of Williams's banishment the lenity of John Winthrop was solemnly rebuked by some of the clergy and rulers as a lax imperiling of the safety of the gospel; and Winthrop, overborne by authority, confessed, explained, apologized, and promised amendment. The Puritans substituted an unformulated belief in the infallibility of "godly" elders acting with the magistrates, for the ancient doctrine of an infallible Church.

In this less scrupulous but more serious age it is easy to hold Williams up to ridicule. Never was a noble and sweet-spirited man bedeviled by a scrupulosity more trivial. Cotton aptly dubbed him "a haberdasher of small questions." His extant letters are many of them vibrant with latent heroism; there is manifest in them an exquisite charity and a pathetic magnanimity: but in the midst of it all the writer is unable to rid himself of a swarm of scruples as pertinacious as the buzzing of mosquitoes in the primitive forest about him. In dating his letters, where he ventures to date at all, he never writes the ordinary name of the day of the week or the name of the month, lest he should be guilty of etymological heathenism. He often avoids

writing the year, and when he does insert it he commits himself
to the last two figures only and adds a saving clause. Thus 1652
appears as "52 (so called)," and other years are tagged with the
same doubting words, or with the Latin "*ut vulgo.*" What
quarrel the tender conscience had with the Christian era it is
hard to guess. So too he writes to Winthrop, who had taken
part in his banishment, letters full of reverential tenderness and
hearty friendship. But his conscience does not allow him even
to seem to hold ecclesiastical fellowship with a man he honors as
a ruler and loves as a friend. Once at least he guards the point
directly by subscribing himself "Your worship's faithful and
affectionate in all *civil* bonds." It would be sad to think of a
great spirit so enthralled by the scrupulosity of his time and his
party, if these minute restrictions had been a source of annoy-
ance to him. But the cheerful observance of little scruples seems
rather to have taken the place of a recreation in his life; they
were to him perhaps what bric-à-brac is to a collector, what a
well-arranged altar and candlesticks are to a ritualist.

Two fundamental notions supplied the motive power of every
ecclesiastical agitation of that age. The notion of a succession of
churchly order and ordinance from the time of the apostles was
the mainspring of the High Church movement. Apostolic primi-
tivism was the aim of the Puritan, and still more the goal of
the Separatist. One party rejoiced in a belief that a mysterious
apostolic virtue had trickled down through generations of bishops
and priests to its own age; the other rejoiced in the destruction
of institutions that had grown up in the ages, and in getting back
to the primitive nakedness of the early Christian conventicle.
True to the law of his nature, Roger Williams pushed this latter
principle to its ultimate possibilities. If we may believe the
accounts, he and his followers at Providence became Baptists that
they might receive the rite of baptism in its most ancient Ori-
ental form. But in an age when the fountains of the great deep
were utterly broken up, he could find no rest for the soles of his
feet. It was not enough that he should be troubled by the Puri-
tan spirit of apostolic primitivism: he had now swung round to
where this spirit joined hands with its twin, the aspiration for
apostolic succession. He renounced his baptism because it was
without apostolic sanction, and announced himself of that sect
which was the last reduction of Separatism. He became a
Seeker.

Here again is a probable influence from Holland. The Seekers had appeared there long before. Many Baptists had found that their search for primitivism, if persisted in, carried them to this negative result; for it seemed not enough to have apostolic rites in apostolic form unless they were sanctioned by the "gifts" of the apostolic time. The Seekers appeared in England as early as 1617, and during the religious turmoils of the Commonwealth period the sect afforded a resting-place for many a weather-beaten soul. As the miraculous gifts were lost, the Seekers dared not preach, baptize, or teach; they merely waited, and in their mysticism they believed their waiting to be an "upper room" to which Christ would come. It is interesting to know that Williams, the most romantic figure of the whole Puritan movement, at last found a sort of relief from the austere externalism and ceaseless dogmatism of his age by traveling the road of literalism, until he had passed out on the other side into the region of devout and contented uncertainty.

In all this, Williams was the child of his age, and sometimes more childish than his age. But there were regions of thought and sentiment in which he was wholly disentangled from the meshes of his time, and that not because of intellectual superiority,—for he had no large philosophical views,—but by reason of elevation of spirit. Even the authority of Moses could not prevent him from condemning the harsh severity of the New England capital laws. He had no sentimental delusions about the character of the savages,—he styles them "wolves endued with men's brains"; but he constantly pleads for a humane treatment of them. All the bloody precedents of Joshua could not make him look without repulsion on the slaughter of women and children in the Pequot war, nor could he tolerate dismemberment of the dead or the selling of Indian captives into perpetual slavery. From bigotry and resentment he was singularly free. On many occasions he joyfully used his ascendency over the natives to protect those who kept in force against him a sentence of perpetual banishment. And this ultra-Separatist, almost alone of the men of his time, could use such words of catholic charity as those in which he speaks of "the people of God wheresoever scattered about Babel's banks, either in Rome or England."

Of his incapacity for organization or administration we shall have to speak hereafter. But his spiritual intuitions, his moral insight, his genius for justice, lent a curious modernness to many of his convictions. In a generation of creed-builders which detested schism, he became an individualist. Individualist in thought, altruist in spirit, secularist in governmental theory, he was the herald of a time yet more modern than this laggard age of ours. If ever a soul saw a clear-shining inward light, not to be dimmed by prejudices or obscured by the deft logic of a disputatious age, it was the soul of Williams. In all the region of petty scrupulosity the time-spirit had enthralled him; but in the higher region of moral decision he was utterly emancipated from it. His conclusions belong to ages yet to come.

This union of moral aspiration with a certain disengagedness constitutes what we may call the prophetic temperament. Bradford and Winthrop were men of high aspiration, but of another class. The reach of their spirits was restrained by practical wisdom, which compelled them to take into account the limits of the attainable. Not that they consciously refused to follow their logic to its end, but that, like other prudent men of affairs, they were, without their own knowledge or consent, turned aside by the logic of the impossible. Precisely here the prophet departs from the reformer. The prophet recks nothing of impossibility; he is ravished with truth disembodied. From Elijah the Tishbite to Socrates, from Socrates to the latest and perhaps yet unrecognized voice of our own time, the prophetic temperament has ever shown an inability to enter into treaty with its environment. In the seventeenth century there was no place but the wilderness for such a John Baptist of the distant future as Roger Williams. He did not belong among the diplomatic builders of churches, like Cotton, or the politic founders of States, like Winthrop. He was but a babbler to his own time; but the prophetic voice rings clear and far, and ever clearer as the ages go on.

Reprinted by consent of the author, and of D. Appleton & Company, publishers, New York.

EGYPTIAN LITERATURE

BY FRANCIS LLEWELLYN GRIFFITH AND KATE BRADBURY GRIFFITH

THE advance that has been made in recent years in the decipherment of the ancient writings of the world enables us to deal in a very matter-of-fact way with the Egyptian inscriptions. Their chief mysteries are solved, their philosophy is almost fathomed, their general nature is understood. The story they have to tell is seldom startling to the modern mind. The world was younger when they were written. The heart of man was given to devious ways then, as now and in the days of Solomon,—that we can affirm full well; but his mind was simpler: apart from knowledge of men and the conduct of affairs, the educated Egyptian had no more subtlety than a modern boy of fifteen, or an intelligent English rustic of a century ago.

To the Egyptologist by profession the inscriptions have a wonderful charm. The writing itself in its leading form is the most attractive that has ever been seen. Long rows of clever little pictures of everything in heaven and earth compose the sentences: every sign is a plaything, every group a pretty puzzle, and at present, almost every phrase well understood brings a tiny addition to the sum of the world's knowledge. But these inscriptions, so rich in facts that concern the history of mankind and the progress of civilization, seldom possess any literary charm. If pretentious, as many of them are, they combine bald exaggeration with worn-out simile, in which ideas that may be poetical are heaped together in defiance of art. Such are the priestly laudations of the kings by whose favor the temples prospered. Take, for instance, the dating of a stela erected under Rameses II. on the route to the Nubian gold mines. It runs:—

"On the fourth day of the first month of the season of winter, in the third year of the Majesty of Horus, the Strong Bull, beloved of the Goddess of Truth, lord of the vulture and of the uræus diadems, protecting Egypt and restraining the barbarians, the Golden Horus, rich in years, great in victories, King of Upper Egypt and King of Lower Egypt, *Mighty in Truth of Ra, Chosen of Ra*,[1] the son of Ra, *Rameses Beloved of Amen*, granting life for ever and ever, beloved of Amen Ra lord of the 'Throne of the Two Lands'[2] in Apt

---

[1] The italicized phrases represent the principal names of the King.
[2] The temple of Karnak.

Esut, appearing glorious on the throne of Horus among the living from day to day even as his father Ra; the good god, lord of the South Land, Him of Edfû[1] Horus bright of plumage, the beauteous sparrow-hawk of electrum that hath protected Egypt with his wing, making a shade for men, fortress of strength and of victory; he who came forth terrible from the womb to take to himself his strength, to extend his borders, to whose body color was given of the strength of Mentu[2]; the god Horus and the god Set. There was exultation in heaven on the day of his birth; the gods said, 'We have begotten him;' the goddesses said, 'He came forth from us to rule the kingdom of Ra;' Amen spake, 'I am he who hath made him, whereby I have set Truth in her place; the earth is established, heaven is well pleased, the gods are satisfied by reason of him.' The Strong Bull against the vile Ethiopians, which uttereth his roaring against the land of the negroes while his hoofs trample the Troglodytes, his horn thrusteth at them; his spirit is mighty in Nubia and the terror of him reacheth to the land of the Kary[3]; his name circulateth in all lands because of the victory which his arms have won; at his name gold cometh forth from the mountain as at the name of his father, the god Horus of the land of Baka; beloved is he in the Lands of the South even as Horus at Meama, the god of the Land of Buhen,[4] King of Upper and Lower Egypt, *Mighty in Truth of Ra*, son of Ra, of his body, Lord of Diadems *Rameses Beloved of Amen*, giving life for ever and ever like his father Ra, day by day." [Revised from the German translation of Professor Erman.]

As Professor Erman has pointed out, the courtly scribe was most successful when taking his similes straight from nature, as in the following description, also of Rameses II. :—

«A victorious lion putting forth its claws while roaring loudly and uttering its voice in the Valley of the Gazelles. . . . A jackal swift of foot seeking what it may find, going round the circuit of the land in one instant, . . . his mighty will seizeth on his enemies like a flame catching the ki-ki plant[5] with the storm behind it, like the strong flame which hath tasted the fire, destroying, until everything that is in it becometh ashes; a storm howling terribly on the sea, its waves like mountains, none can enter it, every one that is in it is engulphed in Duat.[6]»

Here and there amongst the hieroglyphic inscriptions are found memorials of the dead, in which the praises of the deceased are neatly strung together and balanced like beads in a necklace, and passages occur of picturesque narrative worthy to rank as literature

[1] Horus as the winged disk of the sun, so often figured as a protecting symbol over the doors of temples.

[2] The coloration or configuration of his limbs indicated to the learned in such matters his victorious career. Mentu was the god of war.

[3] The southern boundary of the Egyptian empire.

[4] Baka, Meama, Buhen were in Nubia.

[5] The castor-oil plant (*Ricinus communis*).

[6] The underworld.

of the olden time.   We may quote in this connection from the bio-graphical epitaph of the nomarch Ameny, who was governor of a province in Middle Egypt for twenty-five years during the long reign of Usertesen I. (about 2700 B. C.).   This inscription not only recounts the achievements of Ameny and the royal favor which was shown him, but also tells us in detail of the capacity, goodness, charm, dis-cretion, and insight by which he attached to himself the love and respect of the whole court, and of the people over whom he ruled and for whose well-being he cared.   Ameny says:—

«I was a possessor of favor, abounding in love, a ruler who loved his city. Moreover I passed years as ruler in the Oryx nome.   All the works of the house of the King came into my hand.   Behold, the superintendent of the gangs[1] of the domains of the herdsmen of the Oryx nome gave me 3,000 bulls of their draught stock.   I was praised for it in the house of the King each year of stock-taking.   I rendered all their works to the King's house: there were no arrears to me in any of his offices.

«The entire Oryx nome served me in numerous attendances.[2]   There was not the daughter of a poor man that I wronged, nor a widow that I oppressed. There was not a farmer that I chastised, not a herdsman whom I drove away, not a foreman of five whose men I took away for the works.[3]   There was not a pauper around me, there was not a hungry man of my time. When there came years of famine, I arose and ploughed all the fields of the Oryx nome to its boundary south and north, giving life to its inhabitants, mak-ing its provisions.   There was not a hungry man in it.   I gave to the widow as to her that possessed a husband, and I favored not the elder above the younger in all that I gave.   Thereafter great rises of the Nile took place, producing wheat and barley, and producing all things abundantly, but I did not exact the arrears of farming.»

Elsewhere in his tomb there are long lists of the virtues of Amenemhat, and from these the following may be selected both on account of picturesqueness of expression and the appreciation of fine character which they display.

«Superintendent of all things which heaven gives and earth produces, overseer of horns, hoofs, feathers, and shells. . . . Master of the art of causing writing to speak. . . . Caressing of heart to all people, making to prosper the timid man, hospitable to all, escorting [travelers] up and down the river. . . . Knowing how to aid, arriving at time of need; free of planning evil, without greediness in his body, speaking words of truth. . . .

[1] The fellâhîn herdsmen of the time seem to have clubbed together into gangs, each of which was represented by a ganger, and the whole body by a superintendent of the gangs.

[2] Corvée work for the government.

[3] I. e., he did not impress men (wrongfully?) for the government works, such as irrigation or road-making.

Unique as a mighty hunter, the abode of the heart of the King. . . .
Speaking the right when he judges between suitors, clear of speaking fraud,
knowing how to proceed in the council of the elders, finding the knot in the
skein. . . . Great of favors in the house of the King, contenting the
heart on the day of making division, careful of his goings to his equals,
gaining reverence on the day of weighing words, beloved of the officials of
the palace.»

The cursive forms of writing — hieratic from the earliest times,
demotic in the latest — were those in which records were committed
to papyrus. This material has preserved to us documents of every
kind, from letters and ledgers to works of religion and philosophy.
To these, again, "literature" is a term rarely to be applied; yet the
tales and poetry occasionally met with on papyri are perhaps the
most pleasing of all the productions of the Egyptian scribe.

It must be confessed that the knowledge of writing in Egypt led
to a kind of primitive pedantry, and a taste for unnatural and to us
childish formality: the free play and naïveté of the story-teller is too
often choked, and the art of literary finish was little understood.
Simplicity and truth to nature alone gave lasting charm, for though
adornment was often attempted, their rude arts of literary embellish-
ment were seldom otherwise than clumsily employed.

A word should be said about the strange condition in which most
of the literary texts have come down to us. It is rarely that mon-
umental inscriptions contain serious blunders of orthography; the
peculiarities of late archaistic inscriptions which sometimes produce a
kind of "dog Egyptian" can hardly be considered as blunders, for
the scribe knew what meaning he intended to convey. But it is
otherwise with copies of literary works on papyrus. Sometimes these
were the productions of schoolboys copying from dictation as an
exercise in the writing-school, and the blank edges of these papyri
are often decorated with essays at executing the more difficult signs.
The master of the school would seem not to have cared what non-
sense was produced by the misunderstanding of his dictation, so long
as the signs were well formed. The composition of new works on
the model of the old, and the accurate understanding of the ancient
works, were taught in a very different school, and few indeed
attained to skill in them. The boys turned out of the writing-school
would read and write a little; the clever ones would keep accounts,
write letters, make out reports as clerks in the government service,
and might ultimately acquire considerable proficiency in this kind of
work. Apparently men of the official class sometimes amused them-
selves with puzzling over an ill-written copy of some ancient tale,
and with trying to copy portions of it. The work however was be-
yond them: they were attracted by it, they revered the compilations

of an elder age and those which were "written by the finger of Thoth himself"; but the science of language was unborn, and there was little or no systematic instruction given in the principles of the ancient grammar and vocabulary. Those who desired to attain eminence in scholarship after they had passed through the writing-school had to go to Heliopolis, Hermopolis, or wherever the principal university of the time might be, and there sit at the feet of priestly professors; who we fancy were reverenced as demigods, and who in mysterious fashion and with niggardly hand imparted scraps of knowledge to their eager pupils. Those endowed with special talents might after almost lifelong study become proficient in the ancient language. Would that we might one day discover the hoard of rolls of such a copyist and writer!

There must have been a large class of hack-copyists practiced in forming characters both uncial and cursive. Sometimes their copies of religious works are models of deft writing, the embellishments of artist and colorist being added to those of the calligrapher: the magnificent rolls of the 'Book of the Dead' in the British Museum and elsewhere are the admiration of all beholders. Such manuscripts satisfy the eye, and apparently neither the multitude in Egypt nor even the priestly royal undertakers questioned their efficacy in the tomb. Yet are they very apples of Sodom to the hieroglyphic scholar; fair without, but ashes within. On comparing different copies of the same text, he sees in almost every line omissions, perversions, corruptions, until he turns away baffled and disgusted. Only here and there is the text practically certain, and even then there are probably grammatical blunders in every copy. Nor is it only in the later papyri that these blunders are met with. The hieroglyphic system of writing, especially in its cursive forms, lends itself very readily to perversion by ignorant and inattentive copyists; and even monumental inscriptions, so long as they are mere copies, are usually corrupted. The most ridiculous perversions of all, date from the Ramesside epoch when the dim past had lost its charm, for the glories of the XVIIIth Dynasty were still fresh, while new impulses and foreign influence had broken down adherence to tradition and isolation.

In the eighth century B. C. the new and the old were definitely parted, to the advantage of each. On the one hand the transactions of ordinary life were more easily registered in the cursive demotic script, while on the other the sacred writings were more thoroughly investigated and brought into order by the priests. Hence, in spite of absurdities that had irremediably crept in, the archaistic texts copied in the XXVIth Dynasty are more intelligible than the same class of work in the XIXth and XXth Dynasties.

In reading translations from Egyptian, it must be remembered that uncertainty still remains concerning the meanings of multitudes of words and phrases. Every year witnesses a great advance in accuracy of rendering; but the translation even of an easy text still requires here and there some close and careful guesswork to supply the connecting links of passages or words that are thoroughly understood, or the resort to some conventional rendering that has become current for certain ill-understood but frequently recurring phrases. The renderings given in the following pages are with one exception specially revised for this publication, and exclude most of what is doubtful. The Egyptologist is now to a great extent himself aware whether the ground on which he is treading is firm or treacherous; and it seems desirable to make a rule of either giving the public only what can be warranted as sound translation, or else of warning them where accuracy is doubtful. A few years ago such a course would have curtailed the area for selection to a few of the simplest stories and historical inscriptions; but now we can range over almost the whole field of Egyptian writing, and gather from any part of it warranted samples to set before the reading public. The labor, however, involved in producing satisfactory translations for publication, not mere hasty readings which may give something of the sense, is very great; and at present few texts have been well rendered. It is hoped that the following translations will be taken for what they are intended,— attempts to show a little of the Ancient Egyptian mind in the writings which it has left to us.

We may now sketch briefly the history of Egyptian literature, dealing with the subject in periods:[1]—

I. THE ANCIENT KINGDOM, ABOUT B. C. 4500–3000

The earliest historic period — from the Ist Dynasty to the IIId, about B. C. 4500 — has left no inscriptions of any extent. Some portions of the 'Book of the Dead' profess to date from these or earlier times, and probably much of the religious literature is of extremely ancient origin. The first book of *'Proverbs' in the Prisse Papyrus is attributed by its writer to the end of the IIId Dynasty (about 4000 B. C.). From the IVth Dynasty to the end of the VIth, the number of the inscriptions increases; tablets set up to the kings of the IVth Dynasty in memory of warlike raids are found in the peninsula of Sinai, and funerary inscriptions abound. The pyramids raised at the end of the Vth and during the VIth Dynasty are found to contain interminable religious inscriptions, forming almost

---

[1] An asterisk (*) attached to the title of a text indicates that a translation of part or all of it is printed in the following pages.

complete rituals for the deceased kings. Professor Maspero, who has published these texts, states that they "contain much verbiage, many pious platitudes, many obscure allusions to the affairs of the other world, and amongst all this rubbish some passages full of movement and wild energy, in which poetical inspiration and religious emotion are still discernible through the veil of mythological expressions." Of the funerary and biographical inscriptions the most remarkable is that of *Una. Another, slightly later but hardly less important, is on the façade of the tomb of Herkhuf, at Aswân, and recounts the expeditions into Ethiopia and the southern oases which this resourceful man carried through successfully. In Herkhuf's later life he delighted a boy King of Egypt by bringing back for him from one of his raids a grotesque dwarf dancer of exceptional skill: the young Pharaoh sent him a long letter on the subject, which was copied in full on the tomb as an addition to the other records there. It is to the Vth Dynasty also that the second collection of *'Proverbs' in the Prisse Papyrus is dated. The VIIth and VIIIth Dynasties have left us practically no records of any kind.

II. The Middle Kingdom, B. C. 3000 to 1600

The Middle Kingdom, from the IXth to the XVIIth Dynasty, shows a great literary development. Historical records of some length are not uncommon. The funerary inscriptions descriptive of character and achievement are often remarkable.

Many papyri of this period have survived: the *Prisse Papyrus of 'Proverbs,' a papyrus discovered by Mr. Flinders Petrie with the *'Hymn to Usertesen III.,' papyri at Berlin containing a *dialogue between a man and his soul, the *'Story of Sanehat,' the 'Story of the Sekhti,' and a very remarkable fragment of another story; besides the 'Westcar Papyrus of Tales' and at St. Petersburg the *'Shipwrecked Sailor.' The productions of this period were copied in later times; the royal *'Teaching of Amenemhat,' and the worldly *'Teaching of Dauf' as to the desirability of a scribe's career above any other trade or profession, exist only in late copies. Doubtless much of the later literature was copied from the texts of the Middle Kingdom. There are also *treatises extant on medicine and arithmetic. Portions of the Book of the Dead are found inscribed on tombs and sarcophagi.

III. The New Kingdom, etc.

From the New Kingdom, B. C. 1600–700, we have the *'Maxims of Any,' spoken to his son Khonsuhetep, numerous hymns to the gods, including *that of King Akhenaten to the Aten (or disk of the sun), and the later *hymns to Amen Ra. Inscriptions of every kind,

historical, mythological, and funereal, abound. The historical *inscrip-
tion of Piankhy is of very late date. On papyri there are the stories
of the *'Two Brothers,' of the 'Taking of Joppa,' of the *'Doomed
Prince.'

From the Saite period (XXVIth Dynasty, B. C. 700) and later, there
is little worthy of record in hieroglyphics: the inscriptions follow an-
cient models, and present nothing striking or original. In demotic we
have the *'Story of Setna,' a papyrus of moralities, a chronicle some-
what falsified, a harper's song, a philosophical dialogue between a cat
and a jackal, and others.

Here we might end. Greek authors in Egypt were many: some
were native, some of foreign birth or extraction, but they all belong
to a different world from the Ancient Egyptian. With the adapta-
tion of the Greek alphabet to the spelling of the native dialects,
Egyptian came again to the front in Coptic, the language of Christ-
ian Egypt. Coptic literature, if such it may be called, was almost
entirely produced in Egyptian monasteries and intended for edifica-
tion. Let us hope that it served its end in its day. To us the dull,
extravagant, and fantastic Acts of the Saints, of which its original
works chiefly consist, are tedious and ridiculous except for the lin-
guist or the church historian. They certainly display the adjustment
of the Ancient Egyptian mind to new conditions of life and belief;
but the introduction of Christianity forms a fitting boundary to our
sketch, and we will now proceed to the texts themselves.

Francis Le Griffith.
Kate Griffith

LIST OF SELECTIONS

STORIES:

The Shipwrecked Sailor	The Doomed Prince
The Story of Sanehat	The Story of the Two Brothers

The Story of Setna

HISTORY:

The Stela of Piankhy	The Inscription of Una

POETRY:

MORAL AND DIDACTIC:

Songs of Laborers	The Negative Confession
Love Songs	The Teaching of Amenemhat
Hymn to Usertesen III.	The Prisse Papyrus
Hymn to Aten	From the Maxims of Any
Hymns to Amen Ra	Instruction of Dauf
Songs to the Harp	Contrasted Lots of Scribe and Fellâh
From an Epitaph	
From a Dialogue Between a Man and His Soul	Reproaches to a Dissipated Student

THE SHIPWRECKED SAILOR

[One of the most complete documents existing on papyrus is the 'Story of the Shipwrecked Sailor.' The tale itself seems to date from a very early period, when imagination could still have full play in Upper Nubia. In it a sailor is apparently presenting a petition to some great man, in hopes of royal favor as the hero of the marvels which he proceeds to recount.

The Papyrus, which apparently is of the age of the XIth Dynasty, is preserved at St. Petersburg, but is still unpublished. It has been translated by Professors Golenisheff and Maspero. The present version is taken from 'Egyptian Tales,' by W. M. Flinders Petrie.]

THE wise servant said, "Let thy heart be satisfied, O my lord, for that we have come back to the country; after we have long been on board, and rowed much, the prow has at last touched land. All the people rejoice and embrace us one after another. Moreover, we have come back in good health, and not a man is lacking; although we have been to the ends of Wawat[1] and gone through the land of Senmut,[2] we have returned in peace, and our land — behold, we have come back to it. Hear me, my lord; I have no other refuge. Wash thee and turn the water over thy fingers, then go and tell the tale to the Majesty."

His lord replied, "Thy heart continues still its wandering words! But although the mouth of a man may save him, his words may also cover his face with confusion. Wilt thou do, then, as thy heart moves thee. This that thou wilt say, tell quietly."

The sailor then answered: —

"Now I shall tell that which has happened to me, to my very self. I was going to the mines of Pharaoh, and I went down on the Sea[3] on a ship of 150 cubits long and 40 cubits wide, with 150 sailors of the best of Egypt, who had seen heaven and earth, and whose hearts were stronger than lions. They had said that the wind would not be contrary, or that there would be none. But as we approached the land the wind arose, and threw up waves eight cubits high. As for me, I sized a piece of wood; but those who were in the vessel perished, without one remaining. A wave threw me on an island, after that I had been three

[1] Lower Nubia.
[2] District about the first cataract.
[3] A name often applied to the great river Nile.

days alone, without a companion beside my own heart. I laid me in a thicket and the shadow covered me. Then stretched I my limbs to try to find something for my mouth. I found there figs and grapes, all manner of good herbs, berries and grain, melons of all kinds, fishes and birds. Nothing was lacking. And I satisfied myself, and left on the ground that which was over, of what my arms had been filled withal. I dug a pit, I lighted a fire, and I made a burnt-offering unto the gods.

"Suddenly I heard a noise as of thunder, which I thought to be that of a wave of the sea. The trees shook and the earth was moved. I uncovered my face, and I saw that a serpent drew near. He was thirty cubits long, and his beard greater than two cubits; his body was overlaid with gold, and his color as that of true lazuli. He coiled himself before me.

"Then he opened his mouth, while that I lay on my face before him, and he said to me, 'What has brought thee, what has brought thee, little one, what has brought thee? If thou sayest not speedily what has brought thee to this isle, I will make thee know thyself; as a flame thou shalt vanish, if thou tellest me not something I have not heard, or which I knew not before thee.'

"Then he took me in his mouth and carried me to his resting-place, and laid me down without any hurt. I was whole and sound, and nothing was gone from me. Then he opened his mouth against me, while that I lay on my face before him, and he said, 'What has brought thee, what has brought thee, little one, what has brought thee to this isle which is in the sea, and of which the shores are in the midst of the waves?'

"Then I replied to him, and holding my arms low before him,[1] I said to him:—'I was embarked for the mines by the order of the Majesty, in a ship; 150 cubits was its length, and the width of it 40 cubits. It had 150 sailors of the best of Egypt, who had seen heaven and earth, and the hearts of whom were stronger than lions. They said that the wind would not be contrary, or that there would be none. Each of them exceeded his companion in the prudence of his heart and the strength of his arm, and I was not beneath any of them. A storm came upon us while we were on the sea. Hardly could we reach to the shore when the wind waxed yet greater, and the waves rose even

[1] The usual Egyptian attitude of respect to a superior was to stand bent slightly forward, holding the arms downward.

eight cubits. As for me, I seized a piece of wood, while those who were in the boat perished without one being left with me for three days. Behold me now before thee, for I was brought to this isle by a wave of the sea!'

"Then said he to me, 'Fear not, fear not, little one, and make not thy face sad. If thou hast come to me, it is God[1] who has let thee live. For it is he who has brought thee to this isle of the blest, where nothing is lacking, and which is filled with all good things. See now thou shalt pass one month after another, until thou shalt be four months in this isle. Then a ship shall come from thy land with sailors, and thou shalt leave with them and go to thy country, and thou shalt die in thy town. Converse is pleasing, and he who tastes of it passes over his misery. I will therefore tell thee of that which is in this isle. I am here with my brethren and my children around me; we are seventy-five serpents, children, and kindred; without naming a young girl who was brought unto me by chance, and on whom the fire of heaven fell and burnt her to ashes. As for thee, if thou art strong, and if thy heart waits patiently, thou shalt press thy infants to thy bosom and embrace thy wife. Thou shalt return to thy house which is full of all good things, thou shalt see thy land, where thou shalt dwell in the midst of thy kindred!'

"Then I bowed in my obeisance, and I touched the ground before him. 'Behold now that which I have told thee before. I shall tell of thy presence unto Pharaoh, I shall make him to know of thy greatness, and I will bring to thee of the sacred oils and perfumes, and of incense of the temples with which all gods are honored. I shall tell moreover of that which I do now see (thanks to him), and there shall be rendered to thee praises before the fullness of all the land. I shall slay asses for thee in sacrifice, I shall pluck for thee the birds, and I shall bring for thee ships full of all kinds of the treasures of Egypt, as is comely to do unto a god, a friend of men in a far country, of which men know not.'

"Then he smiled at my speech, because of that which was in his heart, for he said to me, 'Thou art not rich in perfumes, for all that thou hast is but common incense. As for me, I am

---

[1] The polytheistic Egyptians frequently used the term «God» without specifying any particular deity: perhaps, too, in their own minds they did not define the idea, but applied it simply to some general notion of Divinity.

prince of the land of Punt,[1] and I have perfumes. Only the oil
which thou saidst thou wouldst bring is not common in this isle.
But when thou shalt depart from this place, thou shalt never
more see this isle; it shall be changed into waves.'

"And behold, when the ship drew near, attending to all that
he had told me before, I got me up into an high tree, to strive
to see those who were within it. Then I came and told to him
this matter; but it was already known unto him before. Then
he said to me, 'Farewell, farewell; go to thy house, little one,
see again thy children, and let thy name be good in thy town;
these are my wishes for thee!'

"Then I bowed myself before him, and held my arms low
before him, and he, he gave me gifts of precious perfumes, of
cassia, of sweet woods, of kohl, of cypress, an abundance of
incense, of ivory tusks, of baboons, of apes, and all kinds of
precious things. I embarked all in the ship which was come,
and bowing myself, I prayed God for him.

"Then he said to me, 'Behold, thou shalt come to thy country
in two months, thou shalt press to thy bosom thy children, and
thou shalt rest in thy tomb!' After this I went down to the
shore unto the ship, and I called to the sailors who were there.
Then on the shore I rendered adoration to the master of this
isle and to those who dwelt therein.

"When we shall come, in our return, to the house of Pha-
raoh, in the second month, according to all that the serpent
has said, we shall approach unto the palace. And I shall go in
before Pharaoh, I shall bring the gifts which I have brought
from this isle into the country. Then he shall thank me before
the fullness of all the land. Grant then unto me a follower, and
lead me to the courtiers of the king. Cast thine eye upon me
after that I am come to land again, after that I have both seen
and proved this. Hear my prayer, for it is good to listen to
people. It was said unto me, 'Become a wise man, and thou
shalt come to honor,' and behold I have become such."

*This is finished from its beginning unto its end, even as it was
found in a writing. It is written by the scribe of cunning fingers,
Ameniamenaa; may he live in life, wealth, and health.*

[1] Punt was the «land of spices» to the Egyptian, and thence, too, the
finest incense was brought for the temple services. It included Somaliland in
Africa, and the south of Arabia.

THE STORY OF SANEHAT

[The story of Sanehat is practically complete. A papyrus at Berlin contains all the text except about twenty lines at the beginning, the whole being written in about three hundred and thirty short lines. Scraps of the missing portion were found in the collection of Lord Amherst of Hackney; and these, added to a complete but very corrupt text of about the first fifty lines, enable one to restore the whole with tolerable certainty. The story was written about the time of the XIIth or XIIIth Dynasty, but was known at a much later period: one extract from the beginning of the tale and one from the end have been found written in ink on limestone flakes or «ostraca» of about the XXth Dynasty (about 1150 B. C.). It seems to be a straightforward relation of actual occurrences, a real piece of biography. At any rate, it is most instructive as showing the kind of intercourse that was possible between Egypt and Palestine about 2500 B. C.]

THE hereditary prince, royal seal-bearer, trusty companion, judge, keeper of the gate of the foreigners, true and beloved royal acquaintance, the attendant Sanehat says:—

I attended my lord as a servant of the king, of the household of the hereditary princess, the greatly favored, the royal wife, Ankhet-Usertesen [?], holding a place at Kanefer, the pyramid of King Amenemhat.[1]

In the thirtieth year, the month Paophi, the seventh day, the god[2] entered his horizon, the King Sehetepabra flew up to heaven; he joined the sun's disk, he attended the god, he joined his Maker. The Residence[3] was silenced, the hearts were weakened, the Great Portals were closed, the courtiers crouching on the ground, the people in hushed mourning.

Now his Majesty had sent a great army with the nobles to the land of the Temehu,[4] his son and heir as their commander, the good King Usertesen.[5] And now he was returning, and had brought away captives and all kinds of cattle without end. The Companions of the Court sent to the West Side[6] to let the king know the state of affairs that had come about in the Audience

---

[1] This paragraph is very difficult to restore and very doubtful.

[2] I. e., the King Sehetepabra Amenemhat I., whose death is recorded in the next clause.

[3] The king's city, and so throughout the story.

[4] The land of the Temehu was in the Libyan desert on the west of Egypt.

[5] Usertesen I., the son and heir of Amenemhat I., reigned ten years jointly with his father.

[6] I. e., the western edge of Lower Egypt.

Chamber.[1]   The messenger found him on the road; he reached him at the time of evening.   " It was a time for him to hasten greatly [was the message]: Let the Hawk[2] fly [hither] with his attendants, without allowing the army to know of it. "   And when the royal sons who commanded in that army sent messages, not one of them was summoned to audience.   Behold, I was standing [near]; I heard his voice while he was speaking.[3]   I fled far away, my heart beating, my arms outspread; trembling had fallen on all my limbs.   I ran hither and thither[4] to seek a place to hide me, I threw myself amongst the bushes: and when I found a road that went forward, I set out southward, not indeed thinking to come to this Residence.[5]   I expected that there would be disturbance.   I spake not of life after it.[6]   I wandered across my estate[7] [?] in the neighborhood of Nehat; I reached the island [or lake] of Seneferu, and spent the day [resting ?] on the open field. I started again while it was yet day,[8] and came to a man standing at the side of the road.   He asked of me mercy, for he feared me.   By supper-time I drew near to the town of Negau. I crossed the river on a raft without a rudder, by the aid of a west wind, and landed at the quay [?] of the quarrymen of the Mistress at the Red Mountain.[9]   Then I fled on foot northward,

[1] Perhaps this refers to the death of the king, or to the deliberations of the royal councilors.

[2] Apparently a term for the king.

[3] Sanehat, accidentally hearing the news of the old king's death, which was kept secret even from the members of the royal family, was overcome with agitation and fled.

[4] It was of course night-time.

[5] The Royal Residence called Athet-taui lay on the boundary of Upper and Lower Egypt, between Memphis and the entrance to the Faiyûm, and so in the direction which Sanehat at first took in his flight from the western edge of the Delta.   One might prefer the word Capital to Residence, but it can hardly be doubted that Thebes and Memphis were then the real capitals of Egypt.

[6] Perhaps the meaning is that Sanehat did not imagine life possible " after the king's death," or it may be " outside the Residence."   The pronoun for " it " is masculine, and may refer either to the palace or to the king.

[7] Or possibly " I turned my course," turning now northward.

[8] Or possibly " the next day."

[9] Here the MS. is injured, and some of the words are doubtful.   The quarries are those still worked for hard quartzite at Jebel Ahmar (Red Mountain), northeast of Cairo.   The positions of most of the places mentioned in the narrative are uncertain.   Doubtless Sanehat crossed the Nile just above the fork of the Delta and landed in the neighborhood of the quarries.   The " Mistress " (Heryt), must be a goddess, or the queen.

and reached the Walls of the Ruler, built to repel the Sati.[1] I crouched in a bush for fear, seeing the day-patrol at its duty on the top of the fortress. At nightfall I set forth, and at dawn reached Peten, and skirted the lake of Kemur.[2] Then thirst hasted me on; I was parched, my throat was stopped, and I said, "This is the taste of death." When I lifted up my heart and gathered strength, I heard a voice and the lowing of cattle. I saw men of the Sati; and an alien amongst them — he who is [now?] in Egypt[3] — recognized me. Behold, he gave me water, and boiled me milk, and I went with him to his camp,— may a blessing be their portion! One tribe passed me on to another: I departed to Sun [?], and came to Kedem.[4]

There I spent a year and a month [?]. But Ammui-nen-sha, Ruler of the Upper Tenu,[5] took me and said to me:—"Comfort thyself with me, that thou mayest hear the speech of Egypt." He said thus, for that he knew my character, and had heard of my worth; for men of Egypt who were there with him bore witness of me. Then he said to me:—"For what hast thou come hither? what is it? Hath a matter come to pass in the Residence? The King of the Two Lands, Sehetepabra, hath gone to heaven, and one knoweth not what may have happened thereon." But I answered with concealment and said:—"I returned with an expedition from the land of the Temehu; my desire was redoubled, my heart leaped, there was no satisfaction within me. This drove me to the ways of a fugitive. I have not failed in my duty, my mouth hath not uttered any bitter words, I have not hearkened to any evil plot, my name hath not been heard in the mouth of the informer. I know not what hath brought me into this country." [And the Ruler Ammui-nen-sha said:][6] "This

---

[1] Asiatics and Bedawin.

[2] Kemur was one of the Bitter Lakes in the line of the present Suez Canal.

[3] Possibly one of the three persons proposed as hostages to Egypt below, p. 5246. The word translated "alien" is uncertain. It may mean a kind of consul or mediator between the tribes for the purposes of trade, etc., or simply a "sheikh." Sanehat himself, returned from Egypt in his old age, is called by the same title, p. 5248.

[4] Or possibly Adim, i. e., Edom; and so throughout.

[5] Later called Upper Retenu: they were the inhabitants of the high lands of Palestine. Ammi was a divine name in Ancient Arabia, and the name Ammi-anshi, found in South-Arabian inscriptions, perhaps of 1000 B. C., is almost identical with that of the king who befriended Sanehat.

[6] These words appear to have been omitted by the scribe.

is like the disposition of God. And now what is that land like if it know not that excellent god,[1] of whom the dread was over the nations like Sekhemt[2] in a year of pestilence?" I spake [thus] to him, and replied to him:—"Nay, but his son hath entered the palace, and taken the heritage of his father, and he is a god without an equal, nor was there any other before him [like unto him]. He is a master of wisdom, prudent in his designs, excellent in his decrees; coming out and going in is at his command. It was he that curbed the nations while his father remained within the palace, and he reported the execution of that which was laid upon him [to perform]. He is a mighty man also, working with his strong arm; a valiant one, who hath not his equal. See him when he springeth upon the barbarians, and throweth himself on the spoilers; he breaketh the horns and weakeneth the hands; his enemies cannot wield their weapons. He is fearless and dasheth heads to pieces; none can stand before him. He is swift of going, to destroy him who fleeth; and none turning his back to him reacheth his home. He is sturdy of heart in the moment [of stress]; he is a lion that striketh with the claw; never hath he turned his back. He is stout of heart when he seeth multitudes, he letteth none repose beyond what his desire would spare. He is bold of face when he seeth hesitation: his joy is to fall on the barbarians. He seizeth the buckler, and leapeth forward; he repeateth not his stroke, he slayeth, and none can turn his lance; without his bow being drawn the barbarians flee from his arms like dogs; for the great goddess hath granted him to war against those who know not his name; he is thorough, he spareth not and leaveth naught behind. He is full of grace and sweetness, a love-winner; his city loveth him more than itself, it rejoiceth in him more than in its own god; men and women go their ways, calling their children by his name. For he is a king that took the kingdom while he was in the egg, and ruled from his birth. He is a multiplier of offspring. And he is One Alone, the essence of God; this land rejoiceth in his government. He is one that enlargeth his borders; he will take the lands of the South, but he will not design to hold the countries of the North: yet he prepareth to smite the Sati, to crush the Wanderers of the Sand. When he cometh here, let him know thy name; dispute not, but

[1] I. e., What does Egypt do without the king?
[2] The goddess of destruction.

go over to his command[1]: for he will not fail to treat well the country that floateth with his stream."

Said he, agreeing to me:—"Verily, Egypt is excellent in its stream[2] beyond anything, and it flourisheth; behold, as long as thou art with me I will do good unto thee." He placed me at the head of his children, he married me with his eldest daughter. He allowed me to choose for myself from his land, and from the choicest of what he possessed on the border of the next land. It was a goodly land; Iaa[3] is its name. Therein were figs and grapes; its wine was more plentiful than water; abundant was its honey, many were its oil-trees, and all fruits were upon its trees; there too was barley and spelt, and cattle of all kinds without end. Great honors also were granted to me, flowing from his love to me; he set me as sheikh of a tribe in a choice portion of his country. There were made for me rations of bread, wine from day to day, cooked meat and roasted fowl, besides wild game snared for me or brought to me, as well as what my hunting dogs caught. They made me many dainties, and milk food cooked in all manner of ways. Thus I passed many years; my children became valiant men, each one the conqueror of a tribe. When a messenger came north or went south to the Residence,[4] he tarried with me; for I gave all men gifts; I gave water to the thirsty, I set the strayed wanderer on his road, and I rescued those who were carried off captive. The Sati who went to war or to repel the kings of the nations, I commanded their expeditions; for this Ruler of the Tenu made me to spend many years as captain of his army. Every land to which I turned I overcame. I destroyed its green fields and its wells, I captured its cattle, I took captive its inhabitants, I deprived them of their provisions, and I slew much people of them by my sword, my bow, my marchings, and my good devices. Thus my excellence was in his heart; he loved me and he knew my valor; until he set me at the head of his sons, when he saw the success of my handiwork.

There came a champion of the Tenu to defy me in my tent; a bold man without equal, for he had vanquished all his rivals. He said, "Let Sanehat fight with me." He thought to overcome

[1] Lit., "stick."

[2] A metaphor for the "policy," "will," of a king or god.

[3] Meaning "reeds" (?).

[4] *I. e.*, of Pharaoh; see above, p. 5238.

me; he designed to take my cattle, being thus counseled by his tribe. This ruler [Ammui-nen-sha] conferred with me. I said:— "I know him not. I assuredly am no associate of his; I hold me far from his place. Have I ever opened his door, or leaped over his fence? It is perverseness of heart from seeing me doing his work. Forsooth, I am as it were a stranger bull among the cows, which the bull of the herd charges, and the strong bull catches! But shall a wretched beggar desire to attain to my fortune? A common soldier cannot take part as a counselor. Then what pray shall establish the assembly?[1] But is there a bull that loveth battle, a courageous bull that loveth to repeat the charge in terrifying him whose strength he hath measured? If he hath stomach to fight, let him speak what he pleaseth. Will God forget what is ordained for him? How shall fate be known?" The night long I strung my bow, I made ready my arrows; I made keen my dagger, I furbished my arms. At daybreak the Tenu came together; it had gathered its tribes and collected the neighboring peoples. Its thoughts were on this combat; every bosom burned for me, men and women crying out; every heart was troubled for me; they said, "Is there yet another champion to fight with him?" Then [he took] his buckler, his battle-axe, and an armful of javelins. But thereon I avoided his weapons, and turned aside his arrows to the ground, useless. One drew near to the other and he rushed upon me. I shot at him and my arrow stuck in his neck; he cried out, and fell upon his nose: I brought down upon him his own battle-axe, and raised my shout of victory on his back. All the Asiatics roared, and I and his vassals whom he had oppressed gave thanks unto Mentu; this Ruler, Ammui-nen-sha, took me to his embrace. Then I took his goods, I seized his cattle. What he had thought to do to me, I did it unto him; I seized that which was in his tent, I spoiled his dwelling. I grew great thereby, I increased in my possessions. I abounded in cattle.

"May[2] the god be disposed to pardon him in whom he had trusted, and who deserted to a foreign country. Now is his

[1] A difficult passage.

[2] Without any pause or introduction Sanehat begins to quote from his petition to the King of Egypt. It is difficult to say whether this arrangement is due to an oversight of the scribe, or is intended to heighten the picturesqueness of the narrative by sudden contrast. The formal introduction might well be omitted as uninteresting. The end of the document with the salutations is preserved.

anger quenched. I who at one time fled away a fugitive, my guarantee is now in the Residence. Having wandered a starved wanderer, now I give bread to those around. Having left my land in rags, now I shine in fine linen. Having been a fugitive without followers, now I possess many serfs. My house is fair, my dwelling large, I am spoken of in the palace. All the gods destined me this flight. Mayest thou be gracious; may I be restored to the Residence; favor me that I may see the place in which my heart dwelleth. Behold how great a thing is it that my body should be embalmed in the land where I was born! Come; if afterwards there be good fortune, I will give an offering to God that he may work to make good the end of his suppliant, whose heart is heavy at long absence in a strange land. May he be gracious; may he hear the prayer of him who is afar off, that he may revisit the place of his birth, and the place from which he removed.

"May the King of Egypt be gracious to me, by whose favor men live. I salute the mistress of the land, who is in his palace; may I hear the news of her children, and may my body renew its vigor thereby. But old age cometh, weakness hasteneth me on, the eyes are heavy, my arms are failing, my feet have ceased to follow the heart. Weariness of going on approacheth me; may they convey me to the cities of eternity. May I serve the mistress of all.[1] Oh that she may tell me the beauties of her children; may she bring eternity to me."

Now the Majesty of the King of Upper and Lower Egypt, Kheper-ka-ra, justified, spake concerning this condition in which I was. His Majesty sent unto me with presents from before the king, that he might make glad the heart of your servant,[2] as he would unto the Ruler of any country; and the royal sons who were in his palace caused me to hear their news.

Copy of the command which was brought to the humble servant to bring him back to Egypt.

"THE HORUS, LIFE OF BIRTHS, LORD OF THE CROWNS, LIFE OF BIRTHS, KING OF UPPER AND LOWER EGYPT, KHEPER-KA-RA, SON OF THE SUN, USERTESEN[3] EVER LIVING UNTO ETERNITY. Royal Command for the attendant, Sanehat.

[1] A phrase for the queen.   [2] The narrator.
[3] The scribe has written Amenemhat by mistake for Usertesen.

"Behold, this command of the king is sent to thee to give thee information: Whereas thou didst go round strange lands from Kedem[1] to Tenu, one country passed thee on to another as thy heart devised for thee. Behold, what thou hast done hath been done unto thee: Thou hast not blasphemed, so also the accusation against thee hath been repelled. So also thy sayings have been respected; thou hast not spoken against the Council of the Nobles. But this matter carried away thy heart; it was not [devised] in thy heart.

"This thy Heaven[2] who is in the palace is stablished and flourishing even now: she herself shareth in the rule of the land, and her children are in the Audience Chamber.[3]

"Leave the riches that thou hast, and in the abundance of which thou livest. When thou comest to Egypt thou shalt visit the Residence in which thou wast, thou shalt kiss the ground before the Great Portals, thou shalt assume authority amongst the Companions. But day by day, behold, thou growest old; thy vigor is lost; thou thinkest on thy day of burial. Thou shalt be conducted to the blessed state; there shall be assigned to thee a night of sacred oils and wrappings from the hands of the goddess Tayt. There shall be held for thee a procession [behind thy statues] and a visit [to the temple] on the day of burial, the mummy case gilded, the head blue, the canopy above thee; the putting in the skin-frame, oxen to draw thee, singers going before thee, the answering chant, and mourners crouching at the door of thy tomb-chapel. Prayers for offerings shall be recited for thee, victims shall be slaughtered at the door portrayed upon thy tablet[4]; and thy mastaba shall be built of white stone, in the company of the royal children. Thou shalt not die in a strange land, nor be buried by the Amu; thou shalt not be put in a sheepskin, thou shalt be well regarded. It is vain [?] to beat the ground and think on troubles.

"Thou hast reached the end.[5]"

---

[1] Or Adim; see above, p. 5239, note.

[2] The queen, his exalted mistress.

[3] Taking part in the councils of the king and in the administration of the kingdom.

[4] This seems to refer to the so-called false door, representing the entrance to the underworld. All that precedes refers to burial with great ceremony.

[5] I. e., of the king's command. The absence of any concluding salutation is noticeable.

When this order came to me, I stood in the midst of my tribe, and when it was read unto me, I threw me on my belly; I bowed to the ground and let the dust spread upon my breast. I strode around my tent rejoicing and saying:—"How is this done to the servant, whose heart had transgressed to a strange country of babbling tongue? But verily good is compassion, that I should be saved from death. Thy *Ka*[1] it is that will cause me to pass the end of my days in the Residence."

Copy of the acknowledgment of this command.

"The servant of the royal house [?], Sanehat, says:—

"In most excellent peace! Known is it to thy *Ka* that this flight of thy servant was made in innocence. Thou the Good God, Lord of both Lands, Beloved of Ra, Favored of Mentu, lord of Uast, and of Amen, lord of the Thrones of the Two Lands, of Sebek, Ra, Horus, Hathor, Atmu and his Ennead, of Sepdu, Neferbiu, Semsetu, Horus of the east, and of the Mistress of the Cave[2] who resteth on thy head, of the chief circle of the gods of the waters, Min, Horus of the desert, Urert mistress of Punt, Nut, Harur-Ra, all the gods of the land of Egypt and of the isles of the sea.[3] May they put life and strength to thy nostril, may they present thee with their gifts, may they give to thee eternity without end, everlastingness without bound. May the fear of thee be doubled in the lands and in the foreign countries, mayest thou subdue the circuit of the sun. This is the prayer of the servant for his master, who hath delivered him from Amenti.[4]

"The possessor of understanding understandeth the higher order of men, and the servant recognizeth the majesty of Pharaoh. But thy servant feareth to speak it: it is a weighty matter to tell of. The great God, like unto Ra, knoweth well the work which he himself hath wrought. Who is thy servant

---

[1] The Ka or "double" was one of the spiritual constituents of man; but "thy Ka" is merely a mode of address to the exalted Pharaoh.

[2] *I. e.*, the uræus or cobra.

[3] In this long array of gods, Mentu and Amen rank next to Ra. They were both worshiped at Thebes, which was then probably capital of the whole country. It certainly was so in the next dynasty, during which this tale was presumably written down. It is curious that Ptah the god of Memphis does not appear.

[4] The place of the dead.

that he should be considered, that words should be spent upon him? Thy majesty is as Horus, and the strength of thy arms extendeth to all lands.

"Then let his Majesty command that there be brought to him Meki of Kedem, Khentiu-aaush of Khent-keshu, and Menus of the Two Lands of the Fenkhu; these are chiefs as hostages that the Tenu act according to the desire of thy *Ka*, and that Tenu will not covet what belongeth to thee in it, like thy dogs.[1] Behold this flight that thy servant made: I did not desire it, it was not in my heart; I do not boast of it; I know not what took me away from my place; it was like the leading of a dream, as a man of Adhu sees himself in Abu,[2] as a man of the Corn-land sees himself in the Land of Gardens.[3] There was no fear, none was hastening in pursuit of me; I did not listen to an evil plot, my name was not heard in the mouth of the informer; but my limbs went, my feet wandered, my heart drew me; a god ordained this flight, and led me on. But I am not stiff-necked; a man feareth if he knoweth [?], for Ra hath spread thy fear over the land, thy terrors in every foreign country. Behold me in thy palace or behold me in this place,[4] still thou art he who doth clothe this horizon. The sun riseth at thy pleasure, the water in the rivers is drunk at thy will, the wind in heaven is breathed at thy saying.

"Thy servant will leave to a successor the viziership which thy servant hath held in this land. And when thy servant shall arrive[5] let thy Majesty do as pleaseth him, for one liveth by the breath that thou givest. O thou who art beloved of Ra, of Horus, and of Hathor! It is thy august nostril that Mentu, lord of Uast, desireth should live for ever."

It was granted that I should spend a day in Iaa,[6] to pass over my goods to my children, my eldest son leading my tribe, and

---

[1] As dogs do the bidding of their master and spare his property.

[2] As a man of Natho (the marshes in the north of the Delta) dreams that he is at Elephantine (the rocky southern frontier).

[3] The second is the name of the southernmost nome of Egypt, that of Elephantine, which has practically no corn-land. It was probably made fruitful by artificial irrigation, with culture of plants, trees, and vines.

[4] So the MS., and it conveys a fair meaning; but perhaps the original ran, "Behold, *thou* art in the palace and I am in this place yet," etc.

[5] Or, "Now thy servant hath finished."

[6] Sanehat's own territory; see p. 5241.

all my goods in his hand, my people and all my cattle, my fruit, and all my pleasant trees. When thy humble servant[1] journeyed to the south, and arrived at the Roads of Horus, the officer who was over the frontier-patrol sent a report to the Residence to give notice. His Majesty sent the good overseer of the peasants of the king's domains, and ships with him laden with presents from the king for the Sati who had come with me to convey me to the Roads of Horus. I spoke to each one by his name, each officer according to his rank. I received and I returned the salutation, and I continued thus[2] until I reached Athtu.[3]

When the land was lightened, and the second day came,[4] there came some to summon me, four men in coming, four men in going,[5] to carry [?] me to the palace. I alighted on the ground between the gates of reception [?]; the royal children stood at the platform to greet [?] me; the Companions and those who ushered to the hall brought me on the way to the royal chamber.

I found his Majesty on the great throne on a platform of pale gold. Then I threw myself on my belly; this god, in whose presence I was, knew me not while he questioned me graciously; but I was as one caught in the night; my spirit fainted, my limbs shook, my heart was no longer in my bosom, and I knew the difference between life and death. His Majesty said to one of the Companions, "Lift him up; let him speak to me." And his Majesty said:—"Behold, thou hast come; thou hast trodden the deserts; thou hast played the wanderer. Decay falleth on thee, old age hath reached thee; it is no small thing that thy body should be embalmed, that thou shalt not be buried by foreign soldiers.[6] Do not, do not, be silent and speechless; tell thy name; is it fear that preventeth thee?" I answered with the answer of one terrified, "What is it that my lord hath said? O that I might answer it! It was not my act: it was the hand of God; it was a terror that was in my body, as it were causing a

---

[1] A frequent phrase for the writer or narrator, especially common in letters.

[2] "Nodding and touching my forehead" is perhaps the real translation of some difficult words here paraphrased.

[3] Probably the Residence; more commonly called Athet-taui, but here abbreviated in name.

[4] Or perhaps "very early."

[5] This probably means "four men behind me and the same number in front," either conducting Sanehat or more probably carrying him in a litter.

[6] Instead of Egyptian priests.

flight that had been foreordained. Behold I am before thee; thou art life; let thy Majesty do what pleaseth him.»

The royal children were brought in, and his Majesty said to the queen, "Behold thou, Sanehat hath come as an Amu, whom the Sati have produced."

She shrieked aloud, and the royal children joined in one cry, and said before his Majesty, "Verily it is not he, O king, my lord." Said his Majesty, "It is verily he." Then they brought their tinkling bead-strings, their wands, and their sistra in their hands, and waved them[1] before his Majesty [and they sang]:—

> "May thy hands prosper, O King;
> May the graces of the Lady of Heaven continue.
> May the goddess Nub[2] give life to thy nostril;
> May the mistress of the stars favor thee, that which is north
>   of her going south and that which is south of her going
>   north.
> All wisdom is in the mouth of thy Majesty;
> The staff [?] is put upon thy forehead, driving away from
>   thee the beggarly [?]
> Thou art pacified, O Ra, lord of the lands;
> They call on thee as on the Mistress of all.
> Strong is thy horn; let fall thine arrow.
> Grant the breath of life to him who is without it;
> Grant thy favor to this alien Samehit,[3] the foreign soldier
>   born in the land of Egypt,
> Who fled away from fear of thee,
> And left the land from thy terrors.
> The face shall not grow pale, of him who beholdeth thy
>   countenance;
> The eye shall not fear which looketh upon thee."

Said his Majesty:—"He shall not fear; let him be freed from terror. He shall be a Companion amongst the nobles; he shall be put within the circle of the courtiers. Go ye to the chamber of praise to seek wealth for him."

When I went out from the Audience Chamber, the royal children offered their hands to me; and we walked afterwards to

---

[1] These instruments rattled or clattered as they were waved or beaten together.

[2] A form of Hathor.

[3] Samehit, "son of the north," is a play on the name Sanehat, "son of the sycamore."

the Great Portals. I was placed in a house of a king's son, in which were fine things; there was a cool bower therein, fruits of the granary, treasures of the White House,[1] clothes of the king's guard-robe, frankincense, the finest perfumes of the king and the nobles whom he loves, in every chamber; and every kind of servitor in his proper office. Years were removed from my limbs: I was shaved, and my locks of hair were combed; the foulness was cast to the desert, with the garments of the Nemau-sha.[2] I clothed me in fine linen, and anointed myself with the best oil; I laid me on a bed. I gave up the sand to those who lie on it; the oil of wood to him who would anoint himself therewith.

There was given to me the house of Neb-mer [?], which had belonged to a Companion. There were many craftsmen building it; all its woodwork was strengthened anew. Portions were brought to me from the palace thrice and four times a day, besides the gifts of the royal children; there was not a moment's ceasing from them. There was built for me a pyramid of stone amongst the pyramids. The overseer of the architects measured its ground; the chief treasurer drew it; the sacred masons did the sculpture; the chief of the laborers in the necropolis brought the bricks; and all the instruments applied to a tomb were there employed. There were given to me fields; there was made for me a necropolis garden, the land in it better than a farm estate; even as is done for the chief Companion. My statue was over-laid with gold, its girdle with pale gold; his Majesty caused it to be made. Such is not done to a man of low degree.

Thus am I in the favor of the king until the day of death shall come.

This is finished from beginning to end, as was found in the writing.

Translation of F. Ll. Griffith.

[1] The treasury containing silver, gold, clothing, wine, and valuables of all kinds.

[2] Meaning «wanderers on the Sand,» Bedawin.

THE DOOMED PRINCE

['The Story of the Doomed Prince' was written at some time during the XVIIIth Dynasty (about 1450 B. C.). The papyrus on which it has been preserved to us, and which is in the British Museum, is much mutilated, and the end is entirely lost.]

THERE was once a king to whom no male child was born; he prayed for himself unto the gods whom he worshiped for a son. They decreed to cause that there should be born to him one. And his wife, after her time was fulfilled, gave birth to a male child. Came the Hathors[1] to decree for him a destiny; they said, "He dies by the crocodile, or by the serpent, or by the dog." Then the people who stood by the child heard this; they went to tell it to his Majesty. Then his Majesty's heart was exceeding sad. His Majesty caused a house to be built upon the desert, furnished with people and with all good things of the royal house, out of which the child should not go. Now when the child was grown he went up upon its roof and saw a greyhound; it was following a man walking on the road. He said to his page who was with him, "What is this that goeth behind the man coming along the road?" He said to him, "It is a greyhound." The child said to him, "Let there be brought to me one like it." The page went and reported it to his Majesty. His Majesty said, "Let there be brought to him a little trotter, lest his heart be sad." Then they brought to him the greyhound.

Now when the days were multiplied after these things, the child grew up in all his limbs, he sent a message to his father saying, "Wherefore should I remain here? Behold, I am destined to three dooms, and if I do according to my desire God will still do what is in his heart." They hearkened to all he said, and gave him all kinds of weapons, and also his greyhound to follow him, and they conveyed him over to the east side and said to him, "Go thou whither thou wilt." His greyhound was with him; he traveled northward following his heart in the desert; he lived on the best of all the game of the desert. He came to the chief of Naharaina.

---

[1] The Hathors were seven goddesses who attended the birth of a child in order to tell its fate. They somewhat correspond to the fairy godmothers of later fairy tales.

Behold, there was no child born to the prince of Naharaina except one daughter. Behold, he built for her a house; its window was seventy cubits from the ground, and he caused to be brought all the sons of all the chiefs of the land of Kharu,[1] and said to them, "He who shall reach the window of my daughter, she shall be to him for a wife."

Now when the days had multiplied after these things, as they were in their daily task, the youth came by them. They took the youth to their house, they bathed him, they gave provender to his horse, they did every kind of thing for the youth; they anointed him, they bound up his feet, they gave him portions of their own food; they spake to him in the manner of conversation, "Whence comest thou, good youth?" He said to them:—"I am the son of an officer of the land of Egypt; my mother is dead, my father has taken another wife. When she bore children, she began to hate me, and I have come as a fugitive from before her." They embraced him and kissed him.

Now when the days were multiplied after these things, he said to the youths, "What is it that ye do here?" And they said to him, "We spend our time in this: we climb up, and he who shall reach the window of the daughter of the prince of Naharaina, to him she will be given to wife." He said to them, "Lo! I desire to try, I shall go to climb with you." They went to climb, as was their daily wont: the youth stood afar off to behold; and the face of the daughter of the prince of Naharaina was turned to him. Now when the days were multiplied after these things, the youth came to climb with the sons of the chiefs. He climbed, he reached the window of the daughter of the prince of Naharaina. She kissed him, she embraced him.

One went to rejoice the heart of her father, and said to him, "A man has reached the window of thy daughter." The prince spake of it, saying, "The son of which of the princes is it?" He said to him, "It is the son of an officer, who has come as a fugitive from the land of Egypt, fleeing from before his stepmother when she had children." Then the prince of Naharaina was exceeding angry; he said, "Shall I indeed give my daughter to the Egyptian fugitive? Let him go back." One came to tell the youth, "Go back to the place from which thou hast come." But the maiden took hold of him; she swore an oath by God, saying, "By the life of Ra Harakhti, if one taketh him from me,

[1] Syria.

I will not eat, I will not drink, I shall die in that same hour.»
The messenger went to tell unto her father all that she said.
Then the prince sent men to slay him, while he was in his
house. But the maiden said, "By the life of Ra, if one slay him
I shall be dead ere the sun goeth down. I will not pass an
hour of life if I am parted from him." One went to tell her
father. Then . . . the prince came; he embraced him, he
kissed him all over, and said, "Tell me who thou art; behold,
thou art to me as a son." · He said to him:—"I am a son of an
officer of the land of Egypt; my mother died, my father took to
him a second wife; she came to hate me, and I fled from before
her." He gave to him his daughter to wife; he gave also to
him people and fields, also cattle and all manner of good things.

Now when time had passed over these things, the youth said
to his wife, "I am destined to three dooms—a crocodile, a
serpent, and a dog." She said to him, "Let one kill the dog
that runs before thee." He said to her, "I will not let my dog
be killed, which I have brought up from when it was small."
And she feared greatly for her husband, and would not let him
go alone abroad.

One did . . . the land of Egypt, to travel. Behold, the
crocodile, . . . he came opposite the city in which the youth
was. . . . Behold, there was a mighty man therein; the
mighty man would not suffer the crocodile to go out, . . .
the crocodile. The mighty man went out to walk when the sun
. . . every day, during two months of days.

Now when the days passed after this, the youth sat mak-
ing a good day in his house. When the evening came he lay
down on his bed; sleep seized upon his limbs; his wife filled a
bowl of milk and placed it by his side. There came out a
serpent from his hole, to bite the youth; behold, his wife was sit-
ting by him; she lay not down. Thereupon the servants gave
milk to the serpent; it drank and became drunk, and lay down,
upside down; his wife cut it in pieces with her hatchet. They
woke her husband; . . . she said to him, "Behold, thy god
hath given one of thy dooms into thy hand; he shall give
. . ." And he sacrificed to God, adoring him, and praising
his mighty spirit from day to day.

Now when the days were multiplied after these things, the
youth went to walk in the pathway in his enclosure, for he went
not outside alone; behold, his dog was behind him. His dog put

his nose to the ground [to pursue some game], and he ran after him. He came to the sea, and entered the sea behind his dog. The crocodile came out, he took him to the place where the mighty man was. . . . The crocodile, he said to the youth, "I am thy doom, following after thee. . . ."

[Here the papyrus breaks off.]

Translation of F. Ll. Griffith.

THE STORY OF THE TWO BROTHERS

['The Story of the Two Brothers' is in places incoherent, but charms throughout by beautiful and natural touches. The copy in which it has been preserved to us is practically complete, but is full of errors of writing and of composition, whole sentences having crept in that are useless, or contradictory to the context. The style is however absolutely simple and narrative, and the language entirely free from archaisms.

The papyrus, which bears the name of Seti II. as crown prince, dates from the XIXth Dynasty. The beginnings of many of the sentences and paragraphs are written in red: this is specially the case when a sentence commences with an indication of time, usually expressed in a fixed formula. In such cases the translation of the passage written in red is here printed in italics.]

ONCE there were two brothers, of one mother and one father; Anpu was the name of the elder, and Bata was the name of the younger. Now, as for Anpu, he had a house and he had a wife. His younger brother was to him as it were a son; he it was who made for him his clothes, while he walked behind his oxen to the fields; he it was who did the plowing; he it was who harvested the corn; he it was who did for him all the work of the fields. Behold, his younger brother grew to be an excellent worker; there was not his equal in the whole land; behold, the strain of a god was in him.

Now when the days multiplied after these things, his younger brother followed his oxen as his manner was, daily; every evening he turned again to the house, laden with all the herbs of the field, with milk and with wood, and with all things of the field. He put them down before his elder brother, who was sitting with his wife; he drank and ate; he lay down in his stable with the cattle.

Now when the earth lighted and the second day came, he took bread which he had baked, and laid it before his elder brother; and he took with him his bread to the field, and he drave his cattle to pasture them in the fields. And he used to walk behind his cattle, they saying to him, "Good is the herbage which is in such a place;" and he hearkened to all that they said, and he took them to the good pasture which they desired. And the cattle which were before him became exceeding excellent, and they became prolific greatly.

Now at the time of plowing, his elder brother said unto him, "Let us make ready for ourselves a yoke of oxen for plowing; for the land hath come out from the water; it is good for plowing in this state; and do thou come to the field with corn, for we will begin the plowing in the morrow morning." Thus said he to him; *and his* younger brother did everything that his elder brother had bidden him, to the end.

Now when the earth lighted and the second day came, they went to the fields with their yoke of oxen; and their hearts were pleased exceedingly with that which they accomplished in the beginning of their work.

Now when the days were multiplied after these things, they were in the field; they stopped for seed corn, and he sent his younger brother, saying, "Haste thou, bring to us corn from the farm." And the younger brother found the wife of his elder brother; [some] one was sitting arranging her hair. He said to her [the wife], "Get up, and give to me seed corn, that I may run to the field, for my elder brother hastened me; be not slow." She said to him, "Go, open the store, and thou shalt take for thyself what is in thy heart; do not interrupt the course of my hair-dressing."

The youth went into his stable; he took a large measure, for he desired to take much corn; he loaded it with barley and spelt; and he went out carrying them. She said to him, "How much of the corn that is wanted, is that which is on thy shoulder?" He said to her, "Three bushels of spelt, and two of barley, in all five; these are what are upon my shoulder;" thus said he to her. And she spake with him, saying, "There is great strength in thee, for I see thy might every day." And her desire was to know him with the knowledge of youth. She arose and took hold of him, and said to him, "Come, lie with me; behold, this shall be to thine advantage, for I will make for thee beautiful garments." Then the youth became like a leopard of the south in fury at the evil speech which she had made to him; and she feared greatly. He spake with her, saying, "Behold, thou art to me as a mother; thy husband is to me as a father; for he who is elder than I hath brought me up. What is this great wickedness that thou hast said? Say it not to me again. For I will not tell it to any man, that it should go forth by the mouth of all men." He lifted up his burden, and he went to the field and came to his elder brother; and they took up their work, to labor at their task.

Now afterwards, at the time of evening, his elder brother was returning to his house; the younger brother was following after his oxen; he loaded himself with all the things of the field; he brought his oxen before him, to make them lie down in their stable which was in the farm. Behold, the wife of the elder brother was afraid for the words which she had said. She took a pot of fat; she made herself as one who had been beaten by miscreants, in order that she might say to her husband, "It is thy younger brother who hath done this wrong." Her husband returned in the even, as his manner was every day; he came unto his house; he found his wife lying down, ill of violence; she did not put water upon his hands as his manner was; she did not make a light before him; his house was in darkness, and she was lying vomiting. Her husband said to her, "Who hath spoken with thee?" Behold, she said, "No one hath spoken with me except thy younger brother. When he came to take for thee seed corn he found me sitting alone; he said to me, 'Come, let us lie together; put on thy wig¹;' thus spake he to me. I would not hearken to him: 'Behold, am I not thy mother, is not thy elder brother to thee as a father?' Thus spake I to him, and he feared, and he beat me to stop me from making report to thee, and if thou lettest him live I shall kill myself. Now behold, when he cometh to-morrow, seize upon him; I will accuse him of this wicked thing which he would have done the day before."

The elder brother became as a leopard of the south; he sharpened his knife; he took it in his hand; he stood behind the door of his stable to slay his younger brother as he came in the evening to let his cattle into the stable.

Now the sun went down, and he loaded himself with all the herbs of the field in his manner of every day. He came; his leading cow entered the stable; she said to her keeper, "Behold, thy elder brother is standing before thee with his knife to

---

¹ The Egyptians shaved their heads and wore wigs, as a matter of cleanliness in a hot climate.

slay thee; flee from before him." He heard what his leading cow had said; the next entered and said likewise. He looked beneath the door of the stable; he saw the feet of his elder brother standing behind the door with his knife in his hand. He put down his load on the ground, he set out to flee swiftly; his elder brother pursued after him with his knife. Then the younger brother cried out unto Ra Harakhti, saying, "My good Lord! Thou art he who distinguishest wrong from right." Ra hearkened to all his complaint; Ra caused to be made a great water between him and his elder brother, full of crocodiles; the one brother was on one bank, the other on the other bank; and the elder brother smote twice on his hands at not slaying him. Thus did he. The younger brother called to the elder on the bank, saying, "Stand still until the dawn of day; when Ra ariseth I shall argue with thee before him, and he giveth the wrong to the right. For I shall not be with thee unto eternity. I shall not be in the place in which thou art; I shall go to the Valley of the Acacia."

Now when the earth lighted and the second day came, Ra Harakhti[1] shone out, and each of them saw the other. The youth spake with his elder brother, saying:—"Wherefore camest thou after me to slay me wrongfully, when thou hadst not heard my mouth speak? For I am thy younger brother in truth; thou art to me as a father; thy wife is to me even as a mother: is it not so? Verily, when I was sent to bring for us seed corn, thy wife said to me, 'Come lie with me.' Behold, this has been turned over to thee upside down." He caused him to understand all that happened with him and his wife. He swore an oath by Ra Harakhti, saying, "Thy coming to slay me wrongfully, having thy spear, was the instigation of a wicked and filthy one." He took a reed knife and mutilated himself; he cast the flesh into the water, and the silurus swallowed it. He sank; he became faint; his elder brother chided his heart greatly; he stood weeping for him loudly, that he could not cross to where his younger brother was, because of the crocodiles. The younger brother called unto him, saying, "Whereas thou hast devised an evil thing, wilt thou not also devise a good thing, or such a thing as I would do unto thee? When thou goest to thy house thou must look to thy cattle; for I stay not in the place where thou art, I am going to the Valley of the Acacia. Now as to what thou

[1] The sun.

shalt do for me: verily, understand this, that things shall happen unto me; namely, that I shall draw out my soul, that I shall put it upon the top of the flowers of the acacia; the acacia-tree will be cut down, it shall fall to the ground, and thou shalt come to seek for it, and if thou passest seven years searching for it, let not thy heart sicken. Thou shalt find it; thou must put it in a cup of cold water that I may live again, that I may make answer to what hath been done wrong. Thou shalt understand this; namely, that things are happening to me, when one shall give to thee a pot of beer in thy hand and it shall foam up: stay not then, for verily it shall come to pass with thee."

He went to the Valley of the Acacia; his elder brother went to his house; his hand was laid on his head; he cast dust on his head; he came to his house, he slew his wife, he cast her to the dogs, and he sat in mourning for his younger brother.

Now when the days were multiplied after these things, his younger brother was in the Valley of the Acacia; there was none with him; he spent the day hunting the game of the desert, he came back in the even to lie down under the acacia, the topmost flower of which was his soul.

Now when the days were multiplied after these things, he built himself a tower with his hand, in the Valley of the Acacia; it was full of all good things, that he might provide for himself a home.

He went out from his tower, he met the Ennead of the gods,[1] who were going forth to arrange the affairs of their whole land. The Nine Gods talked one with another, they said unto him: "Ho! Bata, Bull of the Ennead of the gods, art thou remaining alone, having fled thy village from before the wife of Anpu thy elder brother? Behold, his wife is slain. Thou hast given him an answer to all that was transgressed against thee." Their hearts were sad for him exceedingly. Ra Harakhti said to Khnumu,[1] "Behold, frame thou a wife for Bata, that he may not sit alone." Khnumu made for him a mate to dwell with him. She was more beautiful in her limbs than any woman who is in the whole land. Every god was in her. The seven Hathors

---

[1] Ra Harakhti was the chief of this Ennead. Khnumu, one of his companion gods, was the craftsman, sometimes represented as fashioning mankind upon the potter's wheel.

came to see her: they said with one mouth, "She will die a sharp death."

He loved her very exceedingly, and she dwelt in his house; he passed his time in hunting the game of the desert, and brought what he took before her. He said, "Go not outside, lest the sea seize thee; for I cannot rescue thee from it, for I am a woman like thee: my soul is placed on the top of the flower of the acacia; and if another find it, I shall be vanquished by him." He explained to her all about his soul.

Now when the days were multiplied after these things, Bata went to hunt as his daily manner was. The girl went to walk under the acacia which was by the side of her house; the sea saw her, and cast its waves up after her. She set out to run away from it; she entered her house. The sea called unto the acacia, saying, "Oh, catch hold of her for me!" The acacia brought a lock from her hair, the sea carried it to Egypt, and dropped it in the place of the washers of Pharaoh's linen. The smell of the lock of hair entered into the clothes of Pharaoh. They were wroth with Pharaoh's washers, saying, "The smell of ointment is in the clothes of Pharaoh." The men were rebuked every day; they knew not what they should do. The chief of the washers of Pharaoh went down to the seaside; his soul was black within him because of the chiding with him daily. He stopped and stood upon the sandy shore opposite to the lock of hair, which was in the water; he made one go in, and it was brought to him; there was found in it a smell, exceeding sweet. He took it to Pharaoh; the scribes and the wise men were brought to Pharaoh; they said unto Pharaoh:—"This lock of hair belongs to a daughter of Ra Harakhti; the strain of every god is in her; it is a tribute to thee from a strange land. Let messengers go to every foreign land to seek her: as for the messenger who shall go to the Valley of the Acacia, let many men go with him to bring her." Then said his Majesty, "Excellent exceedingly is what we have said;" and the men were sent.

When the days were multiplied after these things, the people who went abroad came to give report unto the king: but there came not those who went to the Valley of the Acacia, for Bata had slain them; he spared one of them to give a report to the king. His Majesty sent many men and soldiers as well as horsemen, to bring her back. There was a woman among them, into whose hand was put every kind of beautiful ornaments for a woman. The girl came back with her; there were rejoicings for her in the whole land.

His Majesty loved her exceedingly, and raised her to be a princess of high rank; he spake with her that she should tell concerning her husband. She said to his Majesty, "Let the acacia be cut down, and let one chop it up." They sent men and soldiers with their weapons to cut down the acacia; they came to the acacia, they cut the flower upon which was the soul of Bata, and he fell dead upon the instant.

Now when the earth lighted and the second day came, the acacia was cut down. And Anpu, the elder brother of Bata, entered his house; he sat down and washed his hands: one gave him a pot of beer, it foamed up; another was given him of wine, it became foul. He took his staff, his sandals, likewise his clothes, with his weapons of war; he set out to walk to the Valley of the Acacia. He entered the tower of his younger brother; he found his younger brother lying on his bed; he was dead. He wept when he saw his younger brother verily lying dead. He went out to seek the soul of his younger brother under the acacia tree, under which his younger brother used to lie in the evening. He spent three years in seeking for it, but found it not. When he began the fourth year, he desired in his heart to return into Egypt; he said, "I will go to-morrow;" thus spake he in his heart.

When the earth lighted and the second day came, he went out under the acacia, and set to work to seek it again. He found a seed-pod. He returned with it. Behold, this was the soul of his younger brother. He brought a cup of cold water, he dropped it into it: he sat down, as his manner of every day was. Now when the night came his [Bata's] soul absorbed the water; Bata shuddered in all his limbs, he looked on his elder brother; his soul was in the cup. Then Anpu took the cup of cold water in which the soul of his younger brother was; he [Bata] drank it, his soul stood again in its place, he became as he had been. They embraced each other, and they spake with one another.

Bata said to his elder brother, "Behold, I am to become as a great bull, with all the right markings; no one knoweth its history, and thou must sit upon his back. When the sun arises we will go to that place where my wife is, that I may return answer to her; and thou must take me to the place where the king is. For all good things shall be done for thee, and one shall lade thee with silver and gold, because thou bringest me to Pharaoh; for I become a great marvel, they shall rejoice for me in all the land. And thou shalt go to thy village.»

When the earth lighted and the second day came, Bata became in the form which he had told to his elder brother. And Anpu his elder brother sat upon his back until the dawn. He came to the place where the king was; they made his Majesty to know of him; he saw him, and he rejoiced exceedingly. He made for him great offerings, saying, "This is a great wonder which has come to pass." There were rejoicings over him in the whole land. They loaded him with silver and gold for his elder brother, who went and settled in his village. They gave to the bull many men and many things, and Pharaoh loved him exceedingly above all men that are in this land.

Now when the days were multiplied after these things, the bull entered the place of purifying; he stood in the place where the princess was; he began to speak with her, saying, "Behold, I am alive indeed." She said to him, "Who then art thou?" He said to her: "I am Bata. Thou knewest well when thou causedst that they should cut down the acacia for Pharaoh, that it was to my hurt, that I might not be suffered to live. Behold, I am alive indeed, being as an ox." Then the princess feared exceedingly for the words that her husband had spoken to her. And he went out from the place of purifying.

His Majesty was sitting, making a good day with her: she was at the table of his Majesty, and the king was exceeding pleased with her. She said to his Majesty, "Swear to me by God, saying, 'What thou shalt say, I will obey it for thy sake.'" He hearkened unto all that she said. And she said, "Let me eat of the liver of this bull, because he will do nothing;" thus spake she to him. He was exceedingly vexed at that which she said, the heart of Pharaoh was grieved exceedingly.

Now when the earth lighted and the second day came, there was proclaimed a great feast with offerings to the ox. The king sent one of the chief butchers of his Majesty, to have the ox sacrificed. Afterwards it was caused to be sacrificed, and when it was in the hands of the men, it shook its neck, and threw two drops of blood over against the double door of his Majesty. One fell upon the one side of the great door of Pharaoh, and the other upon the other side. They grew as two great Persea trees; each of them was excellent.

One went to tell unto his Majesty, "Two great Persea trees have grown, as a great marvel for his Majesty, in the night, by the side of the great gate of his Majesty." There was rejoicing for them in all the land, and there were offerings made to them.

Now when the days were multiplied after these things, his Majesty was adorned with a blue crown, with garlands of flowers on his neck; he was upon the chariot of electrum; he went out from the palace to behold the Persea trees: the princess also went out with horses behind Pharaoh. His Majesty sat beneath one of the Persea trees, and it spake thus with his wife: — "Oh thou deceitful one, I am Bata; I am alive, though I have suffered violence. Thou knewest well that the causing of the acacia to be cut down for Pharaoh was to my hurt. I then became an ox, and thou hadst me slain."

Now when the days were multiplied after these things, the princess stood at the table of Pharaoh, and the king was pleased with her. She said to his Majesty, "Swear to me by God, saying, 'That which the princess shall say to me I will obey it for her.' Thus do thou." And he hearkened unto all that she said. She said, "Let these two Persea trees be cut down, and let them be made into goodly timber." He hearkened unto all that she said.

Now when the days were multiplied after these things, his Majesty sent skillful craftsmen, and they cut down the Persea trees of Pharaoh, while the princess, the royal wife, stood by and saw it. A chip flew up and entered into the mouth of the princess; and she perceived that she had conceived, and while her days were being fulfilled Pharaoh did all that was in her heart therein.[1]

Now when the days were multiplied after these things, she bore a male child. One went to tell his Majesty, "There is born to thee a son." They brought him [*i. e.*, the child, to the king], and gave to him a nurse and servants; there were rejoicings in the whole land. The king sat making a good day; they performed the naming of him, his Majesty loved him exceedingly on the instant, the king raised him to be the royal son of Kush.

Now when the days were multiplied after these things, his Majesty made him heir of all the land.

Now when the days were multiplied after these things, when he had fulfilled many years as heir of the whole land, his

[1] *I. e.*, in the matter of the trees.

Majesty flew up to heaven. There was command given, "Let my great nobles of his Majesty be brought before me, that I may make them to know all that has happened to me." And they brought to him his wife, and he argued with her before them, and their case was decided. They brought to him his elder brother; he made him hereditary prince in all his land. He was thirty years King of Egypt, and he died, and his elder brother stood in his place on the day of burial.

Excellently finished in peace, for the Ka *of the scribe of the treasury, Kagabu, of the treasury of Pharaoh, and for the scribe Hora, and the scribe Meremapt. Written by the scribe Anena, the owner of this roll. He who speaks against this roll, may Tahuti be his opponent.*

Translation of F. Ll. Griffith.

THE STORY OF SETNA

[The beginning of this tale is lost, but it is clear from what remains of it that Setna Kha-em-uast, son of a Pharaoh who may be identified with Rameses II., of the XIXth Dynasty (about 1300 B. C.), was a diligent student of the ancient writings, chiefly for the sake of the occult knowledge which they were supposed to contain. He discovered, or was told of, the existence of a book which Thoth, the god of letters, science, and magic, had "written with his own hand," and learned that this book was to be found in the cemetery of Memphis, in the tomb of Na-nefer-ka-ptah, the only son of some earlier Pharaoh. Setna evidently succeeded in finding and entering this tomb, and there he saw the *kas* or ghosts of Na-nefer-ka-ptah, his wife (and sister) Ahura, and their little boy Merab; and with them was the book. To dissuade Setna from abstracting the book, Ahura tells him how they had become possessed of it, and had paid for it with their earthly lives; and *it is with her tale that the papyrus begins.* Setna, however, insists upon taking the book; but Na-nefer-ka-ptah challenges him, as a good scribe and a learned man, to a trial of skill in a game, and in the imposition of magical penalties on the loser. Setna agrees; but being worsted, he calls in outside help and succeeds in carrying off the book. Na-nefer-ka-ptah comforts Ahura for its loss by assuring her that Setna shall ignominiously restore it. Setna studies the book with delight; but presently, by the magic power of Na-nefer-ka-ptah, he becomes the victim of an extraordinary hallucination, and the strength of his spirit is broken because (in imagination at least) he is steeped in impurity and crime. When he awakes from this trance, Pharaoh persuades him to return the book to its dead owners. On his return to the tomb, Na-nefer-ka-ptah exacts from him the promise to go to the cemetery of Koptos and bring thence to Memphis the bodies of Ahura and of Merab, which had been buried there, apart from him. Setna duly performs his promise, and so the story ends.

The only known copy of this tale appears to have been written in 251 B. C., the thirty-fifth year of Ptolemy Philadelphus, and it must have been composed at least as late as the Sebennyte Dynasty, early in the fourth century, although it refers to historical characters of a thousand years before.

The story is more elaborate, and its plot is more coherent than is the case with the earlier tales such as that of Anpu and Bata, in which events succeed each other often without natural connection. The language however is in simple narrative style, without any attempt at fine writing.

At the point at which the mutilated papyrus begins, we find that Ahura is telling Setna the story of her life. Apparently he has just been told how she sent a messenger to the king, asking that she may be married to her brother Na-nefer-ka-ptah. The king has refused her request, and the messenger has reproached him for his unkindness; the king replies:—]

" ' IT is thou who art dealing wrongly towards me. If it happen that I have not a child after two children, is it the law to marry the one with the other of them? I will marry Naneferkaptah with the daughter of a commander of troops, and I will marry Ahura with the son of another commander of troops: it has so happened in our family much.'

"It came to pass that the amusement was set before Pharaoh, and they came for me and took me to the amusement named, and it happened that my soul was troubled exceedingly and I behaved not in my manner of the previous day. Said Pharaoh to me, 'Ahura, is it thou that didst cause them to come to me in these anxieties, saying, "Let me marry with Naneferkaptah, my elder brother"?'

"Said I to him, 'Let me marry with the son of a commander of troops, and let him marry with the daughter of another commander of troops: it has happened in our family much.'

"I laughed, Pharaoh laughed, and his soul was exceeding gladdened. Said Pharaoh to the steward of the king's house, 'Let Ahura be taken to the house of Naneferkaptah to-night, and let all things that are good be taken with her.'

"I was taken as a wife to the house of Naneferkaptah in the night named, and a present of silver and gold was brought to me; the household of Pharaoh caused them all to be brought to me. And Naneferkaptah made a good day[1] with me; he received all the heads of the household of Pharaoh. And he found me pleasing, he quarreled not with me, ever, ever: each of us loved his fellow. And when I was about to bear a child, report of it was made before Pharaoh, and his soul was exceeding gladdened,

---

[1] "To make a good day" = to keep holiday, to hold festival.

and Pharaoh caused many things to be taken for me on the instant; he caused to be brought to me a present of silver and gold and royal linen, beautiful exceedingly. Then came my time of bearing; I bore this boy that is before thee, whose name is called Merab, and he was caused to write in the book of the 'House of Life.'[1]

"It came to pass that Naneferkaptah, my brother, had no habit on the earth[2] but to walk in the cemetery of Memphis, reading the writings that were in the catacombs of the Pharaohs, with the tablets of the scribes of the 'House of Life,' and the inscriptions that were on the monuments; and he was eager for writing exceedingly.

"After these things it befell that there was a procession in honor of Ptah; Naneferkaptah went into the temple to worship, and he chanced to be walking behind the procession reading the inscriptions that were in the shrines of the gods. An aged priest saw him and laughed. Naneferkaptah said to him, 'For what art thou laughing at me?'

"And he said:—'I am not laughing at thee; if I laughed, it was that thou art reading writings that no one on earth has any good of. If it be that thou seekest to read writings, come to me, and I will bring thee to the place where that roll is which it was Thoth that wrote with his own hand, and which goes down to fetch the gods. There are two formulas of writing that are upon it, and when thou readest the first formula thou will enchant the heaven, the earth, the underworld, the mountains, and the seas; thou shalt discover all that the birds of the heaven and the creeping things shall say; thou shalt see the fishes of the deep, for there is a power from God brings them into water above them. And when thou readest the second formula, if it be that thou art in Ament[3] thou takest thy form of earth again. Thou wilt see the sun rising in the sky with his circle of gods, and the moon in its form of shining.'

"And Naneferkaptah said, 'As the king liveth! Let a good thing that thou dost desire be told me, and I will have it done for thee, if thou wilt direct me to the place where this roll is.'

[1] This apparently means that he was enrolled as one to be educated as a learned scribe.

[2] *I. e.*, as we should say, "he did nothing in the world but walk in the cemetery of Memphis," etc.

[3] The realm of Osiris as god of the dead.

"Said the priest to Naneferkaptah: 'If it be that thou desirest to be directed to the place where this roll is, thou shalt give me three hundred ounces of silver for my funeral, and provide that they shall make me two coffin cases as a great priest, rich in silver.'

"Naneferkaptah called a lad, and caused to be given the three hundred ounces of silver for the priest, and he caused to be done what he desired for two coffin cases; he caused them to be made as for a great and rich priest.

"Said the priest to Naneferkaptah:—'The roll named, it is in the midst of the Sea of Koptos,[1] in a box of iron. In the iron box is a box of bronze, in the bronze box is a box of *Kedt* wood, in the box of *Kedt* wood is a box of ivory and ebony, in the box of ivory and ebony is a box of silver, in the box of silver is a box of gold in which is the roll. There is a mile of snakes, scorpions, and every kind of reptile surrounding the box in which the roll is; there is a snake of eternity surrounding the box named.'

"At the time of the relation that the priest made before Naneferkaptah, Naneferkaptah knew not what place on earth he was in.[2] And he came out of the temple and related before me all that the priest had said to him. He said to me, 'I shall go to Koptos, I shall fetch this roll thence; I shall not be slow in coming back to the north again.'

"It came to pass that I opposed the priest, saying: 'Beware of this thing that thou hast spoken before him! Thou hast brought to me the strife of the nome of Thebes;[3] I have found it cruel.' I caused my hand to stay[4] with Naneferkaptah, in order not to let him go to Koptos. He did not hearken to me; he went before Pharaoh and related before Pharaoh everything that the priest had said to him—all. Pharaoh said to him, 'What is it that thou desirest?'

"He said to him, 'Cause to be given to me the royal pleasure boat with its equipment: I will take Ahura and Merab her boy to the south with me; I will fetch this roll without delaying.'

[1] It is difficult to locate this lake in accordance with the actual geography of Egypt.

[2] A frequent phrase for extreme delight or amazement.

[3] There seems to be some reference to past history in this.

[4] An idiomatic phrase like "he caused his hand to go after the roll" for "put out his hand to take the roll," p. 5272.

"They gave him the royal pleasure-boat with its equipment, and we went up on board it; we set sail and reached Koptos. And they made report of it before the priests of Isis of Koptos and the high priest of Isis; they came down to meet us, they delayed not to meet Naneferkaptah; their women came down to meet me also. We went up on shore; we went into the temple of Isis and Harpokrates, and Naneferkaptah caused to be brought ox, goose, and wine; he made a burnt-offering and a drink-offering before Isis of Koptos and Harpokrates. We were taken to a house exceeding beautiful, filled with all good things, and Naneferkaptah spent four days making a good day with the priests of Isis of Koptos, the women of the priests of Isis making a good day with myself.

"Came the morning of our fifth day: Naneferkaptah caused to be brought to him pure wax.[1] He made a boat, furnished with its crew and its tackle. He read a spell to them, he caused them to live, he gave them breath, he cast them into the sea. He loaded the royal pleasure-boat of Pharaoh with sand; he caused the boat to be brought, he went on board. I sat by the sea of Koptos, saying, 'I will discover what will become of him.'

"He said, 'Boatmen, row on with me as far as the place in which this roll is.' And they rowed by night as by midday.

"And when he reached it, in three days, he threw sand before him, then there became a space of dry land. And when he found a mile of serpents and scorpions, and every kind of creeping thing encompassing the box in which the roll was, and when he found a snake of eternity encompassing the box, he read a spell to the mile of serpents, scorpions, and every kind of creeping thing that was around the box, and suffered them not to leap up. He went to the place in which was the snake of eternity; he made battle with it, he slew it. It lived; it made its form again. He made battle with it again for a second time; he slew it: it lived. He made battle with it again for a third time; he made it in two pieces; he put sand between one piece and its fellow. It died; it did not make its form ever again.

"Naneferkaptah went to the place where the box was. He found that it was a box of iron; he opened it, he found a box of bronze; he opened it, he found a box of *Kedt* wood; he opened it, he found a box of ivory and ebony; he opened it, he found a

---

[1] Wax was the regular material used for the manufacture of models which were intended to be used in the practice of magic.

box of silver; he opened it, he found a box of gold; he opened it, he found the book in it. He took up the roll from in the box of gold, he read a formula of writing from it. He enchanted the heaven, the earth, the underworld, the mountains, and the seas; he discovered all that the birds of the heaven with the fishes of the deep, the beasts of the mountains said — all. He read another formula of writing, he saw the Sun rising in the sky with all his circle of gods, and the moon rising, and the stars in their shapes; he saw the fishes of the deep, for there was a power from God brought them into the water over them. He read a spell to the sea, and restored it as it was. He embarked. He said to the crew, 'Row on for me as far as the place to which I go.' And they rowed at night like as at midday. When he reached the place where I was, he found me sitting by the sea of Koptos, without drinking or eating anything, without doing anything on the earth, being in the likeness of one who has reached the Good Houses.[1]

"I said to Naneferkaptah, 'O Naneferkaptah, let me see this book, for which we have taken these pains!'

"He put the roll into my hand. I read a formula of writing in it; I enchanted the heaven, the earth, the underworld, the mountains, the seas; I discovered what the birds of the sky, the fishes of the deep, and the beasts of the hills said — all. I read another formula of the writing, and I saw the sun rising in the sky with his circle of gods; I saw the moon shining with all the stars of the heaven in their nature; I saw the fishes of the deep, for it was that a power from God brought them into the water above where they were. As I could not write, it was that I spoke to Naneferkaptah my elder brother, who was a good scribe and a learned man exceedingly; and he caused to be brought before him a piece of new papyrus; he wrote every word that was on the roll before him — all. He dipped it in beer, he melted it in water, he saw that it had been melted, he drank it, he knew that which was in it.[2]

"We returned to Koptos on the day named: we made a good day before Isis of Koptos and Harpokrates. We embarked, we went down to the river, we reached north of Koptos by one mile.

[1] The place of embalmment.

[2] A similar method is still employed by Arab doctors and wizards. To heal a disease a formula is written out and then washed off the paper in a bowl of water, which is given to the patient to drink.

Behold, Thoth had discovered everything that happened to Na-
neferkaptah on account of the roll; Thoth delayed not, he com-
plained before the Sun, saying, 'Know my right, my judgment
with Naneferkaptah the son of Pharaoh Mernebptah! He went
to my place, he robbed it, he took my box containing my book,
he killed my guard who was watching it.'

"It was said to him, 'He is before thee, with every man that
belongeth to him—all.'[1]

"There was sent a power from God down from heaven, saying,
'Let not Naneferkaptah go to Memphis safe, with every man that
belongeth to him—all.'

"An hour passed: Merab, the boy, came out from under the
awning of the pleasure-boat of Pharaoh, he fell into the river, he
did the will of Ra. Everybody that was on board uttered a cry
—all. Naneferkaptah came out from under his cabin, he read a
writing over him, he caused him to come up, for it was that a
power from God in the water was laid on his upper side.[2] He
read a writing over him, he made him relate before him of every-
thing that had happened to him—all, and the accusation that
Thoth made before Ra.

"We returned to Koptos with him. We caused him to be
taken to the Good House and laid in state; we caused him to be
embalmed like a prince and great man; we caused him to rest in
his coffin in the cemetery of Koptos.

"Said Naneferkaptah my brother, 'Let us go down the river,
let us not delay before Pharaoh hear the things that have hap-
pened to us, and his soul be sad therefore.'

"We embarked, we went down-stream, we delayed not; and
traveled to the north of Koptos by one mile. At the place of
the falling of Merab the boy into the river, I came out from
under the awning of the pleasure-boat of Pharaoh, I fell into the
river, I did the will of Ra. Everybody that was on board uttered
a cry—all. They told it to Naneferkaptah, he came out from
under the awning of the pleasure-boat of Pharaoh, he read a
writing over me, he caused me to leap up, for it was that a
power from God in the water rested on my upper side. He
caused me to be taken up, he read a writing over me, he caused
me to relate before him everything that had happened unto me
—all; and the accusation that Thoth had made before Ra. He

[1] Cf. Job i., 12.
[2] I. e., above him.

returned to Koptos with me, he caused me to be brought to the Good House, he caused me to be laid in state, he caused me to be embalmed with the embalmment of a prince and very great person, he caused me to rest in the tomb where Merab the boy lay.

"He embarked, he went down-stream, he hastened north of Koptos by one mile to the place of our falling into the river. He spake with his soul, saying:—'Can I go to Koptos and dwell there? Otherwise, if it be that I go to Memphis, the moment that Pharaoh asks me after his children, what shall I say to him? Can I tell it to him, saying, I took thy children to the nome of Thebes, I killed them, I being alive; I came to Memphis, I being alive still?'

"He caused them to bring a strip of royal linen before him; he made it into a girdle. He bound the roll, he put it upon his stomach, he made it firm. Naneferkaptah came out from under the awning of the pleasure-boat of Pharaoh, he fell into the river, he did the will of Ra. Everybody that was on board uttered a cry—all, saying: 'Great woe! Oppressive woe! Has he gone back,[1] the good scribe, the learned man, to whom there is no equal?'

"The pleasure-boat of Pharaoh went down-stream, without any one on earth knowing where Naneferkaptah was. They reached Memphis, they made report of it before Pharaoh. Pharaoh came down to meet the pleasure-boat of Pharaoh in mourning, the army of Memphis took mourning—all, together with the priests of Ptah, the chief prophet of Ptah, with the officials and household of Pharaoh—all. They saw Naneferkaptah clinging to the rudders of the pleasure-boat of Pharaoh, by virtue of his art of a good scribe. They drew him up, they saw the roll on his stomach. Said Pharaoh, 'Let this roll that is on his stomach be hidden away.'

"Said the officers of Pharaoh, with the priests of Ptah, and the chief prophet of Ptah, before Pharaoh: 'O our great lord the King, may he accomplish the duration of Ra![2] Naneferkaptah was a good scribe, a learned man exceedingly.'

"Pharaoh caused to be given to him entrance to the Good House for sixteen days, wrapping for thirty-five and coffining for seventy; he was caused to rest in his tomb, in his places of rest."

[1] An expression for death, like our "gone home."
[2] *I. e.*, "May he live as long as the Sun god."

[Having finished her story, Ahura proceeds to point out the moral to Setna.]

"I am suffering the ills which have come upon us because of this roll of which thou sayest, 'Let it be given to me!' Thou hast no claim to it: our life on earth has been taken for it."

Said Setna, "Ahura, let this roll be given me which I see between thee and Naneferkaptah, else will I take it by force."

Rose Naneferkaptah on the couch; he said: "Art thou Setna, before whom this woman has told these misfortunes which thou hast not suffered—all? The book named, canst thou take it only by strength of a good scribe? It were sufficient to play draughts with me. Let us play for it at the game of fifty-two points."

And Setna said, "I am ready."

The board and its pieces were put before them. They played at the fifty-two, and Naneferkaptah won a game from Setna. He [Naneferkaptah] read a spell over him; he [Setna] defended himself with the game-board that was before him. He [Naneferkaptah] made him [Setna] go into the ground as far as his feet. He did its like in the second game; he won it from Setna, he made him go into the ground as far as his middle. He did its like in the third game; he made him go into the ground as far as his ears. After these things Setna made a great blow on the hand of Naneferkaptah. Setna called to Anheru, his brother by Anherart,[1] saying: "Make haste and go up upon the earth, do thou relate of everything that has happened to me before Pharaoh, and do thou bring the amulets of Ptah my father,[2] and my rolls of magic."

He hastened up upon earth, he related before Pharaoh of everything that had happened to Setna. Said Pharaoh, "Take to him the amulets of Ptah his father, and his rolls of magic."

Anheru hastened down into the tomb; he laid the talismans on the body of Setna, he [Setna] sprang to heaven at the moment named.[3] Setna caused his hand to go after the roll, he took it. It came to pass that Setna went up from the tomb, Light walking before him and Darkness walking behind him, and Ahura

---

[1] The presence of names compounded with the name of Anher, god of Sebennytus, indicates that the story was written during or after the supremacy of that city, at the end of the native rule.

[2] Setna Kha-em-uast was high priest of Ptah.

[3] Evidently a strong expression, to show the instantaneous and powerful effect of the amulets in drawing him out of the ground.

weeping after him, saying, "Hail to thee, King Darkness! Farewell to thee, King Light! All consolation is gone that was in the tomb."

Said Naneferkaptah to Ahura, "Be not troubled of soul; I will make him bring this book hither, there being a fork for a staff in his hand, there being a pan of fire on his head."[1]

And Setna came up from the tomb, he made it fast behind him in its manner.

Setna went before Pharaoh, he related before him of the thing that had happened to him with the roll. Said Pharaoh to Setna, "Take this roll to the tomb of Naneferkaptah in the manner of a prudent man, else he will make thee bring it, there being a fork for a staff in thine hand, there being a pan of fire on thine head."

Not did Setna hearken to him. It came to pass that Setna had no habit on earth but unrolling the roll and reading it before everybody.

After these things there was a day when Setna passed time in the court of Ptah, and saw a woman beautiful exceedingly, there being no woman of her beauty. There were ornaments of much gold upon her, there were children and women walking behind her, there were fifty-two persons of chiefs of households assigned to her. The hour that Setna saw her he knew not the place on earth where he was. Setna called to his attendant youth, saying, "Go quickly to the place where this woman is; learn what comes under her command."

The attendant youth went quickly to the place where the woman was, he addressed the handmaid who walked behind her, he asked her, saying, "What person is this woman?" She said to him, "She is Tabubua, the daughter of the prophet of Bast, lady of Ankhtaui, she having come hither to pray before Ptah the great god."

The youth went back to Setna, he related before him of everything that she had told him—all.

[In his infatuation for this woman, Setna forgets all decorum and all duty, and follows her home to Bubastis, and "ashamed was every one that was about Setna." To win the favor of Tabubua, he hands over to her all his possessions and the inheritance of his children; and at length she demands that his children should be put to death to prevent disputes.]

Setna said, "Let there be done unto them the abomination that has entered thy heart."

[1] This choice of symbols of submission is not yet explained.

She caused his children to be slain before his face; she caused them to be cast down from the window before the dogs and the cats. They devoured their flesh, he hearing them, he drinking with Tabubua.

[Setna awakens from the trance in which he has in imagination sunk to such depths of wickedness, to find himself lying naked in a strange place.]

An hour it was that passed when Setna saw a great man riding on a chariot, there being many men running at his feet, he being like Pharaoh. Setna came to rise; he could not rise for shame, for there was no clothing upon him. Pharaoh said, "Setna, what has befallen thee in this state in which thou art?"

Said he, "Naneferkaptah is he who hath done this to me — all."

Pharaoh said, "Go to Memphis: thy children they are seeking for thee; they are standing on their feet before Pharaoh."

Setna said before Pharaoh, "My great lord the King, may he accomplish the duration of Ra! What is the manner of going to Memphis that I can do, there being no clothes on earth upon me?"

Pharaoh called to a youth standing by, he made him give clothing to Setna. Said Pharaoh to Setna, "Go to Memphis: thy children, they are alive, they are standing on their feet before Pharaoh."

Setna came to Memphis, he embraced his children with hand, he found them alive. Pharaoh said, "Is it drinking that hath brought thee thus?"

Setna related everything that had happened to him with Tabubua, with Naneferkaptah — all. Pharaoh said: "Setna, I put my hand upon thee before,[1] saying, 'Thou wilt be slain if thou dost not take this roll to the place from which it was brought.' Thou didst not listen to me till this hour. Give this roll to Naneferkaptah, there being a forked stick for a staff in thine hand, there being a pan of fire on thine head."

Setna came out from before Pharaoh, there being a forked stick for a staff in his hand, there being a pan of fire on his head. He went down to the tomb in which was Naneferkaptah. Ahura said to him, "Setna, it is Ptah the great god who hath brought thee back safe."

[1] Compare the expression noted on p. 5265.

Naneferkaptah laughed, saying, "This is a thing that I told thee before."

Setna saluted Naneferkaptah; he found him as it is said, "He is the sun that is in the whole tomb." Ahura and Naneferkaptah saluted Setna greatly. Setna said, "Naneferkaptah, is there aught that is disgraceful?"

Naneferkaptah said, "Setna, thou knowest this, that Ahura and Merab her child, they are in Koptos: bring them here into this tomb by the skill of a good scribe. Let it be commanded before thee, and do thou take pains, and do thou go to Koptos, and do thou bring them hither."

Setna came up from the tomb and went before Pharaoh; he related before Pharaoh of everything that Naneferkaptah had said to him — all.

Pharaoh said, "Setna, go to Koptos, bring Ahura and Merab her child."

He said before Pharaoh, "Let the pleasure-boat of Pharaoh be given to me with its equipment."

The pleasure-boat of Pharaoh was given to him with its equipment; he embarked, he sailed up, he did not delay, he arrived at Koptos.

Information of it was given before the priests of Isis of Koptos, and the chief prophet of Isis. They came down to meet him, they took his hand to the shore. He went up, he went into the temple of Isis of Koptos and Harpokrates. He caused ox, goose, wine to be brought; he made a burnt-offering, a drink-offering, before Isis of Koptos and Harpokrates. He went to the cemetery of Koptos, with the priests of Isis and the chief prophet of Isis; they spent three days and three nights searching in the tombs which were in the cemetery of Koptos — all, turning over the stelæ of the scribes of the House of Life, reading the inscriptions that were on them. They found not the places of rest in which were Ahura and Merab her son.

Naneferkaptah perceived that they found not the places of rest of Ahura and Merab her son. He rose from the dead as an old man, great of age exceedingly. He came to meet Setna, and Setna saw him. Setna said to the old man, "Thou art of the appearance of a man great of age: knowest thou the places of rest in which are Ahura and Merab her child?"

The old man said to Setna, "The father of the father of my father told to the father of my father, and the father of my father told to my father, that the resting-places of Ahura and Merab her child are by the south corner of the house of Pehemato, as his name is."

Said Setna to the old man, "Is it not an injury that Pehemato hath done thee, by reason of which thou comest to cause his house to be brought down to the ground?"

The old man said to Setna, "Let watch be set over me and let the house of Pehemato be taken down. If it be that they find not Ahura and Merab her child under the south corner of his house, may abomination be done to me."

A watch was set over the old man; the resting-place of Ahura and Merab her child was found under the south corner of the house of Pehemato. Setna caused them to enter as great people on the pleasure-boat of Pharaoh; he caused the house of Pehemato to be built in its former manner. Naneferkaptah made Setna to discover what had happened: that it was he who had come to Koptos to let them find the resting-place in which Ahura and Merab her child were.

Setna embarked on the pleasure-boat of Pharaoh, he went down the river, he did not delay, he reached Memphis with all the army that was with him — all. Report was made of it before Pharaoh, he came down to meet the pleasure-boat of Pharaoh. He caused them to be introduced as great persons to the tomb where Naneferkaptah was, he caused dirges to be made above them.

This is a complete writing, relating of Setna Khaemuast, and Naneferkaptah, and Ahura his wife, and Merab her child. This . . . was written in the XXXVth year, the month Tybi.

Translation of F. Ll. Griffith.

THE STELA OF PIANKHY

[THE following inscription, one of the longest in existence, covers both faces and the sides of a large stela of black basalt in the Museum at Gizeh. It was found in the temple of Gebel Barkal, beyond Dongola in Nubia. Here was one of the capitals of a native Ethiopian dynasty, and in the temple dedicated to Amen a number of historical stelæ were set up by different kings, of whom Piankhy (about 800 B. C.) was the earliest. Not improbably he was descended from the priest kings of the XXIst Egyptian dynasty (at Thebes, about 1000 B. C.); at any rate, the name which he bore occurs in that dynasty, and his devotion to Amen agrees with the theory. We learn from the stela that by some means he had obtained the suzerainty over Upper Egypt, which was governed by local kings and nomarchs; while Lower Egypt was similarly divided but independent. Among the princes of the North land the most powerful was Tafnekht, probably a Libyan nomarch of Sais who had absorbed the whole of the western side of Lower Egypt. The stela relates the conflict that ensued when Tafnekht endeavored to unite Lower Egypt in a confederacy and invade the Upper Country. This gave Piankhy, who knew his own strength, an opportunity of which he was not slow to avail himself. The Delta was protected from invasion by its network of canals, and by its extensive marshes. But when the armies and navies of the local kings had been drawn into Upper Egypt and there repeatedly defeated, weakened and cowed, the princes of the North Land were at the mercy of the victorious Ethiopian, who was rewarded for his activity and skill in strategy with an abundance of spoil and tribute, probably also with the permanent subjection of the country.

The inscription is in a very perfect state; with the exception of one lacuna of sixteen short lines the losses are very small. The narrative is far more artistic and sustained than was usual in records of any considerable length. The piety of the Ethiopian and his trust in his god Amen are remarkably indicated; and some passages cannot fail to remind us of the Biblical records of certain Jewish kings and of the prophecies concerning Nebuchadnezzar and Cyrus. There is nothing that suggests the bloodthirstiness and wanton cruelty of the contemporary kings of Assyria. Altogether, when the time and circumstances are taken into account, the impression left is one very favorable to Piankhy. If he seems to insist overmuch on his Divine mission, this exaggeration is perhaps due to the priests of Amen who drafted the document, desirous of thereby promoting the honor both of their god and of their king.

There are numerous indications in the signs composing the inscription that the text was written originally in a cursive character, and afterwards transcribed into hieroglyphics for record on stone.]

[Date.]

YEAR xxi, month Thoth,[1] under the Majesty of the King of Upper and Lower Egypt, Meriamen Piankhy, living forever:—

[Attention demanded.]

Command: My Majesty saith, Hear how I have done more than the ancestors! I am a king, the figure of a god, the living image of Tum, who came forth from the body fashioned as a a ruler, whose elders feared him, . . . whose mother recognized that he would reign [while he was yet] in the egg; the

[1] The first month of the inundation season and of the Egyptian year. This is the date of the first events recorded, not of the dedication of the stela: the «command» is parenthetical.

good God, beloved of the gods, Son of the Sun, working with
his hand,[1] Meriamen Piankhy.

[The narrative.   Report of Tafnekht's invasion received: the king's joy
thereat.]

There came one to tell his Majesty, whereas the ruler of the
West, the nomarch and chief in Neter, Tafnekht, was in the
[Harpoon] Nome, in the Nome of the Bull of the Desert, in Hap,
in . . ., in An, in Per-nub, and in Mennefer,[2] he took unto him-
self the entire West from the sea-coast to Athet-taui, and went
south with a great army; the two lands were united in following
him, the nomarchs and the rulers of fenced cities were as hounds
at his feet.   No fortress was closed [against him]; the nomes of
the South, Mertum, and Per-Sekhem-Kheper-ra, the Temple of
Sebek, Per-Mezed, Tekanesh,[3] and every city of the West, opened
their gates in fear of him.   He turned back to the Eastern
nomes; they opened to him even as the former.   Het-benu,
Tayuzayt, Het-seten, Per-nebt-tep-ah.[4]   Behold [he hath crossed
over to] besiege Henen-seten,[5] he hath ringed it about,[6] not
allowing outgoers to go out, not allowing incomers to enter, by
reason of the daily fighting.   He hath measured it out on every
side, each nomarch gauging his own [length of] wall, that he may
post each one of the nomarchs and the rulers of fenced cities at
his section."

[1] The same expression occurs further on, and evidently refers to the per-
sonal activity of the king.

[2] Neter was probably Iseum in the centre of the Delta, and so a nomarch-
ship quite separate from Tafnekht's extensive territory in the west.   The list
following the name of Tafnekht seems to name localities representative of the
VIIth(?), VIth, Vth, IVth(?), IIId(?), and Ist nomes in Lower Egypt, in
their proper order; the last, Mennefer, being Memphis.   These would form
literally the whole western side of Lower Egypt "from the coast to Athet-
taui."   Athet-taui (Lisht?) was a city marking the boundary of Upper and
Lower Egypt.

[3] Mêdûm, El Lahûn, Crocodilopolis in the Faiyûm, Oxyrhynkhos, Diknâsh,
all — except perhaps the last — in order from north to south.

[4] He crossed over to the east bank and went northward, the cities on his
road throwing open their gates to him.   With the exception of the last, Per-
nebt-tep-ah [Aphroditopolis], the modern Atfîh opposite Mêdûm, they are dif-
ficult to identify positively.

[5] I. e., Heracleopolis Magna, a very powerful city on the edge of the west-
ern desert, left in the rear on Tafnekht's expedition up the river.   Its king
was named Pefaui Bast.   Its modern name is Ahnâs.

[6] Lit., "he hath made himself into a tail-in-the-mouth." [!]

Now [his Majesty heard these things] with good courage, laughing, and with joy of heart.

[Anxiety of the King's governors in Upper Egypt at Tafnekht's progress. Loss of Hermopolis.]

Behold these chiefs, nomarchs, and captains of the host who were in their various cities sent to his Majesty daily, saying: "Hast thou ceased [from action] until thou forgettest the South Country, the nomes of the royal domain[1]? Tafnekht is pushing forward his conquest, he findeth not any to repel his arm. Nemart [the ruler in Hermopolis] and nomarch of Het-Ur[2] hath breached the fortress of Neferus, he hath ruined his own city for fear lest he [Tafnekht] should take it, and then lay siege to another city. Behold, he hath gone to be at his [Tafnekht's] feet;[3] he hath refused allegiance to his Majesty, and standeth with him [Tafnekht] like one of [his retainers. He hath harried] the nome of Oxyrhynkhos,[4] and he giveth to him[5] [Tafnekht] gifts, as his heart inclineth, of all things that he findeth [therein]."

[Piankhy orders the governors to besiege Hermopolis.]

Then his Majesty sent a message to the nomarchs and the captains of the host who were in Egypt, the captain Puarma, with the captain Armersekny, with every captain of his Majesty who was in Egypt, saying: "Make haste in striking, join battle, encircle [Hermopolis], capture its people, its cattle, its ships upon the river. Let not the fellâhîn come out to the field; let not the plowman plow; lay siege to the Hare-city,[6] fight against it daily." Thereupon they did so.

[Piankhy dispatches an army from Ethiopia, bidding them fear not to fight, for Amen is their strength; and to do homage unto the god at Thebes.]

Then his Majesty sent an army to Egypt, urging them very greatly:—"[Spend day and] night as though ye were playing drafts, so that ye fight according as ye see that he hath arrayed battle at a distance. If he say the infantry and cavalry have

---

[1] The precise extent of Piankhy's dominion at this time is uncertain.

[2] Hûr, opposite Beni Hasan.

[3] The notion intended to be conveyed is that of a dog at heel.

[4] Oxyrhynkhos itself was already in the hands of Tafnekht; the Hermopolite nome, including Hûr, Nefrus, etc., lay immediately south of it.

[5] The pronoun "he" is used much too freely in this inscription: occasionally it is impossible to decide to whom it refers.

[6] Hermopolis.

hastened to another city, why then remain ye until his army come, and fight even as he shall say. And if his allies are in another city, hasten ye to them; and the nomarchs, and those whom he bringeth to strengthen him, the Tehenu[1] and his chosen troops, let battle be arrayed against them. One of old saith:—'We know not how to cry unto him, It is the enlistment of troops and the yoking of war-horses, the pick of thy stables, that giveth victory in battle. Thou knowest that Amen is the god that leadeth us.'[2]

"When ye reach Thebes, the approach to Apt-esut,[3] enter ye into the water, wash ye in the river, dress on the bank of the stream, unstring the bow, loosen the arrow. Let no chief boast as possessing might, there being no strength to the mighty if he regard him [Amen] not. He maketh the feeble-handed into strong-handed; a multitude may turn their backs before the few; one man may conquer a thousand. Sprinkle yourselves with the water of his altars; kiss ye the ground before his face; say ye to him, 'Give unto us a way that we may fight in the shadow of thy strong arm. The band that thou leadest, it cometh to pass that it overthroweth that which hath overthrown many.'"

Then they cast themselves on their bellies before his Majesty [saying], "It is thy name that giveth us strength of arm, thy wisdom is the mooring-post[4] of thy soldiers; thy bread is in our bellies on every road, thy beer quencheth our thirst; it is thy valor that giveth us strength of arm; one is fortified at the remembrance of thy name! while the host is lacking whose captain is a vile coward. Who is like unto thee in these things? Thou art a mighty King that worketh with his hands, master of the art of war!"

[The Ethiopian army, after leaving Thebes, defeat the van of Tafnekht's fleet.]

They went down-stream; they reached Thebes; they did according to all the things said by his Majesty.

[1] Libyans, mercenaries or otherwise. The XXIId Dynasty was probably Libyan, and as will be seen from subsequent notes, Libyan influence was still strong in the time of Piankhy.

[2] This would seem to be a quotation taken from some address to an earlier king. Thothmes III., for instance, attributed his successes to Amen.

[5] The great temple of Amen at Karnak.

[4] Our equivalent term would be "sheet-anchor."

They went down-stream upon the river; they found many ships coming up-stream, with soldiers, sailors, levies of troops, every mighty man of the North land, furnished with weapons of war to fight against the host of his Majesty. There was made a great slaughter of them, the number thereof is not known; their troops were captured with their ships, they were brought as live prisoners to the place where his Majesty was.[1]

[Proceeding to attack Heracleopolis, they are met on the river by the confederates under Tafnekht, and defeat them.]

They went to Henen-seten, arraying battle. The nomarchs with the kings of the North land were informed [thereof]. Now the King Nemart with the King Auapeth; the chief of the Me,[2] Sheshenk of Busiris, with the chief of the Me, Zed-Amen-aufankh of Mendes, and his son and heir, who was captain of the host of Hermopolis Parva; the host of the *Erpa* Bakenncfi, with his son and heir, chief of the Me, Nesnakedy in the nome of Hesebka; and every chief wearing the feather[3] who was in the North land, with the King Usorkon who was in Bubastis and in the land of Ra-nefer: every nomarch, and the governors of fenced cities in the West and in the East and in the islands in the midst, assembled with one purpose, as following the feet of the great chief of the West, ruler of the fenced cities of the North land, priest of Neith, mistress of Sais, and Sem-priest of Ptah, Tafnekht.[4]

When they went out against them, a mighty overthrow was made of them, greater than anything, and their ships were captured upon the river; the remainder crossed over and moored on the west side, in the neighborhood of Per-peg.

[1] In Ethiopia.

[2] The title «chief of the Me» seems to mean «captain of the Libyan troops.» The list contains the names of princes of Lower Egypt only, with the exception of Nemart of Hermopolis Magna, in Upper Egypt.

[3] The feather was a Libyan badge of rank.

[4] Tafnekht is here given most of his principal titles, including the sacerdotal ones of high priest of Neith in Sais, and of Ptah in Memphis. With the rise of Sais, Neith had become the leading deity of Lower Egypt, ranking even above Ptah. The priests at Gebel Barkal doubtless took a special pride in the overthrow of the protégé of Neith and Ptah by Piankhy, the worshiper of Amen.

[In a second battle, fought by land on the opposite shore, the enemy is over-
thrown; most escaped northward, but Nemart returns to Hermopolis,
having eluded the besiegers (*i. e.*, the army of the loyal governors).
Hermopolis is more closely besieged.]

When the land lightened very early, the soldiers of his Majesty
crossed over to them. One host met the other. Then they slew
many men of them, and horses without number, in the charge[?].
Those who remained fled to the North land with lamentations
loud and sore, more than anything.[1] Account of the overthrow
made of them: men, persons . . .[2] [But] the King Nemart
went up-stream to the South when it was reported to him,
"Khmenu[3] is in the midst of enemies; the soldiers of his
Majesty are capturing its men and its cattle." Then he [Nemart]
entered into Unu, while the soldiers of his Majesty were at the
port of the Hare-city. Then they heard of it; they surrounded
the Hare-city on its four sides; they allowed not goers out to
go out, nor enterers in to enter in.

[The King, enraged at the escape of the enemy, vows that after the New Year
he will go to Thebes, and having discharged a pious duty there, take the
war in hand himself.]

They sent to report to his Majesty, the King of Upper and
Lower Egypt, Meriamen Piankhy, Giving Life, of every defeat
they had made, and of all the victories of his Majesty. Then
his Majesty raged at it like a leopard:—"Shall one grant unto them
that there be left a remnant of the soldiers of the North land to
permit a goer out to go out from them, to say, 'He commandeth
not to make them die until they be utterly destroyed'? As I live,
as I love Ra, as my father Amen praiseth me, I will go north
myself to ruin that which [Nemart] hath done; I will cause him
to withdraw from battle forever. Verily, after performing the
ceremonies of the New Year, I will sacrifice to my father Amen
in his beautiful festival, when he maketh his fair manifestation of
the New Year. He will lead me in peace to see Amen in the
good feast of the festival of Apt; I shall bring him forth glo-
riously in his divine form unto Southern Apt, in his goodly feast

[1] Or "beaten sorely and grievously."
[2] Here should be the numbers of the slain.
[3] "Khmenu," "Unu," "Hare-city," are all names of Hermopolis Magna, the
capital of Nemart's petty kingdom.

of the feast of Apt at night-time,[1] in the feast established in Thebes, the feast which Ra instituted for him originally. And I will bring him forth gloriously to his own house, to rest upon his throne, on the day of making the god to enter.[2] On the second day of Athyr[3] I will cause the land of the North to taste the taste of my fingers."

[To retrieve their reputation, the army assaults and captures three cities; but the King is not appeased.]

Then the soldiers who were remaining in Egypt heard the rage that his Majesty was in against them. Then they fought against Per Mezed[4] in the nome of Oxyrhynkhos; they took it like a flood of water. They sent a message to his Majesty, but his heart was not appeased thereby.

Then they fought against Tatehen,[5] the very strong; they found it filled with soldiers, and every strong man of the North land. Then there was made a battering-ram for it; its walls were breached and a great slaughter was made of them, the number thereof is not known, including the son of the chief of the Me, Tafnekht.[6] Then they sent word to his Majesty of it, but his heart was not appeased thereby.

Then they fought against Het Benu; its citadel was opened and the soldiers of his Majesty entered into it. Then they sent word to his Majesty, but his heart was not appeased thereby.

[The King comes to Thebes, and thence proceeds to Hermopolis. He chides his troops.]

On the ninth day of Thoth,[7] came his Majesty down the river to Thebes; he completed the feast of Amen in the festival of Apt. His Majesty floated down to the city of the Hare.[8] His Majesty came out of the pavilion of the boat; horses were yoked and chariots mounted. The fear of his Majesty reached unto

[1] Evidently a torchlight procession from Karnak to Luxor (Southern Apt).
[2] The return procession to Karnak.
[3] The third month of the season of inundation. Of course a year would then have elapsed, since the date given in the first line of the inscription.
[4] Oxyrhynkhos.
[5] Tehneh (?)
[6] Tafnekht, stripped of his grandeur after his defeat at Heracleopolis, is reduced to the rank of "Chief of the Me in Sais."
[7] The first month of the season of inundation, and of the Egyptian year.
[8] Hermopolis.

the ends of Asia;[1] his terror was in every heart. Then his Majesty came forth disposed to hate his soldiers, raging at them like a leopard: "Doth it yet remain for you to fight? This is slackness in my business: the year is completed to the end in putting terror of me in the North land."[2] They made a great and grievous lamentation, like one beaten.[3]

He pitched his tent in the Southwest of Khmenu. It [the city] was besieged every day. There was made an earthwork to cover the wall; there was erected a wooden tower to raise the archers shooting arrows, and the slingers slinging stones, slaying the people thereof every day.

[Hermopolis, vigorously attacked, is brought to great straits. It treats with the King, and Nemart's wife prays the Queen to intercede for them.]

The third day came; Unu was abominable to the nose, evil in its smell. Then Unu threw itself on its belly, praying before the face of the King; messengers came out and entered with all things good to behold; gold, every precious mineral, stuffs in a chest. The diadem was on his [Piankhy's] head, the uræus was giving forth its terror; there was no ceasing for many days in praying to his divine crown. His [Nemart's] wife, the royal wife Satnestentmeh, was caused to approach, to pray the royal wives, the royal concubines, the royal daughters, the royal sisters. She cast herself upon her belly in the chamber of the women, before the face of the royal wives: "Come ye unto me, O ye royal wives, daughters, and sisters, that ye may pacify Horus,[4] lord of the palace. Great is his mighty spirit! How grand is his right of victory! Let . . ."[5]

[Presumably the Queen intercedes; Nemart comes out to Piankhy, surrenders, and brings tributes.]

"Who is it that hath led thee?[6] Who is it that hath led thee? Who is it that hath led thee? Who is it that led thee? [Thou hast missed] the road of life. But shall the heaven rain

---

[1] To be taken of course in a general sense, referring to the majestic and terrible aspect of the King.

[2] *I. e.*, "It has taken a full year," etc.

[3] Or, "They were sorely and grievously beaten with blows."

[4] *I. e.*, the King.

[5] Here there is a lacuna of sixteen short lines in the inscription.

[6] Apparently Piankhy is addressing Nemart.

with arrows? I am [satisfied when] the South is in obeisance, and the North lands [cry], 'Put us in thy shadow.' Behold, it is evil . . . with his offerings. The heart is a rudder that wrecketh its owner in that which concerneth the will of God; it looketh on flame as ice. . . . not a prince; see who is his father. Thy nomes are full of children."[1]

Then he cast himself upon his belly before his Majesty [saying]: "Come to me, Horus, lord of the palace! It is thy mighty will that doeth this unto me: I am one of the servants of the King that pay dues to the treasury. . . . Count their dues: I have paid to thee more than they."

Then he offered to him silver, gold, lapis lazuli, malachite, bronze, and minerals of all kinds in great quantity. Behold, the treasury was filled with this tribute. He brought a horse in his right hand, a sistrum in his left, a sistrum of gold and lapis lazuli.

[Piankhy enters Hermopolis and sacrifices to Thoth. Finding the horses in the rebel King's stables starved, he is wroth with Nemart and confiscates his goods.]

Behold, his [Majesty] was brought forth gloriously from his palace, and proceeded to the house of Thoth, lord of Khmenu. He sacrificed bulls, oxen, and fowl to his father Thoth, lord of Khmenu, and the gods in the House of the Eight.[2] The soldiers of the Hermopolite nome rejoiced and sang; they said: "How beautiful is Horus resting in his country, Son of the Sun, Piankhy! Celebrate for us a Sed festival,[3] even as thou hast protected the Hare-name."

His Majesty proceeded to the house of the King Nemart, he went to every apartment of the palace, his treasury and his storehouses; he caused to be brought to him the King's wives and the King's daughters; they praised his Majesty with things

---

[1] The meaning is not clear; but there seems to be a reference to the diminution of the adult population by prolonged wars.

[2] *Khmenu* means eight. Thoth, in late times at any rate, combined the powers of the eight gods who accompanied him. He was sometimes called "twice great," sometimes "eight times great" $=2^3$, an arithmetical term especially indicated by the Greek name Ἑρμῆς Τρισμέγιστος.

[3] A "jubilee" after a thirty-years' reign; the expression is therefore equivalent to wishing the King a thirty-years' reign. The soldiers represent the King as the god Horus come to claim his own land.

that women use;[1] but his Majesty would not amuse himself with them. His Majesty proceeded to the stables of the horses, the stalls of the foals; he beheld that they were starved. He said:—"As I live, as I love Ra, as my nostril is refreshed with life! very grievous are these things to my heart, the starving of my horses, more than any ill that thou hast done in the fulfilling of thine own desire. The fear which thy surroundings have of thee, beareth witness to me of thee. Dost thou ignore that the shadow of God is over me, and he doth not fail in any undertaking of mine? Would that he who did this unto me were another, knowing me not, [then] I would not censure him for it! But I, when I was born from the womb, when I was formed in the egg, the deed of God was in me; and as his *Ka* endureth,[2] I do nothing without him! He it is who commandeth me to act."

Then he counted his [Nemart's] goods to the Treasury, his granary to the sacred store of Amen in Apt-esut.[3]

[The King of Heracleopolis, the siege of which had been raised by the King's troops, brings presents and promises tribute.]

The ruler of Henen-seten, Pefauibast, came with tribute to Pharaoh: gold, silver, every kind of mineral, and horses of the chosen ones of the stable. He cast himself on his belly before his Majesty, and said, "Salutation to thee, Horus, mighty King, bull overthrowing bulls. Duat[4] drew me down, I was overwhelmed in darkness, for which light hath been given unto me.

"I found not a friend on the day of trouble, who would stand in the day of fight, except thee, O mighty King! Thou hast drawn away the darkness from me, and I will be thy servant with all that pertain to me. Henen-seten shall pay tribute to thy storehouse, thou the image of Harakhti, chief of the Akhmu Seku.[5] While he exists, so long shalt thou exist as King; if he be not destroyed thou shalt not be destroyed, O King Piankhy, living for ever!"

[1] Music, dancing, etc.
[2] An oath.
[3] Karnak.
[4] The underworld.
[5] The stars of the northern hemisphere; see Maspero's 'Dawn of Civilization,' p. 94. By Harakhti, the sun is probably meant.

[El Lahûn, prepared to oppose the entry of the King, yields without fighting: the treasuries are confiscated.]

His Majesty went north to the opening of the canal near Rahent[1]; he found Per-sekhem-kheper-ra with its walls raised high, its citadel closed and filled with every valiant man of the North land. Then his Majesty sent to them saying: "Ye who live in death, ye who live in death, miserable ones, wretched ones living in death! If a moment passeth without opening [to me], behold, ye are reckoned as conquered, and that is painful to the King. Close not the gates of your life so as to come to the execution block of this day. Do not love death and hate your life; . . . [embrace] life in the face of all the land."

Then they sent to his Majesty to say: "Behold, the shadow of God is upon thy head; the son of Nut[2] gives to thee his two hands. What thy heart desireth is accomplished immediately, as that which issues from the mouth of a god. Behold thou it! Thou wast born as a god, and thou seest us in thy two hands. Behold thy city, its forts [are open; do as thou wilt with it]; enterers enter in and goers out go out: let his Majesty do as he pleaseth."

Then they came out with the son of the chief of the Me, Tafnekht. The host of his Majesty entered into it; he slew not one of all the people whom he found. [The chancellors came], with the royal seal-bearers to seal its goods, assigning its treasuries to the Treasury, its granaries to the divine offerings of his father Amen Ra, lord of the thrones of the two lands.

[Likewise with Mêdûm and Athet-taui.]

His Majesty floated down-stream, he found that Mêdûm, the Abode of Seker, lord of making light, had been shut up; it could not be reached, it had put fighting into its heart. [But they feared] terror [seized] them; awe closed their mouths. Then his Majesty sent to them saying: "Behold ye, there are two ways before you, choose ye as ye will: open, and ye live; close, and ye die. My Majesty passeth not by a city closed."

---

[1] The mouth of the barrier, *i. e.*, the entrance into the Faiyûm. The name El Lahûn is derived from Rahent; and the city Per-sekhem-kheper-ra, "The house of Usorkon I.," must have been at or close to the modern village of El Lahûn.

[2] Set, the god of physical strength.

Then they opened immediately. His Majesty entered this city; he offered [an oblation] to the god Menhy in Sehez. He assigned its treasury and granaries to the divine offerings of Amen in Apt-esut.

His Majesty floated down-stream to Athet-taui; he found the fortress closed, the walls full of valiant soldiers of the North land. Behold, they opened the forts, they cast themselves on their bellies [singing praises before] his Majesty. "Thy father hath destined for thee his heritage as lord of the two lands; thou art in them,[1] thou art lord of what is upon earth."

His Majesty proceeded [to the temple] to cause to be offered a great offering to the gods who are in this city, of bulls, fat oxen and fowls, and everything good and pure. Then its treasury was assigned to the Treasury, its granaries to the divine offerings [of Amen].

[To Memphis he offers a free pardon, but the city prepares to fight.]

His Majesty went north towards Anbuhez. Then he sent to them, saying, "Do not close, do not fight, O Residence originally of Shu![2] Let the enterers enter and the comers out come out: let none going be stopped. I will offer sacrifice to Ptah and the gods who are in Anbuhez; I will worship Sokaris in the Secret Place; I will behold Res-Anbef.[3] I will go north in peace [for his Majesty loveth that] Anbuhez be safe and sound, and that [even] the children weep not. Ye saw the nomes of the South: not one [soul] was slain therein except the rebels who had blasphemed God. Execution on the block was done to the rebellious."

Then they closed their forts; they caused soldiers to go out against a few of the host of his Majesty, consisting of artisans, of chief builders, and pilots [who had gone towards] the quay of Anbuhez.

---

[1] Athet-taui (Lisht ?) was the boundary of Upper and Lower Egypt, and probably lay in both of them. "The gods who are in this city" of the next paragraph are doubtless kings of the XIIth Dynasty as presiding deities of the place, this royal Residence having apparently been founded by Amenenhat I. Compare p. 5238.

[2] Ra, the first King of Egypt, was fabled to have resided at Heliopolis; Shu his son and successor at Memphis. The city is called sometimes Anbuhez, "white wall," sometimes Men-nefer, after the pyramid of Pepy I.

[3] "South of his wall," an epithet of Ptah, god of Memphis.

[Tafnekht himself visits Memphis in the night, encourages the troops, and departs, promising to return when he has arranged matters with the allies.]

Now that chief of Sais came to Anbuhez in the night, urging its soldiers, its sailors and all the best of its troops, in number eight thousand men, urging them greatly, greatly. "Behold, Mennefer is full of soldiers of all the best of the North land, barley and durra, and all kinds of grain, the granaries are over-flowing, and all kinds of weapons of [war. There is a] wall built, a great battlement made with cunning craft. The river bounds the eastern side, and no way of attack is there. The stalls remain full of fat cattle, the treasury is furnished with all things: silver, gold, copper, bronze, stuffs, incense, honey, oint-ment. I will go, I will give things to the chiefs of Lower Egypt; I will open to them their nomes.[1] I shall be [away traveling] three [?] days until I return." He mounted a horse, he called not for his chariots, he went north in fear of his Majesty.

[Piankhy finds Memphis strongly fortified and the high Nile risen to its walls. The army proposes to bridge it, or attack the city it by elaborate ap-proaches.]

When the earth lightened and it was the second day[2] his Majesty came to Anbuhez. He moored upon its north side, he found the water risen to the walls and ships moored at [the quay of] Mennefer. Then his Majesty saw that it was mighty indeed, the wall raised high with new building, the battlement manned with strength; no way of attacking it was found. Each person fell to saying his say among the hosts of his Majesty of every rule of warfare, and every man said, "Let us lay siege to [Anbuhez]; behold, her soldiers are many." Others said: "Make a causeway unto it; let us raise the ground to its wall; let us construct a wooden work, let us set up ships' masts, let us make its edges of poles. Let us divide it with these things[3] on every side of it, with embankments and . . . upon its north side, in order to raise the ground to its wall that we may find a way for our feet."

---

[1] It is difficult to see what is meant by this. Possibly Tafnekht was pro-posing to bribe the Northern chiefs into continuing the war, by giving up his recently acquired claims as suzerain.

[2] Or "very early."

[3] Perhaps "Let us put these things at intervals."

[The King determines to assault it immediately; he seizes all the boats at the quay, where the houses were comparatively unprotected, and landing his men in them at that point captures the city.]

Then his Majesty raged against it [the city] like a leopard, he said:—"As I live, as I love Ra, as my father Amen who formed me praiseth me, these things have happened unto it by the command of Amen. These things are what men say: '[The North Country] with the nomes of the South they open to him [Tafnekht] from afar; they had not placed Amen in their hearts, they knew not what he had commanded. [Then] he [Amen] made him [Piankhy] in order to accomplish his mighty will, to cause the awe of him to be seen.' I will take it like a water flood; [this] hath [my father Amen] commanded me."

Then he caused his ships and his army to set out to attack the quay of Mennefer. They brought back to him every ferry-boat, every cabin-boat, every dahabiyeh, and the ships in all their number that were moored at the quay of Mennefer, the bows being moored in its houses [on account of the height of the water.[1] Not] the least of the soldiers of his Majesty mourned.[2]

His Majesty came to direct the ships in person in all their number. His Majesty commanded his soldiers: "Forward to it! Scale the walls, enter the houses upon the bank of the stream. If one of you enters upon the wall there will be no stand against him [for a moment], the levies [?] will not bar you. Moreover, it is feeble that we should shut up the South Country, moor at the North land, and sit still at 'the Balance of the two lands.'[3]

Then Mennefer was captured as by a flood of water; men were slain within it in great numbers, and were taken as prisoners to the place where his Majesty was.

[In Memphis Piankhy sacrifices. The neighboring garrisons flee; three Northern chiefs and all the nomarchs submit in person; the treasures of Memphis are confiscated.]

When the [land lightened] and the second day came, his Majesty caused men to go to it to protect the temples of God for him, to guard the sanctuary of the gods from the profane,[4]

---

[1] The boats were floating on a level with the top of the quay.
[2] I. e., no single one of the assailants was injured in the slightest degree.
[3] Meaning of course "at the boundary between Upper and Lower Egypt."
[4] By waving the wand of sanctification therein.

to sacrifice to the royal circle of gods of Hetkaptah,[1] to purify Mennefer with natron and incense, to put the priests on the place of their feet.[2] His Majesty proceeded to the house of [Ptah]; his purification was performed in the Chamber of Early Morning,[3] and all the things prescribed for a king were accomplished. He entered the temple, great offerings were made to his father Ptahresanbef, of fat bulls, oxen, and fowl, and every good thing. His Majesty proceeded to his house.

Then all the villages that were in the region of Mennefer heard, namely, Hery the city, Penynaauaa, the tower of Byu, and the oasis of By; they opened their gates, they fled in flight; one knoweth not the place to which they went.

Came Auapeth with the chief of the Me, Akaneshu, with the *erpa* Pediast, with all the nomarchs of the North land, bearing their tribute, to see the beauties of his Majesty.

Then were assigned the treasuries and the granaries of Mennefer, and made into the second offerings of Amen, of Ptah, of the circle of the gods in Hetkaptah.

[Piankhy crosses over to Babylon, and worships there.]

When the land lightened and the second day came,[4] his Majesty proceeded to the East, and made a purification to Tum in Kheraha,[5] [and to] the circle of the gods in the house of the circle of the gods; namely, the cave in which the gods are, consisting of fat bulls, oxen, and fowls, that they might give Life, Prosperity, and Health to the King Piankhy, living forever.

[He proceeds along the Sacred Way to Heliopolis, visiting the holy places, and enters the sanctuary of Tum in Heliopolis, etc. King Usorkon submits.]

His Majesty proceeded to Anu[6] on that mount of Kheraha, upon the road of the god Sep, to Kheraha. His Majesty pro-

---

[1] The sacred name of Memphis, supposed to be the origin of the name Ἀιγυπτος — "Egypt."

[2] *I. e.*, to re-establish the order of the temple services, etc.

[3] A chamber set apart for the sacred toilet; see also below, p. 5290.

[4] Or "very early."

[5] Kheraha was on the site of old Cairo, known to the classical authors as Babylon. The cave mentioned is not now known.

[6] On, Heliopolis. Here was a sacred well of water ("The Cool Pool"), supposed to spring from Nu, the primeval waters in heaven and earth, and not to be derived from Hapi or the Nile. Tradition relates that it was at this same well, still pointed out at Matariyeh, that the Blessed Virgin washed the Child on her arrival in Egypt.

ceeded to the camp which was on the west of the Atiu canal; he was purified in the midst of the Cool Pool, his face was washed in the stream of Nu, in which Ra washes his face. He proceeded to the sand-hill in Anu, he made a great sacrifice on the sand-hill in Anu, before the face of Ra at his rising, consisting of white bulls, milk, frankincense, incense, all woods sweet-smelling. He came, proceeding to the house of Ra; he entered the temple with rejoicings. The chief lector praised the god that warded off miscreants[1] from the King. The rites of the Chamber of Early Morning were performed, the cloak was put on, he was purified with incense and cold water, flowers for the Het Benben[2] were brought to him. He took the flowers, he ascended the staircase to the great window, to see Ra in the Het Benben. The King himself stood alone, he put the key into the bolt, he opened the double doors, and saw his father Ra in the Het Benben. He sanctified the Madet boat of Ra, the Sektet boat of Tum.[3] The doors were shut, clay was applied and sealed with the King's own seal; and the priests were charged, "I, I have examined the seal; let none other enter therein of all the kings who shall exist."

Then they cast themselves on their bellies before his Majesty, saying, "Unto eternity, Horus[4] loving Anu shall not be destroyed." Returning thence, he entered the house of Tum, and followed the image of his father Tum Khepera, chief of Anu.

Came the King Usorkon to see the beauties of his Majesty.

[Piankhy goes to the vicinity of Athribis and receives the homage of all the Northern princes and nobles. Pediast of Athribis invites him to his city.]

When the land lightened on the second day,[5] his Majesty went to the quay, and the best of his ships crossed over to the quay of Kakem.[6] The camp of his Majesty was pitched on the south of Kaheni, on the east of Kakem. These kings and

---

[1] Or "mishaps." This seems to have been a sort of Te Deum.

[2] The Benben was a pyramidal stone, sacred to Ra or representing him. It was shaped like the top of an obelisk.

[3] The boats in which the Sun god traversed the heavens during forenoon and afternoon respectively.

[4] I. e., the King.

[5] Or "very early."

[6] Athribis.

nomarchs of the North land, all the chiefs who wore the feather, every vizier, all the chiefs, every royal acquaintance[1] in the West and in the East, and in the islands in the midst, came to see the beauties of his Majesty. The *erpa* Pediast threw himself on his belly before his Majesty, and said: "Come to Kakem, that thou mayest see the god Khentkhety; that thou mayest *khu* [?] the goddess Khuyt; that thou mayest offer sacrifices to Horus in his house, consisting of fat bulls, oxen, fowls; that thou mayest enter my house, open my treasury, and load thyself with the things of my father. I will give thee gold unto the limits of thy desire, malachite heaped before thy face, horses many of the best of the stable, the leaders of the stall."

[Piankhy goes to Athribis and worships the local god. Pediast sets the example. of giving up his goods without concealment.]

Proceeded his Majesty to the house of Horus Khentkhety, and caused to be offered fat bulls, oxen, ducks, fowl to his father Horus Khentkhety, lord of Kemur. Proceeded his Majesty to the house of the *erpa* Pediast; he presented him with silver, gold, lapis lazuli, malachite, a great collection of every kind of thing, and stuffs, and royal linen in every count,[2] couches covered with fine linen, frankincense, and unguents in jars, stallions and mares of the leaders of his stable. He [Pediast] cleared himself by the life of God[3] before the face of these kings and great chiefs of the North land:—"Each one of them that hides his horses, that conceals his goods, let him die the death of his father. Thus may it be done to me, whether ye acquit thy humble servant in all things that ye knew of concerning me, or whether ye say I have hidden from his Majesty anything of my father, gold, jewelry, with minerals and ornaments of all kinds, bracelets for the arms, collars for the neck, pendants [?] inlaid with minerals, amulets for every limb, chaplets for the head, rings for the ears, all the apparel of a king, every vessel of royal purification in gold, and every sort of mineral; all these things I have offered

---

[1] The land was divided among kings, nomarchs, and, apparently, Libyan chiefs entitled to wear a feather. The kings had their viziers; the nomarchs and chiefs had their subordinate chiefs, etc. "Royal acquaintances" were persons related to the royal families.

[2] *I. e.*, the linen was of various degrees of fineness, or as we also say technically, of various "counts"; meaning that there are so many threads more or less in any given square of stuff.

[3] An oath.

before the king, stuffs and clothes in thousands of all the best of my looms. I know by what thou wilt be appeased. Go to the stable, choose thou what thou wilt of all the horses that thou desirest.» Then his Majesty did so.

[The princes of Lower Egypt return to their cities to fetch further tribute. A revolt at Mesed is promptly suppressed and the city given as a reward to Pediast.]

Said these kings and nomarchs before his Majesty, «Let us go to our cities, let us open our treasuries, let us select according to the desire of thy heart, let us bring to thee the best of our stables, the chief of our horses.» Then his Majesty did even so. *List of their names :*—

The King Usorkon in Per Bast and the territory of Ranefer;

The King Auapeth in Tentremu and Taanta [?];

The nomarch Zedamenafankh in Mendes and the Granary of Ra;

His son and heir, the captain of the host in Hermopolis Parva, Ankhhor;

The nomarch Akanesh in Thebneter, in Perhebyt, and in Smabehed;

The nomarch and chief of the Me, Pathenf in Per-Sepd and in the Granary of Anbuhez;

The nomarch and chief of the Me, Pamai in Busiris;

The nomarch and chief of the Me, Nesnakedy in Heseb-ka;

The nomarch and chief of the Me, Nckhthornashenut in Pergerer;[1]

The chief of the Me, Pentuart;

The chief of the Me, Pentabekhent;

The priest of Horus, lord of Letopolis, Pedihorsmataui;

The nomarch Hurobasa in the house of Sekhemt mistress of Sa, and the house of Sekhemt mistress of Rohesaut;

The nomarch Zedkhiau in Khentnefer;

The nomarch Pabas in Kheraha and the house of Hapi.

With all their good tribute [consisting of] gold, silver, [lapis lazuli], ma[lachite], [couches] covered with fine linen, frankincense in jars, [and all things that pertain to a man great] in wealth, rich in horses. . . .

[1] First we have two kings, six nomarchs and high Libyan chiefs; after these, two under-chiefs are mentioned, and then four nomarchs in the first and second nomes of Lower Egypt, which are separated as having belonged to Tafnekht's kingdom.

[After] these things came one to say to his Majesty: ["Whereas the nomarch and captain of the] host [. . . hath thrown down] the wall [of . . . and] set fire to his treasury, [and fled away] upon the river, he hath fortified Mesed[1] with soldiers, and hath . . . "

Then his Majesty caused his warriors to go to see what took place therein, as an ally of the *erpa* Pediast. One came to report to his Majesty saying, "We have slain all the people that we found there." His Majesty gave it as a present to the *erpa* Pediast.

[Lastly, Tafnekht begs for mercy: ambassadors receive his presents and sub-
mission to the King, and he is pardoned.]

Then the chief of the Me, Tafnekht, heard it;[2] he caused a messenger to go to the place where his Majesty was, begging his mercy, saying:—"Be gracious! I have not seen thy face in the days of shame; I cannot stand before thy flame; I am terrified at thy awe. Behold, thou art Nubti in the Land of the South, Mentu, the mighty bull.[3] In all these matters to which thou hast given thy attention thou hast not found thy humble servant until I reached the island of the sea. I am afraid of thy mighty spirit according to that saying, 'The flame is my enemy.' Doth not the heart of thy Majesty cool with these things that thou hast done unto me? Verily I am in misery. I am not smitten according to the account of the wickedness. Having weighed with the balance, having reckoned by the ounce,[4] thou multipliest it unto me thrice; having carried away the seed, thou sweepest up [the remnant] at the same time. Do not cut down the grove to its root. As thy *Ka* endureth, thy terror is in my body, thy fear in my bones; I have not sat in the room of carousal,[5] the harp hath not been brought to me. Behold, I eat the bread of hunger, I drink water in thirst, since the day that thou learnedst my name. Pain is in my bones, my head is unshaven, my clothes in rags, in order that Neith may be made gracious unto me. Long is the course that thou hast brought to me; turn thy

[1] Site unknown.

[2] Tafnekht was on an island in the Mediterranean, and therefore heard the news of the surrender of the Northern princes only after some time had elapsed.

[3] Nubti=Set, the god of valor. Mentu was the god of battle.

[4] "*Kedt*-weight," really 140 grains.

[5] *Lit.*, "beer-room."

face unto me now. A year hath cleansed my *Ka* and purified thy servant from his wickedness. Let my goods be taken to the Treasury, consisting of gold with every sort of mineral, and the best of the horses accoutred with everything. Let a messenger come to me in haste, that he may drive fear from my heart. Let me go out to the temple in his sight, let me clear myself with an oath by God.»

His Majesty caused to go the Chief Lector Pediamennestaui, and the captain of the host Puarma. He [Tafnekht] presented him [Piankhy] with silver, gold, stuffs, every valuable mineral. He went out to the temple, he praised God, he cleared himself with an oath by God, saying: "I will not transgress the command of the King. I will not reject the words of his Majesty; I will not sin against a nomarch without thy knowledge; I will act according to the words of the King; I will not transgress what he hath commanded." Then his Majesty was satisfied therewith.

[Crocodilopolis and Aphroditopolis having submitted, the whole country is at the feet of the conqueror, who loads his ships with the tribute and departs homeward.]

One came to say to his Majesty: "The temple of Sebek, they have opened its fort, Metnu hath cast itself upon its belly, there is not a nome that is shut against his Majesty in the nomes of the South, North, West, or East. The islands in the midst are upon their bellies with fear of him, and are causing their goods to be brought to the place where his Majesty is, like the serfs of the palace."

When the land lightened, very early[1] came these two rulers of the South and two rulers of the North, wearing uræi,[2] to smell the ground to the mighty spirit of his Majesty. Behold, moreover, these kings and nomarchs of the North land came to see the beauties of his Majesty; their feet were as the feet of women,[3] they entered not to the King's house, for that they were impure and eaters of fishes, which is an abomination to the King's house. Behold, the King Nemart, he entered to the King's palace, for that he was pure, he ate not fishes. They stood upon their feet, but the one of them entered the palace.

[1] Or «on the second day.»
[2] As symbols of regal power.
[3] Perhaps this means ceremonially unclean.

Then the ships were loaded with silver, gold, bronze, stuffs, all things of the North land, all products of Kharu, all woods of the Divine Land.

His Majesty went up-stream, his heart enlarged, all about him were rejoicing; West and East, they rose high, rejoicing around his Majesty, singing and rejoicing; they said:—"O mighty King! O mighty King! Piankhy! O mighty King! Thou hast come, thou hast ruled the North land. Thou makest bulls into women. Happy is the heart of the mother that bore a male child, that was impregnated with thee amongst the mountains. Praises be given unto her! the cow that hath borne a bull! Thou shalt be to eternity, thy victory remaineth, O Ruler, loving Thebes."

Translation of F. Ll. Griffith.

INSCRIPTION OF UNA

[It is interesting to compare the inscription of Piankhy with an example of the historical texts of the Old Kingdom. Only two are known of any considerable length, and the following is one of them. The biographical inscription of Una, administrator of Upper Egypt, takes one back to 3000 B. C., when almost the only great monuments in Egypt were the pyramids, to the number of which each successive king added.

The inscription was found on a slab in the great cemetery of Abydos, and is now in the Gizeh Museum. The style is somewhat arid, but attracts by its primitive and simple character]

[Una's youth under King Teta, founder of the VIth Dynasty.]

[Una saith] I was tying the girdle,[1] under the majesty of Teta. My grade was that of superintendent of stores, and I acted as overseer of the garden of Pharaoh.

[Una appointed pyramid priest and then judge by Pepy I. He assists at trials in the royal harîm.]

[I was] chief of the *debat* [?] city . . . under the majesty of Pepy: his Majesty put me into the position of royal friend and superintendent of the priests of his pyramid city.[2]

[1] The first words are lost. The girdle was probably assumed at about the age of twelve.

[2] As a rule, each king seems to have built his pyramid in the desert behind his principal residence. The latter was often founded by the king, but might serve for some of his successors, who would then build their pyramids near his. The pyramid field of Memphis is very ancient, and many of the earlier kings must have resided there; but curiously enough the name *Mennefer*, Memphis, is taken from that of the pyramid of Pepy I., here referred to.

Behold I was . . . and his Majesty appointed me judge, and his heart was satisfied with me more than with any of his servants: I heard cases alone with the chief justice and vizier in every secret proceeding [of the palace?] . . . in the name of the King, of the royal *harîm* and of the six great houses,[1] because the King's heart was satisfied with me more than with any of his officers, of his nobles, or of his servants.

[Royal present of a sarcophagus, etc., from the limestone quarries of Turra.]

[Command was given] by the Majesty of my lord to bring for me a sarcophagus of white stone from Ra-au, and his Majesty caused the divine treasurer to cross over [the river] with a band [of soldiers and artificers] under him to bring for me this sarcophagus from Ra-au.[2] He returned with it in the great transport ship of the Residence, together with its lid, and a false door with the lintel, jambs, and foundation block: never was this or the like done to any servant. But I was successful in the heart of his Majesty, I was rooted in the heart of his Majesty; and the heart of his Majesty was satisfied with me.

[Appointment as principal judge in the trial of the queen.]

Now when I was judge, his Majesty made me a sole friend and superintendent of the garden of Pharaoh, and I instructed [?] four [?] of the superintendents of Pharaoh's gardens who were there. I acted according to his Majesty's desire in performing the choosing of the guard [?][3] and making the way of the king and marshaling the nobles [at the court]; I acted altogether so that his Majesty praised me for it more than anything.

When an accusation was brought in the royal *harîm* against the chief royal wife Aamtesi as a secret affair, his Majesty caused me to enter to it and hear the case alone, without there being any chief justice and vizier, or any officer there but me only, on account of my success and rooting in the heart of his Majesty and of his heart being satisfied with me. I drew up [the report] in writing, alone with one judge. Behold, my office

---

[1] Perhaps schools of law, etc.

[2] These quarries, at the modern Turra, have been the source of fine white limestone down to the present day. They were exactly opposite Memphis in the eastern hills.

[3] Probably this means the arrangement of a body-guard or performance of the ritual for the King's amuletic and religious protection.

was that of superintendent of Pharaoh's garden: never before
did one of my grade hear a secret process of the royal *harîm;*
but his Majesty caused me to hear it, because of my success in
the heart of his Majesty above any officer and any noble and any
servant of his.

[Una commander-in-chief of all the native and foreign forces in an expedition
against the Eastern Bedawin.]

When his Majesty chastised the Aamu-Herusha[1] and his Maj-
esty made an army of many tens of thousands out of the whole
of the Upper Country, from Abu[2] in the south to Aphroditopo-
lis [?] in the north, and out of the Lower Country, from the
whole of the two sides,[3] out of Sezer and Khen-sezeru,[4] negroes
from Arertet,[5] negroes from Meza, negroes from Aam, negroes
from Wawat, negroes from Kaau, and foreigners from the land
of Temeh[6]; his Majesty sent me at the head of this host.
Behold, even the *ha*-princes, even the royal chancellors, even
the royal friends of the court, even the nomarchs and governors
of fortresses of the Upper Country and the Lower Country, the
royal friends superintending the frontier, the superintendents of
priests of the Upper and Lower Countries, and the superin-
tendents of domain lands, in command of the contingents from
the Upper and Lower Countries, and from the fortresses [?] and
cities that they ruled, and of the negroes of these tribes — I it
was who planned their procedure, although my grade was that
of superintendent of the garden of Pharaoh, on account of the
preciseness of my disposition: in such a way that no one of them
encroached on any of his fellows, that no one of them took bread
or sandals from the wayfarer, that no one of them stole dough
from any village, and that no one of them took a goat from any
people. I directed them to the Island of the North, the Gate of

---

[1] « The Asiatics who dwell upon the sand »—*i. e.*, Bedawin.

[2] Elephantine.

[3] The Eastern and Western borders of Lower Egypt.

[4] These names probably mean « the halting-station for the night," and « the
bedchamber of halting-station for the night »; evidently garrisoned posts on
the main desert routes.

[5] Arertet, Meza, Aam, Wawat, Kaau, were all in Nubia, and at no great dis-
tance from Egypt. The Meza were afterwards regularly drawn upon for
soldiers and police. The Kaau are more generally called Setu.

[6] *I. e.*, the land of the Libyans.

I-hetep, the *Uart* [?] of Horus Lord[1] of Truth. And behold, although I was of this grade . . . I reviewed the number of these troops which had never been reviewed by any servant.

> This host returned in peace: it had harried the land of the Herusha;
>
> this host returned in peace: it had trampled on the land of the Herusha;
>
> this host returned in peace: it had overthrown its inclosures.
>
> this host returned in peace: it had cut down its figs and vines.
>
> this host returned in peace: it had set fire to all its [camps?];
>
> this host returned in peace: it had slain the troops in it in many tens of thousands;
>
> this host returned in peace: it had [carried off people] from it, very numerous, as prisoners alive:

and his Majesty praised me for it more than anything.

His Majesty sent me to direct [this] host five times, and to smite the land of the Herusha at each of the revolts with these troops, and I acted so that his Majesty praised me for it more than anything. And when it was reported that there were warriors of this tribe in the "Wild-Goat's Nose," I crossed over in boats with these troops, and landed on the coast[2] of Thest, on the north of the land of the Herusha: and behold, when this host had marched by land, I came and smote them all down, and slew every warrior of them.

[Una made governor of the whole of Upper Egypt by the next king, Merenra Mehti-em-saf.]

I was carrier of the chair and sandals at the court, and the king Merenra my lord, who lives [for ever], appointed me *ha*-prince, governor of the Upper Country, from Abu in the south to Aphroditopolis [?] in the north, because of my success in the heart of his Majesty, and my rooting in the heart of his Majesty, and because the heart of his Majesty was satisfied [with me]. And while I was carrier of the chair and sandals, his Majesty praised me for my watchfulness and body-guardianship which I displayed in ushering in nobles [?], which exceeded that of any officer, noble, or servant of his. Never before was this function discharged by any servant.

[1] "Horus Lord of Truth" was the *Ka* name of King Sneferu [the first king of the IVth Dynasty, not much less than 4000 B. C.]. Probably this expedition went toward the Sinaitic peninsula.

[2] Sea-coast, perhaps of the Red Sea.

I performed for him the office of governor of the Upper Country to satisfaction, so that no one there encroached upon his fellow for any work: I paid [?] everything that is paid to the Residence from this Upper Country twice over, and every hour's service that is given to the palace in this Upper Country twice over; and discharged my office in such a way that it established a standard of duty[1] in this Upper Country. Never was the like done in this Upper Country before. I acted altogether so that his Majesty praised me for it.

[Una commissioned to obtain monuments for Merenra's pyramid from Abhat, and granite from the region of Elephantine.]

His Majesty sent me to Abhat to bring the sarcophagus called "Box of the Living Ones," with its cover, and an obelisk, and the costly furniture for my mistress[2] [?] the pyramid Kha-nefer of Merenra. His Majesty sent me to Abu[3] to bring the granite stela and its base, and the granite doors and jambs, and the granite doors and bases of the over-ground temple of my mistress [?] the pyramid Kha-nefer of Merenra. I came down the river with them to the pyramid Kha-nefer of Merenra with six broad boats, three transports, three eight-oars, in one expedition: never was this done, Abhat and Abu [done] in one expedition, in the time of any of the kings. Everything that his Majesty had commanded me came verily to pass just as his Majesty ordered me.

[An altar from the alabaster quarry of Het-nub.]

His Majesty sent me to Het-nub to bring a great table of offerings of the alabaster of Het-nub. I brought him down this table of offerings in seventeen days, quarrying it in Het-nub, and causing it to float down in this broad boat. For I had cut for it a broad boat of acacia-wood, sixty cubits long, thirty cubits broad, and built it — all this [?] in seventeen days, in the third month of harvest,[4] when behold there was no water on the junctions [?] of the channel,[5] and I moored at the pyramid Kha-nefer

[1] *Lit.* "made the officership making the standard."

[2] Or "for the mistress of the pyramid"; *i. e.*, for the queen buried in her husband's pyramid.

[3] Elephantine.

[4] The month Epiphi.

[5] The Nile being low.

of Merenra in peace. All things had come to pass according to the command which the Majesty of my lord had given me.

[A commission to ease the navigation in the region of the cataract, and increase the facilities for procuring granite.]

His Majesty sent me to cut five channels in the South, and make three broad boats and four transports of the acacia of Wawat. Behold, the rulers of Arertet, Wawat, Aam, and Meza were bringing wood for it. All were made in one year, floated, and laden with very great blocks of granite for the pyramid Kha-nefer of Merenra; moreover, I myself gave service to the palace in the whole work of these five channels,[1] on account of my abundance and my wealth [?], and of the loftiness of the mighty spirit of King Merenra, living for ever, beyond that of any god, and because all things came to pass according to the command which his *Ka* ordained.

Translation of F. Ll. Griffith.

SONGS OF LABORERS

THE reapers, represented cutting corn in the tomb of Paheri (XVIIIth Dynasty), are supposed to be chanting a little song, the words of which are engraved above their figures. Such songs are very common among the fellâhîn of the present day, who thus mark time for their work in the fields or on the river. This song is introduced by a phrase which seems to speak of it as being "in answering chant"; and this perhaps gives us the technical Egyptian term for antiphonal singing.

In answering chant they say:—

This is a good day! to the land come out | The north wind is out. The sky works according to our heart | Let us work, binding firm our heart.

The following transcription of the original Egyptian may give some idea of the assonances of words and ordered repetitions which marked the poetical style; the main repetitions are here italicized.

Khen en usheb, zet-sen:—

Hru pen nefer, *per* em ta | Ta mehyt *perta*.
Ta pet her art en *àb-en* | Bek-en mert *àb-en*.

[1] Apparently the passage of the Nile was blocked for boats at five different places about the first cataract, and Una had cleared the channel at his own expense as a free service to the King.

In the same tomb there is another song, already well known but less noticeable in form than the above. It is sung to the oxen on the threshing-floor.

> Thresh for yourselves. Thresh for yourselves.
> Thresh for yourselves. Thresh for yourselves.
> Straw to eat; corn for your masters;
> Let not your hearts be weary, your lord is pleased.

Translation of F. Ll. Griffith.

LOVE SONGS

SOME of the prettiest Egyptian poetry is contained in a papyrus of the XVIIIth Dynasty at the British Museum. The verses are written in hieratic, and are extremely difficult to translate, but their beauty is apparent to the translator even when he cannot fix the sense. A new edition of these and other poems of a kindred nature is being prepared by Professor W. Max Müller of Philadelphia, who kindly permits us to make some extracts from the advance sheets of his publication.

The songs are collected in small groups, generally entitled 'Songs of Entertainment.' The lover and his mistress call each other "brother" and "sister." In one song the girl addresses her lover in successive stanzas under the names of different plants in a garden, and plays on these names. Others are as follows:—

LOVE-SICKNESS

> I WILL lie down within,
> Behold, I am sick with wrongs.
> Then my neighbors come in
> To visit me.
> This sister of mine cometh with them;
> She will make a laughing-stock of the physicians;
> She knoweth mine illness.

THE LUCKY DOORKEEPER

> THE villa of my sister
> Hath its gates in the midst of the estate;
> [So often as] its doors are opened,
> [So often as] the bolt is withdrawn,
> My beloved is angry.

If I were set as the gatekeeper,
I should cause her to chide me;
Then should I hear her voice [when she is] angry:—
A child before her!

LOVE'S DOUBTS

[MY BROTHER] hath come forth [from mine house];
[He careth not for] my love;
My heart standeth still within me.

Behold, honeyed cakes in my mouth,
They are turned into salt;
Even must, that sweet thing,
In my mouth is as the gall of a bird!

The breath of thy nostrils alone
Is that which maketh my heart live.
I found thee! Amen grant thee unto me,
Eternally and for ever!

THE UNSUCCESSFUL BIRD-CATCHER

THE voice of the wild goose crieth,
For she hath taken her bait;
[But] thy love restraineth me,
I cannot loose it.[1]

So I must gather my net together.
What then shall I say to my mother,
To whom I come daily
Laden with wild-fowl?

I have not laid my net to-day,
For thy love hath seized me.

[1] "Loose," i. e., take the bird out of the snare to carry home to her mother.

Translation of W. Max Müller.

HYMN TO USERTESEN III.

[This hymn is the most remarkable example of Egyptian poetry known to us. It was found by Mr. Petrie near the pyramid and temple of Usertesen II., in the town which was founded there for the accommodation of the workmen employed upon these buildings, and for the priestly staff who performed the services for the dead Pharaoh in his chapel. The hymn is addressed to the son and successor of that king,—to Usertesen III.,—an active and warlike prince, who, as the poet also testifies, used his power for the benefit of his country and the pious support of its institutions. It is a marvel that the delicate papyrus on which the hymn is written should have been preserved for nearly 5,000 years. It has not, however, resisted the attacks of time without suffering injury; and the lacunæ, together with the peculiar language employed by the scribe, are baffling to the decipherer. Four stanzas only can be read with comparative completeness and certainty.

The parallelism of the sentences, the rhythm, the balancing of the lines of verse, and the pause in each, recall the style of the Hebrew Psalms. The choice of metaphors, too, is in a similar direction. Unfortunately our limited knowledge of the ancient language does not permit us to analyze closely the structure of the verses, nor to attempt any scansion of them. The radicals only of Egyptian words are known to us; of the pronunciation of the language at the time of the XIIth Dynasty we are entirely ignorant.]

I

HOMAGE to thee, Kha-kau-ra: our "Horus Divine of Beings."[1]
    Safeguarding the land and widening its boundaries: restraining the foreign nations by his kingly crown.
Inclosing the two lands[2] within the compass of his arms: seizing the nations in his grip.
Slaying the Pedti without stroke of the club: shooting an arrow without drawing the bowstring.
Dread of him hath smitten the Anu in their plain: his terror hath slain the Nine Races of Men.[3]
His warrant hath caused the death of thousands of the Pedti who had reached his frontier: shooting the arrow as doth Sekhemt,[4] he overthroweth thousands of those who knew not his mighty spirit.

[1] *Kha-kau-ra,* "Glory of the *Kas* of the Sun," was the principal name that Usertesen III., following the custom of the Pharaohs, adopted on his accession to the throne. "Horus, Divine of Beings," was the separate name for his royal *Ka* assumed at the same time. The *Ka* of a person was his ghostly Double, before and after death, and to the Egyptian this shadowy constituent of the whole being had a very distinct existence.
[2] *I. e.,* Upper and Lower Egypt.
[3] To the Egyptian the world was inhabited by nine races of men.
[4] Sekhemt, a goddess represented with the head of a lioness, the embodiment of the devastating power of the Sun and of the wrath of Ra. See p. 5240.

The tongue of his Majesty bindeth Nubia in fetters: his utterances put to flight the Setiu.

Sole One of youthful vigor, guarding his frontier: suffering not his subjects to faint, but causing the Pat[1] to repose unto full daylight.

As to his timid youth in their slumbers: his heart[2] is their protection.

His decrees have formed his boundaries: his word hath armored the two regions.

II

Twice jubilant are the gods: thou hast established their offerings,

Twice jubilant are thy children: thou hast made their boundaries.

Twice jubilant are thy forefathers: thou hast increased their portions.[3]

Twice jubilant is Egypt in thy strong arm: thou hast guarded the ancient order.

Twice jubilant are the Pat in thine administration: thy mighty spirit hath taken upon itself their provisionment.

Twice jubilant are the two regions in thy valor: thou hast widened their possessions.

Twice jubilant are thy paid young troops: thou hast made them to prosper.

Twice jubilant are thy veterans: thou hast made them to renew their youth.

Twice jubilant are the two lands in thy might: thou hast guarded their walls.

Twice jubilant be thou, O Horus, who hast widened his boundary: thou art from everlasting to everlasting.

III

Twice great is the lord of his city, above a million arms: as for other rulers of men, they are but common folk.

Twice great is the lord of his city: he is as it were a dyke, damming the stream in its water flood.

Twice great is the lord of his city: he is as it were a cool lodge, letting every man repose unto full daylight.

Twice great is the lord of his city: he is as it were a bulwark, with walls built of the sharp stones of Kesem.

[1] «Pat» seems to be a name for mankind, or perhaps for the inhabitants of Egypt.

[2] We speak of the «head» as the seat of the intellect; to the Egyptians it was the «heart.»

[3] Ancestor worship being universal in Egypt, the endowments for funerary services and offerings for the deceased kings must have been very large.

Twice great is the lord of his city: he is as it were a place of refuge, excluding the marauder.

Twice great is the lord of his city: he is as it were an asylum, shielding the terrified from his foe.

Twice great is the lord of his city: he is as it were a shade, the cool vegetation of the flood-time in the season of harvest.

Twice great is the lord of his city: he is as it were a corner warm and dry in time of winter.

Twice great is the lord of his city: he is as it were a rock barring the blast in time of tempest.

Twice great is the lord of his city: he is as it were Sekhemt to foes who tread upon his boundary.

IV

He hath come to us, that he may take the land of the South Country: the Double Crown[1] hath been placed upon his head.

He hath come, he hath united the two lands: he hath joined the Reed to the Hornet. [2]

He hath come, he hath ruled the people of the Black Land: he hath placed the Red Land in his power.[3]

He hath come, he hath protected the two lands: he hath tranquillized the two regions.

He hath come, he hath made the people of Egypt to live: he hath destroyed its afflictions.

He hath come, he hath made the Pat to live: he hath opened the throat of the Rekhyt.[4]

He hath come, he hath trampled on the nations: he hath smitten the Anu who knew not his terror.

He hath come, he hath secured his frontier: he hath delivered him who was stolen away.

He hath come: . . . he granteth reward-in-old-age by what his mighty arm bringeth to us.

He hath come, we nurture our children: we bury our aged ones[5] by his good favor.

Translation of F. Ll. Griffith.

[1] The «Double Crown» was that of Upper and Lower Egypt.

[2] The Reed and the Hornet were the symbols of Upper and Lower Egypt respectively.

[3] The «Black Land» is the alluvial of Egypt, the «Red Land» is its sandy border.

[4] «Rekhyt,» like «Pat,» seems to be a designation of the Egyptians. To «open the throat» of a man is to give him life by enabling him to breathe.

[5] A «good burial» after a «long old age» was a characteristic wish of the Egyptians.

HYMN TO THE ATEN [1]

THE following hymn addressed by King Akhenaten (B. C. 1450) to his one god, the visible Sun itself, was perhaps originally written in ten-line stanzas like the 'Hymn to Usertesen III.,' but the known texts of it are all too mutilated and uncertain for us to attempt any thorough restoration of the composition at present. A good edition of the hymn has been published by Professor Breasted of Chicago, and his text is here followed.

King Akhenaten was one of the most original minds known to us in Egyptian history. His bringing up was probably far more favorable to awakening powers of thought than was usually the case with the Pharaohs. Through his mother, Queen Tiy, he had been in close contact with the religions of Mesopotamia, perhaps even with Israelite monotheism; suddenly he cast off the traditions of his own country and all its multitudinous deities of heaven, earth, and the underworld, and devoted himself to the worship of one god, visible and exalted, before whom all else seemed either petty, gross, or unreal. His motto, as Professor Petrie has remarked, was "living in truth"; and according to his lights he lived up to it. Fervently he adored his god; and we may well believe that the words of this hymn are those which flowed from his own heart as he contemplated the mighty and beneficent power of the Sun.

This heretical doctrine roused the passions of the orthodox, who, triumphing over Akhenaten's reform, condemned his monuments to systematic destruction.

> Beautiful is thy resplendent appearing on the horizon of heaven,
> O living Aten, thou who art the beginning of life.
> When thou ascendest in the eastern horizon thou fillest every land with thy beauties;
> Thou art fair and great, radiant, high above the earth;
> Thy beams encompass the lands to the sum of all that thou hast created.
> Thou art the Sun; thou catchest them according to their sum;
> Thou subduest them with thy love.
> Though thou art afar, thy beams are on the earth;
> Thou art in the sky, and day followeth thy steps.

[1] The Aten is the name of the visible sun rather than of an abstract Sun god. It is pictured as a radiant disk, the rays terminating in human hands, often resting beneficently on the figure of the worshiper, bestowing upon him symbols of life, or graciously accepting his offerings.

When thou settest on the western horizon of heaven,
The land is in darkness like unto death;
They sleep in their chambers;
Their heads are covered, their nostrils are closed, the eye seeth
        not his fellow;
All their goods are stolen from under their heads, and they
        know it not.
Every lion cometh forth out of its cave,
All creeping things bite.
The earth is silent, and he that made them resteth on his
        horizon.

At dawn of day thou risest on the horizon and shinest as Aten
        by day.
Darkness flees, thou givest forth thy rays, the two lands are in
        festival day by day;
They wake and stand upon their feet, for thou hast raised
        them up;
Their limbs are purified, they clothe themselves with their
        garments;
Their hands are uplifted in adoration at thy rising;
The whole land goeth about its several labors.

Flocks rest in their pastures;
Trees and plants grow green;
Birds fly forth from their nests,—
Their wings are adoring thy Ka.[1]
All flocks leap upon their feet;
All flying things and all hovering things, they live when thou
        risest upon them.

Ships pass down-stream, and pass up-stream likewise,
Every way is open at thy rising.
The fishes on the river leap up before thee;
Thy rays are within the great waters.

It is thou who causest women to be fruitful, men to beget.
Thou quickenest the child in its mother's womb;
Thou soothest it that it cry not;
Thou dost nurture it within its mother's womb,
Thou givest breath to give life to all its functions.
It cometh forth from the womb upon the day of its birth.
Thou openest its mouth, that it may speak;
Thou providest for its wants.

[1] See note, p. 5303. The word occurs in these translations often, but not
with any very definite meaning.

When there is a chick within an egg, cheeping as it were
      within a stone,
Thou givest it breath therein to cause thy handiwork to live;
It is full-formed when it breaketh through the shell.
It cometh out of the egg when it cheepeth and is full-formed;
It runneth on its feet when it cometh out thence.

How manifold are thy works,
. . . O one god who hast no fellow!
Thou createdst the earth according to thy will, when thou
      wast alone,—
[Its] people, its herds, and all flocks;
All that is upon earth going upon feet,
All that is on high and flieth with wings,
The countries of Syria, of Ethiopia, of Egypt.
Thou settest each person in his place,
Thou providest for their wants,
Each one his circumstances and the duration of his life,
Tongues distinct in their speech,
Their kinds according to their complexions —
O distinguisher who distinguishest the races of mankind.

Thou makest the Nile in the deep,
Thou bringest it at thy pleasure,   [for thyself —
That it may give life to men, even as thou hast made them
O Lord of them all who art outwearied for them!

O Lord of earth who risest for them!
O Aten of day that awest all distant countries!
Thou makest their life;
Thou placest the Nile in heaven, that it may descend to them,
That it may rise in waves upon the rocks like the sea,
Watering their fields in their villages.
How excellent are thy ways, O Lord of Eternity!
A Nile in heaven poureth down for nations,
For all manner of animals that walk upon feet.
[But] the Nile cometh from the deep to the land of Egypt.
Thy rays nourish every field;
Thou risest and they live for thee.[1]

Thou makest the seasons to bring into existence all that thou
      hast made:
The winter season to refresh them, the heat [to warm them].

[1] The Nile here stands for the main sources of water: that in heaven giving rain on the mountains and fields, that in the "deep" or "underworld" giving rise to springs, wells, and rivers.

Thou madest the heaven afar off, that thou mightest rise
        therein,
That thou mightest see all thou didst make when thou wast
        alone,
When thou risest in thy form as the living Aten,
Splendid, radiant, afar, beauteous —
[Thou createdst all things by thyself]
Cities, villages, camps, by whatsoever river they be watered.
Every eye beholdeth thee before it;
Thou art the Aten of day above the earth.

.   .   .   .

Thou art in my heart.
There is none other that knoweth thee but thy son, Fairest of
        the Forms of Ra, the Only One of Ra[1];
Thou causest him to be exercised in thy methods and in thy
        might.
The whole earth is in thy hand even as thou hast made them;
At thy rising all live, at thy setting they die.

Translation of F. Ll. Griffith.

HYMNS TO AMEN RA[2]

THE following collection of hymns to Amen Ra is from the ortho-
dox worship of the New Kingdom; that is to say, it dates
from the period beginning in the XVIIth Dynasty, about 1700
B. C. The series is contained in a papyrus now preserved in the
museum at Gizeh and in very perfect condition.

In the original, the lines are punctuated with red dots, and the
stanzas are marked by rubrics, a very valuable clue being thus pro-
vided both as to meanings and form.

The first hymn is divided into five stanzas of seven lines each,[3]
but the fourth stanza contains an error of punctuation which has
perhaps prevented this arrangement from being noticed hitherto.
The other hymns do not appear to be so divisible.

[1] "Fairest of the Forms of Ra, the Only One of Ra," is the title which
Akhenaten took when first he ascended the throne, and which he continued
to bear all through his reign, notwithstanding his reform.

[2] Amen was god of Thebes; and under the XVIIIth Dynasty, when Thebes
was the capital of the whole country and Egypt was at the height of her
power, Amen took the first place in the national pantheon. He was then
identified with Ra the Sun god, perhaps to make him more acceptable to the
nation at large. Hence a hymn to Amen Ra was practically a hymn to the
supreme Sun god.

[3] Compare the seven-line stanza in the inscription of Una, above, p. 5298.

The text presents several instances of embellishment by far-fetched, and to our minds very feeble, puns and punning assonances. It is impossible to reproduce these to the English reader, but some lines in which they occur are here marked with asterisks indicating the words in question.

Although these hymns have been much admired, it must be confessed that they are somewhat arid in comparison with the simple expression of Akhenaten's devotion in the 'Hymn to the Aten.' To the Egyptians, however, the mythological references were full of meaning, while to us they are never fully intelligible. Such an enumeration as that of the symbols and insignia of divine royalty which we find in the second hymn, is as empty to us as references to the Stars and Stripes, the White House, the Spread Eagle, the Union Jack, the Rose, the Shamrock, and the Thistle may be to the lords of the world in 5000 to 6000 A. D.

Praise of Amen Ra!
The bull in Heliopolis, the chief of all the gods,
The beautiful and beloved god
Who giveth life to all warm-blooded things,
To all manner of goodly cattle!

I

HAIL to thee, Amen Ra! lord of the thrones of the two
          lands,
Thou who dwellest in the sanctuary of Karnak.
Bull of his mother, he who dwelleth in his fields,
Wide-ranging in the Land of the South.
Lord of the Mezau,[1] ruler of Punt,
Prince of heaven, heir of earth,
Lord of all things that exist!
     Alone in his exploits even amongst the gods,
The goodly bull of the Ennead[2] of the gods,
Chiefest of all the gods,
Lord of truth, father of the gods,
Maker of men, creator of animals,
Lord of the things which are, maker of fruit-trees,
Maker of pasture, who causeth the cattle to live!
     Image made by Ptah,[3] youth fair of love!
The gods give praise unto him;

[1] Mezau and Punt were on and about the east coast of Africa, in Nubia and Somaliland.

[2] The supreme god was surrounded by eight other gods, and together they formed an Ennead, or group of nine.

[3] Ptah was the great god of Memphis, the ancient capital of the country.

Maker of things below and of things above, he illuminateth
      the two lands:
He traverseth the sky in peace.
King of Upper and Lower Egypt, Ra the Justified, chief of
      the two lands.
Great one of valor, lord of awe;
Chief, making the earth in its entirety!
    Nobler in thy ways than any god,
The gods rejoice in his beauties!
To him are given acclamations in the Great House,
Glorious celebrations in the House of Flame;
The gods love his odor when he cometh from Punt.
Prince of the dew, he entereth the land of the Mezau!
Fair of face, coming to the Divine Land[1]!
    The gods gather as dogs at his feet,
Even as they recognize his majesty as their lord.
Lord of fear, great one of terror,
Great of soul, lordly in manifestations,
Flourishing of offerings, maker of plenty,
Acclamations to thee, maker of the gods,
Thou who dost upraise the sky, and press down the ground!

II

    Wake in health, Min-Amen!
Lord of the everlasting, maker of eternity,
Lord of adorations, dwelling in [Khemmis],
Established of two horns, fair of face,
Lord of the uræus crown with lofty double plume,
Beautiful of diadem, with lofty white crown,
The kingly coif with the two uræi are on his forehead.
He is adorned within the palace,
With the Sekhet crown, the Nemes cap, and the Khepersh
      helmet.
Fair of face, he taketh the Atef crown,
Loving its south and its north.
Lord of the Sekhemt sceptre, receiving the Ames sceptre,
Lord of the Meks sceptre, holding the Nekhekh,
    Beautiful Ruler, crowned with the white crown!
Lord of rays, making light!
The gods give praises unto him
Who giveth his two hands [for aid] to him that loveth him,

---

[1] Or the «Land of the Gods,» a name for the lands of the East, and
especially for «Punt.»

Who casteth his enemies in the fire;
His eye it is which overthroweth the wicked;
It casteth its lance at the devourer of Nu;
It causeth the serpent Nak to cast up that which it swal-
          lowed.
    Hail to thee, Ra, lord of truth,
Whose sanctuary is hidden! lord of the gods,
Khepera in the midst of his bark,
He gave command, and the gods were created.
Tum, maker of the Rekhyt,
Distinguishing their kinds, making their lives,
Distinguishing their complexions one from another.
    Hearing the complaint of him who is oppressed,
Kindly of heart when called upon.
He delivereth the timid from him who is of a froward
          heart,
He judgeth the cause of the weak and the oppressed.
    Lord of Understanding, Taste is on his lips,
The Nile cometh at his desire.
Lord of sweetness, great one of love,
He maketh the Rekhyt to live,
He giveth keenness to every eye.
He is made out of Nu,
Creating the rays of light.
The gods rejoice in his beauties,
Their hearts live when they behold him.

III

    Ra, exalted in Karnak!
Great of splendor in the House of the Obelisk
Ani, lord of the New Moon festival,
To whom are celebrated the festival of the sixth day and
          of the quarter month.
Liege lord, to whom Life, Prosperity, Health! lord of all
          the gods,
Who see him [?] in the midst of the horizon,
Chief over the Pat and Hades,
His name is more hidden* than his birth,
In his name of Amen,* the hidden One.
    Hail to thee who art in peace!
Lord of enlargement of heart, lordly in manifestations,
Lord of the uræus crown, with lofty double plume;
Fair of diadem, with lofty white crown!
The gods love the sight of thee,

The Sekhemt* crown is established upon thy forehead.
Thy loveliness is shed* abroad over the two lands;
Thy rays shine forth in the eyes of men; fair for the Pat
        and the Rekhyt is thy rising,
Weary are the flocks when thou art radiant.
Thy loveliness is in the southern sky, thy sweetness in the
        northern sky,
Thy beauties conquer hearts,
Thy loveliness maketh arms to droop,
Thy beautiful form maketh hands to fail;
Hearts faint at the sight of thee.
    Sole figure, who didst make all that is!
One and only one, maker of all that are,
From whose eyes mankind issued,
By whose mouth the gods were created,
Who makest the herbage, and makest to live the cattle,
        goats, swine, and sheep,
The fruit-trees for the Henememt.
He maketh the life of fishes in the river,
The fowl of the air,
Giving breath to that which is in the egg;
Making the offspring of the serpent to live;
Making to live therewith the flies,
The creeping things, and the leaping things, and the like.
Making provision for the mice in their holes;
Making to live the birds in every tree.
    Hail to thee, maker of all these!
One and only one, with many arms!
At night wakeful while all sleep,
Seeking good for his flock.
Amen,* who *establishest all things!
Tum Horus of the horizon!
Praises be to thee in that all say,
"Acclamations to thee, for that thou outweariest thyself
        with us!
Obeisance to thee for that thou didst make us!"
    Hail to thee, from all animals!
Acclamations to thee from every land,
To the height of heaven, to the breadth of earth,
To the depth of the great waters!
The gods bow before thy majesty,
Exalting the mighty spirit that formed them;
They rejoice at the coming of him who begat them;
They say unto thee:—"Come, come in peace!

Father of the fathers of all the gods,
Thou who dost upraise the sky and press down the ground.»
Maker of that which is, former of those which have being,
Liege lord—to whom Life, Prosperity, Health!—chief of
    the gods,
We adore thy mighty spirit even as thou madest us;
Who were made for thee when thou fashionedst us.
We give praises unto thee for that thou outweariest thyself
    with us.
  Hail to thee who didst make all that is!
Lord of truth, father of the gods,
Maker of men, fashioner of animals,
Lord of corn,
Making to live the animals of the desert.
Amen, bull fair of face,
Beloved in Thebes,
Great one of splendors in the House of the Obelisk,
Twice crowned in Heliopolis,
Thou who judgest between the twain in the Great Hall!
  Chief of the great Ennead of the gods,
One and only one, without his peer,
Dwelling in Thebes,
Ani in his divine Ennead,
He liveth on truth every day.
God of the horizon, Horus of the East,
Who hath made the hills that have silver, gold,
Real lapis lazuli, at his pleasure:
Gums and incense are mingled for the Mezau,
Fresh incense for thy nostrils.
Fair of face he cometh to the Mezau,
Amen Ra, lord of the throne of the two lands,
He who dwelleth in Thebes,
Ani in his sanctuary.

IV

  Sole King is he, even in the midst of the gods;
Many are his names, none knoweth their number.
He riseth on the horizon of the east, he is laid to rest on
    the horizon of the west.
He overthroweth his enemies
In the daily task of every day;
In the morning he is born each day;
Thoth raiseth his eyes,
And propitiateth him with his benefits;

The gods rejoice in his beauties,
Exalting him who is in the midst of adorers!
Lord of the Sekti and of the Madet bark,
Which traverse for thee Nu in peace!
   Thy crew rejoice
When they see the overthrow of the wicked one,
Whose members taste the knife;
The flame devoureth him;
His soul is more punished than his body;
That Nak serpent, he is deprived of movement.
The gods are in exultation,
The crew of Ra are in peace,
Heliopolis is in exultation,
The enemies of Tum are overthrown.
Karnak is in peace, Heliopolis is in exultation.
The heart of the uræus goddess is glad,
The enemies of her lord are overthrown;
The gods of Kheraha are in acclamation,
The dwellers in the sanctuaries are in obeisance;
They behold him mighty in his power.
Mighty prince of the gods!
Great one of Justice*, lord of Karnak,
In this thy name, "Doer of Justice*,"
Lord of Plenty, Peaceful Bull*;
In this thy name, "Amen, Bull of his Mother,"
   Making mankind*, creating* all that is,
In this thy name of "Tum* Khepera*,"
   Great hawk, adorning the breast!
Fair of face adorning the bosom.
Figure lofty of diadem.
The two uræi fly on wings before him,
The hearts of men run up to him [like dogs],
The illuminated ones turn towards him.
Adorning the two lands by his coming forth,
Hail to thee, Amen Ra, lord of the throne of the two
       lands!
His city loveth his rising.

This is the end,
in peace,
as it was found.

Translation of F. Ll. Griffith.

SONGS TO THE HARP

[Frequently in the tombs is figured a scene in which a harper plays before the deceased. His song is ever on the same theme: Enjoy life while it lasts, for all things pass away, and are succeeded by others which also perish in their turn. Such were the encouragements to conviviality which the Egyptians put into the mouths of their minstrels.

One of these songs was apparently engraved in front of the figure of a harper in the tomb or pyramid of King Antef (of the XIth or perhaps XIIIth Dynasty, not less than 2000 B. C.), and a copy of·it has been handed down to us on a papyrus of the XVIIIth Dynasty: fragments of the same song are moreover preserved at Leyden on slabs from a tomb of the same period.

Part of another song of the same kind may be read on the walls of the fine tomb of Neferhetep at Thebes (*temp.* XVIIIth Dynasty). This song was a long one, but the latter part of it is now mutilated and hopelessly destroyed; yet enough of the sequel remains to show that it rose to a somewhat higher level of teaching than the first song, and counseled men to feed the poor and to win a good name to leave behind them after death.

The songs seem to fall naturally into stanzas of ten lines each, though the inscriptions and papyri on which they are preserved to us are not punctuated to indicate these divisions. In the first song the ten lines fall readily into pairs, thus producing five-line stanzas.]

I

Songs which are in the tomb of King Antef, justified, which are in front of the singer on the harp

Happy is this good lord! | A goodly fate is spoiled.
One body passeth | and others are set up since the time of the ancestors.
The gods[1] who were aforetime | rest in their sepulchres,
So also the nobles glorified | buried in their sepulchres.
Palaces are built and their places are not | behold what hath been done with them!

I have heard the words of Imhetep and Herdedef | who spake thus continually in their sayings:
« Behold their places, their walls are ruined | their places are not, as though they had not been.
None cometh thence to tell their lot | to tell their estate,
To strengthen our hearts | until ye approach the place to which they have gone.»
Be thou of good cheer thereat | [as for me] my heart faileth me in singing thy dirge.

[1] *I. e.,* the kings, who were always reckoned divine, and as ruling by divine right.

Follow thy heart so long as thou existest | put frankincense on thy
      head;
Be clothed in fine linen, be anointed with pure ben oil | things fit for
      a god.
Enjoy thyself beyond measure | let not thy heart faint.
Follow thy desire and thy happiness while thou art on earth | fret
      not thy heart till cometh to thee that day of lamenta-
      tions.
The Still-of-Heart heareth not their lamentations | the heart of a man
      in the pit taketh no part in mourning.

> With radiant face, make a good day,[1]
> And rest not on it.
> Behold, it is not given to a man to carry his goods
>   with him!
> Behold, there is none who hath gone,
> And cometh back hither again!

II

*[Saith the player on the harp who is in the tomb of the Osirian, the divine
father of Amen,[2] Neferhetep, Justified, he saith: —]*

O how weary! Truly a prince was he!
That good fate hath come to pass.
Bodies pass away since the time of God,
The youthful come in their place,
Ra presenteth himself every morning,
Tum[3] setteth in the Mountain of the West,
Men beget and women conceive;
Every nostril tasteth the breath of sunrise;
Those whom they bring forth — all of them —
They come in their stead.

Make holiday, O divine father!
Set gums and choice unguents of every kind for thy nose,
Garlands of lotuses on the shoulders,
And on the breast of thy sister, who is in thy heart,
Who sitteth at thy side.
Set singing and music before thy face,
Put all sorrow behind thee,
Bethink thyself of joys,

[1] *I. e.*, «make holiday.»
[2] Title of a priest of Amen.
[3] God of the setting sun.

Until there cometh that day on which thou moorest at the land that
       loveth silence,
Before the heart of the son whom thou lovest is still.

Make holiday, O Neferhetep, Justified! | the excellent divine father,
       pure of hands!
There are heard all the things | that have happened to the ancestors
       who were aforetime;
Their walls are ruined | their places are not;
They are as though they had never been | since the time of the god.
May thy walls be established | may thy trees flourish on the bank of
       thy pond!
May thy soul sit beneath them | that it drink their waters!
Follow thy heart greatly | while thou art on earth.
Give bread to him | who is without plot of land.
Mayest thou gain a good name | for the eternal future!
Mayest thou . . .

                        Translation of F. Ll. Griffith.

FROM AN EPITAPH

[In the British Museum there is a memorial tablet of Ptolemaic date for a
lady of highest sacerdotal descent, on her mother's side as well as on her
father's. She was married to the chief priest of Ptah, and on her death she
addresses her male relations and friends among the priests of chief rank with
words and sentiments very different from the orthodox prayers and formulæ
which cover the funerary stelæ of Pharaonic times; though much the same
line of thought found utterance in the songs of the harpers.]

O BROTHER, husband, friend, thy desire to drink and to eat
hath not ceased, [therefore] be drunken, enjoy the love of
women, make holiday. Follow thy desire by night and by
day. Put not care within thine heart. Lo! are not these the
years of thy life upon earth? For as for Amenti, it is a land of
slumber and of heavy darkness, a resting-place for those who
have passed within it. Each sleepeth [there] in his own form;
they never more awake to see their fellows, they behold not
their fathers nor their mothers, their heart is careless of their
wives and children.

The water of life with which every mouth is moistened is
corruption to me, the water that is by me corrupteth me; I know
not what to do[1] since I came into this valley. Give me running

---

[1] An expression of utter bewilderment; *lit.*, "I know not the estate which
is upon me."

water; say to me: " Water shall not cease to be brought to thee."
Turn my face to the north wind upon the edge of the water.
Verily thus shall my heart be cooled, refreshed from its pain.[1]

Verily I think on him whose name is "Come!" All who are
called of him come to him instantly, their hearts terrified with
fear of him. There is none whom he regardeth among gods or
men; with him the great are as the small. His hand cannot
be held back from aught that he desireth; he snatcheth the child
from its mother, as well as the aged who are continually meeting
him on his way. All men fear and pray before him, but he
heedeth them not. None cometh to gaze on him in wonder; he
hearkeneth not unto them who adore him. He is not seen[2] that
propitiatory offerings of any kind should be made to him.

Translation of F. Ll. Griffith.

FROM A DIALOGUE BETWEEN A MAN AND HIS SOUL

[The following is found on a papyrus of the XIIth Dynasty, preserved
at Berlin. After some obscure arguments the man apparently admits that the
present life is full of dissatisfaction, and proceeds.]

DEATH is ever before me [?] like the healing of a sick man, or
like a rise in life after a fall.
Death is ever before me like the smell of frankincense, or like
sitting under an awning on a day of cool breeze.[3]
Death is ever before me like the scent of lotuses, like sitting on the
bank of the Land of Intoxication.[4]
Death is ever before me like a road watered [?], or as when a man
cometh from a campaign to his home.
Death is ever before me like the unveiling of the sky, or as when a
man attaineth to unexpected fortune.
Death is ever before me like as a man desireth to see his house
when he hath spent many years in pulling [the oars?].[5]

[1] To these thinkers, thirst (since the presence of water would induce putre-
faction of the body) and suffocation were the chief material sufferings of the
dead.

[2] From this curious expression it is evident that the Egyptians considered
it necessary that a deity should be visibly represented by statue or animal, in
order that he should receive the offerings presented to him. They never per-
sonified a god of Death, only a god of the Dead.

[3] The sunshine may be taken for granted in Egypt.

[4] Our "on the verge of intoxication" is an almost identical expression,
but without a poetical significance.

[5] A slight correction of the original would give "in captivity" (kidnapped).

Verily he that is therein is as a living god punishing the error of the
    evil-doer.
Verily he that is therein standeth in the boat of Ra and causeth
    choice viands to be given thence to the temples.[1]
Verily he that is therein is as a wizard; he is not prevented from
    complaining to Ra even as he would speak.

My soul said unto me:[2] "Lay aside [?] mourning, O Nessu my
brother, that thou mayest offer upon the altar even as thou fightest
for life, as thou sayest, 'Love me continually.' Thou hast refused
the grave; desire then that thou mayest reach the grave, that thy
body may join the earth, that I may hover [over thee] after thou art
weary. Let us then make a dwelling together."

                        Translation of F. Ll. Griffith.

‹THE NEGATIVE CONFESSION›

[It may be thought that the fundamental ideas of Egyptian morality
would be most succinctly expressed in the so-called 'Negative Confession'
contained in the 'Book of the Dead.' When the deceased appeared before
Osiris he was supposed to recite this confession, in which he alleged his free-
dom from a long catalogue of sins: he repeated it in two forms. After the
XVIIIth Dynasty, B. C. 1500, it was considered as perhaps the most essential
of all the texts deposited in the tomb with the mummy, for the guidance of
the deceased person before his fate was finally settled. It is therefore to be
found in thousands of copies, but unfortunately this much-worn text is as
corrupt as most of the other sections of the Book of the Dead. The hack
scribes and calligraphists were content to copy without understanding it, often
bungling or wresting the sense according to their very imperfect lights. It is
seldom that different copies agree precisely in their readings: often the differ-
ences are very material and leave the true sense altogether uncertain. Again,
even where the reading seems comparatively sure, the meaning remains
obscure, owing to the occurrence of rare words or expressions. All the
phrases begin with the negative "not."]

FIRST CONFESSION

I HAVE not done injury to men.
  I have not oppressed those beneath me.[3]
  I have not acted perversely [prevaricated?], instead of
    straightforwardly.

[1] The advantages of the life beyond seem to consist in being like gods
and in full communion with the greatest of them, Ra.
  [2] This closing speech of the soul is barely intelligible.
  [3] Or perhaps "my kindred."

I have not known vanity.[1]
I have not been a doer of mischief.

.   .   .   .

.   .   .   .

I have not done what the gods abominate.
I have not turned the servant against his master.
I have not caused hunger.
I have not caused weeping.
I have not murdered.
I have not commanded murder.
I have not caused suffering to men.
I have not cut short the rations of the temples.
I have not diminished the offerings of the gods.
I have not taken the provisions of the blessed dead.
I have not committed fornication nor impurity in what was
  sacred to the god of my city.
I have not added to nor diminished the measures of grain.
I have not diminished the palm measure.
I have not falsified the cubit of land.
I have not added to the weights of the balance.
I have not nullified the plummet of the scales.
I have not taken milk from the mouth of babes.
I have not driven cattle from their herbage.[2]
I have not trapped birds, the bones of the gods.
I have not caught fish in their pools.[?]
I have not stopped water in its season.
I have not dammed running water.
I have not quenched fire when burning.[3]
I have not disturbed the cycle of gods when at their choice
  meats.
I have not driven off the cattle of the sacred estate.
I have not stopped a god in his comings forth.

Second Confession

I have not done injustice.
I have not robbed.

[1] Or what is «unprofitable» or «treason.»

[2] This and the two following asseverations seem rather to read: «I have
not caught animals by a bait of their herbage.» «I have not trapped birds
by a bait of 'gods' bones.'» «I have not caught fish by a bait of fishes'
bodies.»

[3] *Lit.*, «in its moment.»

I have not coveted.[?]
I have not stolen.
I have not slain men.
I have not diminished the corn measure.
I have not acted crookedly.
I have not stolen the property of the gods.
I have not spoken falsehood.
I have not taken food away.
I have not been lazy.[?]
I have not trespassed.
I have not slain a sacred animal.
I have not been niggardly in grain.
I have not stolen.   .   .   .
I have not been a pilferer.
My mouth hath not run on.
I have not been a talebearer in business not mine own.
I have not committed adultery with another man's wife.
I have not been impure.
I have not made disturbance.
I have not transgressed.
My mouth hath not been hot.[1]
I have not been deaf to the words of truth.
I have not made confusion.
I have not caused weeping.
I am not given to unnatural lust.
I have not borne a grudge.
I have not quarreled.
I am not of aggressive hand.
I am not of inconstant mind.
I have not spoiled the color of him who washeth the
          god. [??]
My voice has not been too voluble in my speech.
I have not deceived nor done ill.
I have not cursed the king.

·   ·   ·   ·   ·   ·   ·   ·

My voice is not loud.
I have not cursed God.
I have not made bubbles. [?]
I have not made [unjust] preferences.
I have not acted the rich man except in my own things.
I have not offended the god of my city.

                                   Translation of F. Ll. Griffith.

[1] I. e., "I am not hot of speech."

THE TEACHING OF AMENEMHAT

[The advice given by Amenemhat I., the founder of the XIIth Dynasty, to his son and successor Usertesen I. (about B. C. 2500), is a short composition that was much in vogue during the New Kingdom as an exercise for schoolboys. Six copies of portions or of the whole have survived to our day; but with one exception all are very corrupt, and the text is extremely difficult to translate. Our oldest copies appear to date from the middle of the XIXth Dynasty (about B. C. 1300). But the composition itself must be older than this; indeed, it may be a true record of the great King's charge to his son.

The following seems to be the purpose and argument of the work. Amenemhat, who has already virtually associated Usertesen with himself in the kingdom, determines in consequence of a plot against his life to insure his son's succession by announcing it in a formal manner. He has labored strenuously and successfully for his own glory and for the good of his people, but in return he is scarcely saved from ignominious dethronement or assassination through a conspiracy formed in his own household. The moral to be drawn from this is pointed out to his son with considerable bitterness and scorn in the 'Teaching,' in which, however, Usertesen is promised a brilliant reign if he will attend to his father's instructions.

It is perhaps worth while noticing that there is no expression of piety or reference to the worship of divinities either in the precepts themselves or in the narrative. The personified Nile is spoken of in a manner that would be likely to offend its worshipers; but in the last section, the interpretation of which is extremely doubtful, Amenemhat seems to acquiesce in the orthodox views concerning the god Ra.

Usertesen's reign dates from Amenemhat's XXth year, and that his association was then no secret but already formally acknowledged, is amply proved. The King seems to feel already the approach of old age and death, and though he lived on to assist his son with his counsel for no less than ten years, it was apparently in retirement from public life.[1] The work has been considered as a posthumous charge to Usertesen, but although certain expressions seem to support this view, on the whole I think its correctness improbable.

In several copies the text is divided by rubrics into fifteen paragraphs, and the phrases are punctuated by dots placed above the lines. In the following rendering the paragraphs are preserved, and summarized where they are too difficult to translate. The incompleteness of the best text leaves the last two paragraphs in almost hopeless confusion.]

[1] Compare the story of Sanehat (above, p. 5237 seq.) for an indication of the place which Amenemhat retained for himself in the government of the kingdom during the joint rule. "He [Usertesen) curbs the nations while his father remains in his palace, and he [Usertesen] accomplisheth for him what is commanded him."

1. [Title and introduction.]

COMMENCEMENT in the teaching made by the majesty of the King of Upper and Lower Egypt, Sehetepabra, Son of the Sun, Amenemhat, justified, which he spake as a dividing of truth[1] to his Son, the Universal Lord. Said he:—

"Shine forth as a God! Hearken to that I say to thee, that thou mayest be king of the land and rule the territories, that thou mayest excel in all wealth.

2. [Exhortation to caution in associating with subjects.]

"Let one be armored against his associates as a whole; it befalleth that mankind turn their heart to him who inspireth them with fear. Enter not to them singly; fill not thy heart with a brother; know not an honored friend; make not to thyself free-and-easy visitors, by which nothing is accomplished.

3. [Trust not to the aid of friends.]

"When thou liest down, keep to thyself thine own heart; for friends exist not for a man on the day of troubles. I gave to the beggar, and I made the orphan to exist[2]; I caused the man of no position to obtain his purpose even as the man of position.

4. [Continuation of 3: Reward of his beneficence.]

"It was the eater of my food that made insurrection; he to whom I gave a helping hand produced terror therewith; they who put on my fine linen looked on me as shadows[3]; they who were anointed with my frankincense defiled me while using it.

5. [Men forget the heroism of his achievements on their behalf, though their happy condition speaks loudly of it; by forgetting they lose much of the advantages he has procured them.]

"My portraits are among the living, my achievements among men, making for me dirges that none heed, a great feat of combat that none see. Behold, one fighteth for a lassoed ox, that forgetteth yesterday. Good fortune is not complete for one who cannot know it.[4]

---

[1] Compare 2 Timothy ii. 15.

[2] "To exist" often means to have a solid position.

[3] A proverbial word for nullity, worthlessness.

[4] Egypt, the lassoed ox, helpless in the hands of its oppressors, is now free, but fails to appreciate its good fortune.

6. [An attempt upon his life: circumstances of the attack.]

"It was after supper, and night was come on. I took an hour of heart pleasure; I lay down upon my *diwân;* I sank-in-rest, my heart began to follow slumber. Behold! weapons were brandished [?], and there was conversation concerning me; while I acted like the serpent of the desert.[1]

7. [Taken by surprise, he could not defend himself.]

"I awoke to fight; I was alone. I found that it was the stroke of an ally. If I had taken swiftly the arms from his hand I should have caused the cowards to retreat, by dint of smiting round. But there is not a man of valor at night; there is no fighting single-handed; there happens not a successful bout in ignorance. Behold thou me.[2]

8. [Usertesen's association the only safeguard. Amenemhat is not stern enough to rule Egypt longer, but he offers to assist with his counsel.]

"Behold thou, [then ?] abominable things came to pass when I was without thee, because the courtiers had not heard that I had handed on to thee [the kingdom], because I had not sat with thee [on the throne]. Let me [then] make thy arrangements,[3] for I do not confound them.[4] I am not ignorant of them, but my heart does not remember the slackness of servants.

9. [The conspiracy was hatched in the palace itself; the commons were hoodwinked; there was no ground for discontent.]

"Is it the function of women to captain assassins? Is the interior of a house the nursery of insurgents? Is mining done by dint of cutting through the snow?[5] The underlings were kept ignorant of what they were doing. Ill fortunes have not come behind me[6] since my birth; there has not been success like mine in working to the measure of my ability.

[1] Perhaps this means that Amenemhat lay still but ready to rise instantly and fight.

[2] "*Me voilà!*"—after drawing the picture of his helpless state, surprised alone in the night.

[3] *I. e.*, "be thy counselor."

[4] A difficult passage.

[5] Meaning doubtful.

[6] *I. e.*, upon others in consequence of me.

10. [Amenemhat's activity.]

"I pushed up to Elephantine and I turned back to Natho;[1] I stood upon the ends of the earth and saw its edge.[2] I carried forward the boundaries of strength-of-arm[3] by my valor and by my feats.

11. [His beneficent rule.]

"I was a maker of barley, beloved of Nepra[4]; the Nile begged my mercy in every hollow. None were hungry in my years, none were thirsty therein; the people sat [content] in what they did, saying with reference to me, 'Every command is in its right place.'

12. [His valor in war and in the chase.]

"I overcame lions, I captured crocodiles. I seized Wawat, I carried away Mezay; I caused the Setiu to go like hounds.[5]

13. [The house and tomb that he built.]

"I built a house adorned with gold, its ceiling with blue,[6] its walls having deep foundations, the gates of copper, the bolts of bronze, made for everlasting. . . .

14. [Usertesen is the sole guardian of its secrets: he is trusted and beloved by the King and popular in the country.]

"There are numerous intricacies of passages. I know that the successor will seek its beauties, for he knoweth it not without thee. But thou art [?] my son Usertesen, as my feet walk; thou art my own heart as my eyes see, born in a good hour, with mortals who give thee praise.

---

[1] Elephantine and Natho are often named as the extreme north and south points of Egypt; compare the Biblical «from Dan even unto Beersheba.»

[2] Or perhaps «its centre.»

[3] *I. e.*, «surpassed the record,» or perhaps «reached the boundaries.»

[4] The kings of the XIIth dynasty paid much attention to agriculture and irrigation. Barley was the representative cereal, Nepra was the Corn goddess. In the following clause the Nile is represented as a prisoner in the King's power: or possibly as begging him «*for* every hollow» to enter and inundate it.

[5] *I. e.*, «obedient to his commands,» a common figure. The Wawat and Mezay were in Nubia, the Setiu in the Northeast to Syria.

[6] The rendering of this section is very doubtful.

15. [Amenemhat leaves Usertesen with the prospect of a brilliant reign.]

"Behold, what I have done at the beginning thou hast arranged finally. Thou art the haven of what was in my heart. All collectively offer the white crown to [thee], the Seed of God, sealed to its right place. Begin for thee greetings in the bark of Ra.[1] Then a reign cometh of the first order, not of what I did in working to the extent of my powers. Set up monuments and make good thy tomb." . . .

This is its arrival.

THE PRISSE PAPYRUS

[The so-called Prisse Papyrus was obtained at Thebes by the French artist and Egyptologist who gave it the name by which it is now known. It is a celebrated document, though as yet but little understood. The language being difficult and the text in many places corrupt, it is useless to offer a complete translation. In the following, several passages are omitted altogether, and the most uncertain portions are italicized, and even of what remains very little can be guaranteed. The beginning is lost; the first two pages contain the end of a book of proverbs, the text of which falls naturally into sections, although it is not divided by rubrics.]

1. [The first section lays down axioms in regard to discretion in speech.

"THE cautious man succeeds; the accurate man is praised; to the man of silence the sleeping-chamber is opened. Wide scope hath he who is acquiescent in his speech; knives are set against him who forceth his way wrongfully. *Let no one approach out of his turn.*"

2. [In regard to food: abstinence.]

"If thou sittest [at meat] with a company, hate the bread that thou desirest — it is a little moment. Restrain appetite; gluttony is base. . . . A cup of water, it quencheth the thirst; a mouthful of melon, it stayeth the appetite. It is a good thing to make substitute for a luxury [*or*, that which is good can replace a luxury]; a little of a small matter can replace a great thing.

[1] Or, "and the seal to its proper place, even as the acclamations in the bark of Ra ordain for thee." Ra the Sun god was the royal god essentially, and his approval was doubtless required to establish a claim to the throne. He was believed to travel through the sky in a boat.

It is a base fellow who is mastered by his belly, who passeth time that he wotteth not, free ranging of his belly in their houses."

3. [When with a great eater or drinker, offend not by over-abstinence.]

"If thou sittest at meat with a gormandizer and eatest [?], his desire departeth; if thou drinkest with a toper and takest wine, his heart is satisfied. Be not afraid of meat in company with the greedy; take what he giveth thee; refuse it not, for it will humor him."

4. [Against surliness.]

"If there be a man devoid of sociability [*lit.*, making himself known], on whom no word hath power, *sulky* of countenance to *him who would soften* the heart *by being* gracious to him; he is rude to his mother and to his people, every one [crieth]: ' Let thy name come forth! thou art silent with the mouth when spoken to.' "[1]

5. [Against over-confidence in view of the uncertainties of life.]

"Let not thy heart be proud for valor in the midst of thy troops. Beware of overbearingness [?]: one knoweth not what shall happen; what a god will do when he striketh."

[These proverbs were evidently set in a short story, calculated to point the moral that obedience to wise teaching leads to preferment. The introductory part has gone with the beginning of the document; but here at the end of the book there is a passage showing that they were composed by a wazîr, *i. e.*, by the chief administrative official of the kingdom. He read them to his children; one of whom, it seems, named Kagemni, afterwards succeeded to the wazirship. The following is the translation of this concluding text.]

THE wazîr caused his children to be summoned when he had finished the conduct of men;[2] they rejoiced greatly at coming; therefore when he said to them:—"Verily, all things that are in writing on this roll, obey them as I say [them];[3] do not pass beyond what is commanded," they [the children] cast

---

[1] *I. e.*, "Tell us thy name, thou who dost not answer when spoken to," or "Let thy name be henceforth 'Mum-when-spoken-to.'"

[2] *I. e.*, the proverbs; but possibly this expression may mean "on his death-bed."

[3] *I. e.*, obey them strictly.

themselves upon their bellies and read them even as they were written; they were good within them[1] more than anything that is in the whole land; their uprising and their downsitting was according thereto.

Then the majesty of King Huni moored his ship;[2] then was set up the majesty of King Sneferu as the good King in this whole land. Then Kagemni was appointed governor of the royal city, and wazîr.

This is its arrival.[3]

[Huni was the last king of the IIId Dynasty, Seneferu the founder of the IVth Dynasty, and Kagemni is a name found in some of the earliest inscribed tombs; but the language, at least of this last paragraph, betrays the style of the Middle Kingdom. The proverbs themselves may be much earlier.

After a blank the second text begins.]

THE INSTRUCTION OF PTAHHETEP

[This is another collection of proverbs, in sixteen pages, and with the rubrics marked. Small fragments from a duplicate copy of this book of proverbs show considerable variation from the Prisse text, and prove the corruptness and uncertainty of the latter. It is however quite complete. We are able to give a list of the contents of the sections, most of which are very brief, and to append to the headings translations of a considerable proportion of the whole. Further study will doubtless throw light on much that is still obscure.

General Title and Introduction: The wazîr Ptahhetep addresses the King, and recounts the evils of old age.[4] Having received the command to take his son into his office of wazîr, he desires to teach him the rules of conduct observed in the time when the gods reigned over Egypt. The King approves, and bids him commence his instruction.]

Instruction of the governor of the royal city, and wazîr Ptahetep, before the majesty of King Assa, who liveth forever and ever

THE governor of the royal city, and wazîr Ptahhetep, saith:—
"O King my lord, years come on, old age befalleth, decrepitude arriveth, weakness is renewed, he lieth helpless day by day; the two eyes are contracted, the ears are dull, strength diminisheth from weariness of heart; the mouth is silent and

---

[1] *I. e.*, they were pleasing to them.

[2] Arrived at his destination; *i. e.*, died.

[3] = Our "Finis."

[4] From the last paragraph of the book, we learn that he had reached the Egyptian limit of long life, viz.. 110 years: the figure is doubtless to be taken in a general sense.

speaketh not, the heart is closed and remembereth not yesterday;
.   .   .   good becometh evil, all taste departeth; old age is evil
for man in every way: the nose is stopped and breatheth not,
standing and sitting are [alike] weary [?].

"It hath been commanded the servant[1] to make a successor.[2]
Let me tell unto him the sayings of those who obeyed,[3] the
conduct of them of old, of them who obeyed the gods; would
that the like may be done to thee,[4] that ill may be banished
from among the Rekhyt, and the two lands serve thee."

Said the Majesty of this god: —

"Teach him according to the words of former days; let him
do what is admirable for the sons of the nobles, so that to enter
and listen unto his words will be the due training of every
heart; and that which he saith shall not be a thing producing
satiety."

[Title and aim of the proverbs.]

Beginning of the proverbs of good words spoken by the *ha-*
prince,[5] the father of the god who loves the god,[6] the King's
eldest son of his body, the governor of the city and wazîr, Ptah-
hetep, as teaching the ignorant to know according to the rule of
good words, expounding the profit to him who shall hearken unto
it, and the injury to him who shall transgress it.   He saith unto
his son: —

---

[1] *I. e.*, the speaker or writer.

[2] The word for successor seems to read, "staff of old age"; but this is
not quite certain.   Very likely the son would take over the active work of
the viziership, while his father gave him counsel: this was frequently done
in the sovereignty.

[3] Or those who are listened to.

[4] *I. e.*, that the ancient rules may be observed by the present generation
of the King's subjects.   The first kings of Egypt were supposed to have been
the gods.

[5] This high title occurs also in the Inscription of Una, and frequently in
the Piankhy Stela, where it has been translated "nomarch."

[6] "The god" is probably here the King.   The curious title "father of the
god" is well known; it would seem to represent a person who stood cere-
monially in the relation of father to a god or person.   Thus in later times
we have "fathers" of the god Amen, etc.   But at this period "the god"
seems to have meant the King, and the "father of the god" may have been
the guardian or tutor of the King.   Some may even see in it the expression
of an actual paternal relationship, as the principles of the succession to the
Egyptian throne are not understood.

1. [Be not proud of thy learning: there is always more to learn.]

"Let not thy heart be great because of thy knowledge; converse with the ignorant as with the learned: the boundary of skill is not attainable; there is no expert who is completely provided with what is profitable to him: good speech is hidden more than the emeralds[1] that are found by female slaves on the pebbles."

2. [Silence will be the best weapon against a more able debater than thyself.]

"If thou findest a debater[2] in his moment,[3] persuading the heart[4] as more successful than thyself: droop thy arms, bend thy back, *let not thy heart challenge him; then he will not reach unto thee.[5] Be sparing of evil words, as if declining to refute him in his moment. He will be called ignorant of things, while thy heart restraineth its wealth."[6]*

3. [Refute the bad arguments of an equal in debate.]

"If thou findest a debater in his moment, thine equal, who is within thy reach, to whom thou canst cause thyself to become superior: be not silent when he speaketh evil; a great thing is the approval of the hearers, that thy name should be good in the knowledge of the nobles."[7]

4. [A feeble debater can be left to refute himself.]

"If thou findest a debater in his moment, a poor man, that is to say, not thine equal, let not thine heart leap out at him when he is feeble. Let him alone, let him refute himself, question him not overmuch.[8] Do not wash the heart[9] of him who

---

[1] Rather, green feldspar, which was largely used as an ornament.

[2] Perhaps a professional orator, sophist, or the like.

[3] *I. e.*, when he is at his occupation; in the heat of argument.

[4] Perhaps "bold of heart."

[5] Or, "it shall not hurt thee."

[6] This is very uncertain. Its morality hardly accords with that of the rest of the book. Perhaps the youth is recommended to wait, even when he is called ignorant, until his heart has obtained full command of his knowledge and can successfully employ it in his argument.

[7] As we speak of "the education of a gentleman."

[8] Flatter (?).

[9] A frequent phrase, but the meaning of it is obscure.

agreeth with [?] thee: it is painful, despising the poor, . . .
thou strikest him with the punishment of nobles."[1]

5. [A leader of men should use his authority for justice.]
"If thou art a guide, commanding the conduct of a company,
seek for thyself every good aim, so that thy policy may be with-
out error; [?] a great thing is justice, enduring and surviving[2]; it
is not upset since the time of Osiris; he who departs from the
laws is punished and . . . *It is the modest* [?] *that obtain
wealth; never did the greedy* [?] *arrive at their aim; he saith, 'I
have captured for mine own self;' he saith not, 'I have captured
by* [another's] *command.' The end of justice is that it endureth
long; such as a man will say, 'It is from* [?] *my father.'*"

6. [Be not a disturber of the peace.]
"Make not terror amongst men;[3] God punisheth the like.
There is the man that saith, 'Let him live thereby who is with-
out the bread of his lips.' There is the man that saith,
'Strong is he who saith, I have captured for myself what I have
recognized.' There is the man who saith, 'Let him smite
another who attaineth, in order to give to him who is in want:'
never *did violence among men succeed: what God commandeth
cometh to pass. Then*[4] *thou mayest live in a palace; pleasure com-
eth, and people give things freely.*"

7. [Behavior to a patron.]
"If thou art a man of those who sit at the place of a greater
man than thyself, take what he giveth *with thy hand to thy
nose;*[5] thou shalt look at what is before thee; pierce him not
with many glances; it is abomination to the soul for them to be
directed at him. Speak not unto him until he calleth: one know-
eth not the evil at heart [that it causeth]; thou shalt speak when
he questioneth thee, and then what thou sayest will be good to

---

[1] *I. e.*, "in a gentlemanly manner"; but the last half of this section is
obscure.

[2] A remarkable word used here in regard to the contest between justice
and injustice; in the next phrase there is a reference to the myth of Osiris
and Set, in which good, in the persons of Osiris and Horus, survives evil in
the person of Set.

[3] This seems to refer to the profession of brigand and pillager.

[4] By God's favor.

[5] Perhaps a gesture expressing humble acquiescence.

the heart. The noble who hath excess of bread, his procedure
is as his soul[1] commandeth; he will give to him whom he prais-
eth: it is the manner of night-time.[2] It befalleth that it is the
soul that openeth his hands. The noble giveth; it is not that the
man winneth [the gift]. The eating of bread is under the man-
agement of God: it is the ignorant that rebelleth [?] against it."

8. [Behavior of a man sent on business from one lord to an-
other.]
"If thou art a man that entereth, sent by a noble to a noble,
be exact in the manner of him who sendeth thee; do the busi-
ness for him as he saith. Beware of making ill feeling by words
that would set noble against noble, in destroying justice; do not
exaggerate it; but the washing of the heart shall not be repeated
in the speech of any man, noble or commoner: that is abomina-
tion of the soul."

9. [Gain thy living at thy business; do not sponge on rela-
tions, nor hunt legacies.]
"If thou plowest, labor steadily in the field, that God may
make it great in thine hand; let not thy mouth be filled at thy
neighbor's table. *It is a great thing to make disturbance of the
silent.* Verily he who possesseth prudence is as the possessor of
goods: *he taketh like a crocodile from the officials.* [?] Beg not as
a poor man of him who is without children, and make no boast
of him. The father is important when the mother that beareth
is wanting, and another woman is added unto her:[3] *a man may
produce a god such that the tribe shall pray [to be allowed] to
follow him.*"

10. [If unsuccessful, take work under a good master; be re-
spectful to those who have risen in the world.]
"If thou failest, follow a successful man; let all thy conduct
be good before God. When thou knowest that a little man hath
advanced, let not thine heart be proud towards him by reason
of what thou knowest of him; a man who hath advanced, be
respectful to him in proportion to what hath arrived to him;
for behold, possessions do not come of themselves, it is their

---

[1] *Lit.*, *Ka* in Egyptian.
[2] As uncertain as groping in the dark.
[3] Be not sure of the childless man's estate. He can take a second wife and
disappoint you.

[the gods'] law for those whom they love: verily he who hath risen, he hath been prudent for himself, and it is God that maketh his success; and he would punish him for it if he were indolent."

11. [Take reasonable recreation.]

"Follow thy heart the time that thou hast; do not more than is commanded; diminish not the time of following the heart; that is abomination to the soul, that its moment[1] should be disregarded. Spend not [on labor] the time of each day beyond what [is necessary] for furnishing thy house. When possessions are obtained, follow the heart; for possessions are not made full use of if [the owner] is *weary*."

12. [Treatment of a son.]

"If thou art a successful man and thou makest a son by God's grace [?], if he is accurate, goeth again in thy way and attendeth to thy business on the proper occasion, do unto him every good thing: he is thy son to whom it belongeth, that thy *Ka* begat: estrange not thy heart from him; *inheritance* [?] *maketh quarrels.* [?] If he err and transgress thy way, and refuseth [?] everything said while his mouth babbleth vain words. . . ."

13. [Be patient in the law court.]

"If thou art in the council hall, standing and sitting until thy going [forward], that hath been commanded for thee on the earliest day: go not away if thou art kept back, while the face is attentive to him who entereth and reporteth, and the place of him who is summoned is broad.[2] The council hall is according to rule, and all its method according to measure. It is God that promoteth position; it is not done to those who are ready of elbows."

14. [Make friends with all men.]

15. [Report progress, whether good or evil, to your chief.]

16. [A leader with wide instructions should pursue a far-sighted policy.]

17. [A leader should listen to complaints.]

---

[1] The time appointed to it for its own activity, or as we should say, its "day."

[2] Room is made for him.

18. [Beware of women.]

"If thou wishest to prolong friendship in a house into which thou enterest as master, as brother, or as friend, [in fact in] any place that thou enterest, beware of approaching the women: no place in which that is done prospereth. The face is not watchful in attaining it. A thousand men are injured in order to be profited for a little moment, like a dream, by tasting which death is reached." . .

19. [Keep from injustice or covetousness.]

"If thou desirest thy procedure to be good, take thyself from all evil: beware of any covetous aim. That is as the painful disease of colic. He who entereth on it is not successful. It embroileth fathers and mothers with the mother's brothers, it separateth wife and husband. It is a thing that taketh to itself all evils, a bundle of all wickedness. A man liveth long whose rule is justice, who goeth according to its [the rule's] movements. He maketh a property thereby, while a covetous man hath no house."

20. [Be satisfied with a fair share.]

"Let not thine heart be extortionate about shares, in grasping at what is not thy portion. Let not thy heart be extortionate towards thy neighbors: greater is the prayer to a kindly person than force. Poor is he that carrieth off his neighbors [by violence] without the persuasion of words. A little for which there hath been extortion maketh remorse when the blood[1] is cool."

21. [Pay attention to thy wife when thou hast attained a competence.]

"If thou art successful and hast furnished thine house, and lovest the wife of thy bosom, fill her belly, clothe her back. The medicine for her body is oil. Make glad her heart during the time that thou hast. She is a field profitable to its owner." . . .

22. [Entertain visitors with thy means.]

23. [Do not repeat scandal[?].]

24. [Talk not of unfamiliar things in the council.]

25. [Advice to an able speaker.]

"If thou art strong, inspiring awe by knowledge or by pleasing, speak in first command; that is to say, not according to

[1] *Lit.*, belly.

[another's] lead.　The weak man [?] entereth into error.　Raise not thine heart, lest it be cast down.　Be not silent.　Beware of interruption and of answering words with heat [?].　.　.　.　The flames of a fiery heart sweep away the mild man, when a fighter treadeth on his path.　He who doth accounts all day long hath not a pleasant moment; he who enjoyeth himself all day long doth not provide his house.　The archer will hit his mark even as he that worketh the rudder, at one time letting it alone, at another pulling; he that obeyeth his heart [conscience?] shall *command*.»

26.　[Do not add to others' burdens.]

27.　[Teach a noble what will profit him.]

28.　[Deliver an official message straightforwardly.]

29.　[Call not to remembrance favors that you have bestowed, when the recipient has ceased to thank you.]

30.　[Advice to one that has risen in the world.]
"If thou gainest great after small things and makest wealth after poverty, so that thou art an example thereof in thy city, thou art known in thy nome and thou art become prominent: do not wrap up [?] thy heart in thy riches that have come to thee by the gift of God,　.　.　.　another like unto thee to whom the like hath fallen."

31.　[Obedience to chief.]
"Bend thy back to thy chief, thy superior of the king's house, on whose property thine house dependeth, and thy payments[1] in their proper place.　It is ill to be at variance with the chief.　One liveth [only] while he is gracious."　.　.　.

32.　[Against lewdness.]

33.　[Judge a friend's character at first hand.]
"If thou seekest the character of a friend, mind thou, do not ask; go to him, occupy thyself with him alone so as not to interfere with his business.　Argue with him after a season, test [?] his heart with an instance of speech."　.　.　.

34.　[Be cheerful to friends.]
"Let thy face be shining the time that thou hast: verily that which cometh out of the store doth not enter again; but bread is

---

[1] Salary in kind.

for apportionment, and he that is niggardly is an accuser, empty of his belly. It befalleth that a quarrelsome man is a spoiler of things; do it not unto him who cometh unto thee. The remembrance of a man is of his kindliness in the years after the staff [of power ?]." [1]

35. [Importance of credit.]

"Know [2] thy tradesman when thy affairs are unsuccessful; thy good reputation with thy friend is a channel well filled; it is more important than a man's wealth. The property of one belongeth to another. A profitable thing is the good reputation of a man's son to him. The nature is better than the memory."[?]

36. [Punish for an example, instruct for the principle.]

37. [Treat kindly a seduced woman.]

"If thou makest a woman ashamed, wanton of heart, whom her fellow townspeople know to be under two laws, [3] be kind to her a season; send her not away, let her have food to eat. The wantonness of her heart *appreciateth guidance.*"

38. [Advantage of obedience to rule.]

"If thou hearkenest to these things that I tell thee, and all thy behavior is according to what precedeth, [4] verily they have a true course. They are precious, their memory goeth in the mouth of men by reason of the excellence of their phrasing; and each saying is carried on; it is not destroyed out of this land ever; it maketh a rule to advantage by which the nobles may speak. It is a teaching for a man that he may speak to the future. He that heareth them becometh an expert. A good hearer speaketh to the future of what he hath heard. If good fortune befalleth by reason of him who is at the head of affairs, it is to him good forever, and all his satisfactoriness remaineth to eternity. It is he who knoweth that blesseth his soul [5] in

---

[1] The second text gives "Let thy face [be shining] when thou makest a feast. Verily that which cometh out of the store doth not enter [?], but bread is apportioned; he that is niggardly of face is remorseful; [?] his belly is empty. He that remembereth a man is kind unto him in the years after the staff [of power ?]." The last expression may mean "after the loss of authority."

[2] Variant "beseech." The meaning of the section is not certain.

[3] To be in an ambiguous position. (?)

[4] Or "then all thy ways shall have the lead."

[5] *Ba,* in Egyptian: the person who has learned good conduct (the ignorant cannot) pours benediction upon the soul of him who set the example of it, when he finds himself profited on earth by the practice thereof.

establishing his excellence upon earth: he who knoweth hath satisfaction of his knowledge. A noble[1] taketh his right course in what his heart and his tongue provide; his lips are correct when he speaketh, his eyes in seeing, his ears just in hearing; a profitable thing for his son is doing right, free from wrong.

"It is a profitable thing for the son of one who hath hearkened [to instruction] to hearken [to his father], entering and listening to a hearkener. A hearkener becometh a person hearkened to, good in hearkening and good in speech; a hearkener possesseth what is profitable: profitable to the hearkener is hearkening. Hearkening is better than anything: it befalleth indeed that love is good, but twice good is it when a son receiveth what his father saith: old age cometh to him therewith. He who loveth God hearkeneth, he who hateth God doth not hearken: it is the heart that maketh its possessor hearken or not hearken, and the Life, Prosperity, and Health[2] of a man is his heart. The hearkener heareth what is said. He that loveth to hear doeth according to what is said. Twice good is it for a son to hearken to his father. How happy is he to whom these things are told! A son, he shineth as possessing the quality of hearkening. The hearkener to whom they are told, he is excellent in body. He that is pious-and-well-pleasing[3] to his father, his memory is in the mouth of the living who are upon earth, whoever they shall be."

39. [The docile son.]

"If the son of a man receive what his father saith, no plan of his shall fail. [He whom] thou teachest as thy son, or the listener that is successful in the heart of the nobles, he guideth his mouth according to what he hath been told. *He that beholdeth is as he that obeyeth*, i. e., *a son*[4]; his ways are distinguished. He faileth that entereth without hearing. He that knoweth, on the next day is established; he who is ignorant is crushed."[5]

40. [The ignorant and unteachable man is a miserable failure.]

[1] The word presupposes education, as often.

[2] A frequent collocation of words; as for instance, following the mention of a royal person.

[3] *Amakh.* See note to Section 41.

[4] The words "a son" seem inserted.

[5] Or "is fit only for hard manual labor."

41. [The handing down of good precepts.]

"The son of a hearkener is as an Attendant of Horus[1]: there is good for him when he hath hearkened; he groweth old, he reacheth *Amakh*[2]; he telleth the like to his children, renewing the teaching of his father. Every man teacheth as he hath performed; he telleth the like to his sons, that they may tell again to their children.[3] Do what is admirable; cause not thyself to be mocked; [?] establish truth that thy children may live. If virtue entereth, vice departeth: then men who shall see such-like shall say, 'Behold, that man spoke to one who hearkened!' and they shall do the like; or 'Behold, that man was observant.' All shall say, 'They pacify the multitude; riches are not complete without them.'[4] Add not a word, nor take one away; put not one in the place of another. Guard thyself against opening the lacunæ [?] that are in thee. Guard thyself against being told, 'One who knoweth is listening; mark thou. Thou desirest to be established in the mouth of those who hear[5] when thou speakest. But thou hast entered on the business of an expert; thou speakest of matters that belong to us, and thy way is not in its proper place.' "

42. [Speak with consideration.]

"Let thy heart be overflowing, let thy mouth be restrained: consider how thou shalt behave among the nobles. Be exact in practice with thy master: act so that he may say, 'The son of that man shall speak to those that shall hearken. Praiseworthy also is he who formed him.'

"Apply thine heart while thou art speaking, that thou mayest speak things of distinction; then the nobles who shall hear will say, 'How good is that which proceedeth out of his mouth!'"

43. [Obedience to the master.]

"Do according to that thy master telleth thee. How excellent [to a man] is the teaching of his father, out of whom he hath

---

[1] *I. e.*, one of the loyal adherents of Horus the son of Osiris in his war against the evil Set.

[2] The blessed state of well-earned repose and rewards, both in this world and in the next, after faithful service.

[3] This is the reading furnished by the fragments in the British Museum for an unintelligible passage in the Prisse.

[4] "Them" is difficult to assign to any antecedent definitely; perhaps "without their advice how to behave and employ the wealth" is meant.

[5] Or "those who are listened to," "instructors."

come, out of his very body, and who spake unto him while he was yet altogether in his loins! Greater is what hath been done unto him than what hath been said unto him. Behold, a good son that God giveth doeth beyond what he is told for his master; he doeth right, doing heartily [?] in his goings even as thou hast come unto me, that thy body may be sound, that the King may be well pleased with all that is done, that thou mayest spend years of life. It is no small thing that I have done on earth; I have spent 110 years[1] of life while the King gave me praises as among the ancestors, by my doing uprightly to the King until the state of Amakh.[2] »

This is its arrival
like that which was found in the writing.

Translation of F. Ll. Griffith.

[The following extracts are reproduced from the German of Professor Erman's translation.]

FROM THE 'MAXIMS OF ANY'

« KEEP thyself from the strange woman who is not known in her city. Look not upon her when she cometh, and know her not. She is like unto a whirlpool in deep water, the whirling vortex of which is not known. The woman whose husband is afar writeth unto thee daily. When none is there to see her, she standeth up and spreadeth her snare; sin unto death is it to hearken thereto." Hence he who is wise will renounce her company and take to himself a wife in his youth. A man's own house is "the best thing," and also "she will give unto thee a son who shall be as the image of thyself." . . .

[Thy debt to thy mother.]

Thou shalt never forget thy mother and what she hath done for thee, "that she bore thee, and nurtured thee in all ways." Wert thou to forget her then might she blame thee, "lifting up her arms unto God, and he would hearken unto her complaint. For she carried thee long beneath her heart as a heavy burden, and after thy months were accomplished she bore thee. Three long years she carried thee upon her shoulder and gave thee her

---

[1] This was the ideal length of life in Egypt. The figure must not be taken too literally.

[2] See note to Section 41, previous page.

breast to thy mouth." She nurtured thee, nor knew offense from thine uncleanness. "And when thou didst enter the school and wast instructed in the writings, daily she stood by the master with bread and beer from her house."

[Be not drunken with beer.]
Drink not beer to excess! That which cometh forth from thy mouth thou canst no longer speak. Thou fallest down, thou breakest thy limbs, and none stretcheth out a hand to thee. Thy companions drink on; they arise and say, "Away with this one who hath drunken." When one cometh to seek thee, to seek counsel of thee, he findeth thee lying in the dust like a little child.

[Of inward piety.]
"Clamor is abhorrent to the sanctuary of God; let thy prayers for thyself come forth out of a loving heart, whose words remain secret, that he may grant thee thy needs, may hear thy prayer, and accept thine offering."

[Of diligence and discretion.]
Be diligent; "let thine eye be open that thou mayest not go forth as a beggar, for the man who is idle cometh not to honor." Be not officious and indiscreet, and "enter not [uninvited] into the house of another; if thou enter at his bidding thou art honored. Look not around thee, look not around thee in the house of another. What thine eye seeth, keep silence concerning it, and tell it not without to another, that it be not in thee a crime to be punished by death when it is heard." Speak not overmuch, "for men are deaf to him who maketh many words; but if thou art silent thou art pleasing, therefore speak not." Above all be cautious in speech, for "the ruin of a man is on his tongue. The body of a man is a storehouse, which is full of all manner of answers. Wherefore choose thou the good and speak good, while the evil remaineth shut up within thy body."

[Of manners.]
Behave with propriety at table and "be not greedy to fill thy body." And "eat not bread while another standeth by and thou placest not thy hand on the bread for him. The one is rich and the other is poor, and bread remaineth with him who is openhanded. He who was prosperous last year, even in this may be

a vagrant.[?]» Never forget to show respect, "and sit not down while another is standing who is older than thou, or who is higher than thou in his office."

Revised from the German of Adolf Erman.

INSTRUCTION OF DAUF

WHEN Dauf the sage of Sebennytus went up to the Royal Residence with his son Pepy to take him to the "Court Writing-School," he admonished him "to set his heart upon writing, to love it as his mother, for there is naught that surpasseth it." He thereupon composes a poem in praise of *the* profession, to the disparagement of all other callings:—

> "Behold, there is no profession that is not under rule;
> Only the man of learning himself ruleth."

And then,

> "Never have I seen the engraver an ambassador,
> Or the goldsmith with an embassy;
> But I have seen the smith at his work
> At the mouth of his furnace;
> His fingers were as crocodile [hide],
> He stank more than fish-roe.

> "A craftsman who plieth the chisel
> Is wearied more than he who tilleth the soil;
> Wood is his field, and bronze his implement;
> At night — is he released?
> He worketh more than his arms are able;
> At night he lighteth a light."

Etc., etc.

[The praise of learning was a favorite subject with pedagogue and parent. According to other sages] "the unlearned whose name no man knoweth, is like unto a heavy-laden ass, driven by the scribe," while "he who hath set learning in his heart" is exempt from labor "and becometh a wise noble." "The rank of a scribe is princely; his writing outfit and his papyrus roll bring comfort and wealth." "The scribe alone guideth the labor of all men; but if labor in writing is hateful to him, then the goddess of good fortune is not with him."

"O scribe, be not lazy, be not lazy, else thou shalt be soundly chastised; give not thy heart to vain desires, or thou wilt come to ruin. Book in hand, read with thy mouth, and take the advice of those who know more than thyself. Prepare for thyself the office of a noble, that thou mayest attain thereto when thou art become old. Happy is the scribe clever in all his offices. Be strong and diligent in daily work. Pass no day idly, or thou wilt be flogged, for the ears of a boy are on his back, and he heareth when he is flogged. Let thine heart hear what I say; it will bring thee to fortune. Be strong in asking advice; do not overlook it in writing; be not disgusted at it. Therefore let thine heart hear my words; thou shalt find fortune thereby."

Revised from the German of Adolf Erman.

CONTRASTED LOTS OF SCRIBE AND FELLÂH

[The following is a sample of the warnings to young men to stick to the business of the scribe and not be led away by the charms of out-door life, always so dear to the Egyptian.— Date XIXth Dynasty, or earlier.]

IT is told to me that thou hast cast aside learning, and givest thyself to dancing; thou turnest thy face to the work in the fields, and castest the divine words behind thee.

Behold, thou rememberest not the condition of the fellâh, when the harvest is taken over. The worms carry off half the corn, and the hippopotamus devours the rest; mice abound in the fields, and locusts arrive; the cattle devour, the sparrows steal. How miserable is the lot of the fellâh! What remains on the threshing-floor, robbers finish it up. The bronze . . . . are worn out, the horses [oxen?] die with threshing and plowing. Then the scribe moors at the bank who is to take over the harvest;[1] the attendants[2] bear staves, the negroes carry palm-sticks. They say, "Give corn!" But there is none. They beat [the fellâh] prostrate; they bind him and cast him into the canal, throwing him headlong. His wife is bound before him, his children are swung off; his neighbors let them go, and flee to look after their corn.

But the scribe is the leader of labor for all; he reckons to himself the produce in winter, and there is none that appoints him his tale of produce. Behold, now thou knowest!

Translation of F. Ll. Griffith.

[1] That is, for the government.
[2] *Lit.*, doorkeepers — *i. e.*, of the official cabin.

REPROACHES TO A DISSIPATED STUDENT

XIXth Dynasty

THEY tell me that thou forsakest books,
  And givest thyself up to pleasure.
Thou goest from street to street;
Every evening the smell of beer,
The smell of beer, frightens people away from thee,
It bringeth thy soul to ruin.

Thou art like a broken helm,
That obeyeth on neither side.
Thou art as a shrine without its god,
As a house without bread.

Thou art met climbing the walls,
And breaking through the paling:
People flee from thee,
Thou strikest them until they are wounded.

Oh that thou didst know that wine is an abomination,
And that thou wouldst forswear the *Shedeh* drink!
That thou wouldst not put cool drinks within thy heart,
That thou wouldst forget the *Tenreku*.

But now thou art taught to sing to the flute,
      To recite [?] to the pipe,
      To intone to the lyre,
      To sing to the harp,

[and generally to lead a life of dissipation.]

Revised from the German of Adolf Erman.

JOSEPH VON EICHENDORFF

(1788–1857)

HE poetry of the Romantic School is the poetry of longing. It is filled with a spirit of passionate yearning that gives to it its pathos, and makes each poem seem the expression of an undefined but ardent wish. The poet's soul is reaching out for that which no longer is, but which has been and may be again. Novalis has symbolized this yearning in the quest for the mysterious "blue flower." Men longed for the glories of the past, and among the knights and minstrels of mediæval court and castle they sought for that blue flower whose odor is love. In the bleak unfriendliness of the foggy Northern clime, the sunny expansive beauty of the South, where the magnificence of ancient ages still shimmered through a mellow haze, drew all sensitive hearts to Italy. Goethe felt the strong attraction, and fled without leave-taking across the Alps, to recover his genius under Italian skies. He gave to this deep and universal longing for Italy its classic incarnation in the pathetic figure of Mignon. In the very year in which Goethe returned from Rome, Joseph von Eichendorff was born. He was the last and most ardent of the Romanticists, and all the restless longing of those times found in him its typical interpreter.

Eichendorff was born on the family estate at Lubowitz in Silesia, on March 10th, 1788. He was brought up in the Roman Catholic faith, to which thereafter so many of his brother poets were converted. He studied law in Halle, Heidelberg, and Paris. At Heidelberg he took his degree, and at Heidelberg he came definitely under the Romantic influence through his association with Arnim, Brentano, and Görres. In Vienna, where he spent three years, he stood in close relations with Schlegel. His qualities of mind were essentially South German, for he was an Austrian by birth. He was on the point of entering the Austrian service when the famous appeal of February 3d, 1813, from the King of Prussia, roused every German patriot. Eichendorff enlisted as a volunteer in the Prussian army. Throughout that thrilling campaign of the wars for freedom he fought in the cause of the wider Fatherland. He became an officer in the "Lützow Corps," which Körner has made famous in his verse. Scarcely had he obtained his dismissal after the first peace of Paris, when the news of Napoleon's return from Elba summoned him to arms again. In 1816, however, he began his career, after a brilliant showing before the examiners, as an officer in the civil service of Prussia.

IX—335

Henceforth his life was outwardly uneventful. He married soon after his appointment. Intellectually he maintained relations with the finest spirits of his land and time. Having served the State in various capacities for more than a quarter of a century, he was dismissed at his own request in 1844, and retired to private life. He died at Neisse on November 26th, 1857. Heine had died early in the preceding year. With Eichendorff the last great poet of the Romantic School passed away.

It would be fruitless to catalogue the works of Eichendorff that are no longer read. His first independent effort was published at the end of the Napoleonic campaign, under the title of 'Ahnung und Gegenwart' (Presage and Presence). Stories, comedies, tragedies, and excellent translations from the Spanish followed, until now his works fill ten volumes; but of these, only his poems and his tale 'Out of the Life of a Good-for-Nothing' retain their full vitality to-day.

His poems possess enduring beauty. They are full of that profound longing for purer days and fairer realms, and of that dreamy lyric charm, that makes men young again. There is a breath in them of a vanished time; they sing of a golden age in which all men were idle and all women pure. The music of his verse has attracted many composers, from Mendelssohn, his friend, to Robert Franz in our own day. Eichendorff looked down upon the rhetorical ideality of Schiller and the symbolic naturalism of Goethe. He sang of the soul and its homesickness; of its longing for a lost inheritance.

The delightful 'Life of a Good-for-Nothing' appeared in 1824, and it remains to-day one of the most popular tales in German literature. It is the apotheosis of idleness and vagabondism. "In this little book," says Brandes, "all the old charms of romance are shut up, as in a cage, to make music for us. There is the odor of the woods and the song of birds, the longing for travel and the joys of wandering." The book describes the vagabond life of a child of genius, idle with a hundred aptitudes, pure with a hundred temptations, and amid a hundred dangers careless and irresponsible. This Good-for-Nothing illustrates in his roving life the romantic quest of the "blue flower." He lives for pure pleasures and the joys of unremunerative art; his is the infinite longing which never can be stilled, but only rendered endurable by poetry, by music, and by moonlight on forest, field, and stream. The book is an exquisite idyl; it is full of strange adventures and all the romantic machinery of singular disguises, lofty and secluded castles, and mysterious beauties who throw flowers from shaded balconies; and yet it is essentially idyllic, and the beautiful lyrics which are scattered through its pages create an atmosphere of eternal summer in which we are made to forget the work-a-day world where men earn their daily bread and feel the salutary pressure of duty.

Eichendorff himself was a faithful public servant, and in the 'Life of a Good-for-Nothing' we have the confession only of what the author perhaps thought he would have liked to be, rather than of what he was. He was reverent and pious, and one of the most evenly balanced minds in all that circle of madcap poets. He has told us of those early days of the Romantic School and of the deep thrills which agitated the entire German people when Schelling, Novalis, the Schlegels, and Tieck began their life work in literature. And this work was done in the days when the sword of Napoleon hung suspended over Germany; in days when even the poet who was to sing the praises of the *dolce far niente* of Good-for-Nothingness was ready to give three years of his life for the defense of his native land. So far had literature and life lost sight of each other, and the men of vigorous action and solid achievement still sang sweetly of the blue flower and of the pleasures of idleness, leaving behind them a body of literature which, however unreal, will not lose its power to soothe and charm.

FROM 'OUT OF THE LIFE OF A GOOD-FOR-NOTHING'

THE wheel of my father's mill rushed and roared again right merrily, the melting snow trickled steadily down from the roof, the sparrows twittered and bustled about. I sat on the door-sill and rubbed the sleep out of my eyes; I felt so comfortable in the warm sunshine. Just then my father came out of the house. He had worked since daybreak in the mill, and had his tasseled cap awry upon his head. To me he said:—"You Good-for-Nothing! There you are sunning yourself again and stretching and straining your bones tired, and leave me to do all the work alone. I cannot feed you here any longer. Spring is at the door; go out into the world and earn your own bread." "Now," said I, "if I am a Good-for-Nothing, well and good; I will go out into the world and seek my fortune." And really I was very well pleased, for it had shortly before occurred to me too to travel, when I heard the yellow-hammer, who always sung his note in autumn and winter so plaintively at our window, now calling again in the beautiful spring so proudly and merrily from the trees. I went accordingly into the house and got my violin, which I played quite cleverly, down from the wall; my father gave me besides a few groschens to take along, and so I sauntered out through the long village. It gave me in truth a secret pleasure when I saw all my old acquaintances and comrades, right and left, just as yesterday, and day before yesterday, and always, going out to work, to dig and to plow; while I thus wandered out into the free world. I called out to the poor people on all sides proudly and contentedly, Adieu! but nobody paid very much attention to it. In my soul it seemed to me like an eternal Sunday. And when I at last came out into the open fields, I took up my dear violin and played and sang as I walked along the highway. . . .

When I presently looked about, a fine traveling carriage came up quite near to me, that may have been for some time driving along behind me without my having noticed it, since my heart was so full of music; for it went along quite slowly, and two ladies put their heads out of the carriage and listened to me. The one was particularly beautiful and younger than the other, but really both of them pleased me. When I now ceased singing, the elder one had the driver stop and spoke to me kindly: "Ah, you happy fellow, you know how to sing very pretty songs." To which I, not at all backward, answered, "If it please your Excellency, I may have some that are prettier still." Thereupon she asked me again, "Where then are you wandering so early in the morning?" Then I was ashamed that I did not know, myself, and said boldly, "To Vienna." Thereupon both spoke together in a foreign language that I did not understand. The younger one shook her head several times, but the other laughed continuously and finally called out to me, "Spring up behind us: we are also going to Vienna." Who was happier than I! I made a bow, and at a jump was on behind the carriage, the coachman cracked his whip, and we flew along over the glistening road, so that the wind whistled about my hat.

Behind me disappeared village, gardens, and church towers; before appeared new villages, castles, and mountains. Below me grain fields, copse, and meadows flew in many colors past; above me were countless larks in the blue air. I was ashamed to cry aloud, but inwardly I exulted, and stamped and danced about on the footboard of the carriage, so that I had nearly lost my violin which I held under my arm. As the sun, however, rose continually higher, and heavy white noonday clouds came up round about the horizon, and everything in the air and on the broad plains became so empty and close and still over the gently waving grain fields,— then for the first time came into my mind my village, and my father, and our mill, and how it was so comfortable and cool there by the shady pond, and that now everything lay so far, far behind me. I felt so strangely, and as if I must turn back again. I put my violin in between my coat and waistcoat, sat down full of thought upon the foot-board, and fell asleep.

When I opened my eyes the carriage stood still under tall linden-trees, behind which a broad stairway led up between columns into a splendid castle. On one side, through the trees, I saw the towers of Vienna. The ladies, it appeared, had long since got out, and the horses were unharnessed. I was much frightened when I found myself all at once alone. As I sprang quickly up into the castle, I heard somebody above laughing out of the window.

In this castle it fared strangely with me. In the first place, as I was looking about in the wide cool hall, some one tapped me with a stick upon the shoulder. I turned quickly, and there stood a great gentleman in court dress, a broad scarf of gold and silk hanging down to his hips, with a silver-topped staff in his hand, and an extraordinarily long, hooked, princely nose, big and splendid as a puffed-up turkey, who asked me what I wanted there. I was quite taken aback, and for fear and astonishment could not bring forth a sound. Thereupon more servants came running up and down the stairs, who said nothing at all, but looked at me from head to foot. Straightway came a lady's maid (as I afterward learned she was) right up to me and said that I was a charming fellow, and her ladyship desired to ask me whether I would take service here as a gardener. I put my hand to my waistcoat. My couple of groschens, God knows, must have sprung out of my pocket in my dancing about in the carriage, and were gone. I had nothing but my violin-playing, for which, moreover, the gentleman with the staff, as he said to me curtly, would not give a farthing. In my anguish of heart I accordingly said yes to the lady's-maid, my eyes still directed from one side to the uncomfortable figure which continually, like the pendulum of a steeple clock, moved up and down the hall, and just then again came majestically and awfully up out of the background. Last of all the head gardener finally came, growled something to himself about rabble and country bumpkins, and led me to the garden, preaching to me on the way a long sermon — how I should be sober and industrious, should not rove about in the world, should not devote myself to unprofitable arts and useless stuff: in that case I might in time be of some account. There were still more very pretty, well-put, useful maxims, only since then I have forgotten almost all of them again. On the whole, I did not really at all rightly know how everything had come about. I only said yes continually to everything, for I was like a bird whose wings had been wet. Thus I was, God be praised, in possession of my daily bread.

In the garden, life went on finely. I had every day my warm food in plenty, and more money than I needed for wine, — only, alas! I had quite a good deal to do. The temples, too, the arbors, and the beautiful green walks, — all that would have pleased me very well, if I had only been able to walk placidly about and converse rationally, like the ladies and gentlemen who came there every day. As often as the head gardener was away and I was alone, I immediately pulled out my short tobacco pipe, sat down and thought out pretty polite speeches, such as I would use to entertain the young and beautiful lady who brought me along with her into the castle, if I were a cavalier and walked about with her. Or I lay down on my back on sultry afternoons, when everything was so still that one could hear the bees buzzing, and watched the clouds as they floated along to my own village, and the grasses and flowers as they moved hither and thither, and thought of the lady; and then it often happened too that the beautiful lady, with her guitar or a book, really went through the garden at a distance, as gently, as lofty and gracious, as an angel, so that I did not rightly know whether I dreamed or was awake. . . .

Close by the castle garden ran the highway, only separated from it by a high wall. A very neat little toll-keeper's house with a red tile roof was built there, and behind it was a little flower garden, inclosed with a gay-colored picket fence, which, through a break in the wall of the castle garden, bordered on its shadiest and most concealed part. The toll-keeper had just died, who had occupied it all. Early one morning while I still lay in the soundest sleep, the secretary from the castle came to me and called me in all haste to the head steward. I dressed myself quickly and sauntered along behind the airy secretary, who on the way, now here, now there, broke off a flower and stuck it on the lapel of his coat, now brandished his cane skillfully in the air, and talked to the wind all sorts of matters of which I understood nothing, since my eyes and ears were still full of sleep. When I entered the office, where it was not yet wholly light, the steward looked at me from behind a tremendous inkstand and piles of paper and books and a portly wig, like an owl from her nest, and began, "What's your name? Where do you come from? Can you write, read, and cipher?" When I had answered this affirmatively, he added, "Well, her ladyship designs to offer you, in consideration of your good behavior and your particular merits, the vacant toll-keeper's position." I went over quickly in my mind my previous behavior and manners, and I was obliged to confess that I found at the end, myself, that the steward was right. And so I was, then, really toll-keeper, before I was aware of it.

I moved now immediately into my new dwelling, and in a short time was settled. I found a number of things that the late toll-keeper had left behind, among others a splendid red dressing-gown with yellow dots, green slippers, a tasseled cap, and some pipes with long stems. All these things I had wished for when I was still at home, when I always saw our pastor going about so comfortably. The whole day (I had nothing further to do) I sat there on the bench before my house in dressing-gown and cap, smoking tobacco out of the longest pipe that I had found among those left by the late toll-keeper, and looked at the people on the highway as they went to and fro, and drove and rode about. I only wished all the time that people too out of my own village, who always said that nothing would come of me all the days of my life, might come by and see me. The dressing-gown was very becoming to me, and in point of fact all of it pleased me very well. So I sat there and thought of all sorts of things: how the beginning is always hard, how a higher mode of life is nevertheless very comfortable; and secretly came to the decision henceforth to give up all traveling about, to save money, too, like others, and in good time surely to amount to something in the world. In the mean time, however, with all my decisions, cares, and business, I by no manner of means forgot the beautiful lady.

The potatoes and other vegetables that I found in my little garden I threw away, and planted it entirely with the choicest flowers; at which the janitor from the castle, with the big princely nose, who since I lived here often came to me and had become my intimate friend, looked askance and apprehensively at me, and regarded me as one whom sudden fortune had made mad. But I did not allow this to disturb me, for not far from me in the manor garden I heard low voices, among which I thought to recognize that of my beautiful lady, although on account of the thick shrubbery I could see nobody. Then I bound every day a nosegay of the most beautiful flowers that I had, climbed every evening when it was dark over the wall, and placed it on a stone table which stood in the middle of an arbor, and every evening when I brought the new bouquet the old one was gone from the table. . . .

I continually felt as I always feel when spring is at hand,— so restless and glad without knowing why, as if a piece of great good fortune or something else extraordinary awaited me. The hateful accounts, in particular, would no longer get on at all; and when the sunshine through the chestnut-tree before the window fell green-golden upon the figures, and added them up so nimbly from "amount brought forward" to "balance," and then up and down again, very strange thoughts came to me, so that I often became quite confused and actually could not count up to three. For the eight appeared always to me like the stout, tightly laced lady with the broad hat that I knew, and the unlucky seven was wholly like a guide-post always pointing backward, or a gallows. The nine however played the greatest pranks, in that often, before I was aware of it, it stood itself as a six merrily on its head; while the two looked on so cunningly, like an interrogation point; as if it would ask:—"What shall be the outcome of all this in the end, you poor naught? Without her, this slender one-and-all, you will always be nothing!"

Sitting outside before the door, too, no longer pleased me. I took a footstool out with me, in order to make myself more comfortable, and stretched out my feet upon it, and I mended an old parasol of the toll-keeper's and held it against the sun above me, like a Chinese summer-house. But it did not at all avail. It seemed to me as I sat thus, and smoked and speculated, that my legs gradually became longer from very weariness, and my nose grew from idleness, as I looked down on it for hours at a time. And when many a time before daybreak an extra post came by, and I stepped half asleep out into the cool air, and a pretty little face, of which in the dim light only the sparkling eyes were to be seen, bent with curiosity out of the carriage and gave me pleasantly a good-morning, and in the village round about the cocks crew so freshly out over the gently waving grain fields, and between the morning clouds high in the heavens already soared a few too early awakened larks, and the postilion took his post-horn and drove on, and blew and blew — then I stood for a long time still and looked after the coach, and it seemed to me as if nothing else would do, except to go along with them, far, far out into the world.

The nosegays I always placed, in the mean time, as soon as the sun went down, on the stone table in the dim arbor. But that was just it. That was all over now, since that evening; no one troubled himself about them. As often as I, early in the morning, looked after them, the flowers still lay there just as they did the day before, and looked at me in real sorrow with their wilted hanging heads, and the dew-drops standing on them as if they wept. That grieved me very much. I bound no more nosegays. In my garden the weeds might now flourish as they would, and the flowers I let stand and grow until the wind blew away the leaves. My heart was just as waste and wild and disordered. . . .

In these critical times it came to pass that once when I was lying in the window at home and looking gloomily out into the empty air, the lady's-maid from the castle came tripping along the road. When she saw me, she turned quickly toward me and stood still at the window. "His Lordship returned yesterday from his journey," said she briskly. "Is it so?" I replied in astonishment, for for several weeks past I had not concerned myself about anything, and did not even know that his Lordship was away. "Then his daughter, the gracious young lady, has also had, I am sure, a very pleasant time." The lady's-maid looked at me oddly from top to toe, so that I really was forced to consider whether I had not said something stupid. "You don't know anything at all," she finally said, and turned up her little nose. "Now," she continued, "there is going to be a dance and masquerade this evening at the castle in his Lordship's honor. My mistress is also to go in mask, as a flower-girl — do you quite understand? — as a flower-girl. Now my mistress has noticed that you have particularly beautiful flowers in your garden." "That is strange," thought I to myself, "since there are now scarcely any more flowers to be seen on account of the weeds." But she continued: "As my mistress needs beautiful flowers for her costume, but quite fresh ones that have just come out of the flower-bed, you are to bring her some, and wait with them this evening, when it has grown dark, under the great pear-tree in the castle garden. She will come and get the flowers."

I was quite dumbfounded by this news, and in my rapture ran from the window out to the lady's-maid.

"Pah! the nasty dressing-gown!" she cried out when she saw me all at once out-of-doors in my costume. That vexed me. I did not wish to be behind her in gallantry, and made a few pretty motions to catch her and kiss her. But unfortunately the dressing-gown, which was much too long for me, got tangled up at the same time under my feet and I fell my whole length on the ground. When I pulled myself together again the lady's-maid was far away, and I heard her still laughing in the distance; so that she had to hold her sides.

Now, however, I had something to think about and to make me happy. *She* still thought of me and of my flowers! I went into my garden and quickly pulled all the weeds out of the flower-beds, and threw them high up over my head away into the glistening air, as if I drew out with the roots every bit of evil and melancholy. The roses were again like *her* mouth; the sky-blue morning-glories like her eyes; the snow-white lily with its sorrowfully drooping head looked quite like her. I laid them all carefully in a little basket together.

It was a still, beautiful evening, with not a cloud in the heavens. A few stars were already out in the sky; from afar came the sound of the Danube over the fields; in the tall trees in the castle garden near me joyfully sang innumerable birds. Ah, I was so happy!

When night finally came on, I took my little basket over my arm and set out on my way to the great garden. In my basket all lay so bright and pretty together — white, red, blue, and so fragrant that my heart fairly laughed when I looked in.

Full of happy thoughts, I went along in the beautiful moon-light through the quiet paths tidily strewed with sand, over the little white bridges, under which the swans sat sleeping upon the water, and past the pretty arbors and summer-houses. I had soon found the great pear-tree, for it was the same one under which I had lain on sultry afternoons when I was still a gardener.

Here it was so lonely and dark. Only a tall aspen continually whispered with its silver leaves. From the castle sounded now and then the dance music. At times I heard, too, in the garden human voices, which often came quite near to me, and then all at once it was again perfectly still.

My heart beat fast. A strange feeling of dread came over me, as if I intended to steal from somebody. I stood for a long time stock still, leaning against the tree and listened on all sides; but as nobody came, I could no longer endure it. I hung my basket on my arm and climbed quickly up into the pear-tree, in order to breathe again in the open air. . . .

I now directed my eyes immovably toward the castle, for a circle of torches below on the steps of the entrance threw a strange light there, over the sparkling windows and far out into the garden. It was the servants, who were just then serenading their young master and mistress. In the midst of them, splendidly dressed like a minister of state, stood the porter before a music stand, working hard on his bassoon.

Just as I had seated myself aright in order to listen to the beautiful serenade, all at once the doors opened, up on the balcony of the castle. A tall gentleman, handsome and stately in his uniform and with many glittering stars on his breast, stepped out upon the balcony, leading by the hand — the beautiful young lady in a dress all of white, like a lily in the night or as if the moon passed across the clear firmament.

I could not turn my glance from the place, and garden, trees, and fields vanished from my senses; as she, so wondrously illuminated by the torches, stood there tall and slender, and now talked pleasantly with the handsome officer and then nodded kindly down to the musicians. The people below were beside themselves with joy, and I too could not restrain myself at last, and joined in the cheers with all my might.

As she however soon afterward again disappeared from the balcony, and below one torch after the other went out and the music stands were taken away, and the garden now round about also became dark again and rustled as before, — for the first time I noticed all this, — then it fell all at once upon my heart that it was really only the aunt who had sent for me with the flowers, and that the beautiful lady did not think of me at all and was long since married, and that I myself was a great fool.

All of this plunged me truly into an abyss of reflection. I wrapped myself up like a hedgehog in the stings of my own thoughts; from the castle the dance music came more rarely across, the clouds wandered lonely along over the dark garden. And so I sat up in the tree, like a night owl, all night long in the ruins of my happiness.

The cool morning air waked me finally from my dreamings. I was fairly astonished when I looked all at once about me. Music and dance was long over, and in the castle and round about the castle, on the lawn, and the stone steps, and the columns, everything looked so still and cool and solemn; only the fountain before the entrance plashed solitarily along. Here and there in the twigs near me the birds were already awakening and shaking their bright feathers; and while they stretched their little wings they looked with curiosity and astonishment at their strange bedfellow. The joyous beaming rays of morning sparkled along over the garden upon my breast.

Then I straightened myself out up in my tree, and for the first time for a long while, once more looked fairly out into the land, and saw how a few ships were already sailing down the Danube between the vineyards, and how the still empty highways swung themselves like bridges across the glistening country, far out over the mountains and valleys.

I do not know how it came about, but all at once my old desire to travel seized hold of me again: all the old sadness and joy and great anticipation. It came into my mind, at the same time, how the beautiful lady up in the castle was sleeping among the flowers and under silken coverlets, and an angel was sitting beside her on the bed in the stillness of the morning.——"No," I cried out, "I must go away from here, and on and on, as far as the sky is blue!"

And at this I took my basket and threw it high into the air, so that it was very pretty to see how the flowers lay gayly round about in the twigs and on the greensward below. Then I climbed down quickly and went through the quiet garden to my dwelling. Often indeed I stopped still at many a place where I had once seen her, or where lying in the shade I had thought of her.

In and about my house everything still looked just as I had left it yesterday. The garden was plundered and bare; in my room inside, the great account-book still lay open; my violin, which I had almost wholly forgotten, hung covered with dust on the wall. A morning beam, however, from the window opposite fell gleaming across the strings. That struck a true accord within my heart. "Yes," I said, "do thou come here, thou faithful instrument! Our kingdom is not of this world!"

And so I took the violin from the wall, left the account-book, dressing-gown, slippers, pipes, and parasol lying, and wandered, as poor as I had come, out of my little house away on the glistening highway.

I still often looked back. A strange feeling had taken possession of me. I was so sad and yet again so thoroughly joyous, like a bird escaping from its cage. And when I had gone a long way I took up my violin, out there in the free air, and sang.

The castle, the garden, and the towers of Vienna had already disappeared behind me in the fragrance of morning; above me exulted innumerable larks high in the air. Thus I went between the green mountains and past cheerful cities and villages down toward Italy.

Translation of William H. Carpenter.

SEPARATION

Brown was the heather,
    The sky was blue;
We sat together
    Where flowers grew.

Is this the thrilling
    Nightingale's beat?
Are larks still trilling
    Their numbers sweet?

I spend the hours
    Exiled from thee;
Spring has brought flowers,
    But none for me.

Translated for 'A Library of the World's Best Literature,' by Charles Harvey Genung.

LORELEI

'TIS very late, 'tis growing cold;
  Alone thou ridest through the wold?
  The way is long, there's none to see,
  Ah, lovely maid, come follow me.

"I know men's false and guileful art,
And grief long since has rent my heart.
I hear the huntsman's bugle there:
Oh fly,— thou know'st me not,— beware!"

So richly is the steed arrayed,
So wondrous fair the youthful maid,
I know thee now — too late to fly!
Thou art the witch, the Lorelei.

Thou know'st me well,— my lonely shrine
Still frowns in silence on the Rhine;
'Tis very late, 'tis growing cold,—
Thou com'st no more from out the wold!

Translated for 'A Library of the World's Best Literature,' by Charles Harvey
Genung.

GEORGE ELIOT.

GEORGE ELIOT

(1819–1880)

BY CHARLES WALDSTEIN

O GEORGE ELIOT will always have to be assigned a prominent place in the history of the literature of the nineteenth century as a foremost novelist, poet, and social philosopher.

Mary Ann, or, as she subsequently spelt her Christian name, Marian, Evans was born at South Farm, a mile from Griff, in the parish of Calton in Warwickshire, on November 22d, 1819. Her father, the prototype of Adam Bede, was Robert Evans, of Welsh origin; who started life as a carpenter, but soon became a land agent in Warwickshire. This position implies great responsibilities, and demands thorough business capacities as well as firmness and trustworthiness of character, in his relations to his employers as well as his subordinates. He was intrusted with the management of the extensive estates of five great noblemen and land-owners in the county of Warwickshire. He was thus a man of considerable importance and power in the country, and would hold a social position ranking with the highest professional classes of the neighborhood.

This position of her father gave her the opportunity of gaining considerable insight into the lives and characters of English people of every class in the country, and from its neutral height between the great landlord and the farmer, down to the farm laborer, she could command the horizon line of all these lives, realize their habits, their aspirations and sufferings, and command its extent as well as its limitations. The country, the fields, the garden about Griff House, where her childhood was spent, as well as the village with its inhabitants,— with whom, through her mother as well as her father, she came in contact,— all stimulated her loving and sympathetic observation and formed that background of experience in the youthful mind, out of which subsequently rose, with strong spontaneity and truthful precision of design, the characters and scenes of her novels. They will ever remain the classical expositions of English provincial life in literature. The upright strength and pertinacity of her characters, as well as the insight into practical life and the life of men, were no doubt derived from her father, and from the intimate intercourse with him for so many years of the most important formative period of her life.

Her mother was a housewife of the old-fashioned type, whose health was always poor, and who died when Marian was about fifteen years of age. She is supposed to be portrayed in Mrs. Hackit in 'Amos Barton.' She seems to have been a woman with ready wit, a somewhat sharp tongue, an undemonstrative but tender-hearted nature. In many respects she seems also to have been the model for that masterpiece of character-drawing, Mrs. Poyser. Though Marian had two sisters, her brother Isaac Evans was her playmate. The youthful relation between brother and sister was very much like that of Tom Tulliver and Maggie in 'The Mill on the Floss,'—no doubt the most autobiographical of her novels, as regards at least the drawing of Maggie's character.

Marian was at first sent to a school at the neighboring Nuneaton; and at a very early age she taught at Sunday school,—which may have instilled a magisterial bias into her mind from the very outset. At the age of twelve she proceeded to a school at Coventry, kept by the Misses Franklin, which enjoyed considerable reputation in the neighborhood. She remained in this school for three years; beyond elementary school duties she devoted much time to English composition, French and German. Her life was then rather solitary, moved by strong inner religious convictions, upon which she dwelt with passionate fervor. Her religious views were at first simply those of the Church of England, then those of the Low Church, and then became "anti-supernatural." The second phase was no doubt strongly influenced by her aunt. Mrs. Elizabeth Evans, the "Derbyshire Methodist," the prototype of Dinah Morris in 'Adam Bede.' The earnest, almost lugubrious conception of life which she formed in these times, and which subsequent years and experiences only intensified, no doubt gave the keynote to her whole temperament and genius. It produced in her that supreme development of the idea of duty and compassion for human suffering which elevates the tone of her writing with a lofty conception of life, enables her to penetrate into the feelings and aspirations of all classes, and while it widened the range of her sympathy, never did so at the cost of genuineness or intensity of feeling. At the same time this serious keynote, though it was not opposed to humor,—the growth of which it even favored,— led to some limitations in the harmonious development of her artistic nature; notably in that it counteracted the sense for the playful and joyous side of life. The eternal conflict between Hellenism and Hebraism, between the vine-wreath and the crown of thorns, was not reconciled by her, but led to the suppression or defeat of Hellenism. The true, the joyous spirit of Hellenism, with its ideals of beauty and happiness in life, never really possessed her soul. In her own words she has put this eternal dualism:—

«For evermore
With grander resurrection than was feigned
Of Attila's fierce Huns, the soul of Greece
Conquers the bulk of Persia. The maimed form
Of calmly joyous beauty, marble-limbed,
Yet breathing with the thought that shaped its limbs,
Looks mild reproach from out its opened grave
At creeds of terror; and the vine-wreathed god
Fronts the pierced Image with the crown of thorns.»

Only in the tragic manifestation of the Greek mind, above all in an Æschylus, did she find true resonance to the passionate beats of her God-loving and world-renouncing heart. Yet more and more, as her mind grew and severed itself from the traditional beliefs of her childhood,— with which however she ever remained in deepest sympathy,— did this love of God and renunciation of the world mean the love of man and the tolerance of weakness, the pity with suffering and the active effort to help to rectify and to improve. The one element in Hellenism which she adopted and clung to, and which as a supporting wall she added to the whole structure of her more Hebraistic beliefs and ideals, was the worship of Sanity. This worship only intensified the tolerance of the unsound, the pity for the diseased and distorted and miserable. And though she never became a professed Positivist, it was no doubt the response which Comte's philosophy gave to these cravings that made his views ultimately most congenial to her.

The true and independent development of her mind began when after the death of her mother she took charge of Griff House for her father; but especially when in 1841 her father retired from his active duties, and settled at Foleshill near Coventry. It was here, while taking lessons in Latin and Greek from Mr. Sheepshanks, and also devoting herself to music, that she formed the friendship with Mr. and Mrs. Charles Bray of Coventry and their kinsman Mr. Charles C. Hennell, the Unitarian philosopher and writer. These people, deeply interested in philosophy and literature, and important contributors to the philosophico-religious literature of the day, responded fully to the mental needs of George Eliot. Out of this intellectual affinity grew a friendship which lasted through life. They also introduced her to the philosophical and critical literature of Germany, and it was through them that she began in 1843 her first literary task, the translation of David Strauss's 'Life of Jesus,' which had been begun by Miss Brabant, who became Mrs. Charles Hennell. The task of translating Strauss's great work, which occupied three years of her life, was followed by work of the same nature, which, though not as taxing as the life of Christ, must still have called upon thought and perseverance to a high degree: it was 'The Essence of Christianity,' by the German philosopher Ludwig Feuerbach. These works, which stand on the border line between philosophy and religion, led her by a natural development into the domain of pure philosophy; so that the next more extensive task which she undertook, but to our knowledge never completed, was a translation of Spinoza's 'Ethics.'

She was now fairly, at the age of twenty-seven, launched in her literary career; though as yet it was on the side of science and religion and not of art. The essays which belong to the following period, together with her editorial occupation, again formed a transition from the more scientific character of her writing to the domain of pure literature. And though these works belong to the field of criticism, it was criticism as applied to pure literature, fiction, and biography, and thus brought her inherently ponderous and theoretical mind, by natural stages, from analysis and speculation to the more imaginative sphere of synthesis and creation. This early theoretical and scientific direction of her occupation and thought may have produced that fault in her later writing with which she has often been reproached,—it may have made her style and diction clumsy and pedantic. On the other hand, it was a most excellent training for the future writer of even fiction. For it exercised the mind in gaining full mastery over thought; in recognizing and defining the nicest and most delicate shadings of meaning and of expression; in insisting upon their logical sequence, and thus impressing upon the author the rudiments of exposition and composition; in extending and enriching the domain of knowledge and fact; and finally, in producing and training the force of *intellectual* sympathy, which sharpens as well as intensifies insight into life and character, and gives to the mind that pliancy which directs the feeling heart to beat in sympathy with all forms of experiences, desires, and passions,—however far the lives and personalities may be removed from the author who constructs or describes them.

In 1849 the death of her father threw her into a state of deepest depression. It was then that her kind friends the Brays took her for a tour on the Continent, to Italy and Switzerland. She remained at Geneva in the family of the artist D'Albert for eight months, where she no doubt found congenial local associations; for the shores of the Lake of Geneva, haunted by the spirits of Calvin, Rousseau, Voltaire, Madame de Staël, Gibbon, Byron, and Shelley, seem bound up with world-stirring thought as no other place in Europe. Upon her return to England she made her home with the Brays at Rosehill for about a year, and then accepted the offer of Dr. John Chapman to become sub-editor of the Westminster Review and to make her home in his family. She here entered a circle of the most prominent literary men and women of the day, and among these she became an intimate friend of Herbert Spencer, John Oxenford, James and Harriet Martineau, George Henry Lewes, and others. Emerson she had met before at Rosehill. Besides her arduous sub-editorial work, she contributed several remarkable papers to the Review. Among these are: 'Carlyle's Life of Sterling' and 'Margaret Fuller' in 1852; 'Women in France: Madame de Tablé,' 1854; 'Evangelical Teaching: Dr. Cumming,' 1855; 'German Wit: Heinrich Heine,' 'Silly Novels by Lady Novelists,' 'The Natural History of German Life,' 1856; 'Worldliness and Otherworldliness: the Poetry of Young' in 1857.

It was in 1854 that occurred the great event in her life; she joined George Henry Lewes as his wife, though the latter's wife was still alive. Lewes was separated from his first wife, though circumstances made it impossible for him to get a divorce. From that moment George Eliot remained the most faithful and devoted wife to Lewes and mother to his children, until his death in 1878. She united her life with that of Lewes after due and full deliberation, and with a thorough weighing of consequences and duties. But that she felt the deepest regret in that her complete union was not in accordance with the established laws of the society in which she lived, is evident from all her letters and writings; and though it need not have led to her marriage with her late husband Mr. Cross, the opportunity afforded of showing her respect to the established rules of matrimonial life must certainly have made it easier for her to form a new alliance, after the death of her first husband.

With Lewes she went to Germany, living for some time at Berlin and Weimar, while he was writing his 'Life of Goethe' and she was working at her translation of Spinoza's 'Ethics' and was contributing some articles on German literature. Upon their return they settled in London, finally in the Priory, North Bank, in the northwest of the metropolis, which was for many years a *salon* of the London literary world. The Sunday afternoons of this remarkable couple united all the talent and genius, residents or foreign visitors. One might meet in one and the same afternoon Charles Darwin, Robert Browning, Tennyson, Richard Wagner, Joachim the violinist, Huxley, Clifford, Du Maurier, and Turgénieff. Lewes, the most brilliant and versatile conversationalist of his day, gave life and freedom to these meetings; but the intellectual and moral centre always remained George Eliot, with her soft, sweet voice, her clear intonation, her friendly and encouraging smile, lighting up as by a contrast the earnestness of her serious and large features, which resembled those of Savonarola, whose character she has drawn in such strong lines in 'Romola.' But the quality of searching sympathy and benignant humor, so

remarkable in her writings, gave the warmth of kindness and cordial-
ity to these formidably intellectual meetings. The present writer re-
members with grateful piety how, when he was a very young man
struggling to put a crude thought into presentable form before these
giants of thought and letters, she would divine his meaning even in
its embryonic uncouthness of expression, and would give it back to
him and to them in a perfect and faultless garb; so that in admiring
and worshiping the woman, he would be pleased with his own
thoughts and would think well of himself. It is this sympathetic and
unselfish helpfulness of great and noble minds, which gives confidence
and increases the self-esteem of all who come in contact with them.
No wonder that one often saw and heard of a great number of peo-
ple, young girls or young men, who by letter or in person sought
help and spiritual guidance from her, and went away strengthened by
her sympathy and advice.

Her first attempt at fiction was made when in her thirty-seventh
year, in September 1856. The account of this is best shown in her
own words here given among the extracts from her writings. Her
first story was a short one, called 'The Sad Fortunes of the Rev.
Amos Barton.' This was followed by 'Mr. Gilfil's Love Story' and
'Janet's Repentance,' and soon there was that remarkable volume
called 'Scenes of Clerical Life.' Lewes and she and the world all
realized that she was a true novelist, and from that moment she
directed all her energies to the production of those works which will
ever live, in spite of all changes of fashions and modes of story-
telling, classical specimens of English fiction. In rapid succession
now followed 'Adam Bede' in 1858; 'The Mill on the Floss' in 1860;
'Silas Marner' in 1861; 'Romola' in 1863; 'Felix Holt, the Radical,'
in 1866; the poem 'The Spanish Gypsy' in 1868; 'Jubal and Other
Poems' in 1870; 'Middlemarch' in 1872; 'Daniel Deronda' in 1876;
and her last work, 'The Impressions of Theophrastus Such,' which
was not published till after the death of Lewes, which occurred in
1878. She married Mr. Cross in May, 1880. She died on December
22d, 1880.

To lead to the fuller understanding of George Eliot's works, it was
necessary to sketch in broad outlines the growth of her life and per-
sonality. As a writer she was not only a novelist but also a poet,
and above all a social philosopher. Her ethical bias is so strong,
moreover, that one cannot understand her as a novelist or a poet
unless one has grasped her social philosophy and the all-pervading
and ever-present influence it has upon her mind and writing.

In her delineation of character and depiction of scenes, especially
those of rural and domestic life, truthful rendering is to her the
supreme duty; and one need but open the 'Scenes of Clerical Life,'

'Adam Bede,' 'The Mill on the Floss,' 'Silas Marner,' and 'Middlemarch,' on any page, to realize the fullness of truth with which she has painted. At the time of their appearance, not only were the persons and the environment identified with the originals she had in her mind, but as lasting types they tallied exactly with people and local life known to each English reader. This truthful rendering was also conceived by her as a primary duty of the novelist. We would refer the reader to what, in an essay, she says of the English peasant in fiction, and would recall her own words in the same essay:—

"A picture of human life, such as a great artist can give, surprises even the trivial and the selfish into that attention to what is apart from themselves, *which may be called the raw material of sentiment.* . . . Art is the nearest thing to life; it is a mode of amplifying experience and extending our contact with our fellow-men beyond the bounds of our personal lot. All the more sacred is the task of the artist when he undertakes to paint the life of the people. Falsification here is far more pernicious than in the more artificial aspects of life."

Another interesting passage is one containing an estimate of Dickens, in which she considers the Oliver Twists, Joes, and Nancys terrible and pathetic pictures of London life:—

"And if Dickens had been able to give us their psychological character, their conception of life, and their emotions, with the same truth as their idiom and manners, his books would be *the greatest contribution to art ever made to the awakening of social sympathies.*"

George Eliot might thus be classified as one of the greatest if not the greatest realist of the analytical or psychological order. But this would, to our mind, be a one-sided and incomplete estimate of the chief character in her writing and genius. Truthful rendering of life and character may have been one of the chief motives to composition, and a fundamental requisite to the art of her fiction; but it remained a means to a further end—the ultimate end—of her writing, as it no doubt was the fundamental stimulus to her imagination and design. And this end and motive make her an idealist and not a realist in fiction. The direction in which this idealism goes we have indicated in the lines we have italicized in the passages we quote from her, and is to be found in the ethical motive below and beyond all her thought and composition, the predominance of the social philosophy in her fiction and poetry, to which we have already referred.

We will dismiss the coarse and caricatured distinction between realism and idealism, in which the one is supposed to render truthfully *whatever is,* without any principle of selection or composition;

while the other starts with preconceived notions of the *ought to be*,
be it from the point of view of formal beauty or spiritual harmony,
and proves the facts that are.   Art, and the novel above all,— which
deals with life at once so clear and familiar to us, and so perplex-
ingly manifold and varied as constantly to elude choice and design,
— can neither forego truth nor unity of design.

But in the novelist's attitude towards human life there are two
distinct points of view from which a new classification of novelists
might be made: the position given to ethics, the moral laws in the
presentation of life.   The laws of human conduct are so essential to
the relation of man to man, that the fundamental question as to
what position ethics holds in our narrative cannot be ignored.   The
novelist must have decided whether he is going to consider its
claims in the primary structure of his novel, and in the creation and
development of characters, or not.   Is he going to prepare the
groundwork of artistic labor with a view to ethical design, or pure
artistic design?   It may be said that the best work requires both.
But still, in so far as the one is heeded more than the other, will
the writer be an idealist or a realist in this sense.

The idealist will focus his view of the characters, their experi-
ences and sufferings and surroundings, from a view of moral fitness
and design; the realist will find the design and composition, the har-
mony which all art needs, in the characters, in the scenes, in the
life itself, and the inner organic relation of the parts to the whole.
The one leads to the best idealism, the other to the best realism.
The one produces a George Eliot, the other a Guy de Maupassant.
This realist ignores the general fitness of things, the moral law, and
says:—"This character is interesting in itself, this situation is amus-
ing, curious, striking, or terrible,— they are worth depicting, without
any question as to their relation to social or moral ideals."   Guy de
Maupassant takes characters and situations and depicts them with
consummate art; he never troubles himself about general moral fit-
ness,— we never know what his moral and social ideals are, nor
whether he has any at all.   Jane Austen is interested in her charac-
ters, in the tone and range of ideas of the period and the society in
which she lives, the types of life, and she draws them with consum-
mate art; but though we are left in no doubt in her case as to the
good and the bad, and though the good generally prevails and the bad
is defeated, these are not subordinated to a clear conception of an
ideal social order, without which the characters and the story could
not have been conceived and developed — as is always the case with
George Eliot.   Gwendolen Harleth, Felix Holt, Maggie, Dorothea,
Lydgate, the life and surroundings of these figures, all bear a fixed
relation to the social ideals of the author; and it is in this relation

that she conceives and develops them. Nay, it is for the purpose of illustrating and fixing this that she creates them at all. Strange as it may sound, in so far Jane Austen might be called a realist and be classed with Guy de Maupassant; while George Sand, with whom she has so much similarity of spirit, is by contrast an idealist. It is a difference in the initial methods of dealing with life in fiction.

It is not enough for George Eliot to present an interesting character, to follow up its fate and growth, to force the reader into sympathy, to make him hope for success or fear failure; nor even to show the struggle with the surroundings, to depict interesting and complex situations and centres. Her writings always depend upon a primary postulate, and to this postulate all characters, scenes, and situations are ultimately subordinated. This postulate is: The ideal social order as a whole, the establishment of sane and sound social relations in humanity, the development and progress of human society towards such an ideal of general human life. All characters and situations, all scenes of life, whether clerical or provincial, whether of the present or of the past (and this may here be a grave fault), are developed and viewed by her in their relation to this general standard of ideal society; how far they fit into this general harmony, and failing this, how far they can in her stories be made to fit more fully; or they are left to a more tragic end which emphasizes the facts of their unfitness. Herein lies her distinctive character as a novelist, a point in which her delineation differs from most of the other great novelists — from a Balzac and a Flaubert, a George Sand, a Thackeray, and a Dickens, a Turgénieff and an *early* Tolstoy. I do not mean to say that these novelists had not a social ideal at the foundation of their constructive imagination; but it did not play that essential part in their conception and working out of characters and plots, it was not ever present in their minds while they were describing characters, feelings, incidents, and situations, as it appears to have been with George Eliot. Her philosophical and ethical bias thus manifests itself, in that there was an idea of general social fitness and happiness modifying and directing her representation of individual life and character.

To understand this social ideal of a rational and essentially sane world, we must conceive her as an expression of the spirit of the age out of which she grew. And she will thus hold a place not only as a novelist, but as a pregnant and significant exponent of the thought of the third quarter of the nineteenth century.

The time in which her mind was formed is marked on the side of social ethics, in that a broad and powerful humanitarian wave spread over English life and thought. Negatively it manifested itself in that it was a period of storm and stress toward the birth of tolerance —

tolerance with all forms of belief and even unbelief. In the English Church itself, it was the period of clear accentuations of shades of belief that differed to a very marked degree from one another. The Church of Rome was brought nearer to the Anglican believer, and was robbed of its Apocalyptic horrors by a Newman and a Manning; a definite political act was the Irish Church Act. But an especial feature of this tolerance was the social recognition of agnosticism, in its scientific aspect through a Darwin, and in its more ethical aspect through a Mill, a Herbert Spencer, and a Matthew Arnold; while divines of the English Church itself, like Stanley, Maurice, Kingsley, and Jowett, bridged over the gaps between dogmatism and agnosticism. The repeal of the Test Act (according to which the signing of the Thirty-nine Articles was a condition for obtaining a scholarship or fellow-ship) abolished all disqualifications from freethinkers at the great universities. Quakers and Jews had before been admitted to Parliament, and now took prominent and leading places.

But more positively, the philosophy of Auguste Comte with its English exponents, especially Mill, impressed the religious feeling of humanitarianism. There had been a wave of this before, a wave the commotion of which was felt even in our days. It was the humanitarianism of Rousseau, under which George Sand stood. But this differs in a marked manner from that of our friend. With Rousseau it was *deductive*, based upon the inalienable rights of man, of the individual,—a deductive sociology. In our times it was essentially guided by the prevailing spirit and methods of thought of Charles Darwin, Mill, Herbert Spencer, Huxley, Clifford, and Matthew Arnold, with the regenerated and refined sense of truth which they have given to the world. It has thus led to an *inductive* sociology and inductive humanitarianism, freed from all romantic character and admixture, essentially sober and sane, though none the less passionate and deep-seated. The last wave of Rousseauesque feeling filtered through German sources to us in Carlyle and Ruskin. But this mode of thought was foreign to George Eliot. She disliked all forms of exaggeration.

She has always clear in her mind the sane and sober ideals of a society based upon the truthful observation and recognition of its wants and needs. The claims of truth, the claims of charity and unselfishness, are supreme. To this ideal the individual must subordinate himself if he wishes to be happy and noble, beloved and honored; must have "that recognition of something to be lived for beyond the mere satisfaction of self, which is to the moral life what the addition of a central ganglion is to animal life."

Pure applied psychology and knowledge of the *cœur humain*, which have actuated so many great novelists,—the careful and studied development of an individual life and character as such within its surroundings,—were not enough to absorb the desires of George Eliot's efforts in fiction; still less mere striking incidents, and the engrossing consequences and sequences as they push on in the plot of a story; but the *cœur humain* and incidents in life are viewed in their relation to society as a whole, to social ideals. She is thus an idealistic and an ethical novelist.

Even in her poetry this bias manifests itself; and here, from an artistic point of view, the effect is often more disturbing than in her novels. For in poetry the purely artistic, emotional, and lyrical aspect is more important and essential; and any general and impersonal ideal counteracts the reality of the characters, the mood, and the passion. Thus in her longest and greatest poem, 'The Spanish Gypsy,' the feelings and expressions put into the mouth of Fedalma and Zarca are the nineteenth-century thoughts and feelings of a George Eliot, and lose their immediate truthfulness and convincing power from being thus expressed by fictitious persons; while the personalities themselves, their thoughts and feelings, do not strike one with a sense of reality, because they express views which sound anachronistic and have not their proper local coloring. In spite of some beautiful shorter poems, passages, and lines, she fails when criticized as a lyrical poetess; nor will her poems stand faultless when judged from the epic point of view. But if there be any justification (which we hold there is) for didactic poetry,—poetry which calls in artistic emotion to impress truths and moral laws,—then she will always hold a prominent place in this sphere. 'Stradivarius' and the 'Positivist Hymn' will, together with Matthew Arnold's 'Self-Dependence,' rank among the finest types of didactic poems of our age.

Though at times her ethical bias has obtruded itself out of place, and may have counteracted her certainty of touch in drawing lifelike character (as for instance in the construction of Daniel Deronda's personality), it has, on the whole, not prevented her from giving full play to her marvelous power of clear and deep insight into life and of sensuous description.

In studying life she had learned observation in the scientific inductive school, and had thus acquired, with minuteness of perception, the clear-sighted and unprejudiced intellectual justice of vision which enabled her to appreciate fully and to grasp the inner core of all the characters, motives, and passions which her command over her thoughts and language and her docile pen enabled her to fix in so masterly a manner. But these faculties would not have been enough to lead to her creation of human types, had she not possessed to that intense and exalted degree the power of feeling which gave the initial stimulus to her penetration of the human heart and its motives and passions, and which her intellectual control converted into all-encompassing and all-pervading sympathy. She was, after all, what Elizabeth Browning expressed in the pregnant phrase — "a large-brained woman and a large-hearted man."

Nay, this sympathy was so intense and leading a feature of her genius that it again serves to establish a distinct general classification of novelists. Like great actors, great writers of fiction may be classified, according to their mode of rendering the life they study, as subjective and objective interpreters. The former are intellectually so wide and emotionally so responsive, that their great souls and minds grasp and assimilate, absorb for the time being, all the different natures which they portray; they thrill with them — they become them. The objective artists possess more the painter's and sculptor's attitude of mind; they eliminate self completely during the period of observation, and enter, through the fullness and delicacy of their perceptions, into the lives and characters they depict. For the time they see only the object of their study, and reproduce it with clear and dispassionate touch. This is the case with Balzac, Turgénieff, Thackeray, and Dickens. The objective method is the safest and least likely to produce faults in drawing which make the characters at times inconsistent and fall out of their parts; but the subjective method may at times attain depth of insight, and fullness of passion and veracity, which lies hidden from the dispassionate draughtsmen and impersonators. The Brontés had this subjective penetration to the highest degree; but they had not, on the other hand, the inductive and scientific training of George Eliot, which sobered down and made more objective, as it made more humorous, the sympathetic impersonations in her stories. Above all, the purely emotional subjectivity of George Eliot was counteracted by the passion for the general ethical and the social ideal which we have already considered as playing so essential a part in her mind. Upon this we must take our stand in order to appreciate her leading method of composition, which can be traced, we venture to believe, through all her novels.

Starting with a well-defined ideal of social fitness for this world, the harmony in life towards which all action, effort, and individuality must tend, the problem which each novel sets itself to solve is the reconciliation of the conflict arising out of the unfitness of the leading characters (the "hero" or "heroine," as we may call them) as measured by this ideal — the want of harmony between their characters, aspirations, and ambitions, their views of life, and on the other hand the surroundings in which they live. The Greek tragedians, Shakespeare, and all great dramatists, have ever dealt with this central struggle between man and society. But they started with this fact, and had merely the artistic aim of evoking sympathy and pity in the audience because of this tragic struggle, the powerful and perfect representation of which became the final aim of their artistic endeavor. With George Eliot the process of adaptation, the resolution of the discord, and if not the establishment of harmony, then the clear and impressive indication of the best way to its establishment, is the real motive and end of her writing. There is in her no great tragic fatalism, which makes the art of the Greek dramatist so deeply and overwhelmingly tragic. Each one of her leading characters is at fault, when viewed in the light of the healthy social ideal. In the exposition of the character the fault will be shown up strongly; the hero will either be developed into greater social perfection, or the tragic end will impress upon the reader the disease and its remedy, the bane and its antidote.

The social failings and shortcomings which stand in the way of this harmony are grouped by her into two leading faults of a general nature: the discord between the individual and selfish and the general and altruistic; between thoughtless social materialism and conformity, and questioning originality and spiritual revolt; between conventionality and originality; between common-sense and prophetic far-sightedness; between the Philistine and the artistic, the humdrum worker and the world-reformer, the materialist and the dreamer. The one looks down before him on the ground and ignores the heights beyond and the clear sky above, and in his heavy-footed advance shoves the sky-gazer aside and walks over him when he has fallen; the other gazes at the heights and the stars, and spurns the clod and soil, tripping over them,—nay, slipping in the mud. They each ignore one another and the world in which each lives, or they despise each other and their respective goals and aims.

Now, in all her novels this problem is repeated and a solution is attempted. Over and over again she presents this situation as the central point in the composition of her novels, in different layers of society, in most varied characters. And the understanding of this is the key to the understanding of George Eliot's works. She either brings it out in presenting two central figures as the contrasts which represent either faulty extreme, or one figure as opposed to the surroundings, or both these means are used to impress the central fact.

We shall take one pregnant instance to illustrate this: 'Daniel Deronda' has been estimated and criticized chiefly as a novel in which the Jewish question has been discussed by her in a dramatic manner. That it deals powerfully with this question is no doubt true; but the Jewish question is but a side issue—no doubt appealing to her deep sympathies and sense of justice; but it is not the central motive to the story nor the artistic keystone of the novel as

constructed. The central figure in that story is Gwendolen Harleth
(who ought properly to have given her name to the novel). The
contrasting figure at the other extreme is Mordecai the Jew, and
Daniel is the intermediary figure (almost figure-head) between these
two extremes. The personality which, I am sure, set her sympa-
thetic intellect and imagination throbbing into artistic creation was
Gwendolen. As an ordinary though beautiful young lady of English
society (in her rank what Hetty Sorrel and Rosamond Vincy are
in theirs), she is the clod-born, materialistic, and hopelessly selfish
representative of the unsocial member of a society in which ideas
and ideals are unknown, and in which blind impulse, feebly directed
by prejudice and tradition, petty vanity and greed, at most per-
sonal ambition, are the motives to action, and produce the discord
and misery which surround even those who live in affluence. Her
beauty, her position in her family, her whole education, have kept
from her every higher ideal, all semblance of an ideal, and all
altruism and feeling for or with her fellow-men. Her world in the
opening of the story is the most contracted world of a small self,
with a pervading passion out of all proportion to its extent, in
which the desires whirl round and round this little circle in hideous
compression. Now the fundamental problem of the story is: How
can this little, selfish, and materialistic nature, which only realizes
the things before its desiring eyes and grasping touch, be made
large, unselfish, and idealistic, so that it reaches out beyond and
above the world of self into the regions of great ideas, in which the
individual is completely submerged; and that through this whole-
some straining of the heart and of sympathetic power, through this
realization and love of the ideal, it may learn to love and pity, and
think for and in, mankind and all men and women? And this pro-
cess of artistic development of character is sensuously and convin-
cingly represented in this novel. The reader enters sympathetically
into the little soul of that beautiful girl at the very beginning of the
story, and in her he passes through all the phases, until without any
forced hiatus he sees before him at the end the purified and en-
larged Gwendolen, who has learnt her ennobling lesson in the great
school of suffering. It is perhaps the greatest achievement in her art.

The more definite question is: How can such a girl realize the
great world of ideas? The answer is: It must come through the
heart, through the emotions and not the intellect,—the intellect will
be widened and matured after her personality has been thrilled. She
must fall in love with a man who is the impersonation of an idea,
whose whole existence centres round a great desire far removed
from the petty world of self in which she has lived,—nay, opposed
to it, in direct contrast to it.

This impersonation is presented in Daniel Deronda; and the fault in the book is that George Eliot's theoretical bias has been too strong for her, and in her eagerness to make him the bearer of an idea to the central figure of the story she has sacrificed the realistic drawing of Daniel, who is an impersonation at the cost of flesh and blood. Given the fact that Daniel must in his personality represent some unselfish idea, the question was: What actual idea, great in extent and enough to fill a man's mind and soul, should be chosen? The difficulty here arose, that if George Eliot had chosen some purely imaginary topic it would have lacked reality, and would have moved neither Gwendolen nor the reader into sympathy. If on the other hand she had taken some stirring question of the day, the question as such would have engrossed the interest and attention of the reader, and would no longer have been subordinated to the chief artistic purpose it has in the story. As it is, to many, the Jewish question as treated and suggested in the novel has itself engrossed the attention of readers, and has diverted their minds from the main artistic gist of the story. But to the ordinary English reader the subject of Jewish social life and aspirations was sufficiently remote. Nay, so narrow are the sympathies and the intellectual horizon of many cultivated Englishmen, that though they can be interested in the lives of gipsies and farm laborers, they cannot "screw up an interest in those Jews."

To Daniel however it was a real, stirring, and great idea to which he wished to devote his life. Now, in order that Gwendolen should realize in herself such a great impersonal idea, she had to fall in love with the man whose life they filled, and through her heart and her love for him it would reach her mind and raise her thoughts. Daniel, again, the man she loves, is contrasted with the narrow and selfish man, the hardened and crystallized type of another social world, consuming itself in its own self-love.

All Gwendolen's experiences directly or indirectly tend to bring about this development of her soul. A striking scene in this sense is her interview with Klesmer, the genuine and thorough musician devoted to his art and work. And when she comes out of the final soul's tragedy we feel that the woman has stood the test of fire, and has realized the greatness and overwhelming vastness of the spiritual world. G. H. Lewes, to whom the writer communicated this conception of 'Daniel Deronda,' assured him that he had grasped the central idea which George Eliot had in her mind, and the actual history in the story's construction.

Gwendolen's counterpart (and there are many in George Eliot's books) is Dorothea in 'Middlemarch.' She starts with great and extraordinary ideas, and must, through life and suffering, realize the moral justification of the simple and commonplace in life. The contrasting types illustrating this central point can be found in every work: Dorothea and Rosamond on the one side,—original, spiritual, striving as commonplace selfishness,—and Dorothea and Ladislaw as heavy, serious, intellectual morality, and light, playful, artistic freedom, on the other; Lydgate with his great reformatory ideas, slowly enfeebled and annihilated in his Samson-like vigor by the pretty, selfish, shallow-souled Rosamond of provincial worldliness. Gwendolen is also contrasted with Mirah. In 'Adam Bede,' again, Dinah and Hetty present the same contrasts as do Tito Melema and Romola, Esther and Felix Holt. Maggie Tulliver and her brother Tom, the spirit of revolt in Maggie and the hard conventionality of respectability in her brother Tom, are strongly marked types of this kind. Maggie's conflict with her narrow and commonplace surroundings and their conventional respectability are typified in the Mill. It is a wonderful touch of artistic suggestion that she and her brother are finally submerged in the Mill, carried away by the flood. This novel reflects more thoroughly the spirit of Greek tragedy than any other work of modern fiction. The Mill, and the part it plays in the life of the Tulliver family and in Maggie's sorrows, are like great Fate in the Greek tragedy. It is an embodiment of the hard and unrelenting tyranny of the powers that are. Even in 'Silas Marner,' the most artistic and least doctrinaire of her novels, the moral process of remedying Silas's social unfitness and misanthropy is the central idea. Space will not allow us to give further illustrations of this idea in her novels; but enough has been said to enable the reader to test it and follow it up for himself.

The two most striking qualities in George Eliot as a writer are her humor and her sympathy. They are really connected with one another. The power of intellectual observation, when coupled with the power of feeling sympathy, produces humor; the purely intellectual or objective cast of mind produces wit; while the purely subjective habit of mind is unable to produce either.

But with all her wide range of sympathy, upon which we have been dwelling, its limitations can still be discerned. The careful observer will recognize that the subjective attitude of the woman cannot wholly be hidden from view. The chief women into whom she projects herself are after all those that are nearest to herself, and she cannot help treating them as favorites and bestowing the greater attention upon them: Daniel only exists as a creation to develop Gwendolen; nay, Savonarola is really constructed for Romola's spiritual development, Casaubon for Dorothea, and so on. A still more marked and important limitation in her sympathies, arising out of her ethical bias, is her pronounced dislike to all morbid art, all that is fantastic. The poetry of Byron, the music of Chopin, all forms of morbid sentiment, are so repulsive to her nature that she cannot treat them with tolerance or even with humor. Remarks on Esther in 'Felix Holt' bear this out. Probably this is an autobiographical touch, and having freed herself from these morbid tendencies in her youth, she could never look back upon them with tolerance.

Her seriousness and ethical bias may at times also have impaired her style. Her extensive studies in science and philosophy often make her ponderous in thought and in expression. The fondness with which she takes her similes from science is often confusing to the reader who is unfamiliar with the facts and thoughts that are used as illustrations. She never quite overcame the temptation to insert what was new and striking to herself; so that her science and philosophy never reached that mature stage of mental assimilation in which they manifest themselves merely in the general fullness of thought, without ever asserting themselves as science or as philosophy. Still, no writer of fiction has ever introduced reflections and episodes *in propria persona* which are so striking and well worth reading in themselves. When her imitators attempt this they fail signally, and one need but compare such passages with those of George Eliot to realize her greatness as a writer and as a thinker.

To sum up the estimate of George Eliot as a novelist, we would say that she is the greatest representative of the analytical and psychological school, fixing with truth and sensuousness the types of English provincial life; with a final purpose, which she achieved, of illustrating by them the ideals of social ethics for the wider life of humanity.

Cha. Waldstein

THE FINAL RESCUE

From 'The Mill on the Floss'

A T THAT moment Maggie felt a startling sensation of sudden cold about her knees and feet; it was water flowing under her. She started up; the stream was flowing under the door that led into the passage. She was not bewildered for an instant; she knew it was the flood!

The tumult of emotion she had been enduring for the last twelve hours seemed to have left a great calm in her; without screaming, she hurried with the candle up-stairs to Bob Jakin's bedroom. The door was ajar; she went in and shook him by the shoulder.

"Bob, the flood is come! it is in the house! let us see if we can make the boats safe."

She lighted his candle, while the poor wife, snatching up her baby, burst into screams; and then she hurried down again to see if the waters were rising fast. There was a step down into the room at the door leading from the staircase; she saw that the water was already on a level with the step. While she was looking, something came with a tremendous crash against the window and sent the leaded panes and the old wooden frame-work inwards in shivers, the water pouring in after it.

"It is the boat!" cried Maggie. "Bob, come down to get the boats!"

And without a moment's shudder of fear she plunged through the water, which was rising fast to her knees, and by the glimmering light of the candle she had left on the stairs she mounted on to the window-sill and crept into the boat, which was left with the prow lodging and protruding through the window. Bob was not long after her, hurrying without shoes or stockings, but with the lantern in his hand.

"Why, they're both here,—both the boats," said Bob, as he got into the one where Maggie was. "It's wonderful this fastening isn't broke too, as well as the mooring."

In the excitement of getting into the other boat, unfastening it, and mastering an oar, Bob was not struck with the danger Maggie incurred. We are not apt to fear for the fearless when we are companions in their danger, and Bob's mind was absorbed in possible expedients for the safety of the helpless in-doors. The fact that Maggie had been up, had waked him, and had taken the lead in activity, gave Bob a vague impression of her as one who would help to protect, not need to be protected. She too had got possession of an oar and had pushed off, so as to release the boat from the overhanging window frame.

"The water's rising so fast," said Bob, "I doubt it'll be in at the chambers before long,— th' house is so low. I've more mind to get Prissy and the child and the mother into the boat, if I could, and trusten to the water,— for th' old house is none so safe. And if I let go the boat — but *you!*" he exclaimed, suddenly lifting the light of his lantern on Maggie, as she stood in the rain with the oar in her hand and her black hair streaming.

Maggie had no time to answer, for a new tidal current swept along the line of the houses, and drove both the boats out on to the wide water with a force that carried them far past the meeting current of the river.

In the first moments Maggie felt nothing, thought of nothing, but that she had suddenly passed away from that life which she had been dreading; it was the transition of death without its agony,—and she was alone in the darkness with God.

The whole thing had been so rapid, so dream-like, that the threads of ordinary association were broken; she sank down on the seat clutching the oar mechanically, and for a long while had no distinct conception of her position. The first thing that waked her to fuller consciousness was the cessation of the rain, and a perception that the darkness was divided by the faintest light, which parted the overhanging gloom from the immeasurable watery level below. She was driven out upon the flood,— that awful visitation of God which her father used to talk of, which had made the nightmare of her childish dreams. And with that thought there rushed in the vision of the old home, and Tom, and her mother,— they had all listened together.

"O God, where am I? Which is the way home?" she cried out, in the dim loneliness.

What was happening to them at the Mill? The flood had once nearly destroyed it. They might be in danger, in distress, — her mother and her brother, alone there, beyond reach of help! Her whole soul was strained now on that thought; and she saw the long-loved faces looking for help into the darkness, and finding none.

She was floating in smooth water now,— perhaps far on the over-flooded fields. There was no sense of present danger to check the outgoing of her mind to the old home; and she strained her eyes against the curtain of gloom that she might seize the first sight of her whereabouts,— that she might catch some faint suggestion of the spot towards which all her anxieties tended.

Oh, how welcome the widening of that dismal watery level, the gradual uplifting of the cloudy firmament, the slowly defining blackness of objects above the glassy dark! Yes, she must be out on the fields; those were the tops of hedgerow trees. Which way did the river lie? Looking behind her, she saw the lines of black trees; looking before her, there were none; then the river lay before her. She seized an oar and began to paddle the boat forward with the energy of wakening hope; the dawning seemed to advance more swiftly, now she was in action; and she could soon see the poor dumb beasts crowding piteously on a mound where they had taken refuge. Onward she paddled and rowed by turns in the growing twilight; her wet clothes clung round her, and her streaming hair was dashed about by the wind, but she was hardly conscious of any bodily sensations,— except a sensation of strength, inspired by mighty emotion. Along with the sense of danger and possible rescue for those long-remembered beings at the old home, there was an undefined sense of reconcilement with her brother: what quarrel, what harshness, what unbelief in each other can subsist in the presence of a great calamity, when all the artificial vesture of our life is gone, and we are all one with each other in primitive mortal needs? Vaguely Maggie felt this, in the strong resurgent love towards her brother that swept away all the later impressions of hard, cruel offense and misunderstanding, and left only the deep, underlying, unshakable memories of early union.

But now there was a large dark mass in the distance, and near to her Maggie could discern the current of the river. The dark mass must be — yes, it was — St. Ogg's. Ah, now she knew which way to look for the first glimpse of the well-known trees — the gray willows, the now yellowing chestnuts — and above them the old roof! But there was no color, no shape yet; all was faint and dim. More and more strongly the energies seemed to come and put themselves forth, as if her life were a stored-up force that was being spent in this hour, unneeded for any future.

She must get her boat into the current of the Floss, else she would never be able to pass the Ripple and approach the house: this was the thought that occurred to her, as she imagined with more and more vividness the state of things round the old home. But then she might be carried very far down, and be unable to guide her boat out of the current again. For the first time distinct ideas of danger began to press upon her; but there was no choice of courses, no room for hesitation, and she floated into the current. Swiftly she went now, without effort; more and more clearly in the lessening distance and the growing light she began to discern the objects that she knew must be the well-known trees and roofs; nay, she was not far off a rushing muddy current that must be the strangely altered Ripple.

Great God! there were floating masses in it, that might dash against her boat as she passed, and cause her to perish too soon. What were those masses?

For the first time Maggie's heart began to beat in an agony of dread. She sat helpless, dimly conscious that she was being floated along, more intensely conscious of the anticipated clash. But the horror was transient; it passed away before the oncoming warehouses of St. Ogg's. She had passed the mouth of the Ripple, then; *now*, she must use all her skill and power to manage the boat and get it if possible out of the current. She could see now that the bridge was broken down; she could see the masts of a stranded vessel far out over the watery field. But no boats were to be seen moving on the river,—such as had been laid hands on were employed in the flooded streets.

With new resolution Maggie seized her oar, and stood up again to paddle; but the now ebbing tide added to the swiftness of the river, and she was carried along beyond the bridge. She could hear shouts from the windows overlooking the river, as if the people there were calling to her. It was not till she had passed on nearly to Tofton that she could get the boat clear of the current. Then with one yearning look towards her uncle Deane's house that lay farther down the river, she took to both her oars and rowed with all her might across the watery fields, back towards the Mill. Color was beginning to awake now, and as she approached the Dorlcote fields, she could discern the tints of the trees, could see the old Scotch firs far to the right; and the home chestnuts,—oh, how deep they lay in the water,—deeper than the trees on this side the hill! And the roof of the Mill— where was it? Those heavy fragments hurrying down the Ripple,—what had they meant? But it was not the house,—the house stood firm; drowned up to the first story, but still firm;— or was it broken in at the end towards the Mill?

With panting joy that she was there at last,—joy that overcame all distress,—Maggie neared the front of the house. At first she heard no sound; she saw no object moving. Her boat was on a level with the up-stairs window. She called out in a loud piercing voice:—

"Tom, where are you? Mother, where are you? Here is Maggie!"

Soon, from the window of the attic in the central gable, she heard Tom's voice: —

"Who is it? Have you brought a boat?"

"It is I, Tom, — Maggie. Where is mother?"

"She is not here; she went to Garum the day before yesterday. I'll come down to the lower window."

"Alone, Maggie?" said Tom, in a voice of deep astonishment, as he opened the middle window, on a level with the boat.

"Yes, Tom; God has taken care of me, to bring me to you. Get in quickly. Is there no one else?"

"No," said Tom, stepping into the boat, "I fear the man is drowned; he was carried down the Ripple, I think, when part of the Mill fell with the crash of trees and stones against it; I've shouted again and again, and there has been no answer. Give me the oars, Maggie."

It was not till Tom had pushed off and they were on the wide water, — he face to face with Maggie, — that the full meaning of what had happened rushed upon his mind. It came with so overpowering a force, — it was such a new revelation to his spirit of the depths in life that had lain beyond his vision, which he had fancied so keen and clear, — that he was unable to ask a question. They sat mutely gazing at each other, — Maggie with eyes of intense life looking out from a weary, beaten face; Tom pale, with a certain awe and humiliation. Thought was busy though the lips were silent; and though he could ask no question, he guessed a story of almost miraculous, Divinely protected effort. But at last a mist gathered over the blue-gray eyes, and the lips found a word they could utter, — the old childish "Magsie!"

Maggie could make no answer but a long, deep sob of that mysterious, wondrous happiness that is one with pain.

As soon as she could speak, she said: — "We will go to Lucy, Tom; we'll go and see if she is safe, and then we can help the rest."

Tom rowed with untired vigor, and with a different speed from poor Maggie's. The boat was soon in the current of the river again, and soon they would be at Tofton.

"Park House stands high up out of the flood," said Maggie. "Perhaps they have got Lucy there."

Nothing else was said; a new danger was being carried towards them by the river. Some wooden machinery had just given way on one of the wharves, and huge fragments were being floated along. The sun was rising now, and the wide area of watery desolation was spread out in dreadful clearness around them; in dreadful clearness floated onward the hurrying, threatening masses. A large company in a boat that was working its way along under the Tofton houses observed their danger, and shouted, "Get out of the current!"

But that could not be done at once; and Tom, looking before him, saw death rushing on them. Huge fragments, clinging together in fatal fellowship, made one wide mass across the stream.

"It is coming, Maggie!" Tom said, in a deep, hoarse voice, loosing the oars and clasping her.

The next instant the boat was no longer seen upon the water, and the huge mass was hurrying on in hideous triumph.

But soon the keel of the boat reappeared, a black speck on the golden water.

The boat reappeared, but brother and sister had gone down in an embrace never to be parted; living through again in one supreme moment the days when they had clasped their little hands in love, and roamed the daisied fields together.

NATURE repairs her ravages,—repairs them with her sunshine, and with human labor. The desolation wrought by that flood had left little visible trace on the face of the earth, five years after. The fifth autumn was rich in golden cornstacks, rising in thick clusters among the distant hedgerows; the wharves and warehouses on the Floss were busy again, with echoes of eager voices, with hopeful lading and unlading.

And every man and woman mentioned in this history was still living, except those whose end we know.

Nature repairs her ravages, but not all. The uptorn trees are not rooted again; the parted hills are left scarred; if there is a new growth, the trees are not the same as the old, and the hills underneath their green vesture bear the marks of the past rending. To the eyes that have dwelt on the past, there is no thorough repair.

Dorlcote Mill was rebuilt. And Dorlcote church-yard — where the brick grave that held a father whom we know, was found with the stone laid prostrate upon it after the flood — had recovered all its grassy order and decent quiet.

Near that brick grave there was a tomb erected, very soon after the flood, for two bodies that were found in close embrace; and it was visited at different moments by two men who both felt that their keenest joy and keenest sorrow were forever buried there.

One of them visited the tomb again with a sweet face beside him; but that was years after.

The other was always solitary. His great companionship was among the trees of the Red Deeps, where the buried joy seemed still to hover, like a revisiting spirit.

The tomb bore the names of Tom and Maggie Tulliver, and below the names it was written: —

"In their death they were not divided."

THE VILLAGE WORTHIES

From 'Silas Marner'

THE conversation, which was at a high pitch of animation when Silas approached the door of the Rainbow, had as usual been slow and intermittent when the company first assembled. The pipes began to be puffed in a silence which had an air of severity; the more important customers, who drank spirits and sat nearest the fire, staring at each other as if a bet were depending on the first man who winked; while the beer-drinkers, chiefly men in fustian jackets and smock-frocks, kept their eyelids down and rubbed their hands across their mouths, as if their draughts of beer were a funeral duty attended with embarrassing sadness. At last Mr. Snell, the landlord, a man of a neutral disposition, accustomed to stand aloof from human differences as those of beings who were all alike in need of liquor, broke silence by saying in a doubtful tone to his cousin the butcher: —

"Some folks 'ud say that was a fine beast you druv in yesterday, Bob?"

The butcher, a jolly, smiling, red-haired man, was not disposed to answer rashly. He gave a few puffs before he spat, and replied, "And they wouldn't be fur wrong, John."

After this feeble delusive thaw, the silence set in as severely as before.

"Was it a red Durham?" said the farrier, taking up the thread of discourse after the lapse of a few minutes.

The farrier looked at the landlord, and the landlord looked at the butcher, as the person who must take the responsibility of answering.

"Red it was," said the butcher, in his good-humored husky treble,—"and a Durham it was."

"Then you needn't tell *me* who you bought it of," said the farrier, looking round with some triumph: "I know who it is has got the red Durhams o' this country-side. And she'd a white star on her brow, I'll bet a penny?" The farrier leaned forward with his hands on his knees as he put this question, and his eyes twinkled knowingly.

"Well, yes—she might," said the butcher, slowly, considering that he was giving a decided affirmative. "I don't say contrairy."

"I knew that very well," said the farrier, throwing himself backward again, and speaking defiantly; "if *I* don't know Mr. Lammeter's cows, I should like to know who does—that's all. And as for the cow you've bought, bargain or no bargain, I've been at the drenching of her—contradick me who will."

The farrier looked fierce, and the mild butcher's conversational spirit was roused a little.

"I'm not for contradicking no man," he said; "I'm for peace and quietness. Some are for cutting long ribs—I'm for cutting 'em short myself; but *I* don't quarrel with 'em. All I say is, it's a lovely carkiss—and anybody as was reasonable, it 'ud bring tears into their eyes to look at it."

"Well, it's the cow as I drenched, whatever it is," pursued the farrier, angrily; "and it was Mr. Lammeter's cow, else you told a lie when you said it was a red Durham."

"I tell no lies," said the butcher, with the same mild huskiness as before; "and I contradick none—not if a man was to swear himself black; he's no meat o' mine, nor none o' my bargains. All I say is, it's a lovely carkiss. And what I say I'll stick to; but I'll quarrel wi' no man."

"No," said the farrier with bitter sarcasm, looking at the company generally; "and p'raps you aren't pig-headed; and p'raps you didn't say the cow was a red Durham; and p'raps you didn't say she'd got a star on her brow—stick to that, now you're at it."

"Come, come," said the landlord, "let the cow alone. The truth lies atween you; you're both right and both wrong, as I allays say. And as for the cow's being Mr. Lammeter's, I say nothing to that; but this I say, as the Rainbow's the Rainbow. And for the matter o' that, if the talk is to be o' the Lammeters, *you* know the most upo' that head, eh, Mr. Macey? You remember when first Mr. Lammeter's father come into these parts, and took the Warrens?"

Mr. Macey, tailor and parish clerk, the latter of which functions rheumatism had of late obliged him to share with a small-featured young man who sat opposite him, held his white head on one side, and twirled his thumbs with an air of complacency, slightly seasoned with criticism. He smiled pityingly in answer to the landlord's appeal, and said:—

"Ay, ay; I know, I know; but I let other folks talk. I've laid by now, and gev up to the young uns. Ask them as have been to school at Tarley; they've learned pernouncing; that's come up since my day."

"If you're pointing at me, Mr. Macey," said the deputy clerk, with an air of anxious propriety, "I'm nowise a man to speak out of my place. As the psalm says:—

"'I know what's right; nor only so,
　　But also practice what I know.'"

"Well, then, I wish you'd keep hold o' the tune when it's set for you; if you're for practicing I wish you'd prac*tice* that," said a large jocose-looking man, an excellent wheelwright in his week-day capacity, but on Sundays leader of the choir. He winked, as he spoke, at two of the company who were known officially as "the bassoon" and "the key bugle," in the confidence that he was expressing the sense of the musical profession in Raveloe.

Mr. Tookey the deputy clerk, who shared the unpopularity common to deputies, turned very red, but replied with careful moderation:—"Mr. Winthrop, if you'll bring me any proof as I'm in the wrong, I'm not the man to say I won't alter. But there's people set up their own ears for a standard, and expect the whole choir to follow 'em. There may be two opinions, I hope."

"Ay, ay," said Mr. Macey, who felt very well satisfied with this attack on youthful presumption; "you're right there, Tookey: there's allays two 'pinions; there's the 'pinion a man has of himsen, and there's the 'pinion other folks have on him. There'd be two 'pinions about a cracked bell, if the bell could hear itself."

"Well, Mr. Macey," said poor Tookey, serious amidst the general laughter, "I undertook to partially fill up the office of parish clerk by Mr. Crackenthorp's desire, whenever your infirmities should make you unfitting; and it's one of the rights thereof to sing in the choir — else why have you done the same yourself?"

"Ah! but the old gentleman and you are two folks," said Ben Winthrop. "The old gentleman's got a gift. Why, the Squire used to invite him to take a glass, only to hear him sing the 'Red Rovier'; didn't he, Mr. Macey? It's a nat'ral gift. There's my little lad Aaron, he's got a gift — he can sing a tune off straight, like a throstle. But as for you, Master Tookey, you'd better stick to your 'Amens': your voice is well enough when you keep it up in your nose. It's your inside as isn't right made for music: it's no better nor a hollow stalk."

This kind of unflinching frankness was the most piquant form of joke to the company at the Rainbow, and Ben Winthrop's insult was felt by everybody to have capped Mr. Macey's epigram.

"I see what it is plain enough," said Mr. Tookey, unable to keep cool any longer. "There's a consperacy to turn me out o' the choir, as I shouldn't share the Christmas money — that's where it is. But I shall speak to Mr. Crackenthorp; I'll not be put upon by no man."

"Nay, nay, Tookey," said Ben Winthrop. "We'll pay you your share to keep out of it — that's what we'll do. There's things folks 'ud pay to be rid on, besides varmin."

"Come, come," said the landlord, who felt that paying people for their absence was a principle dangerous to society; "a joke's a joke. We're all good friends here, I hope. We must give and take. You're both right and you're both wrong, as I say. I agree wi' Mr. Macey here, as there's two opinions; and if mine was asked, I should say they're both right. Tookey's right and Winthrop's right, and they've only got to split the difference and make themselves even."

The farrier was puffing his pipe rather fiercely, in some contempt at this trivial discussion. He had no ear for music himself, and never went to church, as being of the medical profession, and likely to be in requisition for delicate cows. But the butcher, having music in his soul, had listened with a divided desire, for Tookey's defeat and for the preservation of the peace.

" To be sure," he said, following up the landlord's conciliatory view, "we're fond of our old clerk; it's nat'ral, and him used to be such a singer, and got a brother as is known for the first fiddler in this country-side. Eh, it's a pity but what Solomon lived in our village, and could give us a tune when he liked, eh, Mr. Macey? I'd keep him in liver and lights for nothing — that I would."

"Ay, ay," said Mr. Macey, in the height of complacency; "our family's been known for musicianers as far back as any-body can tell. But them things are dying out, as I tell Solomon every time he comes round; there's no voices like what there used to be, and there's nobody remembers what we remember, if it ain't the old crows."

"Ay, you remember when first Mr. Lammeter's father came into these parts, don't you, Mr. Macey?" said the landlord.

"I should think I did," said the old man, who had now gone through that complimentary process necessary to bring him up to the point of narration; "and a fine old gentleman he was — as fine and finer nor the Mr. Lammeter as now is. He came from a bit north'ard, so far as I could ever make out. But there's nobody rightly knows about those parts; only it couldn't be far north'ard, nor much different from this country, for he brought a fine breed o' sheep with him, so there must be pastures there, and everything reasonable. We heard tell as he'd sold his own land to come and take the Warrens, and that seemed odd for a man as had land of his own, to come and rent a farm in a strange place. But they said it was along of his wife's dying; though there's reasons in things as nobody knows on — that's pretty much what I've made out; though some folks are so wise that they'll find you fifty reasons straight off, and all the while the real reason's winking at 'em in the corner, and they niver see't. Howsom-ever, it was soon seen as we'd got a new parish'ner as know'd the rights and customs o' things, and kep a good house, and was well looked on by everybody. And the young man — that's the Mr. Lammeter as now is, for he'd niver a sister — soon begun to court Miss Osgood, that's the sister o' the Mr. Osgood as now is, and a fine handsome lass she was — eh, you can't think — they pretend this young lass is like her, but that's the way wi' people as don't know what come before 'em. *I* should know, for I helped the old rector, Mr. Drumlow as was, I helped him marry 'em."

Here Mr. Macey paused; he always gave his narrative in installments, expecting to be questioned according to precedent.

"Ay, and a partic'lar thing happened, didn't it, Mr. Macey, so as you were likely to remember that marriage?" said the landlord, in a congratulatory tone.

"I should think there did — a *very* partic'lar thing," said Mr. Macey, nodding sideways. "For Mr. Drumlow — poor old gentleman, I was fond on him, though he'd got a bit confused in his head, what wi' age and wi' taking a drop o' summat warm when the service come of a cold morning; and young Mr. Lammeter he'd have no way but he must be married in Janiwary, which, to be sure, 's a unreasonable time to be married in, for it isn't like a christening or a burying, as you can't help; and so Mr. Drumlow — poor old gentleman, I was fond on him; but when he come to put the questions, he put 'em by the rule o' contrairy like, and he says, 'Wilt thou have this man to thy wedded wife?' says he, and then he says, 'Wilt thou have this woman to thy wedded husband?' says he. But the partic'larest thing of all is, as nobody took any notice on it but me, and they answered straight off 'Yes,' like as if it had been me saying 'Amen' i' the right place, without listening to what went before."

"But *you* knew what was going on well enough, didn't you, Mr. Macey? You were live enough, eh?" said the butcher.

"Lor bless you!" said Mr. Macey, pausing, and smiling in pity at the impotence of his hearers' imagination, — "why, I was all of a tremble: it was as if I'd been a coat pulled by the two tails, like; for I couldn't stop the parson, I couldn't take upon me to do that; and yet I said to myself, I says, 'Suppose they shouldn't be fast married, 'cause the words are contrairy?' and my head went working like a mill, for I was allays uncommon for turning things over and seeing all round 'em; and I says to myself, 'Is't the meanin' or the words as makes folks fast i' wedlock?' For the parson meant right, and the bride and bridegroom meant right. But then when I come to think on it, meanin' goes but a little way i' most things, for you may mean to stick things together and your glue may be bad, and then where are you? And so I says to mysen, 'It isn't the meanin', it's the glue.' And I was worreted as if I'd got three bells to pull at once, when we got into the vestry, and they begun to sign their names. But where's the use o' talking? — you can't think what goes on in a 'cute man's inside."

"But you held in for all that, didn't you, Mr. Macey?" said the landlord.

"Ay, I held in tight till I was by mysen, wi' Mr. Drumlow, and then I out wi' everything, but respectful, as I allays did. And he made light on it, and he says:—'Pooh, pooh, Macey, make yourself easy,' he says, 'it's neither the meaning nor the words—it's the register does it—that's the glue.' So you see he settled it easy; for parsons and doctors know everything by heart, like, so as they aren't worreted wi' thinking what's the rights and wrongs o' things, as I'n been many and many's the time. And sure enough the wedding turned out all right, on'y poor Mrs. Lammeter—that's Miss Osgood as was—died afore the lasses were growed up; but for prosperity and everything respectable, there's no family more looked on."

Every one of Mr. Macey's audience had heard this story many times, but it was listened to as if it had been a favorite tune, and at certain points the puffing of the pipes was momentarily suspended, that the listeners might give their whole minds to the expected words. But there was more to come; and Mr. Snell, the landlord, duly put the leading question:—

"Why, old Mr. Lammeter had a pretty fortin, didn't they say, when he come into these parts?"

"Well, yes," said Mr. Macey; "but I dare say it's as much as this Mr. Lammeter's done to keep it whole. . . . Why, they're stables four times as big as Squire Cass's, for he thought o' nothing but hosses and hunting, Cliff didn't—a Lunnon tailor, some folks said, as had gone mad wi' cheating. For he couldn't ride, Lor bless you! they said he'd got no more grip o' the hoss than if his legs had been cross-sticks: my grandfather heared old Squire Cass say so many and many a time. But ride he would, as if Old Harry had been a-driving him; and he'd a son, a lad o' sixteen; and nothing would his father have him do but he must ride and ride—though the lad was frightened, they said. And it was a common saying as the father wanted to ride the tailor out o' the lad, and make a gentleman on him—not but what I'm a tailor myself, but in respect as God made me such, I'm proud on it, for 'Macey, tailor,' 's been wrote up over our door since afore the Queen's heads went out on the shillings. But Cliff, he was ashamed o' being called a tailor, and he was sore vexed as his riding was laughed at, and nobody o' the gentlefolks here about could abide him. Howsomever, the poor lad got sickly and died,

and the father didn't live long after him, for he got queerer nor
ever, and they said he used to go out i' the dead o' the night,
wi' a lantern in his hand, to the stables, and set a lot o' lights
burning, for he got as he couldn't sleep; and there he'd stand,
cracking his whip and looking at his hosses; and they said it was
a mercy as the stables didn't get burnt down wi' the poor dumb
creaturs in 'em. But at last he died raving, and they found as
he'd left all his property, Warrens and all, to a Lunnon Charity,
and that's how the Warrens come to be Charity Land; though
as for the stables, Mr. Lammeter never uses 'em — they're out o'
all charicter — Lor bless you! if you was to set the doors a-banging
in 'em, it 'ud sound like thunder half o'er the parish."

"Ay, but there's more going on in the stables than what folks
see by daylight, eh, Mr. Macey?" said the landlord.

"Ay, ay; go that way of a dark night, that's all," said Mr.
Maccy, winking mysteriously, "and then make believe, if you
like, as you didn't see lights i' the stables, nor hear the stamping
o' the hosses, nor the cracking o' the whips, and howling too, if
it's tow'rt daybreak. 'Cliff's Holiday' has been the name of it
ever sin' I were a boy; that's to say, some said as it was the
holiday Old Harry gev him from roasting, like. That's what my
father told me, and he was a reasonable man, though there's
folks nowadays know what happened afore they were born better
nor they know their own business."

"What do you say to that, eh, Dowlas?" said the landlord,
turning to the farrier, who was swelling with impatience for his
cue: "here's a nut for *you* to crack."

Mr. Dowlas was the negative spirit in the company, and was
proud of his position.

"Say? I say what a man *should* say as doesn't shut his
eyes to look at a finger-post. I say as I'm ready to wager any
man ten pound, if he'll stand out wi' me any dry night in the
pasture before the Warren stables, as we shall neither see lights
nor hear noises, if it isn't the blowing of our own noses. That's
what I say, and I've said it many a time; but there's nobody
'ull ventur a ten-pun' note on their ghos'es as they make so
sure of."

"Why, Dowlas, that's easy betting, that is," said Ben Win-
throp. "You might as well bet a man as he wouldn't catch the
rheumatise if he stood up to 's neck in the pool of a frosty
night. It 'ud be fine fun for a man to win his bet as he'd

catch the rheumatise. Folks as believe in Cliff's Holiday aren't
a-going to ventur near it for a matter o' ten pound."

"If Master Dowlas wants to know the truth on it," said Mr.
Macey, with a sarcastic smile, tapping his thumbs together, "he's
no call to lay any bet; let him go and stan' by himself — there's
nobody 'ull hinder him; and then he can let the parish'ners
know if they're wrong."

"Thank you! I'm obliged to you," said the farrier, with a
snort of scorn. "If folks are fools, it's no business o' mine. *I*
don't want to make out the truth about ghos'es; I know it
a'ready. But I'm not against a bet — everything fair and open.
Let any man bet me ten pound as I shall see Cliff's Holiday,
and I'll go and stand by myself. I want no company. I'd as
lief do it as I'd fill this pipe."

"Ah, but who's to watch you, Dowlas, and see you do it?
That's no fair bet," said the butcher.

"No fair bet?" replied Mr. Dowlas angrily. "I should like
to hear any man stand up and say I want to bet unfair. Come
now, Master Lundy, I should like to hear you say it."

"Very like you would," said the butcher. "But it's no
business o' mine. You're none o' my bargains, and I aren't
a-going to try and 'bate your price. If anybody'll bid for you
at your own vallying, let him. I'm for peace and quietness, I
am."

"Yes, that's what every yapping cur is, when you hold a
stick up at him," said the farrier. "But I'm afraid o' neither
man nor ghost, and I'm ready to lay a fair bet — I aren't a turn-
tail cur."

"Ay, but there's this in it, Dowlas," said the landlord, speak-
ing in a tone of much candor and tolerance. "There's folks, i'
my opinion, they can't see ghos'es, not if they stood as plain as
a pike-staff before 'em. And there's reason i' that. For there's
my wife, now, can't smell, not if she'd the strongest o' cheese
under her nose. I never seed a ghost myself; but then I says
to myself, 'Very like I haven't got the smell for 'em.' I mean,
putting a ghost for a smell, or else contrariways. And so I'm
for holding with both sides; for as I say, the truth lies between
'em. And if Dowlas was to go and stand, and say he'd never
seen a wink o' Cliff's Holiday all the night through, I'd back
him; and if anybody said as Cliff's Holiday was certain sure for
all that, I'd back *him* too. For the smell's what I go by."

The landlord's analogical argument was not well received by the farrier — a man intensely opposed to compromise.

"Tut, tut," he said setting down his glass with refreshed irritation; "what's the smell got to do with it? Did ever a ghost give a man a black eye? That's what I should like to know. If ghos'es want me to believe in 'em, let 'em leave off skulking i' the dark and i' lone places — let 'em come where there's company and candles."

"As if ghos'es 'ud want to be believed in by anybody so ignorant!" said Mr. Macey, in deep disgust at the farrier's crass imcompetence to apprehend the conditions of ghostly phenomena.

THE HALL FARM

From 'Adam Bede'

EVIDENTLY that gate is never opened; for the long grass and the great hemlocks grow close against it; and if it were opened, it is so rusty that the force necessary to turn to on its hinges would be likely to pull down the square stone-built pillars, to the detriment of the two stone lionesses which grin with a doubtful carnivorous affability above a coat of arms surmounting each of the pillars. It would be easy enough, by the aid of the nicks in the stone pillars, to climb over the brick wall with its smooth stone coping; but by putting our eyes close to the rusty bars of the gate, we can see the house well enough, and all but the very corners of the grassy inclosure.

It is a very fine old place, of red brick, softened by a pale powdery lichen, which has dispersed itself with happy irregularity, so as to bring the red brick into terms of friendly companionship with the limestone ornaments surrounding the three gables, the windows, and the door-place. But the windows are patched with wooden panes, and the door, I think, is like the gate — it is never opened: how it would groan and grate against the stone floor if it were! For it is a solid, heavy, handsome door, and must once have been in the habit of shutting with a sonorous bang behind a liveried lackey who had just seen his master and mistress off the grounds in a carriage and pair.

But at present one might fancy the house in the early stage of a chancery suit, and that the fruit from that grand double row of walnut-trees on the right hand of the inclosure would fall and rot among the grass; if it were not that we heard the booming bark of dogs echoing from great buildings at the back. And now the half-weaned calves that have been sheltering themselves in a gorse-built hovel against the left-hand wall come out and set up a silly answer to that terrible bark, doubtless supposing that it has reference to buckets of milk.

Yes, the house must be inhabited, and we will see by whom; for imagination is a licensed trespasser: it has no fear of dogs, but may climb over walls and peep in at windows with impunity. Put your face to one of the glass panes in the right-hand window: what do you see? A large open fireplace, with rusty dogs in it, and a bare boarded floor; at the far end, fleeces of wool stacked up; in the middle of the floor, some empty corn-bags. That is the furniture of the dining-room. And what through the left-hand window? Several clothes-horses, a pillion, a spinning-wheel, and an old box wide open, and stuffed full of colored rags. At the edge of this box there lies a great wooden doll, which so far as mutilation is concerned bears a strong resemblance to the finest Greek sculpture, and especially in the total loss of its nose. Near it there is a little chair, and the butt-end of a boy's leather long-lashed whip.

The history of the house is plain now. It was once the residence of a country squire, whose family, probably dwindling down to mere spinsterhood, got merged in the more territorial name of Donnithorne. It was once the Hall; it is now the Hall Farm. Like the life in some coast town that was once a watering-place, and is now a port, where the genteel streets are silent and grass-grown, and the docks and warehouses busy and resonant, the life at the Hall has changed its focus, and no longer radiates from the parlor, but from the kitchen and the farm-yard.

Plenty of life there! though this is the drowsiest time of the year, just before hay harvest; and it is the drowsiest time of the day too, for it is close upon three by the sun, and it is half-past three by Mrs. Poyser's handsome eight-day clock. But there is always a stronger sense of life when the sun is brilliant after rain; and now he is pouring down his beams, and making sparkles among the wet straw, and lighting up every patch of vivid green moss on the red tiles of the cow-shed, and turning even the muddy water that is hurrying along the channel to the drain into a mirror for the yellow-billed ducks, who are seizing the opportunity of getting a drink with as much body in it as possible. There is quite a concert of noises: the great bull-dog, chained against the stables, is thrown into furious exasperation by the unwary approach of a cock too near the mouth of his kennel, and sends forth a thundering bark, which is answered by two fox-hounds shut up in the opposite cow-house; the old top-knotted hens, scratching with their chicks among the straw, set up a sympathetic croaking as the discomfited cock joins them; a sow with her brood, all very muddy as to the legs, and curled as to the tail, throws in some deep staccato notes; our friends the calves are bleating from the home croft; and under all, a fine ear discerns the continuous hum of human voices.

For the great barn doors are thrown wide open, and men are busy there mending the harness under the superintendence of Mr. Goby the "whittaw," otherwise saddler, who entertains them with the latest Treddleston gossip. It is certainly rather an unfortunate day that Alick the shepherd has chosen for having the whittaws, since the morning turned out so wet; and Mrs. Poyser has spoken her mind pretty strongly as to the dirt which the extra number of men's shoes brought into the house at din-ner-time. Indeed, she has not yet recovered her equanimity on the subject, though it is now nearly three hours since dinner and the house floor is perfectly clean again; as clean as every-thing else in that wonderful house-place, where the only chance of collecting a few grains of dust would be to climb on the salt-coffer, and put your finger on the high mantel shelf on which the glittering brass candlesticks are enjoying their summer sin-ecure; for at this time of year of course every one goes to bed while it is yet light, or at least light enough to discern the out-line of objects after you have bruised your shins against them. Surely nowhere else could an oak clock-case and an oak table have got to such a polish by the hand: genuine "elbow polish," as Mrs. Poyser called it, for she thanked God she never had any of your varnished rubbish in her house. Hetty Sorrel often took the opportunity, when her aunt's back was turned, of looking at the pleasing reflection of herself in those polished surfaces, for the oak table was usually turned up like a screen, and was more for ornament than for use; and she could see herself sometimes in the great round pewter dishes that were ranged on the shelves above the long deal dinner-table, or in the hobs of the grate, which always shone like jasper.

Everything was looking at its brightest at this moment, for the sun shone right on the pewter dishes, and from their reflecting surfaces pleasant jets of light were thrown on mellow oak and bright brass; — and on a still pleasanter object than these; for some of the rays fell on Dinah's finely molded cheek, and lit up her pale-red hair to auburn, as she bent over the heavy household linen which she was mending for her aunt. No scene could have been more peaceful, if Mrs. Poyser, who was ironing a few things that still remained from the Monday's wash, had not been making a frequent clinking with her iron, and moving to and fro whenever she wanted it to cool; carrying the keen glance of her blue-gray eye from the kitchen to the dairy, where Hetty was making up the butter, and from the dairy to the back kitchen, where Nancy was taking the pies out of the oven. Do not suppose however that Mrs. Poyser was elderly or shrewish in her appearance; she was a good-looking woman, not more than eight-and-thirty, of fair complexion and sandy hair, well-shapen, light-footed; the most conspicuous article in her attire was an ample checkered linen apron, which almost covered her skirt; and nothing could be plainer or less noticeable than her cap and gown, for there was no weakness of which she was less tolerant than feminine vanity, and the preference of ornament to utility. The family likeness between her and her niece Dinah Morris, with the contrast between her keenness and Dinah's seraphic gentleness of expression, might have served a painter as an excellent suggestion for a Martha and Mary. Their eyes were just of the same color, but a striking test of the difference in their operation was seen in the demeanor of Trip, the black-and-tan terrier, whenever that much-suspected dog unwarily exposed himself to the freezing arctic ray of Mrs. Poyser's glance. Her tongue was not less keen than her eye, and whenever a damsel came within earshot, seemed to take up an unfinished lecture, as a barrel organ takes up a tune, precisely at the point where it had left off.

The fact that it was churning day was another reason why it was inconvenient to have the whittaws, and why, consequently, Mrs. Poyser should scold Molly the housemaid with unusual severity. To all appearance Molly had got through her after-dinner work in an exemplary manner, had "cleaned herself" with great dispatch, and now came to ask submissively if she should sit down to her spinning till milking-time. But this blameless conduct, according to Mrs. Poyser, shrouded a secret indulgence of unbecoming wishes, which she now dragged forth and held up to Molly's view with cutting eloquence.

"Spinning, indeed! It isn't spinning as you'd be at, I'll be bound, and let you have your own way. I never knew your equals for gallowsness. To think of a gell o' your age wanting to go and sit with half-a-dozen men! I'd ha' been ashamed to let the words pass over my lips if I'd been you. And you, as have been here ever since last Michaelmas, and I hired you at Treddles'on stattits, without a bit o' character — as I say, you might be grateful to be hired in that way to a respectable place; and you knew no more o' what belongs to work when you come here than the mawkin i' the field. As poor a two-fisted thing as ever I saw, you know you was. Who taught you to scrub a floor, I should like to know? Why, you'd leave the dirt in heaps i' the corners — anybody 'ud think you'd never been brought up among Christians. And as for spinning, why you've wasted as much as your wage i' the flax you've spoiled learning to spin. And you've a right to feel that, and not to go about as gaping and as thoughtless as if you was beholding to nobody. Comb the wool for the whittaws, indeed! That's what you'd like to be doing, is it? That's the way with you — that's the road you'd all like to go, headlongs to ruin. You're never easy till you've got some sweetheart as is as big a fool as yourself: you think you'll be finely off when you're married, I dare say, and have got a three-legged stool to sit on, and never a blanket to cover you, and a bit o' oat-cake for your dinner, as three children are a-snatching at."

"I'm sure I donna want t' go wi' the whittaws," said Molly, whimpering, and quite overcome by this Dantean picture of her future; "on'y we allays used to comb the wool for 'n at Mester Ottley's, an' so I just asked ye. I donna want to set eyes on the whittaws again; I wish I may never stir if I do."

"Mr. Ottley's, indeed! It's fine talking o' what you did at Mr. Ottley's. Your missis there might like her floors dirted wi' whittaws for what I know. There's no knowing what people *wonna* like — such ways as I've heard of! I never had a gell come into my house as seemed to know what cleaning was; I think people live like pigs, for my part. And as to that Betty as was dairymaid at Trent's before she come to me, she'd ha' left the cheeses without turning from week's end to week's end; and the dairy thralls, I might ha' wrote my name on 'em, when I come down-stairs after my illness, as the doctor said it was inflammation — it was a mercy I got well of it. And to think o' your knowing no better, Molly, and been here a-going i' nine months, and not for want o' talking to, neither; — and what are you stanning there for, like a jack as is run down, instead o' getting your wheel out? You're a rare un for sitting down to your work a little while after it's time to put by."

"Munny, my iron's twite told; pease put it down to warm."

The small chirruping voice that uttered this request came from a little sunny-haired girl between three and four, who, seated on a high chair at the end of the ironing-table, was arduously clutching the handle of a miniature iron with her tiny fat fist, and ironing rags with an assiduity that required her to put her little red tongue out as far as anatomy would allow.

"Cold, is it, my darling? Bless your sweet face!" said Mrs. Poyser, who was remarkable for the facility with which she could relapse from her official objurgatory to one of fondness or of friendly converse. "Never mind! Mother's done her ironing now. She's going to put the ironing things away."

"Munny, I tould 'ike to do into de barn to Tommy, to see de whittawd."

"No, no, no; Totty 'ud get her feet wet," said Mrs. Poyser, carrying away her iron. "Run into the dairy and see Cousin Hetty make the butter."

"I tould 'ike a bit of pum-take," rejoined Totty, who seemed to be provided with several relays of requests; at the same time taking the opportunity of her momentary leisure to put her fingers into a bowl of starch and drag it down so as to empty the contents with tolerable completeness on to the ironing-sheet.

"Did ever anybody see the like?" screamed Mrs. Poyser, running towards the table when her eye had fallen on the blue stream. "The child's allays i' mischief if your back's turned a minute. What shall I do to you, you naughty, naughty gell?"

Totty, however, had descended from her chair with great swiftness, and was already in retreat towards the dairy with a sort of waddling run, and an amount of fat on the nape of her neck which made her look like the metamorphosis of a white sucking pig.

The starch having been wiped up by Molly's help, and the ironing apparatus put by, Mrs. Poyser took up her knitting, which always lay ready at hand and was the work she liked best, because she could carry it on automatically as she walked to and fro. But now she came and sat down opposite Dinah, whom she looked at in a meditative way, as she knitted her gray worsted stocking.

"You look th' image o' your Aunt Judith, Dinah, when you sit a-sewing. I could almost fancy it was thirty years back, and I was a little gell at home, looking at Judith as she sat at her work after she'd done the house up; only it was a little cottage, father's was, and not a big rambling house as gets dirty i' one corner as fast as you clean it in another; but for all that I could fancy you was your Aunt Judith, only her hair was a deal darker than yours, and she was stouter and broader i' the shoulders. Judith and me allays hung together, though she had such queer ways, but your mother and her never could agree. Ah! your mother little thought as she'd have a daughter just cut out after the very pattern o' Judith, and leave her an orphan too, for Judith to take care on, and bring up with a spoon when *she* was in the grave-yard at Stoniton. I allays said that o' Judith, as she'd bear a pound weight any day to save anybody else carrying a ounce. And she was just the same from the first o' my remembering her; it made no difference in her, as I could see, when she took to the Methodists, only she talked a bit different, and wore a different sort o' cap; but she'd never in her life spent a penny on herself more than keeping herself decent."

"She was a blessed woman," said Dinah. "God had given her a loving, self-forgetting nature, and he perfected it by grace. And she was very fond of you too, Aunt Rachel. I've often heard her talk of you in the same sort of way. When she had that bad illness, and I was only eleven years old, she used to say, 'You'll have a friend on earth in your Aunt Rachel, if I'm taken from you; for she has a kind heart;' and I'm sure I've found it so."

"I don't know how, child; anybody 'ud be cunning to do anything for you, I think; you're like the birds o' th' air, and live nobody knows how. I'd ha' been glad to behave to you like a mother's sister, if you'd come and live i' this country, where there's some shelter and victual for man and beast, and folks don't live on the naked hills, like poultry a-scratching on a gravel bank. And then you might get married to some decent man, and there'd be plenty ready to have you, if you'd only leave off that preaching, as is ten times worse than anything your Aunt Judith ever did. And even if you'd marry Seth Bede, as is a poor wool-gathering Methodist, and's never like to have a penny beforehand, I know your uncle 'ud help you with a pig, and very like a cow, for he's allays been good-natur'd to my kin, for all they're poor, and made 'em welcome to the house; and 'ud do for you, I'll be bound, as much as ever he'd do for Hetty, though she's his own niece. And there's linen in the house as I could well spare you, for I've got lots o' sheeting, and table-clothing, and toweling, as isn't made up. There's a piece o' sheeting I could give you as that squinting Kitty spun — she was a rare girl to spin, for all she squinted and the children couldn't abide her; and you know the spinning's going on constant, and there's new linen wove twice as fast as the old wears out. But where's the use o' talking, if ye wonna be persuaded, and settle down like any other woman in her senses, i'stead o' wearing yourself out with walking and preaching, and giving away every penny you get, so as you've nothing saved against sickness; and all the things you've got i' the world, I verily believe, 'ud go into a bundle no bigger nor a double cheese. And all because you've got notions i' your head about religion more nor what's i' the Catechism and the Prayer-book."

"But not more than what's in the Bible, Aunt," said Dinah.

"Yes, and the Bible too, for that matter," Mrs. Poyser rejoined rather sharply; "else why shouldn't them as know best what's in the Bible — the parsons and people as have got nothing to do but learn it — do the same as you do? But for the matter o' that, if everybody was to do like you, the world must come to a standstill; for if everybody tried to do without house and home, and with poor eating and drinking, and was allays talking as we must despise the things o' the world, as you say, I should like to know where the pick o' the stock, and the corn, and the best new-milk cheeses 'ud have to go. Everybody 'ud be wanting bread made o' tail ends, and everybody 'ud be running after everybody else to preach to 'em, istead o' bringing up their families, and laying by against a bad harvest. It stands to sense as that can't be the right religion."

"Nay, dear Aunt, you never heard me say that all people are called to forsake their work and their families. It's quite right the land should be plowed and sowed, and the precious corn stored, and the things of this life cared for, and right that people should rejoice in their families, and provide for them; so that this is done in the fear of the Lord, and that they are not unmindful of the soul's wants while they are caring for the body. We can all be servants of God wherever our lot is cast, but he gives us different sorts of work, according as he fits us for it and calls us to it. I can no more help spending my life in trying to do what I can for the souls of others, than you could help running if you heard little Totty crying at the other end of the house; the voice would go to your heart, you would think the dear child was in trouble or in danger, and you couldn't rest without running to help her and comfort her."

"Ah," said Mrs. Poyser, rising and walking towards the door, "I know it 'ud be just the same if I was to talk to you for hours. You'd make me the same answer, at th' end. I might as well talk to the running brook, and tell it to stan' still."

The causeway outside the kitchen door was dry enough now for Mrs. Poyser to stand there quite pleasantly and see what was going on in the yard, the gray worsted stocking making a steady progress in her hands all the while. But she had not been standing there more than five minutes before she came in again, and said to Dinah in rather a flurried, awe-stricken tone:—

"If there isn't Captain Donnithorne and Mr. Irwine a-coming into the yard! I'll lay my life they're come to speak about your preaching on the Green, Dinah; it's you must answer 'em, for I'm dumb. I've said enough a'ready about your bringing such disgrace upo' your uncle's family. I wouldn't ha' minded if you'd been Mr. Poyser's own niece—folks must put up wi' their own kin, as they put up wi' their own noses; it's their own flesh and blood. But to think of a niece o' mine being cause o' my husband's being turned out of his farm, and me brought him no fortin but my savins—"

"Nay, dear Aunt Rachel," said Dinah gently, "you've no cause for such fears. I've strong assurance that no evil will happen to you and my uncle and the children from anything I've done. I didn't preach without direction."

"Direction! I know very well what you mean by direction," said Mrs. Poyser, knitting in a rapid and agitated manner. "When there's a bigger maggot than usial in your head you call it 'direction'; and then nothing can stir you—you look like the statty o' the outside o' Treddles'on church, a-starin' and a-smilin' whether it's fair weather or foul. I hanna common patience with you."

By this time the two gentlemen had reached the palings and had got down from their horses: it was plain they meant to come in. Mrs. Poyser advanced to the door to meet them, curtseying low, and trembling between anger with Dinah and anxiety to conduct herself with perfect propriety on the occasion. For in those days the keenest of bucolic minds felt a whispering awe at the sight of the gentry, such as of old men felt when they stood on tiptoe to watch the gods passing by in tall human shape.

"Well, Mrs. Poyser, how are you after this stormy morning?" said Mr. Irwine with his stately cordiality. "Our feet are quite dry; we shall not soil your beautiful floor."

"Oh, sir, don't mention it," said Mrs. Poyser. "Will you and the captain please to walk into the parlor?"

"No, indeed, thank you, Mrs. Poyser," said the captain, looking eagerly round the kitchen, as if his eye were seeking something it could not find. "I delight in your kitchen. I think it is the most charming room I know. I should like every farmer's wife to come and look at it for a pattern."

"Oh, you're pleased to say so, sir. Pray take a seat," said Mrs. Poyser, relieved a little by this compliment and the captain's evident good-humor, but still glancing anxiously at Mr. Irwine, who she saw was looking at Dinah and advancing towards her.

"Poyser is not at home, is he?" said Captain Donnithorne, seating himself where he could see along the short passage to the open dairy door.

"No, sir, he isn't; he's gone to Rosseter to see Mr. West, the factor, about the wool. But there's father i' the barn, sir, if he'd be of any use."

"No, thank you; I'll just look at the whelps and leave a message about them with your shepherd. I must come another day and see your husband; I want to have a consultation with him about horses. Do you know when he's likely to be at liberty?"

"Why, sir, you can hardly miss him, except it's o' Treddles'on market-day—that's of a Friday, you know. For if he's anywhere on the farm we can send for him in a minute. If we'd got rid of the Scantlands we should have no outlying fields; and I should be glad of it, for if ever anything happens he's sure to be gone to the Scantlands. Things allays happen so contrairy, if they've a chance; and it's an unnat'ral thing to have one bit o' your farm in one county and all the rest in another."

"Ah, the Scantlands would go much better with Choyce's farm, especially as he wants dairy land and you've got plenty. I think yours is the prettiest farm on the estate, though; and do you know, Mrs. Poyser, if I were going to marry and settle, I should be tempted to turn you out, and do up this fine old house, and turn farmer myself."

"Oh, sir," said Mrs. Poyser, rather alarmed, "you wouldn't like it at all. As for farming, it's putting money into your pocket wi' your right hand and fetching it out wi' your left. As fur as I can see, it's raising victual for other folks, and just getting a mouthful for yourself and your children as you go along. Not as you'd be like a poor man as wants to get his bread: you could afford to lose as much money as you liked i' farming; but it's poor fun losing money, I should think, though I understan' it's what the great folks i' London play at more than anything. For my husband heard at market as Lord Dacey's eldest son had lost thousands upo' thousands to the Prince o' Wales, and they say my lady was going to pawn her jewels to pay for him. But you know more about that than I do, sir. But as for farming, sir, I canna think as you'd like it; and this house — the draughts in it are enough to cut you through, and it's my opinion the floors up-stairs are very rotten, and the rats i' the cellar are beyond anything."

"Why, that's a terrible picture, Mrs. Poyser. I think I should be doing you a service to turn you out of such a place. But there's no chance of that. I'm not likely to settle for the next twenty years, till I'm a stout gentleman of forty; and my grandfather would never consent to part with such good tenants as you."

"Well, sir, if he thinks so well o' Mr. Poyser for a tenant, I wish you could put in a word for him to allow us some new gates for the Five Closes, for my husband's been asking and asking till he's tired; and to think o' what he's done for the farm; and's never had a penny allowed him, be the times bad or good. And as I've said to my husband often and often, I'm sure if the captain had anything to do with it, it wouldn't be so. Not as I wish to speak disrespectful o' them as have got the power i' their hands, but it's more than flesh and blood 'ull bear sometimes, to be toiling and striving, and up early and down late, and hardly sleeping a wink when you lie down for thinking as the cheese may swell, or the cows may slip their calf, or the wheat may grow green again i' the sheaf — and after all, at th' end o' the year, it's like as if you'd been cooking a feast and had got the smell of it for your pains."

Mrs. Poyser, once launched into conversation, always sailed along without any check from her preliminary awe of the gentry. The confidence she felt in her own powers of exposition was a motive force that overcame all resistance.

"I'm afraid I should only do harm instead of good, if I were to speak about the gates, Mrs. Poyser," said the captain; "though I assure you there's no man on the estate I would sooner say a word for than your husband. I know his farm is in better order than any other within ten miles of us; and as for the kitchen," he added, smiling, "I don't believe there's one in the kingdom to beat it. By-the-by, I've never seen your dairy: I must see your dairy, Mrs. Poyser."

"Indeed, sir, it's not fit for you to go in, for Hetty's in the middle o' making the butter, for the churning was thrown late, and I'm quite ashamed." This Mrs. Poyser said blushing, and believing that the captain was really interested in her milk-pans, and would adjust his opinion of her to the appearance of her dairy.

"Oh, I've no doubt it's in capital order. Take me in," said the captain, leading the way, while Mrs. Poyser followed.

MRS. POYSER "HAS HER SAY OUT"

From 'Adam Bede'

SOMETHING unwonted must clearly be in the wind, for the old Squire's visits to his tenantry were rare; and though Mrs. Poyser had during the last twelvemonth recited many imaginary speeches, meaning even more than met the ear, which she was quite determined to make to him the next time he appeared within the gates of the Hall Farm, the speeches had always remained imaginary.

"Good-day, Mrs. Poyser," said the old Squire, peering at her with his short-sighted eyes — a mode of looking at her which, as Mrs. Poyser observed, "allays aggravated her: it was as if you was a insect, and he was going to dab his finger-nail on you."

However, she said, "Your servant, sir," and curtsied with an air of perfect deference as she advanced towards him; she was not the woman to misbehave towards her betters, and fly in the face of the Catechism, without severe provocation.

"Is your husband at home, Mrs. Poyser?"

"Yes, sir; he's only i' the rick-yard. I'll send for him in a minute, if you'll please to get down and step in."

"Thank you; I will do so. I want to consult him about a little matter; but you are quite as much concerned in it, if not more. I must have your opinion too."

"Hetty, run and tell your uncle to come in," said Mrs. Poyser as they entered the house, and the old gentleman bowed low in answer to Hetty's curtsy; while Totty, conscious of a pinafore stained with gooseberry jam, stood hiding her face against the clock, and peeping round furtively.

"What a fine old kitchen this is!" said Mr. Donnithorne, looking round admiringly. He always spoke in the same deliberate, well-chiseled, polite way, whether his words were sugary or venomous. "And you keep it so exquisitely clean, Mrs. Poyser. I like these premises, do you know, beyond any on the estate."

"Well, sir, since you're fond of 'em, I should be glad if you'd let a bit o' repairs be done to 'em, for the boarding's i' that state as we're like to be eaten up wi' rats and mice; and the cellar, you may stan' up to your knees i' water in 't, if you like to go down; but perhaps you'd rather believe my words. Won't you please to sit down, sir?"

"Not yet; I must see your dairy. I have not seen it for years, and I hear on all hands about your fine cheese and butter," said the Squire, looking politely unconscious that there could be any question on which he and Mrs. Poyser might happen to disagree. "I think I see the door open there: you must not be surprised if I cast a covetous eye on your cream and butter. I don't expect that Mrs. Satchell's cream and butter will bear comparison with yours."

"I can't say, sir, I'm sure. It's seldom I see other folks' butter, though there's some on it as one's no need to see — the smell's enough."

"Ah, now this I like," said Mr. Donnithorne, looking round at the damp temple of cleanliness, but keeping near the door. "I'm sure I should like my breakfast better if I knew the butter and cream came from this dairy. Thank you, that really is a pleasant sight. Unfortunately, my slight tendency to rheumatism makes me afraid of damp; I'll sit down in your comfortable kitchen. Ah, Poyser, how do you do? In the midst of business, I see, as usual. I've been looking at your wife's beautiful dairy: the best manager in the parish, is she not?"

Mr. Poyser had just entered in shirt-sleeves and open waist-coat, with a face a shade redder than usual, from the exertion of "pitching." As he stood, red, rotund, and radiant, before the small, wiry, cool old gentleman, he looked like a prize apple by the side of a withered crab.

"Will you please to take this chair, sir?" he said, lifting his father's arm-chair forward a little; "you'll find it easy."

"No, thank you, I never sit in easy-chairs," said the old gentleman, seating himself on a small chair near the door. "Do you know, Mrs. Poyser — sit down, pray, both of you — I've been far from contented, for some time, with Mrs. Satchell's dairy management. I think she has not a good method, as you have."

"Indeed, sir, I can't speak to that," said Mrs. Poyser, in a hard voice, rolling and unrolling her knitting, and looking icily out of the window, as she continued to stand opposite the Squire. Poyser might sit down if he liked, she thought: *she* wasn't going to sit down, as if she'd give in to any such smooth-tongued palaver. Mr. Poyser, who looked and felt the reverse of icy, did sit down in his three-cornered chair.

"And now, Poyser, as Satchell is laid up, I am intending to let the Chase Farm to a respectable tenant. I'm tired of having a farm on my own hands — nothing is made the best of in such cases, as you know. A satisfactory bailiff is hard to find; and I think you and I, Poyser, and your excellent wife here, can enter into a little arrangement in consequence, which will be to our mutual advantage."

"Oh," said Mr. Poyser, with a good-natured blankness of imagination as to the nature of the arrangement.

"If I'm called upon to speak, sir," said Mrs. Poyser, after glancing at her husband with pity at his softness, "you know better than me; but I don't see what the Chase Farm is t' us — we've cumber enough wi' our own farm. Not but what I'm glad to hear o' anybody respectable coming into the parish: there's some as ha' been brought in as hasn't been looked on i' that character."

" You're likely to find **Mr.** Thurle an excellent neighbor, I assure you: such a one as you will feel glad to have accommodated by the little plan I'm going to mention; especially as I hope you will find it as much to your own advantage as his."

" Indeed, sir, if it's anything t' our advantage, it'll be the first offer o' the sort I've heared on. It's them as take advantage that get advantage i' this world, *I* think: folks have to wait long enough afore it's brought to 'em."

" The fact is, Poyser," said the Squire, ignoring Mrs. Poyser's theory of worldly prosperity, " there is too much dairy land, and too little plow land, on the Chase Farm, to suit Thurle's purpose — indeed, he will only take the farm on condition of some change in it: his wife, it appears, is not a clever dairywoman like yours. Now, the plan I'm thinking of is to effect a little exchange. If you were to have the Hollow Pastures, you might increase your dairy, which must be so profitable under your wife's management; and I should request you, Mrs. Poyser, to supply my house with milk, cream, and butter, at the market prices. On the other hand, Poyser, you might let Thurle have the Lower and Upper Ridges, which really, with our wet seasons would be a good riddance for you. There is much less risk in dairy land than corn land."

Mr. Poyser was leaning forward, with his elbows on his knees, his head on one side, and his mouth screwed up — apparently absorbed in making the tips of his fingers meet so as to represent with perfect accuracy the ribs of a ship. He was much too acute a man not to see through the whole business, and to foresee perfectly what would be his wife's view of the subject; but he disliked giving unpleasant answers: unless it was on a point of farming practice, he would rather give up than have a quarrel, any day; and after all, it mattered more to his wife than to him. So, after a few moments' silence, he looked up at her and said mildly, " What dost say?"

Mrs. Poyser had had her eyes fixed on her husband with cold severity during his silence, but now she turned away her head with a toss, looked icily at the opposite roof of the cow-shed, and spearing her knitting together with the loose pin, held it firmly between her clasped hands.

" Say? Why, I say you may do as you like about giving up any o' your corn land afore your lease is up, which it won't be for a year come next Michaelmas, but I'll not consent to take

more dairy work into my hands, either for love or money;
and there's nayther love nor money here, as I can see, on'y
other folks' love o' theirselves, and the money as is to go into
other folks' pockets. I know there's them as is born t' own
the land, and them as is born to sweat on 't "—here Mrs. Poyser
paused to gasp a little —" and I know it's christened folks' duty
to submit to their betters as fur as flesh and blood 'ull bear it;
but I'll not make a martyr o' myself, and wear myself to skin and
bone, and worret myself as if I was a churn wi' butter a-coming
in 't, for no landlord in England, not if he was King George
himself."

"No, no, my dear Mrs. Poyser, certainly not," said the Squire,
still confident in his own powers of persuasion; "you must not
overwork yourself; but don't you think your work will rather be
lessened than increased in this way? There is so much milk re-
quired at the Abbey, that you will have little increase of cheese
and butter making from the addition to your dairy; and I believe
selling the milk is the most profitable way of disposing of dairy
produce, is it not?"

"Ay, that's true," said Mr. Poyser, unable to repress an opin-
ion on a question of farming profits, and forgetting that it was
not in this case a purely abstract question.

"I dare say," said Mrs. Poyser bitterly, turning her head half-
way towards her husband, and looking at the vacant arm-chair —
"I dare say it's true for men as sit i' th' chimney-corner and
make believe as everything's cut wi' ins an' outs to fit int' every-
thing else. If you could make a pudding wi' thinking o' the bat-
ter, it 'ud be easy getting dinner. How do I know whether the
milk 'ull be wanted constant? What's to make me sure as the
house won't be put o' board wage afore we're many months older,
and then I may have to lie awake o' nights wi' twenty gallons o'
milk on my mind — and Dingall 'ull take no more butter, let alone
paying for it; and we must fat pigs till we're obliged to beg the
butcher on our knees to buy 'em, and lose half of 'em wi' the
measles. And there's the fetching and carrying, as 'ud be welly
half a day's work for a man an' hoss — *that's* to be took out o'
the profits, I reckon? But there's folks 'ud hold a sieve under
the pump and expect to carry away the water."

"That difficulty — about the fetching and carrying — you will
not have, Mrs. Poyser," said the Squire, who thought that this
entrance into particulars indicated a distant inclination to com-

promise on Mrs. Poyser's part — "Bethell will do that regularly with the cart and pony."

"Oh, sir, begging your pardon, I've never been used t' having gentlefolks' servants coming about my back places, a-making love to both the gells at once, and keeping 'em with their hands on their hips listening to all manner o' gossip when they should be down on their knees a-scouring. If we're to go to ruin, it shanna be wi' having our back kitchen turned into a public."

"Well, Poyser," said the Squire, shifting his tactics, and looking as if he thought Mrs. Poyser had suddenly withdrawn from the proceedings and left the room, "you can turn the Hollows into feeding land. I can easily make another arrangement about supplying my house. And I shall not forget your readiness to accommodate your landlord as well as a neighbor. I know you will be glad to have your lease renewed for three years when the present one expires; otherwise, I dare say, Thurle, who is a man of some capital, would be glad to take both the farms, as they could be worked so well together. But I don't want to part with an old tenant like you."

To be thrust out of the discussion in this way would have been enough to complete Mrs. Poyser's exasperation, even without the final threat. Her husband, really alarmed at the possibility of their leaving the old place where he had been bred and born — for he believed the old Squire had small spite enough for anything — was beginning a mild remonstrance explanatory of the inconvenience he should find in having to buy and sell more stock, with —

"Well, sir, I think as it's rather hard —" when Mrs. Poyser burst in with the desperate determination to have her say out this once, though it were to rain notices to quit, and the only shelter were the workhouse.

"Then, sir, if I may speak — as, for all I'm a woman, and there's folks as thinks a woman's fool enough to stan' by an' look on while the men sign her soul away, I've a right to speak, for I make one quarter o' the rent, and save another quarter — I say, if Mr. Thurle's so ready to take farms under you, it's a pity but what he should take this, and see if he likes to live in a house wi' all the plagues o' Egypt in 't — wi' the cellar full o' water, and frogs and toads hoppin' up the steps by dozens — and the floors rotten, and the rats and mice gnawing every bit o' cheese, and runnin' over our heads as we lie i' bed till we expect

'em to eat us up alive — as it's a mercy they hanna eat the child-
ren long ago.   I should like to see if there's another tenant
besides Poyser as 'ud put up wi' never having a bit o' repairs
done till a place tumbles down — and not then, on'y wi' begging
and praying, and having to pay half — and being strung up wi'
the rent as it's much if he gets enough out o' the land to pay,
for all he's put his own money into the ground beforehand. See
if you'll get a stranger to lead such a life here as that: a mag-
got must be born i' the rotten cheese to like it, I reckon.   You
may run away from my words, sir," continued Mrs. Poyser, fol-
lowing the old Squire beyond the door — for after the first mo-
ments of stunned surprise he had got up, and waving his hand
towards her with a smile, had walked out towards his pony.   But
it was impossible for him to get away immediately, for John was
walking the pony up and down the yard, and was some distance
from the causeway when his master beckoned —

"You may run away from my words, sir, and you may go
spinnin' underhand ways o' doing us a mischief, for you've got
Old Harry to your friend, though nobody else is; but I tell you
for once as we're not dumb creatures to be abused and made
money on by them as ha' got the lash i' their hands, for want
o' knowing how t' undo the tackle.   An' if I'm th' only one as
speaks my mind, there's plenty o' the same way o' thinking i'
this parish and the next to 't, for your name 's no better than a
brimstone match in everybody's nose — if it isna two-three old
folks as you think o' saving your soul by giving 'em a bit o' flan-
nel and a drop o' porridge.   An' you may be right i' thinking
it'll take but little to save your soul, for it'll be the smallest
savin' y' iver made, wi' all your scrapin'."

There are occasions on which two servant-girls and a wagoner
may be a formidable audience, and as the Squire rode away on
his black pony, even the gift of short-sightedness did not pre-
vent him from being aware that Molly and Nancy and Tim were
grinning not far from him.   Perhaps he suspected that sour old
John was grinning behind him — which was also the fact.   Mean-
while the bull-dog, the black-and-tan terrier, Alick's sheep-dog,
and the gander hissing at a safe distance from the pony's heels,
carried out the idea of Mrs. Poyser's solo in an impressive
quartet.

Mrs. Poyser, however, had no sooner seen the pony moved
off than she turned round, gave the two hilarious damsels a look

which drove them into the back kitchen, and unspearing her knitting, began to knit again with her usual rapidity, as she re-entered the house.

" Thee'st done it now," said Mr. Poyser, a little alarmed and uneasy, but not without some triumphant amusement at his wife's outbreak.

" Yes, I know I've done it," said Mrs. Poyser; " but I've had my say out, and I shall be th' easier for 't all my life. There's no pleasure i' living if you're to be corked up forever, and only dribble your mind out by the sly like a leaky barrel. I shan't repent saying what I think, if I live to be as old as th' old Squire; and there's little likelihoods — for it seems as if them as aren't wanted here are th' only folks as aren't wanted i' th' other world."

" But thee wutna like moving from th' old place, this Mich-aelmas twelvemonth," said Mr. Poyser, " and going into a strange parish, where thee know'st nobody. It'll be hard upon us both, and upo' father too."

" Eh, it's no use worreting; there's plenty o' things may hap-pen between this and Michaelmas twelvemonth. The captain may be master afore then, for what we know," said Mrs. Poyser, inclined to take an unusually hopeful view of an embarrassment which had been brought about by her own merit, and not by other people's fault.

" *I'm* none for worreting," said Mr. Poyser, rising from his three-cornered chair, and walking slowly towards the door; " but I should be loath to leave th' old place, and the parish where I was bred and born, and father afore me. We should leave our roots behind us, I doubt, and niver thrive again."

THE PRISONERS

From 'Romola'

IN 1493 the rumor spread and became louder and louder that Charles the Eighth of France was about to cross the Alps with a mighty army; and the Italian populations, accustomed, since Italy had ceased to be the heart of the Roman empire, to look for an arbitrator from afar, began vaguely to regard his coming as a means of avenging their wrongs and redressing their grievances.

And in that rumor Savonarola had heard the assurance that
his prophecy was being verified. What was it that filled the ears
of the prophets of old but the distant tread of foreign armies,
coming to do the work of justice? He no longer looked vaguely
to the horizon for the coming storm: he pointed to the rising
cloud. The French army was that new deluge which was to pu-
rify the earth from iniquity; the French King, Charles VIII., was
the instrument elected by God as Cyrus had been of old, and all
men who desired good rather than evil were to rejoice in his
coming. For the scourge would fall destructively on the impeni-
tent alone. Let any city of Italy, let Florence above all — Flor-
ence beloved of God, since to its ear the warning voice had been
specially sent — repent and turn from its ways like Nineveh of
old, and the storm cloud would roll over it and leave only refresh-
ing rain-drops.

Fra Girolamo's word was powerful; yet now that the new
Cyrus had already been three months in Italy, and was not far
from the gates of Florence, his presence was expected there with
mixed feelings, in which fear and distrust certainly predominated.
At present it was not understood that he had redressed any
grievances; and the Florentines clearly had nothing to thank him
for. He held their strong frontier fortresses, which Piero de'
Medici had given up to him without securing any honorable terms
in return; he had done nothing to quell the alarming revolt of
Pisa, which had been encouraged by his presence to throw off
the Florentine yoke; and "orators," even with a prophet at their
head, could win no assurance from him, except that he would
settle everything when he was once within the walls of Florence.
Still, there was the satisfaction of knowing that the exasperating
Piero de' Medici had been fairly pelted out for the ignominious
surrender of the fortresses, and in that act of energy the spirit
of the Republic had recovered some of its old fire.

The preparations for the equivocal guest were not entirely
those of a city resigned to submission. Behind the bright dra-
pery and banners symbolical of joy, there were preparations of
another sort made with common accord by government and
people. Well hidden within walls there were hired soldiers of
the Republic, hastily called in from the surrounding districts;
there were old arms duly furbished, and sharp tools and heavy
cudgels laid carefully at hand, to be snatched up on short notice;
there were excellent boards and stakes to form barricades upon

occasion, and a good supply of stones to make a surprising hail
from the upper windows.   Above all, there were people very
strongly in the humor for fighting any personage who might be
supposed to have designs of hectoring over them, they having
lately tasted that new pleasure with much relish.   This humor
was not diminished by the sight of occasional parties of French-
men, coming beforehand to choose their quarters, with a hawk,
perhaps, on their left wrist, and metaphorically speaking, a piece
of chalk in their right hand to mark Italian doors withal; espe-
cially as creditable historians imply that many sons of France
were at that time characterized by something approaching to a
swagger, which must have whetted the Florentine appetite for a
little stone-throwing.

And this was the temper of Florence on the morning of the
17th of November, 1494.

The sky was gray, but that made little difference in the
Piazza del Duomo, which was covered with its holiday sky of
blue drapery, and its constellations of yellow lilies and coats of
arms.   The sheaves of banners were unfurled at the angles of
the Baptistery, but there was no carpet yet on the steps of the
Duomo, for the marble was being trodden by numerous feet that
were not at all exceptional.   It was the hour of the Advent ser-
mons, and the very same reasons which had flushed the streets
with holiday color were reasons why the preaching in the Duomo
could least of all be dispensed with.

But not all the feet in the Piazza were hastening towards the
steps.   People of high and low degree were moving to and fro
with the brisk pace of men who had errands before them; groups
of talkers were thickly scattered, some willing to be late for the
sermon, and others content not to hear it at all.

The expression on the faces of these apparent loungers was
not that of men who are enjoying the pleasant laziness of an
opening holiday.   Some were in close and eager discussion; others
were listening with keen interest to a single spokesman, and yet
from time to time turned round with a scanning glance at any new
passer-by.   At the corner looking towards the Via de' Cerretani —
just where the artificial rainbow light of the Piazza ceased, and
the gray morning fell on the sombre stone houses — there was a
remarkable cluster of the working people, most of them bearing

on their dress or persons the signs of their daily labor, and almost all of them carrying some weapon, or some tool which might serve as a weapon upon occasion. Standing in the gray light of the street, with bare brawny arms and soiled garments, they made all the more striking the transition from the brightness of the Piazza. They were listening to the thin notary, Ser Cioni, who had just paused on his way to the Duomo. His biting words could get only a contemptuous reception two years and a half before in the Mercato; but now he spoke with the more complacent humor of a man whose party is uppermost, and who is conscious of some influence with the people.

"Never talk to me," he was saying in his incisive voice, "never talk to me of bloodthirsty Swiss or fierce French infantry; they might as well be in the narrow passes of the mountains as in our streets; and peasants have destroyed the finest armies of our condottieri in time past, when they had once got them between steep precipices. I tell you, Florentines need be afraid of no army in their own streets."

"That's true, Ser Cioni," said a man whose arms and hands were discolored by crimson dye, which looked like blood-stains, and who had a small hatchet stuck in his belt; "and those French cavaliers who came in squaring themselves in their smart doublets the other day, saw a sample of the dinner we could serve up for them. I was carrying my cloth in Ognissanti, when I saw my fine Messeri going by, looking round as if they thought the houses of the Vespucci and the Agli a poor pick of loadings for them, and eyeing us Florentines, like top-knotted cocks as they are, as if they pitied us because we didn't know how to strut. 'Yes, my fine *Galli*,' says I, 'stick out your stomachs; I've got a meat-axe in my belt that will go inside you all the easier;' when presently the old cow lowed,* and I knew something had happened — no matter what. So I threw my cloth in at the first doorway, and took hold of my meat-axe and ran after my fine cavaliers towards the Vigna Nuova. And, 'What is it, Guccio?' said I, when he came up with me. 'I think it's the Medici coming back,' said Guccio. *Bembè!* I expected so! And up we reared a barricade, and the Frenchmen looked behind and saw themselves in a trap; and up comes a good swarm

---

* "*La vacca muglia*" was the phrase for the sounding of the great bell in the tower of the Palazzo Vecchio.

of our *Ciompi*,* and one of them with a big scythe he had in his hand mowed off one of the fine cavaliers' feathers: — it's true! And the lasses peppered a few stones down to frighten them. However, Piero de' Medici wasn't come after all; and it was a pity; for we'd have left him neither legs nor wings to go away with again."

"Well spoken, Oddo," said a young butcher, with his knife at his belt; "and it's my belief Piero will be a good while before he wants to come back, for he looked as frightened as a hunted chicken when we hustled and pelted him in the piazza. He's a coward, else he might have made a better stand when he'd got his horsemen. But we'll swallow no Medici any more, whatever else the French king wants to make us swallow."

"But I like not those French cannon they talk of," said Goro, none the less fat for two years' additional grievances. "San Giovanni defend us! If Messer Domeneddio means so well by us as your Frate says he does, Ser Cioni, why shouldn't he have sent the French another way to Naples?"

"Ay, Goro," said the dyer; "that's a question worth putting. Thou art not such a pumpkin-head as I took thee for. Why, they might have gone to Naples by Bologna, eh, Ser Cioni? — or if they'd gone to Arezzo — we wouldn't have minded their going to Arezzo."

"Fools! It will be for the good and glory of Florence," Ser Cioni began. But he was interrupted by the exclamation, "Look there!" which burst from several voices at once, while the faces were all turned to a party who were advancing along the Via de' Cerretani.

"It's Lorenzo Tornabuoni, and one of the French noblemen who are in his house," said Ser Cioni, in some contempt at this interruption. "He pretends to look well satisfied — that deep Tornabuoni — but he's a Medicean in his heart; mind that."

The advancing party was rather a brilliant one, for there was not only the distinguished presence of Lorenzo Tornabuoni, and the splendid costume of the Frenchman with his elaborately displayed white linen and gorgeous embroidery; there were two other Florentines of high birth, in handsome dresses donned for the coming procession, and on the left hand of the Frenchman was a figure that was not to be eclipsed by any amount of

---

* The poorer artisans connected with the wool trade — wool-beaters, carders, washers, etc.

intention or brocade — a figure we have often seen before.   He
wore nothing but black, for he was in mourning; but the black
was presently to be covered by a red mantle, for he too was to
walk in procession as Latin Secretary to the Ten.   Tito Melema
had become conspicuously serviceable in the intercourse with the
French guests, from his familiarity with Southern Italy and his
readiness in the French tongue, which he had spoken in his early
youth; and he had paid more than one visit to the French camp
at Signa.   The lustre of good fortune was upon him; he was
smiling, listening, and explaining, with his usual graceful unpre-
tentious ease, and only a very keen eye bent on studying him
could have marked a certain amount of change in him which
was not to be accounted for by the lapse of eighteen months.
It was that change which comes from the final departure of
moral youthfulness — from the distinct self-conscious adoption of
a part in life.   The lines of the face were as soft as ever, the
eyes as pellucid; but something was gone — something as in-
definable as the changes in the morning twilight.

The Frenchman was gathering instructions concerning cere-
monial before riding back to Signa, and now he was going to
have a final survey of the Piazza del Duomo, where the royal
procession was to pause for religious purposes.   The distinguished
party attracted the notice of all eyes as it entered the Piazza,
but the gaze was not entirely cordial and admiring; there were
remarks not altogether allusive and mysterious to the French-
man's hoof-shaped shoes — delicate flattery of royal superfluity in
toes; and there was no care that certain snarlings at "Mediceans"
should be strictly inaudible.   But Lorenzo Tornabuoni possessed
that power of dissembling annoyance which is demanded in a
man who courts popularity, and Tito, besides his natural disposi-
tion to overcome ill-will by good-humor, had the unimpassioned
feeling of the alien towards names and details that move the
deepest passions of the native.

Arrived where they could get a good oblique view of the
Duomo, the party paused.   The festoons and devices placed over
the central doorway excited some demur, and Tornabuoni beck-
oned to Piero di Cosimo, who, as was usual with him at this
hour, was lounging in front of Nello's shop.   There was soon an
animated discussion, and it became highly amusing from the
Frenchman's astonishment at Piero's odd pungency of statement,
which Tito translated literally.   Even snarling onlookers became

curious, and their faces began to wear the half-smiling, half-humiliated expression of people who are not within hearing of the joke which is producing infectious laughter. It was a delightful moment for Tito, for he was the only one of the party who could have made so amusing an interpreter, and without any disposition to triumphant self-gratulation he reveled in the sense that he was an object of liking — he basked in approving glances. The rainbow light fell about the laughing group, and the grave church-goers had all disappeared within the walls. It seemed as if the Piazza had been decorated for a real Florentine holiday.

Meanwhile in the gray light of the unadorned streets there were on-comers who made no show of linen and brocade, and whose humor was far from merry. Here too the French dress and hoofed shoes were conspicuous, but they were being pressed upon by a large and larger number of non-admiring Florentines. In the van of the crowd were three men in scanty clothing; each had his hands bound together by a cord, and a rope was fastened round his neck and body in such a way that he who held the extremity of the rope might easily check any rebellious movement by the threat of throttling. The men who held the ropes were French soldiers, and by broken Italian phrases and strokes from the knotted end of the rope, they from time to time stimulated their prisoners to beg. Two of them were obedient, and to every Florentine they had encountered had held out their bound hands and said in piteous tones: —

"For the love of God and the Holy Madonna, give us something towards our ransom! We are Tuscans; we were made prisoners in Lunigiana."

But the third man remained obstinately silent under all the strokes of the knotted cord. He was very different in aspect from his two fellow prisoners. They were young and hardy,. and in the scant clothing which the avarice of their captors had left them, looked like vulgar, sturdy mendicants. But he had passed the boundary of old age, and could hardly be less than four or five and sixty. His beard, which had grown long in neglect, and the hair which fell thick and straight round his baldness, were nearly white. His thick-set figure was still firm and upright, though emaciated, and seemed to express energy in spite of age — an expression that was partly carried out in the dark eyes and strong dark eyebrows, which had a strangely

isolated intensity of color in the midst of his yellow, bloodless,
deep-wrinkled face with its lank gray hairs.   And yet there was
something fitful in the eyes which contradicted the occasional
flash of energy; after looking round with quick fierceness at
windows and faces, they fell again with a lost and wandering
look.   But his lips were motionless, and he held his hands reso-
lutely down.   He would not beg.

This sight had been witnessed by the Florentines with grow-
ing exasperation.   Many standing at their doors or passing
quietly along had at once given money — some in half-automatic
response to an appeal in the name of God, others in that unques-
tioning awe of the French soldiery which had been created by
the reports of their cruel warfare, and on which the French
themselves counted as a guarantee of immunity in their acts of
insolence.   But as the group had proceeded farther into the
heart of the city, that compliance had gradually disappeared, and
the soldiers found themselves escorted by a gathering troop of
men and boys, who kept up a chorus of exclamations sufficiently
intelligible to foreign ears without any interpreter.   The soldiers
themselves began to dislike their position, for with a strong
inclination to use their weapons, they were checked by the
necessity for keeping a secure hold on their prisoners, and they
were now hurrying along in the, hope of finding shelter in a
hostelry.

"French dogs!"   "Bullock-feet!"   "Snatch their pikes from
them!"   "Cut the cords and make them run for their prisoners.
They'll run as fast as geese — don't you see they're web-footed?"
These were the cries which the soldiers vaguely understood to
be jeers, and probably threats.   But every one seemed disposed
to give invitations of this spirited kind rather than to act upon
them.

"Santiddio! here's a sight!" said the dyer, as soon as he had
divined the meaning of the advancing tumult; "and the fools do
nothing but hoot.   Come along!" he added, snatching his axe
from his belt, and running to join the crowd, followed by the
butcher and all the rest of his companions except Goro, who
hastily retreated up a narrow passage.

The sight of the dyer, running forward with blood-red arms
and axe uplifted, and with his cluster of rough companions be-
hind him, had a stimulating effect on the crowd.   Not that
he did anything else than pass beyond the soldiers and thrust

himself well among his fellow-citizens, flourishing his axe; but he served as a stirring symbol of street-fighting, like the waving of a well-known gonfalon. And the first sign that fire was ready to burst out was something as rapid as a little leaping tongue of flame; it was an act of the conjurer's impish lad Lollo, who was dancing and jeering in front of the ingenuous boys that made the majority of the crowd. Lollo had no great compassion for the prisoners, but being conscious of an excellent knife which was his unfailing companion, it had seemed to him from the first that to jump forward, cut a rope, and leap back again before the soldier who held it could use his weapon, would be an amusing and dexterous piece of mischief. And now, when the people began to hoot and jostle more vigorously, Lollo felt that his moment was come: he was close to the eldest prisoner; in an instant he had cut the cord.

"Run, old one!" he piped in the prisoner's ear, as soon as the cord was in two; and himself set the example of running as if he were helped along with wings, like a scared fowl.

The prisoner's sensations were not too slow for him to seize the opportunity; the idea of escape had been continually present with him, and he had gathered fresh hope from the temper of the crowd. He ran at once; but his speed would hardly have sufficed for him if the Florentines had not instantaneously rushed between him and his captor. He ran on into the Piazza, but he quickly heard the tramp of feet behind him, for the other two prisoners had been released, and the soldiers were struggling and fighting their way after them, in such tardigrade fashion as their hoof-shaped shoes would allow — impeded, but not very resolutely attacked, by the people. One of the two younger prisoners turned up the Borgo di San Lorenzo, and thus made a partial diversion of the hubbub; but the main struggle was still towards the Piazza, where all eyes were turned on it with alarmed curiosity. The cause could not be precisely guessed, for the French dress was screened by the impending crowd.

"An escape of prisoners," said Lorenzo Tornabuoni, as he and his party turned round just against the steps of the Duomo, and saw a prisoner rushing by them. "The people are not content with having emptied the Bargello the other day. If there is no other authority in sight they must fall on the *sbirri* and secure freedom to thieves. Ah! there is a French soldier; that is more serious."

The soldier he saw was struggling along on the north side of
the Piazza, but the object of his pursuit had taken the other
direction.   That object was the eldest prisoner, who had wheeled
round the Baptistery and was running towards the Duomo, de-
termined to take refuge in that sanctuary rather than trust to
his speed.   But in mounting the steps, his foot received a shock;
he was precipitated towards the group of signori, whose backs
were turned to him, and was only able to recover his balance as
he clutched one of them by the arm.

It was Tito Melema who felt that clutch.   He turned his head,
and saw the face of his adoptive father, Baldassarre Calvo, close
to his own.

The two men looked at each other, silent as death: Baldas-
sarre, with dark fierceness and a tightening grip of the soiled
worn hands on the velvet-clad arm; Tito, with cheeks and lips
all bloodless, fascinated by terror.   It seemed a long while to
them — it was but a moment.

The first sound Tito heard was the short laugh of Piero di
Cosimo, who stood close by him and was the only person that
could see his face.

" Ha, ha! I know what a ghost should be now."

" This is another escaped prisoner," said Lorenzo Tornabuoni.
" Who is he, I wonder ? "

"*Some madman, surely*," said Tito.

He hardly knew how the words had come to his lips: there
are moments when our passions speak and decide for us, and we
seem to stand by and wonder.   They carry in them an inspira-
tion of crime, that in one instant does the work of premeditation.

The two men had not taken their eyes off each other, and it
seemed to Tito, when he had spoken, that some magical poison
had darted from Baldassarre's eyes, and that he felt it rushing
through his viens.   But the next instant the grasp on his arm
had relaxed, and Baldassarre had disappeared within the church.

«OH, MAY I JOIN THE CHOIR INVISIBLE»

OH, MAY I join the choir invisible
    Of those immortal dead who live again
        In minds made better by their presence; live
In pulses stirred to generosity,
In deeds of daring rectitude, in scorn
For miserable aims that end with self,
In thoughts sublime that pierce the night like stars,
And with their mild persistence urge man's search
To vaster issues.

            So to live is heaven:
To make undying music in the world,
Breathing as beauteous order, that controls
With growing sway the growing life of man.
So we inherit that sweet purity
For which we struggled, failed, and agonized,
With widening retrospect that bred despair.
Rebellious flesh that would not be subdued,
A vicious parent shaming still its child,—
Poor anxious penitence,— is quick dissolved;
Its discords, quenched by meeting harmonies,
Die in the large and charitable air;
And all our rarer, better, truer self,
That sobbed religiously in yearning song,
That watched to ease the burthen of the world,
Laboriously tracing what must be,
And what may yet be better — saw within
A worthier image for the sanctuary,
And shaped it forth before the multitude
Divinely human, raising worship so
To higher reverence more mixed with love —
That better self shall live till human Time
Shall fold its eyelids, and the human sky
Be gathered like a scroll within the tomb
Unread for ever.

            This is life to come,
Which martyred men have made more glorious
For us who strive to follow. May I reach
That purest heaven; be to other souls
The cup of strength in some great agony;
Enkindle generous ardor; feed pure love;
Beget the smiles that have no cruelty—

Be the sweet presence of a good diffused,
And in diffusion even more intense.
So shall I join the choir invisible
Whose music is the gladness of the world.

R. W. EMERSON.

RALPH WALDO EMERSON

(1803–1882)

BY RICHARD GARNETT

NOTEWORTHY also," says Carlyle, "and serviceable for the progress of this same Individual, wilt thou find his subdivision into Generations."

It is indeed the fact that the course of human history admits of being marked off into periods, which, from their average duration and the impulse communicated to them by those who enter upon adolescence along with them, may be fitly denominated generations, especially when their opening and closing are signalized by great events which serve as historical landmarks. No such event, indeed, short of the Day of Judgment or a universal deluge, can serve as an absolute line of demarcation; nothing can be more certain than that history and human life are a perpetual Becoming; and that, although the progress of development is frequently so startling and unforeseen as to evoke the poet's exclamation,—

> "New endless growth surrounds on every side,
> Such as we deemed not earth could ever bear,"—

this growth is but development after all. The association of historical periods with stages in the mental development of man is nevertheless too convenient to be surrendered; the vision is cleared and the grasp strengthened by the perception of a well-defined era in American history, commencing with the election of Andrew Jackson to the Presidency in 1828 and closing with the death of Abraham Lincoln in 1865,— a period exactly corresponding with one in English history measured from the death of Lord Liverpool, the typical representative of a bygone political era in the prime of other years, and that of Lord Palmerston, another such representative, in the latter. The epoch thus bounded almost precisely corresponds to the productive period of the two great men who, more than any contemporaries, have stood in the conscious attitude of teachers of their age. With such men as Tennyson and Browning, vast as their influence has been, the primary impulse has not been didactic, but artistic; Herbert Spencer, George Eliot, Matthew Arnold, and others, have been chiefly operative upon the succeeding generation; Mill and the elder Newman rather address special classes than the people at

large; and Ruskin and Kingsley would have willingly admitted that
however eloquent the expression of their teaching, its originality
mainly consisted in the application of Carlyle's ideas to subjects
beyond Carlyle's range. Carlyle and Emerson, therefore, stand forth
like Goethe and Schiller as the Dioscuri of their period; the two men
to whom beyond others its better minds looked for guidance, and
who had the largest share in forming the minds from which the suc-
ceeding generation was to take its complexion. Faults and errors
they had; but on the whole it may be said that nations have rarely
been more fortunate in their instructors than the two great English-
speaking peoples during the age of Carlyle and Emerson. Of Carlyle
this is not the place to speak further; but writing on Emerson, it
will be necessary to exhibit what we conceive to have been the spe-
cial value of his teaching; and to attempt some description of the
man himself, in indication of the high place claimed for him.

It has been said of some great man of marked originality that he
was the sole voice among many echoes. This cannot be said of
Emerson; his age was by no means deficient in original voices. But
his may be said with truth to have been the chief verbal utterance
in an age of authorship. It is a trite remark, that many of the men
of thought whose ideas have most influenced the world have shown
little inclination for literary composition. The president of a London
freethinking club in Goldsmith's time supposed himself to be in pos-
session of the works of Socrates, no less than of those of "Tully and
Cicero," but no other trace of their existence has come to light.
Had Emerson lived in any age but his own, it is doubtful whether,
any more than Socrates, he would have figured as an author. "I
write," he tells Carlyle, "with very little system, and as far as
regards composition, with most fragmentary result—paragraphs in-
comprehensible, each sentence an infinitely repellent particle." We
also hear of his going forth into the woods to hunt a thought as a
boy might hunt a butterfly, except that the thought had flown with
him from home, and that his business was not so much to capture it
as to materialize it and make it tangible. This peculiarity serves to
classify Emerson among the ancient sages, men like Socrates and
Buddha, whose instructions were not merely oral but unmethodical
and unsystematic; who spoke as the casual emergency of the day
dictated, and left their observations to be collected by their disciples.
An excellent plan in so far as it accomplishes the endowment of
the sage's word with his own individuality; exceptionable when a
doubt arises whether the utterance belongs to the master or the dis-
ciple, and in the case of diametrically opposite versions, whether
Socrates has been represented more truly by the prose of Xenophon
or the poetry of Plato. We may be thankful that the spirit of Emer-
son's age, and the exigencies of his own affairs, irresistibly impelled

him to write: nevertheless the fact remains that with him Man
Thinking is not so much Man Writing as Man Speaking, and that
although the omnipotent machinery of the modern social system
caught him too, and forced him into line with the rest, we have in
him a nearer approach to the voice, apart from the disturbing and
modifying habits of literary composition, than in any other eminent
modern thinker. This annuls one of the most weighty criticisms
upon Emerson, so long as he is regarded merely as an author,—his
want of continuity, and consequent want of logic. Had he attempted
to establish a philosophical system, this would have been fatal.
But such an undertaking is of all things furthest from his thoughts.
He does not seek to demonstrate, he announces. Ideas have come to
him which, as viewed by the inward light, appear important and
profitable. He brings these forward to be tested by the light of
other men. He does not seek to connect these ideas together, except
in so far as their common physiognomy bespeaks their common par-
entage. Nor does he seek to fortify them by reasoning, or subject
them to any test save the faculty by which the unprejudiced soul
discerns good from evil. If his jewel will scratch glass, it is suffi-
ciently evinced a diamond.

It follows that although Emerson did not write most frequently
or best in verse, he is, as regards the general constitution of his
intellect, rather to be classed with poets than with philosophers.
Poetry cannot indeed dispense with the accurate observation of
nature and mankind, but poetic genius essentially depends on intu-
ition and inspiration. There is no gulf between the philosopher and
the poet; some of the greatest of poets have also been among the
most powerful of reasoners; but their claim to poetical rank would
not have been impaired if their ratiocination had been ever so illogi-
cal. Similarly, a great thinker may have no more taste for poetry
than was vouchsafed to Darwin or the elder Mill, without any im-
peachment of his power of intellect. The two spheres of action are
fundamentally distinct, though the very highest geniuses, such as
Shakespeare and Goethe, have sometimes almost succeeded in making
them appear as one. To determine to which of them a man actually
belongs, we must look beyond the externalities of literary form, and
inquire whether he obtains his ideas by intuition, or by observation
and reflection. No mind will be either entirely intuitive or entirely
reflective, but there will usually be a decided inclination to one or
other of the processes; and in the comparatively few cases in which
thoughts and feelings seem to come to it unconsciously, as leaves to
a tree, we may consider that we have a poet, though perhaps not a
writer of poetry. If indeed the man writes at all, he will very
probably write prose, but this prose will be impregnated with poetic

quality. From this point of view we are able to set Emerson much higher than if we regarded him simply as a teacher. He is greater as the American Wordsworth than as the American Carlyle. We shall understand his position best by comparing him with other men of genius who are poets too, but not pre-eminently so. In beauty of language and power of imagination, John Henry Newman and James Martineau, though they have written little in verse, yield to few poets. But throughout all their writings the didactic impulse is plainly the preponderating one, their poetry merely auxiliary and ornamental; hence they are not reckoned among poets. With Emerson the case is reversed: the revealer is first in him, the reasoner second; oral speech is his most congenial form of expression, and he submits to appear in print because the circumstances of his age render print the most effectual medium for the dissemination of his thought. It will be observed that whenever possible he resorts to the medium of oration or lecture; it may be further remarked that his essays, often originally delivered as lectures, are very like his discourses, and his discourses very like his essays. In neither, so far as regards the literary form of the entire composition, distinguished from the force and felicity of individual sentences, can he be considered as a classic model. The essay need not be too severely logical, yet a just conception of its nature requires a more harmonious proportion and more symmetrical construction, as well as a more consistent and intelligent direction towards a single definite end, than we usually find in Emerson. The orator is less easy to criticize than the essayist, for oratory involves an element of personal magnetism which resists all critical analysis. Hence posterity frequently reverses (or rather seems to reverse, for the decision upon a speech mutilated of voice and action cannot be really conclusive) the verdicts of contemporaries upon oratory. "What will our descendants think of the Parliamentary oratory of our age?" asked a contemporary of Burke's, "when they are told that in his own time this man was accounted neither the first, nor the second, nor even the third speaker?" Transferred to the tribunal of the library, Burke's oratory bears away the palm from Pitt and Fox and Sheridan; yet, unless we had heard the living voices of them all, it would be unsafe for us to challenge the contemporary verdict. We cannot say, with the lover in Goethe, that the word printed appears dull and soulless, but it certainly wants much which conduced to the efficacy of the word spoken:—

> «Ach wie traurig sieht in Lettern,
> Schwarz auf weiss, das Lied mich an,
> Das aus deinem Mund vergöttern,
> Das ein Herz zerreissen kann!»

Emerson's orations are no less delightful and profitable reading than his essays, so long as they can be treated as his essays were intended to be treated when they came into print; that is, read deliberately, with travelings backward when needed, and frequent pauses of thought. But if we consider them as discourses to be listened to, we shall find some difficulty in reconciling their popularity and influence with their apparent disconnectedness, and some reason to apprehend that, occasional flashes of epigram excepted, they must speedily have passed from the minds of the hearers. The apparent defect was probably remedied in delivery by the magnetic power of the speaker; not that sort of power which "wields at will the fierce democracy," but that which convinces the hearer that he is listening to a message from a region not as yet accessible to himself. The impassioned orator usually provokes the suspicion that he is speaking from a brief. Not so Emerson: above all other speakers he inspires the confidence that he declares a thing to be, not because he wishes, but because he perceives it to be so. His quiet, unpretending, but perfectly unembarrassed manner, as of a man with a message which he simply delivers and goes away, must have greatly aided to supply the absence of vigorous reasoning and skillful oratorical construction. We could not expect a spirit commissioned to teach us to condescend to such methods; and Emerson's discourse, whether in oration or essay, though by no means deficient in human feeling nor of the "blessed Glendoveer" order, frequently does sound like that of a being from another sphere, simply because he derived his ideas from a higher world; as must always be the case with the man of spiritual, not of course with the man of practical genius. It matters nothing whether this is really so, or whether what wears the aspect of imparted revelation is but a fortifying of the natural eye, qualifying it to look a little deeper than neighboring eyes into things around. In either case the person so endowed stands a degree nearer to the essential truth of things than his fellows; and the consciousness of the fact, transpiring through his personality, gives him a weight which might otherwise seem inexplicable. Nothing can be more surprising than the deference with which the learned and intelligent contemporaries of the humble and obscure Spinoza resort to his judgment before he has so much as written a book.

This estimate of Emerson as an American Wordsworth, one who like Wordsworth not merely enforced but practically demonstrated the proposition that

> "One impulse from a vernal wood
>   May teach you more of man,
> Of moral evil and of good,
>   Than all the sages can,"

is controverted by many who can see in him nothing but a polisher
and stringer of epigrammatic sayings. It is impossible to argue with
any who cannot recognize the deep vitality of 'Nature,' of the two
series of Essays first published, and of most of the early orations and
discourses; but it may be conceded that Emerson's fountain of inspira-
tion was no more perennial than Wordsworth's, and that in his latter
years his gift of epigrammatic statement enabled him to avoid both
the Scylla and the Charybdis of men of genius whose fount of
inspiration has run low. In some such cases, such as Wordsworth's,
the author simply goes on producing, with less and less geniality at
every successive effort. In others, such as Browning's, he escapes
inanity by violent exaggeration of his characteristic mannerisms.
Neither of these remarks applies to Emerson: he does not, in ceasing
to be original, become insipid, nor can it be said that he is any more
mannered at the last than at the first. This is a clear proof that his
peculiarity of speech is not mannerism but manner; that consequently
he is not an artificial writer, and that, since the treatment of his
themes as he has chosen to treat them admits of no compromise
between nature and rhetoric, he has the especial distinction of sim-
plicity where simplicity is difficult and rare. That such is the case
will appear from an examination of his earlier and more truly pro-
phetic writings.

Of these, the first in importance as in time is the tract 'Nature,'
commenced in 1833, rewritten, completed, and published in 1836.
Of all Emerson's writings this is the most individual, and the most
adapted for a general introduction to his ideas. These ideas are
not in fact peculiar to him; and yet the little book is one of the
most original ever written, and one of those most likely to effect an
intellectual revolution in the mind capable of apprehending it. The
reason is mainly the intense vitality of the manner, and the transla-
tion of abstract arguments into concrete shapes of witchery and
beauty. It contains scarcely a sentence that is not beautiful,—not
with the cold beauty of art, but with the radiance and warmth of feel-
ing. Its dominant note is rapture, like the joy of one who has found
an enchanted realm, or who has convinced himself that old stories
deemed too beautiful to be true are true indeed. Yet it is exempt
from extravagance, the splendor of the language is chastened by
taste, and the gladness and significance of the author's announce-
ments would justify an even more ardent enthusiasm. They may be
briefly summed up as the statements that Nature is not mechanical,
but vital; that the Universe is not dead, but alive; that God is not
remote, but omnipresent. There was of course no novelty in these
assertions, nor can Emerson bring them by a hair's-breadth nearer
demonstration than they had always been. He simply re-states them

in a manner entirely his own, and with a charm not perhaps surpassing that with which others had previously invested them, but peculiar and dissimilar. Everything really Emersonian in Emerson's teaching may be said to spring out of this little book: so copious, however, were the corollaries deducible from principles apparently so simple, that the flowers veiled the tree; and precious as the tract is, as the first and purest draught of the new wine, it is not the most practically efficient of his works, and might probably have passed unperceived if it had not been reinforced by a number of auxiliary compositions, some produced under circumstances which could not fail to provoke wide discussion and consequent notoriety. The principles unfolded in 'Nature' might probably have passed with civil acquiescence if Emerson had been content with the mere statement; but he insisted on carrying them logically out, and this could not be done without unsettling every school of thought at the time prevalent in America. The Divine omnipresence, for example, was admitted in words by all except materialists and anti-theists; but if, as Emerson maintained, this involved the conception of the Universe as a Divine incarnation, this in its turn involved an optimistic view of the universal scheme totally inconsistent with the Calvinism still dominant in American theology. If all existence was a Divine emanation, no part of it could be more sacred than another part,—which at once abolished the mystic significance of religious ceremonies so dear to the Episcopalians; while the immediate contact of the Universe with the Deity was no less incompatible with the miraculous interferences on which Unitarianism reposed its faith. Such were some of the most important negative results of Emerson's doctrines; in their positive aspect, by asserting the identity of natural and spiritual laws, they invested the former with the reverence hitherto accorded only to the latter, and restored to a mechanical and prosaic society the piety with which men in the infancy of history had defied the forces of Nature. Substantially, except for the absence of any definite relation to literary art, Emerson's mission was very similar to Wordsworth's; but by natural temperament and actual situation he wanted the thousand links which bound Wordsworth to the past, and eventually made the sometime innovator the patron of a return towards the Middle Ages.

Emerson had no wish to regress, and, almost alone among thinkers who have reached an advanced age, betrays no symptom of reaction throughout the whole of his career. The reason may be, that his scrupulous fairness and frank conceptions to the Conservative cast of thought had left him nothing to retract or atone for. He seems to have started on his journey through life with his Conservatism and Liberalism ready made up, taking with him just as much of either as he wanted. This is especially manifest in the discourse 'The Conservative' (1841), in which he deliberately weighs conservative against progressive tendencies, impersonates each in an imaginary interlocutor, and endeavors to display their respective justification and shortcomings. Nothing can be more rigidly equitable or more thoroughly sane than his estimate; and as the issues between conservatism and reform have broadened and deepened, time has only added to its value. It is a perfect manual for thoughtful citizens, desirous of understanding the questions that underlie party issues, and is especially to be commended to young and generous minds, liable to misguidance in proportion to their generosity.

This celebrated discourse is one of a group including one still more celebrated, the address to the graduating class of Divinity College, Cambridge, published as 'The Christian Teacher' (1838). This, says Mr. Cabot, seems to have been struck off at a heat, which perhaps accounts for its nearer approach than any of his other addresses to the standard of what is usually recognized as eloquence. Eloquent in a sense Emerson usually was, but here is something which could transport a fit audience with enthusiasm. It also possessed the power of awakening the keenest antagonism; but censure has long since died away, and nothing that Emerson wrote has been more thoroughly adopted into the creed of those with whom external observances and material symbols find no place. Equally epoch-making in a different way was the oration on 'Man Thinking, or the American Scholar' (1837), entitled by Dr. Holmes "our intellectual Declaration of Independence," and of which Mr. Lowell says: "We were socially and intellectually moored to English thought, till Emerson cut the cable and gave us a chance at the dangers and glories of blue water." In these three great discourses, and in a less measure in 'The Transcendentalist' and 'Man the Reformer' (both in 1841), America may boast of possessing works of the first class, which could have been produced in no other country, and which — even though, in Emerson's own phrase, wider circles should come to be drawn around them — will remain permanent landmarks in intellectual history.

These discourses may be regarded as Emerson's public proclamations of his opinions; but he is probably more generally known and more intimately beloved by the two unobtrusive volumes of Essays, originally prefaced for England by Carlyle. Most of these, indeed, were originally delivered as lectures, but to small audiences, and with little challenge to public attention. It may be doubted whether they would have succeeded as lectures but for the personal magnetism of the speaker; but their very defects aid them with the reader, who, once fascinated by their beauty of phrase and depth of spiritual

insight, imbibes their spirit all the more fully for his ceaseless effort
to mend their deficient logic with his own. Like Love in Dante's son-
net, Emerson enters into and blends with the reader, and his influ-
ence will often be found most potent where it is least acknowledged.
Each of the twenty may be regarded as a fuller working out of
some subject merely hinted at in 'Nature,'—statues, as it were, for
niches left vacant in the original edifice. The most important and
pregnant with thought are 'History,' where the same claim is pre-
ferred for history as for the material world, that it is not dead but
alive; 'Self-Reliance,' a most vigorous assertion of a truth which
Emerson was apt to carry to extremes,—the majesty of the individual
soul; 'Compensation,' an exposition of the universe as the incarnation
of unerring truth and absolute justice; 'Love,' full of beauty and
rapture, yet almost chilling to the young by its assertion of what is
nevertheless true, that even Love in its human semblance only sub-
serves ulterior ends; 'Circles,' the demonstration that this circum-
stance is no way peculiar to Love, that there can be nothing ultimate,
final, or unrelated to ulterior purpose,—nothing around which, in
Emersonian phrase, you cannot draw a circle; 'The Over-Soul,' a
prose hymn dedicated to an absolutely spiritual religion; 'The Poet,'
a celebration of Poetry as coextensive with Imagination, and in the
highest sense with Reason also; 'Experience' and 'Character,' valu-
able essays, but evincing that the poetical impulse was becoming
spent, and that Emerson's mind was more and more tending to ques-
tions of conduct. The least satisfactory of the essays is that on
'Art,' where he is only great on the negative side, Art's inevitable
limitations. The æsthetical faculty, which contemplates Beauty under
the restraints of Form, was evidently weak in him.

'Representative Men,' Emerson's next work of importance (1845),
shows that his parachute was descending; but he makes a highly suc-
cessful compromise by taking up original ideas as reflected in the
actions and thoughts of great typical men, one remove only from
originality of exposition on his own part. The treatment is neces-
sarily so partial as to exercise a distorting influence on his represent-
ation of the men themselves. Napoleon, for example, may have
been from a certain point of view the hero of the middle class, as
Emerson chooses to consider him; but he was much besides, which
cannot even be hinted at in a short lecture. The representation of
such a hero, nevertheless, whether the character precisely fitted Napo-
leon or not, is highly spirited and suggestive; and the same may be
said of the other lectures. That on Shakespeare is the least satisfy-
ing, the consummate art which is half Shakespeare's greatness making
little appeal to Emerson. He appears also at variance with himself
when he speaks of Shakespeare's existence as "obscure and profane,"

such a healthy, homely, unambitious life being precisely what he else-where extols as a model. The first lecture of the series, 'Uses of Great Men,' would seem to have whispered the message more vocifer-ously repeated by Walt Whitman.

Emerson was yet to write two books of worth, not illumed with "the light that never was on sea or land," but valuable complements to his more characteristic work, and important to mankind as an indisputable proof that a teacher need not be distrusted in ordinary things because he is a mystic and a poet. 'The Conduct of Life' (1851), far inferior to his earlier writings in inspiration, is yet one of the most popular and widely influential of his works because con-descending more nearly to the needs and intelligence of the average reader. It is not less truly Emersonian, less fully impregnated with his unique genius; but the themes discussed are less interesting, and the glory and the beauty of the diction are much subdued. Without it, we should have been in danger of regarding Emerson too exclu-sively as a transcendental seer, and ignoring the solid ground of good sense and practical sagacity from which the waving forests of his imagery drew their nutriment. It greatly promoted his fame and influence by coming into the hands of successive generations of readers who naturally inquired for his last book, found the author, with surprise, so much nearer their own intellectual position than they had been led to expect, and gradually extended the indorse-ment which they could not avoid according to the book, to the author himself. When the Reason and the Understanding have agreed to legitimate the pretensions of a speculative thinker, these may be con-sidered stable. Emerson insensibly took rank with the other Amer-ican institutions; it seemed natural to all, that without the retractation or modification of a syllable on his part, Harvard should in 1866 confer her highest honors upon him whose address to her Divinity School had aroused such fierce opposition in 1838. Emerson's views, being pure intuitions, rarely admitted of alteration in essence, though supple-ment or limitation might sometimes be found advisable. The Civil War, for instance, could not but convince him that in his zeal for the independence of the individual he had dangerously impaired the necessary authority of government. His attitude throughout this great contest was the ideal of self-sacrificing patriotism: in truth, it might be said of him, as of so few men of genius, that you could not find a situation for him, public or private, whose obligations he was not certain to fulfill. He had previously given proof of his insight into another nation by his 'English Traits,' mainly founded upon the visit he had paid to England in 1847–48: a book to be read with equal pleasure and profit by the nation of which and by the nation for which it was written; while its insight, sanity, and kindliness justify what has been said on occasion of another of Emerson's writings: « The ideologist judges the man of action more shrewdly and justly than the man of action judges the ideologist.» This was the secret of Napoleon's bitter animosity to «ideologists»: he felt instinctively that the man of ideas could see into him and through him, and recognize and declare his place in the scheme of the universe as an astronomer might a planet's. He would have wished to be an incalculable, original, elemental force; and it vexed him to feel that he was something whose course could be mapped and whose constitution defined by a mere mortal like a Coleridge or a De Staël, who could treat him like the incarnate Thought he was, and show him, as Emerson showed the banker, « that he also was a phantom walking and working amid phantoms, and that he need only ask a question or two beyond his daily questions to find his solid universe proving dim and impalpable before his sense.»

The later writings of Emerson, though exhibiting few or no traces of mental decay, are in general repetitions or at least confirmations of what had once been announcements and discoveries. This can scarcely be otherwise when the mind's productions are derived from its own stuff and substance. Emerson's contemporary Longfellow could renovate and indeed augment his poetical power by resort in his old age to Italy; but change of environment brings no reinforcement of energy to the speculative thinker. Events however may come to his aid; and when Emerson was called before the people by a momentous incident like the death of President Lincoln, he rose fully to the height of the occasion. His last verses, also, are among his best. We have spoken of him as primarily and above all things a poet; but his claim to that great distinction is to be sought rather in the poetical spirit which informs all his really inspired writings, than in the comparatively restricted region of rhyme and metre. It might have been otherwise. Many of his detached passages are the very best things in verse yet written in America: but though a maker, he is not a fashioner. The artistic instinct is deficient in him; he is seldom capable of combining his thoughts into a harmonious whole. No one's expression is better when he aims at conveying a single thought with gnomic terseness, as in the mottoes to his essays; few are more obscure when he attempts continuous composition. Sometimes, as in the admirable stanzas on the Bunker Hill dedication, the subject has enforced the due clearness and compression of thought; sometimes, as in the glorious lines beginning «Not from a vain or shallow thought,» he is guided unerringly by a divine rapture; in one instance at least, ' The Rhodora,' where he is writing of beauty, the instinct of beauty has given his lines the symmetry as well as the sparkle of the diamond. Could he have always written like this, he would have been supreme among American poets in metre; as it is, comparison seems unfair both to him and to them.

What we have to learn from Emerson is chiefly the Divine immanence in the world, with all its corollaries; no discovery of his, but re-stated by him in the fashion most suitable to his age, and with a cogency and attractiveness rivaled by no contemporary. If we tried to sum up his message in a phrase, we might perhaps find this in Keats's famous 'Beauty is Truth, Truth Beauty'; only, while Keats was evidently more concerned for Beauty than for Truth, Emerson held an impartial balance. These are with him the tests of each other: whatever is really true is also beautiful, whatever is really beautiful is also true. Hence his especial value to a world whose more refined spirits are continually setting up types of æsthetic beauty which must needs be delusive, as discordant with beauty contemplated under the aspect of morality; while the mass never think of bringing social and political arrangements to the no less infallible test of conformity to an ideally beautiful standard. Hence the seeming idealist is of all men the most practical; and Emerson's gospel of beauty should be especially precious to a country like his own, where circumstances must for so long tell in favor of the more material phases of civilization. Even more important is that aspect of his teaching which deals with the unalterableness of spiritual laws, the impossibility of evading Truth and Fact in the long run, or of wronging any one without at the same time wronging oneself. Happy would it be for the United States if Emerson's essay on 'Compensation' in particular could be impressed upon the conscience, where there is any, of every political leader; and interwoven with the very texture of the mind of every one who has a vote to cast at the polls!

The special adaptation of Emerson's teaching to the needs of America is, nevertheless, far from the greatest obligation under which he has laid his countrymen. His greatest service is to have embodied a specially American type of thought and feeling. It is the test of real greatness in a nation to be individual, to produce something in the world of intellect peculiar to itself and indefeasibly its own. Such intellectual growths were indeed to be found in America before Emerson's time, but they were not of the highest class. Franklin was a great sage, but his wisdom was worldly wisdom. Emerson gives us, in his own phrase, morality on fire with emotion,— the only morality which in the long run will really influence the heart of man. Man is after all too noble a being to be permanently actuated by enlightened selfishness; and when we compare Emerson with even so truly eminent a character as Franklin, we see, as he saw when he compared Carlyle with Johnson, how great a stride forward his country had taken in the mean time. But he could do for America what Carlyle could not do for Great Britain, for it was done already: he could and did create a type of wisdom especially national, as distinctive of the West as Buddha's of the East.

R. Garnett.

All the following citations from Emerson's works are reprinted by special arrangement with, and the kind permission of, Mr. Emerson's family, and Messrs. Houghton, Mifflin & Co., publishers, Boston, Mass.

THE TIMES

From the Lecture on 'The Times,' 1841

BUT the subject of the Times is not an abstract question. We talk of the world, but we mean a few men and women. If you speak of the age, you mean your own platoon of people, as Dante and Milton painted in colossal their platoons, and called them Heaven and Hell. In our idea of progress we do not go out of this personal picture. We do not think the sky will be bluer, or honey sweeter, or our climate more temperate, but only that our relation to our fellows will be simpler and happier. What is the reason to be given for this extreme attraction which *persons* have for us, but that they are the Age? They are the results of the Past; they are the heralds of the Future. They indicate — these witty, suffering, blushing, intimidating figures of the only race in which there are individuals or changes — how far on the Fate has gone, and what it drives at. As trees make scenery, and constitute the hospitality of the landscape, so persons are the world to persons. . . . These are the pungent instructors who thrill the heart of each of us, and make all other teaching formal and cold. How I follow them with aching heart, with pining desire! I count myself nothing before them. I would die for them with joy. They can do what they will with me. How they lash us with those tongues! How they make the tears start, make us blush and turn pale, and lap us in Elysium to soothing dreams and castles in the air! By tones of triumph, of dear love, by threats, by pride that freezes, these have the skill to make the world look bleak and inhospitable, or seem the nest of tenderness and joy. I do not wonder at the miracles which poetry attributes to the music of Orpheus, when I remember what I have experienced from the varied notes of the human voice. They are an incalculable energy which countervails all other forces in nature, because they are the channel of supernatural powers. There is no interest or institution so poor and withered but if a new strong man could be born into it he would immediately redeem and replace it. A personal ascendency,— that is the only fact much worth considering. I remember, some years ago, somebody shocked a circle of friends of order here in Boston, who supposed that our people were identified with their religious denominations, by declaring that an eloquent man — let him be of what sect soever — would be ordained at once in one of our metropolitan churches. To be sure he would; and not only in ours but in any church, mosque, or temple on the planet: but he must be eloquent, able to supplant our method and classification by the superior beauty of his own. Every fact we have was brought here by some person; and there is none that will not change and pass away before a person whose nature is broader than the person whom the fact in question represents. And so I find the Age walking about in happy and hopeful natures, in strong eyes and pleasant thoughts, and think I read it nearer and truer so than in the statute-book, or in the investments of capital, which rather celebrate with mournful music the obsequies of the last age. In the brain of a fanatic; in the wild hope of a mountain boy, called by city boys very ignorant, because they do not know what his hope has certainly apprised him shall be; in the love-glance of a girl; in the hair-splitting conscientiousness of some eccentric person who has found some new scruple to embarrass himself and his neighbors withal,— is to be found that which shall constitute the times to come, more than in the now organized and accredited oracles. For whatever is affirmative and now advancing contains it. I think that only is real which men love and rejoice in; not what they tolerate, but what they choose; what they embrace and avow, and not the things which chill, benumb, and terrify them.

And so why not draw for these times a portrait gallery? Let us paint the painters. Whilst the daguerreotypist, with camera-obscura and silver plate, begins now to traverse the land, let us set up our camera also, and let the sun paint the people. Let us paint the agitator, and the man of the old school, and the member of Congress, and the college professor, the formidable editor, the priest, and reformer, the contemplative girl, and the fair aspirant for fashion and opportunities, the woman of the world who has tried and knows — let us examine how well she knows. Could we indicate the indicators, indicate those who most accurately represent every good and evil tendency of the general mind, in the just order which they take on this canvas of time, so that all witnesses should recognize a spiritual law, as each well-known form flitted for a moment across the wall, we should have a series of sketches which would report to the next ages the color and quality of ours.

Certainly I think if this were done there would be much to admire as well as to condemn; souls of as lofty a port as any in Greek or Roman fame might appear; men of great heart, of strong hand, and of persuasive speech; subtle thinkers, and men of wide sympathy, and an apprehension which looks over all history and everywhere recognizes its own. To be sure, there will be fragments and hints of men, more than enough; bloated promises, which end in nothing or little. And then, truly great men, but with some defect in their composition which neutralizes their whole force. Here is a Damascus blade, such as you may search through nature in vain to parallel, laid up on the shelf in some village to rust and ruin. And how many seem not quite available for that idea which they represent! Now and then comes a bolder spirit, I should rather say, a more surrendered soul, more informed and led by God, which is much in advance of the rest, quite beyond their sympathy, but predicts what shall soon be the general fullness; as when we stand by the sea-shore, whilst the tide is coming in, a wave comes up the beach far higher than any foregoing one, and recedes; and for a long while none comes up to that mark; but after some time the whole sea is there and beyond it.

FRIENDSHIP

FRIENDSHIP may be said to require natures so rare and costly, each so well tempered and so happily adapted, and withal so circumstanced (for even in that particular, a poet says, love demands that the parties be altogether paired), that its satisfaction can very seldom be assured. It cannot subsist in its perfection, say some of those who are learned in this warm lore of the heart, betwixt more than two. I am not quite so strict in my terms, perhaps because I have never known so high a fellowship as others. I please my imagination more with a circle of godlike men and women variously related to each other, and between whom subsists a lofty intelligence. But I find this law of *one to one* peremptory for conversation, which is the practice and consummation of friendship. Do not mix waters too much. The best mix as ill as good and bad. You shall have very useful and cheering discourse at several times with two several men, but let all three of you come together and you shall not have one new and hearty word. Two may talk and one may hear, but three cannot take part in a conversation of the most sincere and searching sort. In good company there is never such discourse between two, across the table, as takes place when you leave them alone. In good company the individuals merge their egotism into a social soul exactly coextensive with the several consciousnesses there present. . . .

Unrelated men give little joy to each other, will never suspect the latent powers of each. We talk sometimes of a great talent for conversation, as if it were a permanent property in some individuals. Conversation is an evanescent relation,— no more. A man is reputed to have thought and eloquence; he cannot, for all that, say a word to his cousin or his uncle. They accuse his silence with as much reason as they would blame the insignificance of a dial in the shade. In the sun it will mark the hour. Among those who enjoy his thought he will regain his tongue.

Friendship requires that rare mean betwixt likeness and unlikeness that piques each with the presence of power and of consent in the other party. Let me be alone to the end of the world, rather than that my friend should overstep, by a word or a look, his real sympathy. I am equally balked by antagonism and by compliance. Let him not cease an instant to be himself. The only joy I have in his being mine, is that the *not mine* is *mine*. I hate, where I looked for a manly furtherance or at least a manly resistance, to find a mush of concession. Better be a nettle in the side of your friend than his echo. The condition which high friendship demands is ability to do without it. That high office requires great and sublime parts. There must be very two before there can be very one. Let it be an alliance of two large, formidable natures, mutually beheld, mutually feared, before yet they recognize the deep identity which beneath these disparities unites them.

He only is fit for this society who is magnanimous; who is sure that greatness and goodness are always economy; who is not swift to intermeddle with his fortunes. Let him not intermeddle with this. Leave to the diamond its ages to grow, nor expect to accelerate the births of the eternal. Friendship demands a religious treatment. We talk of choosing our friends, but friends are self-elected. Reverence is a great part of it. Treat your friend as a spectacle. Of course he has merits that are not yours, and that you cannot honor if you must needs hold him close to your person. Stand aside; give those merits room; let them mount and expand. Are you the friend of your friend's buttons, or of his thought? To a great heart he will still be a stranger in a thousand particulars, that he may come near in the holiest ground. Leave it to girls and boys to regard a friend as property, and to such a short and all-confounding pleasure instead of the noblest benefit.

Let us buy our entrance to this guild by a long probation. Why should we desecrate noble and beautiful souls by intruding on them? Why insist on rash personal relations with your friend? Why go to his house, or know his mother and brother and sisters? Why be visited by him at your own? Are these things material to our covenant? Leave this touching and clawing. Let him be to me a spirit. A message, a thought, a sincerity, a glance from him, I want; but not news, nor pottage. I can get politics and chat and neighborly conveniences from cheaper companions. Should not the society of my friend be to me poetic, pure, universal, and great as nature itself? Ought I to feel that our tie is profane in comparison with yonder bar of cloud that sleeps on the horizon, or that clump of waving grass that divides the brook? Let us not vilify, but raise it to that standard. That great defying eye, that scornful beauty of his mien and action, do not pique yourself on reducing, but rather fortify and enhance. Worship his superiorities; wish him not less by a thought, but hoard and tell them all. Let him be to thee forever a sort of beautiful enemy, untamable, devoutly revered, and not a trivial conveniency to be soon outgrown and cast aside. The hues of the opal, the light of the diamond, are not to be seen if the eye is too near. To my friend I write a

letter and from him I receive a letter. That seems to you a
little. It suffices me. It is a spiritual gift, worthy of him to
give and of me to receive. It profanes nobody. In these warm
lines the heart will trust itself, as it will not to the tongue, and
pour out the prophecy of a godlier existence than all the annals
of heroism have yet made good. . . .

The higher the style we demand of friendship, of course the
less easy to establish it with flesh and blood. We walk alone in
the world. Friends such as we desire are dreams and fables.
But a sublime hope cheers ever the faithful heart, that elsewhere,
in other regions of the universal power, souls are now acting,
enduring, and daring, which can love us and which we can love.
We may congratulate ourselves that the period of nonage, of
follies, of blunders and of shame, is passed in solitude, and when
we are finished men we shall grasp heroic hands in heroic hands.
Only be admonished by what you already see, not to strike leagues
of friendship with cheap persons, where no friendship can be. Our
impatience betrays us into rash and foolish alliances which no
god attends. By persisting in your path, though you forfeit the
little you gain the great.

NATURE

THERE are days which occur in this climate, at almost any sea-
son of the year, wherein the world reaches its perfection;
when the air, the heavenly bodies, and the earth, make a
harmony, as if nature would indulge her offspring; when, in these
bleak upper sides of the planet, nothing is to desire that we
have heard of the happiest latitudes, and we bask in the shining
hours of Florida and Cuba; when everything that has life gives
sign of satisfaction, and the cattle that lie on the ground seem
to have great and tranquil thoughts. These halcyons may be
looked for with a little more assurance in that pure October
weather which we distinguish by the name of the Indian Sum-
mer. The day, immeasurably long, sleeps over the broad hills
and warm wide fields. To have lived through all its sunny
hours seems longevity enough. The solitary places do not seem
quite lonely. At the gates of the forest, the surprised man of
the world is forced to leave his city estimates of great and
small, wise and foolish. The knapsack of custom falls off his
back with the first step he takes into these precincts. Here is

sanctity which shames our religions, and reality which discredits our heroes. Here we find nature to be the circumstance which dwarfs every other circumstance, and judges like a god all men that come to her. We have crept out of our close and crowded houses into the night and morning, and we see what majestic beauties daily wrap us in their bosom. How willingly we would escape the barriers which render them comparatively impotent, escape the sophistication and second thought, and suffer nature to intrance us. The tempered light of the woods is like a per- petual morning, and is stimulating and heroic. The anciently reported spells of these places creep on us. The stems of pines, hemlocks, and oaks almost gleam like iron on the excited eye. The incommunicable trees begin to persuade us to live with them, and quit our life of solemn trifles. Here no history, or church, or state, is interpolated on the divine sky and the immortal year. How easily we might walk onward into the opening landscape, absorbed by new pictures and by thoughts fast succeeding each other, until by degrees the recollection of home was crowded out of the mind, all memory obliterated by the tyranny of the present, and we were led in triumph by nature.

These enchantments are medicinal; they sober and heal us. These are plain pleasures, kindly and native to us. We come to our own, and make friends with matter which the ambitious chatter of the schools would persuade us to despise. We never can part with it; the mind loves its old home: as water to our thirst, so is the rock, the ground, to our eyes and hands and feet. It is firm water; it is cold flame: what health, what affinity! Ever an old friend, ever like a dear friend and brother when we chat affectedly with strangers, comes in this honest face, and takes a grave liberty with us, and shames us out of our nonsense. Cities give not the human senses room enough. We go out daily and nightly to feed the eyes on the horizon, and require so much scope, just as we need water for our bath. There are all degrees of natural influence, from these quarantine powers of nature, up to her dearest and gravest ministrations to the imagination and the soul. There is the bucket of cold water from the spring, the wood fire to which the chilled traveler rushes for safety,—and there is the sublime moral of autumn and of noon. We nestle in nature, and draw our living as parasites from her roots and grains; and we receive glances from the heavenly bodies, which

call us to solitude, and foretell the remotest future. The blue
zenith is the point in which romance and reality meet. I think
if we should be rapt away into all that we dream of heaven, and
should converse with Gabriel and Uriel, the upper sky would be
all that would remain of our furniture.

It seems as if the day was not wholly profane, in which we
have given heed to some natural object. The fall of snowflakes
in a still air, preserving to each crystal its perfect form; the
blowing of sleet over a wide sheet of water, and over plains; the
waving rye field; the mimic waving of acres of houstonia, whose
innummerable florets whiten and ripple before the eye; the re-
flections of trees and flowers in glassy lakes; the musical steam-
ing odorous south wind, which converts all trees to wind-harps;
the crackling and spurting of hemlock in the flames, or of pine
logs, which yield glory to the walls and faces in the sitting-
room,—these are the music and pictures of the most ancient
religion. My house stands in low land, with limited outlook, and
on the skirt of the village. But I go with my friend to the
shore of our little river, and with one stroke of the paddle I
leave the village politics and personalities,—yes, and the world of
villages and personalities,—behind, and pass into a delicate realm
of sunset and moonlight, too bright almost for spotted man to
enter without novitiate and probation. We penetrate bodily this
incredible beauty; we dip our hands in this painted element; our
eyes are bathed in these lights and forms. A holiday, a villeggi-
atura, a royal revel, the proudest, most heart-rejoicing festival
that valor and beauty, power and taste, ever decked and enjoyed,
establishes itself on the instant. These sunset clouds, these deli-
cately emerging stars, with their private and ineffable glances,
signify it and proffer it. I am taught the poorness of our inven-
tion, the ugliness of towns and palaces. Art and luxury have
early learned that they must work as enchantment and sequel to
this original beauty. I am over-instructed for my return. Hence-
forth I shall be hard to please. I cannot go back to toys. I am
grown expensive and sophisticated. I can no longer live without
elegance; but a countryman shall be my master of revels. He
who knows the most, he who knows what sweets and virtues are
in the ground, the waters, the plants, the heavens, and how to
come at these enchantments, is the rich and royal man. Only
as far as the masters of the world have called in nature to their
aid, can they reach the height of magnificence.

COMPENSATION

A MAN cannot speak but he judges himself. With his will or against his will, he draws his portrait to the eye of his companions by every word. Every opinion reacts on him who utters it. It is a thread-ball thrown at a mark, but the other end remains in the thrower's bag. Or rather, it is a harpoon thrown at the whale, unwinding, as it flies, a coil of cord in the boat; and if the harpoon is not good, or not well thrown, it will go nigh to cut the steersman in twain or to sink the boat.

You cannot do wrong without suffering wrong. "No man had ever a point of pride that was not injurious to him," said Burke. The exclusive in fashionable life does not see that he excludes himself from enjoyment, in the attempt to appropriate it. The exclusionist in religion does not see that he shuts the door of heaven on himself, in striving to shut out others. Treat men as pawns and ninepins, and you shall suffer as well as they. If you leave out their heart, you shall lose your own. The senses would make things of all persons; of women, of children, of the poor. The vulgar proverb "I will get it from his purse or get it from his skin," is sound philosophy.

All infractions of love and equity in our social relations are speedily punished. They are punished by fear. Whilst I stand in simple relations to my fellow-man, I have no displeasure in meeting him. We meet as water meets water, or as two currents of air mix,— with perfect diffusion and interpenetration of nature. But as soon as there is any departure from simplicity, and attempt at halfness, or good for me that is not good for him, my neighbor feels the wrong; he shrinks from me as far as I have shrunk from him; his eyes no longer seek mine; there is war between us; there is hate in him and fear in me.

All the old abuses in society, universal and particular, all unjust accumulations of property and power, are avenged in the same manner. Fear is an instructor of great sagacity, and the herald of all revolutions. One thing he teaches,— that there is rottenness where he appears. He is a carrion crow; and though you see not well what he hovers for, there is death somewhere. Our property is timid, our laws are timid, our cultivated classes are timid. Fear for ages has boded and mowed and gibbered over government and property. That obscene bird is not there for nothing. He indicates great wrongs which must be revised.

Of · the like nature is that expectation of change which instantly follows the suspension of our voluntary activity. The terror of cloudless noon, the emerald of Polycrates, the awe of prosperity, the instinct which leads every generous soul to impose on itself tasks of a noble asceticism and vicarious virtue, are the tremblings of the balance of justice through the heart and mind of man.

Experienced men of the world know very well that it is best to pay scot and lot as they go along, and that a man often pays dear for a small frugality. The borrower runs in his own debt. Has a man gained anything who has received a hundred favors and rendered none? Has he gained by borrowing, through indolence or cunning, his neighbor's wares, or horses, or money? There arises on the deed the instant acknowledgment of benefit on the one part and of debt on the other; that is, of superiority and inferiority. The transaction remains in the memory of himself and his neighbor, and every new transaction alters according to its nature their relation to each other. He may soon come to see that he had better have broken his own bones than to have ridden in his neighbor's coach, and that " the highest price he can pay for a thing is to ask for it."

A wise man will extend this lesson to all parts of ׅlife, and know that it is the part of prudence to face every claimant and pay every just demand on your time, your talents, or your heart. Always pay; for first or last you must pay your entire debt. Persons and events may stand for a time between you and justice, but it is only a postponement. You must pay at last your own debt. If you are wise, you will dread a prosperity which only loads you with more. Benefit is the end of nature. But for every benefit which you receive, a tax is levied. He is great who confers the most benefits. He is base — and that is the one base thing in the universe — to receive favors and render none. In the order of nature we cannot render benefits to those from whom we receive them, or only seldom. But the benefit we receive must be rendered again, line for line, deed for deed, cent for cent, to somebody. Beware of too much good staying in your hand. It will fast corrupt and worm worms. Pay it away quickly in some sort.

LOVE

HERE let us examine a little nearer the nature of that influence which is thus potent over the human youth. Beauty, whose revelation to man we now celebrate, welcome as the sun wherever it pleases to shine, which pleases everybody with it and with themselves, seems sufficient to itself. The lover cannot paint his maiden to his fancy poor and solitary. Like a tree in flower, so much soft, budding, informing loveliness is society for itself; and she teaches his eye why Beauty was pictured with Loves and Graces attending her steps. Her existence makes the world rich. Though she extrudes all other persons from his attention as cheap and unworthy, she indemnifies him by carrying out her own being into somewhat impersonal, large mundane, so that the maiden stands to him for a representative of all select things and virtues. For that reason the lover never sees personal resemblances in his mistress to her kindred or to others. His friends find in her a likeness to her mother, or her sisters, or to persons not of her blood. The lover sees no resemblance except to summer evenings and diamond mornings, to rainbows and the song of birds.

The ancients called beauty the flowering of virtue. Who can analyze the nameless charm which glances from one and another face and form? We are touched with emotions of tenderness and complacency, but we cannot find whereat this dainty emotion, this wandering gleam, points. It is destroyed for the imagination by any attempt to refer it to organization. Nor does it point to any relations of friendship or love known and described in society; but as it seems to me, to a quite other and unattainable sphere, to relations of transcendent delicacy and sweetness, to what roses and violets hint and foreshow. We cannot approach beauty. Its nature is like opaline dove's-neck lustres, hovering and evanescent. Herein it resembles the most excellent things, which all have this rainbow character, defying all attempts at appropriation and use. What else did Jean Paul Richter signify when he said to music, "Away! away! thou speakest to me of things which in all my endless life I have not found and shall not find." The same fluency may be observed in every work of the plastic arts. The statue is then beautiful when it begins to be incomprehensible, when it is passing out of criticism and can no longer be defined by compass and measuring wand, but demands an active imagination to go with it and· to say what it is in the act of doing. The god or hero of the sculptor is always represented in a transition *from* that which is representable to the senses, *to* that which is not. Then first it ceases to be a stone. The same remark holds of painting. And of poetry the success is not attained when it lulls and satisfies, but when it astonishes and fires us with new endeavors after the unattainable. Concerning it Landor inquires "whether it is not to be referred to some purer state of sensation and existence."

In like manner personal beauty is then first charming and itself when it dissatisfies us with any end; when it becomes a story without an end; when it suggests gleams and visions and not earthly satisfactions; when it makes the beholder feel his unworthiness; when he cannot feel his right to it, though he were Cæsar; he cannot feel more right to it than to the firmament and the splendors of a sunset.

Hence arose the saying, "If I love you, what is that to you?" We say so because we feel that what we love is not in your will, but above it. It is not you, but your radiance. It is that which you know not in yourself and can never know.

This agrees well with that high philosophy of Beauty which the ancient writers delighted in; for they said that the soul of man, embodied here on earth, went roaming up and down in quest of that other world of its own out of which it came into this, but was soon stupefied by the light of the natural sun, and unable to see any other objects than those of this world, which are but shadows of real things. Therefore the Deity sends the glory of youth before the soul, that it may avail itself of beautiful bodies as aids to its recollection of the celestial good and fair; and the man beholding such a person in the female sex runs to her and finds the highest joy in contemplating the form, movement, and intelligence of this person, because it suggests to him the presence of that which indeed is within the beauty, and the cause of the beauty.

If however, from too much conversing with material objects, the soul was gross, and misplaced its satisfaction in the body, it reaped nothing but sorrow; body being unable to fulfill the promise which beauty holds out; but if, accepting the hint of these visions and suggestions which beauty makes to his mind, the soul passes through the body and falls to admire strokes of character, and the lovers contemplate one another in their discourses and their actions, then they pass to the true palace of beauty, more and more inflame their love of it, and by this love extinguishing the base affection, as the sun puts out fire by shining on the hearth, they become pure and hallowed. By conversation with that which is in itself excellent, magnanimous, lowly, and just, the lover comes to a warmer love of these nobilities and a quicker apprehension of them. Then he passes from loving them in one to loving them in all, and so is the one beautiful soul only the door through which he enters to the society of all true and pure souls. In the particular society of his mate he attains a clearer sight of any spot, any taint which her beauty has contracted from this world, and is able to point it out; and this with mutual joy that they are now able without offense to indicate blemishes and hindrances in each other, and give to each all help and comfort in curing the same. And beholding in many souls the traits of the divine beauty, and separating in each soul that which is divine from the taint which it has contracted in the world, the lover ascends to the highest beauty, to the love and knowledge of the Divinity, by steps on this ladder of created souls.

CIRCLES

THE eye is the first circle; the horizon which it forms is the second; and throughout nature this primary figure is repeated without end. It is the highest emblem in the cipher of the world. St. Augustine described the nature of God as a circle whose centre was everywhere and its circumference nowhere. We are all our lifetime reading the copious sense of this first of forms. One moral we have already deduced in considering the circular or compensatory character of every human action. Another analogy we shall now trace, that every action admits of being outdone. Our life is an apprenticeship to the truth that around every circle another can be drawn; that there is no end in nature, but every end is a beginning; that there is always another dawn risen on mid-noon, and under every deep a lower deep opens. . . .

There are no fixtures in nature. The universe is fluid and volatile. Permanence is but a word of degrees. Our globe, seen by God, is a transparent law, not a mass of facts. The law dissolves the fact and holds it fluid. Our culture is the predominance of an idea which draws after it this train of cities and institutions. Let us rise into another idea; they will disappear. The Greek sculpture is all melted away as if it had been statues of ice; here and there a solitary figure or fragment remaining, as we see flecks and scraps of snow left in cold dells and mountain clefts in June and July. For the genius that created it creates now somewhat else. The Greek letters last a little longer, but are already passing under the same sentence and tumbling into the inevitable pit which the creation of new thought opens for all that is old. The new continents are built out of the ruins of an old planet; the new races fed out of the decomposition of the foregoing. New arts destroy the old. See the investment of capital in aqueducts, made useless by hydraulics; fortifications by gunpowder; roads and canals by railways; sails by steam; steam by electricity.

You admire this tower of granite, weathering the hurts of so many ages. Yet a little waving hand built this huge wall, and that which builds is better than that which is built. The hand that built can topple it down much faster. Better than the hand and nimbler was the invisible thought which wrought through it; and thus ever behind the coarse effect is a fine cause, which, being narrowly seen, is itself the effect of a finer cause. Everything looks permanent until its secret is known. A rich estate appears to women and children a firm and lasting fact; to a merchant, one easily created out of any materials, and easily lost. An orchard, good tillage, good grounds, seem a fixture like a gold mine, or a river, to a citizen; but to a large farmer, not much more fixed than the state of the crop. Nature looks provokingly stable and secular, but it has a cause like all the rest; and when once I comprehend that, will these fields stretch so immovably wide, these leaves hang so individually considerable? Permanence is a word of degrees. Everything is medial. Moons are no more bounds to spiritual power than bat-balls.

The key to every man is his thought. Sturdy and defying though he look, he has a helm which he obeys, which is the idea after which all his facts are classified. He can only be reformed by showing him a new idea which commands his own. The life of man is a self-evolving circle, which from a ring imperceptibly small, rushes on all sides outwards to new and larger circles, and that without end. The extent to which this generation of circles, wheel without wheel, will go, depends on the force or truth of the individual soul. For it is the inert effort of each thought, having formed itself into a circular wave of circumstance,—as for instance an empire, rules of an art, a local usage, a religious rite,—to heap itself on that ridge and to solidify and hem in the life. But if the soul is quick and strong it bursts over that boundary on all sides and expands another orbit on the great deep, which also runs up into a high wave, with attempt again to stop and to bind. But the heart refuses to be imprisoned; in its first and narrowest pulses it already tends outward with a vast force and to immense and innumerable expansions.

Every ultimate fact is only the first of a new series,—every general law only a particular fact of some more general law presently to disclose itself. There is no outside, no inclosing wall, no circumference to us. The man finishes his story,—how good! how final! how it puts a new face on all things! He fills the sky. Lo! on the other side rises also a man and draws a circle around the circle we had just pronounced the outline of the sphere. Then already is our first speaker not man, but only a first speaker. His only redress is forthwith to draw a circle outside of his antagonist. And so men do by themselves. The result of to-day, which haunts the mind and cannot be escaped, will presently be abridged into a word, and the principle that seemed to explain nature will itself be included as one example of a bolder generalization. In the thought of to-morrow there is a power to upheave all thy creed, all the creeds, all the literatures of the nations, and marshal thee to a heaven which no epic dream has yet depicted. Every man is not so much a workman in the world as he is a suggestion of that he should be. Men walk as prophecies of the next age.

Step by step we scale this mysterious ladder; the steps are actions, the new prospect is power. Every several result is threatened and judged by that which follows. Every one seems to be contradicted by the new; it is only limited by the new. The new statement is always hated by the old, and to those dwelling in the old, comes like an abyss of skepticism. But the eye soon gets wonted to it, for the eye and it are effects of one cause; then its innocency and benefit appear, and presently, all its energy spent, it pales and dwindles before the revelation of the new hour.

SELF-RELIANCE

Trust thyself: every heart vibrates to that iron string. Accept the place the Divine providence has found for you, the society of your contemporaries, the connection of events. Great men have always done so, and confided themselves child-like to the genius of their age, betraying their perception that the absolutely trustworthy was seated at their heart, working through their hands, predominating in all their being. And we are now men, and must accept in the highest mind the same transcendent destiny; and not minors and invalids in a protected corner, not cowards fleeing before a revolution, but guides, re-deemers, and benefactors, obeying the Almighty effort and advancing on Chaos and the Dark.

What pretty oracles nature yields us on this text in the face and behavior of children, babes, and even brutes! That divided and rebel mind, that distrust of a sentiment because our arithmetic has computed the strength and means opposed to our purpose, these have not. Their mind being whole, their eye is as yet unconquered, and when we look in their faces we are disconcerted. Infancy conforms to nobody; all conform to it: so that one babe commonly makes four or five out of the adults who prattle and play to it. So God has armed youth and puberty and manhood no less with its own piquancy and charm, and made it enviable and gracious and its claims not to be put by, if it will stand by itself. Do not think the youth has no force, because he cannot speak to you and me. Hark! in the next room the voice is sufficiently clear and emphatic! It seems he knows how to speak to his contemporaries. Bashful or bold then, he will know how to make us seniors very unnecessary.

The nonchalance of boys who are sure of a dinner, and would disdain as much as a lord to do or say aught to conciliate one, is the healthy attitude of human nature. A boy is in the parlor what the pit is in the play-house: independent, irresponsible, looking out from his corner on such people and facts as pass by, he tries and sentences them on their merits, in the swift summary way of boys, as good, bad, interesting, silly, eloquent, troublesome. He cumbers himself never about consequences, about interests; he gives an independent, genuine verdict. You must court him; he does not court you. But the man is, as it were, clapped into jail by his consciousness. As soon as he has once acted or spoken with éclat he is a committed person, watched by the sympathy or the hatred of hundreds, whose affections must now enter into his account. There is no Lethe for this. Ah, that he could pass again into his neutrality! Who can thus avoid all pledges, and having observed, observe again from the same unaffected, unbiased, unbribable, unaffrighted innocence, must always be formidable. He would utter opinions on all passing affairs, which being seen to be not private but necessary, would sink like darts into the ear of men and put them in fear.

These are the voices which we hear in solitude, but they grow faint and inaudible as we enter into the world. Society everywhere is in conspiracy against the manhood of every one of its members. Society is a joint-stock company, in which the members agree, for the better securing of his bread to each shareholder, to surrender the liberty and culture of the eater. The virtue in most request is conformity. Self-reliance is its aversion. It loves not realities and creators, but names and customs.

Whoso would be a man must be a nonconformist. He who would gather immortal palms must not be hindered by the name of goodness, but must explore if it be goodness. Nothing is at last sacred but the integrity of your own mind. Absolve you to yourself, and you shall have the suffrage of the world. I remember an answer which when quite young I was prompted to make to a valued adviser, who was wont to importune me with the dear old doctrines of the Church. On my saying, "What have I to do with the sacredness of traditions, if I live wholly from within?" my friend suggested, "But these impulses may be from below, not from above." I replied, "They do not seem to me to be such; but if I am the Devil's child, I will live then from the Devil." No law can be sacred to me but that of my nature. Good and bad are but names very readily transferable to that or this: the only right is what is after my constitution; the only wrong what is against it. A man is to carry himself in the presence of all opposition as if everything were titular and ephemeral but he. I am ashamed to think how easily we capitulate to badges and names, to large societies and dead institutions. Every decent and well-spoken individual affects and sways me more than is right. I ought to go upright and vital, and speak the rude truth in all ways. If malice and vanity wear the coat of philanthropy, shall that pass? If an angry bigot assumes this bountiful cause of Abolition, and comes to me with his last news from Barbadoes, why should I not say to him:—" Go love thy infant; love thy wood-chopper; be good-natured and modest; have that grace; and never varnish your hard, uncharitable ambition with this incredible tenderness for black folk a thousand miles off. Thy love afar is spite at home." Rough and graceless would be such greeting, but truth is handsomer than the affectation of love. Your goodness must have some edge to it, else it is none. The doctrine of hatred must be preached, as the counteraction of the doctrine of love, when that pules and whines. I shun father and mother and wife and brother when my genius calls me. I would write on the lintels of the door-post, *Whim*. I hope it is somewhat better than whim at last, but we cannot spend the day in explanation. Expect me not to show cause why I seek or why I exclude company. Then again, do not tell me, as a good man did to-day, of my obligation to put all poor men in good situations. Are they *my* poor? I tell thee, thou foolish philanthropist, that I grudge the dollar, the dime, the cent I give to such men as do not belong to me and to whom I do not belong. There is a class of persons to whom by all spiritual affinity I am bought and sold; for them I will go to prison if need be: but your miscellaneous popular charities; the education at college of fools; the building of meeting-houses to the vain end to which many now stand; alms to sots, and the thousandfold relief societies;—though I confess with shame I sometimes succumb and give the dollar, it is a wicked dollar, which by-and-by I shall have the manhood to withhold. . . .

What I must do is all that concerns me, not what the people think. This rule, equally arduous in actual and in intellectual life, may serve for the whole distinction between greatness and meanness. It is the harder because you will always find those who think they know what is your duty better than you know it. It is easy in the world to live after the world's opinion; it is easy in solitude to live after our own; but the great man is he who in the midst of the crowd keeps with perfect sweetness the independence of solitude.

HISTORY

CIVIL and natural history, the history of art and of literature, must be explained from individual history, or must remain words. There is nothing but is related to us, nothing that does not interest us; kingdom, college, tree, horse, or iron shoe, —the roots of all things are in man. Santa Croce and the Dome of St. Peter's are lame copies after a divine model. Strassburg Cathedral is a material counterpart of the soul of Erwin of Steinbach. The true poem is the poet's mind; the true ship is the ship-builder. In the man, could we lay him open, we should see the reason for the last flourish and tendril of his work; as every spine and tint in the sea-shell pre-exists in the secreting organs of the fish. The whole of heraldry and of chivalry is in courtesy. A man of fine manners shall pronounce your name with all the ornament that titles of nobility could ever add.

The trivial experience of every day is always verifying some old prediction to us, and converting into things the words and signs which we had heard and seen without heed. A lady with whom I was riding in the forest said to me that the woods always seemed to her *to wait*, as if the genii who inhabited them suspended their deeds until the wayfarer had passed onward; a thought which poetry has celebrated in the dance of the fairies, which breaks off on the approach of human feet. The man who has seen the rising moon break out of the clouds at midnight, has been present like an archangel at the creation of light and of the world. I remember one summer day in the fields, my companion pointed out to me a broad cloud, which might extend a quarter of a mile parallel to the horizon, quite accurately in the form of a cherub as painted over churches,—a round block in the centre, which it was easy to animate with eyes and mouth, supported on either side by wide-stretched symmetrical wings. What appears once in the atmosphere may appear often, and it was undoubtedly the archetype of that familiar ornament. I have seen in the sky a chain of summer lightning which at once showed to me that the Greeks drew from nature when they painted the thunderbolt in the hand of Jove. I have seen a snowdrift along the sides of the stone wall, which obviously gave the idea of the common architectural scroll to abut a tower.

By surrounding ourselves with the original circumstances we invent anew the orders and the ornaments of architecture, as we see how each people merely decorated its primitive abodes. The Doric temple preserves the semblance of the wooden cabin in which the Dorian dwelt. The Chinese pagoda is plainly a Tartar tent. The Indian and Egyptian temples still betray the mounds and subterranean houses of their forefathers. "The custom of making houses and tombs in the living rock," says Heeren in his 'Researches on the Ethiopians,' "determined very naturally the principal character of the Nubian Egyptian architecture to the colossal form which it assumed. In these caverns already prepared by nature, the eye was accustomed to dwell on huge shapes and masses, so that when art came to the assistance of nature it could not move on a small scale without degrading itself. What would statues of the usual size, or neat porches and wings, have been, associated with those gigantic halls before which only Colossi could sit as watchmen or lean on the pillars of the interior?"

The Gothic church plainly originated in a rude adaptation of the forest trees, with all their boughs, to a festal or solemn arcade; as the bands about the cleft pillars still indicate the green withes that tied them. No one can walk in a road cut through pine woods without being struck with the architectural appearance of the grove, especially in winter, when the barrenness of all other trees shows the low arch of the Saxons. In the woods in a winter afternoon one will see as readily the origin of the stained-glass window, with which the Gothic cathedrals are adorned, in the colors of the western sky seen through the bare and crossing branches of the forest. Nor can any lover of nature enter the old piles of Oxford and the English cathedrals without feeling that the forest overpowered the mind of the builder, and that his chisel, his saw and plane still reproduced its ferns, its spikes of flowers, its locust, elm, oak, pine, fir, and spruce.

The Gothic cathedral is a blossoming in stone, subdued by the insatiable demand of harmony in man. The mountain of granite blooms into an eternal flower, with the lightness and delicate finish as well as the aerial proportions and perspective of vegetable beauty.

In like manner all public facts are to be individualized, all private facts are to be generalized. Then at once History becomes fluid and true, and Biography deep and sublime.

EACH AND ALL

LITTLE thinks, in the field, yon red-cloaked clown
      Of thee from the hill-top looking down;
      The heifer that lows in the upland farm,
Far-heard, lows not thine ear to charm;
The sexton tolling his bell at noon,
Deems not that great Napoleon
Stops his horse, and lists with delight,
Whilst his files sweep round yon Alpine height;
Nor knowest thou what argument
Thy life to thy neighbor's creed has lent.
All are needed by each one;
Nothing is fair or good alone.
I thought the sparrow's note from heaven,
      Singing at dawn on the alder bough;
I brought him home, in his nest, at even;
      He sings the song, but it cheers not now,
For I did not bring home the river and sky;—
He sang to my ear,—they sang to my eye.
The delicate shells lay on the shore;
The bubbles of the latest wave
Fresh pearls to their enamel gave,
And the bellowing of the savage sea
Greeted their safe escape to me.
I wiped away the weeds and foam,
I fetched my sea-born treasures home;
But the poor unsightly, noisome things
Had left their beauty on the shore
With the sun and the sand and the wild uproar.
The lover watched his graceful maid,
As 'mid the virgin train she strayed,
Nor knew her beauty's best attire
Was woven still by the snow-white choir.
At last she came to his hermitage,
Like the bird from the woodlands to the cage;
The gay enchantment was undone—
A gentle wife, but fairy none.
Then I said, "I covet truth:
      Beauty is unripe childhood's cheat;
I leave it behind with the games of youth:"—
      As I spoke, beneath my feet
The ground-pine curled its pretty wreath,

Running over the club-moss burrs;
I inhaled the violet's breath;
Around me stood the oaks and firs;
Pine-cones and acorns lay on the ground;
Over me soared the eternal sky,
Full of light and of deity;
Again I saw, again I heard,
The rolling river, the morning bird;—
Beauty through my senses stole;
I yielded myself to the perfect whole.

THE RHODORA

On Being Asked, Whence is the Flower?

In May, when sea-winds pierced our solitudes,
I found the fresh Rhodora in the woods,
    Spreading its leafless blooms in a damp nook,
To please the desert and the sluggish brook.
The purple petals, fallen in the pool,
    Made the black water with their beauty gay;
Here might the red-bird come his plumes to cool,
    And court the flower that cheapens his array.
Rhodora! if the sages ask thee why
This charm is wasted on the earth and sky,
Tell them, dear, that if eyes were made for seeing,
Then Beauty is its own excuse for being:
Why thou wert there, O rival of the rose!
    I never thought to ask, I never knew;
But in my simple ignorance suppose
The self-same Power that brought me there brought you.

THE HUMBLE-BEE

BURLY, dozing humble-bee,
  Where thou art is clime for me.
    Let them sail for Porto Rique.
Far-off heats through seas to seek;
I will follow thee alone,
Thou animated torrid zone!
Zigzag steerer, desert cheerer,
    Let me chase thy waving lines;
Keep me nearer, me thy hearer,
    Singing over shrubs and vines.

Insect lover of the sun,
Joy of thy dominion!
Sailor of the atmosphere;
Swimmer through the waves of air;
Voyager of light and noon;
Epicurean of June;
Wait, I prithee, till I come
Within earshot of thy hum,—
All without is martyrdom.

When the south wind, in May days,
With a net of shining haze
Silvers the horizon wall,
And with softness touching all,
Tints the human countenance
With a color of romance,
And infusing subtle heats,
Turns the sod to violets,—
Thou in sunny solitudes,
Rover of the underwoods,
The green silence dost displace,
With thy mellow, breezy bass.

Hot midsummer's petted crone,
Sweet to me, thy drowsy tone
Tells of countless sunny hours,
Long days, and solid banks of flowers;
Of gulfs of sweetness without bound,
In Indian wildernesses found;
Of Syrian peace, immortal leisure,
Firmest cheer, and bird-like pleasure.

Aught unsavory or unclean
Hath my insect never seen;
But violets and bilberry bells,
Maple-sap and daffodels,
Grass with green flag half-mast high,
Succory to match the sky,
Columbine with horn of honey,
Scented fern, and agrimony,
Clover, catchfly, adder's-tongue
And brier-roses, dwelt among;
All beside was unknown waste,
All was picture as he passed.

Wiser far than human seer,
Yellow-breeched philosopher!
Seeing only what is fair,
    Sipping only what is sweet,
Thou dost mock at fate and care,
    Leave the chaff, and take the wheat.
When the fierce northwestern blast
Cools sea and land so far and fast,
Thou already slumberest deep;
Woe and want thou canst outsleep;
Want and woe, which torture us,
Thy sleep makes ridiculous.

THE PROBLEM

I LIKE a church; I like a cowl;
    I love a prophet of the soul;
    And on my heart monastic aisles
Fall like sweet strains, or pensive smiles:
Yet not for all his faith can see
Would I that cowlèd churchman be.
Why should the vest on him allure,
Which I could not on me endure?

Not from a vain or shallow thought
His awful Jove young Phidias brought;
Never from lips of cunning fell
The thrilling Delphic oracle;
Out from the heart of nature rolled
The burdens of the Bible old;
The litanies of nations came,
Like the volcano's tongue of flame,

Up from the burning core below,—
The canticles of love and woe:
The hand that rounded Peter's dome
And groined the aisles of Christian Rome
Wrought in a sad sincerity;
Himself from God he could not free;
He builded better than he knew;—
The conscious stone to beauty grew.

Know'st thou what wove yon wood-bird's nest
Of leaves, and feathers from her breast?
Or how the fish outbuilt her shell,
Painting with morn each annual cell?
Or how the sacred pine-tree adds
To her old leaves new myriads?
Such and so grew these holy piles,
Whilst love and terror laid the tiles.
Earth proudly wears the Parthenon,
As the best gem upon her zone,
And Morning opes with haste her lids
To gaze upon the Pyramids;
O'er England's abbeys bends the sky,
As on its friends, with kindred eye;
For out of thought's interior sphere
These wonders rose to upper air;
And Nature gladly gave them place,
Adopted them into her race,
And granted them an equal date
With Andes and with Ararat.

These temples grew as grows the grass;
Art might obey, but not surpass.
The passive Master lent his hand
To the vast soul that o'er him planned;
And the same power that reared the shrine
Bestrode the tribes that knelt within.
Ever the fiery Pentecost
Girds with one flame the countless host,
Trances the heart through chanting choirs,
And through the priest the mind inspires.
The word unto the prophet spoken
Was writ on tables yet unbroken;
The word by seers or sibyls told,
In groves of oak, or fanes of gold,

Still floats upon the morning wind,
Still whispers to the willing mind.
One accent of the Holy Ghost
The heedless world hath never lost.
I know what say the Fathers wise,—
The Book itself before me lies,
Old Chrysostom, best Augustine,
And he who blent both in his line,
The younger Golden Lips or mines,—
Taylor, the Shakespeare of divines.
His words are music in my ear,
I see his cowlèd portrait dear;
And yet, for all his faith could see,
I would not the good bishop be.

DAYS

DAUGHTERS of Time, the hypocritic Days,
        Muffled and dumb like barefoot dervishes,
        And marching single in an endless file,
Bring diadems and fagots in their hands.
To each they offer gifts after his will,
Bread, kingdoms, stars, and sky that holds them all.
I, in my pleached garden, watched the pomp,
Forgot my morning wishes, hastily
Took a few herbs and apples, and the Day
Turned and departed silent. I, too late,
Under the solemn fillet saw the scorn.

MUSKETAQUID

BECAUSE I was content with these poor fields,
  Low open meads, slender and sluggish streams,
    And found a home in haunts which others scorned,
The partial wood-gods overpaid my love,
And granted me the freedom of their state,
And in their secret senate have prevailed
With the dear dangerous lords that rule our life,
Made moon and planets parties to their bond,
And through my rock-like, solitary wont
Shot million rays of thought and tenderness.
For me, in showers, in sweeping showers, the Spring
Visits the valley;—break away the clouds,—
I bathe in the morn's soft and silvered air,
And planted world, and full executor
Of their imperfect functions.
But these young scholars who invade our hills—
Bold as the engineer who fells the wood,
And traveling often in the cut he makes—
Love not the flower they pluck, and know it not,
And all their botany is Latin names.
The old men studied magic in the flowers,
And human fortunes in astronomy,
And an omnipotence in chemistry,
Preferring things to names; for these were men,
Were unitarians of the united world,
And wheresoever their clear eye-beams fell,
They caught the footsteps of the SAME.   Our eyes
Are armed, but we are strangers to the stars,
And strangers to the mystic beast and bird,
And strangers to the plant and to the mine.
The injured elements say, "Not in us;"
And night and day, ocean and continent,
Fire, plant, and mineral say, "Not in us;"
And haughtily return us stare for stare.
For we invade them impiously for gain;
We devastate them unreligiously,
And coldly ask their pottage, not their love.
Therefore they shove us from them, yield to us
Only what to our griping toil is due;
But the sweet affluence of love and song,
The rich results of the divine consents

Of man and earth, of world beloved and lover,
The nectar and ambrosia, are withheld;
And in the midst of spoils and slaves, we thieves
And pirates of the universe, shut out
Daily to a more thin and outward rind,
And loiter willing by yon loitering stream.
Sparrows far off, and nearer, April's bird,
Blue-coated,— flying before from tree to tree,
Courageous sing a delicate overture
To lead the tardy concert of the year.
Onward and nearer rides the sun of May;
And wide around, the marriage of the plants
Is sweetly solemnized. Then flows amain
The surge of summer's beauty; dell and crag,
Hollow and lake, hillside and pine arcade,
Are touched with genius. Yonder ragged cliff
Has thousand faces in a thousand hours.

Beneath low hills, in the broad interval
Through which at will our Indian rivulet
Winds mindful still of sannup and of squaw,
Whose pipe and arrow oft the plow unburies;
Here in pine houses built of new-fallen trees,
Supplanters of the tribe, the farmers dwell.
Traveler, to thee perchance a tedious road,
Or it may be, a picture; to these men,
The landscape is an armory of powers,
Which, one by one, they know to draw and use;
They harness beast, bird, insect, to their work;
They prove the virtues of each bed of rock,
And, like the chemist mid his loaded jars,
Draw from each stratum its adapted use
To drug their crops or weapon their arts withal.
They turn the frost upon their chemic heap,
They set the wind to winnow pulse and grain,
They thank the spring-flood for its fertile slime,
And, on cheap summit-levels of the snow,
Slide with the sledge to inaccessible woods
O'er meadows bottomless. So, year by year,
They fight the elements with elements
(That one would say, meadow and forest walked,
Transmuted in these men to rule their like),
And by the order in the field disclose
The order regnant in the yeoman's brain.

What these strong masters wrote at large in miles,
I followed in small copy in my acre;
For there's no rood has not a star above it;
The cordial quality of pear or plum
Ascends as gladly in a single tree
As in broad orchards resonant with bees;
And every atom poises for itself,
And for the whole. The gentle deities
Showed me the lore of colors and of sounds,
The innumerable tenements of beauty,
The miracle of generative force,
Far-reaching concords of astronomy
Felt in the plants and in the punctual birds;
Better, the linkèd purpose of the whole,
And — chiefest prize — found I true liberty
In the glad home plain-dealing Nature gave.
The polite found me impolite; the great
Would mortify me, but in vain; for still
I am a willow of the wilderness,
Loving the wind that bent me. All my hurts
My garden spade can heal. A woodland walk,
A quest of river grapes, a mocking thrush,
A wild rose, or rock-loving columbine,
Salve my worst wounds.
For thus the wood-gods murmured in my ear:
"Dost love our manners? Canst thou silent lie?
Canst thou, thy pride forgot, like nature pass
Into the winter night's extinguished mood?
Canst thou shine now, then darkle,
And being latent, feel thyself no less?
As, when the all-worshiped moon attracts the eye,
The river, hill, stems, foliage, are obscure,
Yet envies none, none are unenviable."

FROM THE 'THRENODY'

THE South-wind brings
  Life, sunshine and desire,
    And on every mount and meadow
Breathes aromatic fire;
But over the dead he has no power,
The lost, the lost, he cannot restore;
And looking over the hills, I mourn
The darling who shall not return. . . .

O child of paradise,
Boy who made dear his father's home,
In whose deep eyes
Men read the welfare of the times to come,
I am too much bereft.
The world dishonored thou hast left.
O truth's and Nature's costly lie!
O trusted broken prophecy!
O richest fortune sourly crossed!
Born for the future, to the future lost!

The deep Heart answered, "Weepest thou?
Worthier cause for passion wild
If I had not taken the child.
And deemest thou as those who pore,
With agèd eyes, short way before,—
Think'st Beauty vanished from the coast
Of matter, and thy darling lost?
Taught he not thee—the man of eld,
Whose eyes within his eyes beheld
Heaven's numerous hierarchy span
The mystic gulf from God to man?
To be alone wilt thou begin,
When worlds of lovers hem thee in?
To-morrow, when the masks shall fall
That dizen Nature's carnival,
The pure shall see by their own will,
Which overflowing Love shall fill,
'Tis not within the force of fate
The fate-conjoined to separate.
But thou, my votary, weepest thou?
I gave thee sight—where is it now?
I taught thy heart beyond the reach
Of ritual, Bible, or of speech;

Wrote in thy mind's transparent table,
As far as the incommunicable;
Taught thee each private sign to raise
Lit by the supersolar blaze.
Past utterance, and past belief,
And past the blasphemy of grief,
The mysteries of Nature's heart;
And though no Muse can these impart,
Throb thine with Nature's throbbing breast,
And all is clear from east to west.

"I came to thee as to a friend;
Dearest, to thee I did not send
Tutors, but a joyful eye,
Innocence that matched the sky,
Lovely locks, a form of wonder,
Laughter rich as woodland thunder,
That thou might'st entertain apart
The richest flowering of all art:
And, as the great all-loving Day
Through smallest chambers takes its way,
That thou might'st break thy daily bread
With prophet, savior, and head;
That thou might'st cherish for thine own
The richest of sweet Mary's Son,
Boy-Rabbi, Israel's paragon.
And thoughtest thou such guest
Would in thy hall take up his rest?
Would rushing life forget her laws,
Fate's glowing revolution pause?
High omens ask diviner guess;
Not to be conned to tediousness.
And know my higher gifts unbind
The zone that girds the incarnate mind.
When the scanty shores are full
With thought's perilous, whirling pool;
When frail Nature can no more,
Then the Spirit strikes the hour:
My servant Death, with solving rite,
Pours finite into infinite.
Wilt thou freeze love's tidal flow,
Whose streams through Nature circling go?
Nail the wild star to its track
On the half climbed zodiac?

Light is light which radiates,
Blood is blood which circulates,
Life is life which generates,
And many-seeming life is one,—
Wilt thou transfix and make it none?
Its onward force too starkly pent
In figure, bone, and lineament?
Wilt thou, uncalled, interrogate,—
Talker!—the unreplying Fate?
Nor see the genius of the whole
Ascendant in the private soul?
Beckon it when to go and come,
Self-announced its hour of doom?
Fair the soul's recess and shrine,
   Magic-built to last a season;
Masterpiece of love benign,
   Fairer that expansive reason
Whose omen 'tis, and sign.
Wilt thou not ope thy heart to know
What rainbows teach, and sunsets show?
Verdict which accumulates
From lengthening scroll of human fates,
Voice of earth to earth returned,
Prayers of saints that inly burned,—
Saying, *What is excellent,*
As God lives, is permanent;
Hearts are dust, hearts' loves remain;
Heart's love will meet thee again.
Revere the Maker; fetch thine eye
Up to his style, and manners of the sky.
Not of adamant and gold
Built he heaven stark and cold;
No, but a nest of bending reeds,
Flowering grass and scented weeds;
Or like a traveler's fleeing tent,
Or bow above the tempest bent;
Built of tears and sacred flames,
And virtue reaching to its aims;
Built of furtherance and pursuing,
Not of spent deeds, but of doing.
Silent rushes the swift Lord
Through ruined systems still restored,
Broad-sowing, bleak and void to bless,
Plants with worlds the wilderness;

Waters with tears of ancient sorrow
Apples of Eden ripe to-morrow.
House and tenant go to ground,
Lost in God, in Godhead found.»

CONCORD HYMN

SUNG AT THE COMPLETION OF THE BATTLE MONUMENT, APRIL 19, 1836

BY THE rude bridge that arched the flood,
    Their flag to April's breeze unfurled,
Here once the embattled farmers stood,
    And fired the shot heard round the world.

The foe long since in silence slept;
    Alike the conqueror silent sleeps;
And time the ruined bridge has swept
    Down the dark stream which seaward creeps.

On this green bank, by this soft stream,
    We set to-day a votive stone;
That memory may their deed redeem,
    When, like our sires, our sons are gone.

Spirit, that made those heroes dare
    To die, and leave their children free,
Bid Time and Nature gently spare
    The shaft we raise to them and thee.

ODE

SUNG IN THE TOWN HALL, CONCORD, JULY 4, 1857

O TENDERLY the haughty day
    Fills his blue urn with fire;
One morn is in the mighty heaven,
    And one in our desire.

The cannon booms from town to town,
    Our pulses beat not less,
The joy-bells chime their tidings down,
    Which children's voices bless.

For He that flung the broad blue fold
    O'er mantling land and sea,
One third part of the sky unrolled
    For the banner of the free.

The men are ripe of Saxon kind
     To build an equal state,—
To take the statue from the mind
     And make of duty fate.

United States! the ages plead,—
     Present and Past in under-song,—
Go put your creed into your deed,
     Nor speak with double tongue.

For sea and land don't understand,
     Nor skies without a frown
See rights for which the one hand fights
     By the other cloven down.

Be just at home; then write your scroll
     Of honor o'er the sea,
And bid the broad Atlantic roll,
     A ferry of the free.

And henceforth there shall be no chain,
     Save underneath the sea
The wires shall murmur through the main
     Sweet songs of liberty.

The conscious stars accord above,
     The waters wild below,
And under, through the cable wove,
     Her fiery errands go.

For He that worketh high and wise,
     Nor pauses in his plan,
Will take the sun out of the skies
     Ere freedom out of man.